D1348733

0 589 558 8

SEÁN JENNETT

THE MAKING OF BOOKS

FABER & FABER

First published in 1951
by Faber & Faber Limited
3 Queen Square, London W.C.1
Second edition 1956
Third edition 1964
Reprinted 1966
Fourth edition 1967
Fifth edition 1973
Printed in Great Britain
The text and the half-tone plates
by Robert MacLehose & Co. Ltd., Glasgow
the auto-lithograph by the Baynard Press, London
the collotype plates
by the Cotswold Collotype Co. Ltd.
the photo-lithography and Plastocowell plates
by W. S. Cowell & Sons Ltd., Ipswich
and the photogravure plates
by Clarke & Sherwell, Northampton
The line and half-tone blocks
made by Fine Art Engravers Ltd.
Printed on paper supplied by
Gerald Judd Ltd.
and bound
by James Burn & Co. Ltd., Esher
The type is Monotype Baskerville

ISBN 0 571 04786 6

PREFACE

When this book was first published in 1951 it embodied my attempt to explain to authors and others in the field of publishing the practice and aesthetics of book design and the technologies of printing, binding, process-engraving, and the various other trades that contributed their share to the business of turning an author's manuscript or typescript into a book printed and bound and ready for publication. It turned out that publishers themselves found interest in my book and in addition it became a standard work for students of bibliography, typography, and printing.

In the following twenty years the aesthetic bases of book design have not changed to any important extent, but the technologies of the manufacturing trades that serve publishing, and especially that of printing, have changed a great deal. Conscious that my book is now read by many people in one or other of the fields of printing and publishing, I have sought from edition to edition to keep the work up to date. Now I have to do more than this. The pace of development has been so accelerated that I have had to try to foresee the future at least to the extent of considering machines and processes that are not yet in common use but which, it seems, are likely to be in use during the currency of this edition. While donning this mantle of prophecy I have kept in mind that many of my readers may have little understanding of technical matters and less of the jargons that serve their purpose for initiates but appear to others as a wall of incomprehension. Yet technical jargon is not to be despised. It comes about because common language is not always competent to express succinctly the details and functions of new technologies and new inventions. The computer field is especially rich in jargon and consequently equally rich in incomprehension and misunderstanding. I have done my best to cut a clear path through the thicket of thorny neologisms, to explain and to describe in clear English, and if in this I may have been only partially successful I believe that it is better to have conveyed a grain of knowledge rather than to baffle by polysyllabic technicalities that may be no more expressive to the layman than Sanskrit to an Eskimo.

I have also kept in mind that this is a book about the making of books as it is, that my attempts at prophecy must rest upon current practice. New techniques and technologies, new machines and materials do not commonly at once dismiss the old, certainly not in printing and binding. A good deal that may appear old-fashioned remains in these trades and survives not because of backwardness but simply because it remains efficient for its purpose. In this connection it should be understood that book-publishing, in Great Britain at least, despite mergers and takeovers, is still essentially an industry of small units producing goods in quantities that would be regarded in other fields as absurdly uneconomic. The appearance of book-publishing may be that of a mass-production industry, and it uses, and was among the first to use, a mass-production technique, for that is what printing is, but the average book is not one selling tens of thousands of copies, but one selling decidedly less than ten thousand copies. A number of large firms plan and tailor books for mass consumption, for sale by mail order, and these will seek out the best use of the manufacturing trades and their new technologies; but though they may be successful such publishers are partially parasite—it is not through these that new authors come into view, it is not these that find and nurture new creative writers through small editions towards wider popularity.

Yet, since printing and publishing are my field, I have taken notice of their needs, I have sought to understand and to evaluate what is new and different and progressive. There are many differences between this fifth edition and the previous one. Here and there throughout the text a paragraph has been changed or rewritten to evaluate or describe change. I have completely rewritten the chapter on photo-composition and on the place of computers in type composition generally. The progress of printing and process-engraving is reflected in four additional pages of half-tone illustrations and in a number of other illustrations replaced by more modern equivalents. The number of text type faces available to the printer continues to increase and the specimens of text type faces in this book have been increased in number from twenty to thirty-seven. The changes in the measurements of paper sizes consequent upon the conversion to metric sizes have been noted, together with the new methods of buying paper. The bibliography has been revised and extended and now represents a very creditable library and source of information on typography and publishing. Finally, I have corrected a few errors in the polyglot glossary that had crept in from my fault, and I have added further words.

CONTENTS

PREFACE *page* 5

PART ONE
PRINTING AND BINDING

I. A SURVEY OF DEVELOPMENT *page* 23
II. TYPE, SPACES, AND FURNITURE 36
III. COMPOSING AND THE COMPOSITOR 49
IV. COMPOSING MACHINES: THE LINOTYPE, THE INTERTYPE, AND THE MONOTYPE 66
V. DEVELOPMENTS IN TYPESETTING: PHOTO-SETTING AND COMPUTERS 81
VI. THE PAGE TAKES SHAPE: MAKE-UP AND IMPOSITION 99
VII. THE PRINTER'S READER 111
VIII. PRINTING MACHINES AND THE WORK OF THE PRESSMAN 118
IX. ILLUSTRATING THE BOOK: PROCESS ENGRAVING 132
X. ILLUSTRATING THE BOOK: PHOTOGRAVURE, LITHOGRAPHY, AND COLLOTYPE 154
XI. PAPER: ITS MANUFACTURE AND VARIETIES 171
XII. BINDING: HAND-BINDING AND MACHINE-BINDING 188

PART TWO
THE DESIGN OF BOOKS

XIII. THE DEVELOPMENT OF TYPE DESIGN 217
XIV. THE TYPOGRAPHER AND HIS WORK 256
XV. TEXT TYPES OF TO-DAY 268
XVI. PAGE 314

CONTENTS

XVII. PART-TITLES AND CHAPTER-HEADS *page* 343
XVIII. ODDMENTS 367
XIX. THE TITLE-PAGE 383
XX. THE USE OF ILLUSTRATION 425
XXI. ENDPAPERS 467
XXII. BINDING DESIGN 472
XXIII. THE BOOKJACKET 490
XXIV. HARMONY AND THE WHOLE 509

A SELECTION OF BOOKS 517
A POLYGLOT GLOSSARY OF TECHNICAL TERMS 524
ACKNOWLEDGEMENTS 540
INDEX 543

ILLUSTRATIONS

1. Page from *Ars Memorandi*, a block book printed in Germany about 1470 *page* 27
2. The shape of type in the fifteenth century: a pulled letter showing in *La Lèpre morale* by Jean Nider, printed at Cologne about 1476 *page* 31
3. Section of the Diamond Sutra, printed from wood blocks in China in A.D. 868; reduced *facing page* 32
4. Indulgence printed from movable type by Gutenberg in 1455; reduced *facing page* 33
5. The parts of type *page* 37
6. Examples of kerned letters 40
7. A page of Caslon to show the progression of type sizes from 6 point to 72 point *page* 45
8. Types of various sizes, with four sorts to show nicks, pin marks, and the arched casting of larger sizes *facing page* 48
9. Leads, quotations of several sizes, and metal furniture, with a 72-point letter to show scale and type height *facing page* 48
10. A compositor setting type from a double case 49
11. A closer view of the compositor's hands, to show the action in detail *facing page* 49
12. An early printing house *page* 50
13. A pair of cases, showing the lay 52
14. A printing house in the sixteenth century 55
15. A galley of type, ready for proofing 59
16. A printing house in the seventeenth century 61
17. A double case and its lay 64
18. The Young-Delcambre composing machine 67
19. A Linotype machine in operation *facing page* 68
20. The assembly slide of a Linotype with a line of matrices being composed *facing page* 68
21. A punch-cutting machine 69
22. A Linotype matrix *page* 69

23. Diagram of a standard Monotype keyboard laid out for bookwork (seven alphabets) *page* 73
24. Punched paper strip from the Monotype keyboard 75
25. A Monotype keyboard in operation *facing page* 76
26. A Monotype composition caster 76
27. Matrix case or die-case from a composition caster 77
28. Type emerging from a composition caster 77
29. Monophoto matrix case and matrix 84
30. Monophoto studio-lettering machine 84
31. Monophoto photo-lettering machine and matrices 85
32. Lumitype character disk 85
33. Diagram of light-path of a Monophoto composing machine *page* 85
34. Computer tape, 6-level 86
35. K. S. Paul computer keyboard *facing page* 92
36. A Linotron installation: keyboard, control cabinet with keyboard, and photo-unit *facing page* 92
37. A compositor making up a thirty-two page forme on an imposition surface 93
38. Half-sheet imposition for two-page leaflet *page* 102
39. Sheet-imposition (two formes) for four-page folder 103
40. Sheet imposition for sixteen-page sheet to fold in octavo *page* 105
41. Sheet imposition for sixty-four pages to fold into four octavo sections of sixteen pages each *page* 107
42. Section of a thirty-two page forme, showing the arrangement of furniture and quoins *page* 108
43. Proof-reader's marks and corrected page *pages* 114–15
44. A nineteenth-century iron hand-press *page* 120
45. Diagram of a Koenig and Bauer press 121
46. A Miehle two-revolution machine *facing page* 132
47. A view under the feeding-board of a two-revolution machine, showing the impression of the cylinder upon the forme *facing page* 132
48. A wood-engraving by Reynolds Stone and an electrotype made from it *facing page* 133
49. A line block and half-tone block 133
50. A simple wood-cut of the fifteenth century (*c.* 1497) *page* 133
51. White-line wood-engraving by Thomas Bewick 134

52. Modern wood-engraving by Eric Ravilious (from *Poems* by Thomas Hennell, O.U.P., 1936) *page* 135
53. The progress of a line block: original, negative, block, and print *page* 137
54. A selection of mechanical tints 139
55. A Magnacolor camera with its control unit *facing page* 140
56. The back of a process camera, with the operator measuring the image on the focusing screen. *facing page* 140
57. Klischograph electronic engravers 141
58. Crosfield Magnascan electronic scanner 141
59. Part of a half-tone screen enlarged; enlarged portion of a half-tone print showing the varying size of the dots; and a diagram representing a half-tone block in section, also enlarged *page* 142
60. A powderless-etch machine *facing page* 144
61. A routing machine in operation on a line block *facing page* 144
62. Half-tone blocks of various screens 145
63. A four-colour half-tone block sectioned to show the separate colours and the order in which they are printed *facing page* 148
64. A photogravure screen, with a diagram showing the varying depth of the cells on the plate or cylinder; and a print showing the effect of the variation of depth of cell; all greatly enlarged *facing page* 160
65. A sheet-fed gravure machine 161
66. The printed web emerging from a rotary gravure machine *facing page* 161
67. A Roland Ultra four-colour litho machine 164
68. The plate cylinder with the blanket cylinder below, showing the transfer of the image *facing page* 164
69. Coating a metal collotype plate on an upright whirler *facing page* 165
70. Operator wiping a metal collotype plate on a rotary press *facing page* 165
71. A flat-bed collotype machine in operation 165
72. Effects possible in drawing on a litho stone; and a litho stone with a drawing on it *facing page* 168
73. Pulp in a beater 172
74. The wet end of a paper-making machine 172

75. General view of two paper-making machines from the wet end *facing page* 173
76. A supercalender machine 173
77. Paper-making in the sixteenth century (woodcut from Jost Amman) *page* 174
78. A paper-making machine in the nineteenth century *page* 179
79. Theoretical evolution of the codex 189
80. The parts of a hand-bound book 190
81. A sewing-frame 193
82. Hand-binder working at a sewing-frame *facing page* 196
83. Glueing the spine of the book after sewing 196
84. Making the joint after rounding the spine 196
85. Lacing the boards on 197
86. Trimming the edges with a plough 197
87. Lettering the spine of the book with leaf gold 197
88. Three kinds of spine: a flexible spine; a fast spine; and a hollow back *page* 198
89. Book-binding tools: a burnisher; a fillet, with a section of a decorated fillet; a letter Z; a gouge; an ornament; a rule; and an ornamental stamp *page* 199
90. Methods of inserting plates: four-page sections for wrapping round or inserting; plates hooked in; plates tipped in *page* 204
91. Four rows of octavo sections issuing from a quad folding machine *facing page* 204
92. A gathering machine 204
93. A girl operating a book-sewing machine 204
94. A nipping machine 205
95. A book-pressing machine 205
96. A wrappering machine 205
97. Elaborate decoration of gothic lettering (from *Fundamentbuch*, Strasbourg, 1579); reduced *page* 218
98. Five varieties of gothic: lettre de forme (Turrecremata, *Meditationes*, Mainz, 1497); lettre de somme (*Martyrologium Viola Sanctorum*, Strasbourg, 1499); lettre bâtarde (*Evangelien und Episteln*, Strasbourg, *c.* 1485); modern Schwabacher and Fraktur (Monotype) *page* 219
99. The first roman type, used by Adolf Rusch at Strasbourg, *c.* 1464 *page* 220

100. A romanized gothic type (from *Biblia Latina*, Mentelin, Strasbourg, *c.* 1460) *page* 221
101. Type used by Sweynheim and Pannartz at Subiaco (from Cicero, *De Oratore*, 1465) *page* 221
102. Type used by Sweynheim and Pannartz at Rome (from Rhodericus, *Speculum Vitae Humanae*, 1468) *page* 221
103. The da Spira type (from Juvenal, *Satyrae*, 1469) 221
104. Nicolas Jenson's roman (from Cicero, *Rhetorica Nova et Vetus*, 1470) *page* 223
105. Type used by Aldus in *De Aetna*, Venice, *c.* 1495 225
106. Griffi's type from *Hypnerotomachia Poliphili* (Aldus, Venice, 1499) *page* 225
107. The Aldine italic (from Virgil, *Opera*, 1501) 225
108. Garamond's roman, *c.* 1540 228
109. Type used by Christopher Plantin (from *Biblia Polyglotta*, Antwerp, 1572) *page* 230
110. Baskerville's type (from *The Works of Congreve*, Birmingham, 1761) *page* 232
111. Bodoni's type (from *Manuale Tipografico*, Parma, 1818) *page* 234
112. Revived types selected to show theoretically the transition from old face to modern face: Caslon, Baskerville, Bell, Bodoni, and Scotch Roman *page* 235
113. William Morris's roman, the Golden Type (from *The Poems of William Shakespeare*, Kelmscott Press, 1893) *page* 239
114. William Morris's Chaucer type (from *The Works of Geoffrey Chaucer*, Kelmscott Press, 1896) *page* 239
115. The Riccardi type (from Swinburne, *Atalanta in Calydon*, 1923) *page* 242
116. The King's Fount, Vale Press, 1896 243
117. The Vale Fount, Vale Press, 1896 243
118. The Doves Press type, 1901 243
119. The Ashendene type, 1902 243
120. Decorative letters, probably cut on wood (from the title-page of Pater's *Typis literarum*, Leipzig, 1710) *page* 245
121. Nineteenth-century frivolities 247
122. A fine example of a nineteenth-century decorated letter (reproduced from proofs taken from the original wood type); reduced *page* 248

123. The Gill Sans family *page* 249
124. Display types in use to-day *pages* 252–55
125. Opening page (*Incipit*) from Euclid's *Elementa* (Ratdolt, Venice, 1482); reduced *page* 317
126. Page from *Hypnerotomachia Poliphili* (Aldus, Venice, 1499); reduced *page* 319
127. Page from *Horae*, with borders by Geofroy Tory (printed by Simon de Colines, Paris, 1524); reduced *page* 321
128. Page from Basinius, *Opera* (Albertiniana, 1793); reduced *page* 323
129. Page from Davison's *Poetical Rhapsody* (Lee Priory Press, 1814) *page* 325
130. Page from William Morris's *News from Nowhere* (Kelmscott Press, 1892) *page* 326
131. Page from *The Odyssey*, translated by Alexander Pope (Nonesuch Press, 1931); reduced *page* 328
132. Page from the Tiptoft Missal (English manuscript, before 1332); reduced *facing page* 330
133. Opening page from the 42-line Bible (Mainz, 1456); reduced *facing page* 331
134. Page from *The Four Gospels*, with wood-engravings by Eric Gill (Golden Cockerel Press, 1931); reduced *page* 333
135. Page with engraved chapter-head illustration (from d'Ussieux, *Le Décaméron françois*, Paris, 1774) *facing page* 334
136. Engraved chapter-head ornaments (eighteenth-century; source unknown; from a scrapbook in the author's possession); reduced *facing page* 335
137. A selection of headline styles *page* 337
138. Diagram to show 55 per cent type area and 58 per cent type area *page* 338
139. Diagram to show proportions and margins of pages calculated on the diagonal *page* 339
140. Diagram to show margins in the proportion 1½, 2, 3, and 4 *page* 340
141. Chapter head from *La Mer des Histoires*, Paris, 1488; border and initial cut on wood; reduced *page* 345
142. Page from *The Works of Congreve* (Baskerville, Birmingham, 1761) *page* 347

143. Chapter head with printers' flowers (from P. S. Fournier, *Dissertation sur l'origine et les progrès de l'art de graver en bois*, etc., *c.* 1758–60) *page* 351
144. Chapter head from Bodoni's *Manuale Tipografico* (Parma, 1818); reduced *page* 353
145. Chapter head from *The Bible designed to be Read as Literature* (Heinemann, 1937); reduced *page* 355
146. Wood-cut initial used by Johann Landen, Cologne, 1496 *page* 356
147. Wood-cut initial used by Ulrich Zell, Cologne, *c.* 1500 357
148. Initial used by Erhard Ratdolt, Augsburg, 1499 358
149. Initial used by Johann Schoeffer, Mainz, 1518 358
150. Initial used for a title-page by Pierre le Caron (c. 1489–1500), Paris; reduced *page* 359
151. Initial used by Erhard Ratdolt, Augsburg, 1486 360
152. Initial used by Robert Estienne, Paris, 1544 360
153. Initial, one of a set in J. R. Wood's type catalogue, U.S.A., 1869 *page* 361
154. Initial U, wood-engraved, from a nineteenth-century novel (reproduced from scrap used to wrap a parcel sent to the author); reduced *page* 361
155. Initial designed by Eric Gill for the Golden Cockerel Press *page* 364
156. Initial designed by Edward Bawden for the Curwen Press *page* 364
157. Initial, one of a set, designed by Barnett Freedman for the Baynard Press *page* 365
158. Typical 'Here beginneth' (Cologne, 1485) 385
159. The first displayed title-page (from *Calendarium*, Ratdolt, Venice, 1476); reduced *page* 387
160. Title-page showing typical mixture of gothic and roman, and division of words, also typical wood-cut border (from *A Pronostycacyon practysed by Master Mathias Brothyel of Ravensburgh*, London, 1545); reduced *page* 389
161. Title-page of *Il Libro del Cortegiano del Conte Baldessar Castiglione*, Venice, 1545; reduced *page* 391
162. Poster title-page (from *Cabala*, London, 1663); reduced *page* 393
163. Baskerville title-page (from *Juvenalis*, Birmingham, 1761); reduced *page* 397

164. Bodoni title-page (from Horace, *Opera*, Parma, 1791); reduced *page* 399
165. Bodoni title-page (from *Oratio Dominica*, Parma, 1806); reduced *page* 401
166. Title-page from *The Holy War* (Pickering, London, 1840) *page* 403
167. Title opening from *The Works of Geoffrey Chaucer*, with borders by William Morris and a drawing by Sir Edward Burne-Jones (the Kelmscott Press, 1896); reduced *pages* 406–7
168. Title-page designed by D. B. Updike for *Stephen Crane* (Merrymount Press, Boston, U.S.A., 1923) *page* 409
169. Title-page of *The Iliad* (Nonesuch Press, 1931); reduced *page* 411
170. Title-page cut on wood by Eric Gill for Chaucer's *Troilus and Criseyde* (Golden Cockerel Press, 1927); reduced *page* 415
171. Title-page from *Four Victorian Ladies*; the border is enlarged from the device in Figure 151 (Faber & Faber, 1945) *page* 417
172. Title-page engraved on wood by Joan Hassall for *Cranford* (Harrap, 1940) *page* 419
173. Engraved title-page (from *Theatrum Praecipuarum Urbium*, Amsterdam, 1657); reduced *facing page* 420
174. Title-page with engraved lettering (from *Le Décaméron françois*, Paris, 1774) *facing page* 421
175. Title-page from *Realms of Silver* (Routledge & Kegan Paul, 1954) *page* 423
176. Nineteenth-century ornamental rules 424
177. A page from *Hypnerotomachia Poliphili* (Aldus, Venice, 1499); reduced *page* 427
178. Engraved illustration by Moreau le Jeune (from *Œuvres de Molière*, Paris, 1773) *facing page* 428
179. Engraving made for Rupert Brooke's poems by Ru van Rossem (1948; not previously published); reduced *facing page* 429
180. Wood-cut from *Quadriregio*, Florence, 1508 *page* 430
181. Wood-cut by Albrecht Dürer, from *The Great Passion*, Nuremberg, *c.* 1510; reduced *page* 432
182. Wood-cut from *Theuerdanck*, 1517; reduced 433

183. Wood-engraving from a drawing by F. Sandys (from 'Amor Mundi', *Shilling Magazine*, 1865); reduced *page* 435

184. Wood-engraving by Dalziel from a drawing by A. Hughes (from Christina Rossetti, *Sing-song*, 1872) *page* 436

185. Laurence Olivier as Romeo; oil painting by Harold Knight; four-colour photo-offset from colour separation negatives (from *Theatre*, Britain in Pictures series, Collins, 1948) *facing page* 436

186. Chiswick Reach at Low Tide—oil painting by Gwen Herbert (photo-offset reproduction from *Ports of London*, Britain in Pictures series, Collins, 1948) *facing page* 437

187. Wood-engraving from a drawing by Gustave Doré for *The Rime of the Ancient Mariner*, 1877; reduced *page* 438

188. Line drawing by Aubrey Beardsley for *The Rape of the Lock*, 1896; reduced *page* 441

189. Scraperboard drawing by C. F. Tunnicliffe (from *Farm on the Hill*, Faber & Faber, 1949) *page* 442

190. Plastocowell drawing by Gordon Noel Fisher to illustrate *The Castle of Otranto* by Horace Walpole *facing page* 444

191. Plastocowell drawing by Anthony Gross for the *Forsyte Saga* (Heinemann) *facing page* 445

192. Wood-engraving by Reynolds Stone for a part-heading for *Apostate* (Faber & Faber, 1946) *page* 446

193. Line drawing by Mervyn Peake for *The Rime of the Ancient Mariner* (Chatto & Windus, 1943); reduced *page* 448

194. Etching by Henri Matisse for *Poésies de Stéphane Mallarmé* (Skira, Lausanne, 1932); reduced *page* 450

195. Fourteenth-century jewelled gold binding of German origin for a manuscript of the Gospels written in letters of gold between A.D. 1000 and 1020 (in the Bibliothèque Nationale, Paris) *facing page* 480

196. Binding made for Grolier for *Origenis Adamantii Directa in Deum*, *c.* 1535 *facing page* 481

197. Cottage binding, Book of Common Prayer, 1678 *facing page* 484

198. Binding by Monnier of Baudello, *La Prima Parte de le Novelle*, London *facing page* 485
199. Cloth binding for *The Poems of Jean Ingelow*, London, 1867 *facing page* 492
200. Modern fine-edition binding by Paul Bonet (Paris, 1946) for *L'Apocalisse*, Milan, 1941 *facing page* 493
201. Printed bindings: *A Book of English Clocks*, King Penguin, 1947, and *Poems of Death*, Frederick Muller, 1945 *facing page* 496
202. Cloth bindings: *Moby Dick*, Cresset Press, 1946; *Roland*, Faber & Faber, 1937; *The Fool*, Faber & Faber, 1935; *Stephen Hero*, New Directions, New York, 1944; *Pride and Prejudice*, Chatto & Windus, 1946; *Swift*, Nonesuch Press, 1939 *facing page* 497
203. Lettered jacket by Dr. Akke Kumlien for *Postludium* (P. A. Norstedt & Söner, Stockholm, 1946) *facing page* 500
204. Design by Mogens Zieler for *Den Lille Aesop* (Gyldendal, Copenhagen, 1945) *facing page* 501
205. Wood-cut jacket design by Robert Sessler for *Dr. Dokter us Dr. Sunnegas* (H. R. Sauerlender & Co., *Aarau*, 1945) *facing page* 501
206. Lithographic jacket drawn on the stone by Pierre Gauchat for *Auf dem Amazonas* (Eugen Rentsch, Zurich, 1946) *facing page* 508
207. Jacket by Leonard Weisgard for *Mystery Tales for Boys and Girls* (Lothrop, Lee & Shepherd Co. Inc., New York, 1946) *facing page* 508
208. Jacket reproduced from a print by Thomas Malton for *Dublin* (Batsford, London, 1949) *facing page* 509
209. Jacket design by Mariette Lydis for *Le Lys de Brooklyn* (Hachette, Paris, 1946) *facing page* 509

PART ONE

*

PRINTING AND BINDING

I

A SURVEY OF DEVELOPMENT

JOHANN GUTENBERG of Mainz is usually credited with the invention of printing, and great honour has been accorded him on that account; but it is a rare thing for an invention to be the work of a single man, and in spite of the history books and the important service rendered by Gutenberg, printing is no exception to the rule: Gutenberg did not invent it.

The principle of the transfer of an image by impression is almost as ancient as the known history of man. The merchants of Babylonia and Sumeria and the noblemen of Egypt knew the use of seals, and perhaps used them as signatures, as rubber stamps are sometimes used to-day. The Babylonians impressed bricks with relief stamps perhaps carved out of wood, or else moulded in clay afterwards fired. They even reached the stage of impressing a whole 'page' of characters in one operation. They got no further. If it was not beyond their ingenuity to develop 'printing' of this kind, quantities of documents large enough to make the labour worth while were no doubt beyond their need.

The need apparently existed in China, for it was here that true printing began. The earliest printed book that survives was produced in China in A.D. 868, and contains an imprint giving the equivalent of this date. It was found with a quantity of manuscripts in 1900 in a sealed chamber in a cave in Szechuan, where it had apparently lain concealed since the eleventh century. So early a date may appear incredible to a European, and yet printing had been practised in Japan a century earlier for the mass production of paper charms; further, it is considered that printing was introduced into Japan from China, where it may have been known in the seventh century. To these achievements we of the West must pay humble tribute. To such an extent was printing advanced in China that in the year 932 the Chinese could put in hand an immense and ambitious project of printing a collection of the classics, and complete it in a hundred and thirty volumes in 953. They used the process called block printing, by which books were printed in Europe during the fifteenth century. Some time in the eleventh century a man called Pi-Sheng introduced separate, or movable, types. Chinese, however, not being written alphabetically and like most non-alphabetic scripts having an enormous number of characters, is among the scripts least suited to the use of movable type, and Pi-Sheng's invention expired with his death.

It is difficult to say how much influence Chinese printing could have had upon that of Europe, for the Far East was not altogether unknown to the men of the West in the fifteenth century A.D.; but it is interesting to remark that printing did not appear in Europe until after Marco Polo and other enterprising travellers had visited China and brought back with them tales full of impossibilities, improbabilities, and incredible actualities; and not until after the Golden Horde had swept half across Europe, bringing with it not only destruction but also knowledge and ideas.

With the close of the middle ages three kinds of book printing appeared in Europe, evidence of men's growing eagerness for books. Until this time books had been supplied by the labours of scribes, generally in monasteries, but their efforts could not result in large numbers of copies. With the advent of the press the days of the scribes were numbered, and the production of books, immensely increased, passed from the scriptorium into the hands of the lay craftsman.

The three kinds of printing were: that from wooden blocks, *à la Chine*; that from movable type attributed to Janszoon Coster; and Gutenberg's method, also using movable type. There is a difference among scholars about the precedence of these (and a question of the validity of Coster's work), some affirming that block books did not precede movable type, others that they did. We need not enter into the controversy here. It cannot be proved that block printing came first, as no European block book survives that is certainly earlier than the earliest book printed from movable type; but it is certain that it did not survive very long in competition with Gutenberg's process. From the standpoint of development, block printing is certainly the most primitive; and the Coster method of printing from movable type is cruder than Gutenberg's.

The block printer began with a planed piece of wood a little larger than the type area he intended to print on the page, and on the smooth surface he wrote the letters that comprised his text, or transferred them from a written sheet. It was necessary to have the letters on the wood in reverse, to obtain a print the right way round. When the writing was complete the surface of the wood was cut away wherever it was not covered by ink, so that finally only the letters stood, in relief, at the original level. This must have taken a great deal of time and a great deal of exacting labour, for a separate block had to be made for every page contained in the book it was intended to print. When the cutting was finished the block was ready for the press, and was capable of printing thousands of copies—certainly more than were likely to be required by the reading public of the time. The disadvantages of the process were numerous. If any error crept into the text in the cutting—and no printer is immune from misprints and the sins of omission and repetition—the block concerned could not be altered easily or satisfactorily. The initial cost of the blocks was high, because of the amount of labour that had to be expended on them, and that cost could not be spread over several books (as it can be with type); when the demand for the book was exhausted the blocks were of no more use than firewood.

Janszoon Coster is said to have begun experimenting with movable types at some unknown date in the fifteenth century. It may have occurred to him that if each letter were cut on a separate block, and a mould made from it so that a large number of replicas could be cast, the letters could be assembled to correspond with the text of the book to be printed, and after printing could be taken apart and reassembled for another book. There are many advantages in doing this. In any book each letter of the alphabet occurs many times over; in block printing no use can be made of this repetition, whereas it is the very factor that makes movable type advantageous. It is easier and cheaper to cast a number of letters than to carve them one by one, and the cost of assembling, or composing, type does not outweigh the saving. Again, correction is made easy, since only that portion of the page in which the offence lies need be altered, and that with far more facility than in block printing. Finally, type can be used repeatedly, until it wears out.

It is not certain how Coster made his type. If he did make moulds and cast his letters in metal, it was revolutionary enough, in all conscience; but his craftsmanship was poor and aesthetically the productions claimed for him cannot compare with those of Gutenberg and his followers.

Apparently about the same time Gutenberg, first in Strasbourg and later in Mainz, was working on the same problem. It is impossible to say when he first began, or whether he owed anything of his inspiration to the Dutchman of Haarlem, of whom he may or may not have heard. The existence of Coster as a printer is questionable; that Gutenberg existed and was a printer is certain, but what his contribution to printing was is not known. He did not invent the printing press or discover the principle of transfer by impression; he was not the first to think of making books mechanically. It seems possible, however, that his invention was the type mould and a method of making punches to produce matrices for use with the mould. If this is so it is no small thing, for the mould and the matrix are the basis on which the whole edifice of printing has been erected, and on which in large part it still stands. Without these two components neither composing machine nor printing press could have grown as they have. They represent the only way of making type. Without an efficient mould practicable types cannot be cast, and without type the progress of the whole world must have been inconceivably retarded. Whatever uncertainty there may be concerning Gutenberg's invention, there is ample evidence

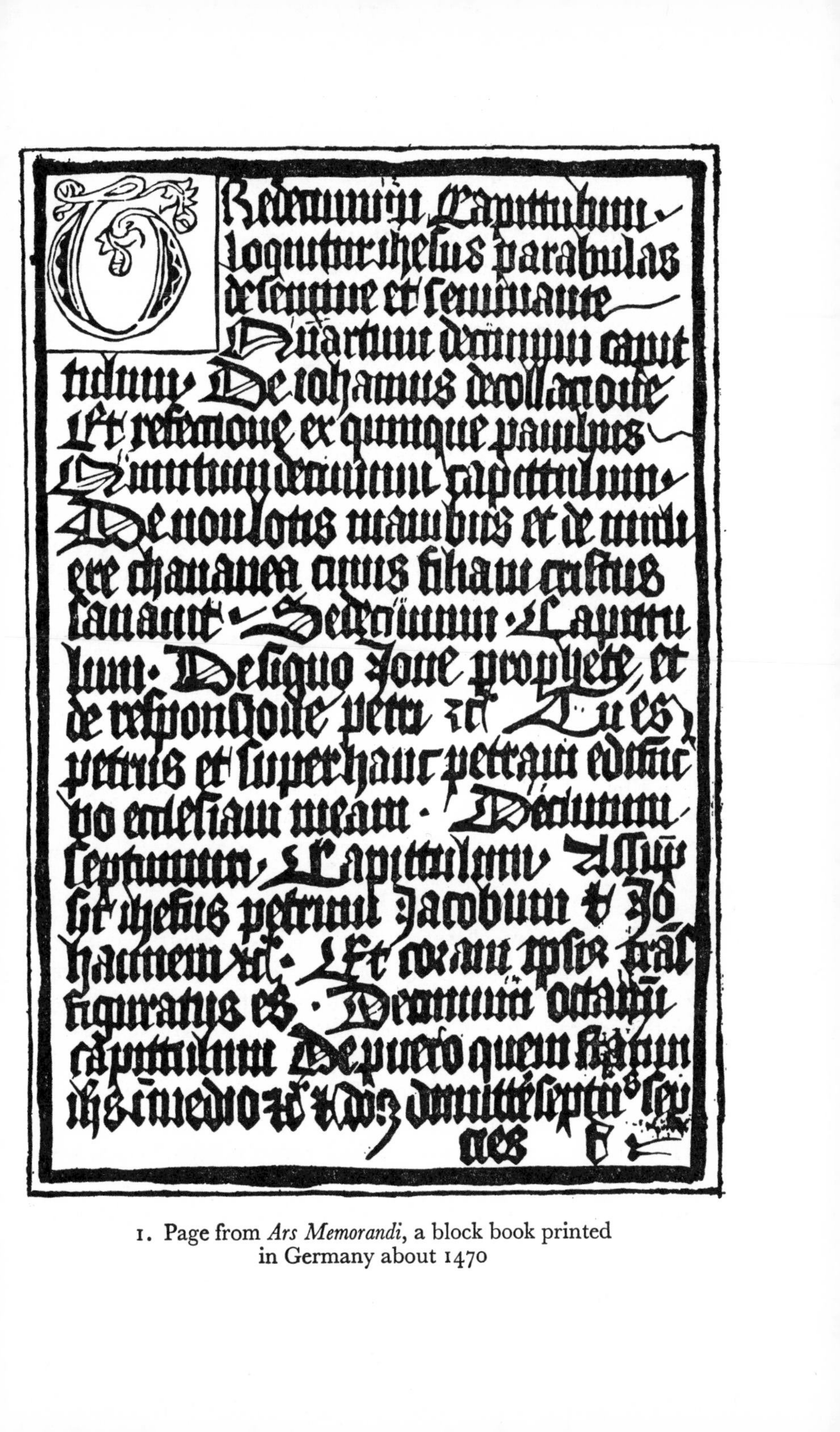

1. Page from *Ars Memorandi*, a block book printed in Germany about 1470

in his products that he had found a way of making type with a sufficient degree of precision and of printing from it competently. With his work printing as we know it to-day began.

Gutenberg was familiar with the work of goldsmiths and silversmiths, if he was not one himself. He must have known something of their methods of casting metal, and this knowledge would have been useful to him in dealing with the problem of casting type. He was backed financially by a goldsmith called Fust, who appears, over a period of years, to have spent a considerable amount of money on Gutenberg's ideas for little return up to 1454. In that year and in the following one Gutenberg printed some indulgences remarkable for the neatness and clarity of comparatively small sizes of type. They mark the first astonishing flowering of his work. In these years he was working also on the famous 42-line Bible, but he was handicapped by lack of funds and had to apply to Fust for further support. The goldsmith was now becoming impatient of the dilatory printer, and although he lent him the money, he later sued him for it, perhaps despairing of ever receiving a return on his capital. A couple of indulgences were not enough to satisfy Fust. The unfortunate Gutenberg lost the case and found himself sold up by his backer, who took over his apparatus and entered into partnership with one Peter Schoeffer, who may have been one of Gutenberg's assistants. This was in 1455, and in the following year the great Bible appeared, the fruit of Gutenberg's labours gathered by his former collaborators.

For a while Gutenberg disappeared into obscurity, during which he possibly printed another Bible in Bamberg, but later he emerged with another book, the *Catholicon*, conjecturally printed at Mainz in 1460. Eventually the Archbishop of Mainz gave him a pension that sufficed to make his last years comfortable; but no doubt he found it galling to see Fust and Schoeffer carrying his invention from success to greater success.

If Gutenberg did not invent printing, and though, in fact, we do not know exactly what he did invent, it is clear that with his work printing as we know it to-day commenced. His was the first successful venture in mass production, and, unlike those of the manufacturers of a later day, his products lost little in appearance and quality compared with the hand product that had gone before. He was fortunate enough to appear at the right time, when all over Europe a subtle air was clearing away the fogs and vapours of the middle ages; and as the medieval conception dissolved before a new type of mind, a demand for books arose that the scribes, copying books one by one, must eventually have found impossible to cope with. The infant craft of printing grew all at once mature to supply the demand; and in doing so it first impoverished the scribes and eventually put them out of business altogether.

With surprising rapidity in an age of uneasy transport printing spread throughout Europe. Men learned the mystery in Germany and then trekked over frontiers and set up their presses in typographically virgin lands; or they came from their own countries and carried the knowledge away with them. Gutenberg lived to see printing established in Italy (1465) and in Switzerland (1468), as well as in various towns of Germany; and after his death in 1468 the process of expansion continued with the setting up of presses in France (1470), the Netherlands (1470), Belgium (1473), Spain (1474), England (1476), Denmark (1482), Sweden (1483), and Portugal (1489).

The early printers were their own typefounders—was not typefounding the essence of the thing?—and indeed manufacturers of almost everything they required; but specialization soon appeared and separate workshops came into existence for the founding of type. Printing houses one by one closed down their foundries and allowed themselves to depend on the specialists for their material. This tendency led to a gradual improvement of the technical quality of type, and no doubt cheapened the cost of its manufacture; it also left the printers free to concentrate on their business of printing. The founders held their field from the end of the sixteenth century until the early part of the twentieth.

The history of printing from the sixteenth century to the end of the eighteenth is mainly a record of the development of type design, and with this I shall deal in a later chapter. Technically, various minor improvements during this period made printing more certain in its results and increased its capacity—the art of punch-cutting, for example, reached a high stage of development, and moulds for casting type were greatly improved—but there was nothing evident of the brilliant flare of invention that made the fifteenth century remarkable. The press of the year 1700 was in all essentials the same as that used by the printers of the incunabula, and a hundred years later no serious advance had been made other than to build the machine of iron instead of wood, of which it had been made hitherto. Certainly presses became larger, with many minor improvements, and their use in batteries to make printing cheaper and more expeditious was developed. The iron hand-press possessed distinct advantages over its wooden prototype, but it was out of date almost as soon as it appeared, despite the fact that it has continued in use into our time, for a new factor had entered the workshop and was about to invade the press room. It was the incalculable power of steam.

Steam was first used in a printing office in 1814 in the production of *The Times* newspaper. *The Times* obtained the services of two German engineers, Koenig and Bauer, who set up in *The Times* office a new machine that for the first time utilized in printing the power of steam coupled with rotary motion. It was an undoubted success, and though it was soon superseded by an improved version, it was the ancestor of the presses of the present day. The stop-cylinder and two-revolution machines used for printing books are derived from it, as well as those vast and ingenious affairs that turn out the morning papers in millions, already folded and counted. Later, steam too was superseded, and the presses were linked to the new power of electricity.

Type seems to have altered very little during all this time. There is no direct evidence to show what Gutenberg's type looked like, but there is something to show the shape of that used by a slightly later printer. About 1476 a book called *La Lèpre morale* was printed at Cologne, and an accident annoying for the printer but delightful for the historian caused one of the letters to be drawn from its fellows, to lie broadside upon them, and to be printed in this way. The impression shows plainly that the type of the fifteenth century looked very much like the type of the twentieth. The length of the shank has varied from time to time and from country to country, but the basic shape has remained. Early type may not have been cast with the precision of the modern typefounder, but it was precise enough to serve its purpose. No revolution in the character of type has occurred;

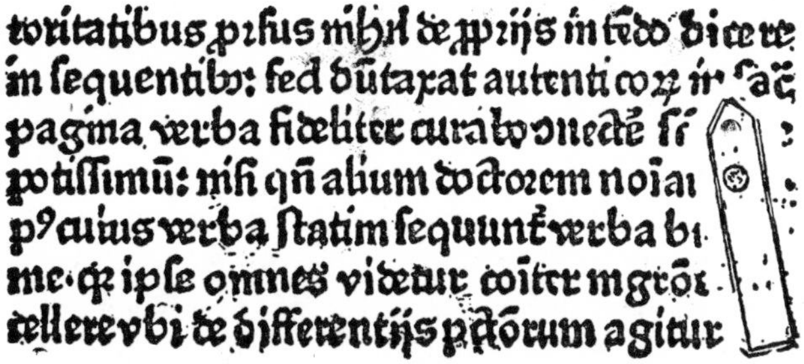

2. The shape of type in the fifteenth century

the revolution, when it came, and it was a long time coming, affected, not the type, but the manner of manufacturing and of composing it.

The basis of the alloy from which type is cast seems from the first to have been lead. By itself this metal is too soft to allow of many impressions, and at some early date tin and antimony were added to make an alloy that can be cast easily and that is hard and tough and resistant to wear.

For four centuries type was composed solely by hand. To compose a book meant picking up each letter singly and assembling it with others in an instrument called a composing stick according to the wording of the manuscript, which the compositor read phrase by phrase as he went along. Compositors achieve considerable dexterity in this work, but there is a limit to the speed of the fingers, and in the nineteenth century ingenious men were trying to devise a machine that would perform this operation more quickly. Various models were built and put to use in printing houses, but with little real success. There were several difficulties, and two in particular seemed insuperable. These were justification, or the spacing out of the line to the full width of the measure, and the problem of what to do with the type the machine composed after the book was printed and it was no longer needed. If the machine could compose the type, it was unable to distribute it again and to fill its own magazines, and this fact imposed a distinct limit upon its usefulness, upon the amount of time and labour it dispensed with.

The solution of the problem lay in an unexpected direction and was demonstrated by the invention of the Linotype composing machine, the first commercial model of which appeared in 1886. The magazine of this machine does not hold type, but matrices, or moulds, for casting the typeface; these matrices are assembled by the operation of a keyboard, and in conjunction with a mould for casting the body of the type, are used for casting a whole line in one piece. Justification is achieved by a system of wedges, and distribution is simply provided for—the used type going back into the melting-pot for re-use in the machine. The unexpectedness of the process lay in the combination of type-casting with composing.

In the nineties Tolbert Lanston of Washington was perfecting his Monotype machine. Despite its undoubted advantages there has for many printers always been something a little unsatisfactory in the Linotype method; for example, letter design has to be accommodated to the exigencies of the machine, and this is not always in the interest of the design; again, in the opinion of many, a solid line of type is not as satisfactory for printing as a line made up of separate types, in which each letter makes its own individual impression. The Monotype machine imposes the minimum of restriction on the designer or the design, and it produces separate types. This machine is also operated from a keyboard, and uses matrices and a mould for casting the type, as it is composed, from a crucible of molten metal. With the Monotype, as with the Linotype, one man can do in an hour as much work as six or seven hand-compositors can do in the same time; unlike the product of the Linotype, the completed Monotype page presents on the printing machine the same proposition as hand-set type, with this important difference, that every

3. Section of the Diamond Sutra, printed from wood blocks in China in A.D. 868

4. Indulgence printed from movable type by Gutenberg in 1455

letter is new and sharp. Monotype offers, too, all the advantages of easy correction and manipulation, and does not demand a procedure in handling different from that confirmed by the tradition of four centuries of printing.

Other composing machines appeared and achieved enough success to retain their hold on the market; notably there is the Intertype, a machine resembling the Linotype, and the now rare Typograph, which works on rather a different principle but casts a slug, or line of type all in one piece, as the Linotype does. Nothing, however, has successfully challenged Tolbert Lanston's invention in the composing and casting of movable type.

The Linotype and the Monotype have undergone much improvement since they first appeared, and are now much more effective machines than they once were. To some extent their uses are divergent, the Linotype being used principally in magazine and newspaper offices, where its solid slug is a distinct asset in the rush and bustle of getting out a newspaper, while the Monotype is used in book printing, for which the better design of its type faces and the convenience of movable type suit it. This is a generalization, however, and in no way exclusive; Monotype machines are found in some newspaper offices (*The Times* has a battery of them), and a great many books have been composed on the Linotype. In America the Linotype appears to be the staple machine for all purposes.

Among the models of the Monotype used by the printer is the super-caster. This is not a composing machine at all, but simply an instrument for casting large sizes of type for hand-composition, and it brings the printer back to the position in which his predecessors of the fifteenth century stood: he becomes his own founder again—though with the difference that he casts his type automatically and easily, and with precision.

The fact that such a machine as the super-caster should be necessary is evidence of the importance of the hand-compositor in modern printing. He has by no means been superseded. Where a large quantity of matter is to be set all in one size of type he cannot compete with the machine; but the machine is restricted in the setting of display matter in which several sizes of type are used, and to-day there is more display matter than ever. In the setting of books the compositor is responsible for title-pages, chapter headings, part titles, and so forth; and it is he who arranges the type produced by the machine in the columns or pages required for a newspaper or book.

Another machine for the compositor is the Ludlow. The compositor sets matrices, not type, by hand, in a special kind of composing stick and inserts them line by line in this machine, to cast from each one a solid line of type resembling a Linotype slug.

It will be seen from this account that we are to-day in the second of two periods of great technical advance in the craft of printing, the years between 1500 and 1800 approximately being barren of technical invention of great importance. During this interval there was much improvement in the manufacture and use of printing implements and materials—it contained, for instance, the experiments of John Baskerville with the printing qualities of paper, and the advent of the iron hand-press—but it was no more than modification of existing ideas. The fifteenth century was, typographically, a period of intense and brilliant revolution, and there has been nothing like it until comparatively modern times. With the industrial revolution came steam power and a fervent exploration and application of the principles of mechanics. We are still in the midst of the ferment. It is possible that in the future metal type will disappear, from the printing of books and periodicals, if not from all kinds of printing. Photographic composing machines, which produce lines of letter images on film, have appeared on the scene and are taking over increasing quantities of typesetting. Photo-set type on film may be used to produce lithographic plates for printing on lithographic machines, flat or curved relief plates for letterpress machines, or intaglio surfaces for gravure. Many prophets have foretold the ultimate disappearance of metal type, and any dispassionate examination of the future of printing will appear to confirm the forecast. On the other hand, as metal typesetting allows for considerable flexibility and adaptability in use and can be corrected more easily and cheaply than photo-typesetting, it is likely to be many years yet before the method of printing perfected by Gutenberg becomes quite obsolete.

That amiable, slow-moving proto-printer would be astounded by the development of printing in our time. If he perceived a ferment of ideas in his day, he would see nothing but a violent ebullition in ours. The technology of printing has been moving forward perceptibly since at least the year 1800, but since the Hitler war a sudden upsurge of technological development in nearly every field of printing has overlaid the simple business of putting ink on paper with so many new techniques and so many new jargons that there can be very few printers who know clearly what printing is now all about.

II

TYPE, SPACES, AND FURNITURE

APART from the products of slug-composing machines, with which I shall not deal in this chapter, there are two kinds of type in use in the printing house to-day, and these are founders' type and monotype.[1] The difference between them lies more in the manner of their manufacture than in their use by the printer, though there are superficial points of dissimilarity, and I shall mention them in a moment. In the meantime a description of founders' type will apply equally well to monotype.

I remarked in the previous chapter that the founding of type early became a specialized trade, separate from that of printing, and founders still exist to-day. It might have seemed that with the introduction of the Monotype, and particularly of the super-caster, the foundries were doomed, and perhaps they are. It is true that many founders have closed down and that their numbers have been further reduced by amalgamation, but those that remain, and in particular Continental founders, are competing strenuously with the threat to their existence. Foundry type is no longer used to any appreciable extent in the setting of text matter in books, but for display work it has peculiar advantages. In many printing houses display sizes of type are not returned to the melting-pot after use, as are text sizes, but are distributed back into type cases for further use, and the superior quality of the alloy of founders' type allows for harder and longer wear. Another factor, and perhaps the most important one in the survival of type foundries, is type design. Type de-

[1] It should be noted that the word 'Monotype' designates the machine as well as its product: monotype is produced by the Monotype. I have used the capital initial for the machine and lower-case for the type.

signs are copyright, and if a printer wishes to use a particular design of type issued by a founder it is only by buying that founder's type that he can do so.

Figure 5 shows a piece of founder's type with the various parts indicated and named. It will be noticed that the parts of type are named after parts of the human anatomy—an odd thing, though apt enough.

The body (or shank or stem) is all that part of the type from the feet to the flat surface at the upper end from which the

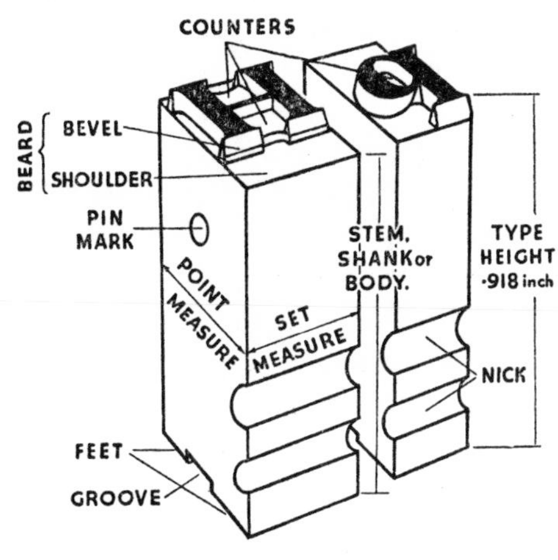

5. The parts of type

moulded letter rises. It is the foundation on which the letter rests, and it is more than that: for the body is precisely rectangular in section, and this fact allows large numbers of types to be placed side by side in words, and above and below in lines, as on this page, when the whole assembly can be put into a frame and held so rigidly by a system of wedges that type and frame can be lifted and transported in one piece. This would not be possible if the body were not rectangular and accurately made.

At the base of the body is the groove, between the feet. When type is cast a fragment of metal, the tang, is left adhering at the base from the orifice in the mould through which the molten metal is injected. This tang is broken off and the resulting roughness of the fracture ground down; the grinding produces the groove, and the groove inevitably produces the feet. The groove has no particular value in printing. Monotype has no groove.

Like any cubic form a piece of type has six surfaces. One of these is occupied by the feet and the groove. Of the vertical surfaces two are sides and one the back and one the front. In the front is a group of horizontal furrows, known collectively as the nick, and this has a twofold purpose. When he is setting type the compositor has no time to look at the face of every individual piece to see which is the right way up, and the nick, which in English and American types is in the front and level with the base of the letter, tells him at a glance, in whatever attitude the type may be lying, or he feels it with his finger as he picks it up. The nick also serves the purpose of identification. Wide furrows are combined with narrow ones, and square ones with round ones, to make a compound nick that is characteristic for every letter of the particular size and design of type, thus distinguishing it from other founts. This system is particularly useful when there are two type faces of similar appearance in the composing room, when the difference in nicks prevents, or should prevent the type faces, from becoming mixed. It should be remarked that although there may be no difficulty in distinguishing between two types on the printed page it is not at all as easy to distinguish them in metal. Nevertheless, the days when the nick system was really invaluable have passed with the advent of the Monotype. When type had to be distributed back into the cases from which it was composed the nick saved much inconvenience and annoyance arising from the mixture of types—a calamity that sometimes happened in the best regulated of printing houses because of the number of people who had access to the cases, and among them apprentices of varying skill and experience, who had to have access, and perhaps had to make mistakes, if they were to learn their craft properly; at such times the atmosphere of the composing room was blue. Nowadays book sizes of type are not founders', but monotype, and this is not distributed but melted down for the further use of the machine; while those display sizes that are distributed are large enough to be recognized easily without any assistance from the nick. All that is necessary now, and all that the Monotype provides, is a simple nick to distinguish the front from the back. The back of the type is the surface opposite the front, and it is blank. Continental types, however, have the nick in the back.

Blank, too, is one of the sides. The other, in foundry type, bears the pin-mark, or occasionally two pin-marks. This mark is of no sort of use to the printer, except that in larger sizes of type, where the mark is larger, it sometimes bears the name of the founder, and reminds him, when he wishes to be reminded, where he got the fount.

The remaining surface, the upper end, is the business end. On this surface the letter is moulded, and it is the face of the letter that is inked—Figure 5 shows the face black, as it would look after the inking roller has passed over it. The face of type is the part that demonstrates itself to the reader, and on its shape depends the character of the letter on the printed page, by which the type is judged aesthetically. The quality of the metal of which the type is cast and the manner of its casting, the finish and accuracy of the body, and the nick system are technical matters subserving the purpose of type, which is the impression of ink in a predetermined pattern upon paper; but the design of the face enters into the field of aesthetics besides that of utility, and it is all important. This is so well understood among printers and people having to do with print that type designs are more often spoken of as type faces than otherwise—in fact, it may be said that the purpose of the type designer is to produce type faces. A printer may have a particular design in a dozen different sizes, but it is all one face. A type-founder's catalogue is seldom called a list of type designs, but nearly always a list of type faces.

Between the surface and the edge of the body are a steeply sloping portion and a flat portion, and these together are the beard. That part of the beard below the lower serifs is called the shoulder, and is occupied in the case of such letters as the g and y by the descender.

In italic founts of type these descenders often project beyond their own body and rest on the shoulder of the adjacent letter (see Figure 6); the same thing happens with other letters in italics, for instance the right arms of *W* and *V*, the tail of *Q*, the head and tail of *f*, and many others. These projecting parts are called kerns, and on the printed page their presence may be detected in letters that extend over or under their neighbours.

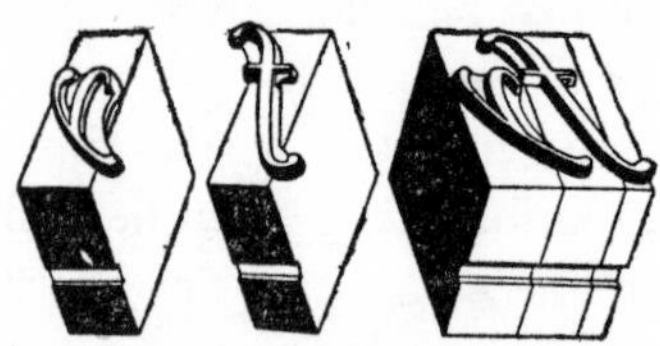

6. Examples of kerned letters

If it were not for kerns proper spacing of italic letters in a word would be impossible, and what we may term the 'calligraphy' of the face would be seriously affected, because the design would have to be altered to confine the letters concerned to the area of their own bodies. The sweep and freedom of italics must thereby be lost. This shift has had to be resorted to in the italic faces of the line-casting machines.

Type in any particular country is a standard height from foot to face, and in England and America and some other countries it is ·918 of an inch—nearly the height of a 5p piece. There is no magic in this figure—it seems merely to have been that adopted by a group of founders influential enough to make their figure the standard. All sizes of type are the same height, so that when assembled together they present an even, plane surface to the paper; thus any combination of type sizes may be used, and the reader may refer for examples to the large initial at the head of each chapter in this book, standing cheek by jowl with the letters of the text.

A distinction should be noted here to prevent possible confusion later on. Type height, or height to paper, is not the same thing as height of face. The latter is the measurement of the printed character from the serif at the foot to the serif at the head.

Type height, since it is standard, does not concern the printer in itself; though he may be concerned with departures from it caused by wear of the face or by foreign bodies under the feet, the one causing the letter affected to print too lightly and the other too heavily. Type, however, is measured in two other ways that concern him a great deal, and these are point-wise and set-wise measurements.

Type sizes are measured in points, a point equalling 0·013837 inch—which is near enough for most matters to one seventy-second of an inch; the odd decimal figure is out of all reason, the expression of a standard that is pragmatic rather than logical. The measurement is taken from the front of the body to the back, and since, naturally, the face is proportionate to the size of the body, point size is an indication of the size of the face. It is a sufficient statement of the distance from the tail of the longest descender, generally p or q, to the top of the longest ascender, the letter l, say. It is not, however, a reliable indication of x-height, which is the size of the letter x and other such letters as a, e, r, w, etc., that have neither ascender nor descender. It is by these letters that the apparent size of type is judged, and in different faces they are not in the same proportion to the ascenders and the descenders. An example will make this clear:

This is a line of 11 point Perpetua
and this is set in 11 point Times New Roman

These two lines appear to be set in two quite different sizes of type, yet they are both the same point size and a dozen lines of either would occupy exactly the same depth of space. Perpetua, having long descenders and ascenders, and a small x-height, would appear to have more space between the lines than Times, which has short descenders and ascenders and a large x-height. A type like Times, which is 'large on the body', must sacrifice something to achieve its effect, and what it sacrifices is the just proportion between the x-height and the length of descenders and ascenders. A type that is large on the body may not be very legible if it is set without leading. It will be clear from this that point size is not a good indication of the apparent size of type, and in fact there is no ready-made rule that can be relied on; the only way of knowing whether a type is large or small on the body is to know what that particular face looks like—in other words, by experience.

Standardization in point sizes is young in the history of printing, for it was not until after 1900 that it began to overset the English system, although in the United States, from which it came, it had been adopted some time before. Nevertheless, there was nothing new in the idea. The French—that 'logical people'—had adhered to the Didot system, which is much the same thing in principle, a hundred and fifty years before the English determined upon standardization of type sizes. The Didot system now extends throughout most of Europe.

Standardization, more, rationalization, was sorely needed. The question was a bone of contention between printers and typefounders; the latter, reasonably enough, since they did not have to use the types that they themselves cast, balked at the expenditure of capital necessary if they were to adapt their plant. But they could not uphold for ever the manifestly absurd English system. What has come to be called the English system of type sizes was indeed irrational, and nothing could have been more undependable. The sizes went by charming names, hallowed by long custom, and rooted in the past; but they were woolly in meaning. Below is a list of the names, with the nearest point equivalent of the sizes they indicate:

English	*Point*	*English*	*Point*
Minikin	3	Nonpareil[1]	6
Brilliant	3½	Minion	7
Gem	4	Brevier[1]	8
Diamond	4½	Bourgeois[1]	9
Pearl	5	Long Primer[1]	10
Ruby	5½	Small Pica	11

[1] Pronunciation is not what might be expected. Brevier is pronounced 'breveer'', nonpareil 'non'prel', bourgeois 'burjoy'ce', and primer 'prim'mer'.

English	*Point*	*English*	*Point*
Pica[1]	12	Great Primer	18
English	14	Double Pica	22
2-line Brevier	16	2-line Pica	24

The progression of type sizes in this list is very good, and we have not bettered it; indeed, it would have been perfect if the sizes had borne any real mathematical relation to each other, but they did not do so, for there was no common unit on which they could be based. The rubs were multitudinous. As the sizes were not accurately related, the compositor could not count on two lines of pica, for instance, occupying the same amount of space as one line of two-line pica, and this made any combination of type sizes unnecessarily difficult and troublesome. Even the names were a snare. Double pica was the equivalent of neither two lines of pica nor of one of two-line pica; nor could it be depended on to be exactly twice the size of small pica. These confusions might have been supposed to have been enough, but the type-founders thought otherwise. Each had his own idea of the meaning of each name, and the small pica of one founder was not necessarily the same size as the small pica of another; indeed, it was much more likely to be different. A printer using types from two different foundries had to keep them separate, a task in which even the nick could not always help him, many of the accessories of type having no nick—spaces, for instance. Spaces supplied with the fount might have the nick of the fount; then if he had several different founts of the same size from the same founder, he would have a quantity of spaces all of the same size but with a variety of nicks. Mixing of founts in the case was very liable to occur, a calamity not to be despised, as I have indicated; while the compositor, endeavouring to justify his types, became a skilful bodger, introducing strips of card or paper to make up the difference.

People who ought to know better, journalists, for instance, may still talk glibly about minion, nonpareil, english, etc., as though these were current technical terms. In fact they are as dead as they are ever likely to be; only the words nonpareil and

[1] Pica is pronounced 'py'ka'.

pica have survived, and any other of the English names in the mouth of a printer is a sort of hoary joke—another printer will know what he means, and what he means is the nearest point equivalent. Nonpareil to-day means exactly six points, and pica is twelve.

The English system has given way to the point system completely. To-day it is very rare to find any of the older sizes in use: the compositor can now count upon his type being exactly the size it is stated to be, from whatever founder it may have come, and count upon the sizes being in strict point relation one with another. The result is that what were once annoying and time-consuming difficulties, involving precarious bodging for their solution, are now reduced to problems in simple arithmetic.

Type faces are classified into three kinds among printers, and this classification depends partly upon size and partly upon the design of the face. The three kinds are book faces, jobbing faces, and poster types. There are no hard edges in these divisions. Book faces are those that are suitable for the text of books, jobbing faces those that are suitable for display, and poster types the large types used for placards. The larger sizes of book faces can be used as jobbing faces, the smaller sizes of some jobbing faces for bookwork, and the largest sizes of either for posters.

The smallest type in ordinary use to-day is 6 point, though smaller sizes are available and are used for special purposes—in timetables and small ads, for example; and the largest size ordinarily used in bookwork is 72 point—larger sizes are found on wrappers. Page 45 shows the progression of type sizes from 6 point to 72 point. This range is the one usually available, but not all series are complete. Some differ in not possessing a 16 point, while a few include 20 point or 22 point—these two sizes indicate that the type face in which they are found is of Continental origin. The largest size of type capable of being cast by the Monotype is 72 point.

Above 60 point the body of the type is usually made hollow, the groove being deepened and widened until the body is

6 pt. This page shows specimens of Caslon Old Face in sizes ranging from 6 point to 72 point. This face was cut in 1722 by William Caslon, who had been an engraver of the stocks and barrels of guns.

8 pt. Its appearance marked the end of the supremacy in England of Continental type designers as founders. Caslon Old Face is a type of excellent moderation and good proportion.

10 pt. The ascenders and descenders are not unusually long nor are they unusually short, and Caslon can be described as a face of average

11 pt. or medial line. From the foundry started by William Caslon

12 pt. in London at the beginning of the eighteenth century

14 pt. nearly every other English foundry of importance

16 pt. was derived in one way or another, and the

18 pt. Caslon Letter Foundry itself continued in

24 pt. existence until 1937, when it

30 pt. was merged with that of

36 pt. Stephenson, Blake

42 pt. which also owes

48 pt. its origin to the

60 pt. Caslon

72 pt. house.

7. A page of Caslon to show the progression of type sizes from 6 point to 72 point. Other sizes may be found in other faces—4½, 7, 9, 13 point, for instance.

no more than an arch of metal on which the face is supported; this cutting away is done to reduce weight, for it should be remembered that type metal is mostly lead, and is consequently heavy. Large sizes of Monotype have outsize nicks back and front—see Figure 8.

Beyond about 96 to 108 point type ceases to be made of metal, and boxwood takes its place. This also helps to reduce weight. Though wood cannot be worked to the accuracy of metal, it is of little moment, as extreme accuracy is unnecessary in poster sizes. Because of this it would be misleading, besides being cumbrous, to denote the sizes as so many points, and they are measured in lines: a 'line' is roughly twelve points, and a twelve-line type is therefore (approximately) 144 points deep.

Besides being measured from back to front, type is also measured from side to side, and this measurement is termed set. It is essential to the estimator if he is to work out with any degree of accuracy the space a certain amount of copy will occupy when set in a particular type. It will be noticed that as x-height differs in two different faces, so too does the width of each letter differ in the two faces, as the following example shows:

This type is 11 point 9½ set (Bembo)
This type is 11 point 11 set (Times New Roman)

Set measurement is obtained by assuming—and it is a reasonable assumption—that the letters of a face are in fairly constant proportion to the widest letter of the fount, and the width of the widest letter—usually M or W—is measured in points to give the set figure.

SPACES

Under this heading I include all spacing material used in conjunction with type, though in fact only one kind of spacing material is properly called spaces. The others are leads, clumps, reglets, quotations, and furniture.

Spaces have no representation on the printed page, unless a blank can be called representation, but to the printer they are something solid and tangible. The gaps between the words you are reading, as well as the large voids of blank pages and chapter endings, are in type so much solid metal. Type, as I have indicated, is held together when assembled, or composed, by lateral pressure, and there must be something to occupy the blanks or the pressure could not operate. That something is the space, under whatever name it may go.

Examples of the kind of space used between words can be seen clearly in Figure 8; it needs little description, for it looks very much like a piece of type, except that it has no face and is not as high as type and therefore neither receives ink nor touches the paper.

Founders' spaces are made in nine different thicknesses for each size of type, and each thickness is based on the thickness of the em quad. An em quad is a space as thick as the type size it belongs to is deep; thus a ten-point em is ten points wide, a twelve-point em twelve points wide. The en[1] quad is half this thickness; next there are thick spaces, equal to a third of an em; middles, equal to a quarter; thins, equal to a fifth; and hair spaces, which vary with the type size from half a point to one point thick. Wider than the em quad are two-em, three-em, and four-em quads, which are used for filling up the short lines at the ends of paragraphs.

Monotype spaces do not conform to these proportions, and I will deal with them in the chapter on composing machines. The largest space available on the Monotype is the em quad, which is not always a true square, but equals in width the set of the face.

It frequently happens that more space is required between the lines of type than the type itself allows when set solid, and when this is so the compositor inserts a lead. This is a flat piece of metal, a space of a special kind, as long as the line is wide and varying in thickness; leads are made 1, 1½, 2, 3, and 4 points thick. Leads six and twelve points thick or more change their

[1] The names are said to come from the letters m and n, which are cast on bodies of (approximately) em and en width respectively. In a busy and noisy composing room there is no time to distinguish between the closely similar sounds of em and en and printers call these spaces muttons and nuts.

names and become clumps—why 'clumps' I do not know, but there is something endearing in the older technical terms of printing (Figure 9).

Clumps are also made of wood, when they are called reglets.

Very large quads, used for filling up large areas of space, are termed quotations. They are usually hollow, simply four walls, sometimes strengthened by one or more internal girders.

Quotations are nowadays included under the heading furniture, but furniture proper is still larger than quotations. Metal furniture is made on a girder principle, and can be had in almost any multiple of 12 point ems long and wide. Wooden furniture is, of course, solid; it is also made in sizes of multiples of twelve-point ems. Both kinds are used for filling up large blanks such as blank pages and the wide open spaces of dedications, half-titles, etc.

The pica was once the unit by which furniture, length of line of type, depth of page, and many other things were measured; now the unit is the twelve-point em, which has assumed the name 'pica'. In this book, as in the printing house, the words em and en with no qualification of size will invariably mean the twelve-point em and en. The twelve-point em is nearly equal to a sixth of an inch, since seventy-two points are just a shade under an inch.

8. Types of various sizes, with four sorts to show nicks, pin marks, and the arched casting of larger sizes

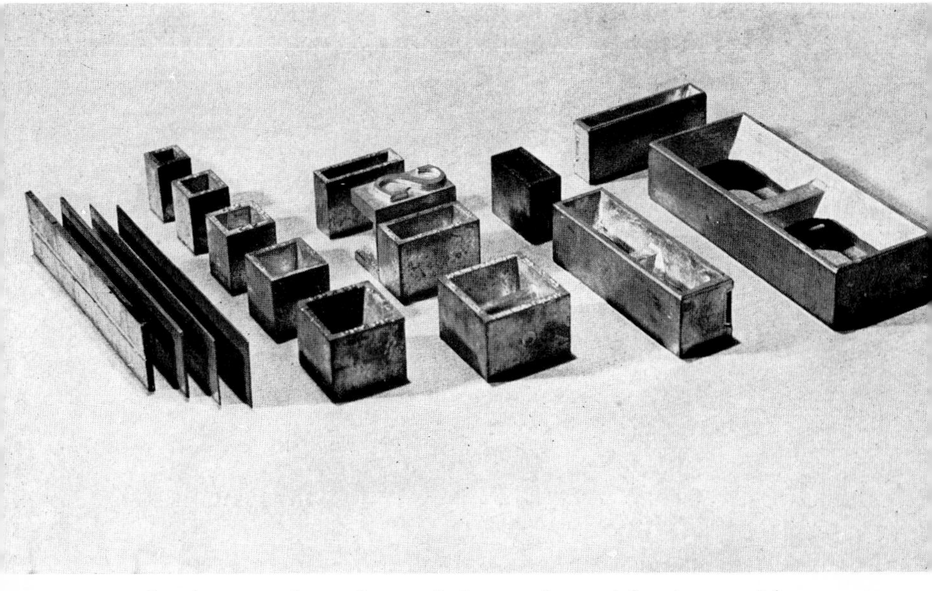

9. Leads, quotations of several sizes, and metal furniture, with a 72-point letter to show scale and type height

10. A compositor setting type from a double case

11. A closer view of the compositor's hands to show the action in detail

III

COMPOSING AND THE COMPOSITOR

A PIECE of type is a unit designed to combine with other units to make a composite whole. The act of assembling the units is called composing, and the man who performs the operation is the compositor.

He is an ancient figure in the history of printing. The conception of movable type presupposed his coming into existence. From the first he had to have special qualities. Nimble fingers and strong, sure hands are necessary, but they are among the least of his qualifications. In an age when to be able to read at all was to be counted something of a scholar, he had to be able to read more quickly and more accurately than most people; further, he had to be able to spell, and literacy and orthography are not the same thing. Nowadays—and it is in no small degree due to the printer—it is no uncommon thing to be able to read; but accurate reading is by no means common, and by comparison the ability to spell is rare. Orthography appears to be innate, a gift of birth, and if you do not possess it you will have to labour greatly to achieve it, and possibly fail.

In some of the incunabula there are woodcuts showing scenes inside printing houses, and in these woodcuts there often appears a compositor working at the case that holds his types. The alteration and decay of centuries have turned the bones of these men to dust and erased their memory, but they have not vanished utterly, for in the modern comp at his frame they labour still. Essentially there is little change. The costume is different, the tools and materials are infinitely improved, but the compositor of to-day is doing the same kind of work, in recognizably the same way, as his fifteenth-century predecessors.

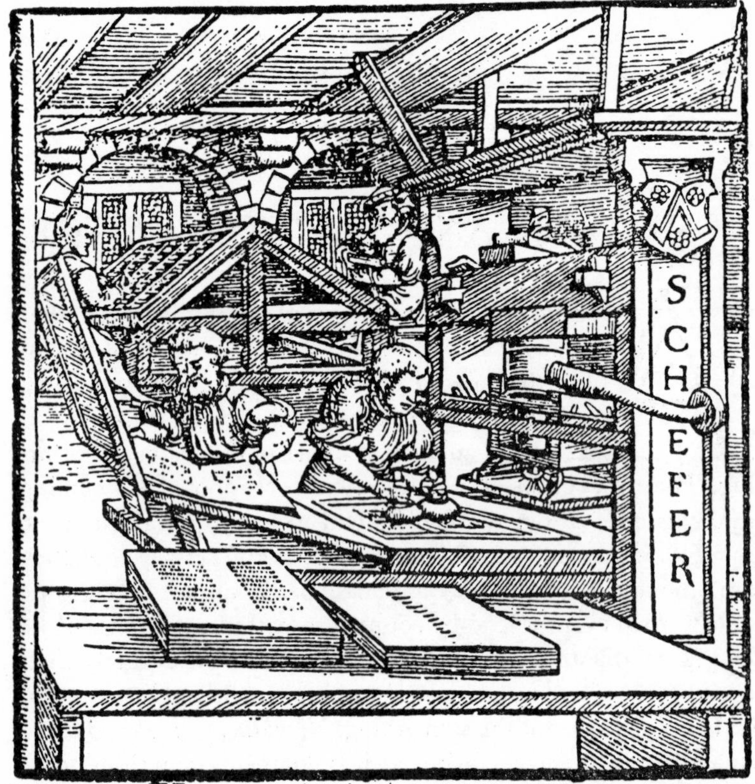

12. An early printing house. In the background are the compositors at their cases. In the foreground are two pressmen, one taking off the sheet, while the other inks the forme with a pair of ink-balls.

He has lost something in prestige, no doubt, because literacy is common now, and the responsibility of design has been mainly taken from him; but he can, if he wills, be a craftsman still, and no mere labourer. And his craft is still a mystery to the layman.

So far as the type and implements with which the old compositor worked are concerned, we have more than contemporary woodcuts to go by. In the Musée Plantin-Moretus at Antwerp a whole printing house has survived, arranged as it was in 1576. It is the office of the famous printer, Christopher Plantin. A modern compositor would not, I think, find it altogether unfamiliar; even a modern pressman, working in a way that might seem to have progressed out of all recognition compared with the sixteenth century, would need no introduction to the primitive presses.

The compositor's work is to compose the separate letters of type in accordance with the author's manuscript or typescript, which he has before him as he works. With his coat off and his shirt sleeves rolled up so that they cannot brush against the type and upset it, and with his clothes protected by a white apron with a bib, he stands before a frame on which are two cases resting at an angle, one behind and above the other (Figure 13). A case is not what is ordinarily meant by the word, but a tray a little over an inch deep and 32½ inches wide by 14½ inches from back to front. Each of the two cases is divided by partitions into a number of boxes, the upper case into boxes all of the same size, and the lower case into boxes of various sizes. The two cases together contain a fount of type, which is made up of the following characters:

A B C D E F G H I J K L M N O P Q R S T U V
W X Y Z Æ Œ

A B C D E F G H I J K L M N O P Q R S T U V
W X Y Z Æ Œ

a b c d e f g h i j k l m n o p q r s t u v
w x y z æ œ fi ff fl ffi ffl

á à ä â é è ë ê í ì ï î ó ò ö ô ú ù ü û

1 2 3 4 5 6 7 8 9 0 £ &

- , ; : . ? ! — ' ( ) [ ] * † ‡ § ‖ ¶

In practice, not all the fount is kept in the pair of cases, and room is made wherever possible for characters outside the fount but used with it, such as fractions and arithmetical signs. To include some of these the accented letters must often give up their boxes in the upper case and be stored elsewhere. Spacing material must, of course, be easily available, and spaces of the various thicknesses are kept in boxes in the upper and lower cases.

The manner in which the characters are distributed among the boxes of the pair of cases is termed the lay of the case, and is shown in Figure 13, which also shows the relative positions of the two cases in use. The upper case contains the capitals and small capitals and a number of the less frequently used

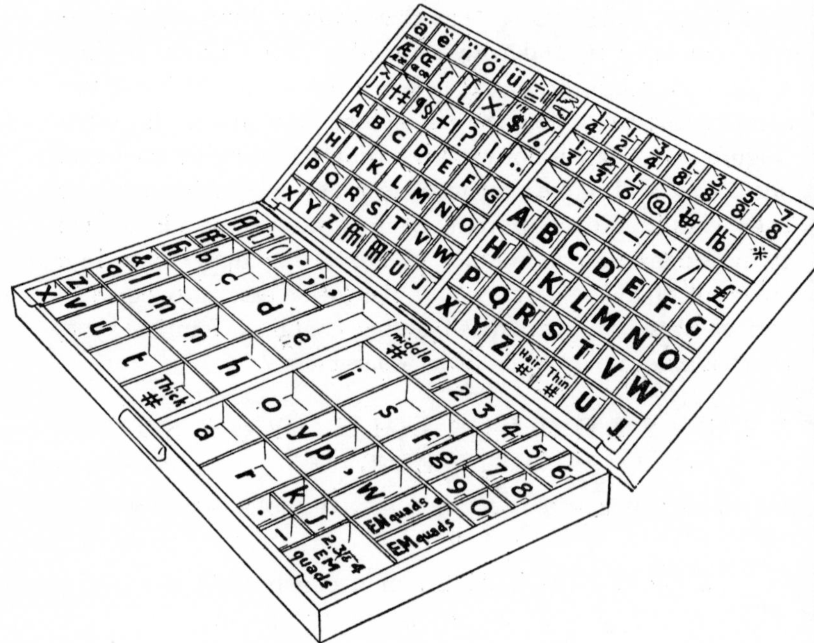

13. A pair of cases, showing the lay

signs and fractions, etc. The arrangement of the alphabet is conventional except for one peculiarity, the expulsion of J and U from their normal positions and their addition after Z, like an afterthought. And in fact, it is an afterthought. In the early days of printing J and U did not exist, I and V doing their work; but the distinction of sound was beginning to be indicated in writing by a distinction of character, which in time was introduced in type. By that time, however, compositors had become used to a lay without J and U, and to insert them in the upper case in their alphabetical order would have meant altering the relative position of every letter after I, and confusing the case. So J and U were put in at the end of the alphabet, and there they have remained.

The peculiar arrangement of the lower case, with its boxes of different sizes and its alphabet completely out of order, is in fact no more peculiar than the arrangement of the keys on a typewriter. Both arrangements are attempts to solve what is fundamentally the same problem, and it seems to me that the typographical (and very much earlier) solution is less arbitrary and more efficient than that of the designer of the typewriter keyboard; nevertheless, it is not perfect. In any language the several letters of the alphabet are used in widely varying proportions, and in English and most European languages the letter most frequently used is e; therefore e must have a large box to hold a large number of types, and it must be placed in the case so that it will be convenient for the compositor's hand. The other letters are apportioned boxes of position and size according to their frequency of use, and the result is the lower case shown.

In some printing houses one of the boxes in the case is set aside for the reception of defective or battered types, which can be resold to the founder as scrap metal; this box is known as the hell box, because it is where the bad type goes.

This lay is in the main standard throughout the English-speaking world. There are minor variations from printer to printer—infrequent letters like k and z and some of the signs are apt to be unsettled of habitation in either case, but the main arrangement is always the same. A compositor may go from one printer to another with no fear of having to learn a new lay at each remove. This is important, because the act of composing type becomes ingrained as a habit; and habits are notoriously difficult to alter. If the lay of the case were unique in each printing house the compositor would have to learn it when he went there and at the same time disengage himself from the lay he had worked with before. It would be weeks perhaps months, before he became an efficient workman with the new lay.

Because they are kept in the lower case small letters are invariably known among printers as lower-case letters, or more simply, lower-case; and capitals, for a similar reason, but not invariably, are known as upper-case. A printer will speak of upper and lower-case, or caps and lower-case; a man who spoke of caps and small letters would at once be suspected of knowing very little about printing. The phrase 'caps and smalls' does exist in typographical language, but it means capitals and small capitals.

The frame on which the pair of cases rests at working level was once nothing more than a framework of timber, and from this the name is derived; but for many years these frames have been utilized as racks for storing cases of type, and modern ones are made of steel and so designed that they are almost completely dustproof when they are full of cases—they are really cabinets, but they are still popularly called frames. The top case in a frame at which a compositor works is used by him for storing the tools of his trade and papers appertaining to the job; and some manufacturers of the cabinet kind of frame recognize this and provide a drawer for the purpose; otherwise each frame usually contains cases of one face of type in various sizes, and italics.

When composing, the compositor stands rather to the left of the middle of the case so that his right hand shall have unhindered access to all parts. In his left hand he holds a composing stick set to the measure of the line required. The stick is really a small, three-sided tray, five-eighths of an inch deep, about two inches wide, and for bookwork about eight inches long (see Figure 11). One of the side walls is adjustable as a slide and can be fixed firmly in any position along the stick by means of a simple screw or wedge mechanism. The measure the stick is set to is the width of the line required, and this is calculated in ems—the line you are reading now, for instance, is twenty-four ems wide. The stick is held as in the photograph, with the thumb inside, and a brass setting rule is used inside the stick

14. A printing house in the sixteenth century

so that there is a smooth hard surface on which the type can slide.

The copy to be set rests on the upper case, over the small capitals, where it can be easily seen and need not often be disturbed. The compositor reads the first few words, memorizing the wording and punctuation exactly, and proceeds to compose the type. Just as a typist knows the keyboard of a typewriter so that she can type without looking at it, so the compositor knows his case. His right hand goes without hesitation to the boxes holding the letters required, and the left hand follows with the stick. As each letter is picked up it is conveyed to the stick and the thumb of the left hand holds it in position in the growing line. At the end of each word a space is added and the following word commenced. The type is not inspected as it is picked up to see which is the right way round of the face; the compositor can tell by the shape of the type on which end the face is, and the nick shows the right way round of the letter.

When the measure of the stick is all but full the compositor must pause and take stock of the line. If he is in the middle of a word he must consider whether he has room to complete it, or whether it must be divided and a hyphen inserted; or if he has completed the last word he must consider whether it is possible to get another word into the line. In any case the line must be justified—it must be spaced out until it is a firm fit in the measure. If there is a little room left at the end of the line, but not enough to include another word or part of a word, the spaces between the words are removed one by one and wider ones inserted, until the line fits the measure to which the stick has been set. If another word can be included the spaces are reduced to make room for it. This is the solution of that subtle mystery that puzzles every small boy—how the lines of a printed book come to be all exactly of the same length. It is unlikely that the line can be spaced out with spaces all of the same width, and the compositor spaces—or should space—unevenly but in such a way that the eye is persuaded that the spacing is equal. More space can be inserted between letters with vertical strokes, for example between a word ending in d and one beginning in h; and neighbouring words ending and beginning with rounded letters can do with less space.

Not only should the spaces be optically equal in the line, they should be equal, or more or less so, over the whole book. This is not always easy to achieve, and is particularly difficult in narrow measures, but there is no doubt that text matter looks better evenly spaced.

At the beginning of a paragraph an em quad is inserted to give the paragraph indention, and at the end two-em, three-em, and four-em quads are set as necessary after the full point to bring the final short line out to the full measure. It should be remembered that it is essential that all lines should be the same length in type metal, even though they may not appear so on the printed page.

When the line is completed the setting rule is transferred from the back to the front and the composing of the next line is commenced.

Type cannot be composed by hand as quickly as words can be read, nor even as quickly as they can be written. The speed of hand composing on straightforward matter is between one thousand and fourteen hundred ens per hour, which is, roughly, that number of letters and spaces. The economy of printing is not in the setting up of the type, but in the facility, once it is set up, with which large numbers of copies can be printed.

If more space is required between the lines than the type itself allows for, a lead of the appropriate thickness and length is inserted after each line.

When the stick is full the compositor reads it before emptying it, to discover any errors he may have made. If there are any they are corrected—the offending letter is abstracted and the correct one put in its place, and any difference in width made up by respacing the line as necessary.

The way in which a compositor reads type is apt to strike the layman as something marvellous. The compositor sets the type with the face upside down; and this is how he reads it. Besides being upside down, it is also, as is to be expected, in reverse. The paragraph you have just read appears like this to the compositor:

the compositor:
reverse. The paragraph you have just read appears like this to
Besides being upside down, it is also, as is to be expected, in
type with the face upside down; and this is how he reads it.
the layman as something marvellous. The compositor sets the
The way in which a compositor reads type is apt to strike

Reading in this way becomes a mere question of habit, and, like swimming and riding a bicycle, once it is acquired it is seldom lost again. After many years' absence from printing I find myself still able to read, without effort, as a compositor reads.

Type is not read with the face upside down for any idle reason. By reading in this way the lines can be taken in their proper order, and, what is important, the normal habit of reading from left to right is preserved. The compositor's way of reading, which seems at first so very strange, in fact is the way involving the least disturbance of the normal manner of reading. Anyway, the custom is fixed in the compositor's subconscious, and if he were handed a page of type 'top side up' he would do what any other man would do if he were handed a book upside down—turn it round.

An apprentice learning to read type must mind not only his p's and q's, according to the maxim, but also his d's and b's as well, and other letters too. The letters p and q, as they are reversed, are particularly liable to be confused by the unwary lad who has not altogether acquired the habit of reading type; worse still, if he forgets that he is reading upside down, his confusion will be increased by his taking them for d and b.

After reading and correction the type in the stick is lifted out. Compositors achieve great dexterity in the lifting of hundreds of separate pieces of type with no more support than a couple of leads and the pressure of their fingers, and can carry or move type around in a way that might seem highly precarious to the layman.

When, as occasionally does happen even with the best of comps, a disaster occurs and the type falls or collapses, the resulting disordered heap is the famous printer's pi. Formerly, when all type was founders', pi was given to an apprentice to sort out and distribute back into the case; to-day, with monotype, it is simply shot into a box to be melted down for the caster.

The type from the stick is placed on a galley, a shallow, three-sided tray of zinc or steel—one of them may be seen resting on the frame in Figure 10. Galleys are made in a multitude of different sizes for different purposes, a book galley being about two feet long and six to eight inches wide and rather more than half an inch deep. Each stickful of type is placed on the galley as it is completed, until at last there is a slab of type about eighteen or twenty inches long (Figure 15). This is the equivalent of three or more pages, but the exact length is no matter yet—the galley is only a temporary receptacle.

When there is sufficient type on the galley a piece of metal furniture is set against the last line to prevent it from falling over and a long strip of wooden furniture is placed down the whole length of the free edge; between this strip and the side of

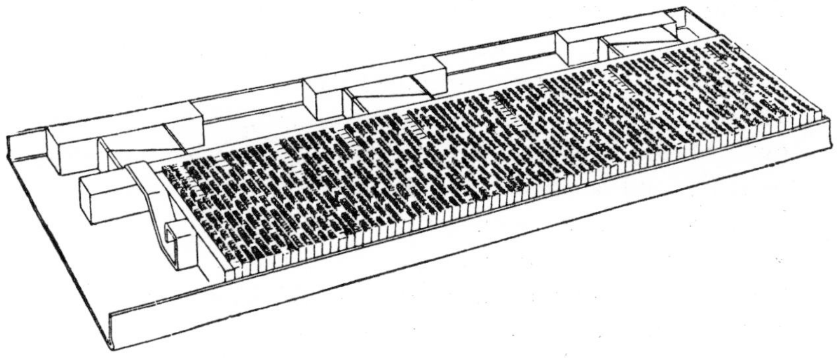

15. A galley of type ready for proofing

the galley, wedges (quoins, pronounced 'coins') are inserted and tightened up so that a firm pressure is applied to every line. The galley is now ready for proofing, and is set down on the proofing press, inked, and printed on to a long strip of paper. This is the galley proof or slip proof. Proofs of several galleys are gathered together in their right order and sent with the appropriate copy to the reading room for checking. Any errors found by the reader are marked by him in the margin of the slip, and are attended to by the compositor when the slips return to the composing room, the corrections being made in the type in the same way as the errors the compositor himself discovered were corrected in the stick.

Correction in galley is very much easier than after the type has been made up into page form, and consequently cheaper; if the publisher or author has foreseen that there is likely to be a large number of amendments in the text he will have asked for galley proofs. In this case, after the type has been corrected, new slips together with the copy are sent out to the publisher, who will pass them on to the author: and eventually they return to the printer with the author's alterations marked. Correction of the type is made as before. It was formerly the custom for publishers to have galley proofs of nearly all books, but today many publishers prefer to economize by editing the author's typescript as carefully as possible so that the need for galley proofs may be avoided for all but difficult books; the first proofs the publisher sees for most books nowadays are page proofs.

Authors, who, in the printer's eyes, are often the most inconvenient of people, sometimes take it into their heads to add three or four words, or delete them, here and there throughout the proofs. No doubt the alteration changes what was before ordinary and mediocre English into great and memorable language, ensuring the author's fame to furthest posterity; but when it comes to paying for it he is apt to argue. Now, adding a word or more in a line means, since all the lines must be of the same length, that the word at the end of the line must come out and be placed at the beginning of the next, while the word at the end of that line is in turn transposed to the beginning of the following one, and so on to the end of the paragraph, every line affected having to be respaced. If the correction occurs at the beginning of a paragraph it may be necessary to reset the entire paragraph. The cost of adding a single word may thus amount

16. A printing house in the seventeenth century. The man kneeling on the left is damping paper for the press. On top of the press is a griffin with a pair of ink-balls in its talons—an heraldic device traditionally appropriated to printing

to many more pence than there are letters in the line, and the question whether it is really worth while should be carefully considered.

The type is now ready to be divided into pages, and when this is done it is proofed again and once more sent out to the publisher and author for correction, and finally corrected according to their instructions, when it is ready for the press. It goes from the composing room into the machine room, and so vanishes for a while from the scope of this chapter.

Later, when the edition has been printed off, and it has been decided that no more editions will be needed, the type comes back to the composing room for distribution. It is placed again on galleys and each compositor takes his share of them and begins the business of putting the letters back in the appropriate boxes.

Distribution is a gentle, apparently leisurely, affair, and requires very little effort of mind from the expert compositor—though not less than is sufficient to ensure that the type is being distributed into the right case. Half a dozen or more lines are picked up in the left hand (with the face upside down, as usual), with a lead behind the lower line for support, and with the other hand a word with the space in front of it is picked up between forefinger and thumb, with the second finger under the feet of the type. The compositor reads the word and then moves his hand across the case, dropping first the space and then the letters into the proper boxes as he goes. While this is going on the forefinger and thumb are engaged in moving the types forward letter by letter, so that each one may be dropped surely and separately at the right time. It is done very quickly, so much so that it may not be apparent to an onlooker that anything at all is being done other than a few vague movements of the hand above the case. Leads, rules, ornaments, etc., are collected together later and returned to their racks or cases.

Distribution is done very much more quickly than composing, but nevertheless it always presented an awkward problem for those people who wished to find some way of speeding up printing. If it could be eliminated a large proportion of the cost of composition would be eliminated too. It defeated the inventors of the first composing machines, though at least one of them got nearly on the right track by sending all used type back to the foundry and using only new type on his machine. The solution was the one adopted by Ottmar Mergenthaler in his Linotype machine, and that solution has been adopted by every subsequent designer of machines for composing metal types.

Because it will be of assistance in understanding composing machines and much else in composing, I have described in this chapter the composition of a book by hand as though this were still the practice. It is not so. Composing machines have captured the setting of text matter from the compositor almost entirely; when there are large quantities of matter to be set all in one size of type, it is not profitable to set it by hand when it can be done by machine more quickly and cheaply and just as well, and with other advantages too. Nevertheless, the compositor is not ousted entirely; he still exists, and moreover is indispensable to printing. Machines are supreme in the setting of text matter, but they cannot set displayed matter in several sizes of type and perhaps in several faces, nor will they deal with text matter when they have set it. The dividing up into pages and all that goes with it is done by the compositor. Chapter heads, part titles, and title-pages and such things as advertisements may be best set by hand. Even minor corrections of machine-set type are more cheaply done by hand.

The fact that compositors are no longer called upon to set text matter means that they need less type of any one kind. Only sufficient is required for text correction and the small number of words in displayed matter, and this has led to a different kind of case. The pair of cases has disappeared from the composing room, and in their place there is a case looking like the diagram on the following page. This contains the capitals and lower-case letters in one case, and therefore occupies just half as much room as the pair of cases. Small capitals and accents, etc., are kept in special cases in racks where they can be easily got when required.

Compositors used to work in groups of five or more called

companionships, or 'ships', under the charge of a clicker, who was also a compositor, and was responsible to the foreman of the composing room. The clicker received the work to be done and apportioned it among the members of his ship, watched its progress, and advised on any difficulties that occurred, and generally supervised operations.

The companionship was an organization principally directed to the satisfactory performance of the compositor's work. There is another organization that concerns itself with the conditions

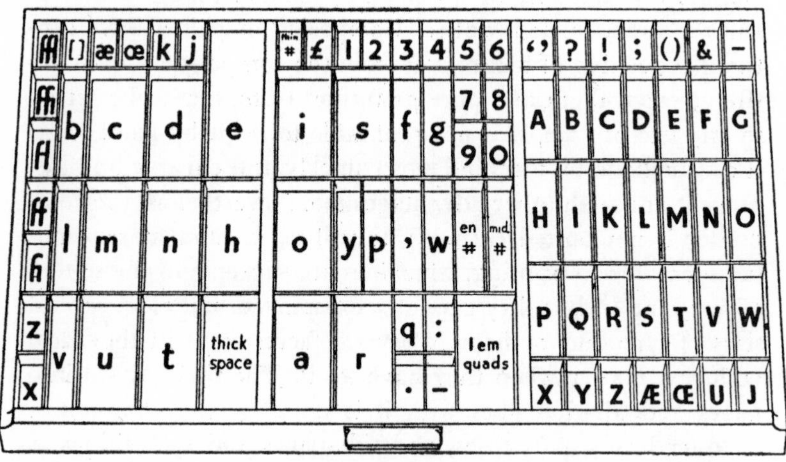

17. A double case and its lay

in the printing house, with the fraternity of the men engaged there, with the regulation of apprentices, and generally with the common interests of the men. This is the chapel; its name is said to be derived from the fact that the first printing press in England was set up in the precincts or in a chapel of Westminster Abbey—Caxton's press. The head of the chapel is the father, who is elected by the free vote of the journeymen, and its members are the firm's journeymen compositors and those apprentices near the end of their apprenticeship. It is purely an employee's organization, and though its meetings take place in the composing room, the employer does not attend unless invited by the chapel. Its powers are wide. It can arraign any craftsman or apprentice who in his conduct makes himself odious or obstructive to his fellows, and can punish him by suitable fines; it makes rules for the conduct of the men in the composing room, and may be the court that deals with any infringement of the rules. It is a trade union in embryo, and can object to any procedure of the master printer and suggest what that procedure should be (though it cannot enforce them, he would be a foolish employer who ignored the chapel's wishes). To-day the chapel is an important element in the printer's trade-union organization, but is not necessarily dominated by the union. The father of the chapel is a person of consequence in the composing room, and his position is one that commands respect and not a little affection. On the benevolent side it is the chapel that assists any man in difficulties through illness or other fault not his own, that sends him flowers, fruit, and magazines if he is in hospital; and it was the chapel that arranged the annual outing—the spree that printers called so curiously a 'wayz-goose', and which seems now to be a dying custom.

Machine-minders usually have a chapel of their own.

IV

COMPOSING MACHINES

The Linotype, the Intertype, and the Monotype

A GREAT deal of inventive ingenuity was expended during the nineteenth century in attempts to construct a machine that would do the work of the compositor more quickly and more cheaply than the compositor himself could do it: or, it would be more accurate to say, that would do the composing, for no machine has ever been designed or, as far as I know, attempted, that could do the whole of the compositor's work. The main problems inventors found presented to them were those of justification, the supply of type to the machine, and the recurrent question of distribution. There seemed to be insuperable difficulties in the way of successful mechanical justification, and with the first machines brought out the problem was abandoned and the mechanically set lines of type were handed over to a compositor for justification by hand. The saving of time and effort cannot have been great, if it existed at all, and these machines never became commercially practicable, although *The Times* ran one of them for a while.

Composing machines based on the use of founders' type left the operation of distribution quite untouched. Type had still to be distributed by hand, and in addition the letters had to be arranged in rows after or during distribution, ready for reinsertion into the magazine of the machine.

What was required, therefore, was a machine that would compose type, justify the lines, and do away with the necessity for distribution. It appeared, and perhaps it was, impossible that any machine could do all this while still using founders' type. It was essential to get quite away from the conception of typesetting as the compositor understood it, and in consequence the

18. The Young-Delcambre composing machine. The girl on the left is justifying the lines

first workable machine incorporated many ideas that were altogether foreign to the compositor of the time, though they would not, paradoxically, have been quite as strange to the craftsman of the fifteenth century. This new machine was the

Linotype, and it has been claimed that it inaugurated as great a revolution in the history of printing as did the invention of movable type.

THE LINOTYPE

After several attempts and failures, Ottmar Mergenthaler brought out the first commercially practicable model of the Linotype in 1890. It must have astonished the printers of the day, not only because it incorporated a type-foundry in itself, but also because it seemed to abandon the principle of movable type; for the product of the Linotype is not a line of separate letters, but a solid metal strip, or 'slug', bearing on one of the long edges the characters that go to make up the whole line. It was not truly an abandonment, however, but a development, as the following concise account will show.

The modern Linotype is in principle essentially the same as Mergenthaler's machine of 1890. The early machine solved at once the three problems of composition, justification, and distribution, but as might be expected there was room for improvement, and improvement has been brought about. As a result of the experience and development of the last seventy years or so the Linotype is now a machine of great flexibility and wide scope. To-day, while in the printing of books it is not as widely used in Britain as a later comer, the Monotype, in the production of newspapers and magazines it is supreme, and there is little likelihood of the Monotype's being able to oust it from this field. For where time is scant and type must be handled with great speed and perhaps little care, the slugs of the Linotype are easier and safer than the separate types of the Monotype.

The modern Linotype is a tall, gaunt machine, but its shape is dictated by the work it does (Figure 19). Low down in front is a keyboard, at which the operator sits; the keys are similar to those of a typewriter, but the arrangement of the alphabet in the banks is very different. As far as I know there is no particular reason why the Linotype keyboard should be different from the

19. A Linotype machine in operation

20. The assembly slide of a Linotype with a line of matrices being composed

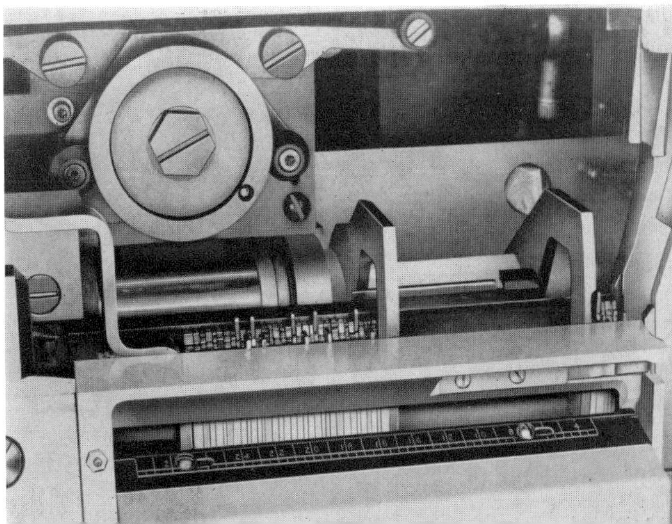

21. A punch-cutting machine; the operator traces the master letter with the pointer, and the punch is automatically cut in the upper part of the machine

universal keyboard adopted by the typewriter companies and also by the manufacturers of the Monotype; the universal keyboard may not be perfect, and the Linotype keyboard may have, as is claimed, special advantages, but the fact that it is peculiar may well be a disadvantage in itself. Above the keyboard is the magazine containing in channels the matrices for the various characters, a matrix being a mould for casting the face of type (Figure 22). At the touch of a key in the keybank a matrix for the letter indicated by the key falls from the magazine on to an endless belt, which delivers it into a slide (Figure 20) that may be said to represent the composing stick of the compositor. Matrix follows matrix as the words are spelled out by the operator's tapping on the keys, and fall in their correct order into the slide. At the end of each word the space key is depressed and a space-band is delivered into the box. It will be seen from this that although the Linotype produces a solid line of type, the principle of movable type is retained in the composition of separate matrices. When sufficient matrices have been gathered in the slide to fill up the line almost completely the operator depresses a handle beside the keybank and commences the next line. The line he has just composed is henceforth dealt with automatically. The matrices are transferred from the slide and brought in front of a mould designed to cast the body of the line to the right point size and em measure; at this juncture the space-bands, which are opposed wedges, are expanded sufficiently to make the line of matrices the full width of the measure by increasing the spaces between the words. The matrices are clamped tightly against the mould, molten metal is injected from a crucible, and immediately solidifies in the form of the slug familiar to all printers. The slug is then trimmed to the correct type height and ejected upright on to a galley. The matrices are collected by an arm and returned to the magazine, where each one is made to fall into its proper channel by means of a revolving spiral and an ingenious system of notched teeth on

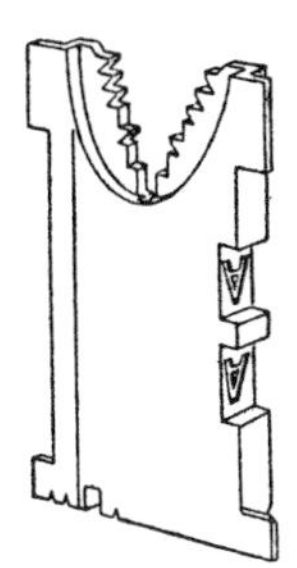

22. A Linotype matrix

the matrix. The space-bands are picked up separately by a grabber and transferred to the space-box, ready for use again. In this way the magazine is kept supplied with matrices and the space-box with space-bands, so that neither can ever run short; for each matrix and space-band is used over and over again, constantly circulating from magazine to assembly slide, from assembly slide to mould, and from the mould back to the magazine again, and there is no hindrance to continuous composition by the operator.

Distribution is provided for very simply: after use on the press the slugs are returned to a melting pot and melted down into ingots, which in turn are fed into the pot of the Linotype as required. Thus the metal also has a continuous circulation: from the Linotype to the press, from the press to the melting pot, and from the melting pot to the Linotype again.

The operator is paid more than a compositor, but he can do as much in an hour as six or more men working at the case, and moreover the slugs produced represent new type for each job. Then, as I have already said, in an office where speed is the primary consideration slugs can be handled with more ease and dispatch than masses of separate types. Nevertheless, the Linotype has some disadvantages for ordinary book printing. The metal of which the slugs are cast is usually of a softer alloy than that used for separate types, and will not withstand as much wear without tending to lose some of its freshness. Then the method of casting from assembled matrices imposes a definite restriction on the free design of the letter, and some characters have to be crushed and squeezed unnaturally—no kerns are possible, for instance, and the result is that the graceful italic *f* becomes this: *f*. As type designs are matters of tradition and long development, this malformation is a distinct drawback. A not very satisfactory solution of this problem has been achieved by producing compound matrices of the kerned letter and its neighbour; appearance is all right, but the number of matrices required for the fount is increased, usually beyond the capacity of the keyboard, when the operator must stop to insert the required combination in the assembly slide by hand; and he has then to be constantly on the watch for these combinations. Corrections in Linotype matter, however slight, cannot be made by a compositor; the line affected must be reset entirely on the machine and recast. Even the alteration of a full point to a comma entails the resetting of the whole line, with the possibility, which the best of operators cannot altogether avoid, of perpetrating fresh errors. Finally, the slug, or solid line of letters, it has been argued with some reason, is not as suitable a printing surface for the best work as the line of separate types.

Despite these arguments, the Linotype machine is considered by many competent persons a suitable machine for bookwork. In Britain, at least, it is not always operated to the best advantage, but in America it is the machine used above all others, and there is no doubt that in the hands of capable operators fine work can be done with it. Preference to some extent depends on personal opinion. Nevertheless, it is undeniable that in England the consensus of the best opinion is against using the Linotype for better classes of bookwork. There the Monotype, with its separate types, continues to hold the field.

There is another machine similar to the Linotype, the Intertype. It looks very much the same, and it works in the same way, but it has features that may be considered advantages —notably a system of standardization.

With the introduction and development of the Linotype one form of mechanical composition was provided and the compositor had largely to abandon a field in which he had had no rival. Nevertheless, the Linotype could not set movable types, as could the compositor, and there was something desirable, and indeed essential, in certain circumstances, in movable types, as I have indicated. A young man in America, Tolbert Lanston, was working on the problem in the eighties and nineties, and in 1897 he brought out a machine that proved successful. It was the Monotype.

THE MONOTYPE

The modern Monotype must, I think, be the sort of machine an engineer delights in; even the layman would be impressed by this mechanical wonder, as he would not be impressed by the Linotype or the Intertype. The Linotype (and the Intertype) is large and untidy-looking, as though it might have grown thus rather than have been designed by an engineer, and its operations are not difficult to understand. The Monotype, on the other hand, is compact and comparatively small, and such a mass of intricate mechanism and simultaneous operations that it is difficult to comprehend without study.

It is really two machines (Figures 25 and 26). One is the keyboard, on which the words to be set are tapped out as on a typewriter, and the other machine, quite separate, is the caster, which casts the letters and lines of type in the order dictated by the operator's fingers on the keyboard. Perhaps the best way to describe the machine is to take a phrase and follow it through the keyboard to its casting in movable types on the caster. For the phrase we want there is the typefounder's favourite—'The quick brown fox jumps over the lazy dog'—typefounders love it because it contains all the letters of the alphabet.

The keyboard has 306 keys—which may seem an enormous quantity compared with the number on an ordinary typewriter. It is, however, no more complicated or difficult to learn, for the characters are arranged on exactly the same system, except that there are seven alphabets instead of one only, with some additional characters, such as fi, ff, fl, ffi, ffl, œ, æ, and so forth, that do not occur on the typewriter at all. The kinds of type represented by the seven alphabets vary with the sort of matter for which the keyboard has been arranged, but for ordinary bookwork the alphabets are: capitals and lower-case of roman, italics, and bold face; together with small capitals. There are also keys for figures, for points of punctuation, for the ligatures mentioned above, and several for spaces of fixed widths. In the upper part of the keybank are two rows of red keys, shown solid black on the diagram (Figure 23), each row numbered 1 to 15, and these are used in justifying the lines as they are completed.

Above the keybank is the paper-tower, in which is a reel of paper perforated along the edges like ciné film; sprockets,

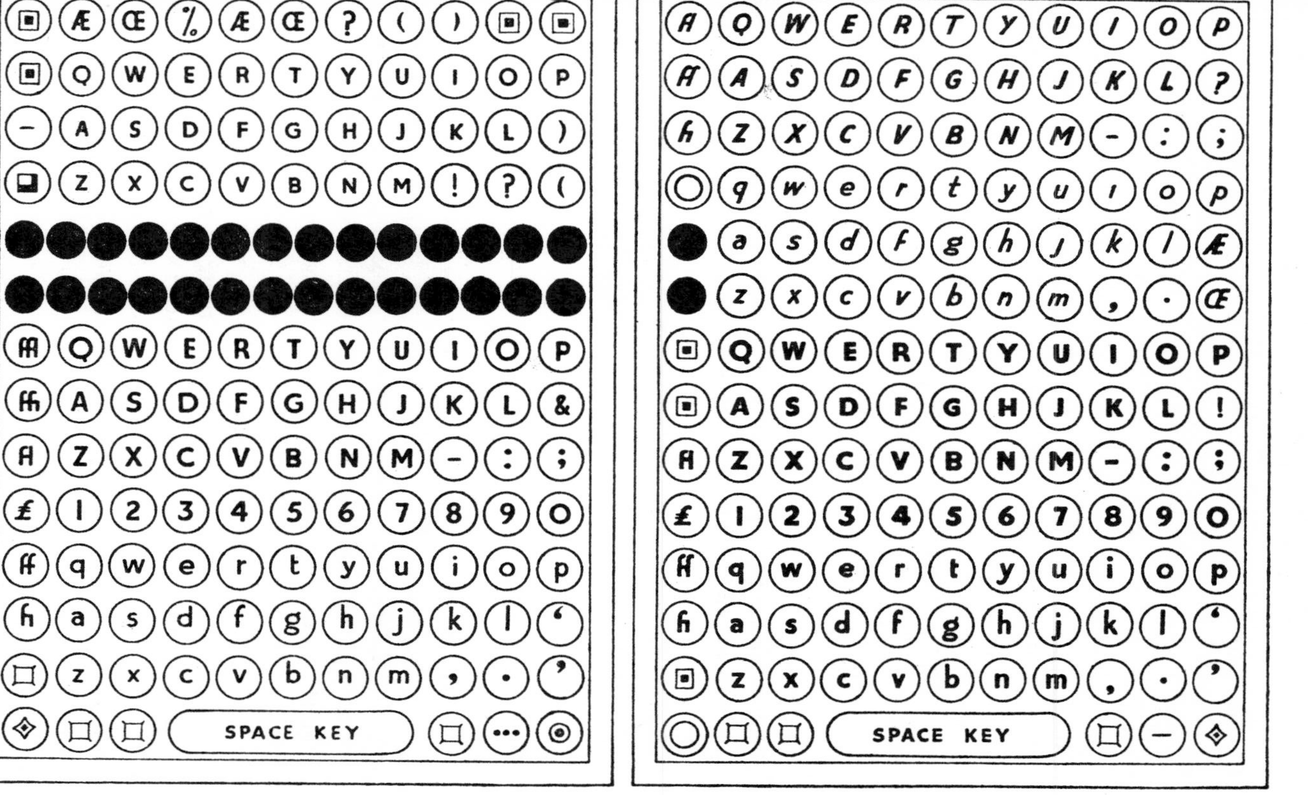

23. Diagram of a standard Monotype keyboard, laid out for bookwork (seven alphabets)

engaging in the perforations, move the paper along one step at a time over a row of punches stretching across the width of the paper. The operator begins by adjusting his keyboard for the length of line to be used and the set of the type specified—these factors in computer terms, which we shall come to later, would be called 'parameters'. They are necessary because the keyboard contains a kind of calculating or computing system that operates on the basis of these factors or parameters. The operator, sitting at the keyboard and setting our phrase, depresses first the key for the em quad, to obtain the paragraph indention, and the paper strip in the tower is moved along one step. Next the key for T is depressed, and two of the punches in the row in the tower rise and perforate the paper (Figure 25), after which the strip is moved on another step by the sprockets engaging in the marginal holes. The same process is followed for each key the operator depresses, two punches—which are operated by compressed air released by the key—rising to perforate the paper.

As each key is depressed a calculating mechanism notes the width of the character it represents and adds it to the total of characters already set in the line; each time the space key is depressed a pointer moves a step up the surface of a revolving drum engraved with figures.

There are thirty-one punches in the row in the paper tower. Two perforations are made in the paper strip for each letter, and each letter possesses its own combination of two of the punches different from the combination for any other letter. The strip unwinds from a reel, passes over the punches and is perforated, and is wound up again on another reel as the sprockets drive the strip forward.

With 'The' accounted for, the next thing required is a space. This is obtained by depressing the space bar, a long key at the foot of the keybank, very like the space-bar of a typewriter. The space is also recorded as a combination of punch-holes in the paper strip, and is taken into account by the calculating mechanism; but for the present it has no absolute value.

Tapping on the keys, the operator travels across the width of

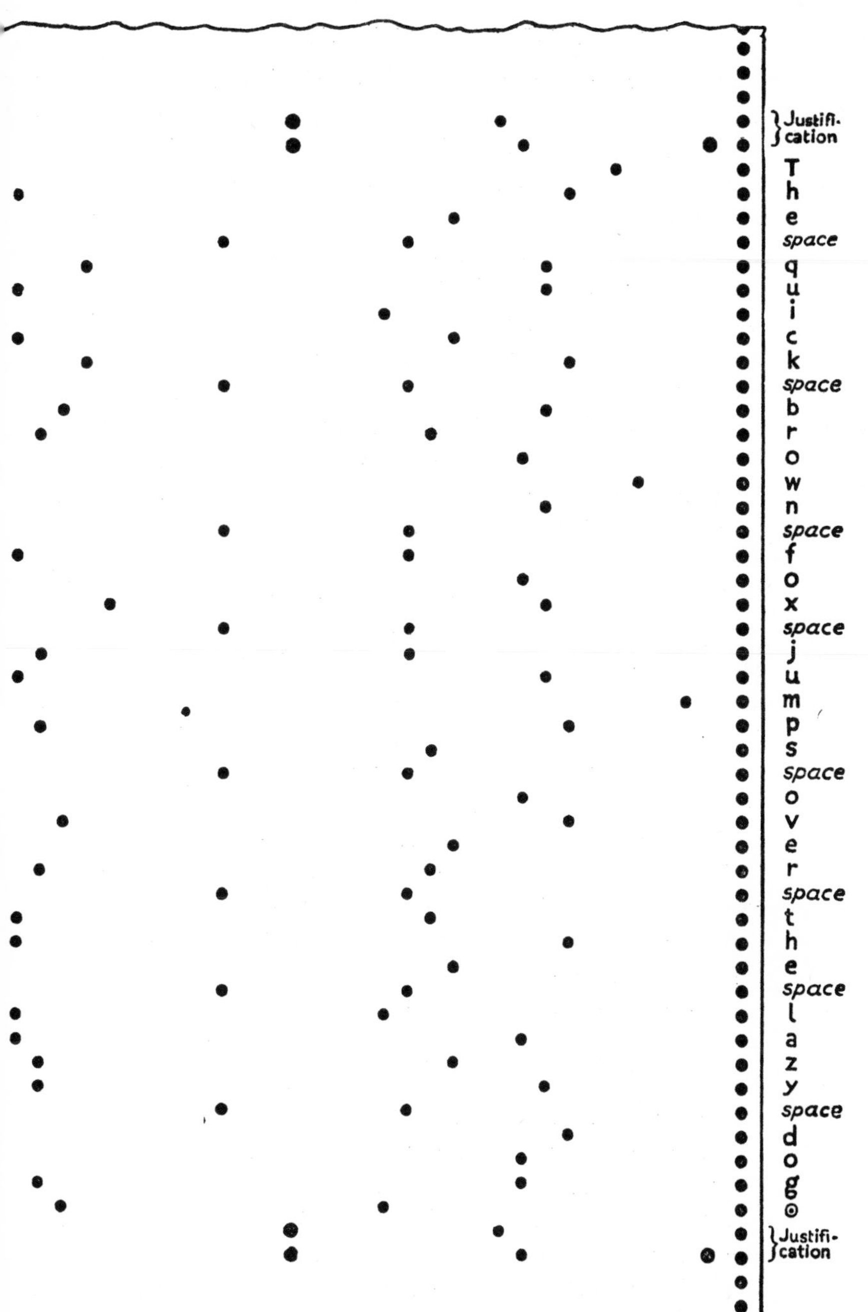

Punched paper strip from the Monotype keyboard. The letters on the right are those represented by the holes

the measure until he is warned by a bell that the line is nearly full and will hold only five or six more letters—which is sufficient to complete the word he is engaged on or to divide it in a correct manner. He must now look at the pointer, which while he has been depressing the space keys has been rising up the surface of the revolving drum. On the end of the pointer is a small L-shaped frame, through which are visible two pairs of figures on the drum. These figures are the result arrived at by the calculating mechanism, which has recorded the width of each letter, and the number of spaces in the line, and now indicates how the space remaining at the end of the line should be divided among the spaces between the words in order to complete the justification. All that is necessary is to note the figures and to depress the corresponding red justification keys. This completes the line. This operation should be remembered because it is a step to the understanding of one of the most important functions of the computer in typesetting. The Monotype keyboard has automatically calculated or computed the total number of units of the characters and has shared the difference between that and the total number of units in the measure among the word spaces. On the Monotype it is necessary for the operator to transfer the information manually to the keyboard, and so to the paper ribbon, by pressing the red justification keys. In computer typesetting this manual transfer is not required, the machine itself performing the equivalent operation.

A reversing key returns the em-scale pointer and a new line can now be commenced.

An electronic keyboard, or 'perforator', is available to serve both Monotype and Monophoto machines. It provides for automatic justification at the touch of a button, without any need to read and transfer scale figures.

When the last word of the copy has been set and the last line justified the part of the roll of paper that has been punched is torn from the remainder and taken to the caster. The punched paper is the only link between the caster and the keyboard; and it is the master of the heavy and powerful caster, which it directs in every one of its operations.

25. A Monotype keyboard in operation; the justification drum and the paper tower are above the keys

26. A Monotype composition caster

27. Die case from a composition caster

28. Type emerging from a composition caster; a new line is nearly complete

The formative parts of the caster are the matrix case (Figure 27), the mould, and the wedges controlling the mould blade, and thus the width of the mould opening. The matrix case is rectangular, with fifteen rows of seventeen matrices each, so that there are 255 in all. The point size of the mould is fixed, and a different mould is needed for each size of body; but it is adjustable setwise between the width of the narrowest space and that of the widest character—generally the M or W.

There is a paper-tower on the caster as there is on the keyboard, but there are no punches. The paper strip passes between a duct of compressed air and a row of small holes corresponding in number, size, and spacing to the punches on the keyboard. At any moment in the operation of the caster the paper obscures all but two of these holes, those corresponding to the holes made in the paper by the punches when the operator depressed the key. As I have shown, each letter is represented by two punch holes made by two of a line of punches, each combination being peculiar to a particular letter. The punched paper thus bears the message in a cipher of punch-holes, and some operators can read it. The small holes opposite the air duct in the caster are the entrances to air-pipes. The paper is drawn across the air-pipes step by step as the sprockets engage and the compressed air is thus allowed at each step to pass down two of the pipes, and two only. This air causes the caster to centre the appropriate matrix over the mould, and to open the mould to the correct width; molten metal is pumped in, cooled at once, and the type is ejected into the line being set.

Our phrase, then, is a roll of paper bearing so many punch-holes. On the keyboard this was rolled up as it was punched; the caster now commences unrolling the paper, and it comes first to the end of the last line. The first holes to come opposite the air-pipe are those made by the justification keys on the keyboard, and these set the width of the space to be used after each word in the coming line. Next the holes for the full point come opposite the air-pipes, causing the matrix case to move so that the appropriate matrix is centred over the mould, while the mould blade drives in or out to make the aperture the right width for the shank of the character. Thus as each pair of punch-holes is positioned opposite the air-pipes the appropriate matrix is centred over the mould and the mould-blade determines the correct width of the body of the type. Spaces are dealt with in the same way, except that a mechanism comes into action to make the space the non-printing lower height, the mould blade making each space exactly the thickness predetermined by the justification holes. This instruction holds good for the whole line, and is only cancelled by the presentation of the justification holes for the next line.

The mould is cooled by a constant circulation of water, so that the molten metal is chilled and solidified immediately it is pumped in. Each letter is cast correct in point size and type height, and after a tang that is cast with it is automatically broken off it is fully finished too, and is ejected from the mould into a channel adjoining a galley. The letter remains always on its feet, and it and its fellows dance out from the machine in a continuous vibrating stream. As each line is completed it is pushed forward automatically on to the galley while the next one is being cast.

The operation of the caster is entirely automatic; once started, it will continue to cast type until the paper strip is finished, when the caster automatically stops. Thus the caster attendant may look after more than one machine at once, and he usually does.

The caster is also a type foundry, from which the compositor can draw supplies of type to fill up his cases for hand composition and for hand correction of machine-set type; and in addition it will supply many border units, rules, and ornaments.

The only limit to the speed at which the operator can compose on the keyboard is the agility of his own fingers; he cannot hope to overtake the limits of the mechanism, which are estimated at somewhere in the neighbourhood of forty thousand ens per hour. A good average speed is about eight or nine thousand ens an hour; less if the work is involved or the manuscript difficult to decipher, more, perhaps, if everything is clear and straightforward. On the latest models of the caster letters are cast at speeds up to eleven thousand per hour.

When the paper strip is finished or the galley holds as much type as convenient, the galley is handed over to the compositor, who deals with it as described in the next chapter. Corrections can be made by hand from monotype stored like founders' type in double cases, unless they are so extensive or awkward that it is cheaper or quicker to reset the whole paragraph or a substantial part of it; in this event it is reset on the machine and the new matter put in place of the old on the galley.

Distribution is carried out in the simple and effective manner adopted by Mergenthaler—the used type goes back into the melting pot and is melted down to make new supplies of ingots for the caster.

The type produced by the Monotype is of excellent quality, and in use is indistinguishable from founders' type. Compared with founders' type it presents the advantage of a newly cast, sharp face for every job. The metal used, while not quite as hard as the alloy used by founders, is nevertheless hard enough to withstand many thousands of impressions. There are few restrictions on the free design of the face, kerns are possible where required, and no type design need be altered essentially to suit the machine.

The Monotype is the only machine of its kind, and is the present limit of mechanical progress in the composition of separate types. A certain amount of simple display matter can be set by it, as it can be by the Linotype, but it is seldom worth while to use the machine for this; and there is very much more display that it cannot do at all. Where several sizes or kinds of type are to be used together the compositor is essential, and, it seems, is likely to continue so.

Composing machines have had the effect of enormously increasing the demand for matrices, and this in turn implies an increase in the demand for punches, from which matrices are made. The ambitious programmes of expansion of the ranges of faces available on the machines, in which all the companies indulged, only increased the demand still further. Punch-cutting was not a business that could be pursued on a mass-production basis, however. The punch-cutter required long and careful training and no small amount of innate ability, and even at best could not produce punches quickly. The supply could not conceivably fill the rising demand, and the usefulness of composing machines might have been very seriously curtailed from the first had not a method of cutting punches mechanically been developed. The Benton punch-cutting machine, which works on the pantograph principle, reduced the cutting of punches to a rapid and comparatively unskilled process, quite capable of keeping up with the demands made on it. It was invented in 1884 for his own purposes by Linn Boyd Benton of Milwaukee. By sheer accident it came to the notice of the directors of the Linotype Company at the moment when their new composing machine, already in action, but not yet perfected, threatened to prove useless for lack of matrices (see Figure 21).

V

DEVELOPMENTS IN TYPESETTING

Photo-composition and Computers

A FERMENT of invention and experiment has been going on for many years in the background of the printing industry and its effects have been felt in a proliferation of new machines, new processes, and new jargons. Revolutionary techniques for typesetting have emerged and have passed beyond the stage of theory and development to become commercially available. The compositor, handling solid metal types at the case, and the composing-machine operator, who always knew that the tapping of his fingers on the keys was a vicarious handling of metal types, now find themselves faced with the hitherto alien techniques of photography and the mystery of computers and the need to understand whole new areas of language. There are today several techniques through which the typesetting of books may be channelled where before there was only the conventional composition of metal types through line-casting or separate-type composing machines.

These various developments have occurred unrecognized by the ordinary reader of books. They have very rarely changed the appearance of books or disturbed the conventions by which books and typography are appreciated. On the contrary, the aim of the designers of new equipment has been powerfully controlled by the conventions of book-production and of printing in general.

PHOTO-COMPOSITION

The use of photography to replace hot metal in composing machines was developed between the wars but did not become common in printing-houses until after the Hitler war, when the Monotype Corporation's Monophoto machine was put on the market. Photography has not driven the hot-metal machines out of use, however, as some enthusiasts supposed it would, and it is not likely to do so for many years to come. There are many kinds of printing in which metal type remains more economical and more convenient.

The advantages of photo-setting are many, however. A page of metal type is heavy, bulky, and precarious, and the metal is expensive, so that storage against a reprint entails not only considerable space but also the locking up of capital. A photo-set page is a negative or positive on film, occupying no more space than a leaf of a book, and no heavier. A printer can store the films for a whole book in a single box or file, and the films are ready at any time to make new printing surfaces for letterpress, litho, or gravure with no possibility of introducing typographical errors.

The principle of photo-composition rests on a series of images on film of the letters of the alphabet, or alphabets, which may be called photo-matrices (Figures 29 and 32), since they are the equivalent of the recessed matrices from which the face of metal type is cast. These photo-matrices are presented, under command from a keyboard, between a light-source and a lens and the projected image is received on photographic film, which is afterwards developed. Provision for justification must of course be incorporated before the matrices are photographed on to the film, and the film itself must be in a holder capable of advancing it as required to obtain the required spacing or leading between lines. It will be seen that, since the matrix is photographed in order to transfer its image to the film, enlargement or reduction of the image on the film is possible by altering or exchanging the lenses, and photo-composition machines make provision for this, in most instances at keyboard command.

In general photo-matrices are of negative form, that is a clear letter on opaque black, and the film made from them is therefore positive, that is with black letters on a clear ground. Negative film may be required for some purposes, e.g. for process engraving, and this can be produced by using positive matrices, by photographic reversal, or by printing positive film on to new film. Paper prints may be preferred for pasting-up and these can be made from the films, or alternatively may be made directly in the photo-setting machine by using bromide paper or stabilization paper in place of film. Paper or film may be required right-reading, as on the printed page, or reverse or wrong-reading, and these variants may be produced also.

The exposed film or paper must be developed to convert the latent image into a visible one. Development has to be done with care and with control of time and of the temperature of the solutions; variations in the length of development or the temperature affect the density of the image, making it either lighter or heavier. Not only should the films representing the entire book be consistent in development, but so too should any films developed perhaps several weeks later as a result of resetting due to author's or publisher's corrections. Differences of density can show quite clearly on the final printed page, and this is obviously undesirable. The easiest way to achieve accuracy and consistency is to use an automatic film-processor, in which the film is fed in at one end and emerges at the other developed and ready for washing. Stabilization materials are also processed in machines, to emerge ready for use.

All three hot-metal composing-machine companies in Britain, and others abroad, have introduced photo-composing machines. The Monophoto filmsetter was adapted from the Monotype hot-metal caster. The Intertype Fotosetter was also an adaptation, of the Intertype line-casting machine. Linotype set foot on the same road, but then produced the Linofilm, a machine based upon the use of electronics. All subsequent machines have been electronic.

The Monophoto filmsetter. The division between keyboard operation and type-casting that we saw in the Monotype is preserved in the Monophoto filmsetter system—as it is in nearly every other photo-composing machine. A Monotype keyboard, in fact, needs little alteration to serve a Monophoto filmsetter and the operator does not have to learn a new technique. A small number of new keys are introduced to control functions possible on the filmsetter that are not possible in hot metal, such as low and high alinement of characters, useful in the setting of mathematics and in the composition of fractions. Interlinear leading may also be controlled from the keyboard in increments of one point independently of the body size selected for the job. The produce of the keyboard is a 31-channel paper ribbon indistinguishable in appearance from that produced for hot-metal casting.

The filmsetter resembles a Monotype caster and much of its procedure is similar. The paper ribbon is fed into it over a duct of compressed air, allowing the air to pass along pipes to the mechanism that positions the matrix case. From this point the operation differs from that of the hot-metal machine. The matrix case, superficially resembling the matrix case of the Monotype caster (Figures 27 and 29), is made up of photographic negatives of the characters. There is no mould, no metal-pot, etc. Instead there is a system of lens and prisms and a drum that carries a length of photographic film. A lamp illuminates the matrix and a shutter controls the exposure while the character is projected through the lens and through prisms and an angled mirror on to the drum (Figure 33). The drum does not move during the composition of a line; the mirror moves laterally and proportionately so that each character is reflected and photographed in turn in its correct place. The amount of movement of the mirror and the word-spacing to produce justified lines is controlled by the perforations in the paper ribbon. When the end of the line is reached the drum revolves by an amount equivalent to the body size of the type being set, plus any leading required. This movement is known in photo-setting terms as 'film advance'.

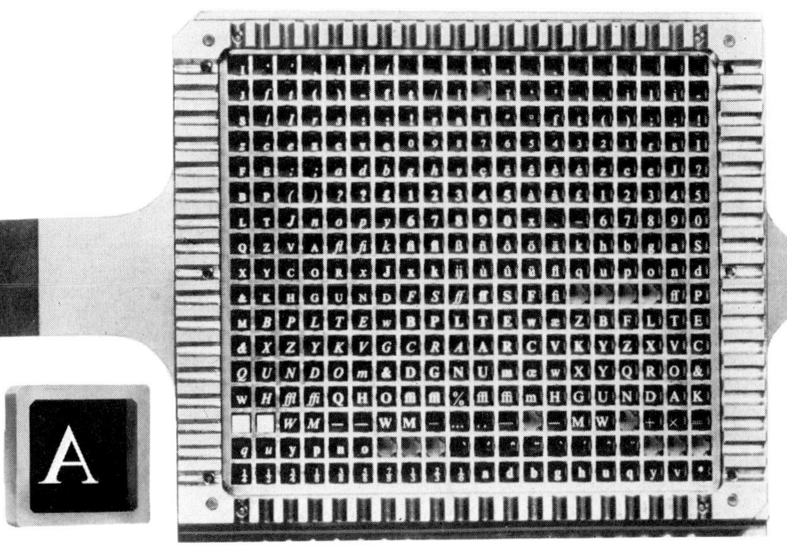

29. Monophoto matrix case and matrix

30. Monophoto studio lettering machine

31. Monophoto photo-lettering machine. *Inset*, matrices

32. Part of a Lumitype character disk

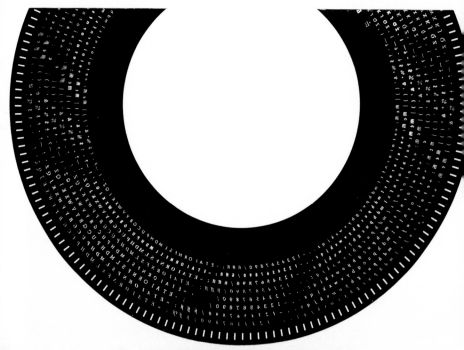

The lens and prisms of the filmsetter may be moved towards or away from the matrix to enlarge or reduce the size of the image conveyed to the film. Theoretically, any size of type is available from only one size of matrix, and types designed for photo-setting make use of this facility—Apollo and the sanserif Univers are examples. Type-faces originally designed to be cast in metal may need two, and in a few instances three, sets of matrices to match the appearance of the equivalent sizes in metal. It is possible to produce fractional point sizes on the filmsetter, but in practice there are fixed settings of the lens and prisms to obtain established point sizes, which are not variable at keyboard command.

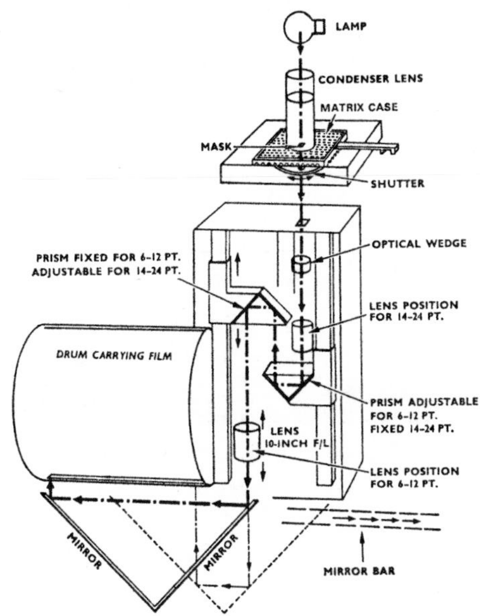

33. Diagram of light-path of a Monophoto composing machine

The mechanical Monophoto may be called a first-generation photo-composing machine. It is the only such machine to remain in production and it is a tribute to its quality and its performance, and to its convenience to the printer, that it is still the most numerous and widely used of photo-composing machines. But it begins to appear old-fashioned when its complex and cacophonous mechanism and untidy shape are compared with the sleek proportions and comparative quiet of its younger electronic competitors, which are of simple cabinet appearance, while its maximum speed of about 11,000 characters per hour is much slower. The Monotype Corporation have themselves brought out an electronic machine, the Monophoto 600.

Electronic photo-composing machines. The later generations of composing machines, the electronic generations, have become a family of bewildering numbers and complexity. The simplest machines are designed to be served by counting or justifying keyboards, as the Monotype and the two Monophotos are served. Most electronic photo-composing machines, however, operate from punched tape only about an inch wide, with six to nine levels or rows of perforations divided by a single row of small sprocket-holes, similar to computer tape (Figure 34)—the Linofilm, taking tape of fifteen levels, is a notable exception.

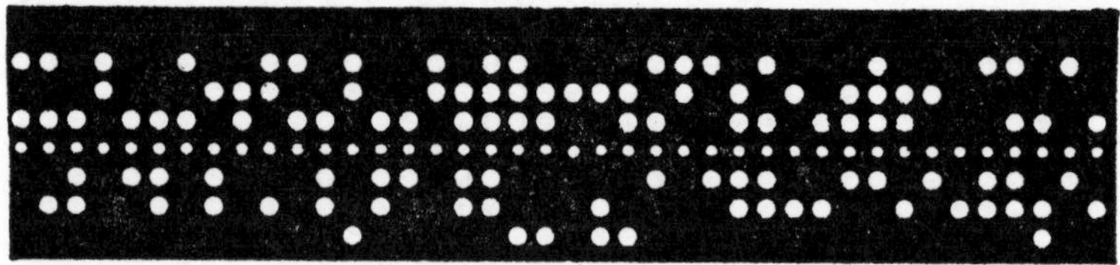

34. Computer tape, 6-level. The small perforations along the centre are sprocket holes.

Any number of perforations up to the maximum in a transverse row may be used as a code for a character or a machine function. Many machines, including the Monophoto 600, will accept magnetic tape also. This magnetic tape looks like that used on a tape-recorder; instead of the holes of paper tape, it carries combinations of magnetized spots or bars that are the codes for the characters and for the photo-setter functions. The function codes on either kind of tape specify type size and set, line width, film advance, various spacing requirements, character delete and line-kill to cancel wrong letters or other errors, high and low alinement, justification, etc., all tapped by the operator at the keyboard, with a final code to stop the photo-setter at the end of the piece. The matrices in the Monophoto 600, to the number of 397, are carried on four disks, which are automatically selected and positioned, and the characters may be reproduced in various sizes from 6 to 28 point. The operating speed of the Monophoto 600 is 100,000 characters per hour, ten times the speed of the mechanical Monophoto. Fast as this appears, it is positively leisurely in comparison with the speeds claimed for more complex machines, which in some instances extend to more than a million characters per hour.

There is a diversity in the manner in which various composing machines carry their photo-matrices. The mechanical Monophoto has a matrix-case, the Monophoto 600 has disks, the Linofilm and the Linotron use square grids, different Lumitypes use strips, hollow drums, or a disk, and the Crosfield Magnaset has a drum carrying several strips of characters. The Lumitype 540 is of interest for the fact that its disk does not stop to be photographed; the spinning disk is illuminated by a very brief flash, quoted as one millionth of a second, for each letter as required as it comes into position, and this is short enough to avoid blur.

A number of photo-composing machines embody computer functions. Before we consider these we need to understand the place of computers in type composition.

COMPUTERS IN TYPE COMPOSITION

The application of computers to the problems of typesetting is now an established technique, though it was only in 1964 that computer typesetting equipment became commercially available to printers. Until then there had been confusion in the minds of most printers about exactly what a computer could do in typesetting and what advantages it could offer. It was supposed by many that these miraculous machines might do away with compositors altogether and somehow set type straight from the author's copy. This was not then true (but it is true today, given certain essential conditions—see pages 96 seq.). The compositor survives, however, as necessary in the computer age as he was before—or at least it is necessary to have someone to tap the keys of a keyboard to convert the author's text into a code of perforations or spots on magnetic tape that is the language the computer understands.

The first thing to be understood is that computers do *not* set type—the term 'computer-aided typesetting', abbreviated to CaT, is preferred by some writers on the subject because it expresses more accurately the function of the computer in typesetting. In order to serve the purpose of typesetting the computer has to be programmed, and in addition it can work only in conjunction with a number of other machines, which are known as peripherals. The peripherals include a tape-reader at the input stage and a tape-punch at the output.

Programming, which is a human operation achieved by the use of pen and paper and a computer keyboard, equips a computer with the formulae to solve the problems it will encounter in the work it is set to do. Programming is a skilled business and it may take weeks to programme and test a computer, but once the work is complete it will serve indefinitely. A computer working in typesetting also has to be 'informed' of the details of each job—in computer terms it must be supplied with the 'parameters' of the work. In typesetting these parameters include type size and set, line length, line advance, style of word-spacing, and so forth.

Two kinds of computer are applied to typesetting, the general-purpose computer and the special-purpose computer. The first is the versatile machine applied to difficult calculations and to various kinds of data processing. When programmed for typesetting it is capable of performing automatically all the functions of justification and of hyphening words as necessary at the ends of lines. It achieves hyphenation by means of a programmed logic system, or, when this logic does not apply, by automatic reference to an exception dictionary of words stored in the computer on magnetic tape, on magnetic disks, or in a core store of wire lattices. It hunts through this dictionary at high speed to find the word and the word-division required. Even so, the English language being what it is, the machine is likely to produce a small percentage of word-divisions that are not acceptable and these have to be put right by a correction routine (see page 95). The data-processing function of the computer makes it invaluable in such things as directories, in which names have to be set in a particular order. Large general-purpose computers, however, have a high rate of cost, which has to be reflected in the charges for typesetting. The machines have not proved economically advantageous in typesetting where suitable work is not available in sufficient quantities. There are, in fact, few such installations in operation. The right kind of work would be that which makes use of the data-processing capacity of the computer. A telephone directory is an example: the computer would sort the entries and it would also deal with revisions for new editions economically and expeditiously, up-dating the text with a minimum of human labour, and process the results at high speed.

Since the justification function is programmed into the computer, no justification codes are required in the tape input to it. Nor, since typographical parameters are also in the computer, is there need to punch codes for these in the tape. The tape may be produced on a non-counting or non-justifying keyboard. The operator can start setting at the beginning of chapter one and continue to the end of the last chapter, setting the book as it were in one long line. He will punch codes for new paragraphs, for line centring, for italics or bold face, and other textual requirements, but he does not pause to justify the lines. What he produces is known as primary tape, or primitive word-string, or more picturesquely as 'idiot tape'.

The tape is fed into a tape-reader, which is linked by cable to the computer. The tape-reader senses the perforations and passes its reading to the computer in the form of electrical impulses. Since it is the computer that stores the typographical parameters, and they are not on the tape, it will be seen that the computer can be changed to a new set of parameters to set the same tape in a quite different typographical form—in a different size and style of type, a different line length, and so on. In fact, the same tape may be used at any time for any number of different formats.

In addition to the tape-reader, which senses the perforations at speeds of over a thousand characters per second, the computer peripherals include a magnetic tape station and a high-speed printer. As the input tape is read the codes are stored on magnetic tape and the high-speed printer produces a print-out. The print-out is a line-for-line equivalent of the type eventually to be set and it may be used as a proof; but as it is all in capitals, with marks or diacritics to indicate actual capitals, italics, etc., it is an uncomfortable proof to read and unlikely to be accepted by authors.

Corrections marked by a reader are set on the keyboard and fed into the computer through the tape-reader. The corrections may be made by a tape-merging process or by changes in the magnetic tapes (see pages 95–6).

The output of the computer is either punched paper tape or magnetic tape embodying, with the text, all the signals for justification, hyphenation, line advance, etc. This tape is fed into the tape-reader of a composing machine to produce either metal type or photo-set films. Computer paper tape is narrow tape, however, and it will not serve Monotypes or Monophotos, nor the Linofilm. For these machines the computer tape must be fed through a converter to perforate another tape of the appropriate width and levels.

Special-purpose computers are machines specifically designed for typesetting and they therefore lack the versatility of general-purpose computers and cannot perform some of the functions, such as data-processing. The simplest special-purpose computers will justify lines to produce tapes with the necessary codes to control typesetting machines. One of the Linasec models, for example, does not automatically divide words. When this machine comes to a word it cannot get into the measure, it displays the word on a cathode-ray screen above a row of buttons with indicator lines to the spaces between the letters. The operator has only to press the appropriate button and the machine continues until the next word-break occurs. This monitor-hyphenation reduces the complexity of the computer and therefore its cost, and it has the advantage that all word-divisions ought to be correct. Some other machines, used principally for newspaper work, make no provision for hyphenation.

The present tendency is for computers to be built into or to be supplied in conjunction with photo-composing machines as a unified installation. There are many such installations available. The Linofilm is an example, as also are the later-comer the Linotron 505C, various models of the Lumitype, and the Harris Intertype Fototronic. These installations bring nearer, if they do not yet achieve, the computer engineer's dream, an installation in which the various peripherals, the keyboards, and the composing-machine are in line, connected by cable rather than by the transfer of reels of tape from one element to another. The problem to be solved is the development of peripherals and composing machines that can keep up with the computer.

Keyboards. The place of keyboards in the setting of type has been familiar for nearly a hundred years and there is little in their application to computer use or for photo-setting that is very different. There are additional keys for new functions and facilities made possible by photo-setting machines, such as the alteration of the size of type by simple keyboard command, which brings a lens of different focal length into operation in the photo-setter, and in most instances there is a wider variety of characters available to the keyboard. The operator also has more control over line advance, which he can vary from the keyboard. A few photo-composition machines will allow the keyboard operator to condense or to extend the type image projected on to the film, or to make it lean forwards or backwards as a sloped roman or a reverse-sloped roman.

There are basically two kinds of keyboards. Non-counting keyboards have no calculating apparatus and their product is primary tape or primitive word-string intended to be put through a computer. Justifying or counting keyboards embody a calculating or computing system that adds up the unit-values of the letters as they are set and records the number of word spaces. At the end of a line the operator presses a button and the keyboard automatically performs the operation of justification, adding a code to the tape to instruct the composing machine how much space to set between the words.

Many keyboards provide the operator with no visual evidence, other than tape, of what he has typed—Monotype keyboards, of course, have always been of this kind. Others produce a typewritten copy at the same time as the tapes are punched. This typewritten copy is known as 'hard copy'. It is divided into lines, as with any kind of typewritten copy, but with a non-counting keyboard the lines will not correspond in length with those eventually printed; they may correspond on a counting keyboard, but they will not be justified. Hard copy may be read as a proof by the printer's reader, and even by the publisher and the author, and marked up in the usual way.

Photo-composing machines incorporating computers. The modern tendency is towards installations designed to be complete in themselves, with the computing operation performed in a control unit that may or may not be incorporated in the photo-setter. The Linotron illustrates such an installation (Figure 35). It comprises: 1, the keyboard, which may be of the counting or non-counting variety producing punched tape, which is the link between the keyboard and the control unit; 2, the control console, with an accessory keyboard through which the operator can instruct the computer which is in effect a small general-purpose unit; 3, the photo-unit, which accepts the text as coded and justified by the computer and in operation positions the appropriate matrices in the light-path to expose them on to film.

One keyboard, however, would not be sufficient to keep the installation occupied. No keyboard operator could keep up with an electronic photo-composing machine, much less with a computer. The installation will serve up to eight keyboards.

The photo-unit contains four character grids each with 238 characters, which can be projected in sizes ranging from 4 point

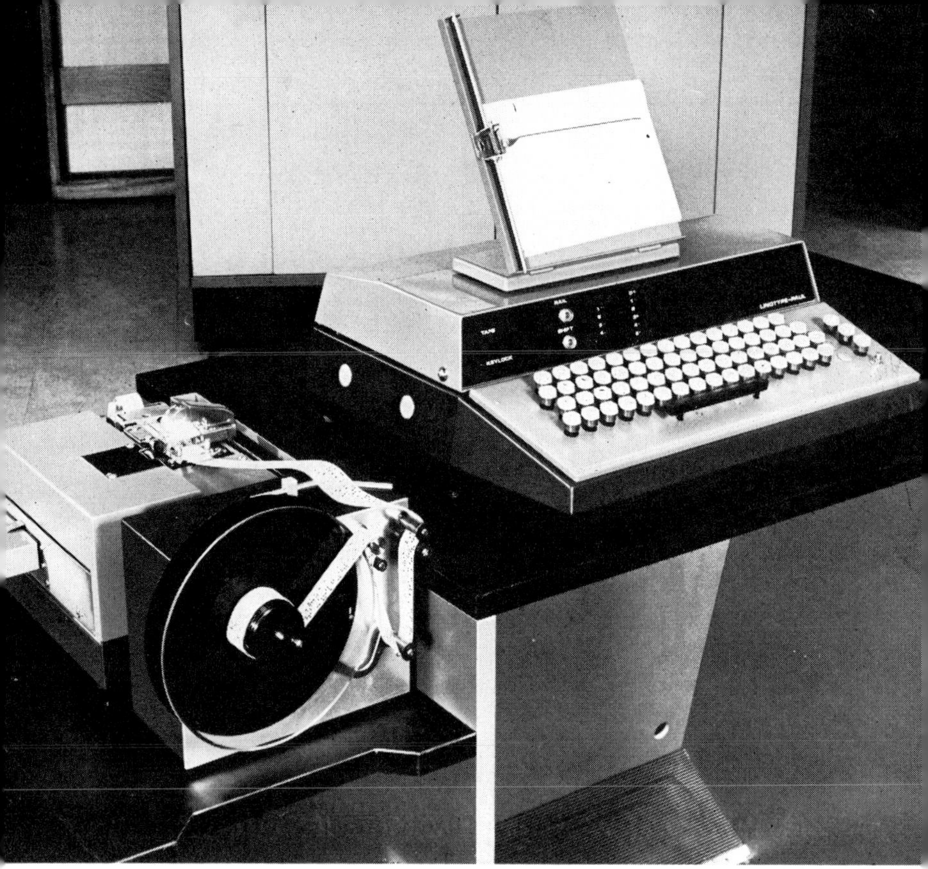

35. K. S. Paul computer keyboard; the perforating unit is seen at the left

36. A Linotron installation: keyboard, control unit with keyboard, and photo-unit

37. A compositor locking up a 32-page forme on an imposing surface

to 28 point, or to 72 point in an alternative version. In addition, there is what is called a pi system, found also in other machines, in which the printer may have matrices of special signs or symbols or other characters outside the normal complement of the grids; these characters are represented on the keyboard and can be set to keyboard command as required.

Accessory magnetic read/write units allow the machine to work with magnetic tape.

CRT photo-setters. A number of machines are now on the market that utilize a cathode-ray tube in the formation of the image photographed on to the film. The character derived from the matrix is presented on the face of the tube as on a television screen. There are raster lines, but they are much finer than on a television screen. In addition the image is larger than it will finally be and is reduced through a lens to the size required; the result is a letter sufficiently sharp when printed on paper, and indeed indistinguishable from any photographed directly from a photo-matrix. The Linotron 505 is one of these machines. CRT machines also include a remarkable variety, the window- or area-composition photo-composing machines. These are rare for the present, but no doubt they will become more common. All the machines we have so far considered set type in what we have always supposed to be the logical manner, that is following the order of the letters in the author's copy. That order, however, may not be the one most convenient mechanically or electronically and the newer area-composition machines achieve fantastic speeds by doing things differently. They put down the characters over an area of a number of lines or of a whole page; they could put down all the a's at once, to be followed by all the b's, scattered across the area but in the right places for the meaning and the justification of the lines to turn out correct. To do this the machine embodies a storage facility in which it stores the codes of the characters of the area and from which it selects as it requires. Examples of these machines include the Linotron 1010, the Fototronic CRT, the Digiset, and the Crosfield Magnaset. The Magnaset is perhaps the easiest to understand. Its matrices are carried on eight tracks around a drum, each track illuminated from the interior by a flash tube, which flashes for each character selected on its track. The composition area is a window two inches deep by up to ten inches wide, in which the characters are laid down as best suits the machine and not necessarily in orthographical sequence. The matrices are presented to an 'image orthocon camera', which converts the images into video signals and at the same time amplifies them. The signals pass to a cathode-ray tube, from the surface of which the images are projected through a lens on to film or paper. The speed claimed is up to a million characters per hour in sizes ranging from 5 point to 72 point. The machine works from computer-generated magnetic tape or unjustified perforated paper tape.

Very few of these complex machines are at present in service, but they are perhaps a portent of what the future holds for text composition in the printing industry.

CORRECTIONS IN PHOTO-COMPOSITION AND IN COMPUTER-AIDED TYPESETTING

Correction of photo-set type. One of the problems of photo-composition is the correction of the type subsequent to the exposure and development of the film. The film may be altered but at the cost of resetting and rephotographing the lines affected, cutting out the erroneous lines from the film, and fixing the new lines in their place. This work must be done with precision in order to preserve the alinement and the accuracy of interlinear spacing of the text. The operation is less convenient, especially for minor corrections, than is the correction of metal type, and consequently more costly, and this will be a factor governing the publisher's choice of hot metal or photo-composition for any particular book. A certain number of errors may be avoided in photo-composition by pre-photography correction. Errors perceived during composition may be corrected at the keyboard by killing words or lines so that they are not perforated in the tape, or if they are perforated the composing machine ignores them. Hard copy from the keyboard may be read as a proof and the tape corrected either by splicing in a new section in place of the erroneous one or by tape-merging. By such means it may be possible to produce, before photography, a tape that is correct and accurate according to the author's copy so that the film is free of the kind of errors the printer calls literals—i.e. mispellings, omissions, doublings, etc. This work, however, can take no account of subsequent emendations, additions, or deletions made in proof by the author or the publisher. Authors and publishers still want to see type-set proofs of books, with good reason, and will not be satisfied with hard copy as a proof to be passed for press. So we come back to corrections *after* photography, at the time when they are least convenient to carry out, and it will not be until some means has been found of carrying out such corrections economically that photo-composition will be able to compete with metal in the matter of correction costs.

Correction of computer-set text. Text that has been set on a computer or on a photo-composition machine embodying a computer may be corrected by the method of tape-merging. For this method it is essential that each word should have an 'address', and this is provided by automatic numbering of the lines on the hard copy, or on the proof, as they are set. The keyboard operator scans the copy corrected by the printer's reader or the author and for each correction he perforates in a new tape codes for the co-ordinates or 'address' of the word affected. This address is the line number and the number of the word in the line. He taps out this word as corrected and passes on to the next correction. We have then two tapes, the original or master tape and a second or correction tape, the latter carrying only the corrections with their corresponding addresses. The two tapes are fed through the computer (or a tape-merger), which follows the master tape, automatically perforating a third tape, until it comes to the first correction on the correction tape; it takes in this corrected word instead of the erroneous one and returns to follow the master tape until the next correction. The third tape, or merged tape, represents the text with all the corrections properly made and any justification (where justified tapes are being merged) adjusted accordingly. A revised hard copy may be produced during this process, which may be checked as a further precaution. Tapes may be merged as many times as required, the aim being to produce a final tape entirely free of errors and ready to set type on a composing machine without the expense of correcting machine-set type or film.

Magnetic tape may be corrected in a different way. Everyone with a tape recorder knows that a recording on tape can be cancelled or replaced with ease. With magnetic tape in a computer, storing the text in the form of magnetized spots on the coating, it is only necessary to be able to identify the precise position of a word to alter it as required. This is done by coding the address on a keyboard as for paper tape and retyping the word concerned.

THE FUTURE OF TEXT COMPOSITION

The field of general-purpose and special-purpose computers and their relation to typesetting, and especially to photo-composition, is for the present confused. There are too many kinds of justifying and non-justifying keyboards, of computers, and of photo-composing machines designed to be linked with computers. It seems probable that the market cannot support them all and sooner or later there will be a weeding out. Nor is it easy to see what will happen in relation to the complex and for the present expensive machines that set text at very high speeds. The question is not how fast or how much faster these machines may be made to work, but of the magnitude of our requirements in relation their enormous output.

The future may see the disappearance of the perforating keyboard or its relegation to a less important role. It is possible at the present time for a typescript to be read by a machine and for that reading to be converted automatically into tape to be fed into a computer, or indeed by cable directly into a computer without the intervention of tape. This system, called optical character recognition, or OCR, is well advanced, but it is apparent that it requires a perfect typescript. Authors will never supply perfect typescripts, and OCR may come into operation only when publishers take upon themselves the responsibility of supplying perfect typescripts to printers. This suggests that the keyboarding, which is what the preparation of a perfect typescript represents, will tend to be transferred from the printing-house to the publisher's office. Any such development would present another possibility. The printing unions have always jealously guarded the operation of typographical keyboards as a male preserve; in these new circumstances they might experience difficulty in preventing the work from passing to women.

A perfect typescript, in the sense of one entirely free of errors, is not essential if the retyping is done for optical reading on a machine such as the Crosfield Compuscan. A typewriter with a key for a special delete symbol is required. The typist types her copy in the conventional manner until she perceives that she has made an error. She does not try to erase the error. Instead she types the delete symbol immediately after the wrong letter. If she wishes to cancel the whole word she types two delete symbols, if a line three delete symbols. The typed sheets are then placed in the Compuscan, which optically reads the characters, omitting any letter, word, or line followed by delete symbols.

Any publisher will recognize that this is not enough. It must be possible for the typescript to be read editorially before it goes through the machine and there must be provision for hand-corrections. This is provided for. The Compuscan will stop when it encounters a hand-correction and the corrected word or insertion of additional matter may be typed on a keyboard built into the machine. Further, a cathode-ray tube may be used to display blocks of text and this allows for yet a further check.

In the machine the edited and corrected text is processed to a paper-tape punch or a magnetic-tape deck. The resulting tape may then be processed through a computer or a computing photo-composition machine.

PHOTO-SETTING FOR DISPLAY

The compositor setting larger sizes of metal type for display work—that is, in books, for such things as chapter openings, for title-pages, and for book-jackets—is paralleled in photo-composition by operators using special machines for photo-setting display sizes. There are several machines on the market designed for this work. Some are simple, little more than adapted photographic dark-room enlargers and they must be used in a dark-room. Others may be used in full light, are more sophisticated in design, and allow greater ease and accuracy in operation. All will enlarge or reduce from their photo matrices, which are carried on strips, slides, or disks, the letters being projected one by one and positioned more or less manually before being exposed to film or paper. Accessories make most of them capable of extraordinary things—they will compress or expand characters, make them slope forwards or backwards, set them in a circle or a multiple curve, or apply tints over them to produce grey effects. The Starsettograph and the Monotype studio-lettering machine (Figure 30) are examples of the simpler kind, the Monotype photo-lettering machine (Figure 31) of the more sophisticated variety. The Hadego, among those longest established, is rather different; it may be compared with the hot-metal Ludlow; with the Hadego the photo-matrices are set in a 'stick' by hand, to be put into the machine as a line to be photographed all at once.

VI

THE PAGE TAKES SHAPE

Make-up and Imposition

WHETHER the type has been set by hand or by machine, it is not in the shape of a book, and cannot be printed as a book, while it still lies in slabs, each two or three pages long, on galleys. The slabs will first have to be divided up into page lengths and then to each page length must be added whatever accessories in the way of page headings, folios, and footnotes that may be required.

Paging is a manual operation carried out by compositors working in the composing room. Each man has his share of slip proofs, and receives the corresponding galleys after the proofs have been read and the type corrected, and instructions have been given to go ahead with paging. First the lines of type on the galley are divided into sections each with the exact number of lines for a page. This is straightforward and easy, but there are certain conventions that introduce a little extra work; for instance, a page must not begin with the half-line at the end of a paragraph, and if the division results in this, then the paging will have to be recast slightly, or the spacing of some lines widened or reduced in order to gain or save a line, to prevent the defect. But some printers and publishers do not object to it. Then, too, it looks silly and niggling to end a chapter with a page of only two or three lines, and if this happens the paging must be revised to produce more lines for this last page or to absorb them into the previous one. Footnotes are included in the page depth, and these have to be added wherever they are indicated, and the appropriate reference numbers or signs inserted in the text and at the beginning of the note. Any line blocks that are to be printed with the text must also be inserted, and if the text is to run round them the lines affected must be rearranged and respaced; legends for the blocks must be included too, and properly leaded. Then the page heading and the folio number are added.

Page headings, footnotes, legends, and folios are usually set on the machine, and the compositor has them by him on galleys ready for use. If there are only a few of any of these items, it is not worth while to set them mechanically, and then they are set by hand. Any displayed matter, such as part titles, chapter titles, etc., is also usually set by hand.

The positioning and spacing of half-titles and chapter titles needs careful attention and each must be given the correct drop from the top of the page.

If leading of the text is required this has to be done at the make-up stage if it has not already been done on the machine. Usually it is done on the composing machine very simply and efficiently by using a mould of a larger point size than that normally required for the size of type in use. Thus an eleven-point type cast on a twelve-point body will appear as though it has one point extra space between the lines. Almost without exception type faces look better and are easier to read if they are leaded, so much so that it is generally preferable to use a smaller size of type and to lead it than to use a larger one and to set it solid. I am aware that this statement flatly contradicts the teachings of many book designers, especially of those inspired by William Morris.

If leading has not been done on the machine, leads must be inserted between the lines by the compositor. With founders' type this is the only way leading can be done. It is not a good way, because leads are bought by the printer in long lengths and cut up by him into the measures required, and no amount of care seems able to ensure that every lead is exactly the right length. If the lead is too long it will endanger whole masses of type at the imposition stage later on; and if it is too short it will not support narrow letters at the ends of the lines, and these will slip and assume an aloof or drunken appearance. The reader will have noticed this intoxication at one time or another.

There is a tale, often repeated, that leading articles in newspapers are called leaders because they are usually leaded. Why anyone should choose to believe this when it seems more reasonable to assume that they are called leaders because they lead I cannot tell. Anyway, the newspaper leader is a 'leeder' and the printers leads are 'leds'—for the very good reason that they are made chiefly of lead.

Any half-page blanks or whole blanks that are to appear in the book are made up by the compositor. Although nothing is printed on a page, it does not mean that that page is represented by nothing in type metal: and the same thing applies to the half blanks at the end of the chapters, and to the open spaces of part-titles. All these must be made up in leads and furniture to the right measure and page depth.

It will be seen from this account that the process of make-up is the assembly of all the parts of type, furniture, etc., that are required for the complete book, and their proper arrangement in page lengths. I showed that it was essential that each line of type should be exactly the same measure, and it is equally essential that every page should be the same depth. We shall see why in a moment.

As each page is completed it is tied up with cord so that it may be moved about, to a limited extent, without falling to pieces. It is then ready for imposition.

IMPOSITION

Imposition is the name given to the work of arranging a number of pages so that they will print together on a sheet of paper in such a way that when the sheet is folded in a particular manner the pages appear in correct sequence; and it is also the name for the arrangement itself.

A leaf of a book is a sheet of paper printed on both sides. The simplest way to print this is to print one page first on one side and the second page afterwards on the other; and this would be the only possible way if the only size of paper available were that of the leaf. Each side would have to be imposed and printed separately in what is called sheet imposition.

If, however, paper double the size of the leaf is at hand, half-sheet imposition can be used and a great deal of labour saved. The two pages would be laid down together as in Figure 38, and the two printed at once on one side of the double-size sheet of paper, which would then be turned over and printed

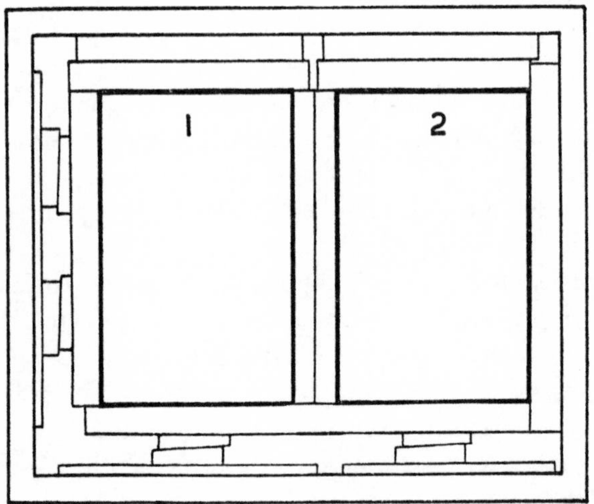

38. Half-sheet imposition for two-page leaflet

on the other side—page 1 printing on the back of page 2 and page 2 on the back of page 1. It is now only necessary to divide the sheet down the middle to give two complete copies of the leaf.

These are the two simplest forms of imposition; and while they will do for an example here, they will not in fact do for the printing of a book, since the leaves they produce are all separate and cannot be bound in the ordinary way.

It is essential in the making of a book that the minimum size of paper used should be twice as large as a leaf and that it must remain that size when complete. Thus, instead of printing pages 1 and 2 in half-sheet imposition as in the foregoing example, and then printing them again on the back of the paper to produce two identical copies, it will be necessary to go about it in another way. Assuming that the paper is twice the size of the leaf, we shall have to print four different pages on it to produce a copy capable of being bound, and the imposition would be (sheet imposition) as in Figure 39. Pages 1 and 4 are

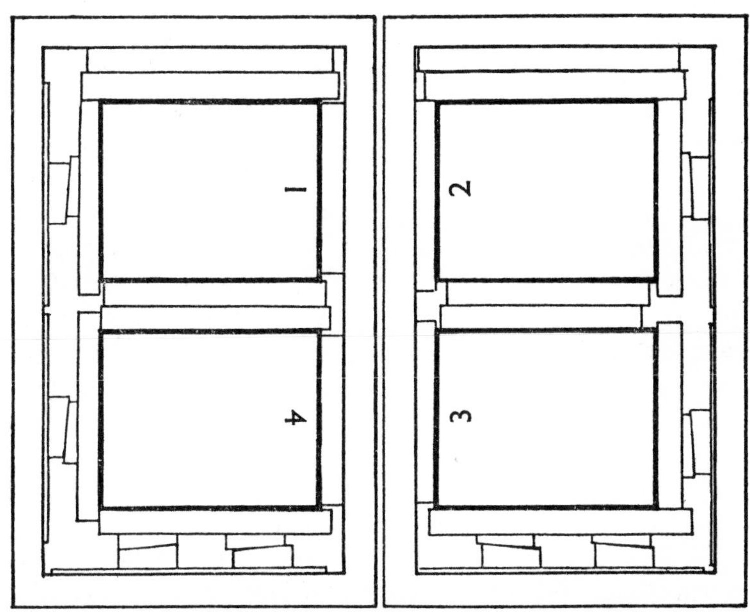

39. Sheet imposition (two formes) for four-page folder

printed on one side of the sheet and pages 2 and 3 on the other side; if the sheet is now folded down the middle a four-page section of four consecutive pages is obtained, and this can be bound by stitching through the fold.

Time and labour can again be saved if paper twice as large as the double page is used. Then the two impositions above can be combined and half-sheet imposition resorted to.

These impositions were once used for the printing of books, but are now used no longer, except for oddments of a few pages at the end. To-day larger and more powerful machines are available, more pages can be printed at once, and more complicated impositions have been worked out. If you look along the top edge of this book you will see that it has been bound in sections of eight leaves, or sixteen pages (some of the sections have additional pages of illustrations, which are added as explained in a later chapter), and you will find if you refer to other books that this is by far the most usual arrangement. These eight leaves represent the size of the sheet used in printing (or, it would be better to say, as I will show later, the basic size); and the size of the leaf obtained in this way is octavo.

The sheet is therefore eight times the size of the leaf of the book, and eight pages are printed on each side, giving sixteen in all. The imposition would be as in Figure 40. One set of pages is printed on one side of the paper and the other on the other side (sheet imposition). The sheet can then be folded to give sixteen consecutive pages. The resulting section or signature (one is the binder's name for it, the other the printer's) will have folds at the head and on the foredge and cannot be read until these have been cut or trimmed off. This is the solution of the profound mystery that puzzles most children when they receive an uncut book—how the 'writing' was done in those inaccessible places.

The intricacy of imposition does not stop here, for to-day sheets four times the size of the basic sheet, or even eight times, are in general use, and sheet or half-sheet imposition can be used with any of these sizes. These impositions contain 64 and 128 pages respectively. Books are commonly printed on sheets four times the size of the basic sheet (quad size). There are several ways of folding such a sheet, and therefore several different schemes of imposition. A frequent imposition is the one shown in Figure 41. The quad sheet is cut into four by the binder's folding machine during folding.

The imposition of the pages of type is the business of the stone-hand, who works at a table with a top of smoothly planed steel (Figure 37). This table is the imposing surface. Formerly the top was made of stone, and because of this the whole table was known as the 'stone' and the man who worked at it the 'stone-

40. Sheet imposition for sixteen-page sheet to fold in octavo

hand'. Stones are now anachronisms in the composing room, but the name 'stone-hand' remains, and the steel-surfaced table is itself still often called the stone, though this name tends to give way now to 'the surface'.

In the traditions of printing the stone plays an important part, for around it once or twice a year, or whenever special circumstances warrant it, the meeting of the chapel is held. The stone forms the table of the meeting, and at it the father of the chapel stands, with a wooden mallet in his hand as a gavel, with which he beats upon the stone to keep order.

The surface is machined accurately flat, so that type standing on its feet upon it will all stand at the same level. The pages for the particular imposition are gathered together from the galleys—it will be remembered that they were tied up with cord so that they could be moved about—and arranged on the surface in the correct order and in approximately the correct position. Next the stone-hand places around the group of pages a chase—a steel frame with two crossbars. Metal or wooden furniture, reglets, and leads are inserted between the pages to give the margins required in the finished book, and also between the outside pages and the edge of the chase, where about half an inch of space is left, in which are inserted metal double wedges or expansion devices called quoins. Quoins were originally wooden wedges as shown on pages 102, 103; though old-fashioned these are by no means obsolete. A later kind of quoin is shown on page 105; this is made of iron and the wedges are moved one against the other by means of a toothed key; these quoins in turn tend to be replaced by patented devices consisting essentially of two pieces forced apart by an eccentric, again turned by a key, or spread by a wedge lifted by a screw; examples of such quoins are shown in Figure 37.

The diagrams show the arrangement plainly, and it will now be clear why every line of type must be exactly the same length and why each page must be the same depth. The pressure of the wedges against the chase squeezes the type up against the crossbars, so that every single piece of type receives its share of pressure and is held in a vice-like grip. Type, furniture, and

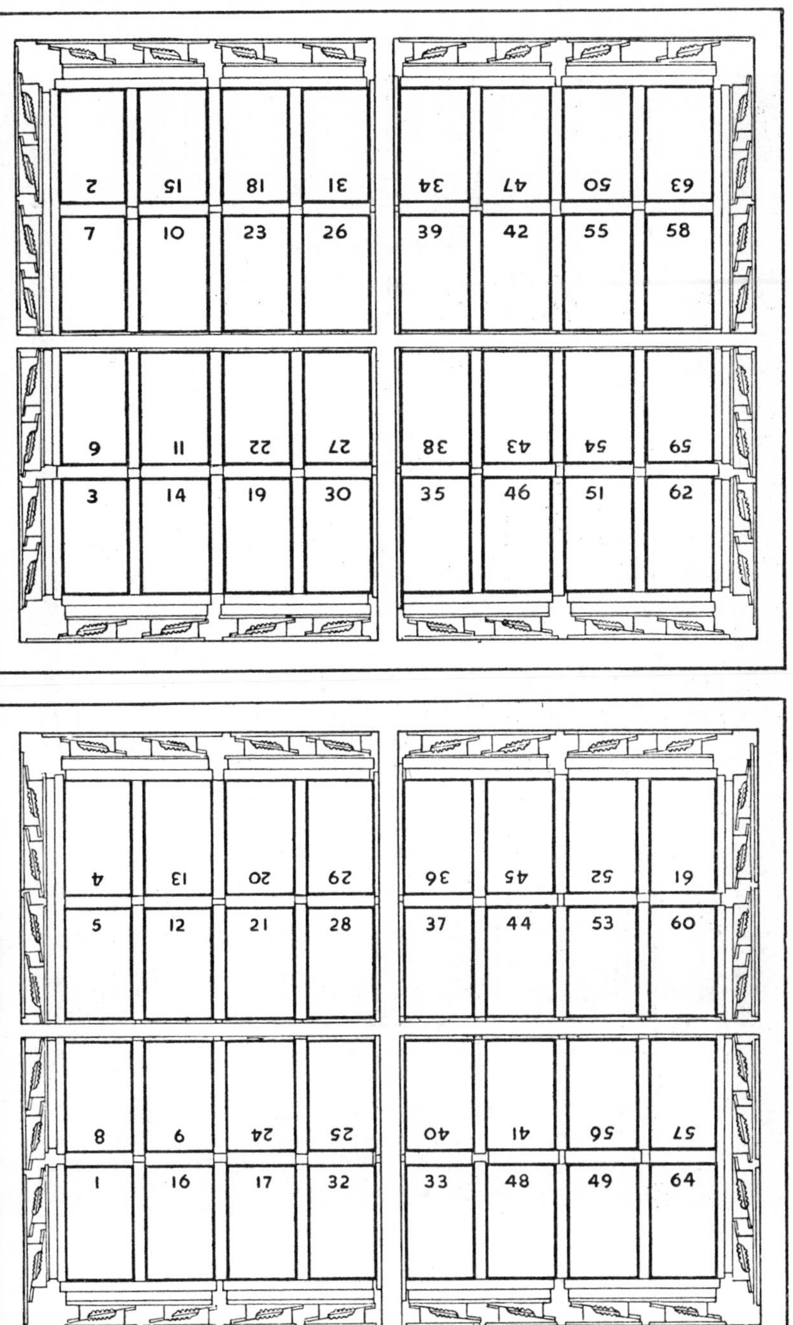

41. Sheet imposition for sixty-four pages to fold into four octavo sections of sixteen pages each

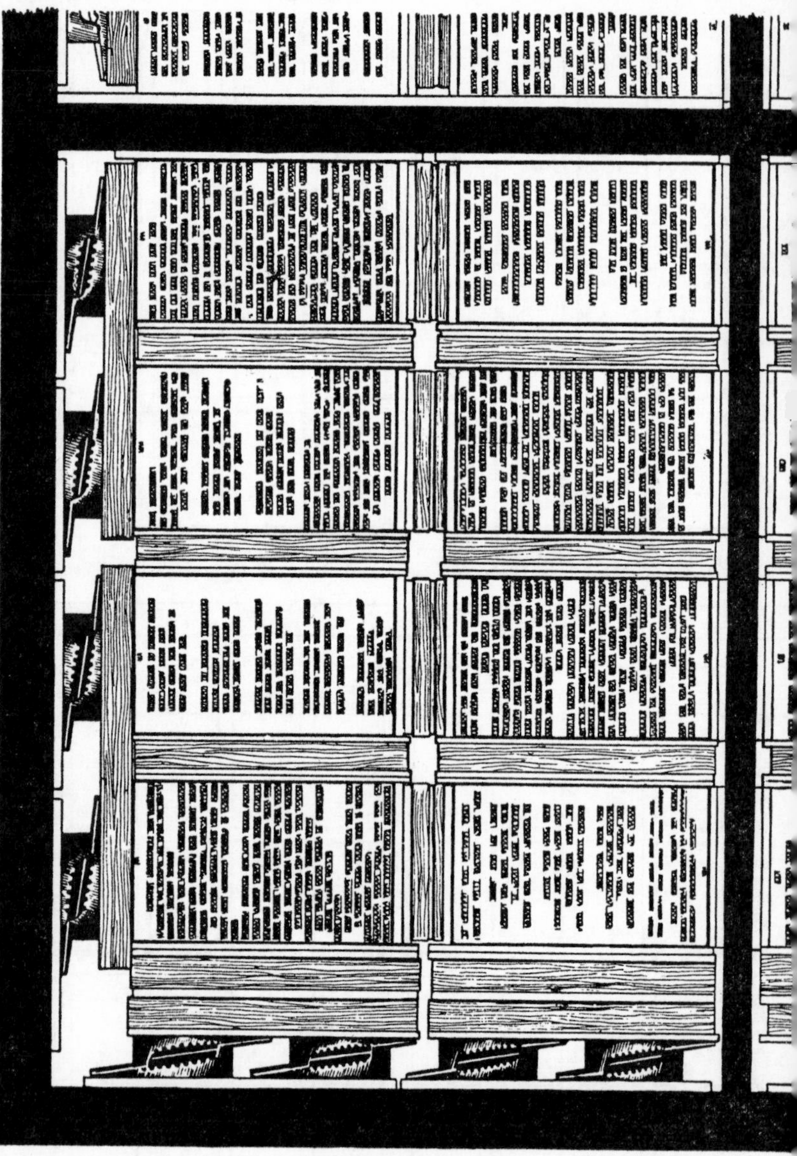

42. Section of a thirty-two page forme, showing the arrangement of furniture and quoins

the chase are converted by the pressure of the quoins alone into a solid unit that can be lifted and transported with no danger, if the work has been properly done, of any part falling out. The type is, in the printer's phrase, locked up, and the whole assembly is called a forme (Figures 38–42).

Proofs of the forme are made on a proofing press, folded, and sent for reading by the printer's reader, by the publisher, and by the author, and the forme is stored away to await the return of the proofs. When they are returned the forme is lifted back on to the surface, the quoins are loosened, and any corrections necessary are made in much the same way as the compositor made them on the galley at an earlier stage. After correction the forme is locked up again, checked yet once more, and sent to the machine room, ready for printing.

STEREOTYPING

In some circumstances—for example, when a book is to be printed in a larger edition than can be obtained from type—stereotypes may be made from the pages of type. A stereotype is a cast of the type face and to produce it a mould is required. The mould or matrix for casting a metal stereotype plate is made of a card-like material called 'flong' which is forced firmly upon the type in a heavy press, so producing indentations of the shape of every letter. The mould is then placed in a casting-box and molten metal is poured in to produce a plate of metal bearing upon one side reliefs of the letters of the original type. This plate is shaved level on the reverse side and is mounted on wood or special mounts to bring it to type height. Metal stereos are still made but thermoplastics are increasingly used for the mould, while rubber or plastics, the latter either thermosetting or thermoplastic, are used for the plate. Plastics and rubbers are lighter to handle than metal stereotypes and give good service; for very long runs two or more sets of stereos may be made. Stereotypes may be curved to fit the cylinders of rotary machines, as happens regularly in newspaper offices.

MAKE-UP AND IMPOSITION OF PHOTO-SET TYPE

The principle of making up formes of photo-set matter is basically the same as for metal type. The aim is to prepare a forme of a group of pages of text—eight, sixteen, thirty-two, or sixty-four pages—and the operator has to observe the same rules of imposition, the same regard for margins and positions, but he works at a light-table instead of an imposing-surface. The table is surfaced with glass and illuminated from below. If he is working with film, he lays a sheet of transparent plastic on the table and on this he attaches in the positions required all the various pieces of film representing text, folios, headlines, chapter titles, and so forth, which may have come to him from several text composing machines and lettering machines, together with film of any illustrations the book is to have in the text. Some computers can be programmed to produce 'fully formatted' pages, that is text divided into page lengths complete with page numbers and headlines, and when this is the case the work of make-up is a little easier. The end product is the equivalent of a forme of metal type as a positive or negative that can be printed down on to metal to produce printing surfaces for letterpress, litho, or gravure. The operator may work with paper prints instead of film, in which case he will produce a paste-up for rephotographing.

VII

THE PRINTER'S READER

THE printer's reader is too often an undervalued employee the cost of whose services is liable to be thought of as an overhead. In many printing houses he is relegated to a small and stuffy closet or room that cannot be put to other good use, or is incarcerated in a wooden box made by partitioning off one corner of the composing room. Ideally the conditions he requires are those of light and air, everything that conduces to mental alertness and the avoidance of eye-strain; and sometimes he gets the ideal, or something near it.

It is a mistake, and a serious and silly mistake, to undervalue the reader, for on him depends no small amount of the reputation of the printing house; and he may, too, be instrumental in preventing legal actions for libel and damages.

Readers commonly work together in one room, each with his own desk, and in some houses his own little compartment. Assisting the readers are a number of girls or boys, who are called copyholders. It is the reader's business to discover any errors that may have been made in the setting of the type and to give instructions for their correction; and also to look out for mistakes made by the author himself, and if necessary to call his attention to them.

First, as we saw earlier, the galley proofs come into the reading room together with the appropriate copy. Preferably, any book should be read in its entirety by one reader. A copyholder is called in to read aloud from the author's manuscript or typescript while the reader follows the wording of the proof, checking it with what the copyholder is reading, watching out for errors both of compositor and copyholder, and also for those of the author, watching for wrong-fount letters that may have crept into the text, and keeping a weather eye open for libel and defamation, or anything that might bring the printing house into bad repute or actual legal complications.

Any errors that are found are indicated by special marks, of which a number are shown on pages 114–15. Every printer understands the meaning of these marks, and when the galley returns to the compositor the latter will carry out the corrections thus indicated.

When proofs are returned corrected from the author, it is the reader's job to incorporate the author's corrections with his own on one set of galleys, and if necessary to convert the author's markings (which may be very queer indeed) into something that can be more correctly understood. If the corrections are numerous it may be necessary to have revised galley proofs before going into page, but otherwise instructions to go ahead with the pagination are passed on now.

In due course the page proofs come to the reader, and must be checked against the corrected galleys, to see that all the corrections have been carried out and that no new errors have been made. At this stage there will be new matter to be read and corrected, page headlines, for example, chapter heads, the legends of illustrations, etc., and care must be taken to see that any displayed matter is set in the types and sizes specified and properly spaced.

After this check the proofs are returned to the composing room for the correction of the forme.

Lastly, a new set of proofs comes to the reading room. This is the machine proof, which is pulled immediately before the forme goes on the press, or while it is actually on the press; and while the press is being prepared for printing the machine proof is read by a particularly experienced and capable reader, the press reader. This is the last opportunity there is for discovering any errors that have so far escaped detection, and for this reason a reliable man is chosen for this work.

If anything goes wrong with the text of a book after it is

printed—if errors are found in it, or something has been done that should not have been done, or not done that should have been done—it is the reader who is blamed. Poor man, he lives under the responsibility of proving his innocence. And he is in a sense the Cinderella of printing, constantly fighting for a higher wage and better conditions, and not greatly succeeding; his basic wage is the same as that of a compositor. The composing room envies him because he sits at a desk and does not have to dirty his fingers with type, or detests him because he seems to point out its shortcomings—which is his work, after all; the machine-minders perhaps see no reason why he should exist.

The qualifications required of him are extensive. He must have a sharp eye and an alert mind to recognize at once the subtlest of misspellings; and he should be able to recognize every type face presented to him, even to a single letter. He must be able to spell almost anything without referring to a dictionary—a team of readers would make hay of any opponents in a spelling bee. He must be able to read the most crabbed and illegible hand-writing, and read it correctly—and authors, like doctors, possess notoriously untidy and unreasonable fists. Ideally he should know every date in the history book, and have besides an intimate acquaintance with the meaning and shape of every word in or out of the Oxford English Dictionary. He should know every phrase in Shakespeare and the Bible and be able to pick out misquotations as they occur. He should know all about comparative religion and as much about economics, politics, and science as possible—and art too, of course. In fact he should have the widest possible general knowledge, and his value is enhanced if he can speak and write, say, a dozen languages.

If such a paragon as this exists he would be a fool if he did not at once find a job more lucrative than reading for a printing house. The reader does his best, and very often he does surprisingly well. He is not necessarily an old man, bowed with the weight of years, experience, and university degrees. He is more likely a compositor who has shown aptitude and been translated from the composing room; or he has served an

THE READER'S MARKS

The marks in the margins of this page are such as the reader makes in painting out the sins of the compositor. It is a sign language of ancient lineage, understood by *all* printers. The double twirl with a tail signifies delete, i.e. take out, the letter crossed word or through in the text. The delete sign is no more than a simplified d (or possibly δ) combined with a stroke following it. Where a word has left out it is inserted as shown here; or where has it been put in the wrong place, transposed.

Perhaps a space is missing, andif so the place is indicated and the grating marked in the margin; or a space may have been put in where there should be none, when two little curved lines serve to re move it. where a lower-case letter is to be changed to a capital, it can be crossed through and the word 'cap' written in the margin or it can be done by writing the capital letter there, together with three underlinings, which mean cap. Where the Reverse is required, l.c. is written.

The signs are really self-explanatory, as may be seen by comparing the facing page which is a corrected version of this with the reader's marks on this one. It is important that any corrections should be indicated in the margin, for the compositor doesread through the proof, and cannot be expected to see an alteration in the middle of the text that is not signposted in the margin. Printers do not usually make as many errors as may be suggested by this page

Note that the strokes used in the text and between the marks in the margin are not the same for a replacement and an insertion. The stroke to cross out a letter is a mere line; that used to insert a letter or a word is a line with a small branch, a 'caret', at the foot.

THE READER'S MARKS

THE marks in the margins of this page are such as the reader makes in pointing out the sins of the compositor. It is a sign language of ancient lineage, understood by all printers. The double twirl with a tail signifies delete, i.e. take out, the letter or word crossed through in the text. The delete sign is no more than a simplified d (or possibly δ) combined with a stroke following it. Where a word has been left out it is inserted as shown here; or where it has been put in the wrong place, transposed. Perhaps a space is missing, and if so the place is indicated and the grating is marked in the margin; or a space may have been put in where there should be none, when two little curved lines serve to remove it. Where a lower-case letter is to be changed to a capital, it can be crossed through and the word 'cap' written in the margin; or it can be done by writing the capital letter there, together with three underlinings, which mean capital. Where the reverse is required, l.c. is written. Note that the strokes used in the text and between the marks in the margin are not the same for a replacement and an insertion. The stroke to cross out a letter is a mere line; that used to insert a letter or a word is a line with a small branch, a 'caret', at the foot.

The signs are really self-explanatory, as may be seen by comparing the facing page, which is a corrected version of this, with the reader's marks on this one. It is important that any corrections should be indicated in the margin, for the compositor does not read through the proof, and cannot be expected to see an alteration in the middle of the text that is not sign-posted in the margin.

Printers do not usually make as many errors as may be suggested by this page!

43. The opposite page shows a selection of marks made by a proof-reader, and this page shows the type after correction by the compositor.

apprenticeship to reading, and learned by hard experience what he ought to do. He should, and usually does, know a great deal about printing, because such knowledge is useful, more, essential, in his work; and he possesses also a heterogeneous store of facts learned from books he has read, or picked up here and there, for every fact he can master is potentially useful.

It might be thought that the reader is superfluous and that what he does should be done by the author, who ought to know what he wants to say and how to say it. In practice the author is seldom a trustworthy person to pass his own proofs. He may have, probably has, gone through life with the fixed belief that he can spell, when in fact he has never been able to spell at all. He may be dimly aware that many words in English can be correctly spelled in two or more ways, and use every variety of spelling without realizing it. Nearly always he has no notion of the proper use of capital letters. The reader silently sets him right, and receives precious little credit for it.

Authors, who, as many of them do, hate the sight of their own typescripts and never refer to them again once they have proofs in type, are sometimes appalled by what they have written when they see it in print, and believe, perhaps, that the printer has been improvising on their work; the reader sometimes wishes that he could.

Nevertheless, many authors are greatly indebted to the printer's reader, and some of them acknowledge the debt. The reader may not rewrite the author's sentences, nor alter his ideas, but he can, when he considers a statement untrue, or ambiguous, or merely silly, call attention to the matter by inserting a query in the margin of the proof that is to be sent out to the author. He must do it tactfully, however, for authors are notoriously touchy, and the reader often has no idea what sort of man he is dealing with. If the author accepts the suggestion, he will amend or correct the sentence concerned, and, we hope, be duly grateful; if he does not accept it he should cross out the query, but sometimes he succumbs, lamentably, to the temptation to write a sarcastic reply.

Besides his other qualifications the reader should know

something of the law of libel and the laws relating to indecency. If anything libellous or indecent is printed the printer is liable to the same extent as the author and publisher, and he cannot legally shuffle off the responsibility on to them. Any successful action for damages reflects on him, and indeed there have been occasions when the printer was the only person able to pay, since he was the only one of the three parties to the publication of a book who had any capital—and that in the form of plant. The reader must, as well as he can, protect his employer against these risks by calling attention to any defamatory or indecent matter he finds, when the printer can refuse to print the book unless it is amended. This is particularly difficult in the case of libel, because it is not always possible to know when words that would be defamatory if applied to real people can be applied to real people. It is not usually possible, for example, for the reader to know that the double-dyed villain has been drawn from real life, and if there is any doubt about it the best course is safety first.

VIII

PRINTING MACHINES AND THE WORK OF THE PRESSMAN

THE word 'printing', it seems, means to the layman simply the impression of type on paper, and he understands very little, or nothing at all, of composing. The compositor, if he has heard of him, is an individual who does something shadowy and vague in a printing house, but is not, perhaps, the real printer. There is, however, no such thing as a 'printer' in modern printing, if by this term is meant someone who operates the process from beginning to end. Division of labour began very early in the history of the industry, and is to-day practically complete. The average compositor can no more do the work of the pressman than the pressman can do that of the compositor; and even if he could the regulations of one of the strongest trade unions in the country forbid him to do so. He must be one or the other and he cannot be both together.

Just as the compositor is a skilled man, the product of a careful apprenticeship and a long tradition, so too is the pressman; and his history may be even longer, for while there could be no compositors before the invention of movable type, pressmen were necessarily concerned in the printing of woodcuts and block books.

The first presses were heavy, cumbersome affairs, perhaps converted cheese presses, or, what may be thought more likely, bookbinders' or papermakers' screw presses adapted or modified, but some very good work was done on them despite their deficiencies. They were soon refined for their purpose, and by the later part of the fifteenth century a principle had been worked out that was to remain fundamentally the same for the next three hundred years, and which still survives to-day.

A printing press is essentially an appliance by means of which a sheet of paper is pressed against the inked surface of a forme of type, so that the ink is transferred from the type to the paper. This was all that the hand-press could do. A modern press is power-driven, and provides for the automatic inking of the type, for the feeding of the paper into the machine, and for its removal afterwards, as well as for the fundamental business of impression, but all these complications are comparatively recent.

The hand-press evolved in the fifteenth century was made of wood, and made massively, not only because it was the custom of the time to make most things massive, but also to secure rigidity and to withstand the wear and tear of constant heavy use. For the sake of rigidity it was fixed not only to the floor, but to the ceiling also, as will be seen in Figure 12. The first iron press appeared in 1800, and thenceforward wood was superseded; the principle, however, remained the same (though the ceiling attachment had been abandoned long ago). Some iron hand-presses were highly ornamented (see Figure 44). Iron hand-presses were manufactured until late in the nineteenth century, and in many printing offices there survives a specimen, still valiantly at work, in use as a proofing press or for the printing of small quantities of posters, etc. Occasionally some enthusiastic amateur gets hold of one and, following in the revered footsteps of William Morris, sets up a private press to produce 'real hand-printed books'—with what advantage only he and the handicraft enthusiast can tell.

The hand-press consists of a flat plate, the bed, on which the forme is laid. Hinged to the bed is a frame, the tympan, holding a stretched canvas or vellum sheet, on which the paper to be printed is fixed in a predetermined position. The forme used to be inked by dabbing it with an ink-covered ball made of leather and filled with sand; now it is done by rolling with a hand roller made of a rubber-like composition. After the type is inked, the tympan is lowered on to the forme. The bed is set on runners, so that by turning a handle it can be made to slide under the upright part of the press, where it comes to rest immediately below a ponderous iron plate, the platen. Then a

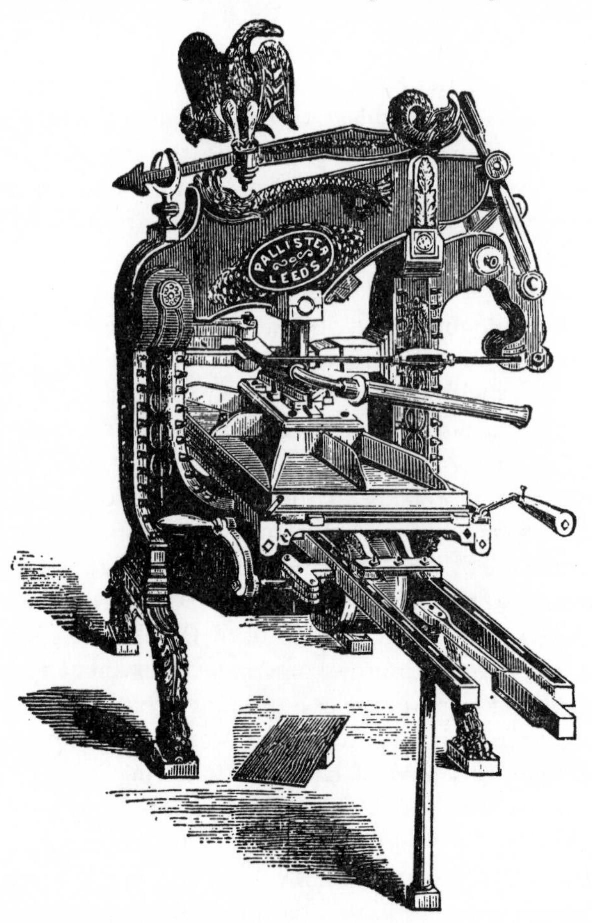

44. A nineteenth-century iron hand-press—the Columbian

lever is pulled over to bring the platen down with considerable, but gradual, pressure on the tympan, the lever is released, the bed withdrawn, and the tympan raised. The sheet of paper, now printed, is removed and hung over a line like a piece of washing for the ink to dry. The cycle of operations is repeated for the next sheet, and so on until the edition is complete.

This kind of machine was slow by our standards and incapable of printing great quantities in a reasonable time, but it satisfied printers and the demand for books for nearly four centuries, until the discovery of steam power and the extension of literacy inaugurated an era both of inventive mechanical genius and the demand to stimulate it.

The first steam press was one built by two Saxon engineers, Koenig and Bauer, in London in 1812. Their invention,

45. Diagram of a Koenig and Bauer double-cylinder press built for *The Times* in 1814. This machine printed two sheets at once. The sheets were fed in from the upper-feeding boards at left and right, passed round the cylinder, and were taken off on to the lower boards.

revolutionary in character, was a success. The principle on which they worked had been put forward by an Englishman, William Nicholson, at the end of the previous century, but not put into practice; it is the principle on which all book presses work to-day, and, indeed, that on which the great presses of modern newspaper offices are based, though these have developed out of all recognition.

In this new machine the platen was no longer a flat plate, but a cylinder that rolled over a reciprocating bed on which the forme lay. As the bed travelled under the cylinder, the latter revolved, taking with it a sheet of paper and pressing it against the type, which had been inked by passing under inking rollers before engaging with the cylinder. The sheets were fed to the machine one by one by hand, several operatives being required in constant attendance. It worked much faster than a hand-press could do, and produced up to eight hundred copies per hour. The machine provided automatic inking. It so impressed John Walter, of *The Times*, that he ordered two machines on the spot.

I need not go further into the development of printing machines than this. Newspaper presses went their own way and have become enormous contraptions into which paper is fed at one end from a reel, while at the other end are delivered completed newspapers ready folded and counted; and book presses became versatile and more compact, more efficient, and more automatic.

There are to-day two kinds of press in general use in the printing of books, the stop-cylinder press and the two-revolution press. Both kinds are capable of the best quality of work. The two-revolution machine is the later comer and it seems destined to oust the stop-cylinder, at least in the larger sizes.

THE STOP-CYLINDER PRESS

The type of this machine is the Wharfedale, so called because it was first made more than ninety years ago in that part of Yorkshire—Otley, to be exact—still a centre of printing machinery manufacture. The word 'Wharfedale' is in this connection a trade name, but for the printer it has become so familiar that it is used to denote, not merely a particular make of machine, but a particular kind, as who should say 'Wharfedale' says 'stop-cylinder', though to-day this kind of machine is made by several firms in different parts of the world.

The principle of the Wharfedale is the principle of the Koenig and Bauer press—an impression cylinder lying horizontally above a flat reciprocating bed. The bed is attached to an ink table, which reciprocates with the bed, and at each reciprocation passes under a duct to receive a supply of ink, which is evenly distributed over the table by rollers. The ink table then passes under another system of rollers, the inking rollers. These pick up an even layer of ink, and as the bed with the forme on it in turn reciprocates, impart the ink to the type in a thin film. All this happens during the forward and backward strokes of the bed. On the forward stroke the bed passes under the cylinder without affecting it, and while it does so a sheet of paper is fed to guides close to the cylinder. On the backward stroke the bed engages with the cylinder and causes it to revolve, grippers in the cylinder take hold of the edge of the sheet and draw it in, and it is pressed against the inked surface of the type. When the cylinder has completed about half the revolution the grippers release the sheet, which is taken up by a roller and then conveyed on endless tapes to the rear of the machine, where it is dropped on a delivery board. With the completion of one revolution the cylinder stops and the bed reciprocates towards the front of the machine again, ready for the next printing stroke.

At the front of the machine is the feeding board, a large wooden surface sloping gently down towards the base of the cylinder. On this board the paper is placed in a pile, and the feeder takes it, one sheet at a time, and slides it down the incline to gauges that mark the correct position in which the sheet must lie at the moment the cylinder grippers take hold of it. Feeding must be done in a definite, deliberate rhythm that does not tire the feeder and yet keeps pace with the machine. A new hand will scramble and fumble to get each sheet to the gauges in time, and then not succeed in getting them straight; but an expert will feed the same machine with an appearance of leisure in the regular, quite slow movements of hands and arms, and will be able to go on feeding all day. Feeders, where they are employed, are generally women, but the machines are in charge of a man, who regulates the ink supply, sees that the machines are running properly, and oversees the operation generally.

The stop-cylinder press prints only one side of the sheet at once. The other side is printed later, either by turning the paper over and printing the same forme on it (half-sheet imposition), or printing a new forme on the second side (sheet imposition).

These machines will produce 1,000 to 1,500 impressions per hour. They are made in several sizes, to print paper from crown size (15 × 20 inches) to quad demy (35 × 45 inches) or even double quad demy (70 × 45 inches).

THE TWO-REVOLUTION MACHINE

This is fundamentally similar in many respects to the stop-cylinder press, and it prints in the same manner, by means of a cylinder revolving over a reciprocating bed on which is the forme; but there is an obvious difference in that the cylinder does not stop when the bed returns on the non-printing stroke, but continues to revolve, rising slightly so that it cannot come in contact with the type and descending again for the printing stroke. It is claimed for this principle that it does away with the jar resulting from the continual braking and stopping of the heavy cylinder found in the stop-cylinder press, and it is certainly true that the two-revolution press has less vibration. I have seen a machine-minder demonstrating the stability of his press by standing a pencil on end on the feeding board while the machine was running, a feat that would be impossible with a large stop-cylinder. The minimum of vibration makes for quieter running, too.

Because the cylinder does not stop, the two-revolution press can work at a greater speed than the stop-cylinder, and commonly does so, producing 2,000 or more impressions per hour. It is in no way inferior in results, the extra speed being mainly possible because of the continual revolution of the cylinder.

We saw that the sheets fed to the stop-cylinder press are fed to the base of the cylinder, and the feeder stands at floor level, or only slightly above it. With the two-revolution press the sheets are fed over the top of the cylinder, and the feeder stands on a platform half-way up the side of the machine.

I need make no special reference to other points of working

of this machine, because the differences between it and the stop-cylinder are ones for experts to wrangle over. In both machines the bed is joined with the ink table, and the assembly shuttles or reciprocates under the cylinder, making a printing impression while travelling one way and not when travelling the other. Rollers pick up ink from the ink table and apply it to the face of the type, while the ink table itself receives constant supplies from a fount or duct.

The commonest type of the two-revolution machine is the Miehle, made by the Linotype & Machinery Company, or the American Miehle, made by the American Miehle Company; but there are several other makes on the market.

While the ordinary stop-cylinder and two-revolution presses print only one side of the sheet at a time, there are other presses made to print both sides of the sheet, not indeed in one operation, which would be impossible, but during the single travel of the sheet through the machine. These machines are in effect two presses combined in one, printing one side of the sheet first and the other side immediately afterwards. They are called perfectors, from the fact that the printing of the second side of the sheet is known as perfecting. Two-colour and four-colour presses print two or four colours in a single travel of the sheet through the machine, with obvious advantages in colour work. Both perfectors and multi-colour machines bring the engineer and the pressman sharply up against the problem of set-off, which is all too likely to occur when a sheet receives ink on both sides or two or four lots of ink on one side. One solution actually in use is a spray, an apparatus that is attached to the machine and timed to bathe each sheet immediately after impression in a cloud of vapourized wax or powder, which forms a layer over the ink to separate the sheets. Extended delivery systems on some machines also assist drying by keeping the sheet exposed to the air a little longer before it is deposited on the pile. Another method is the application of heat to drive off solvents in special inks.

AUTOMATIC FEEDING

Hand-fed machines (and all machines were hand-fed until the last fifty years or so) require each a workman or woman to take the sheets one by one and feed them to the gauges, so that the cylinder picks up one sheet on each printing stroke. Hand-feeding, however, has become obsolete, except for certain difficult kinds of paper, and machines are now available that can be attached to the press and will feed the paper reliably and as quickly as necessary.

With the later printing machines the automatic feeder is built in as part of an integral whole, but it is nevertheless a sort of separate machine, accessory, but independent.

Automatic feeders are remarkable machines, and perhaps deserve the name of robot, though they are anything but anthropomorphic in form. They separate each sheet from the pile and guide it carefully to the feed gauges, and see that the grippers take safe hold of it. If anything untoward happens—if, for instance, two sheets are stuck together and will not be separated, or if the sheet is torn or incomplete, or if it jams anywhere in the feeder because it has been crumpled or damaged, or if the cylinder fails to take hold of it—if any of these things happen the press must be prevented from printing and the automatic feeder provides for this. It also stops the press when the last sheet in the pile has been fed.

The use of automatic feeders allows machines to be run at much higher speeds, which may be regulated according to the need of the work being printed. Speeds up to four thousand impressions per hour are possible with large machines while small lithographic machines may achieve eight thousand sheets or more per hour.

PRINTERS' INK AND PRINTING ROLLERS

I feel I should say something here about printers' ink because so few people know what it is. Many laymen seem to imagine that it is something like ordinary ink, though occasionally someone may wonder how it comes to be so very black; and I have at times been asked how blotting paper is printed, as it is, without blots ensuing.

First, printer's ink is nothing whatever like ordinary ink of the kind used with pens; nor is it anything like the odorous preparation that is poured on stamp pads. Red or black or yellow, or whatever the colour, printer's ink is like nothing so much as thick paint. Black ink looks like solid black treacle. The base of the ink may be linseed oil boiled until it attains a glue-like consistency, and freed from the fats it contains when raw. The modern solvents and plastics industries have brought new base materials to the manufacture of printing inks. The colouring matter varies with the colour, that for black ink being usually lamp black. With any ink the particles must be exceedingly fine—even the soot of lamp black is too coarse—and the colouring matter is ground and reground until not the slightest knobble or lump remains to clog the counters of the smallest of letters.

The great rollers of printing machines are descendants of the leather dabbers or ink balls used for many centuries for inking type. No doubt the hand rollers that superseded the dabbers were also made of leather, and trouble must have been experienced from the inevitable seam, which would leave a white or under-inked mark across the form.

The solution of this problem was the invention of a substance that could be melted and cast on the roller shafts, without any seam or irregularity, and that substance must be the very first artificial rubber. It was made of nothing more recondite than treacle and glue. This composition got rid of the seam and made continuous rolling practicable, but it would only work satisfactorily under certain climatic conditions. The more torrid the weather the more the rollers tended to behave like treacle toffee in the process of being sucked, and printing with them must sometimes have been a sore trial.

The glue and treacle roller has long given place to rollers of a composition in which gelatine and glycerine are the principal ingredients. This compound is more stable and more rubber-like than the former one, is reasonably unaffected by ordinary climatic variations, and holds and transfers ink with complete efficiency.

Ordinary rubber itself is not used for inking rollers, though it may at first seem a likely material. Special rubbers and rubber compounds, which must be adapted to resist oils, make excellent and durable rollers, though more expensive than composition rollers. Rollers made of special kinds of rubbers or plastics are now popular.

MAKE-READY

The conjunction of forme, printing press, and ink will not alone produce perfectly printed copies; this mere conjunction is not even likely to produce legible copies. It is not enough to dump the forme on the bed, see that there is ink in the fount, and start the machine.

Theoretically it might appear that if the bed were absolutely level and smooth, if every piece of type were absolutely of the same height, and if the cylinder gave absolutely even impression, there would be nothing else that need be done but start up. In practice, even if these perfections of engineering were attainable, the result would not be satisfactory: the printed sheet would be here too black, there too grey, and only in places approximately right. The reason for this is that the forme does not respond best to an even impression, but to a discriminatingly uneven one, and a deal of handwork must be done on the cylinder and on the type before the ideal is achieved. This preparation is make-ready, and is a skilled business, proficiency in it marking all the difference between good presswork and poor.

Before commencing at all there is the question of the ink to be decided. Not any ink will print well on any paper. If the paper is loose in texture, too stiff an ink will pluck pieces from its surface, and these will be rolled into dirty little pellets that will encumber the type; the ink must be thinned to just the consistency that will not pluck the paper and will not, on the other hand, be so liquid that it will not dry readily—if it does not oxidize quickly enough on the surface it will come off (or 'set off') on the back of the next sheet in the printed pile. If the paper has a hard surface, a stiffer ink can be used, and it must have an even better drying capacity, since little of it can soak into the paper and prevention of set-off depends mostly on the airing the paper gets as it goes over the tapes or flyers between impression and delivery to the pile at the back of the machine—a mere matter of seconds (complete drying is not, of course, possible in this time; all that is required is sufficient to form an impervious skin on the surface). When the ink is satisfactory in consistency and quality, the ink duct must be adjusted so that ink is supplied to the different parts of the forme in exactly the quantity required.

The cylinder is wrapped in a blanket and layers of paper to increase the pressure, as it is set for the lightest impression likely to be required, and for a book-size forme it will need some reinforcement. A proof is pulled with this arrangement, and inspected. It will probably be a sorry example of printing, grey and uneven in colour, but it gives the pressman a guide to what is required. First there is the position of the type on the paper to be determined, and this can be adjusted very simply by shifting the forme on the bed or by altering the position of the feed gauges, whichever seems best. Then the make-ready proper can begin.

First, the proof will probably show that any large area or large size of type will be too grey; while, on the other hand, small or isolated areas will be too black and heavy and may even be embossing the paper—this may happen in the case of a dedication or a half-title isolated in the middle of an otherwise blank page. These two kinds of page must be printed together, and the cylinder, giving an even impression, cannot itself discriminate between them.

In order to make the large areas or large sizes of type print properly it is necessary to give them more pressure, and this is done by pasting pieces of thin paper over that part of the cylinder on which they fall during impression—the forme is allowed to print on the cylinder covering to show exactly where these areas are. In some cases several layers of paper may have to be pasted on before the correct weight is obtained.

In the places where the type is printing too strongly a fragment of the paper covering is cut away until the impression has been so reduced in that part that the letters print properly.

The forme itself receives some attention too. Heavy areas and large letters such as initials or chapter heads may have a layer of paper, cut to the correct shape and size, pasted under them, or more layers as required.

The aim of the pressman is an impression that will be even all over the sheet and will bite just sufficiently into the paper to impress the type properly, but not enough to show the impression on the other side. As the paper to be printed may be no more than one two-hundredth of an inch thick, and may even be less, this is a delicate job calling for accuracy of judgement. It can take a great deal of time too, for it must be remembered that there may be up to sixty-four pages to be printed at once, and every single letter in every page must be made to print exactly as required. A good pressman is therefore a man to be prized and respected.

Make-ready on the machine immobilizes the machine for hours. Non-productive machine time is avoided by doing as much as possible of the make-ready before the forme goes to press. A proof pulled on an accurate proofing press will show what is required. Weak areas that need more impression are strengthend by having underlays of tissue paper pasted beneath them. Blocks are tested for accuracy and underlaid or interlaid as needed. Half-tones may be provided with overlays to paste on to the machine cylinder.

The modern tendency is to make the general impression as light as possible consistent with a satisfactory general colour. Many typographers deplore this very light impression—kiss-impression, it is called—and it is quite wrong for many type faces. Certainly it is entirely a modern development, for it is only with the greater accuracy of modern machines that it became possible. The result, it seems to me, is slightly effeminate. Such precise control of the impression is impossible on a hand-press, and books printed by hand therefore tend to show stronger impression than do those printed on a modern power press; hand-press books look masculine and vigorous compared with those printed with a light impression. Certainly the impression should not be so heavy that the type embosses the paper, which it often does in hand-printed books, but it should be heavy enough, it seems to me, to make the type bite into, rather than merely deposit ink on, the surface.

When the make-ready is completed and the machine is ready to start its run the automatic feeder is charged and brought into position and adjusted as necessary. The run then commences, and while the sheets are going through, the pressman inspects them at intervals as they come from the machine to ensure that they are being printed correctly, and adjusts the ink supply as required. He must also keep the machine running properly, and see, as well as he can, that it does not break down, but he hardly needs to watch it to do this. Like any other engineer, he is aware at once of an audible difference when some part is not joining properly in the concert.

The composition of the type and the make-ready on the machine are the two principal preliminary charges of printing. Both must be incurred before a single sheet can be printed, and if the edition is a small one the cost will seem disproportionate on each copy. This is one of the reasons why limited editions are expensive, and it may push up their price considerably (though it should be remembered that this does not necessarily apply to limited 'de luxe' editions printed at the same time as a larger number of a cheaper edition). It is more laborious, more troublesome, and more expensive to print one copy of a book than it is to write the whole thing out by hand or on a typewriter; but if *one* can be printed, thousands of others can be printed too at great speed. The economy of printing lies entirely in its capacity to duplicate.

IX

ILLUSTRATING THE BOOK

Process Engraving

MEN have made pictures from the dawn of time, but it is only comparatively recently that they have discovered how to multiply copies of a picture. Some of the processes that have been developed, though successful in what they set out to achieve, are not, nevertheless, bibliographical, and do not come within the scope of this book. Examples of these are etching, mezzotinting, and steel-engraving—the first the oldest and still surviving as a medium for the artist. They have, indeed, been used in books, steel-engraving particularly, but they are essentially artist processes and severely restricted in output. A typographical process was in existence when Gutenberg was working out the principle of movable type and was very well adapted to become a partner in the making of books. This was wood-cutting.

Wood-cuts and wood-engravings are familiar to modern readers, for they have enjoyed a revival in our time. The methods by which they are produced differ, and the results are distinctive. Both are letterpress processes, which means that the print is taken from the surface; any part of the block that is not required to print must be cut away so that neither the ink nor the paper will come in contact with it in the press. In a wood-cut the cutting is done with a knife, and the effect is usually broad and akin to a line drawing, but it is eminently typographical and consorts well with type. Wood-engraving, on the other hand, is done with engraving tools on the end grain of

46. A Miehle two-revolution press. At the far end the machine minder checks the operation of the automatic feeder; his assistant inspects the printed sheets as they are delivered

47. A view under the feeding board of a two-revolution machine, showing the impression of the cylinder upon the forme

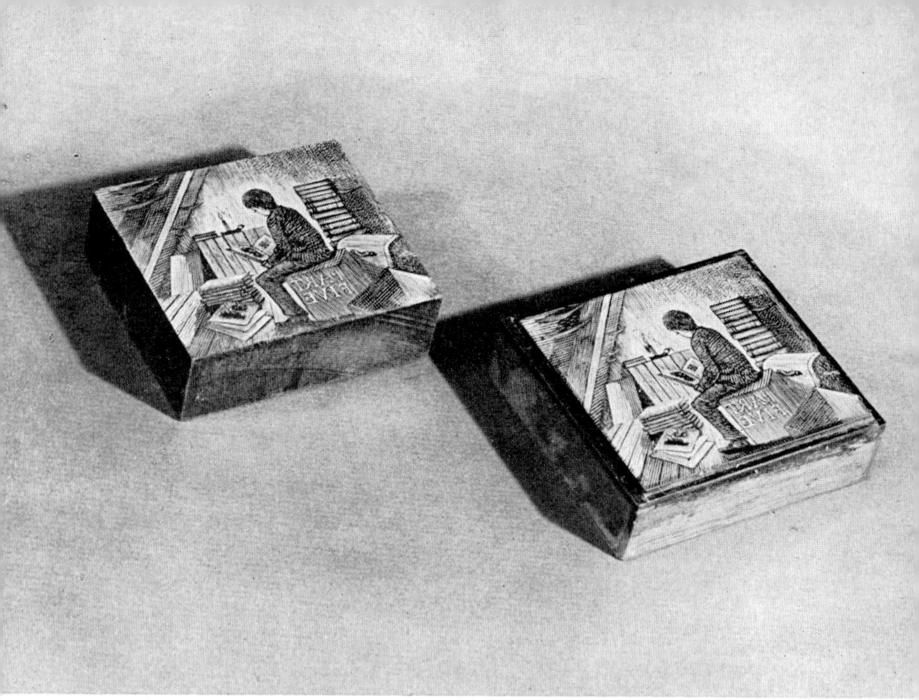

48. A wood-engraving by Reynolds Stone and an electrotype made from it

49. A line block and a half-tone block

the wood, and more subtle and elaborate effects are obtainable. With a wood-cut only one tone is possible, that of the black line, and this is true also of wood-engraving; but half-tones or greys can be simulated by means of fine shading and cross-hatching.

Wood-engraving received its first honours at the hands of Thomas Bewick late in the eighteenth century. Although it was

50. A simple wood-cut of the fifteenth century

known before Bewick's time it was little practised, and he enlivened it by the introduction of a fresh technique and a consummate mastery of the medium. His pastorals and pictures of animals and birds were widely popular, and, since he was a prolific artist, his work appears in many books of the period. He was, perhaps, the first artist of note to become specifically a book illustrator.

After Bewick's day wood-engraving developed in technique, acquired virtuosity, in fact, but tended to lose in imagination. The great newspapers that came into existence in the nineteenth century demanded, not imaginative interpretation, but factual illustrations of real events and people. Wood-engravers tried to cope with this demand, and for a time flourished because there was no process that could compete with them; but in the end they vanished in the face of a new invention, process engraving. Wood-engraving was too slow, one block taking perhaps hours or even days to prepare, and the time was coming when news and topical illustrations were stale if they were more than a few hours old.

Wood-engraving has disappeared from the news columns of the daily paper, but in our day it has undergone a revival in connection with book illustration. It has, too, attracted the

51. White-line wood-engraving by Thomas Bewick

attention of some fine artists, among whom one of the foremost was Eric Gill, who also revived the wood-cut with effect.

Wood-engravings and wood-cuts are not nowadays printed direct from the wood blocks, in ordinary book printing at least. The wood is too fragile and too much time and effort have been expended on it to risk it on the bed of the modern power press. A facsimile block is made by electrotype, and used instead.

To make an electrotype an impression of the engraving is made either on a wax-coated foil or on a sheet of thermoplastic material. The mould made by this impression is polished with graphite or sprayed with metallic silver to make it conduct an electric current. The mould is then immersed in a solution containing copper sulphate and sulphuric acid and a layer of copper is deposited on it by electrolysis. When a sufficient thickness, about fifteen-thousandths of an inch, has been grown the copper shell is separated from the mould and is given a backing of lead-based alloy. The backing is trimmed and planed level and finally the resulting plate is mounted to bring

52. Modern wood-engraving by Eric Ravilious
(*printed from an electrotype*)

it to type height. When properly made an electro will give a print indistinguishable from that from a wood block.

The development of photography as a practical process after the middle of the nineteenth century provided a new way of making pictures, and, what is more, a completely different kind of picture. There was no other way of making pictures so quickly and there was no other way of obtaining them so factually accurate. There was, too, at least later in the history of the process, the possibility of obtaining unlimited numbers of copies of each picture. Yet there was nothing in this to interest the printer of books. Photographs could not be printed together with type, and if they were bound into books they had to be mounted and were awkward and bulky, and gave no guarantee of permanence.

A number of ingenious men interested themselves in the possibilities of devising a means whereby photographs could be printed on a letterpress machine. The problem was to make a black ink give grey tones, or the semblance of grey, in any shade in selected parts of the plate. The black ink of printing is black and only black, and it will not print grey; printed paper bears either black marks or no marks at all. How then could grey be obtained? Fox Talbot made a valuable contribution towards the achievement of this aim when in 1852 he suggested the use of a gauze or muslin screen to break up the image into dots. Following up this suggestion, many experimenters devised various screens, but without real success. It was not until the eighteen-eighties that a satisfactory method was achieved through the introduction of the cross-line screen, which is still in use to-day. This I shall describe shortly.

Experiments in photographic reproduction had led to a process by means of which line drawings could be reproduced on the printing machine without the intervention of the wood-engraver. The process is now in extensive use throughout the world, in all kinds of letterpress printing, and scarcely any newspaper can appear without somewhere in its columns an illustration or a diagram or a map printed from a line block.

THE LINE BLOCK

By this process any drawing in black and white can be reproduced in unlimited quantities on the printing press. Further, the reproduction may be smaller or larger than the original, and still, in everything but size, a faithful reproduction. The original itself, from which the line block is to be made, may be a drawing, a diagram, a map, a manuscript, or a page of type—anything one can think of, provided it does not contain tones. For the convenience of this description let us call the original a drawing.

It is set up on a copyboard and lighted brightly and evenly.

The copyboard is part of a large camera; the most modern examples are built against a wall so that the copyboard and its lights are in one room and the back of the camera, with most of the controls, in another room. This second room is a darkroom, with facilities for developing the plates exposed in the camera. In front of the lens is a system of prisms and a mirror, whose function is to introduce an additional reversal of the image from left to right. In ordinary photography a lens reverses an image in this way, but in printing the negative on to bromide paper a second reversal occurs to cancel out the first, and the result is a picture the right way round. In making a block, however, there is an additional stage to be taken into account, i.e. from subject to negative, from negative to block, and from block to paper. To obtain a final print the right way round we must start with a negative the right way round too, and this is what the additional reversal is for. The negative the right way round gives a block the wrong way round, and this gives a print that is correct. Figure 53 will help to make this clear.

53. The progress of a line block. On the left is the original; this gives a negative as in the second picture; from this is made a line block as in the third picture; from which is obtained a print as the fourth picture

The plate or film exposed in the camera is developed to produce a negative in which the drawing appears as clear lines on an opaque black ground. This negative is now printed down on to a metal plate—usually zinc—coated with a sensitive emulsion that has the property of hardening under the action of light and of becoming insoluble wherever it is thus hardened. Development removes the unexposed emulsion and leaves the drawing represented by lines of hardened emulsion on the surface of the bare metal. The plate is now treated to convert the emulsion into an acid resist, and it is then ready for etching. Etching with acid eats away the surface of the metal wherever it is not protected, leaving the resist-protected lines standing in relief.

Until only a few years ago etching was a tedious process requiring several stages, the plate having to be withdrawn from the etch bath at intervals so that a red powder, known as dragon's blood, could be brushed and fused against the sides of the lines to prevent the acid from undercutting them. This method is now little used, for a revolution in the technique of etching has made it obsolescent. This has been brought about by a new kind of machine, the powderless-etch machine.

There are several varieties of powderless-etch machines, but they work on the same principle. The powder they dispense with is dragon's blood. The plate, prepared as already described, is fixed in the machine. It should be said that it may not carry only one picture; for economy several pictures are printed down on to one large sheet of metal and etched together. The machine is now started. Paddles or sprays project an etching emulsion of nitric acid and oil and other ingredients against the surface of the plate. Additives in the etch fluid protect the sides of the relief as the etch proceeds while allowing the acid to bite into the metal between the lines of the image. The operation is complete in about fifteen minutes, compared with perhaps three hours by the older process. The plate is not withdrawn from the etch for treatment, but is etched to completion in the single operation. The block that results is superior to one produced by the older method, with sharper edges to the relief and better depth.

Large areas of white space within the drawing will need additional treatment to deepen them, and this is done with a high-speed revolving cutter known as a routing machine. The plate is now ready for mounting and printing.

Another modern development is the electronic engraving

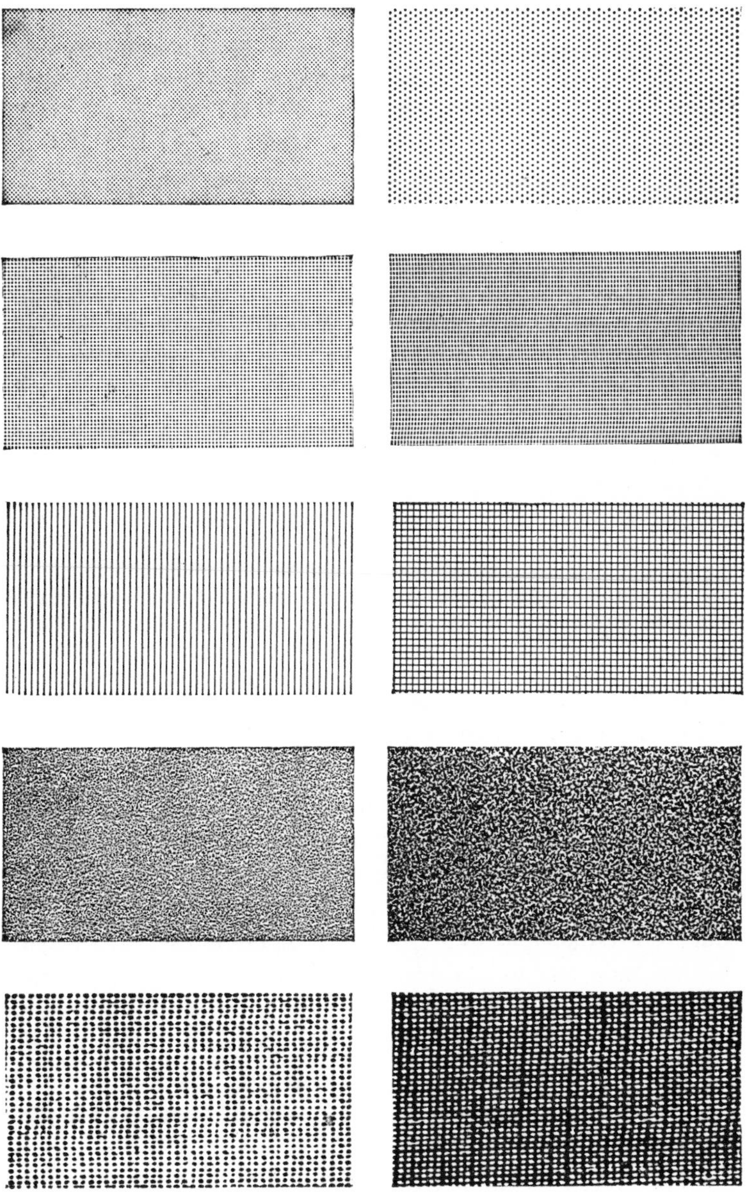

54. A selection of mechanical tints

machine (Figure 57). It can produce both line work and half-tone. Its method is true engraving, whereas the process for so long called process engraving or photo-engraving is not really engraving at all, but a form of etching.

The electronic engraver obtains relief in the printing plate by cutting away those parts of the surface of the plate that are not required to print. The original drawing or photograph is placed in the machine, where it is scanned by a photo-sensitive cell or 'eye' in fine parallel lines, much as a television image is scanned. The impulses received by the cell are led through amplifiers to control a stylus. This stylus travels across the plate in the same scanning rhythm as the photo-sensitive cell, cutting away the surface wherever the original shows white space. The plate may be of metal or of plastic.

The finished plate from either process is now mounted on wood or other material and it is ready for the press. Printing on a letterpress machine will produce many thousands of copies.

For many purposes metal is giving way to plastic. Dycril is a thin layer of hard, photo-sensitive polymer bonded to metal. It is exposed in the same way as metal and after exposure is etched by a wash-out process to produce a relief printing plate. Nyloprint and Kodak relief plates are similar materials.

Drawings in colour can also be reproduced by line block, providing that they have been made with an understanding of the limitations of the process, and that, as before, no tone is expected in any part of the reproduction. A separate block is necessary for each colour, and the colours are printed one at a time. The colour blocks are made in precisely the same way as the monochrome block, and look and are exactly the same, except, of course, for the difference of image. There is a difference in the handling of the process camera, however, and the separate blocks have to be carefully made so that the colours fall into their proper places (or register) when they are printed.

Let us say that the colours of the original drawing are yellow and red. The camera will not normally discriminate between these and will reproduce both on the plate. To prevent this a

55. A Magnacolor enlarger camera with its control unit

56. The back of a dark-room process camera, with the operator measuring the image on the focusing screen. The circular disk is a half-tone screen

57. Klischograph electronic engravers; a plate is seen under the engraving head on the nearest machine

58. Scanning a transparency on a Crosfield Magnascan electronic scanner

filter is used on the lens to eliminate one colour while the other is being dealt with, and when this has been done another filter is used to eliminate the latter colour and allow the former to affect a second negative. From these two negatives two line blocks are made in the manner already described and printed in their respective colours, one impression over the other.

Colour separation by means of filters means that colour-sensitive photographic material must be used, and even so the separation may not always be all that is desired; when this happens the defects must be remedied by handwork. In extreme cases separation by the camera may have to be abandoned and black tracings made of the colours.

I have said that tone cannot be obtained by means of the line block, but this is not altogether true. In certain cases a simulation—a rough one, certainly—of tone can be obtained by means of mechanical tints. These vary in pattern, but the most common one is made up of tiny dots in regular rows, and may be noticed in almost any newspaper cartoon. A selection of mechanical tints is shown in Figure 54. The tints may be applied to the original drawing in the form of preprinted adhesive cellophane, cut to the shape required, or by means of pressure-sensitive materials such as Letraset; they then appear automatically on the negative. Alternatively they may be printed down on to the negative from a separate photographic tint negative; in this case those parts of the image that are not to be tinted must be covered with some kind of masking or stopping-out material, which is removed before the negative is printed down on to the plate. The plate is then etched in the ordinary way.

THE HALF-TONE BLOCK

The effort to obtain a picture in true tone from the letter-press machine was doomed to failure from the first, and inventors realized this and set their minds to work to devise a successful conjuring trick to persuade the eye that there was tone where in fact there was no such thing. A photograph may be made up of a subtle and almost infinite range of tones from black through every shade of grey to white. Printers' ink is black and paper is white, and the problem was how to mix these two to produce various tones of grey. The answer lay in the synthesizing quality of the human eye. The mechanical tints used with line blocks show that the eye can be persuaded to accept an arrangement of small dots on white paper as representing grey; in effect, the eye mixes the black of the dots and the white of the paper. Large dots closely spaced give dark grey, and small dots widely spaced a much lighter tone. With this understood, what was required was some way of breaking up the tones of a photograph into black dots of different size to simulate the range of tones. This is done by the cross-line screen.

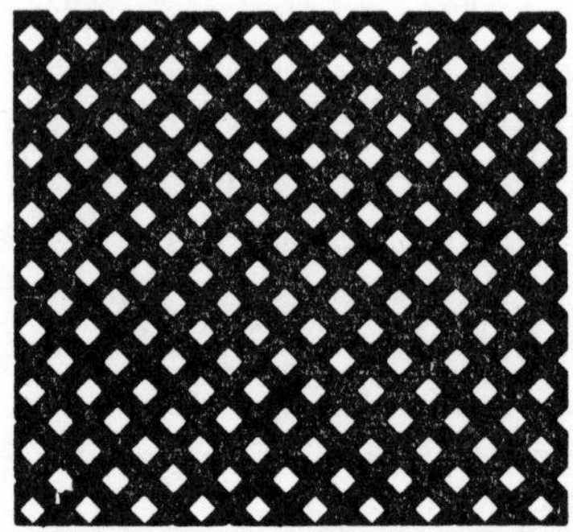

59. On the left is part of a half-tone screen, enlarged; on the right is an enlarged portion of a half-tone print showing the varying size of the dots; below is a diagram representing a half-tone block in section, also enlarged, with the dots ranging from the darkest areas on the left to the lightest on the right

The screen is a fine mesh of diagonal lines at right angles on glass (see Figure 59). With its aid anything that can be photographed may be reproduced by means of a half-tone block. The original to be reproduced may be a painting or a photograph, or any other kind of picture. It is laid on the copyboard of the camera, and the screen is set in place in front of the sensitive film. The image formed by the lens passes through the screen and is broken up by it into thousands of small points of light, which are strongest where the original is lightest in tone and weakest where it is dark. The result is that when the film is developed into a negative, the light areas of the original are represented by dark areas of negative pierced by tiny apertures of clear film, and where the original is darkest the negative is clear with only small black dots.

The negative is now printed down to a zinc or copper plate coated with a sensitized emulsion—zinc is used for coarser screens for coarser papers. This plate is treated to convert the image into an acid resist. Etching may be done in powderless-etch machines or by the older method. In the older method the plate is withdrawn from the bath at intervals, and areas that are considered sufficiently etched are painted over with a resist to prevent further action, after which the plate is returned to the bath for another 'bite'; this operation is known as 'fine etching'.

Dycril polymer and other proprietary polymer materials may also be used for half-tone plates in monochrome or colour.

The finished plate is mounted to bring it to type height, and it is then ready for the press.

Blockmakers send at least two proofs of each block for approval by the customer. The publisher uses these proofs to judge the quality of the reproduction, and if he is not satisfied, he may ask for alterations and reproofing.

Electronic engraving machines cut half-tones by physical engraving, as we saw for line blocks. Some machines will cut only coarse-screen blocks, but others will cut blocks up to 150 screen, the finest in normal use. The original is scanned by an electronic eye, and the tone under the scanning eye is converted into an impulse controlling an engraving tool, which cuts or burns a hole in the plate the size of which is directly related to the tone of the original under examination at that moment. Where the original is light in tone the tool makes larger holes, with little material in relief between them; where it is dark, it cuts smaller holes, or none. The engraved block may be given a slight etch in an acid bath to remove any burrs left by the cutting tool.

A printer's rough proof of a half-tone block is apt to be disappointing to the photographer who made the original picture and who does not understand the treatment necessary to make the block print properly. This treatment is laborious and costly, and it is not worth while to do it for a proof when both printer and publisher understand that better results will be obtained in the final printing. The process is not carried out until instructions are given to go ahead with the printing of the edition.

It is no more than make-ready. Make-ready used to be done when the forme was on the press, and consequently presses might stand idle for periods while this work was in progress. Printers now avoid the wastefulness of this method by using a system of what is called 'pre-make-ready'. As far as possible all blocks are prepared for printing in a special pre-make-ready department or section, with the aid of sensitive measuring instruments and gauges. Overlays to be pasted on the cylinder of the press are prepared in this department, leaving the minimum of make-ready for the machine-minder to do, and so reducing as much as possible interruptions in the running of the presses.

Half-tone illustrations do not normally contain either clear white or total black areas. The darkest areas still have minute dots of white to reduce the depth of the colour, and the lightest areas have a very fine screen of black dots; but the total impression is that of a photograph in continuous tone.

If you take up a newspaper and examine the pictures through a magnifying glass, the screen will be obvious in the dot formation of the tones; indeed, it is visible without the aid of a glass if your sight is normal. It will be clear that the dots are arranged in diagonal rows in two directions, and these rows of dots represent the ruling of the screen. Turn now to the half-tones in this book: the dots are not apparent without a magnifying-glass, though they are there, nevertheless. The reason for this is that half-tones are made in different degrees, coarse to fine, through different qualities of screen, to suit different kinds of paper. For good quality, every dot must print, and if the screen

60. A powderless-etch machine. The operator places the printed metal plate in position on the lid, which is then turned downwards over the tank, which contains the etching fluid

61. A routing machine in operation on a line-block

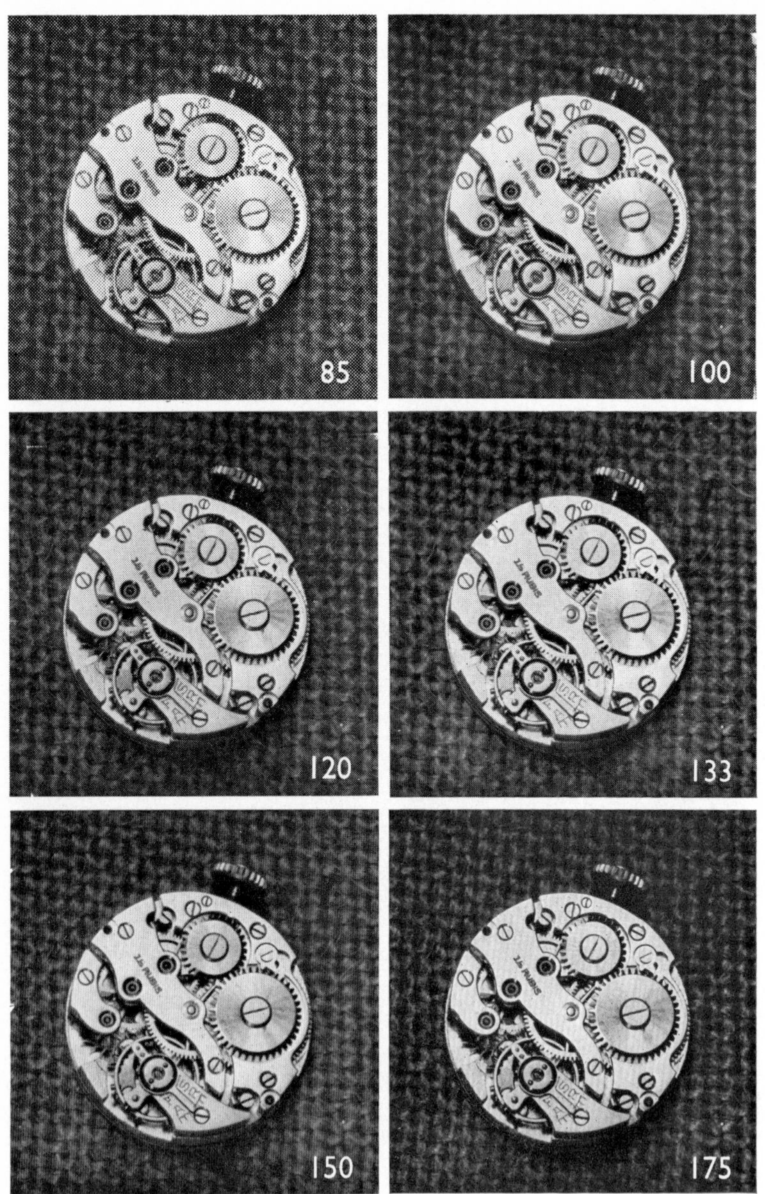

62. Half-tone blocks of various screens

is fine and the paper coarse, some of the dots are bound to fall on irregularities in the paper and misfire; besides which some of the fluff from the paper will get mixed up with the ink and clog the block. So for a rough-surfaced paper a screen with lines comparatively widely spaced (fifty to sixty lines to the inch) is used, and the dots are in consequence hefty and able more or less to overcome paper irregularities if they happen to hit them; while for a block intended to be printed on smooth paper a finer screen (100 to 175 lines to the inch) is used.

It is certainly better to use a smooth paper and a fine screen than a rough paper and a coarse screen, as you will see for yourself if you compare the plates in this book with the illustrations in a newspaper. Newspapers must be printed on cheap paper if you are to have them at the price you are accustomed to pay, and so they present pictures that are manifestly imperfect in every particular, but are no doubt better than no pictures at all. A book is produced in less haste, and at a price consonant with its cost of production, and the fact that its illustrations are more perfect is because you pay for them and enable the publisher to use a special paper and to have that paper inserted in its proper place in the book by the binder.

There is no doubt that for sheer brilliance of result a fine-screen half-tone properly printed on suitable paper is unsurpassed; yet half-tones have peculiar and special disadvantages. The screen itself is a disadvantage on occasions, when, for instance, it is desirable that the reproduction should bear examination through a glass. Where the subject is as interesting in detail as it is entire, as in the case of a photomicrograph of germs, it is essential that it should yield further detail on magnification. This the half-tone will not do, the glass revealing only a formless arrangement of dots. Again, the half-tone depends very much on the contrast between the black ink and the paper, and is seldom wholly satisfactory if printed in any colour other than black—the result tends to be flat.

Another disadvantage, and to my mind a serious one, is that if the picture is to be well reproduced the screen must be fine, and consequently the paper must be smooth. No paper made is smooth enough in itself to do full justice to a fine-screen half-tone block, and in order to present a suitable surface the paper must be loaded (imitation art paper) or coated (real art) with china clay and rolled smooth. The result is a kind of paper that many people consider unpleasant because of its objectionable shine and peculiar feel.

Many ideas and suggestions have been put forward to abolish the necessity for art paper, but none of them has come to anything. If a successful invention ever appears, publishers will welcome it, for every one of them would prefer to print illustrations on the same paper as the text—apart from any aesthetic considerations, it would be cheaper and easier to do this.

COLOUR ILLUSTRATIONS

THE TRICHROMATIC HALF-TONE PROCESS

A good reproduction of a picture in full colour can be achieved in more ways than one, but most of such reproductions in books are printed by the trichromatic half-tone process. Like the ordinary half-tone process, it depends on the inability of the human eye to distinguish the truth, provided the truth is small enough. Just as the tones of the half-tone reproduction are an optical illusion, so too, except for the three primaries, are the colours of the trichromatic process. A coloured reproduction of a painting—I have before me at the moment one of Titian's 'Bacchus and Ariadne'—does not really contain all those subtle shades and tones of colour the eye of the beholder sees. There really are colours present, but there are only three of them, the primaries yellow, red, and blue, or variations of them. With these three colours the engraver and the printer bamboozle the beholder into thinking that there are also present green, brown, purple, orange, black—almost anything in the colour circle.

Whether the colours the reader thinks he sees are the same as those of the original painting is another matter. Colour reproduction has improved immensely in recent years, but there are conditions that cannot be fulfilled, and are not likely to be fulfilled. Ideally the engraver and the printer should have beside them for reference as they work the original painting itself, if the print is to be true, and no one is going to trust a valuable picture to such circumstances. The next best thing is a colour transparency, and good as these are they are not entirely accurate. These statements can be tested by comparison of two different reproductions of the same picture—the variations will be found to be surprising. Even when the original is not of great value it is not customary to send it to the printer.

The trichromatic process is a development of the monochrome half-tone, the only complication being the colour. Three blocks have to be made, one to print each of the primaries, yellow, red, and blue, and the first requirement is to analyse the original into its relative values of each of these primaries. The analysis is expressed in the making of the negatives and is obtained by the use of filters on the lens of the camera. These are similar to the filters used in ordinary photography, that is, coloured gelatine, or optical flats of glass, and their purpose is to restrain or prevent those colours that are not required from affecting the negative. Thus to obtain the block to print the yellow primary a dark blue or blue-violet filter is used that prevents the yellow in the picture from affecting the film and emphasizes the other two colours. The developed negative shows the pure yellow part of the picture as clear glass and the red and blue parts opaque. These are the extremes, and between them there are tones of light to dark grey representing the colours of the original in which yellow has a share—orange and green, for example.

This negative, it will be remembered, having been taken through a screen, is broken up into dots like an ordinary half-tone negative. It will be printed down on to a sensitized copper plate, the emulsion of which is hardened by the action of light. This plate is prepared and etched as we have seen, and finally is mounted.

For the red block a green filter is used to exclude red and emphasize yellow and blue, and, what is important, the screen is moved in a circular direction so that the dots on the negative fall in a slightly different position relative to those on the yellow block. For the blue block a red filter is used and the screen moved a little farther round, so that the dots fall in yet another position. The negatives of both these colours are printed down on to copper as before, and the plates etched and mounted, when, subject to approval of the proofs by the customer, they are ready to be sent to the printer.

The preparation of colour plates calls for considerable skill and care to ensure that each colour contributes its correct quota to the hues in the picture. Though in theory it should be possible to split any colour into its primaries by means of filters, in practice no perfect analysis can be made. The defects of colour analysis may be made good on the plate by delicate fine etching, but the tendency today is to reduce the need for fine etching as much as possible, or to abolish it altogether, by means of photographic manipulations of negatives and positives in the darkroom, and the use of photographic masks designed to correct tonal renderings. These masks are in effect weak positives or negatives on film, made through filters and printed down with the negatives to control the final colour values.

A set of proofs called progressives is sent with the blocks to the printer. These are clipped together in a particular order, and consist of (i) a proof of the yellow block; (ii) a proof of the red block; (iii) a proof of the yellow with the red superimposed; (iv) a proof of the blue block; (v) a complete proof showing the three colours printed one over the other to form the finished picture (Figure 63). The progressives show the exact shades of colour necessary for the correct result, and also the order in which the printer should print the colours—which is nearly always the lightest colour first and the others in the order of lightness—in our case, yellow, red, and blue.

It should be stated here that although the printer may speak in general terms of the primaries yellow, red, and blue, the process engraver and the inkmaker more correctly speak of yellow, magenta, and cyan, these being the standard colours of inks that give the best result in the half-tone process. The yellow block is termed the yellow printer, the magenta the

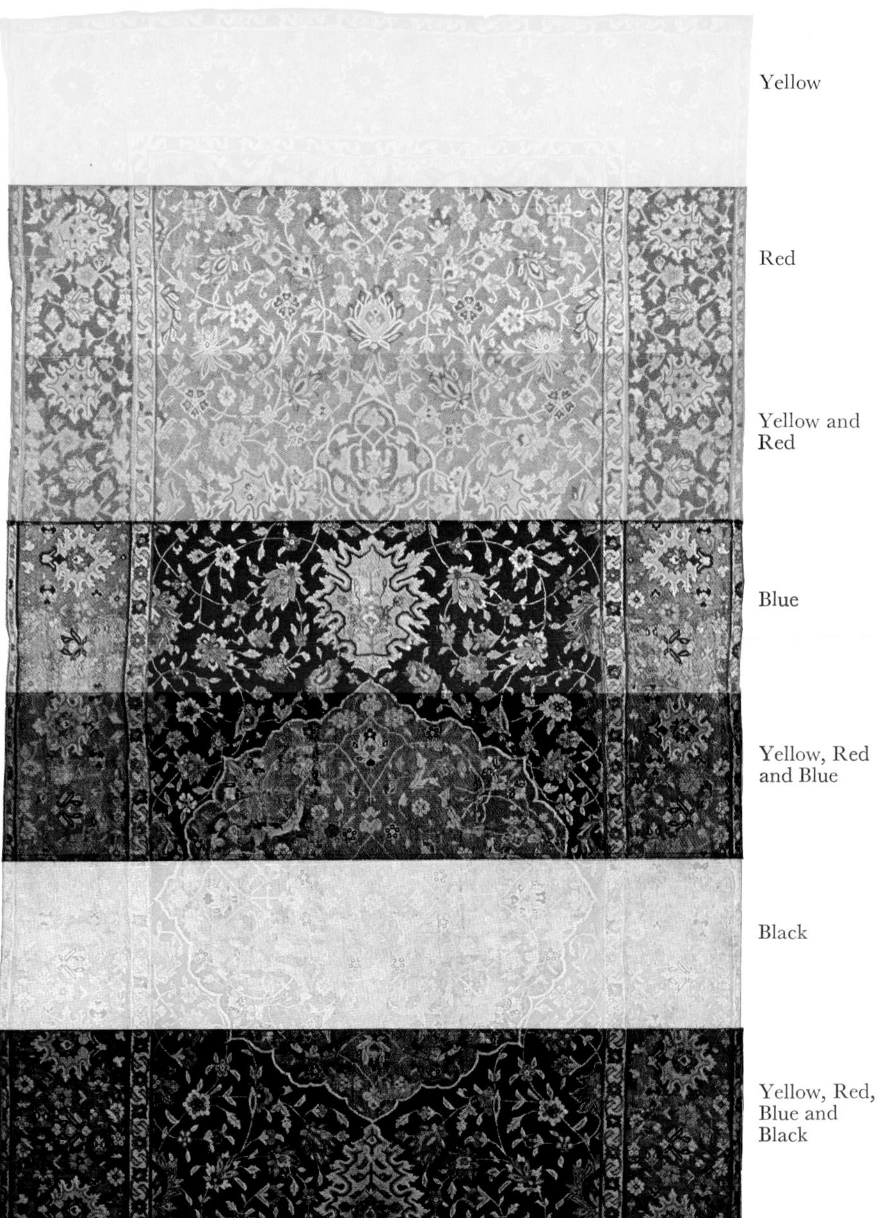

63. A four-colour half-tone block sectioned to show the separate colours and the order in which they are printed

magenta printer, and the cyan the cyan printer. These ink colours are by no means perfect for their purpose, and in effect photographic masking of negatives or positives and fine etching of plates are carried out partly to compensate for the short-comings of colour inks.

In the printer's hands each block is treated exactly as an ordinary half-tone, except that it is printed in its proper colour. Only one colour can be printed at a time on an ordinary machine, so that for a three-colour reproduction the paper must go through the machine three times—a detail that contributes to the cost of the process.

In printing the second and third colours care must be taken to obtain exact register on the colours preceding. It will be remembered that the process-engraver moved his screen so that the dots of each colour fell in a position different from that of the dots of the other colours: this was done so that the dots should print side by side, and not one on top of the other. It is this juxtaposition of the primary colours that produces the impression of complementary colours and neutral tints. This can be seen with a magnifying-glass if an area of the reproduction is examined. If, for example, this area appears green, it will be found through the glass that it is composed of yellow and cyan dots in a rose pattern, with, perhaps, a few magenta ones interspersed here and there. Other tints and hues are formed in the same way. The paper is a palette on which the printer mixes, not inks, but light rays; and the eye—an inveterate generalizer—is unable to distinguish, because of their minute size, one element from another, and cheerfully accepts them for the sum of their union.

I have already said that theoretically it should be possible to produce any colour from the three primary colours, but that in practice certain disadvantages prevent perfection. Some colours and neutral shades are difficult to obtain from the three primaries—mauve and pure grey being examples. Where these colours are present in the original a further block is made by the engraver, usually to print black. This block strengthens the shadows, provides the greys and some other colours, and generally helps towards a richer quality in the reproduction. Most good colour half-tone printing, these days, is in four workings.

Much more colour work is printed today than used to be the case, and this is partly the result of a cross-fertilization of demand and technology. Colour printing has always been expensive, and will continue to be so as long as we have to print four separate workings to achieve a full-colour result, but much has been done to facilitate the preparatory work represented by the making of the plates. One simple system of producing colour plates more quickly is the direct-screen process, which is used principally in conjunction with new types of cameras that are also enlargers, such as the Magnacolor (Figure 55). Direct-screen, however, is not satisfactory for every kind of job. The original, a transparency, is copied to produce a mask to control the colour rendering and the density range—colour transparencies usually show a much wider range of densities than can be obtained on paper and the range therefore has to be compressed. Original and mask, in register, are placed directly in the enlarger head and projected on to the enlarger baseboard to the size required. A sheet of photographic film is laid down on the baseboard and over it is laid a contact screen, the two being brought into close contact by vacuum pressure. Exposure through the transparency/mask combination and an appropriate trichromatic filter down on to the screen/film combination produces a separation negative ready screened to be printed down on to metal.

A contact screen is a sheet of plastic material with a screen pattern printed on it—in grey for colour work and in magenta for other purposes.

The enlarger-camera may be used also for reproducing reflection originals, e.g. colour prints, by laying the original on the baseboard, where it is illuminated, and putting the photographic film in the enlarger head. The whole machine is considerably taller than a man, but it takes far less floor space than a horizontal or vertical camera, and its facilities include a considerable range of enlargement and reduction. Some examples, such as the Pawo, have a sophisticated kind of computer control.

The most revolutionary machine in the field of colour reproduction is without doubt the electronic scanner. Its function is to produce colour separation sets from colour transparencies or reflection copy—the latter must be flexible enough to be wrapped round a cylinder. There are several types of electronic scanner, e.g. the Linoscan, the Crosfield Diascan and Magnascan, and the Hell Chromograph, with various differences, but the following account summarizes the general principle and function.

The mechanical parts of the machine include two drums or cylinders (conjoined on the Diascan) that revolve in concert on their axes. One of these cylinders is of glass or perspex and the transparency to be reproduced is fixed on this (Figure 58). A light shines through the cylinder and illuminates the transparency. A minute disk of the illuminated transparency is observed by a lens, which is on a carriage moving parallel with the cylinder. As the cylinder revolves and the lens traverses, the transparency is scanned in a series of parallel lines rather like the raster of a television screen, though much finer—the pitch may be from 250 to 2000 lines to the inch. At any moment the lens is projecting into the machine a fine pencil of light that carries the tone and the colour of a particular point on the transparency. The first requirement is to split the light into its components. This may be done by passing the beam through a prism (Linoscan) or a set of dichroic mirrors (Diascan and Magnascan). In either case the result is three diverging rays of coloured light, green, blue, and red, the intensities of which vary in accord with the tone and the amount of each primary in the spot of colour scanned. These three rays represent the magenta, yellow, and cyan printers. The rays are received by photo-multipliers, which convert the modulations of the light into electrical impulses. The impulses are passed to a computer.

From this point we need follow only one of these colour elements, say that for the yellow printer. In the computer the values of the other two colours are taken into account to modify the output of the yellow signal. The signal is now converted once more into light values through a lamp the intensity of which varies in accordance with the values of the tones of yellow in the original transparency as modified and corrected by the computer. The light is projected as a fine beam upon a sheet of photographic film wrapped round the second cylinder, which is thus exposed in a series of lines similar to the scan of the transparency.

When the scan is finished the film is taken off and developed to produce a separation negative (or positive—many machines can be switched over to produce positives instead of negatives). The other two colours are dealt with in a similar manner. A negative (or positive) for a black printer can also be produced, its densities being controlled by the signals of the three separation colours.

A full set of separations can be completed by the scanner in a very short time—the precise period depends upon the size of the picture to be scanned and the pitch of the scan—about one minute per lateral inch is quoted for a 1000-line scan.

The advantage of the scanner does not lie only in the speed of its operation, but also in the control and selection that are possible from what at first sight seems a bewildering array of knobs and switches. The effect of any colour may be reduced or enhanced or selectively controlled. The black printer may be made to any degree of density or contrast. The effect of masking may be expressed automatically in the separations, as also may be what is called detail-contrast or unsharp-masking, which sharpens the boundaries between continuous tones. Another facility is undercolour removal, the need for which has been emphasized with the arrival of high-speed multi-colour presses, such as web-offset machines, that print the colours in such rapid succession that wet ink goes over wet ink. In conventional four-colour work certain passages of the printed picture, where the colours are dark or rich, may be obtained by overprinting near solids in each of the four workings; the total result is a thick layer of ink. To forestall troubles that come from printing too much wet ink on wet the scanner may be adjusted to produce separations to give plates that print less solidly in these dark passages; the required strength is obtained by an increase in the black, with a reduction in the total of the ink. Some letterpress printers, printing conventionally, also like to have undercolour removal to help in preventing set-off.

Most scanners will produce separations only to the same size as the original, the finished size being achieved from the separations in an enlarger. The Crosfield Magnascan is an example of a machine that can reduce or enlarge within a broad range to provide separations to the final size. The separations may be screened at the same time by means of a contact screen wrapped round the exposing cylinder over the photographic film. A bright light is needed to penetrate a contact screen and the Magnascan provides this by taking its exposing light from a xenon lamp used to illuminate the transparency and conducting it along a fibre-optic channel (which looks like a length of electric cable) to a crystal, in which it is modified by signals from the computer to expose the film as required.

Some scanners have two exposing cylinders to make two separations at once, and others have four exposing cylinders to produce a full set of four separations at a single operation.

X

ILLUSTRATING THE BOOK

Photogravure, Lithography, and Collotype

THERE are three important processes other than process-engraving by which books may be illustrated. Two of them, photogravure and lithography, may be used to print the text as well as the illustrations. Lithography and collotype are planographic processes—that is they work from a plane surface, not a relief surface like letterpress—and photogravure is an intaglio process, the reverse of letterpress, working from the hollows of the plate rather than from the relief.

PHOTOGRAVURE

Photogravure began as a closely guarded secret known only to a few firms, but gradually experimenters working along the same lines arrived at similar results, and details of the process became known. It is an elaborate and intricate process, capable alike of cheap printing in enormous quantities and indifferent quality, and of fine work fit for the best kind of book. It is in common use to-day for the printing of magazines.

It should be kept in mind throughout this section that photogravure is an intaglio process, printing, like an etching, from the hollows of the plate. The printing surface is not flat like a half-tone block, but takes the form of a cylinder with a facing of copper. The transference of the matter to be printed to the surface of the cylinder begins with a material called carbon tissue (because black carbon was formerly used in its manufacture); it is essentially a thin sheet of gelatine on a paper backing. The tissue is sensitized to light and is then exposed under a screen. This screen is not to be confused with that used in process engraving, for it serves a different purpose and takes no part in the illusion of tone—it is simply a mechanical convenience. After exposure to the screen the tissue is exposed to positives made from the matter to be printed; in the case of type matter these may be positives direct from a photo-composition machine. The action of light on the gelatine of the carbon tissue is to harden or tan it proportionately in relation to the tonal range of the positive.

The carbon tissue is now pressed into contact with the gravure cylinder and its paper backing is peeled away, leaving the gelatine attached to the cylinder. The cylinder is now ready for etching. The length of time the gelatine will withstand the etching fluid is important. Where the original is white the gelatine representing it on the cylinder is sufficiently thick to protect the copper against the action of the acid. Where, on the other hand, the original is grey, the gelatine is thinner and protects the copper only for the limited period it withstands the acid, after which the copper too is attacked and eroded. Other areas of the subject are etched proportionately. Thus, when the etch first reaches the copper in the grey tones, the dark tones have been etching for some time, while the light tones are still protected. The result is a surface on different levels, the areas and depths of the levels corresponding to the tones of the picture to be reproduced.

The screen used in photogravure is the reverse of that used in process engraving. Instead of being a clear glass plate ruled with opaque lines, it is an opaque plate ruled with clear lines. The screen, printed down with the subject matter, forms a mesh of thick gelatine through which the etching acid cannot penetrate; the finished cylinder shows the screen as lines of copper standing at the original level of the surface, breaking up the varying depths of the etched cylinder into myriads of tiny cells (see Figure 64).

Although these cells vary in depth they are all of the same

size and shape. The reproduction of tone is dependent not on the area of the cell, but on the thickness of the film of ink it can impart. A shallow cell imparts to the paper in printing only a thin film of ink and the white of the paper shines through it with small impairment of its brilliance; a deep cell imparts a thicker film that obscures the paper more or less completely. Between these two extremes there is a wide tonal range produced by a varying thickness of ink film corresponding to the varying levels of the cylinder surface.

This will be clearer when the method of printing is understood. The etched cylinder is mounted in the printing machine in contact with another cylinder, which is faced with rubber; between the two the paper travels in a continuing strip or 'web' from a reel—a washerwoman's nightmare of an eternal sheet going through an immense mangle. The etched cylinder is flooded with ink as it revolves, and the ink is immediately scraped off again by a flexible blade called a 'doctor'. This blade has a straight edge, and cannot penetrate into the cells, each one of which remains full to the brim after the passage of the doctor. It is in connection with the doctor that the screen achieves its full use, for it provides a surface for the blade to ride on, besides breaking up the hollow areas into cells from which the ink is not likely to be dragged out by the scraping action. Revolving from the doctor blade the cylinder next comes in contact with the paper, which is pressed tightly against it by the opposing rubber-faced cylinder. Continuing its revolution the etched cylinder is continuously being inked, scraped, and pressed against the travelling web of paper, the sequence proceeding without pause. As the two cylinders revolve one against the other, with the paper between them, the paper is pressed in close contact with the ink-bearing cells, and the ink adheres to the paper, here a mere film, there a comparatively thick layer, according to the depth of cell. At each revolution the cylinder prints one complete copy of the subject or subjects engraved upon it. As the paper is a length unwound from a reel, there are printed on it thousands of copies, which are later separated by cutting.

This kind of machine, working from the reel and at high speed, is known as a rotogravure machine. A rather better quality of work, more suitable for books, is obtainable from slower-running sheet-fed photogravure machines, which print separate sheets as does a Wharfedale or a Miehle press.

A magnifying-glass showed a half-tone print to be made up of dots of varying size and shape, but all uniformly black; the same glass will show that the dots (i.e. the cells) of the photogravure print are all of the same size and uniformly square, but unequal in depth of colour. It may also show that the spaces between the cells (the screen) are not white, as might be expected, but faintly toned. This tone is caused by ink spreading from the cells under pressure, and it is valuable because it assists in the illusion of continuous tone.

Much gravure work in colour is now printed from cylinders made with a half-tone dot screen. The cells are not regular in area, as they are with conventional gravure, but vary in size and shape as do the dots of a half-tone block. There are two varieties of this kind of invert or intaglio half-tone. In one the cells are all of the same depth, in the other a combination of the conventional gravure method and the half-tone dot screen produces cells that vary in depth from shallow in the highlights to deep in the shadows. Intaglio half-tone allows better control in colour printing, but has little advantage in monochrome. Consequently monochrome work continues to be printed in the conventional manner while colour work is increasingly in intaglio half-tone. The combination may be seen in the newspaper colour supplements.

Intaglio half-tone cylinders may be produced by electronic scanning engravers, which work after the manner of the electronic engraving machines and colour scanners used for letterpress and lithography. The machine, scanning the original picture, chips out diamond-shaped recesses in the cylinder surface varying in depth and area according to the tone and colour content of the original.

Cylinders may also be made by the powderless-etch process.

Photogravure is capable of a wide range of tone, from the

richest of shadows to the most delicate of highlights, and very beautiful results can be obtained from it. There is, however, a large initial cost in the preparation of the cylinder, and for this reason photogravure is only occasionally used for printing the illustrations of books. The usual edition of two to six thousand copies is not large enough to be economic. On the other hand, the cylinder will print enormous quantities with little deterioration, and if more than twenty or thirty thousand copies are required, photogravure may be the cheapest method of printing them. So we have the paradox of photogravure illustrations in a cheap Penguin while they are too expensive for more costly books that have smaller editions.

The process is excellent for certain types of magazines, and in these cases the text also is printed by photogravure at the same time as the illustrations. It cannot be expected that a weekly magazine, printed in a limited time, and at as low a price as possible, should show the best results the process can give, but remarkable results are obtained in mass-production publications. *Woman* is an example of a weekly magazine with a large circulation printed by photogravure.

Type matter printed by photogravure is not as satisfactory as that printed direct from the type by letterpress. For gravure printing the type is set and proofed as usual, and the proof finally photographed and transferred to the copper cylinder; but unfortunately the screen must be used with it, and this gives to the printed letter a microscopic raggedness and woolliness that is undesirable.

LITHOGRAPHY

Under the heading of lithography there are a number of related processes, but I need notice only two of them here. These two are artist or auto-lithography and photo-lithography.

Lithography is a planographic process—which is to say that the printing surface is neither raised, as in letterpress, nor recessed, as in photogravure, but quite flat. The printing surface is divided into printing and non-printing parts by an ingenious application of the well-known phenomenon that grease and water do not mix.

AUTO-LITHOGRAPHY

The first lithographic printing surface was Bavarian limestone, and it is from the use of this material that the process receives its name. This kind of limestone has the same absorptive affinity to grease as it has to water. The surface is ground smooth and perfectly level, and may then be given any variety of fine or coarse grain to suit the taste of the artist who is to do the drawing. The artist may himself do this graining, and indeed will if he is particular—only his own labour will give him exactly what he wants. He has probably roughed out the work on paper beforehand, and now he proceeds to do the finished drawing on the stone. It is done in greasy crayon, in greasy ink with a pen or brush, or by airbrush, or in any combination of these methods. The ink need not be used with a pen or brush; it can be applied with anything the artist cares to use—with a chewed matchstick, a piece of cloth or leather, or even the finger. It depends on what effect is wanted (Figure 72). The texture of the stone can be varied, within limits, from part to part, so that one drawing may have several different grain effects. The ink or crayon, by the way, is black, but this is only so that the artist can see what he is doing; the pigment has no influence on the printing—only the grease is important.

Some erasure and emendation is possible, but not a great deal, and the drawing must in the main be done surely at the first effort; it must also be done in reverse from left to right, but this is no hardship to an artist used to the process—no more than it is to the etcher or the engraver. In any case, a mirror may be kept handy so that the work can be seen the right way round as it progresses.

It will be realized that this form of lithography differs from other processes so far described in that the artist is employed intimately in the manufacture of the printing surface. By no other process can the individuality and idiosyncrasy of the artist be as completely preserved through thousands of copies; and no other printing process allows so much scope for individual expression.

The finished stone shows the picture in black grease on a polished or grained surface (Figure 72). The surface must be absolutely free from grease apart from the drawing. Absolutely means exactly that, for grease that is quite invisible and unsuspected will, when the printing stage is reached, come up as black as any part of the drawing. An apparently clean finger may leave an invisible mark containing enough natural grease from the skin to show clearly on the printed sheet.

When the drawing is complete the stone is treated to ensure that it is chemically clean and free from unwanted grease, and afterwards to fix the grease of the drawing in the porous surface of the stone. As soon as this process is complete the stone is ready for printing.

The machine for printing lithography direct is in some ways similar to a letterpress machine, but it has an additional set of rollers, which distribute water, not ink. The stone is placed on the bed of the machine, and during the operation passes first beneath the damping rollers and afterwards under the inking rollers. The damping rollers charge the stone with water, which damps the surface wherever it is not covered with grease; where there is grease the water is rejected. Under the inking rollers the reverse happens—the ink is greasy, and it is attracted to the grease on the stone, but repelled from the damp parts. The stone next passes under the impression cylinder, which presses the sheet of paper into contact with the damp stone and inked image and the paper comes forth bearing a faithful print of the drawing made on the stone.

Very fine colour work can be done by this form of lithography. There is no trichromatic principle, as in photo-reproduction, to reduce the number of printings to three or four, and a different working is necessary for every colour. There may be as many as sixteen or seventeen different stones to prepare, and as many separate printings, to produce the effect desired; though in practice it is more usual for the artist to accept the limitations

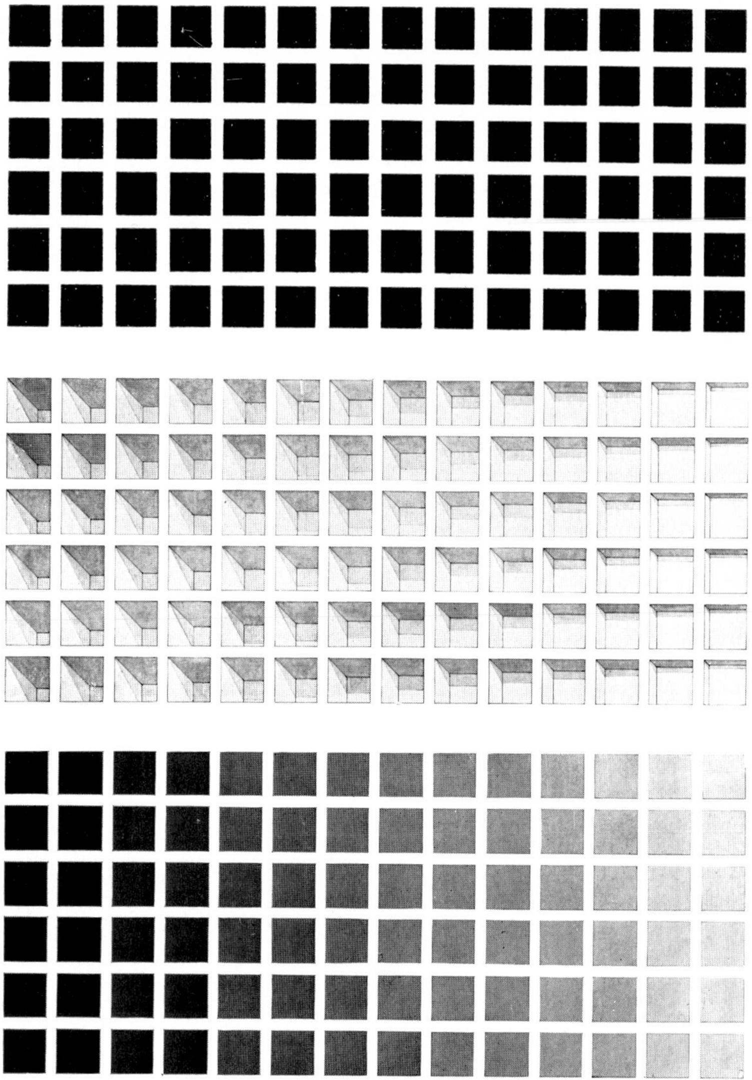

64. Above, a photogravure screen; centre, a diagram showing the varying depth of cells on the plate or cylinder; and below, a print showing the effect of the variation of depth of cell; all greatly enlarged

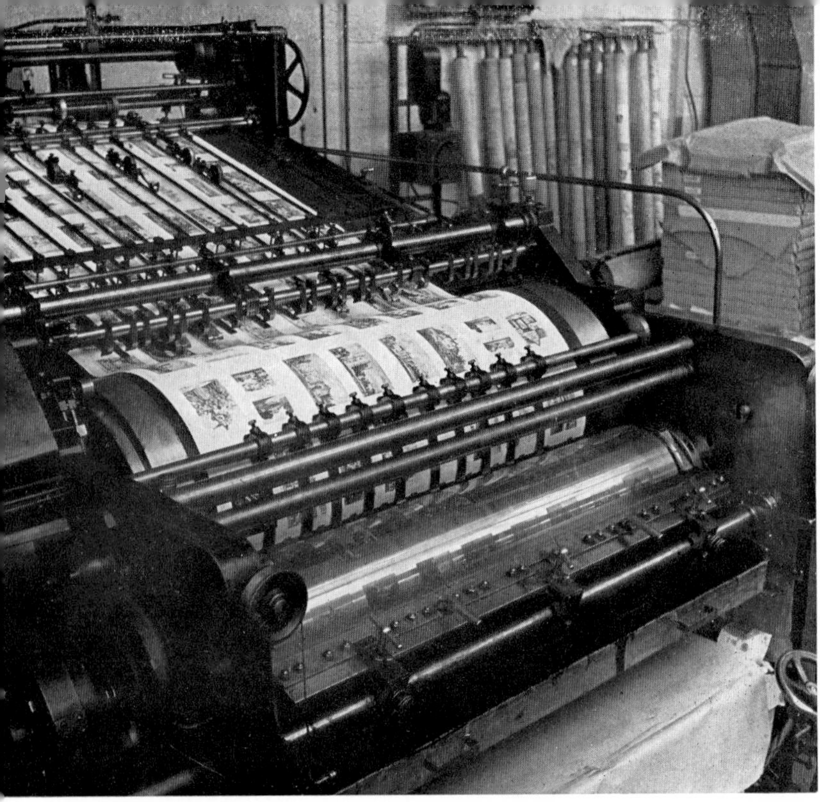

65. A sheet-fed gravure machine; the sheets shown are being backed up, or perfected

66. The printed web emerging from a rotary gravure machine; the cylinder is seen revolving in a bath of ink

of expense and time and to do his work within the compass of two to six colours. An impression of tone in each colour can be obtained to some extent by means of stippling and chalking, and no lack of variety is noticeable in a good lithograph of two or three colours.

For examples of colour lithography the reader should refer to book-jackets and illustrations by Barnett Freedman and Anthony Gross; and, where they are available, nineteenth-century ballet prints will show what can be done in rather a different way.

While Bavarian limestone is the original material used in lithography, and by some artists is still thought to be the best material for their purpose, its use has declined. Zinc or aluminium plates have displaced stone widely, among their many advantages being lightness of weight, cheapness, and the small amount of space they occupy in storage. Further, they can be grained mechanically, though not with the same variety of grain as stone. They are grained in a box containing water, sand, and hundreds of glass marbles of the sort that used to be found in lemonade bottles. The box is agitated by a motor so that the marbles perform a wild and ear-splitting jig among the sand and water over the surface of the plate. Graining is also done by sand blasting and by etching.

The kind of lithography described is known as direct lithography because the paper comes directly in contact with the stone or plate. There is another form of lithography, known as offset, in which there is no direct contact and which allows the artist to make his drawing the right way round. It is described in the next section.

Instead of zinc or stone, the artist may draw on a special kind of paper called transfer paper. This has the advantage of ease and portability; but it also has some disadvantages, among which is a slight deterioration in the quality of the image. A much superior method was introduced in 1948 by W. S. Cowell Ltd., of Ipswich. Transparent plastic materials, in sheet form and grained on one side, have been used for some kinds of drawing for years, principally by the printer's own lithographic artists. The drawing can be printed straight down on to a metal plate coated with a sensitive solution, and a lithographic image prepared from this. Cowell's have developed this method a good deal further. They introduced a plastic that can be worked in many ways to produce countless textures and effects, and they encouraged a number of artists to experiment with it, as a form of auto-lithography. The plastic can be engraved like a copper plate; it can be drawn upon with a pen or a pencil or a crayon; it can be painted; and it can be knifed or scratched with a needle. All these effects may be used together, if required, giving the artist enormous scope. The drawing must be the same size as the reproduction is intended to be. Illustrations reproduced by this process face pages 444 and 445.

OFFSET PHOTO-LITHOGRAPHY

Artist or auto-lithography is a medium involving the direct participation of the artist. Photo-lithography, on the other hand, is to lithography what process engraving is to letterpress—except that the term includes the actual printing as well. The offset method of printing is a variant of the ordinary method and I shall come to it in detail in a moment.

The printing surface is a metal plate. When metal plates are employed the term 'lithography' is strictly inaccurate, but is still used.

Photography goes hand in hand with offset litho to make the printing process known as photo-lithography. By means of the camera anything that can be photographed can be printed lithographically. Line subjects are printed clearly and entire, but for tone subjects a screen similar to that of process engraving, and serving the same purpose, must be used. Like letterpress, and unlike photogravure, photo-litho can print only an even film of ink, and in tone reproduction the dots of the finished picture vary in size exactly as do those of the half-tone block.

Except for the imposition of the screen, printing surfaces for line and tone are prepared in much the same way. A photographic negative of the subject is made, and this is printed down on to a plate of aluminium or zinc sensitized with a bichromated coating, which is hardened by exposure to light. The plate is next rolled with a greasy ink, and then washed to remove the unexposed coating and its ink layer. The design is left standing in tanned or hardened inked coating on an otherwise clean metal surface. After further treatment to ensure the chemical cleanliness of the plate and to fix the image, the printing is proceeded with.

Printing is done essentially as in direct lithography, the plate being damped and inked at every revolution. There is a flat-bed machine, but machines made for faster running have a cylinder in place of a bed, and this allows a much greater output. The plate is wrapped round this cylinder, and fastened on with clamps. Next to this is another cylinder, covered with rubber, and next to this still a further one, the impression cylinder. Between the last two the paper passes to be printed. The operation of printing is as follows: the cylinder carrying the plate is damped and inked; it revolves in contact with the rubber, or offset, cylinder, transferring an impression of the subject to the rubber; the offset cylinder in turn revolves against the paper and the impression cylinder, and transfers the ink to the paper.

The advantages of offset printing are attributable to this use of an offset cylinder with a resilient covering. The rubber presses gently but firmly against the plate, contacting every dot, and in turn presses as gently and as firmly on the paper. Because the pressure is even and from a smooth surface, art papers are not essential for the printing of screen illustrations. These can be printed even on a coarse paper, but a smooth paper nevertheless gives the best results.

Photo-lithography is satisfactory for the reproduction of line subjects, and it is used by publishers for reprinting books of which the type has been distributed; it saves the cost of resetting, and allows a reprint to be made which resetting would otherwise make uneconomic. Line drawings or diagrams, and maps, too, may be printed in this way.

The kind of litho plate we have been discussing is capable of printing only a thin layer of ink. A better result and a longer-lasting plate may be obtained by a deep-etch process. In this process the printing plate is exposed under a positive, not a negative, made from the original. The result is a plate with the non-printing surfaces represented by hardened coating and the printing areas, that is the image, represented by coating unaffected by light. This is the opposite of the system previously described: the method is adopted so that the hardened coating may be utilized as a stencil. The unexposed coating is removed from the image areas and the plate is then subjected to a slight etch to deepen the image. This etch produces a depth microscopic in measurement but sufficient to make the process worth while. The image is now made ink-attractive, and after this the hardened coating is removed from the non-image area and the plate is ready to be printed. The method is applicable to both line and tone.

For many years litho printers prepared and coated their own plates. They had to, because the coatings then in use, principally of dichromated albumen, had a very short storage life before exposure. Various manufacturers now formulate coatings much more durable and have applied them to plates that the printer can buy ready made and can store for a considerable time. Presensitized plates are available in a range of sizes to suit different machines, and in various qualities and fineness of grain. They can be used for negative working, in the older manner, or for positive working for deep-etch, and they will of course serve for both line and half-tone.

Conventional litho plates, however coated, present on the press an image composed of hardened coating. On a cylinder revolving at high speed against inking and damping rollers and against the impression cylinder, this coating is subject to friction; eventually it wears down and the plate begins to print badly. The press life of a plate depends on the skill of the pressman, but other factors such as the sort of ink in use and the nature of the paper printed have a bearing upon it. For very long runs the kinds of plate called bi-metallic and tri-

67. A Roland Ultra four-colour litho machine

68. The plate cylinder with the blanket cylinder below showing the transfer of the image

69. Coating a metal collotype plate on an upright whirler

70. Operator wiping a metal collotype plate on a rotary press

71. A flat-bed collotype machine in operation; the sheet is being fed for the printing of a further colour; the plate can be seen on the bed of the machine

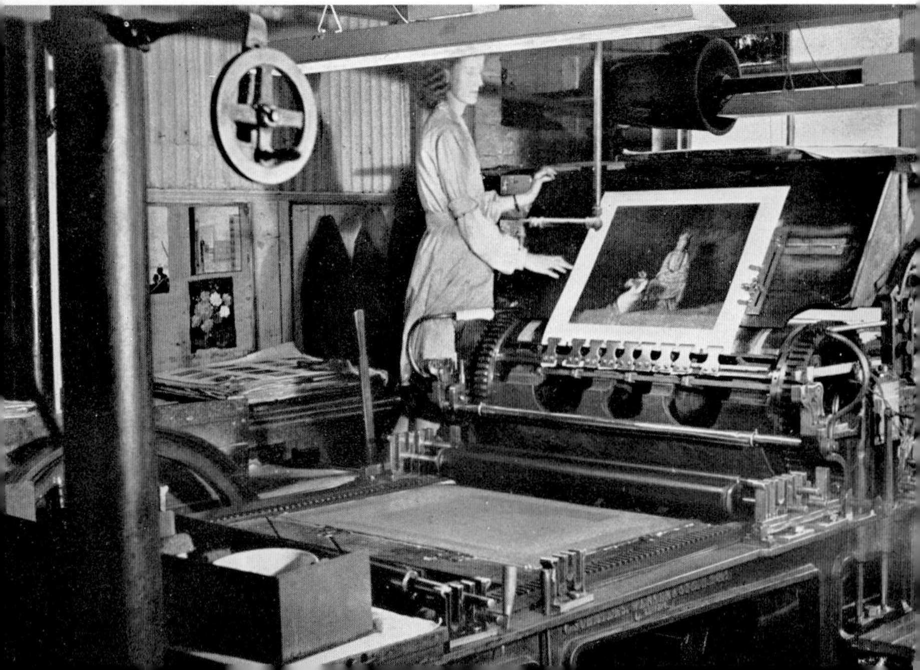

metallic are more serviceable. The terms are misleading: all these plates may be considered as bi-metallic. Certain metals have affinities for water and others for grease. Copper, for instance, will take grease and stainless steel and chromium will accept water, in each case as an even covering. Copper and one of these other two metals may therefore be used as coating and base. A copper image on a stainless-steel background makes an all-metal plate that is highly resistant to wear. Metals may also be used to produce deep-etch plates, the surface of which is chromium over copper. Plates of these kind will print millions of copies. Tri-metallic plates are nothing more than plates on which two metals—copper and chromium—are electro-plated on to a base of sheet steel or other metal. The base is simply a support, with no other printing function.

Bi-metallic and tri-metallic plates are more costly to produce than coated plates of aluminium or zinc and so they are not used for every job. They have, however, no grain and so are capable of printing more sharply and cleanly than a grained plate. For this reason some printers regularly use them for half-tone work, where the sharp quality of the dot is important in the result.

A mention should be made of paper plates. These are plates of a tough kind of paper given a presensitized coating. They are cheap and easy to use, but they have only a very short press life and so are employed for jobs of which the quantity required is not much more than a thousand.

Yet another kind of plate has appeared, and it is one that bids to revolutionize the lithographic method. It is the driographic plate. The novelty of this plate is that it is coated with a substance that is permanently antipathetic to grease and does not need to be refreshed with water at every printing stroke, or indeed at all. It therefore allows the whole damping system of the machine to be abolished, together with all the consequent problems of the proper balance of ink and water. The driographic plate is for the moment in its infancy, but it has been successfully demonstrated.

Photo-litho in colour in tone or line needs no detailed explanation here. A separate plate is made for each colour and printed separately in its appropriate colour on the machine. In essentials the principles of colour printing in photo-litho are similar to those of letterpress. Art paper is not essential, and this is an advantage not to be belittled. Again, the peculiar character of lithography, its softness and delicacy, gives its own special pleasure.

In the last decade or two a great deal of progress has been made in the development of web-offset machines. These are machines that print, as a newspaper press does, from reels of paper, which after printing are cut into sheets to be folded as required. A number of books, mostly paperbacks, are printed by this kind of machine, but the application is essentially for large editions rather than for the general run of books, and for acceptable rather than high quality in the result. The primary application is for newspapers and periodicals. Four-colour web-offset seems to promise the old dream of newspapers in full colour, and a few brave provincial newspapers are using it for this purpose: but the fortress of Fleet Street remains unconquered.

The more common kind of four-colour web-offset machine prints the colours from units arranged in tandem, through which the web of paper passes in sequence. A different kind of machine is designed on a planetary system, with the impression cylinder as the sun revolving in contact with four blanket cylinders, each with its plate cylinder and train of inking rollers and dampers. The four colours are printed in one revolution of the impression cylinder. The system is designed for a saving of space and for better control of register.

Indirect letterpress or letterset are terms used for letterpress printing on to a blanket cylinder and then on to paper, after the manner of litho offset; the printing surface is a shallow etched metal or plastic plate curved round the plate cylinder. Some machines are designed to print litho or letterset as required.

Lithography was invented at the beginning of the nineteenth century by Alois Senefelder, whose books on the process remained applicable even until our own day. There are several stories of the manner in which he stumbled on the idea. A story told by Senefelder himself is that he was experimenting with the etching of limestone when he was called upon to make out his mother's laundry list. To write it he used the materials nearest to his hand, which happened to be a slab of limestone and a stick of grease crayon. Afterwards it occurred to him to try to etch the stone with the writing on it, but it was not a success; then he tried printing from it as it was, and evolved the lithographic process more or less complete.

Offset lithography, invented much later, was, strangely enough, known for some time before its advantages for printing on paper were realized. It was first used for printing tinware with the choice designs we find on the lids of boot-polish containers and such things, and it is still used for this purpose. In the early years of this century it was used for the first time for printing paper, and there began then what has developed into a considerable industry.

COLLOTYPE

This, like lithography, is a planographic process. As with process engraving, photogravure, and lithography, anything that can be photographed can be reproduced; but collotype is more purely photographic than other printing processes. The printing surface is a photographic positive on glass or metal. Glass plates are used on flat-bed machines. Metal plates may be used on flat-beds or on rotary presses.

The plates are prepared by coating with an emulsion of bichromated gelatine—different from that used in other processes in that it is not soluble in water at ordinary temperatures. Glass plates are coated and then dried in an oven. Metal plates are coated and dried on a perpendicular whirler (Figure 69)—the whirling of metal plates produces a more even coating than may be obtained on glass and this allows improved reproduction of line work and of type. When it is dry the coating is sensitive to light.

Reversed negatives of the picture to be reproduced—which may be line or tone—are made, and these negatives are laid down in prearranged positions on the sensitized plate. Any portions round the negatives that are intended to remain white on the final printed page—the margins, for instance—are covered with a layer of foil.

The plate is now exposed to light through the negatives. It should be recalled here that white areas in the original are represented on the negative by black or dark gelatine, and black areas by clear places; while middle tones are represented by intermediate transparencies. This effect is familiar to everyone who has used a camera. As a result of the exposure through the negatives the sensitized plate is affected by light in those areas representing the shadows of the original, and is not affected where the dark portions of the negative, representing the lightest parts of the original, prevent the light from reaching the coating; between these two extremes the gelatine is affected according to the density of the negative. The effect is to harden the gelatine in proportion to the amount of illumination it receives; where most light is transmitted it is hardened most, where little is transmitted it remains proportionately soft and absorbent.

The negatives are now lifted off and the plate is washed in water to remove the unexposed bichromate and render the coating insensitive to any further exposure. It must be understood that the soft gelatine is not washed off the plate with the bichromate, as in other processes; the gelatine remains a continuous layer over the whole surface. After washing, the plate is dried and allowed to 'mature' for several hours. Next it is soaked in a mixture of water and glycerine, which is absorbed by the gelatine in proportion to its hardness, the softest parts absorbing most. The plate is then ready for printing.

The method of printing is similar to that of direct lithography, except that damping rollers are not used, as the gelatine retains sufficient water. The inking rollers deposit on the plate an ink that, because of its greasy nature, is rejected in proportion as the plate is damp, and is deposited mostly thickly on the hardened gelatine, which has absorbed little or no moisture

72. Effects possible in drawing on a litho stone, and (below) a litho stone with the drawing on it

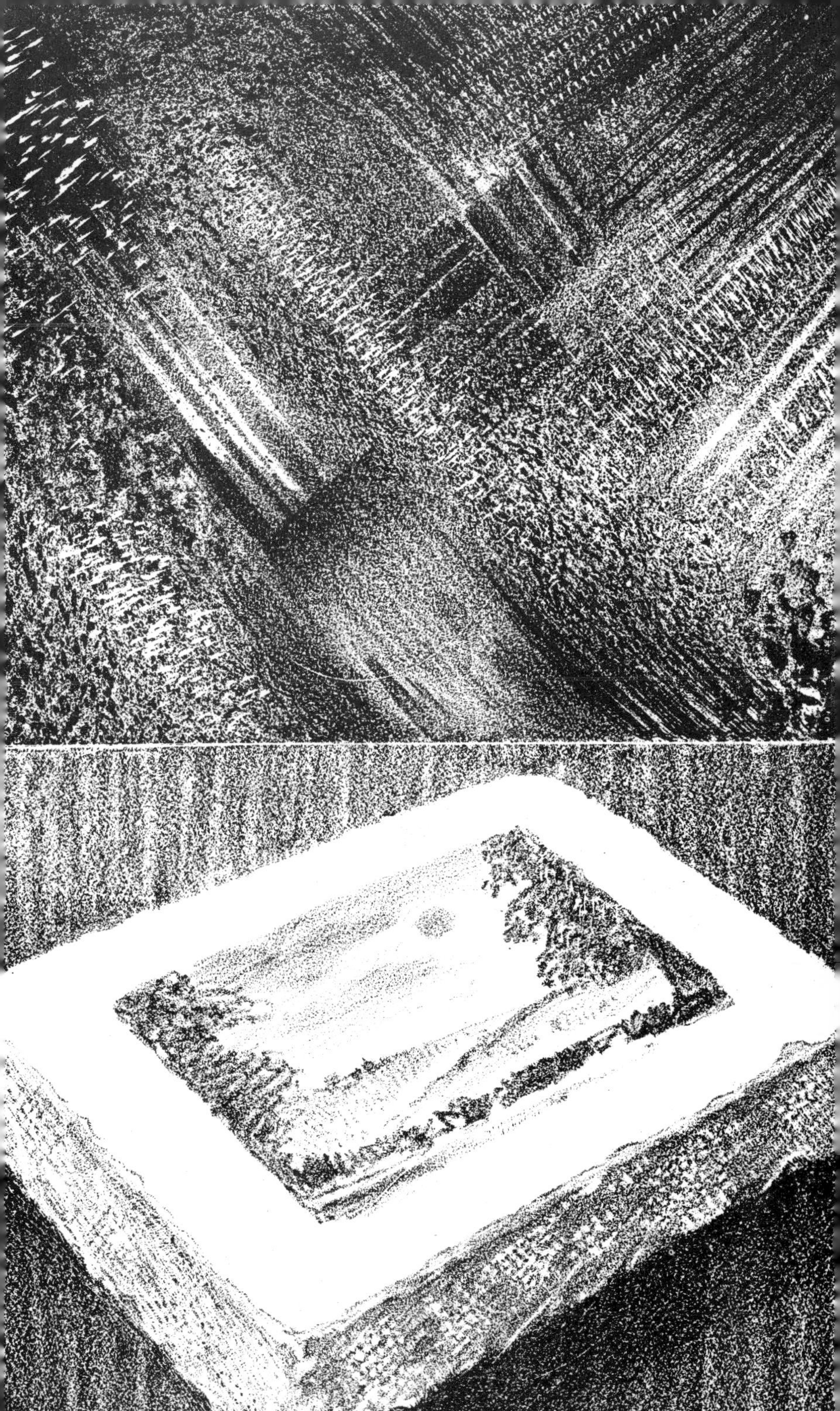

and represents the shadows of the picture. Impression of the plate on paper now transfers the ink as a reproduction of the original picture.

The tonal range is wide, and consists of true tones, as there is no visible grain or screen to break them up. Technically, collotype has a grain—not a screen grain, but the natural irregularity of the gelatine. It is so fine that it is not visible under an ordinary magnifying-glass, and alone among tone reproductions pictures printed by collotype will stand examination in this way. This quality makes the process invaluable for scientific reproductions of such things as photomicrographs and geological specimens, but this is by no means its only use. No other process gives quite the same delicacy and yet also the same strength of tone as collotype, and many competent people consider that collotype reproduction is the best that can be obtained by any commercial process.

Many kinds of paper can be used, provided they are of good quality, though one with a moderately smooth surface is best. Paper with a soft surface is unsuitable.

Collotype in colour can be very beautiful. It is not restricted by the trichromatic principle and from five to eight workings may be used, without fear of screen clash, to obtain a faithful reproduction of the original. The quality is high and the cost is in line with it, and for this reason full-colour collotype seldom appears in books. There are, however, some notable exceptions. Full-colour collotype is more often used for printing wall pictures, and to possess a fine example of these prints is next only to the possession of the painting from which it is reproduced.

The comparative simplicity of the method of making the printing plates gives the process an economic advantage in monochrome in editions up to about 5000 copies. In larger quantities the advantage of economy of plate-making is lost in the slow speed of the press, and collotype becomes too costly for general use.

There are only a few firms in the world capable of printing in collotype, and one of these, the Cotswold Collotype

Company, is in the British Isles, at Wotton-under-Edge, in Gloucestershire.

EXAMPLES OF PROCESSES

The illustrations in this book serve as examples of printing processes as follows:

Photogravure: Figures 132, 133, 135, 136
Auto-lithography: Figure 72
Lithography (from Plastocowell): Figures 190, 191
Photolithography (four-colour process): Figures 185, 186
Collotype: Figures 173, 174, 178, 179, 197, 198, 199, 200
Letterpress half-tone (four colour process): Figure 63
Letterpress half-tone: all the tone illustrations other than those listed above
Line-blocks: all the line illustrations in the text

XI

PAPER

Its Manufacture and Varieties

THE Egyptians seem to have been the first to make a material that might, though it stretches the meaning of the word, be called paper; and from the Greek name for their invention, *papyros*, comes our own word, *paper*. There is, however, no real relation between the two substances, other than that they are both composed of vegetable material. Papyrus was made by laying split sections of reed side by side in layers at right angles, and cementing them together in some manner not perfectly understood. The resulting sheet was durable (it has endured four thousand years or more), if brittle. Paper, on the other hand, is composed of plant fibres broken down to microscopic proportions and then felted together.

History does not show, as might be expected, a continuous development from papyrus to paper. The Chinese are credited with the invention of paper as long ago as the second century A.D., but it can scarcely be claimed that they received any inspiration from ancient Egypt; as far as we know, the two countries might have been on different planets for all they knew of each other. A specimen of Chinese paper of the second century is in the British Museum. From China paper-making was carried in the seventh century to Korea and Japan, but it had started on its westward march long before that time. The Arabs, in their conquest of Tartary, came upon this new craft, new to them but already ancient to the Chinese, and brought examples of its product back to Mecca in A.D. 707; and in 793

Caliph Haroun al Raschid brought Chinese paper-makers to Baghdad.

Europe was slow to discover and use paper; and perhaps it had little use for it. Vellum and parchment, and various other kinds of skin, were the writing surfaces in use. Not until the twelfth century do we hear of a European paper mill, and this was set up at Játiva by, or under the influence of, the Moors, who had held and continued to hold a monopoly of paper in the western world. The first paper mill in Christendom seems to have been that founded at Fabriano in Italy about 1270, where fine papers are still made. With the Renaissance the supply of parchment and vellum must have begun to prove inadequate and perhaps too costly for the increasing numbers of readers, and paper began to come more into use. The invention of printing and the consequent enormous increase in the production of books made it at last the common basis of literary exchange.

Early paper was made of linen, jute, or flax, and if we may judge by what has survived, some of it was very good paper indeed. The earliest English specimen known is in the Public Record Office, and is a letter from Raymond, son of the Duke of Navarre, to Henry III.

Paper was still being made of rags in the seventeenth century and the demand was outstripping the supply. The position was serious enough to attract the attention of Parliament, which, as an amelioration, prohibited the burial of the dead in shrouds made of linen or cotton, because the paper mills needed the material.

Paper-making continued with little development until the eighteenth century, when John Baskerville, wanting something smoother and more even than he had been able to obtain, in order to bring out the full quality of his fine new type, introduced wove paper, free of the watermarked rulings that had hitherto been characteristic. To-day by far the greater part of all paper is wove—it suits modern printing techniques better than laid paper. Laid paper is used for a comparatively small number of books, especially for those aiming at an antique or special effect.

73. Pulp in a beater

74. The wet end of a paper-making machine; bubbles on the surface of the pulp, which might cause flaws, are dispersed by steam jets

75. General view of two paper-making machines from the wet end

76. A supercalender machine, showing the web of paper travelling between the rollers, which give it a smooth surface

The scarcity of rag inspired a search for alternative materials, and in 1800 Matthias Koops was granted a patent for making paper from straw. In 1801 he produced a book printed half on paper made from straw and half on paper made from wood. The straw paper is brownish in colour and is inferior to the wood paper, which appears to have been produced by what is now called the chemical wood process. Straw paper was unsuccessful and was forgotten, but in his use of wood Koops founded what is to-day one of the great industries of the world.

Forty years later a Saxon watchmaker, Keller, produced a wood paper made by mechanical means. It was an inferior paper, as mechanical wood paper is to-day, but it was cheap, and is so still; and of the sections of the industry, that for making paper mechanically from wood is by far the largest. Mechanical wood paper is used for newsprint all over the world, and huge forests have fallen, and are falling hourly, into the maw of the paper-making machine.

Experiments directed towards the use of esparto grass in the manufacture of paper were in progress in 1839, but this material achieved no commercial value until after 1860. The American Civil War restricted the supply of cotton and necessity made esparto more popular than otherwise it might have been. In other countries esparto is little used, but in Great Britain its popularity has increased consistently, and large quantities of this grass are imported yearly from the Mediterranean littoral.

Since the beginning of the nineteenth century considerable changes have occurred in the methods by which paper is manufactured. It would be strange if the far-reaching mechanization of the industrial revolution had not affected the manufacture of paper, and in fact it has changed it utterly. Until that time paper had been made by hand by methods that had not altered throughout the centuries, and the process, though it produced excellent paper, was slow and cumbersome. The world needed paper, and it was to need more and more paper, beyond all competence of the labouring hand. The introduction of machinery into various industries could only exaggerate the demand for paper, and paper at a low price. If the Renaissance was founded on paper, the industrial revolution needed it much more. The paper-making machine was invented in 1798 by Louis Robert of Essonnes, in France. It was introduced into England in 1803 by Henry Fourdrinier, who was bankrupted by his efforts to promote the sale of the machine, but at least had the

77. Paper-making in the sixteenth century; in the background water-wheels operate a row of hammers to beat the pulp, and behind the vatman is a screw press

satisfaction of seeing it called by his name. Improvements were made by several people subsequently, bringing the machine to its present high level of efficiency and economy. Paper is made by this machine in sheets quite impossible by hand, and very much more rapidly and cheaply. True, it may not be entirely as good as hand-made paper, but it can be very good paper indeed, and only by machine can the even quality and character required by the modern printing press be maintained. To-day huge, but not very complicated, structures, make paper in vast ribbons yards wide and miles in length for the ceaseless service of the press.

It is interesting to follow the materials through the mill from the moment when they enter, as bales of dried grass, wood, or rags, until they emerge in the form of finished paper ready for the printer.

Rags are first sorted and cleared of any buttons, clips, or zips, or other objects that might have been useful in clothing but can have no part in a book, and are then cut into small pieces and boiled and bleached in a solution of lime and caustic soda. Next they are washed, to remove the chemicals and any remaining dirt, and beaten in a machine designed to separate the fibres and to prepare them for felting. At this stage other kinds of pulp may be added, according to the kind of paper required, or a loading of kaolin or other substance may be mixed in, or size as a hardening agent.

Wood is pulped in either of two ways, mechanically or chemically. Mechanical wood pulp is produced by pressing the wood against a grindstone revolving in water, and so reducing it to shreds, with which, however, are mixed many impurities resulting from the grinding, and unwanted substances natural in the wood. The process is a cheap one, and is used for the manufacture of newsprint. Mechanical wood pulp is undesirable as an ingredient in any paper that is expected to endure; its presence makes the paper turn yellow and brittle sooner or later.

Chemical wood pulp is a very different product. The wood is first broken into chips and is then chemically treated to reduce it to pulp suitable for further working. Three different chemicals are in ordinary use, and each produces a distinct kind of fibre and paper. With caustic soda a soft, fluffy fibre is obtained, out of which are manufactured various kinds of cover and writing papers. Calcium bisulphite (or magnesium bisulphite) produces a stronger and harder fibre that is much used as an ingredient in various kinds of printing papers. Pulp made with sodium sulphate produces a paper of exceptional toughness, not suitable for books; it is used for good qualities of wrapping paper.

Esparto grass arrives in bales containing some dust and foreign matter, and is cleared of this in a special machine, out of which the grass passes to boilers containing caustic soda, where it is boiled under pressure. From this it goes to the breaking machine, where the grass is kept in continual movement past a revolving cylinder or paddle-wheel, which breaks it up into fine shreds, and beats the mass into a thick pulp, a constant stream of water flowing through to remove any dirt or impurities that remain. The pulp now goes into the potchers, where it is bleached and the last foreign matter removed, so that nothing remains but fibres and water, the fibres being so fine that they are invisible, singly, to the eye.

The final stage in the making of the pulp is the beating machine, in which the reducing process is continued still further, and quantities of other pulps are added to produce particular kinds of paper. There may also be added a small quantity of colouring matter, to ensure that the paper will be white, much as blue powder is added to certain detergents to whiten clothes. Or if coloured paper is required, suitable colouring is added at this stage.

The pulp now goes to the stuff chest, which is nothing more than a great vat, a reservoir, in which the pulp is kept constantly in motion, to prevent the fibres from settling, until it is required.

Before the days of machines all these operations were done by hand, or with simple engines of one kind or another, but nothing is gained by reverting to the old methods now. Hand-made paper is still manufactured, but as far as the stage we have reached the pulp is made in much the same way for both hand-made and machine-made papers. The hand work of modern hand-made paper follows from this stage.

Making paper by hand is laborious and slow, and entails considerable training and practice and a nice judgement of weight. A tank about five feet by six is filled with pulp, which is kept constantly agitated, and at this the vat man works. His tool is a tray of the same size as the sheet to be made. The bottom of the tray is formed of parallel wires, with others running at right angles, and it is these wires that form the laid marks in paper—more common in writing and ledger papers these days than in printings. If wove paper is being made, the bottom of the tray is formed of a fine metal mesh, closely woven. The sides of the tray are separate, and come apart, as a frame, from the bottom. A mould is made to produce one size of paper only, and a different mould is required for each size. Watermarks, first introduced at Fabriano in the thirteenth century, are made by a wire pattern woven into the mould (Figure 77).

The tray is dipped into the vat and exactly the right amount of pulp is taken up to make a sheet of paper of the thickness and weight required. It is here that fine judgement of weight is necessary, for the vat man has no other indication than his own experience of the amount of pulp required for the sheet. Lifting the mould with the pulp on it, he shakes it first forwards and backwards and then from side to side, while water escapes through the interstices of the wire. The purpose of this shaking is to make the fibres cross in all directions, and so give strength to the paper: and it is the distinguishing mark of hand-made paper that the fibres do cross like this—the machine cannot do it so well. As the water escapes from the mould it leaves a matted layer of fibre on the wire, and this is the sheet of paper. The mould is now taken apart and the paper transferred to a sheet of felt; on top of this another felt is placed, and on this the next sheet of paper to be made; and so on until a pile of felts interleaved with sheets of paper has accumulated. The pile is placed in a press and subjected to pressure for a while, after which the paper is separated from the felts and pressed separately for some hours. If a smooth finish is required, further pressings are necessary. Drying of the paper is done in a loft, where it is hung like so much washing over lines.

At this stage the paper has the absorbent qualities of blotting. To make it harder and less absorbent it is sized, that is, it is passed through a bath of gelatine or other solution, which permeates the surface of the paper as starch does a collar. The paper is then again dried, and glazed perhaps, and after counting and packing it is ready for the printer.

Because of the cost of making paper by hand it is not worth while to use any but the best materials for it, and practically all hand-made paper to-day is made of rags. From this fact has arisen a belief that hand-made paper is always the best paper obtainable. This is usually true in fact because the best materials are used for it; but it is not true in theory. Paper made by hand of esparto pulp should be better for some purposes than the same kind of paper made by machine; but it is unlikely that it would be better than machine-made rag paper.

The manufacture of paper by machine is the hand process mechanized, though the resulting paper is different in texture and in other qualities. The machine is not capable of the same lateral shake of the mould, with the result that the fibres do not interlink to the extent they do in hand-made paper. Machine-made paper therefore has a more distinct grain, a direction in which the fibres run. Such paper is stiffer in the direction of the grain, but it will also tear more easily that way; and it may be liable to uneven shrinkage and expansion. This is of little moment except in colour printing, where expansion or contraction can make the registration of colours difficult.

The paper-making machine is a long affair, composed of many cylinders, an endless belt of woven wire, and another one of felt. At one end is a chest, to which the pulp, or stuff, is led from the stuff chest; and from which it enters the machine in a stream that can be regulated according to the thickness and weight of the paper to be made. The pulp first passes over sand tables that are intended as a final trap for any foreign matter or hard particles that may have escaped so far, and then runs on to the belt of woven wire. This corresponds with the mould of the hand worker, and is agitated in two directions as the water falls through the mesh of the wire. Most of the water has fallen away, and some more has been removed by suction, when the pulp, now so much soggy fibre, but beginning to look like paper, passes under rollers, which remove more water by pressure. Emerging from the rollers, the paper—for it can now be called paper—is just strong enough to stand the strain of being transferred from the wire to the felt, on which it is carried through further sets of rollers, where more moisture is removed and the fibres are pressed into closer contact. It next passes over heated cylinders, to remove the last of the water, and finally between sets of cold iron rollers to give it the finished surface.

78. A paper-making machine in the nineteenth century

It is then wound into reels whose length is only limited by the quantity of the pulp available or the ability of the mill to handle them. A reel of paper may be anything up to five miles long and 230 inches wide.

Paper made in this way goes through no separate sizing process. The size is mixed with the pulp in the beater, and permeates every fibre. This is cheaper than separate sizing, but the result is not quite as good. Certain superior kinds of machine-made paper are sized after manufacture, and are known as tub-sized papers.

Hand-made paper, as we saw, is made in sheets of definite dimensions—the various standard sizes, in fact; and all four edges of each sheet have the natural edge of manufacture—the gradual thinning and unevenness that forms the now much vaunted and certainly pleasant deckle. Our ancestors thought it a disfigurement, and were in the habit of cutting it off. Whatever one may think of it personally, our appreciation of it to-day is partly the result of snobbishness. Machine-made paper, being made in long strips, has to be cut to size, so that each edge is a cut edge, and a genuine deckle is impossible. The deckle therefore became a distinguishing mark of hand-made paper, and I think there is no doubt that it was first retained just to show that the paper really was 'ye olde' genuine hand-made. Nowadays it is regarded as almost a crime to cut off the deckle.

Newsprint is not cut into sheets, as the newspaper press prints direct from the reel and cuts the paper for itself. Newsprint is therefore rewound, and as it moves from one reel to another is slit into widths required for the press. It is at the same time examined for blemishes, and when one is found the reeling is stopped, the defective portion cut out and the two ends joined, and the re-reeling and slitting continued.

Watermarks and laid marks are not necessary productions of the paper-making machine. They are illogical and extraneous. The wire mesh on which the pulp flows plays no part in marking the paper, and to obtain watermarks and laid marks the damp web passes under a roller—the dandy roller—which impresses the marks on the paper. This is a further difference between machine-made and hand-made paper, the markings of the latter resulting from the structure of the mould. Nevertheless, I doubt that the difference of method is discernible in the result.

VARIETIES OF PAPER

Paper is not, of course, all of one kind, and the following list gives some details of the more important varieties used in books, together with definitions of some relevant terms.

Wove and Laid Papers. It may be said that all papers are either wove or laid. Wove paper, if held to the light, shows an even, characterless, structure. Laid paper shows a series of closely spaced parallel lines with bolder and more widely spaced lines running at right angles. These lines are more transparent because at these places the paper is slightly thinner; a water-mark is produced in a similar way. Laid papers are not as frequently used in the production of books as they were formerly, but are common in writing and wrapping papers.

Engine-sized Papers are those in which the size is mixed with the pulp to become an integral part of the paper.

Tub-sized Papers are sized, like hand-made papers, after being made. They are generally superior to parallel sorts of engine-sized paper; and certainly the size is where it is wanted, in the surface. They are, too, harder and tougher than engine-sized papers.

Antique Papers. This name means very little except that papers so designated have a comparatively rough, and not a smooth, surface—i.e. not machine-finished or supercalendered. The name is perhaps intended to convey that the paper has a surface similar to that of old hand-made papers, but the resemblance is remote. It covers a wide range of papers, some comparatively smooth, others very rough; and comprises qualities from the very worst to the best. Some antiques are remarkable in their relation of weight to thickness, being very thick and at the same time very light indeed. Such papers are loosely compacted, have very little strength, and in use rapidly become woolly and soiled. Their only recommendation—if it is one—is that they can be used to make a book with only a few pages as thick as one with a great many—and such a book may be as much as fifty per cent nothing but air. For a reason only they can tell, some publishers appear to consider feather-weight antiques the most suitable papers for children's books, although nothing could be less calculated to withstand the rough usage a child's book is liable to receive.

Many antiques are very good papers indeed, and to-day perhaps more books are printed on this kind of paper than on any other. The best are strong, even, handle well, and are of good substance; they take type and line blocks excellently.

Cartridge Paper is used occasionally for books. It is a strong, tough paper, originally used in the manufacture of cartridges, and still liable to disappear from the market in time of war. The surface is rather like that of a good antique, but is harder. Cartridge paper, like other papers, has a wrong side and a right side, the wrong side, usually the rougher of the two, being the one formed against the wire mesh of the paper-making machine. Two different sides are undesirable in a book with illustrations on both sides of the paper, and to allow satisfactory printing of such books twin-wire cartridges are made. These cartridges have two right sides, formed by bonding two thin webs of paper back to back.

SUPERCALENDERED PAPERS are given a smooth finish by repeated rolling between hot and cold rollers. They are sometimes used for books where fine-line blocks or half-tones are included in the text; and sometimes for no particular reason at all other than that some misguided printer or publisher takes a fancy to them. They give good results from type, and passable ones even from half-tones; but they are unpleasant in a book because their shine is uncomfortable to the eye.

MACHINE-FINISHED PAPERS (or M.F.) have the normal finish of the paper-making machine. The surface is moderately smooth and shiny, but not glossy. It prints well. There is a wide range of grades, the best being pleasant and useful, the worst unpleasant.

MOULD-MADE PAPERS are a paradox. They are in effect hand-made papers made by machine. They have the feathery deckle characteristic of hand-made papers, but rather different in formation. They are not quite as strong as hand-made, but none the less a good mould-made paper is a very good paper indeed, and fit for the limited editions for which so often hand-made paper is considered indispensable. It is expensive, but cheaper than hand-made.

OFFSET PAPERS. Offset lithography works best with a paper that has a smooth surface, free from fluff, and with a particular kind of sizing. Good offset paper is very pleasant, and is used at times in letterpress books.

COATED PAPERS. Art paper is given a special coating of glazed china clay to present the smoothest possible surface on which to print half-tone blocks of fine screen. It gives the best results obtainable from these, but as a paper it has serious disadvantages. The coating weakens the paper considerably, and makes it so brittle that a fold quickly becomes a crack, and eventually a fracture—which is one of the reasons why plates come out of books. Because of the coating the paper is very heavy, and a book printed on art paper throughout, as some books are, may feel like so much lead. Glazed art paper has a high polish; if the glazing operation is omitted, the paper remains as matt art, smooth but not glossy. The coating is applied by different methods. In one process the coating is controlled and smoothed by an air-knife, in another by a trailing blade. Machine-coated papers are cheaper varieties in which the coating is applied, not separately, but as the web emerges from the paper-making machine. Blade-coated cartridges are coated papers with a stronger base material and a smooth matt finish designed for printing illustrations by litho.

IMITATION ART PAPERS. Real art paper is coated after the paper is made, so that the coating forms a layer on the surface. For imitation art the clay is mixed in with the pulp, a proceeding that saves an operation and reduces cost, but produces a paper inferior to real art. Imitation art is used for the printing of half-tone blocks, and gives good results. A simple test serves to distinguish real from imitation art paper: if a silver coin is rubbed on real art, it will leave a distinct mark like a pencil; imitation art gives no response, or only a faint one.

LOADED PAPERS. This is not a separate class of paper; most kinds of paper are loaded in some way or other. Loading means the addition to the pulp of substances, for example kaolin or french chalk or titanium, designed to make the paper smoother or more opaque. The process is the same as that for imitation art, but much less of the loading substance is introduced. It was first practised in the nineteenth century, apparently surreptitiously, to save pulp and reduce the cost to the manufacturer, but it was found that restricted quantities of loadings improved the paper rather than otherwise.

INDIA PAPER. This paper has for long been connected with the Oxford University Press, who were the first to have it made. It is a very good paper, but its best-known quality is its amazing thinness and, for its weight, its opacity. It is useful when a book contains many pages and would bulk too much on ordinary paper. The Bible, if printed on featherweight antique, might be more than a foot thick; on India paper it might be no more than an inch.

PATTERNED PAPERS. Many papers used for jackets or bindings are patterned in relief with some design or other—a favourite one simulating leather. It is done very simply by passing the paper as it comes from the machine through rollers engraved with the pattern. For linen or crash patterns the rollers may be wrapped with the material itself.

The terminology of paper is inexact and at times woolly. There are many more varieties than I have given here, and in addition there are special kinds of paper peculiar to particular manufacturers and possessing names unto themselves. Other papers, such as those called parchments and printings, differ among themselves to a degree that defeats any attempt to discover the common relationship. Some may be placed in one of the categories given above, others show differences of one sort or another. Some are good, some moderate, some bad. The only way of knowing what any paper is like is to see it.

BOOK SIZES OF PAPER

Until metrication was adopted in 1968 a series of standard sizes of sheets of paper was in use in Britain, giving a variety of finished book sizes. These sizes, which may be called imperial sizes, went by names derived from ancient usage, in some instances traceable back to medieval watermarks (e.g. foolscap, crown). Millions of books exist in the imperial sizes given in the following table. Note that these sizes are untrimmed, that is, they represent the sheets as folded by the binder before the edges are guillotined or trimmed.

The broadside sizes were the sizes of the basic sheets. Paper was made in multiples of these basic sizes for economy of printing many pages at once. Thus, for example, double crown was 30 × 40 inches, quad crown 60 × 40 inches. Double quad sizes were also available from the paper-maker for very large printing machines.

Other countries used similar ranges of sizes, but not necessarily of the same proportions. American paper sizes, for instance, give squarer books than English usage.

Imperial sizes are still made, but it is probable that they will disappear before the advance of metrication.

Imperial book sizes in inches

Broadside	*Folio*	*Quarto*	*Octavo*	*Sixteenmo*
Royal				
20 × 25	20 × 12½	10 × 12½	10 × 6¼	5 × 6¼
Medium				
18 × 23	18 × 11½	9 × 11½	9 × 5¾	4½ × 5¾
Demy				
17½ × 22½	17½ × 11¼	8¾ × 11¼	8¾ × 5⅝	4⅜ × 5⅝
Large crown				
16¼ × 21½	16¼ × 10¾	8⅛ × 10¾	8⅛ × 5⅜	4$\frac{1}{16}$ × 5⅜
Crown				
15 × 20	15 × 10	7½ × 10	7½ × 5	3¾ × 5

On the Continent standardized metric sizes have been in use for some years. Based on the recommendations of the International Standards Organization and consequently known as ISO sizes, they are also called DIN sizes, from their adoption by the German standards organization, Deutsche Industrie Normen. The A group of these sizes applies to books. The basic sheet is A0, 841 × 1189 mm (33$\frac{1}{10}$ × 46⅘ inches). This sheet is designed to produce the same proportions for each sub-division across the longer dimension. Each sub-division is numbered. A1, half of A0, measures 841 × 594 mm, A2 = 420 × 594 mm, and so forth. Multiples of A0 are given a figure in front of them, e.g. 2A0 = 1189 × 1682 mm.

British publishers were not satisfied with the limitations of the A sizes and a conference between the Publishers' Association and the British Federation of Master Printers produced an additional range of standard metric paper sizes that may be said to be the imperial sizes converted to the nearest convenient millimetre. The old names are retained for these new sizes. The intention is to produce a series of book sizes standard *as trimmed.* Because of the method of trim, the quarto sizes are slightly larger than double the octavo sizes. The quarto and octavo formats are shown below:

Metric paper sizes in millimetres

	Equivalent in inches	*Quarto*	*Octavo*
A sizes A0: 841 × 1189	$33\frac{1}{10} \times 46\frac{4}{5}$	A4: 210 × 297	A5: 148 × 210
Quad royal 960 × 1272	$37\frac{3}{4} \times 50$	237 × 312	234 × 156
Quad demy 888 × 1128	$35 \times 44\frac{3}{8}$	219 × 276	216 × 138
Quad large crown 816 × 1056	$32\frac{1}{8} \times 41\frac{5}{8}$	201 × 258	198 × 129
Quad crown 768 × 1008	$30\frac{1}{4} \times 39\frac{5}{8}$	189 × 246	186 × 123

BUYING PAPER

Paper is sold in reams. A ream was originally 480 sheets, a figure that allowed easy sub-division. An attempt was made to standardize on 500 sheets, but a third size of ream arrived, of 516 sheets. The additional sixteen sheets were intended to allow for spoils and so for calculation in even 500s. In general, publishers prefer the ream of 516 sheets, but the ream of 500 is also marketed and no doubt it accords more neatly with the theory of metrication, if not with printing and publishing practice.

The thickness or substance of paper was formerly expressed, in Britain, as the weight of the ream. This meant a different figure for different sizes of the same paper—for example crown 12 lb. was the same as royal 20 lb. and demy 16 lb. On the

Continent the much more sensible method of measuring the weight of a square metre of paper is used, and this has been adopted in Britain also. The gramme weight per square metre, written gsm or g/m², is the same for any specified paper, whatever the size of the sheet actually used in printing. As part of the metrication of paper manufacture and use, a range of gsm substances related one to another in geometrical progression is recommended. Papers for bookwork range from 40 gsm for a thin Bible paper to 136 gsm or more for a sturdy offset cartridge. Boards such as those used for the covers of paper-back books may go as high as 280 gsm.

Publishers buy paper by weight in kilograms per ream and in quantities of imperial tons or metric tonnes; the price is quoted at so much per kilogram or so much per ton or tonne. Publishers frequently have paper specially made for them by paper-mills in order to obtain particular qualities of furnish or colour, in standard or non-standard weights, or to provide a required bulk for a stated number of pages. It is not economical to order special makings for quantities of less than a thousand kilograms, and some mills require even larger minimum quantities to be ordered.

XII

BINDING

Hand-binding and Machine-binding

THE kind of book with which we are familiar to-day, composed of a number of leaves fastened together down one side and known to scholars as a 'codex', is a development of the scroll of the ancients. Scrolls were from three to twelve inches deep or more and might be several feet long. At first the lines were written the full length of the material; the reader began at one end and, as he read, unrolled the scroll with one hand and rolled it up again with the other; when he reached the end of the line, he might, according to the language, be able to start on the next line at once, reading it in the reverse direction and rolling and unrolling accordingly, or he might have to go all the way back to the beginning to commence the second line. This meant a great deal of rolling and unrolling, and considerable wear of the scroll, not to speak of wear of the reader. Later the lines were broken into short lengths and arranged in columns, which were set in a row along the length of the scroll. This must have been an improvement, making reading easier, and saving much wear and tear; but it was still necessary to rewind the scroll when the last page was reached, or when any other page than that being read was referred to.

It occurred to some inventive intelligence that if the paged scroll were folded in concertina fashion, instead of being wound on a roller, it would be more accessible; and perhaps the same person thought of fastening the back folds together, to give the contraption better mechanical unity. This form of book was much used throughout the East, and is known as an orihon. There was some waste of material, since only one side could be written on, the other being hidden inside the folds; but once the spine was securely fastened, the foredge could be cut, and both sides of the leaf utilized.

A stitch through one layer of material is not as strong a fastening as one made through several layers, and experience

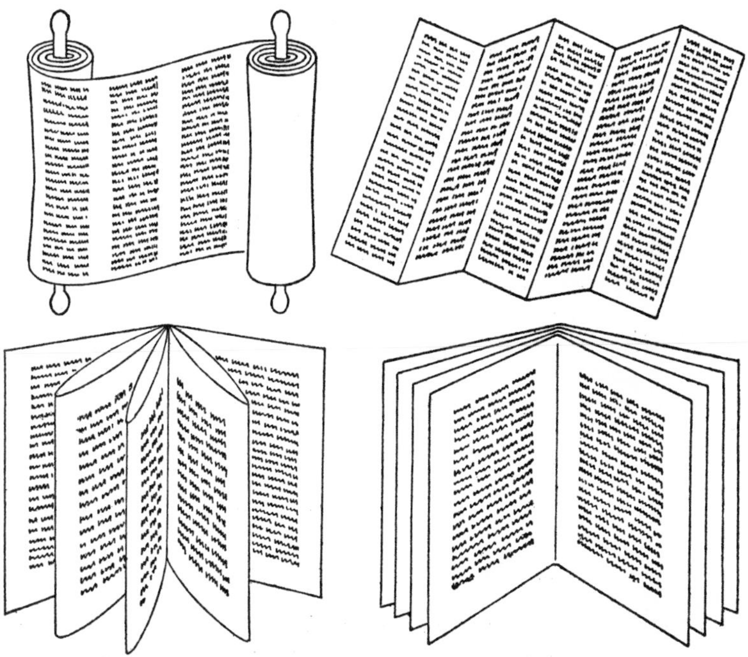

79. Theoretical evolution of the codex

must soon have made this clear. To provide extra strength several folded sections were placed one within the other and stitched together, the assembly being fastened to its neighbour by another stitch.

Books were precious things, made with great expenditure of labour and time, and a cover of some kind was required to protect and preserve them. At first it was perhaps only an envelope or some sort of separate wrapping; this would give adequate protection while the book was on the shelf, but not while it was being read, which was when it needed protection most. To give constant protection the cover was joined to the pages, and the book reached the form we know to-day.

Before I proceed further it will be useful to name the various parts of a book, as the terms will crop up again.

Figure 80 shows a bound book with the parts indicated and named. The spine is that portion, often called the back, that

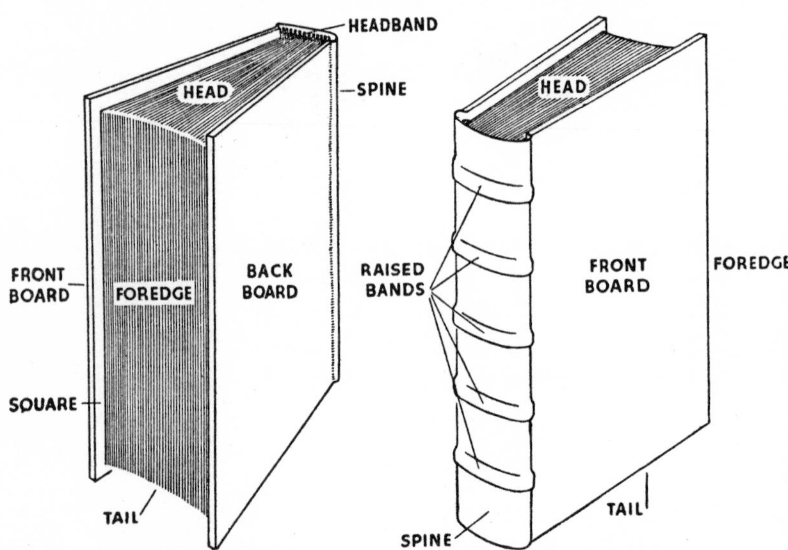

80. The parts of a hand-bound book

shows when the book is on the shelf. It bears the title and the author's name, and usually the publisher's name too, and often some decoration. Projecting from the spine of most hand-bound books are a number of transverse swellings, usually five—the bands or cords. The board covering the title-page is the front board, and that at the end is the back board. The edge of the book opposite the spine is the foredge, that at the top is the head, and that at the bottom the tail. At each end, inside the board, is an endpaper, sometimes decorated or printed with a map or an illustration; one half of the endpaper is pasted on to the board, and the other half is free, to form the first leaf, or flyleaf. In a machine-bound book the assembly of spine and boards is known as a case, its manufacture being different from that of the hand-bound book.

BINDING BY HAND

Books are still bound by hand, though now it is only limited editions or single copies that are bound in this way: the machine cannot compete with the hand-worker in the binding of single copies. It is usually the private press that is responsible for limited editions of hand-bound books. It chooses hand-binding for its own reasons—the snobbish appeal of craftsmanship in these machine-ridden days, perhaps; or because there is a tradition that hand-bound books are stronger and more durable than those bound by machine. Whatever it may be that guides its choice, some of the hand-bound books that appear on the market are little, if at all, stronger or better than those produced commercially by machine, though they may contain more expensive materials.

Certainly, if the materials are equal and the work is properly done, hand-binding produces a better and more durable book than can be got from the machine; but machine quality is maintained throughout an edition, and I doubt if the same could be said of hand-binding. None the less, given a fine book and a craftsman interested in his business and devoted to it, willing to spend time and energy upon a single work (and with a customer willing to pay for it), nothing is more fine and satisfying than a book well bound by hand. Such books are rare these days; but they are made, and their manufacture provides a living for a small number of craftsmen, whose work is to be found in the libraries of bibliophiles and in the archives of great institutions and national states; in public libraries, where there are manuscript lists of those who have fallen in war; and even in some bookshops, where a few sumptuously bound books await in glass cases the customers who can afford them.

The hand-binder is no longer accustomed, as he was before the days of binding machines, to receiving flat sheets fresh from the press, to be folded and bound; more often he is given a machine-bound book and asked to take it to pieces and to put it together again in a richer cover. But sometimes, as in the case of the limited editions of the private press, he does receive sheets and has to fold them.

Folding is done by girls, who achieve by continual practice great speed and accuracy. The sheet is printed with the pages in a particular arrangement (cf. the chapter on imposition), so that when it is correctly folded the pages will appear in sequence. For hand folding the pages are imposed in what is called a right-angle imposition, which means that the sheet must be folded so that each fold is at right-angles to the previous one. The girl takes hold of one end of the sheet and folds it towards the other, taking care that the pages that are brought to face each other are in alinement, and then with a bone folding-stick the fold is made neat and sharp; subsequent folds are made in the same manner, to complete the section.

In some books the sections are of eight pages, in others of thirty-two, and in many old books they contain twelve; but in the majority of books they contain sixteen pages. If a book is examined at the head close to the spine, these sections can easily be distinguished. At the foot of the first page of each section there will be found a small letter and perhaps also a figure. These are the signatures placed there by the printer for the guidance of the binder. Each section has its own letter, and they follow in alphabetical order, except for J, V, and W, which are not used. Section A consists of pages 1 to 16, section B of pages 17 to 32, and so on. Section A, however, bears no signature letter, because it would have to be placed on the bastard title, where it would be obtrusive and unsightly, and unnecessary too, the bastard title itself being sufficient indication that here is the beginning of the book. When there are more than twenty-three sections in a book the alphabet is commenced again and doubled or used with a figure 2. Thus after section Z comes section AA or Aa or A2 or 2A.

When folding is finished, the sections are gathered together in correct sequence according to the signatures—the binder does not look at the page numbers to see that they follow on because if the signature sequence is correct the pagination also should be correct.

After gathering, the sections are sewn together. Sewing is done on a frame of the kind shown in Figure 81. The vertical cords stretched on this frame are primarily intended to fasten the book to the boards, as will be seen shortly, and they are responsible

81. A sewing-frame

for the projections on the spine of the hand-bound book. Formerly the cords were leather thongs, but now a kind of stout string is more usual. The binder has the set of sections before him, and he takes them one at a time and sews each to its neighbour on the frame, turning the thread round the cords as it emerges from the section, and using a series of stitches of a kind hallowed by tradition. The final result is that each section, sewn through the middle, is attached to its neighbour at head and tail by special stitches called kettle stitches and also to the cords. When all the sections are sewn the cords are cut, leaving a short length projecting at each side; these ends are called slips and will be used later in attaching the book to its boards. But first the book must be consolidated. This is done by hammering the edges where the folds lie and is completed by putting the book between boards and screwing it down in a standing-press for a while. Before consolidating, the book is a loose, floppy collection of sections; afterwards it has the firm, solid feeling familiar to everyone.

The spine is now given a coating of glue, which is applied with a brush and well worked in so that it penetrates between the sections and helps to hold them together. The glue is allowed to dry until it is elastic, when the rounding of the spine is done. Rounding is carried out with a hammer, the book being laid on a firm surface and tapped with the hammer until it assumes the correct shape, after which it is placed in a press between backing boards and the outer sections are tapped over to form the joint. Next the spine is covered with paste and left to soak until the glue is soft enough to be scraped off, leaving a surface clear and clean again except for hair lines of glue showing where the adhesive has been forced between the sections.

The boards in which the book is to be bound are cut to size so that they will project in the familiar way on the foredge, head, and tail when the edges of the book are trimmed later. They are lined with thin white paper, which as it dries causes the boards to be drawn inwards—this helps to counteract a contrary pull when the cover is drawn on later. Where they come against the spine the boards are pierced and through the holes the slips are threaded, and hammered flat on the board, and there glued in position. After this the book is ready for covering with cloth or leather.

The edges of the book are trimmed after the boards are on. In hand-bound books often only the head is trimmed, but for special purposes or tastes all three edges may be trimmed. Trimming is done with a special plane, or plough, first at the head, then at the tail, and finally at the foredge. In order to trim the foredge the rounding must be temporarily cancelled out, so that a level surface is provided for the plough.

The materials used for covering are of many kinds, but leather principally, with vellum a poor second, appear to be the most popular in hand-binding. Cloth takes a lower place. Both cloth and leather are obtainable in wide variety of substance, finish, and colour, as well as quality. In half- and quarter-bound books the two may be used together.

When leather is chosen a rectangle is cut large enough to cover the book in one piece and to leave a clear margin all round for turning in. It must be pared thin on all turn-in edges, and for slim books down the spine as well. The leather is damped on the outside to prevent staining from the paste which is now applied on the inner surface (glue is used for cloth), and after soaking for a few minutes the cover is carefully drawn on over the spine and boards. The spine is attended to first, and here the leather is moulded round the cords and smoothed down neatly between them. The cords are considered as part of the fundamental shape of the book and are made an integral part of any decoration the spine receives after binding; their size may be enhanced by strips of card or leather pasted over them under the cover. After the spine, the leather is smoothed over the boards, turned in over the edges, and pasted down on the inside, where the edges are later trimmed square. The book is then left to dry, with a length of string tied tightly round it close to the spine and in the joint. The string is supposed to help in the formation of the joints, but it is also responsible for those small dimples at the top and bottom of the hinges.

There is much finesse about the addition of endpapers to hand-bound books, but I need not deal with it here. The ordinary endpaper is simply a sheet of strong paper, twice the size of one leaf of the book; half of it is pasted down on the inner surface of the board and the other half is left free so that in effect it becomes the first leaf of the book. Technically it serves to conceal the mechanics of binding; for the reader it is like a theatre curtain, the lifting of which commences the show.

The book is now ready for lettering and tooling. There may be lettering only, perhaps nothing more than the title and the author's name; on the other hand, the whole effect may be altered and enhanced by the addition of tooling, either simple and restrained, or demonstrating any nuance of richness or exuberance through the scale to the sumptuous and magnificent. The amount and kind of decoration advisable is at the discretion of the bookbinder or his designer, and some books, very old ones, are gorgeous in their display of masterly tooling and inset jewels and metal studs. In this bankrupt age jewels are no longer used, but gold is. On all but the shoddiest examples gold lettering and tooling is done in real gold—and this is true of the better class of machine-bound books also. Nothing has been found that can take the place of the precious metal: substitutes have a way of tarnishing, while gold stays bright.

Binding tools are similar to pieces of type, but with longer shanks and made of brass instead of lead (Figure 89). Each is set in a wooden handle. A separate tool is required for each item of the design, and the bookbinder's collection usually includes (*a*) an assortment of conventionalized flowers and leaves; (*b*) gouges, with which curved lines are made; (*c*) fillets, which are wheels and are used for impressing continuous lines; and (*d*) several alphabets of different sizes and design. Other tools are used occasionally for special purposes. Binding design therefore consists of the ingenious combination and use of existing units of pattern.

Blind tooling consists simply of impressions in the leather, without gold. It is done by impressing the heated tool on the material, when an impression is made corresponding to the pattern on the tool. It is an effective method of design, either alone or in conjunction with gold tooling.

For gold tooling the design is first blinded in. If it is intricate it is worked out on paper and the tools are impressed through this. After blinding-in, the material is treated with glair, a preparation of egg albumen, which is the adhesive that fastens the gold to the surface. A gold leaf is then laid on and the heated tool impressed again, through it, into the blind impression, exact judgement being necessary to make the second impression register on the first. The metal adheres wherever it has received heat and pressure. The surplus leaf gold is cleaned

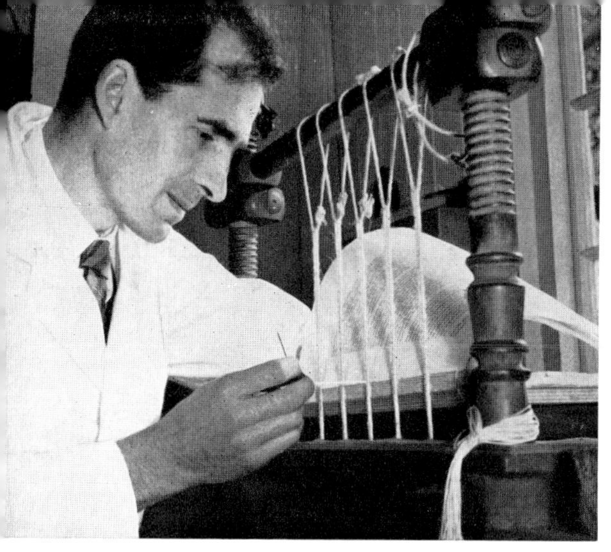

82. Hand-binder working at a sewing frame

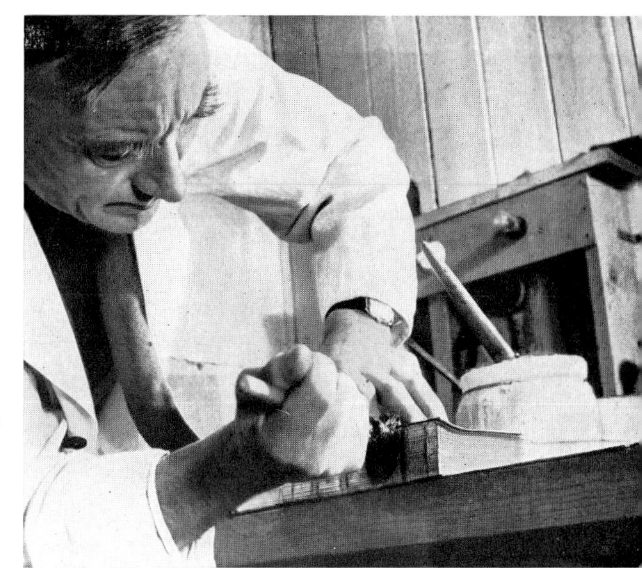

83. Glueing the spine of the book after sewing

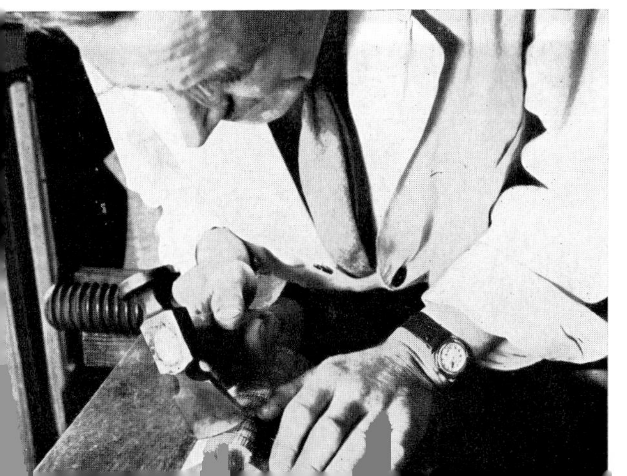

84. Making the joint after rounding the spine

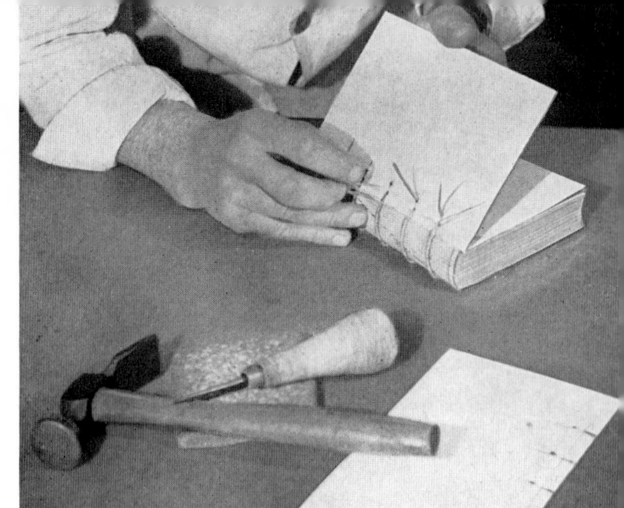

85. Lacing the boards on

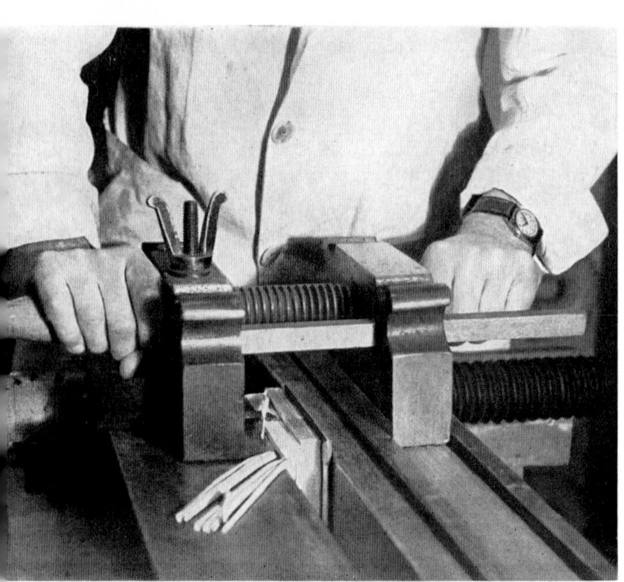

86. Trimming the edges with a plough

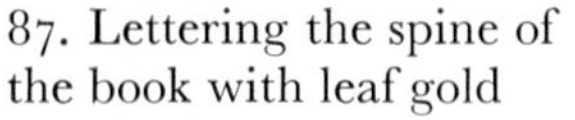

87. Lettering the spine of the book with leaf gold

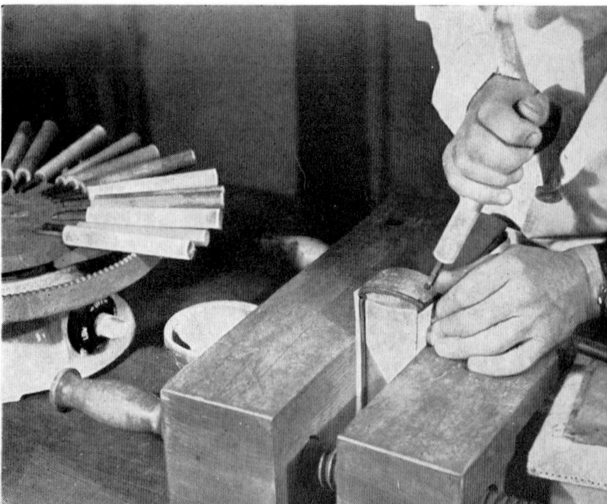

away with soft rubber, which picks up the metal and can later be sent to the assayer for its extraction. In this way each part of the design, letter by letter and flower by flower, is gone over, until the whole is completed. With lettering, care and experience are necessary to obtain even alinement of the characters.

Inlaying of different colours of leather is another method of design, and it is sometimes used in conjunction with blind or gold tooling, or both.

Polishing or varnishing follows and the book is complete.

There are additional processes through which the book may have to go for particular effects. For instance, it may be thought desirable to gild or colour the edges. For edge gilding, the book, after trimming, is squeezed in a press and the edges washed over with a preparation of red chalk, which is said to enhance the colour of the gold that will be laid on top of it. The edges are now brushed briskly until they shine; size is then applied, and the gold is put on immediately. Finally the gold is burnished. Apart from aesthetic considerations, gilding is of practical value because it provides a non-absorptive metal surface that can easily be cleaned; and it is of particular value on the head, on which dust inevitably collects. Many people like gilt edges at the head, but I personally object to having them on the foredge and tail as well—it makes the book far too metallic in appearance and to the touch.

For coloured edges the book is pressed as I have described and washed over with liquid colour until the proper shade is obtained.

The treatment for silver tooling and silver edges is the same as I have outlined for gold, but while the gold is real gold, a white base metal such as aluminium is used instead of silver. Aluminium retains its brightness for many years, but silver turns black very quickly. Nevertheless, the monetary-minded need not worry: it makes little difference in value what metal is employed. Gold leaf is so extremely thin that not all the books of the British Museum and the Bodleian could provide a paying gold mine.

A spine produced in the manner I have described is strong

and lasting, but it has a serious disadvantage. The leather of the cover is fixed firmly to the spine and must bend inwards when the book is opened, and constant usage is likely to cause the gold to scale off—a disaster when the spine has had much labour expended on it. One way of avoiding this is to make the spine so stiff that it cannot bend, which will preserve the integrity of

88. Three kinds of spine—left, a flexible spine; centre, a fast spine; right, a hollow back

the tooling but has the effect of preventing the book from opening properly. A combination of the two methods produces the hollow back, which allows free opening and yet does not spoil the tooling. The three kinds of binding are shown end-on in Figure 89. In the hollow back the spine of the book is kept separate from the spine of the cover, so that while the first bends the second retains its shape. It is necessary to get the cords out of the way, and to do this saw-cuts are made across the spine just deep enough for the cords to lie in; as the sewing is drawn tight the cords are pulled down into the saw-cuts, leaving a level surface for the attachment of the paper tube that is an important part of a hollow back. Machine-bound books invariable have hollow backs, but made in rather a different way, without the paper tube and of course without any necessity for sawing, as there are no cords.

The strength of hand-bound books is not always as great as it may appear, and this is particularly so when inferior leather is used for the binding. If the materials are good and they are handled by a competent craftsman, the book will be good; but modern leather may be bad, and some of it is very bad indeed. It is no modern deterioration, for it seems to have begun about the middle of the eighteenth century, and to have continued unchecked until comparatively recently, when the question received attention and efforts were made to deal with it. There are leathers available now that are excellent and equal to the

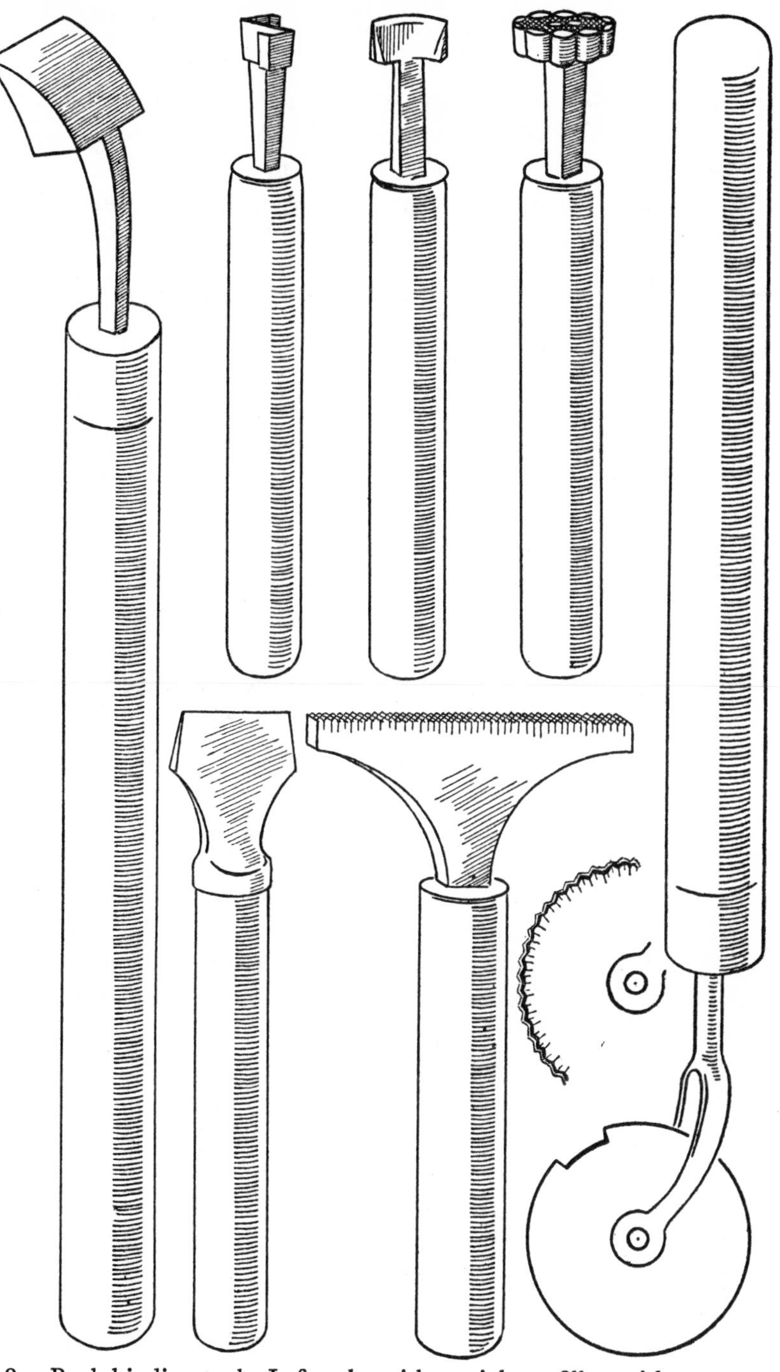

89. Book-binding tools. Left, a burnisher; right, a fillet, with a section of a decorated fillet. Above, a letter Z, a gouge, and an ornament. Below, a rule and and an ornamental stamp

best of former periods, and which are, as far as we can tell, as durable: but there are also others. Defective preparation of leather destroys its durability, and on top of this a reprehensible habit arose in the eighteenth century, and has continued, of splitting the leather into skivers, or of shaving it so thin that there is practically no strength left in it. In this state it will tear more easily than paper, even paper of indifferent quality. It is not altogether the fault of the binders, many of whom would prefer to work only with the best materials. There are people who blindly believe that there is nothing like leather, but who are not prepared to pay a reasonable price for it, and cheap and inferior material is manufactured for their especial benefit. As a binder said to me, you get what you pay for, and deception creeps in when gumption is away from home.

Half-binding and quarter-binding are the result of the idea, valid when the materials are good, that leather is stronger and will wear better, and should therefore be used at the points of greatest wear. In fact some books partly bound in leather in these styles would be more durable if they were wholly bound in the less pretentious of the two materials used.

MACHINE BINDING

Those who bind books by hand sometimes affect to despise machine binding. They say that machine-bound books cannot receive individual attention, which is true, and that they are not strong enough to endure as they should, which is only conditionally true. They think in terms of many years, perhaps centuries. But no-one expects or hopes that an ephemeral novel will withstand the wear of generations, to show our descendants what fools we were, and machine binding is all very well for such as these. What of good books, of works of original genius? Surely they should be made to last? But wiser men than bookbinders have found it difficult to recognize genius when it appears, and no one can really tell what our children will find precious among our accumulated goods.

Is there so very much in the contention that machine

binding cannot produce durable books? I do not think so. I have shown that the hand-binder may be misled and may mislead others into thinking that a book bound in trashy leather is well bound, and the machine-binder may also use inferior material and fall into the same error. He is more likely to use cloth than leather, and there are good cloths and bad ones.

The use of cloth, begun as an experiment in the nineteenth century, has extended across the world, until to-day an enormous quantity of books is bound in one variety or another of this material. It is to be had in a multitude of qualities and kinds and in as many colours, surfaces, and finishes, and to the book designer it offers wider scope than can be calculated. In strength and durability some cloths, good buckram, for example, may be as good as leather and certainly superior to some sorts of it. The test, however, is time itself, and cloth has not been used long enough to prove its worth conclusively. Admittedly, many cloth-bound books of the nineteenth century are falling asunder to-day—but others survive intact and as sound as the day they were made. A great deal depends on use, and it should be remembered that no book, in leather or in cloth, will survive treatment it was never designed to resist: it is not really good for a book to use it as a missile, or as a door-stop, or to prop up the leg of a chair from which the castor is missing.

Bookbinders' cloths are available in a wide range of quality and in colours that extend from the dark and dismal, the feeble and faded, to brilliant and exciting colours that glow in the bookcase. So-called 'white-back' cloths are coloured only on the surface and wear causes the colour to come off and the white to show through; these cloths are cheaper than others and inferior. Most cloths are dyed right through and so retain their colour, if they are not subject to fading under the action of light. Better qualities are lightfast to a considerable degree. Most cloths are made of cotton. Cotton and linen are used in buckram; the better class buckrams are all linen.

Between the wars substitutes for cloth began to be used for the bindings of cheaper books. Because of the increased price of cloth, such substitutes are now employed extensively so that probably at least fifty per cent of the hard-backed books issued in Great Britain are bound in cloth substitutes. The trade names of these materials include Linson, Glindura, Arlin, Duralin, Fabroleen, etc. Known as non-woven materials, they are all forms of paper, and considerably cheaper than cloth. Nearly all of them are embossed to imitate woven cloth. The imitation is excellent and many people who buy books bound in these materials probably suppose that they are getting books bound in cloth. It would be naive to suppose that these embossings are not meant to deceive: they are. That is a pity, because non-woven binding materials, as special kinds of paper, do have intrinsic value and could have aesthetic characteristics of their own, derived from their substance. With less imitation they might have a more honourable place in the edition-binding of books. They take blocking in gold or in ink, or even blind blocking, very well, and each of the several manufacturers offers a range of attractive colours. The white and lighter colours may be printed in monochrome or colour by letterpress or litho, or by silk-screen, and to facilitate this the material is available in sheet form as well as in rolls. Non-woven materials are not as strong as cloth and do not resist wear quite as well, and they ought not to be used for a large and heavy book, nor for one, such as a reference book, that is expected to withstand a great deal of use.

A different kind of covering material, also non-woven, is represented by Balacuir and Balatron, which are made in Holland. These are vinyl materials lined with paper. They are available in a range of beautiful colours, block excellently, and present a smooth, impermeable surface that can be sponged clean. These vinyl materials are also embossed to imitate cloths, as well as various leathers. More expensive than paper-based materials, they are unlikely to be used extensively on ordinary books.

Binding by machine involves several kinds of complex apparatus, and it includes also a great deal of handling of each individual book. Mechanization of the industry is far from complete, and perhaps it never will be complete. Much of the handwork is not skilled, and is done by girls after a short period of instruction and practice; but some operations require apprenticeship and training.

The sheets reach the binder flat, in single, double, or quad size, as the case may be, with the pages arranged in an imposition suitable for one of the several types of folding machine, and the first business is to fold them. Perhaps the most common size of sheet in use in book printing is the quad sheet, and if the book is to be folded in sixteen-page octavo sections, which is also usual, the sheet must be cut into four. In practice, this cutting is not done separately, but is part of the operation of the folding machine.

Occasionally sections of thirty-two or sixty-four pages are used in cheap books or in those printed on very thin paper; these larger sections save sewing and with thin paper give more grip to the stitch, but they are not as satisfactory for general use as sections of sixteen pages.

Each kind of folding machine is designed to fold sheets in a particular manner that proved mechanically convenient for its inventor, and they will not fold in any other way. Folding machines, therefore, do not all fold alike, and it is to suit their idiosyncrasies that different impositions have been arranged. A score or more of impositions are in use, and are distinguished by letters of the alphabet. Sheets imposed to imposition B and folded on the B folder will show the pages in correct sequence; the same sheet folded on a machine designed for imposition N would not have the pages in correct sequence.

Folding machines are not very large, but they are fairly complex, and appear larger than they really are because they have automatic feeders attached to them or built into the machine. The feeder, separating the sheets, presents each one accurately to the gauges of the folder, when it is taken up by revolving wheels, which draw the sheet into the machine and into position for the first fold. Here it lies on a metal 'table' across which runs a slot; a 'knife' (but it doesn't cut) descends on the paper at the point where the fold is to be and pushes it through the slot, where rollers make the fold good. The sheet then passes to a further table, knife, and rollers, where another fold is made, and so on until the sheet is completely folded. Some folders make one or more of their folds by a buckle method, the sheet travelling through the machine until it comes against a stop, when a buckle forming across the sheet is drawn through rollers to make the fold. Slitting of double and

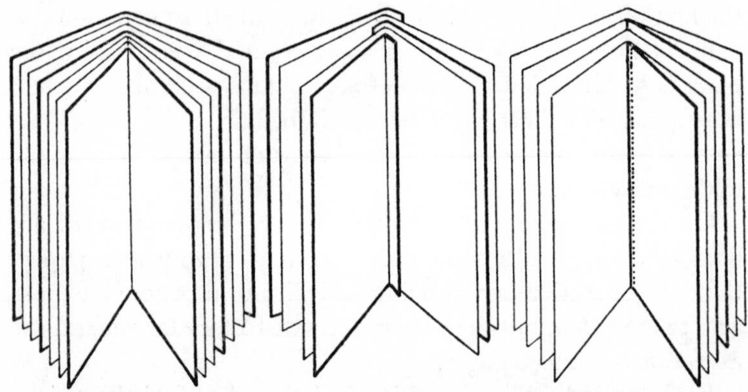

90. Methods of inserting plates. Left, four-page sections for wrapping round or inserting; centre, plates hooked in; right, plates tipped in. The heavy outlines represent the pages of plates, and the light ones the pages of text

quad sheets into singles is done during the travel of the sheet through the machine.

The next operation is insertion of the plates. Much of this is hand work. How the plates are inserted depends on the provision the publisher has made for them. If he has been willing to sacrifice exact positioning of the plates opposite their references in the text for the sake of convenience in binding and durability in use, he will have arranged for the plates to be printed in four-page sections to bind in with the sections of the book. In this way, the plates are sewn in with the sections and are firmly anchored; further, the work of inserting them is simple and can be done rapidly. If, on the other hand, exact positioning is important, many or all of the plates will have to be inserted as single leaves. Such leaves are usually fixed in by a line of paste along the inner edge, by means of which they adhere to the text page next to them: or they can be printed on

91. Four rows of octavo sections issuing from a quad folding machine

92. A gathering machine; the arms can be seen drawing out sections along the length of the machine, and below them is the moving belt on which the sections are gathered

93. A girl operating a book-sewing machine

94. A nipping machine

95. A book-pressing machine

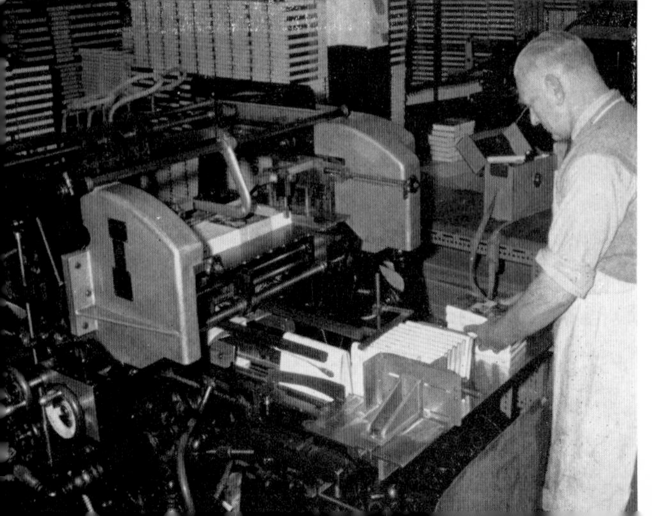

96. A wrappering machine

paper slightly wider than the page and the surplus folded over to form a fold that may be hooked over the fold of the text page and sewn in. Folding maps and charts may be either hooked or pasted in.

All sections of the same signature are folded at once, as the sheets come from the printer in this way, so that when folding is complete there are so many stacks of sections, here a stack of signature A, next a stack of signature B, and so on. To obtain a complete book it is necessary to take one section from each stack and put the collection in the right order. In the bindery the stacks may be arranged in sequence on a bench and the gatherer then walks the length of the bench, taking a section from each stack as she passes, so that at the end she has a complete set of sections in her hand. For each set this little jaunt must be taken, and no doubt a good many miles are covered in the course of a day's gathering.

This method of gathering by hand is not much used now, the first attempts to mechanize the operation having been made long ago. One of the earliest ideas was to make the bench move instead of the gatherer. A round table, on which the stacks of sections were arranged in sequence, was made to revolve, and several girls sat around the table, each taking a section from each stack as it reacher her, until a set was complete, when she began again without pause. Thus as many books were gathered at once as there were girls working round the table.

Modern gathering machines are very different; they may be large and appear ungainly, but they work well. The sections are placed in sequence in boxes along a sort of counter or bench. Before each box is an arm with a pair of jaws on the end of it, and below the arms is a conveyor belt. The operation at each box is the same: the bottom section in the stack is separated from the rest by suction, and the arm with its jaws comes forward, grips the section, and carries it back about a foot to drop it face down on the conveyor belt, when the arm swings forward for the next section. While it is returning, the conveyor brings the section level with the next in the row of boxes, which contains, say, section B, and section B is dropped on top of section A. The conveyor, still moving, carries the two sections forward to receive section C, and so for as many sections as are required. There are about twenty boxes on one of these machines and as many books are being gathered at once. If anything goes wrong—if, for example, the jaws fail to hold the section, or pick up two sections at once, the machine stops dead, and a signal springs up to show at which box the fault has occurred. It is put right in a moment and the machine is started again.

The book has begun to look vaguely like a book, though it is still only a pile of loose sections. The next step is to join the sections together on the sewing machine. This is nothing at all like the domestic sewing machine. It is operated by a girl, who takes up the section open at the middle and lays it astride a metal saddle, which then conveys it to a set of needles in the upper part of the machine, where the section is pierced and sewn through with thread, and pushed on to a tray behind the needles. The next section is laid on the saddle, brought up to the needles, and sewn to the previous one, the needles going right through the section as before to make the stitches that can be seen in any sewn book. During this operation lengths of tape may be laced in with the stitches across the spine, and this tape will later be used to attach the book to its case. The sections are sewn in this way one after the other, until the delivery tray can hold no more, when they are taken off. There are now several copies of the book sewn together, and they have to be cut apart before the next stage is proceeded with.

The modern tendency is to omit tapes in sewn books. Books without tapes are described as French sewn.

The next stage is the machine appropriately called the smasher or the bumper, and also, inappropriately, the nipper. It is in effect an automatic clamp capable of some hundreds of pounds of pressure, and the books are fed in stacks at one end and delivered at the other properly smashed, bumped, or nipped. This means that they have been consolidated and compacted.

If the edges of the book are to be cut, this is the next operation, and the machine used for the purpose bears the grim name of 'guillotine'. Printers use a kind of guillotine for cutting paper, but theirs has only one knife, powerful though it is; the binder's guillotine has three knives, and is capable of making three cuts in rapid succession. The books are placed under a clamp and the first knife descends to cut the foredge, and as it withdraws two other knives come down at right angles to cut the head and the tail.

Trimming is another method of cutting the edges, employing a revolving knife. It is used when a slightly rough or apparently 'untrimmed' edge is required, usually on the foredge or the tail, or both (if cut, the head should always be cut smooth). A book designed for this effect will have been imposed and folded so that the bolts, that is the folds along the edges of the pages, project from the cut edges of the sheet. The revolving knife cuts away the folds without leaving a smooth cut edge to the book. The three-knife guillotine cannot be used for such effects, and consequently trimmed books cost a little more to produce.

Now the books are ready for the first coat of glue on the spine. Each is placed spine down in a narrow channel and is conveyed over a roller running in a bath of hot glue; and immediately afterwards over a hard stubby brush, which removes the surplus glue and drives the rest well in between the sections, where it will help to hold them together.

After standing in stacks until the glue is partly dry the books are rounded and the joint formed. The machine that performs the operation is massively built, but is not intricate. The book is placed in a narrow channel, this time foredge down, and is drawn along until it arrives over a forming bar, where it is gripped between facing rollers revolving in opposite directions while the bar is pushed up against the foredge. The two sides of the book are dragged downwards while the middle is being pushed up, and the spine assumes the familiar curve. From this the book, gripped between jaws that perform the function of the backing boards used by the hand-binder, travels under a rocker that finishes off the rounding and makes the joints. The rocker is a heavy piece of metal with a concave edge, which is brought down until the concave is in contact with the spine, when the rocker moves quickly from side to side, giving shape to the curve and bending over the outer sections for the joint. The book is then delivered from the machine.

Our book looks now very much like the sort of book that sits on our shelves, except that it seems naked and incomplete; and so it is, for it lacks a cover yet. Before it can be supplied with one another machine must be traversed.

This, the lining machine, is perhaps the most complicated mechanism in the bindery; and it is certainly the most amusing to watch. The books are placed one by one in a channel or slide, and are picked up by conveyors, each of which carries one book, with the spine exposed. Along the machine are a number of stations, and at each of these the conveyors stop while the machine goes into action. The conveyors are spaced so that when one of them is stopped at any station there is another at each of the other stations. At each station a particular operation is performed, and while each book goes successively through all the stations, other stations are simultaneously performing the operation appropriate to them on the book stopped there.

At the first station a glue roller swoops along and gives the spine a coating of glue, after which the conveyor carries the book on to the following station, where a length of mull (the open-weave material that can be seen through the endpapers of most books) of the right length and width is cut off a roll and deposited on a carrier, which shoots into the machine, rises to press the mull into contact with the glued spine, and returns empty for another piece for the next book. The next station is like the first, with a roller carrying glue, but here two arms come into play to hold the surplus mull and the slips away from the glue. The following station is like the mull station, except that here a length of paper is cut off and carried to the spine. Finally there is another station with rollers to press the paper into contact, and then the book is delivered, ready for casing.

The conveyors are on the endless belt system, and as many of them are in action at once as there are stations on the machine.

If for any reason any one of the conveyors fails to pick up a book and travels along empty, the operation at each station it arrives at is cut out, so that nothing happens for that conveyor; but the other conveyors proceed as usual, and so do the stations they arrive at.

When the books reach the casing machine, the cases should be ready waiting for them if there is to be no delay, and while the work I have described is proceeding the cases are made by a case-making machine. I showed how, in a hand-bound book, the cover is built on the book to become an integral part of it; in machine binding there is no analogous process. The boards are not laced on to the book with thongs or cords, and this fact allows the case to be made separately and by machine, to be affixed to the book later.

The case starts with a roll of cloth, cardboard, and stiff paper of the width required on a reel. The cardboard is cut into boards of a size to suit the book, and these are loaded into the case-making machine on either side of the reel of paper. The roll of cloth, also cut to the width required, is loaded in also. As the cloth is unwound it is drawn over a roller running in a bath of hot glue, and receives from this a coating of adhesive; next it passes below the board and stiffener magazines, and two boards are dropped on to the sticky cloth with a length of the stiff paper for the spine between them, each in its correct relative position. After this knives make two v-shaped cuts in the edges of the cloth on opposite sides, and another knife slits the cloth across, between the apexes of the v's. The cloth is then automatically turned in over the edges of the boards and stiffener and pressed home, and the case emerges from the machine complete except for the lettering.

Another type of machine makes cases in a similar manner, but from cloth previously cut to size and loaded into the machine as piles of sheets.

The hand-binder, we saw, impressed his tools one by one, laboriously and lovingly, but such a process would not do for commercial binding on the scale it has reached in our day. Editions are probably larger now than they used to be, and the saving of labour is more than enough to pay for a specially cut brass block by means of which all the lettering and tooling can be done at one impression (if it is in only one colour or metal). Blocking of a kind was done by the old binders for the coats of arms of their noble customers, but was seldom applied to lettering and decoration. For the coat of arms the device was cut in relief in brass, heated, and laid on top of the book in a press. At first probably the ordinary standing press was used, and no doubt it was heartily cursed by the workman who had to apply it to a purpose for which it was never intended. Later a press on the lines of the printer's hand-press was specially made for the operation and was called the arming press; and by this name this type of press is still known. It has given way to-day to a more powerful and speedier machine for the blocking of the edition, but it has survived, as has the hand-press, for proofs and odd copies.

The brass from which the lettering and decoration is blocked on a modern book is made by a skilled engraver, who is capable of cutting in this hard metal practically any kind of letter that can be printed in ink on paper, or he can reproduce line drawings with exactitude, reducing or enlarging them as required. A good brass is clean cut with vertical walls, so that the impression will be sharp and clear. Brass is used because it is hard enough to withstand the pressure of blocking, but not too hard to engrave; and in addition, its surface can be given a high polish, which is imparted to the impression in the binding. At first, too, the fact that brass has the property of retaining heat was important, but this does not matter so very much to-day, when blocking machines are mostly heated by electricity controlled by a rheostat.

Line blocks and electros may also be used for blocking. They do not have the endurance of brass, nor the depth of cut that allows a brass to emboss deeply, and they should therefore not be used for other than small editions and smooth cloths.

The blocking press is a development of the platen machine used by printers for small work such as cards and leaflets; essentially it consists of two flat tables of metal, which are arranged one facing the other and are made to open and close together mechanically. One surface is the bed on which the brass is fixed in position, and the other is the platen, on which the case is laid. When gold blocking is being done, a reel of gold tape is used in the machine. This reel is composed of cellophane bearing an opaque layer of fine gold dust and over the gold a layer of some resinous material corresponding to glair. The reel is fixed above the bed and the tape joined to a take-up spool below it, the intervening strip covering the brass. Behind the bed is a heating element. In operation the platen bearing the case closes up to the bed and sandwiches the gold tape between the brass and the case. The heat from the element passes through the bed into the brass, and the raised portions of the brass fuse gold and adhesive on to the case, so that when platen and bed part the case bears the design in gold. As the opening takes place the tape is drawn down one step to present a new surface for the next case, and the blocked case is taken off and another one fed in. The feeding and the taking off are done automatically by metal arms with suction cups at the end. With this kind of machine an output of something like fifteen hundred cases an hour is possible.

Real gold is not now used as much as it was. It is probably true to say that most books now blocked in gilt exhibit an imitation rather than the genuine metal. Earlier imitation golds were poor stuff that tarnished towards black in a short time, so that on a dark cloth the lettering became invisible. Much more durable gilt materials are now available.

For silver blocking the process is the same, except that silver tape (aluminium) is used; and tapes with foils of various colours can be used in the same way when coloured blocking is required. If ink is to be employed instead of foil, tapes are dispensed with and inking rollers fitted to the machine, the ink being supplied automatically from a duct like that of a printing machine.

The book is complete, only waiting for its case, and the case is ready for the book, and the two are brought together by the casing machine. A stack of cases is placed in a magazine on this machine and the books are fed in one by one. As each book is carried through, a case is carried as well, until the two arrive over a paste box and paste rollers. Here the endpapers, the mull, and the slips are given a coating of paste, and the case is laid on and pressed into position, when the book is delivered into a trough.

The book is now finished and complete except for a final pressing, which is done in a tall press in which the books are stacked foredge to spine and left for some hours.

There are, of course, variations in blocking and casing according to the book and the wishes of the customer, and some of these can be done by machine and some by hand. Edge gilding is done by hand with gold leaf, and so is colouring; these are comparatively expensive processes, therefore, and their results are not usually found in cheap books. Blind tooling is done by the blocking machine exactly as any other tooling, except that no tape or ink is used. Blocking in two colours or more, or in colours and a metal, is also done by machine, the case being blocked separately for each colour or metal. Yapp edges and chamfered edges need special treatment, partly mechanical and partly manual.

Jackets are put on by the binder. This work is done by hand, by girls, who achieve great dexterity and speed in wrapping the books so that the spine and boards are accurately placed. Finally, other girls rapidly flick over the pages of each book to check that it has been correctly made, and after this the books are packed in bales of twenty to a hundred and delivered to the publisher, in time for the publication date he has already fixed.

Mechanization and automation have for long occupied the minds of the directors of large binderies, and recent developments have gone some way towards achieving the ideal—a system in which sheets enter at one end of the factory and emerge as bound books at the other, with little or no handling in the interval. This is perhaps an impossible pipe-dream, but certainly it is not so for the later part of the journey, which has been made automatic by linking various machines together by endless bands that carry the books from the delivery of one machine to the feed of the next in the line. This would not have been possible without the introduction of two new machines, a book-forming and pressing unit and a jacketing machine, to fill what would have been gaps in the system.

The automatic system begins after the books have been sewn and the cases have been made and blocked. The books are fed into a rounding and backing machine to form the curve of the spine and the joints, and from this they pass to a lining machine such as has already been described. From the lining machine they go on to a casing-in machine, where they meet the blocked cases, and book and case are united by paste applied to the endpapers. At this stage the books would have to be pressed in standing presses for several hours were it not for the introduction of the pressing unit. This takes the books and clamps each between metal plates, and sends it so clamped on a circular journey, stopping at each of several stations; at each station heated bars bearing ridges or rims move in from each side to press the cover material down into the joints, forming the familiar channels, known as French grooves, along each side of the spine. The books now want only their jackets to be ready for delivery, and for this they pass to a jacketing machine, which lifts the front and back boards of the book and applies the jacket, tucking the flaps neatly under the boards. Books emerge from this system at the rate of about two thousand an hour.

The whole edition is not usually bound at once, unless preliminary orders prove encouraging. More often, the binder is instructed to bind only a portion of the edition, and to retain the remainder in sheets pending further instructions. If the book sells well enough the remainder is bound before the first binding is exhausted; if, on the other hand, the book proves a failure, the publisher has at least saved the cost of binding the rest. Binding is the most expensive item the publisher has to meet in book production, and it may easily cost more than all the other costs of the book together. If the first half of the edition fails to sell, something may be saved from the wreck by binding the second half in a cheaper form either for sale as a cheap edition or for the remainder market.

The immense expansion of the paper-back market has made this kind of book an important factor in the bookshop and in the binding industry. The printing of paper-backs is achieved by conventional methods, but new kinds of machinery have been developed to deal with them in the bindery. Most paper-backs are now bound by a method called 'perfect' or unsewn binding. Folding and collating are done in the same way as for other books, but the sections are not sewn together. Instead, the books are fed into a machine that saws off the folds on the spine, leaving a rough edge to receive an adhesive applied to hold the leaves together, the spine being bent first one way and then the other so that the adhesive penetrates slightly between the leaves. The machine then applies a strip of glued paper or linen to the spine. Finally the cover is drawn on and the head and tail and foredge are trimmed in a guillotine. Unsewn books, it will be seen, are bound in much the same way as a writing-pad is, though, of course, more strongly. This kind of binding is also used for many hard-cover books, especially the cheaper kinds bound in paper-covered boards.

In the early days of this process the adhesives used were not always satisfactory and books were liable to fall apart. This trouble has been overcome and modern unsewn binding is usually sufficiently firm for normal use if the paper on which the book is printed is suitable for the binding process. Art paper, which has a relatively fragile surface, will not hold satisfactorily, and stiff or heavy papers may lever themselves out of the joint.

PART TWO

*

THE DESIGN OF BOOKS

XIII

THE DEVELOPMENT OF TYPE DESIGN

When Gutenberg began his experiments towards the mass-production of books he was not, perhaps, influenced by aesthetic considerations. He seems to have been rather an unworldly person, who spent a great deal of other people's money in pursuit of his end, the perfection of his process. His technical ability can scarcely be doubted, but he was not an original artist; rather he was an imitator who set out to produce mechanically the kind of books that had hitherto been made by hand in scriptoria. He aimed at no revolution in their appearance, and he achieved none. He was fortunate in that he appeared at a time when the art of the scribe was at a high level, and that he had before him models that were among the best of their kind. He copied them as faithfully as his process would allow, and if we admire the books he and his immediate successors produced, the credit for their excellence is not altogether the printer's, but belongs in part to the scribe. What the printer aimed at was, in fact, the production of 'manuscripts' in larger numbers and comparatively cheaply.

Since this was so, we have not far to look for the origin of the kind of letter Gutenberg, and Fust and Schoeffer after him, used in the indulgences and books they printed: it is to be found in the manuscripts of the period. The letter in use among scribes in Germany in the fifteenth century, as in most other countries, was one variety or another of what we have come to call gothic. It is a letter of magnificent decorative potentiality. This was seized upon in both manuscript and printed book, the best of which possess beauty and glory not equalled elsewhere in the history of books, except in Ireland, where monkish scribes of an earlier day had spent much care and loving labour on the illumination of such manuscripts as the Book of Kells. Gothic had the drawback of not being easily legible, and least so in its most formal and decorative phase, but this was perhaps of little moment in an age when books were scarce and precious and were read slowly and repeatedly; or, on the other hand, not read at all, but bought to be looked at and admired, like a

Fundament Buch
inhaltende mancherley wolgeform
Teutsche vnd Lateinische schrifften: Wie die inn Cantz-
leien vnd inn gemeyn begert/ vnd löblich inn brauch gezogen
werden. Dises M. D. LXXVIII. Jars künstlich vnd
leicht begreifflich fürgeben vnd geschriben.
Durch Jacob Jacobelln vom New-
marck auß Schlesienn. Jetziger zeit Teutscher
Schulmeyster zu Heydelbergk.
Getruckt zu Straßburg/bei Bernhard Jobin. Anno 1579.

97. Elaborate decoration of gothic lettering, from *Fundamentbuch*, Strasbourg, 1579

picture book, in the library of some rich but illiterate noble. Such a letter was not a suitable vehicle for the vast amount of information and ideas that was even now beginning to stream from the rising spirit of the Renaissance. It is probable that gothic would have passed out of use even without the assistance of the press, for men were turning away from or condemning all those things that savoured of the age that was closing and were seeking in the remote past for models and ideas through

ũ ergo tres videns unum adoraret in
gura trium iuvenum unum deũ in tri
itate adorãdum intellexit, Verum quo
iam incomprehensibile est sancte trinita

Lettre de forme

Ircũcisio dñi nostri iesu xpi. Nam sicut dicitur Luce
ij. Postq̃ consummati sunt dies octo. Glosa.a natiuite dñi computando vtramqꝫ extremitatem vt circum
cideretur puer. Sic em̃ preceptum fuerat. Gen.xvij.
Infans octo dierꝫ circũcidetur in vobis. vocatum est nomen
eius iesus idest saluator ad significandumqꝫ spiritualiter cir

Lettre de somme

Koeder wisse dat nu dye vre is van dem slaiff vp
tzo stain. want nu is naer vnser heill dan wyr gelo
ueden. die nacht is vergangen. mer der dach neckt
Dair vm sollen wyr van vns werpen dye werken
der duysternisse. ind soellen aen doen dye waeppen
des liechts. alsus dat wyr in dem dach eerlich wã

Lettre bâtarde

Die Erfindung des Buchdrucks mit beweglichen Lettern war eines der wichtigsten Ereignisse in der Geschichte der Zivilisation, denn die originalgetreue Vervielfältigung von Schriften war unmöglich, ehe Gutenberg den Gelehrten seine einheitlichen Typen zur Verfügung gestellt hatte. Voreingenommene Fachleute des fünfzehnten Jahrhunderts bedauerten

Modern Schwabacher (Monotype)

Die Erfindung des Buchdrucks mit beweglichen Lettern war eines der wichtigsten Ereignisse in der Geschichte der Zivilisation, denn die originalgetreue Vervielfältigung von Schriften war unmöglich, ehe Gutenberg den Gelehrten seine einheitlichen Typen zur Verfügung gestellt hatte. Voreingenommene Fachleute des fünfzehnten Jahrhunderts bedauerten

Modern Fraktur (Monotype)

98. Five varieties of gothic

which they might express their new vision. True, a contest between the dispossessed and the dispossessing raged for some time to come, the advantage now going to this side, now to that. It was expressed in the making of books by the abandonment of the gothic character for the roman, by its readoption and reabandonment; until at last, in all countries other than the Germanic, gothic was discarded and the manner of reading it forgotten. The roman letter became the vehicle of the new civilization, inspired by the culture of ancient Greece and Rome.

The press did not merely follow the fashion, it to some extent directed it; because of its very capacity to multiply books it also

latitūdo. Apricis. Sole gaudentibꝫ Sane apricus dicitur & locꝰ ſole calēs qđ eſt opaco & abdito contrariū. Et apricos dicimus locis apricis gaudētes. Virgilius ducēt apricis in collibus vua calorē. Perſius vt noſtra foralia poſſint aprici meminiſſe ſenes. Apricū autē

99. The first roman type, used by Adolf Rusch at Strasbourg, *c.* 1464

multiplied readers, and brought to them the literature of which men talked, that literature that was at once as aesthetically impatient of gothic elaboration as it was psychologically of unreasoning faith. Then, too, as men read more, they desired to read more easily and without impediment, and they found the roman character a readier and smoother vehicle.

Typographically, the movement away from gothic began when two German printers, who for reasons best known to themselves had migrated to Subiaco in Italy, found themselves in the midst not only of the Renaissance but of a revival by the scribes of a kind of letter that it was believed had been used in ancient Rome. This letter was in fact one that had been developed under Charlemagne by the monks of the scriptoria for the writing of new editions of the classics and the holy books, but it was certainly based on Roman originals. Scholars, seeking in the fresh enthusiasm of discovery for editions of ancient works,

thaas·et maacha. Capłm q̄ · xxiij·
Vixit autē ſara centū viginti ſeptē annis·
et mortua ē in ciuitate arbee·q̄ ē hebron
ī terra chanaan. Venitq; abrahā ut plāgeret
et fleret eā. Cūq; ſurrexiſſet ab officio funeris:
locutus eſt ad filios heth dicēs. Aduena ſū·&

100. A romanized gothic type, *c.* 1460

compata. Ergo item inqt illa quę ſepe diſerte agēda ſunt: &
quę ego paulo ante cū eloquentiam laudarem dixi oratoris
eſſe: neq; habent ſuum locū ullum in diuiſione partium neq;
certū pręceptoꝝ genus: et agenda ſunt nō minus diſerte q̄

101. Type used by Sweynheim and Pannartz at Subiaco, 1465

genſ: ſi plebeo nupſerit ignobiliſ effitiatur. Et idem i
:qui propter delictum nobilitatem perdit. Quo fiet.
aliqua tēporiſ parte infelix homo ſit nobiliſ: & alia
nobiliſ. & eueſtigio. Rurſuſ nec omni loco nobilitaſ
eſt. Sarracenuſ enī nobiliſ a nobiſ captuſ: ꝑculdubio

102. Type used by Sweynheim and Pannartz at Rome, 1468

C ruraq; totius facient tibi lęuia gentis.
H orrida uitanda eſt hyſpania: gallicus axiſ
I lliricumq; latus. parce & meſſoribus illiſ
Q ui ſaturant urbem circo: ſcęneq; uacantem.
Q uanta autem inde feres tam dirę premia culpę

103. The da Spira type, 1469

found them in Carolingian manuscripts in the Carolingian script, and revived not only the old texts but the script as well. Sweynheim and Pannartz, the two exiles at Subiaco, entered into the spirit of the revival by cutting a new type in what they conceived to be the fashion. It was not successful. It was not a very good type, and neither was it a very bad one. It was neither gothic nor roman, but a hybrid of the two. This was in 1464 or 1465. They came, it seems, to realize something of its deficiencies, for two years later we find them working in Rome with a different type again, distinctly roman this time, but still tainted with the gothic flavour.

An easy, if merely theoretical, development from gothic to roman is shown on page 221. Unfortunately, history is seldom as neat as this. The first distinctly roman type appeared in Germany, of all places, at Strasbourg, in 1464, before Sweynheim and Pannartz brought out their Subiaco type. The printer was for long known as the R-printer, because his type has a peculiar R; he has been identified as Adolf Rusch. See Figure 99.

The first roman type that appears completely roman to us was used in a book printed at Venice in 1469 by Johann and Wendelin da Spira. It was the first of a kind now known as Italian or Venetian. It is a letter of good quality and proportion, and it is legible and clear. Johann da Spira thought so much of it that he obtained a patent to exclude other printers from the use of any similar face; but he died in the following year and the patent expired with him, leaving the way clear for a greater type-cutter, Nicolas Jenson.

Jenson, like many printers an exile from his native land, had been sent by the French government to Germany to learn there the principles of the new craft, with the intention that he should return and introduce printing into France. He did return in due time, only to find that the old king was dead, and dead with him was the royal interest in printing. The new king, Louis XI, was apparently not interested, and may even have been hostile. Whatever the reason, Jenson appears to have decided that France was no longer fertile soil for his genius and he took himself off to Italy.

& absolutam conclusionem : tum uero uehementer id quod opus est oratori: comprobat cõtraria re: & ex eo quod dubium nõ est expedit illud quod dubium ẽ: ut aut dilui non possit: aut multo difficilliẽ possit.

De Membro:

MEmbrum orõnis appellatᵉ res breuiter absoluta sine totius orõnis demonstratione: quæ denuo alio mẽbro orõnis excipitᵉ hoc modo. Et iimico ꝓderas. idest unum quod appellatᵉ mẽbrum. deinde hoc excipiatur: oportet ab altero & amicum lædebas. Ex duobus mẽbris suis hæc exornatio potest constare. Sed commodissima & absolutissĩa est: quæ ex tribus cõstat hoc pacto. & iimico ꝓderas: & amicũ lædebas: & tibi ipsi non consulebas. Itẽ nec rei. p. consuluisti: nec amicis profuisti : nec inimicis restitisti.

Articulus grauis.

ARticulus dicitur cum singula uerba interuallis distinguẽtᵉ cæsa orõne hoc modo. Acrimonia: uoce: uultu aduersarios ꝑteruisti. Itẽ inimicos inuidia: iniuriis: potentia: ꝑfidia sustulisti. inter huius generis & illius superioris uehementiã hoc interest: ꝙ illud tardius & rarius uenit: hoc crebrius & celerius ꝑuenit. itaq; in illo genere ex remotione brachii & cõtortione dextræ gladius ad corpus afferri. in hoc autẽ crebro et celeri corpus uulnere insaciari uidetᵉ.

Continuatio Mediocris.

COntinuatio est densa & continens frequẽtatio uerboꝝ cum assolutione sententiaꝝ. ea utemur commodissime tripartito: in sententia: in contrario: in cõclusione. In sẽtẽtia hoc pacto. ei nõ multũ põt obesse

104. Nicholas Jenson's roman, 1470. The initials are drawn

It has been claimed that Jenson was responsible for the type the da Spira brothers used and which Johann patented. This may have been so, but for his own use Jenson cut a new and yet finer face. It appeared for the first time in the *De Praeparatione Evangelica* of Eusebius, which was issued in 1470. It is an open, dignified letter, clear and legible, of even colour and perfect harmony, subtly plain and simple. The contrast between thick stroke and thin is small; the serifs are blunt, with only slight brackets. The capitals are beautifully proportioned, and have no obtrusive or intrusive peculiarities of design to mar the harmony. This type has been acclaimed as the finest that has ever been made, and certainly many of Jenson's contemporaries thought so too, for they lauded it and envied it, and some of them attempted to copy it. These attempts were not successful, and others made in our own time, even by means of the camera (as was Morris's Golden type), have met with no better fortune. Bruce Rogers' Centaur is a version based on photography, but it is not like Jenson, as a moment's comparison will show. Some of this difficulty in copying is due to Jenson's defective press work, but that is not the entire obstacle; the type possesses something beyond definition, an individuality and humanism that defy reproduction.

Jenson's type face did not drop from the skies, as something new. Like earlier printers, he was attempting to copy manuscripts and his letters were based on those to be found in manuscripts, though they were informed by an excellence and character seldom present in the originals. Individually, his letters are not perfect, and this is as it should be. Perfection of form is something that might conceivably be fatal in a type design; the humanity of imperfection, of divergence from the ideal, appears essential. As we are more comfortable with a person who is imperfect as we ourselves are, and could not tolerate the perfect man if we found him, so we are more comfortable with a type that is human and warm; harmony is all.

Though Jenson's roman and similar types came to typography later than gothic, because they were derived from a

eum feci. PETRVS BEMBVS FILI
VS. Diu quidem pater hic ſedes: & certe
ripa haec uirens; quam populi tuae iſtae
denſiſſimae inumbrant; & fluuius alit; ali
quanto frigidior eſt fortaſſe, q̄ ſit ſatis.

105. Type used by Aldus in *De Aetna*, *c.* 1495

HOEBO IN QVEL HORA MANAN
do, che la fronte di Matuta Leucothea candi-
daua, fora gia dalle Oceane unde, le uolubile
rote ſoſpeſe non dimonſtraua, Ma ſedulo cum
gli ſui uolucri caballi. Pyroo primo, & Eoo al-
quanto apparendo, ad dipingere le lycophe
quadrige della figliola di uermigliante roſe, ue

106. Griffi's type from the *Hypnerotomachia Poliphili*, 1499

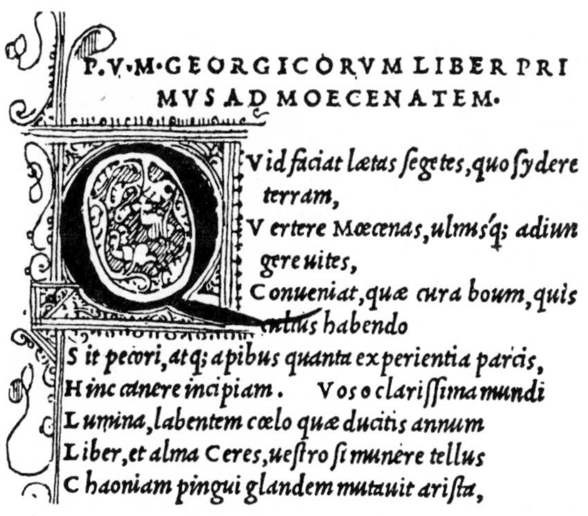

P. V. M. GEORGICORVM LIBER PRI
MVS AD MOECENATEM.

Vid faciat lætas ſegetes, quo ſydere terram,
Vertere Mœcenas, ulmiſq; adiungere uites,
Conueniat, quæ cura boum, quis cultus habendo
Sit pecori, atq; apibus quanta experientia parcis,
Hinc canere incipiam. Vos o clariſſima mundi
Lumina, labentem cœlo quæ ducitis annum
Liber, et alma Ceres, ueſtro ſi munere tellus
Chaoniam pingui glandem mutauit ariſta,

107. The Aldine italic, 1501. The initial is drawn.

tradition older than gothic they were known as antiqua; and in some type lists they are labelled 'antiqua barbaricus'. To-day it is the other way round: it is roman that is characteristic of our modern world, and gothic that is considered antique and barbarous.

Some type-cutters did not follow Jenson but struck out for themselves towards new conceptions of type design. Of these was Francesco Griffi, or Francesco da Bologna, who cut types for the great Venetian printer and publisher, Aldus Manutius. Griffi cut an irregular, highly individual character, but none the less based on a manuscript form, that was first used in the *Hypnerotomachia Poliphili* of Francesco Colonna. It was revived under the name Poliphilus by the Monotype Corporation before the war, and has been used with effect in various kinds of modern books.

Griffi went on to cut a kind of letter altogether new in typography but well known in the scriptorium—chancery italic, a typographical version of the hand used in the papal chancery. Italics take up less room than do roman letters, chancery italics especially so, and Aldus used them for small and compact editions of the classics published at a low price, the famous Aldine editions. They were issued in large numbers, and many of them have survived, so that copies may occasionally be obtained at no prohibitive cost in second-hand bookshops.

At first, only the lower-case of chancery was cut, the capitals used with it being those of a roman face of suitable size, the two going together very well. Otherwise the whole text of the book was set in this italic. This is a practice that has sunk out of knowledge, and italic faces have so declined in favour, and have become so emasculated, that to-day no typographer would consider them suitable for the text of a book. It is no modern degeneration, for few printers after Aldus's press ceased to function used italics in this way; and none do it in our day, though a number of revivals of chancery italics are available for use on composing machines. It seems that italics are forever doomed to be no more than servants and handmaids to roman.

The influence of Jenson and of Griffi spread abroad with their fame and the circulation of the books they printed or cut the types for, and most countries that turned to roman adopted first a letter after the Jenson model, and later, as Griffi did, began to experiment for themselves. As native designers and cutters arose, type faces began to alter in appearance. Letters were made sharper, the serifs were given fuller and more graceful brackets, the contrast between thin and thick strokes was accentuated. The Venetian flavour that had once distinguished the printed page diminished and at last disappeared. It is not altogether true to say that it was replaced by national influences; certainly the style of script that had been in vogue in any country to which printing came tended to affect the types used by the printer, as the manner of their display affected the printer's manner. To this extent French printing, let us say, became recognizably French. As once the printer had depended on Germany for his methods and technique, so he came to depend upon Italy for his type faces, or the inspiration that informed those he cut for himself; and so later he came to depend upon whatever country produced brilliant or capable type designers and cutters, either out of its native stock or by providing a haven for the talented exile. Indeed, type-cutters and printers were likely to be of any nationality other than that of the country they worked in. Sweynheim and Pannartz were Germans, Nicolas Jenson was a Frenchman, the first printers in France (who, incidentally, began with a roman type) were Germans, and the leading light of Dutch typography, Christopher Plantin, was a Frenchman. Wherever he may have worked, the influence of a great type-cutter or a great printer was carried abroad and affected the style of other countries, bringing the exile, in a manner of the spirit, back to his own land. Seen in this way, typography became not so much national as international. French printers bought type in Italy, Dutch printers bought type in France, and English printers bought type in the Netherlands. What is distinctive of different countries is not so much the type faces they used, as the manner in which they used them.

Even before the appearance of the *Hypnerotomachia*, Aldus had used in the *De Aetna* of Cardinal Bembo a type nearer to the kind we are familiar with to-day. Johann Schoeffer in 1520 was using a roman type that prefigured Garamond's of twenty years later and showed the tendency to enhanced sharpness, contrast, and grace; and Fröben was using a similar type at Basle in 1526. The tendency was brought to maturity in France about the year 1540 by Garamond in a type that has perhaps no equal of its kind. Conventionally it is based on the pen-written character, as are all old face types, but it does not imitate or emulate

Vn Roy, tant ſoit il grand en terre ou en proüeſſe,
Meurt comme vn laboureur ſans gloire, ſ'il ne laiſſe
Quelque renom de luy, & ce renom ne peut
Venir apres la mort, ſi la Muſe ne veut
Le donner à celluy qui doucement l'inuite,
Et d'honneſte faueur compenſe ſon merite.

108. Garamond's roman, *c.* 1540

anything produced by the scribe. Here is a letter specifically designed for the press and the printed page, and not intended to be used in the manufacture of counterfeit manuscripts. Claude Garamond learned his craft under Geofroy Tory, a famous printer who was, in fact, more of an illuminator than a printer. Garamond was familiar with the Italian kind of letter from Tory's use of it, but he did not follow it in his own type. Nor, as I have shown, did he create something entirely new. He expressed something that was in the air, and he did it with such excellence that gothic, venetian, and chancery were finally thrust out of favour and never again recovered their former position. From this time on the course of type design flowed from Garamond.

Garamond finally freed type design from the influence of the manuscript, and indeed in his day printed books had lost the impetus that the inspiration of the manuscript had once provided. The press no longer produced magnificent and ambitious masterpieces such as those that had been brought out by Gutenberg and Fust and Schoeffer in emulation or imitation of the scriptoria. Printing houses had become more numerous and were no longer supported by wealthy patrons as once they had been. They were now commercial ventures, expected not only to support the workmen who laboured in them, but also to provide a livelihood and the prospect of fortune for their owners. Printed books, once rarities among manuscripts, were now common, and it was the manuscript that was rare. The press had destroyed its mentor, and henceforward it must depend upon itself and create its own traditions.

In France, Garamond's influence was strong for many years, but the high level of his achievement was never reached again; and as the sixteenth and seventeenth centuries wore on, his influence waned and at last ceased. French types entered a period of emasculation and degeneration from which they have only recently recovered. The decline can be traced through Jannon, whose type long passed and still passes as Garamond's, and through Grandjean and the Didots. First it was towards a lighter or more delicate letter, and this was exaggerated until in the eighteenth century types were produced that were so weak they scarcely coloured the paper and were anything but readable. Fournier attempted to redress the balance with types that were firmer and more vigorous, though not possessing the excellence of the earlier time, but he did not stem the flow. Nor, as we see it now, could he hope to do so, for there seems to be something in the French character inimical to good book faces, and it was later to treat modern faces as it had treated old faces, to emasculate and condense until nothing in the world was as wretched as the ordinary run of French books up to the outbreak of war in 1939.

Christopher Plantin began to print at Antwerp in 1555, and later set up a foundry in connection with his press. Assault, official obstruction, religious intolerance, and the depredations of mutinous soldiery repeatedly retarded him, but he persevered and at the zenith of his career his printing house was the greatest in Europe, which is also to say the greatest in the world. He was not a type designer or type cutter, but a printer who knew a good type when he saw one, and more, how to use it. He was a Frenchman and procured much of his material in Paris, so that his work is more typical of France, or was so at first, than of the Netherlands or of Spain, under whose domination the Low Countries then were. He owned the rights of printing a number

CAPVT PRIMVM.

A IN principio creauit Deus cælum & terrã. * Terra autem erat inanis & vacua : & tenebræ erant ſuper faciẽ abyſsi: & ſpiritus Dei ferebatur ſuper aquas. * Dixitq; Deus, Fiat lux. Et facta eſt lux. * Et vidit Deus lucem quòd eſſet bona: & diuiſit lucem à tenebris. * Appellauitq; lucem diem; & tenebras noctẽ. Factumq; eſt veſpere

109. Type used by Christopher Plantin, 1572

of liturgical works for the Spanish Church, for the Netherlands, and for Hungary and Germany, as the right of printing Bibles is now held by a group of privileged printers, and these monopolies kept him and his successors in affluence for many years. He brought out a famous polyglot Bible, but he is better known for the pocket editions that are typical of his press. He employed first François Guyot, then Robert Granjon, and later Henric van der Keere to cut types for him, and also bought founts from other foundries or other printers as occasion offered. Few printers were as enterprising and at the same time as excellent as Plantin, and at his death in 1589 he had, in spite of adversity, established a reputation and a business for his press that were to stand his successors in good stead for a hundred years or more; and he had placed the Netherlands in a position of supremacy in the world of printing.

In England little of typographical importance had happened during these years, little of importance, that is, when seen against the background of Europe. True, the craft of printing had been introduced and had flourished, and had once suffered curtailment so that it could be strictly controlled by the Star Chamber. English printers had plodded on, following the style in vogue on the Continent, obtaining their materials there, and even importing their workmen from Holland or France. This dependence upon the Continent continued through the sixteenth century and through the seventeenth century also. Printing came to England through the Netherlands, and it was the Netherlands that for long influenced this country most; an influence that was confirmed by the rise of Dutch printing under the genius of Christopher Plantin. There were, it seems, some founders in this country in the seventeenth century, but they were of little account and were held in scorn by the better printers of the day; they could not produce types that technically or aesthetically equalled those brought from abroad.

At the beginning of the eighteenth century this state of affairs attracted the attention of William Caslon, an engraver of gun stocks and barrels. Encouraged by certain influential printers, he began to cut types himself, and by 1720 had started a foundry to cast them commercially.

Caslon's type was an immediate success in England, and one of the first effects of his new foundry was to make English printers independent of the Continent for their types and type ornaments. Yet Caslon's was not an original design. It showed a distinct Continental influence, and that influence was, as might be expected, particularly attributable to the Netherlands. It does not possess the superlative qualities of Garamond and Jenson, but it was a better type than any that had been made in England up to that time. Caslon was a superb craftsman, and his type was of excellent technical quality, well cut and alined and balanced. In design it is a graceful, delicate, and subtle old face, with the serifs fully bracketed, and the now familiar variation between thick and thin strokes. The letters vary in different sizes, showing the divergences inevitable in any repetition of work by hand, as well as nice adjustments made to preserve the character of the face. Taken individually, the letters show imperfections, as do those of any good type, but they marry without disharmony to make a page easy and comfortable to read, as well as pleasing in appearance.

Caslon enjoyed little influence abroad, where what he had achieved was nothing new and offered no fresh excitement or inspiration. Continental type-cutters were looking ahead of the style Caslon represented, and were awaiting a very different kind of type. The first English type-cutter to have any influence

IT is with a great Deal of Pleaſure, that I lay hold on this firſt Occaſion, which the Accidents of my Life have given me, of writing to your Lordſhip: For ſince at the ſame Time, I write to all the World, it will be a Means of publiſhing (what I would have every Body know) the Reſpect and

110. Baskerville's type, 1757

on European printing was John Baskerville, a writing master, who, having made a fortune in japanning, proceeded to spend some of it on the improvement of printing. He declared admiration for Caslon's work, but the type of the book in which he made this statement was very different from anything imagined by Caslon. It expressed admirably the eighteenth-century passion—or should we use so strong a word as that? rather, the eighteenth-century inclination—towards grace and gentility. It was conscious of its own virtues, as was the dandy or the fop, or the fine ladies who spent their days in the salon or at fashionable resorts, but it was not artificial. Baskerville was well aware of what he attempted, and he expended unexampled care in the printing of his books, such care and judgement as have made them things to be prized and loved. His first great book, a Virgil issued in 1757, astonished by its general excellence of type, paper, printing, and design. Alas for the nobly born and the delicately nurtured! Baskerville's type is to-day used very widely in the ordinary run of book production; not for fine editions only, but also for the common cheap novel printed with no care or forethought. For the excellent typographic qualities of Baskerville have made it a stock face, now too commonplace for self-consciousness, and few printers dare be without some version of it. This book is printed in Monotype Baskerville.

None the less, there is no doubt that it is a good type, indeed a very good one. English printers were impressed, but not stimulated, but those of the Continent saw in it an advance-guard of a new style and welcomed it. The books in which it appeared were also something new and different: Baskerville invented blacker ink and a smoother paper to give full value to his type, and further he glazed his paper between sheets of hot metal after printing, to increase the contrast and enhance the surface. The type itself is legible, firm, and of remarkable printing quality; it possesses dignity and restraint, and when suitably printed that delicacy I have already mentioned, which was achieved by fining away the thin strokes of the letters and by an alteration of the stress nearer the vertical. The result is certainly impressive and attractive, but it pointed the way towards snares that were to entrap lesser men in a later age.

Baskerville's type and his books were regarded with particular interest by Giambattista Bodoni of Parma, who was a type designer, as was Baskerville, but was more of a printer than his English contemporary ever became. Baskerville would have liked to make money from his press, but he complained that he did not; he was an amateur, desiring, as he said himself, to print only a few books, and those the classics. Bodoni, on the other hand, was head of a large printing house possessed of government monopolies and producing great quantities of printed matter every year. By means of this press Bodoni could disseminate his ideas of letter form far and wide.

He aimed at blocks of rich black type on dazzling white paper, but he carried the theory to an extreme quite foreign to Baskerville, and indeed showed everywhere the exaggerated contrast of a more brilliant climate. Bodoni's books are beautiful, but they are not among those that are most comfortable for the eye. The typographer has become fully self-conscious at last, aware of his own excellence, and not a little intolerant. The characteristics of Bodoni's types are a vertical stress, a further whittling away of the thin strokes, coupled with an exaggeration of the thick ones, and an upright emphasis generally that is at once the source of its charm and of its weakness. It is a type based ultimately on the use of the engraving tool rather than on that of the pen.

ECCOVI i saggi dell'industria e delle fatiche mie di molti anni consecrati con veramente geniale impégno ad un'arte, che è compimento della più bella, ingegnosa, e giovevole inven-

111. Bodoni's type, 1788

Bodoni brought this style of letter to its greatest excellence, but it was not, in fact, confined to Italy. Printers and type-cutters of other countries were travelling the same road, and arrived sooner or later at a similar stage. Notably, the Didots in France and William Martin, Alexander Wilson, and John Bell in England showed the influence and progress of the movement; and by the turn of the century what was to be called modern face was firmly established, indeed, had begun to oust the old faces.

From this time onwards text faces can be divided into two clear categories, known to the printer as 'old faces' and 'modern faces'; such types as had appeared up to and including Caslon, and Baskerville too, for that matter, are grouped under the term 'old face', of which Italians such as Jenson, though really a class of their own, may be regarded as members. The chief characteristic of old-face types is the fundamental relation of the line to that made by the pen. The stress is tilted in more or less degree, and the accent diminishes gradually into the thin

QUOUSQUE TANDEM ABUTERE, CATILINA, patienta nostra? quamdiu nos etiam furor iste tuus eludet? quem ad finem sese effrenata jactabit audacia? nihilne te nocturnum praesidium palatii, nihil urbis

Caslon, 12 pt.

QUOUSQUE TANDEM ABUTERE, CATALINA, patientia nostra? quamdiu nos etiam furor iste tuus eludet? quem ad finem sese effrenata jactabit audacia? nihilne te nocturnum praesidium palatii,

Baskerville, 12 pt.

QUOUSQUE TANDEM ABUTERE, CATILINA, patientia nostra? quamdiu nos etiam furor iste tuus eludet? quem ad finem sese effrenata jactabit audacia? nihilne te nocturnum praesidium palatii, nihil urbis

Bell, 12 pt.

QUOUSQUE TANDEM ABUTERE, CATILINA, patientia nostra? quamdiu nos etiam furor iste tuus eludet? quem ad finem sese effrenata jactabit audacia? nihilne te nocturnum praesidium palatii,

Bodoni, 12 pt.

QUOUSQUE TANDEM ABUTERE, CATILINA, patientia nostra? quamdiu nos etiam furor iste tuus eludet? quem ad finem sese effrenata jactabit audacia? nihilne te nocturnum praesidium palatii,

Scotch Roman, 12 pt.

112. Revived types selected to show theoretically the transition from old face to modern face

stroke without obvious junction; exaggeration and artificial emphasis are generally avoided. Modern faces, on the other hand, are typical of the practice of the engraver rather than of the scribe, and their relationship to the engraved form remains close. The stress is vertical and the change of accent is apt to be abrupt, a heavy thick line suddenly and precipitately becoming the thinnest of hair lines. The general effect is sharper and more rigorous than is that of old face.

A few transitional types appeared and have survived—or, rather, have been revived, for if they were not dead they were very much like it. Bell and Walbaum are examples. Transitional faces may be very pleasant types, possessing characteristics that old faces do not possess, without the attendant disadvantages of out and out moderns.

The heyday of modern faces was reached within the years 1780 to 1820—rather in the earlier part of the period than in the later; and after this they began to decline rapidly, bringing with them in their fall the whole practice of printing. Excellent as were the types of Bodoni and the Didots, they held within them the seed of such degeneration as the history of printing had not yet known. The development of modern was typical of the eighteenth century, but the tendency that suddenly sprang up and flowered as the century closed was not a new one. A type prefiguring modern had appeared in a book printed at Florence as early as 1691, and others more pronounced in character had come out between that date and the appearance of Baskerville's new letter; but no such great designer or cutter had set his hand to modern faces before Baskerville brought out his transitional face and, unwittingly, helped to impel Bodoni to what he considered was the logical conclusion.

There is nothing objectionable in a good modern face properly used; it can be a very good letter indeed, readable, sensible, and practical; but there is a good deal that is objectionable in the spawn of mean and anaemic offspring that issued from this source. The earlier half of the nineteenth century was a low ebb of typography, though technically it was a period of great advance. New type faces appeared in greater numbers than ever, issuing from the foundries without distinction to recommend them or promise of useful service; and like a horde of locusts they overwhelmed the good things that had been in the land before them. The old faces had vanished before the novelty and conscious excellence of the early moderns; and now Baskerville, Bodoni, Didot, Bell, and the rest of them were cast into limbo by the crowd of nonentities they had fathered.

Not everything was bad, not all the world was dark; here and there a printer or a publisher kept the flag of good craftsmanship aloft and flying. The fine editions (in modern faces) of Bulmer and Bensley continued until 1830, and Charles Whittingham of the Chiswick Press and the publisher William Pickering carried on the tradition of good work, producing editions that are increasing in value, though occasionally one may be found at a modest price. They are treasured by those who collect books for their own sake, and not because they are rarities.

It was Whittingham and Pickering who began the movement that was to result in the revival of old-face types and bring back again something of their pristine glory. Printer and publisher co-operated in a proposed edition of Juvenal, and for some reason of their own persuaded the Caslon foundry to cast type for it from William Caslon's hundred-year-old matrices, then stored away among the dirt and debris that seem always to accumulate about anything to do with type. For one reason or another the edition of Juvenal hung fire, and in the meantime it occurred to Whittingham and Pickering that Caslon's type was the very thing for a new book Pickering was about to publish, the diary of a fictive lady of the seventeenth century, which they thought might be suitably printed in a contemporary style. *The Diary of Lady Willoughby* was thus the first book of the Caslon revival; it appeared in 1844, and the Juvenal the year after.

Lady Willoughby was a success not only as fiction but as a piece of printing as well. It seems nothing wonderful to us now, but it was novel to the printers of the time because they had forgotten such things, much as Morris's types were to appear novel and strange in a later generation to those who did not know from what they were derived. Everyone was tired of lack-lustre moderns, and a flash of enthusiasm for Caslon followed the publication of the diary. It was not necessarily accompanied by any spurt of imagination, and though printers set out to follow the new fashion and bought Caslon, many of them used the good type very badly, as before they had used bad types atrociously. Nor does it seem to have occurred to anyone to revive other old-face types, though there were enough of them to choose from had they only looked. But it was unlikely, it must in fairness be pointed out, that in other instances the punches or matrices should have survived so conveniently as those of Caslon.

Towards the end of the seventeenth century Dr. John Fell, Dean of Christ Church at Oxford, had imported some interesting types and matrices from Holland and presented them to the Oxford University Press, where they were used for a time until Caslon swept everything before it. When Whittingham and Pickering brought out *Lady Willoughby* these types had long lain unused and almost forgotten, and they continued so for some thirty years more, until they attracted the attention of the Reverend C. H. O. Daniel, who had been Provost of Worcester College, and who had for a number of years supervised a small private press that he had founded at Frome. He revived the Fell types, and after 1877 used them with fine judgement in small editions of small books; setting an example that the University Press itself was to find of value later.

It seemed that typography, the designing of type faces and of books, was in the air, that more and more it was beginning to be understood that printed matter should be designed to the best effect, and development might have gone on smoothly, if slowly, had not a disturbing influence taken a hand in the revival of printing; and not merely taken a hand, but seized the reins and driven it into a blind alley. William Morris had begun to take a practical interest in printing towards the end of the eighties, as he took a practical interest in so many things—always with the best of intentions. In 1889 he had one of his books printed for him by the Chiswick Press—and no doubt he made himself a nuisance to the worthy successors of Charles Whittingham; no craftsman can object more strongly to interference from outside than the printer—is not his craft a mystery still, and the layman meddling with it the equivalent of a bull in a china shop? I can imagine something of the pungent dialogue that must have passed between the compositors and the clickers, between the stone-hands and the machine-minders,

SO am I as the rich, whose blessed key
Can bring him to his sweet up-locked treasure,
The which he will not ev'ry hower survay,
For blunting the fine point of seldome pleasure.
Therefore are feasts so sollemne and so rare,
Since, seldom comming, in the long yeare set,
Like stones of worth they thinly placed are,

113. William Morris's roman, the Golden type, 1890

And the ryver that then I sat upon,
Hit made suche a noyse as hit ther ron,
Acordaunt to the foules ermonye,
Methoght hit was the beste melodye
That myghte be herd of eny lyvyng man.

114. William Morris's Chaucer type, 1893

as they considered Morris's unprecedented demands. But they printed his book for him, as near to his ideals as he could bring them. Perhaps it did not altogether satisfy him, for in 1891 he founded the Kelmscott Press in a house by the river at Hammersmith, and began to print his books for himself, issuing *The Story of the Glittering Plain* as the first fruits of the new printing house. The typography of this book, like the story, was sham medieval, but it was magnificent, none the less; what did it matter if to read it was almost beyond the bounds of human endurance? It was thrown upon a peaceful world like an anarchist's bomb, and among those who were fortunate enough to see it, it demolished the ideals and preconceptions of many. D. B. Updike says of Morris's work: 'The effect on printing in general that Morris was to have through his types and typesetting entirely escaped most printers, as did the source from which he derived his methods. Because they knew very little about early manuscripts or early books, about the characters of one or the types of the other, the Kelmscott books appeared to them to have fallen from the sky—either very new and very wonderful or else very freakish and senseless—just as they would to anybody who knew nothing whatever about it.'

Morris, when he set out to provide a roman for his press, hit upon Jenson as a model, and aspired to design a type face that would be an improvement on Jenson's. It was good to introduce Jenson to a public that had never heard of him, but Morris's conception of what Jenson's types should be was far from what Jenson himself seems to have thought, and in his Golden type Morris reintroduced what Jenson had sought to escape—the influence of gothic. The relationship and the difference between the two faces are perceptible at once. For Morris was travelling in a direction antithetically opposite to that taken by Jenson. Jenson had succeeded in freeing himself from the influence of gothic, while Morris was rapidly returning to it; and indeed Morris shortly designed a gothic face for himself, and used it concurrently with his Jenson pastiche—an offence he must have found difficult to explain in those elysian fields to which typographers and printers are at last inevitably wafted.

Morris, labouring in his private press, had really little effect on the commercial printing and book production of his time; but if he did not make printers print as he did, what he did achieve was of immense value. Fine as it is, his own printing was a sport, a freak in history, an example of decorative art rather than of typography; his press vanished, and of his precepts and practice hardly anything remains; but he set afoot a new interest in the making of books, he aroused a controversy that made men pause to examine what they were doing and to ask if it could not be done better, if there was any reason why the result of their labour should not avoid ugliness and carelessness, and attain beauty.

A number of amateurs, such as Morris himself was, were

inspired by his example to set up private presses of their own; and if some of these presses, as Morris's did, led taste in the wrong direction, or took it up the garden path, they did serve to enhance the increasing interest in book production. People at last began to ask whether the books they read were well made and well designed, and they discovered more often than not that they were not well made and were not designed at all. Among the presses that succeeded the Kelmscott were the Vale Press, with three bad founts of type; the Doves Press, with another type based on Jenson, and the best up to this time; the Ashendene Press, with a version of the romano-gothic type used by Sweynheim and Pannartz at Subiaco: the Eragny Press, with yet another Italian type, debased and effeminate and fussy; the Riccardi Press, which was the name under which the Medici Society published various books set in a peculiar but not ineffective type called Riccardi designed by Herbert Horne; and the Golden Cockerel Press, which for forty years produced limited editions of which the typography is sometimes very fine. The Golden Cockerel confined itself to no special type, but was wisely content with those available from the commercial founder or the composing machine, suitably selected. All these presses flourished for a while, publishing their quota of books, and then, either because money had run out, or their sponsors were tired of them, or for any other reason that came into their capricious heads, they one by one closed their doors and put up the shutters. Their day faded and the need for them waned with the approach to a new period of typographical awareness which they had themselves helped to inaugurate. If some of them worked in the wrong way towards the right end, they nevertheless made their mark.

Too much attention, I believe, has been focused on the peculiar types used by the private presses; it seems to me that what is important is the manner in which those types were used rather than the types themselves. They were generally used with skill and taste, and to good advantage, and the result was an object lesson for printers, publishers, and readers alike. If the private presses could use their odd types to such purpose, then

the commercial printer should be able to use what types were available to him at least equally well; and in the latter days of the private presses type faces were available commercially that were far better than anything that had ever issued from the private press. The lead was not ignored, but it was some time in being followed.

CHORUS
When the hounds of spring are on winter's traces,
The mother of months in meadow or plain
Fills the shadows and windy places
With lisp of leaves and ripple of rain:
And the brown bright nightingale amorous
Is half assuaged for Itylus,
For the Thracian ships and the foreign faces,
The tongueless vigil, and all the pain.

115. The Riccardi type, 1909

It was not until well into the twentieth century, when the influence of Morris and his disciples had faded and begun to look a little tawdry, that type and typography came into their own, type in a revival of faces from the dusty lumber-room of history, and typography in a new manner of their use. The revival received its greatest impetus from the manufacturers of the Linotype and the Monotype, but particularly from the Monotype Corporation, who initiated an ambitious policy of revival of old types and coupled it with the issue of newly designed faces of a great many varieties. The taste of both companies has proved erratic, and both include in their lists not only grotesque and often repulsive display faces, but doubtful and inharmonious book faces as well; though it must perhaps be admitted for their defence that they were doing no more than serve the demand of the public. On the other hand, they combed the centuries for fine old types, and either copied them facsimile or used them as models for the cutting of new faces related to the originals.

The change that came upon printing as a result of the appearance and use of these types extended at last even to the newspapers, which until the early nineteen-thirties had held

in templum, et votum fecit, si ad eloquentiam pervenisset? quis, si philosophiæ fontem atticisset? Ac ne bonam quidem valetudinem petunt: sed statim, antequam limen Capitolii tançant, alius donum promittit, si propinquum divitem extulerit: alius, si thesaurum effo-

116. The King's Fount, Vale Press, 1896

Apollo pueri umbram revocavit in florem, et omnes fabulæ quoque habuerunt sine æmulo complexus. At ego in societatem recepi hospitem, Lycurgo crudeliorem. Ecce autem, ego dum cum ventis litigo, intravit pinacothecam senex canus, exercitati vultus, et qui videretur nescio

117. The Vale Fount, Vale Press, 1896

¶ These Books printed, as a first essay, the whole field of literature remains open to select from. To-day there is an immense reproduction in an admirable cheap form, of all Books which in any language have stood the test of time. But such reproduction is not

118. The Doves Press type, 1901

nono apparve a me, ed io la vidi quasi alla fine del mio nono. Apparvemi vestita d'un nobilissimo colore umile ed onesto, sanguigno, cinta ed ornata alla guisa che alla sua giovanissima etade si convenia. In quel punto dico veracemente che lo spirito

119. The Ashendene type (cf. Figure 101), 1902

on to their nineteenth-century moderns. Of these moderns *The Times* had undoubtedly the best, but most of them, those used by the large London dailies and evening papers and by provincial journals also, were a wretched set, the product of a bad period of type design. *The Times* led the way to reform by coming out in a type specially designed for it, with harmonious titlings for use in the column headings. Times Roman is a type designed for a special and very limited purpose, the printing of a newspaper, and it achieved an immediate success. In character Times is a heavy old style, inclining towards modern, with fully bracketed serifs and a general sturdiness of construction that makes it efficient for its purpose. But it is more than this. It attracted the attention of book printers and of publishers and soon began to appear in all kinds of books, in which—particularly when leaded—it performs very well. A certain stubby quality due to the short descenders was evident in the longer line of the book; but when alternative long descenders were made available this disability vanished.

There have never before been so many and such a variety of good type faces at the service of the printer as there are to-day, though they are set among a horde of bad, illegible, cramped, tortured, and ill-designed types that make good choice a trial for the printer and the typographer. The composing machine companies have brought out failures as well as successes, and both have remained on the market, the successes, we hope, because they are good, the failures because once a type is broadcast among printers it is very difficult to kill it even if you want to—Cheltenham is the persistent example.

DISPLAY FACES

Alongside the development of book faces there has gone, since the beginning of the nineteenth century, a development of types intended for display, and some of these are used in books for chapter headings or title-pages, or for book jackets. Display types were, to begin with, nothing more than large sizes of book faces; but after the year 1700, or thereabouts, there began to be a difference. Types began to assume the form of things alien to them, the shapes of twigs or branches, for example. It was not done to any great extent in the eighteenth century, and when it was it was only for a word or two on a title-page or in a chapter heading. It is possible, indeed probable, that these words were not printed from type at all, but from wood blocks cut for the

DE
GERMANIÆ MIRACVLO
OPTIMO, MAXIMO,

TYPIS
literarum,

120. Decorative letters, probably cut on wood, from the title-page of Pater's *Typis Literarum*, Leipsig, 1710

particular purpose, like the decorated *lettres de forme* of the fifteenth and sixteenth centuries. Used discreetly in this manner, and not often, ornamental lettering does possess a charm and a novelty not open to more normal types; but used frequently and without discretion it becomes boring and irritating and defeats its end. This was what happened in the nineteenth century.

Bewick's success as a book illustrator caused type designers to contrive type faces that would match with wood-engravings, and consequently an invasion of fat faces laid waste the typographical landscape of this country; and through this country that of other countries also, when Britain, as a result of the Napoleonic Wars, became the envied great power and arbiter of taste and everything else throughout Europe. And shortly occupying forces of fanciful and fantastic designs took over the land. Type faces sprouted every kind of excrescence imaginable, or attempted to imitate or simulate anything and everything that inspired the misguided ingenuity of the designer. Never was there such a wilderness of leaves and flowers and trees, of streams and ice and snow, of railway trains and horse carriages. Letters were made so that they looked like twigs, like pieces of string, or like contorted animals or insects; they bore burdens of snow or frost, or trailing blossoms, or birds' nests with eggs or chicks. They were designed so that they could be joined together to look as though they were strung on telegraph wires, or on the bars of a fence, or borne on the wagons of a railway train. They melted like wax in heat, or they were extended like soft toffee until they were four or five times their normal width, or compressed until they were only a fourth or fifth of it. They were knock-kneed, bow-legged, and pot-bellied. Nothing was too strange or too far-fetched to be made into the letters of the alphabet. All that came was grist, however grisly.

Most of these queer types were mania types; they were produced to satisfy a demand for novelty, and when the taste cloyed they wore away in disgrace and a later novelty took their place. What appetites our grandfathers and our great-grandfathers had! We are now busy reviving some of the things they did.

Some of these fancy types, the less monstrous and strange, remained, or were revived again in our own day. Amid the welter of worthless preciosities a few types achieved genuine extension of type design, as if they had stumbled on it by accident. If many sanserifs that appeared were poor and ill formed, the idea of dispensing with the serifs was of value; on the other hand, putting emphasis on the serifs, as in the egyptians, was also useful. Thorne's shadowed bold fat face is a good letter when properly used, and even lateral compression and expansion, within reason, are of service.

Printers and typographers to-day sometimes laugh at their predecessors who doted on these things, but they are often no better themselves. They have the same thirst for novelty, and the same facility for tiring of their pets. Typefounders' catalogues are strewn with the dead corpses of types that flourished exotically for a day and then drooped and were forgotten. Kino, Modernistic, Gallia, Vesta, Chic, Braggadocio, Ashley Craw-

FADING SUN

Another Disaster

THE HEBRIDES.

NEATEST

FANCIFUL

FANCY TYPE.

CHIME.

AMERICAN

RURAL ARCHITECTURE

MAGNIFICENT

A FANCY LETTER

BRITISH BALLADS.

121. Nineteenth-century frivolities

ford, Chisel, Festival, are examples. They do not show the unrestricted imagination of the nineteenth century, but many do demonstrate the same disregard for the fundamentals of good letter form and the long tradition of printing.

None the less, the passion for novelty and the enthusiasm of the type designer combine to-day, as they did so long ago, to throw up occasional type faces that are excellent in themselves and of permanent value; and variations are played upon a basic design to produce a family of type faces the members of which are all different, but all bear the family resemblance. The first notable type family was Cheltenham, but for our time an illustrative example is Gill Sans, of which twelve varieties are shown in Figure 123. Not all types exhibit the same range as

122. A fine example of a nineteenth-century decorated letter

Gill Sans, but there are few display faces that have not offspring of some kind, even though they may masquerade under another name. Nor is Gill the only sanserif that can be had; it is one of the best-known but it is a question of opinion whether it is the best. Others are Cable, Futura, Erbar, Nobel, Tempo, Vogue, and Metro. All these are monotone sanserifs of a mechanical character, based on the drawing board and geometry. Modern taste tends towards sanserifs of a more 'humane' kind, that is to say, more freely drawn and with some variety of stroke. Examples are Monotype series 215 and 216 and the elaborate family called Univers.

There are many egyptians. Well known were Beton, Cairo, Karnak, Rockwell. Like the sanserifs of the same period, these are rather mechanical and humourless designs, and they have been displaced by faces of nineteenth-century origin or inspiration, of which Consort is an excellent example.

Gill Sans Light *and Italic*

Gill Sans Medium *and Italic*

Gill Sans Medium Condensed

Gill Sans Bold

Gill Sans Bold Italic

Gill Sans Extra Bold

GILL SANS BOLD CONDENSED TITLING

GILL SANS SHADOW NO. 1

GILL SANS SHADOW LINE

123. Some of the Gill Sans family of related type faces

Among 'fancy' faces the inlined or tooled must be mentioned, and the list may commence with the graceful Old Face Open, one of the most successful and beautiful (as well as the most conservative) of display faces, and continue through Dominus and Goudy Hand-tooled to the more novel Pharos, Adastra, Prisma, Colonna, and Castellar.

Decorated faces also returned, though few in number. One of Fournier's graceful ornamental letters was revived under the name June; Fry's tooled and jewelled capitals were reissued by Stephenson Blake as Fry's Ornamental; and the same founder reissued the first of ornamental types, the seventeenth-century Union Pearl.

French antiques, thickened top and bottom and compressed laterally, were popular during the last century, but fell into disuse until they were revived through new designs in this. Plinth and Playbill are examples.

Condensed and elongated modern faces also came back in Bessemer, Slimback, Onyx, and Elongated Roman; but they came to be used in a manner very different from that in which they had been of service before. Once they were resorted to when it was difficult to get the matter into one line; now they are used for their own sake, and so far from reasons of space economy that they are more often than not set with wide letter-spacing.

At the other extreme fat faces have enjoyed a new vogue, and each founder has brought out his own particular kind. Ultra Bodoni, Falstaff, and Thorowgood are examples.

There is a range of script faces of every conceivable variety, some of them decidedly repulsive, but others possessing grace and delicacy; or others still originality or humour. Among the more conventional are Bernhard Cursive (the English version was called Madonna Ronde), Bernhard Tango, and Trafton. Less conventional, and based on individual handwriting, rather than on an ideal copperplate, are Holla, Legend, Francesca Ronde, Mistral, and Reiner. Holla, which looks, perhaps, as though it comes from the fist of a paralytic calligrapher, is peculiarly effective, but must be used with discretion; and this is true also of Legend, which is among the oddest of the odd—and yet not so odd when its descent from the French *civilité* types and manuscript hands is understood. A few display scripts are farther from handwriting and nearer to bold italics—for example, Klang, Salto, and the scratchy Stop.

We still have, of course, the larger sizes of text faces for use in display. These are reinforced by other decorative or display romans, examples of which are Forum Titling, Marathon, Elizabeth Roman, Weiss Roman, and Vendôme; and transitional between the traditional and modern display the Albertus series, Steel, and such curiosities as Jacno.

As there is no end to the making of books, so there is no end to the making of types with which to print them. Each period develops its own tastes, and the next winnows from the result those faces that most accord with its own particular preferences. Good faces that endure through the centuries are rare, and they arise like things of genius first in this country and then in that. At no time, I believe, have there been as many good type faces in current use as there are to-day, but whether among our new designs there is one that will outlast our own fickleness and fancy it is hard to say.

There have been various attempts to classify type faces. A system proposed by the British Standards Institution is largely based on that of Maximilien Vox of France, as follows (the names devised by Vox are in parentheses):

1. Humanists (*Humanes*): venetians.
2. Garaldes (*Garaldes*): old faces.
3. Transitionals (*Réales*): Baskerville, Bell, Walbaum, etc.
4. Didones (*Didones*): faces with vertical stress and flat serifs with or without brackets, e.g. Bodoni.
5. Slab-serifs (*Mécanes*): egyptians.
6. Lineales (*Linéales*): sanserifs.
7. Glyphics (*Incises*): letters based on the chisel rather than on the pen, e.g. Albertus, Othello.
8. Scripts (*Scriptes*): scripts.
9. Graphics (*Manuaires*): scripts carefully drawn rather than derived from writing, e.g. Libra, Cartoon, Jacno.

ABCDEFGHIJK

June—Stephenson, Blake

ABCDEFGHIJKLM

Old Face Open—Stephenson, Blake

ABCDEFGHIJKL

Fry's Ornamented No. 2—Stephenson, Blake

ABCDEFGHIJKL

Thorne Shaded—Stephenson, Blake

ABCDEFGH

Molé Foliate—Stephenson, Blake

ABCDEFGHIJKLMNOP

Delphian—Ludlow

ABCDEFGHIJKLMNOPQ

abcdefghijklmnopqrstuvwxyz ſbſtſ Qu&,.

Union Pearl—Stephenson, Blake

ABCDEFGHIJKLM

Castellar—Monotype

ABCDEFGHI

Profil—Haa'sche Schriftgiesserei

124. Display types

ABCDEFGHIJKLMNOP

abcdefghijklmnopqrstuvwxyz.,':;?!

Legend—Bauer

A B C D E F G H I J K L M N O P Q R

a b c d e f g h i j k l m n o p q r s t u v w x y z th tz sz tt ß e s t

Reiner Script—Amsterdam Type Foundry

A B C D E F G H I

abcdefghijklmnopqrstuvwxyzæœ

Society Script—Stephenson, Blake

ABCDEFGHIJKLMNOPQRSTUVW

XYZabcdefghijklmnopqrstuvwxyz

Mistral—Amsterdam Type Foundry

ABCDEFGHIJKLMNOPQRSTUVWXYZ

abcdefghijklmnopqrstuvwxyz

Klang—Monotype

ABCDEFGHIJKLMNOPQRSTUVWXYZ

abcdefghijklmnopqrstuvw123456&£

Studio—Amsterdam Type Foundry

ABCDEFGHIJKLMNOPQRSTUVW

XYZabcdefghijklmnopqrstuvwxyz& £123456

Holla—Klingspor

124. Display types

ABCDEFGHIJKLMN
abcdefghijklmnopq

Stop—Ludwig & Mayer

ABCDEFGHIJKLMNOP
abcdefghijklmnopqrstuv

Vendôme—Amsterdam Type Foundry

ABCDEFGHIJKLMNOP
abcdefghijklmnopqrstu

Craw Modern—Soldans

ABCDEFGHIJKLMNOPQRST
abcdefghijklmnopqrstuvwxyz

Consort—Stephenson, Blake

ABCDEFGHIJKLMNOPQRST
abcdefghijklmnopqrstuvwxyz

Antique No. 3

ABCDEFGHIJKLMNOPQRSTUVWXYZ
abcdefghijklmnopqrstuvwxyz&£1234567890

Playbill—Stephenson, Blake

ABCDEFGHIJKLMNOPQRSTUVWXYZ&£

Slim Black—Deberny et Peignot

124. Display types

ABCDEFGHIJKLMNOPQRSTUVWX
abcdefghijklmnopqrstuvwxyz£123456
Albertus

ABCDEFGHIJKLMNOPQRSTU
Albertus Bold Titling

ABCDEFGHIJKLMNOPQRSTUV
abcdefghijklmnopqrstuvwxyz
Falstaff

ABCDEFGHIJKLMNOPQRST
abcdefghijklmnopqrstuvwxyz
Falstaff italic

ABCDEFGHIJKLMNOPQRSTUVWXY
abcdefghijklmnopqrstuvwxyzæœ
Mercurius

ABCDEFGHIJKLMNOPQRSTUVWXYZ
abcdefghijklmnopqrstuvwxyz£1234567890
Condensa

ABCDEFGHIJKLMNOPQRSTUV
Perpetua Titling

ABCDEFGHIJKLMNOPQRSTUVWX
Times Titling

ABCDEFGHIJKLMNOPQRSTUVWXYZ
abcdefghijklmnopqrstuvwxyz123456
Sans 215

ABCDEFGHIJKLMNOPQR
Times Extended Titling

124. Display types
Monotype display faces

XIV

THE TYPOGRAPHER AND HIS WORK

THE typographer is a phenomenon principally of this century, but in effect typographers have existed since the first days of printing, though they have not always been persons distinct from the printer and the printing house. Independence of the printer is the attribute of the typographer of our time, independence, that is, not only of control by the printer, but independence as a separate person. There was a time when printer and typographer were aspects of the individual craftsman. The man who designed the great Bible that came belatedly from Gutenberg's press was a typographer, and a good one, though derivative; and the compositor of any period who set type to a pattern of his own conception was also a typographer.

Is there here some confusion of sense? The word means, in essence, no more than a man who manipulates types, and any compositor does that; but it has lost that essential meaning in acquiring another, and now means a man who uses type as a material of design, handling the physical matter only, so to speak, at second hand, through the directed fingers of the printer. It is a usurptive sense and it denotes a usurpation; but life is always a usurper and history is nothing but his story.

The time when any man, or group of men, working in concert, performed all the operations of a process, from the initial concept to the finished product, has passed away, and with it, usually, has gone the individuality of the worker as a craftsman. The curdling influence of specialization did not leave the printing and kindred trades unaffected. Technique increased in complexity and extent, and absorbed more and more of the printer's time and thought, and in the welter of new machines and new technical ideas that burst upon him with the advance of the nineteenth century, continuing in spate into our own day, he forgot the art of choosing and of using type. But if the artist in him was overwhelmed by the mechanic, he did not necessarily cease to think of himself as capable of design; he did think so. His taste became crude and the subtlety of good design escaped him; he saw nothing in design that did not blatantly proclaim itself as such. It was a progressive disease. The more his taste declined, the more degenerate became the type faces offered to him by the founders, and the more inept his use of them; until at last he played like a delighted child with the crowds of gimcrack faces and fantastic ornaments that descended like gaudy balloons upon him.

The type designer and the typefounder were not led into the dance unwillingly. They had to make their living by giving the printer what he wanted, but there seems to be no doubt that they helped to confuse the printer's taste. And the printer's customers, the publishing houses, must share the responsibility. The printer had to give them what they wanted, or what he conceived they would like, for often what they wanted was indicated in the haziest of terms. The outline was filled in, and filled in to some purpose, by the printer's foreman or the comp at the frame.

When through the influence of artists and calligraphers a new renaissance was begun and a demand arose for a new kind of typography, a demand that was later to be intensified out of all proportion by the realization that well designed printed matter succeeds better than that which is badly designed, the printer, still in his doldrums, was unable to respond. If he tried, he could not successfully compete with men who had spent their lives in the study of fine lettering and its use and brought to it taste and mental equipment superior to his own. Typography, the use of type in design to a definite end, became the attribute of a new kind of artist, the typographer; new because he is a specialist. He does not set type, nor does he operate the press; very likely he is incapable of doing either of these things. But he studies his materials and technical requirements, and selects with care and purpose the elements that are to go towards an ordered whole. His knowledge and experience should not be limited to letterpress printing, but should extend over the whole field of book production to include other printing processes, process engraving, and binding, and the subtleties of type design and of paper quality and kind. He chooses and directs artists to illustrate or decorate particular books, or to design jackets for them, keeping, in the case of the jacket, an eye on the psychology of sales appeal. In short, the book typographer's work is, in part—and in good part—a collation, with all the elements of that collation flowing in an ordered stream in space and time towards the completion of the book.

Some of the fun was lost by the printer when the right of design was taken away; but where that right had not been much exercised, or was enjoyed in the practice of ingenuity, the subtraction was perhaps not felt, might indeed be some relief because with it went responsibility. Not all printers accepted it as inevitable, however, though they were compelled to recognize that the compositor's taste could no longer be relied on. Seeking to be in advance of others and to attract to their offices the kind of work they preferred to do, they employed typographers, finding them sometimes in unlikely places. A few such printing houses, like the Curwen, Baynard, and Shenval presses, became well known and brought out work of which they had every reason to be proud. Others found that it did not pay, or that the typographer they had employed at such expense was rejected by their customers, some of whom preferred doggedly to stick to the style that was good enough for their fathers; others preferred their own designers.

The result is that the position is little relieved. A few printers have created individual styles that distinguish their work to their advantage, but the majority prefer either to depend upon the customer for instructions or, where there are no such instructions, to follow whatever style or lack of style may prove most convenient. This, at least, may be said, that however bad a printed book may be to-day, typographically, it is seldom bad for the reasons that applied in the nadir of production in the last century: facile ingenuity and over-elaboration are largely gone.

Though the parallel is not exact, it may be said that a typographer is to a book what an architect is to a building. The typographer's conception is the unifying force that directs towards a common end the diverse trades and multitudinous operations concerned in the making of a book; so the architect's ideas, embodied in plans and specifications, control the materials and operations of building. Several printers may be involved in the printing of a book, and they may be far apart and unknown to each other; with binders, process engravers, brass-cutters, and others in still other parts of the country. None of these is aware of what the others are doing, nor would it be likely to interest them if they were told; each is intent upon his own particular business. Their diverse contributions to the projected whole are made under the direction of the typographer, who in instructing each trade or craft works within his conception of the complete book.

In a publishing house he starts with a manuscript placed in his hands by the editorial department. The fact that it has passed through the editorial and reached him usually means that the book has been accepted for publication by that department, but not invariably: acceptance may be conditional upon the cost of production. A script by the time it has reached this stage is not always the tidy, fresh stack of sheets that books on authorship suggest are the only things likely to appeal to the publisher. A new author, under the influence of the textbook or correspondence colleges, may produce such a script, neatly and professionally typed, without correction, and possibly bound in cloth; but the old hand is more apt to send in a slightly dog-eared collection of variegated folios held together by a piece of string, more or less emended, erased, and re-emended, and showing many signs of second thoughts and new ideas. There is no virtue or sovereign specific in such untidiness, however. It does not impress anybody; and everyone who has to read a script would prefer it clean and legible.

In the publisher's office a manuscript or typescript receives some wear and tear as it passes through the hands of perhaps half a dozen readers, and this is inevitable; any of these readers may suggest alterations or improvements, which, if the author accepts them, will be incorporated in the script. The result that finally reaches the typographer's desk is often the reverse of inspiring.

In a busy publishing house it is unlikely that the script will arrive at that desk alone; it will have companions, probably, the products of the editorial's merciless mill, and it may be accompanied by various odds and ends of illustrations, diagrams, charts, etc.; or some indication that such things are to come. The components of a book are liable to be flung at the unfortunate typographer at various times, with or without explanation, and he is expected to put them together, and to have everything printed and the books bound by the time they are wanted.

The question of the size of the book our manuscript or typescript will make is the first thing to decide. There is no rule about it unless the typographer has created one for himself, or the accumulated precedents of his firm weigh upon him. The presence or absence of illustrations may have some bearing upon the decision, and the quality or kind of book may also affect it. Generally—and it must be emphasized that it is no more than a generalization—frivolous or ephemeral books tend to be smaller, while those that are grave or serious or are expected to be of permanent interest are mostly larger.

Choice of type and the design of the book as a whole are interdependent: one influences the other. The layout may be completed in major detail at a sitting, but it is often more convenient to do it piecemeal. The title-page and any other displayed element must be designed in relation to the text, and there is little point in designing them at this stage, when they may have to be changed to suit any change made in the setting of the text as a result of dissatisfaction with the specimen page.

A specimen page is the first thing that is required from the printer. Set in the type face and size selected by the typographer, and showing details of page area, headlines, and chapter opening according to his instructions, it is in effect an advance sample showing how the opened book would appear. If it does not please in any way it can be altered until it is satisfactory, a new, revised specimen being obtained to show the alterations in practice. When it is finally approved it is returned to the printer, who takes it as his guide in setting the text of the book, which is now proceeded with.

The specimen is usually accompanied by an estimate of twofold character showing (*a*) the number of pages the book will make set in the style of the accompanying specimen; and (*b*) the cost of the composition of the type, either stated for the book or per sixteen or thirty-two pages. With these details a publisher's estimate can be made, to show what will be the profit on the sale of the edition. Machining and binding costs, which are included in this estimate, may be obtained from printer and binder at the same time, but can equally well be worked out from schedules of fixed charges. Any other charges, for blockmaking and printing of illustrations, for example, are included in it also.

In giving the printer instructions for the specimen page the typographer will also have given him instructions or layouts for the setting of chapter titles and part titles, and these are settled with the approval of the specimen. This approval is a signal in advance showing that the printer will shortly need a layout for the preliminary pages, which he must have before he commences paging, unless he can be informed of the exact number of pages the prelims will occupy. Prelims, or preliminary pages, are all those pages that precede the commencement of the text proper of a book—half or bastard title, title-page, preface, list of contents, and list of illustrations, etc. A set of page proofs commencing with a section of blank pages representing the prelims is a nuisance from everybody's point of view, and so it is better to do the layout in time for the prelims to be included in the proofs.

At some stage the margins of the page must be settled. They require some thought, though there are systems that may be followed, and which, if they are followed blindly, require no thought whatever. No system is entirely satisfactory: the placing of two rectangles of text upon the pages is a matter of aesthetics, and not amenable to rule. A process of trial and error is better, aimed at an arrangement that 'looks right'. Much the best time to fix the margins is when the specimen page is approved; from the printer's point of view a belated settlement of margins is likely to be a confounded nuisance, and from the publisher's a waste of money, for the printer naturally charges for details that absorb time and cause trouble in his composing-room.

It is the business of a production department, of which a typographer forms part, to send out proofs to the author as they come from the printer; and though the typographer himself may not be concerned in this, he is concerned in their return from the author. He is responsible for the transmission of the author's corrections to the printer, together with any corrections of his own or of the publisher's proof-reader, all of which are included in the set of proofs returned for press.

Illustrations make no small demands on the typographer's time and patience. It is not often that they can be dealt with *en masse*, a general instruction covering them all; it is much more usual to find that each illustration, no matter of what kind, needs individual consideration, not only in selection, but also at each stage of production. Selecting illustrations is a matter not only for the publisher and the artist or photographer, but for the author too, and often the author is made responsible for supplying the material to illustrate his book. When the selection is complete it may be found that a number of the photographs are not the author's copyright and that no steps have been taken to obtain permission to use them. Some authors, though they may be capable of writing excellent books, appear to have the mentality of an imbecile in matters of simple business, and it is useless to insist that they should fulfil their responsibilities. The production department must obtain permissions and arrange the fees to be paid for them. It is no real part of its job, but it must be done if indignant protests, and even legal action, are to be avoided after publication.

Where a book is to have drawings especially made for it an artist must be selected who can be depended on to produce drawings showing not only sympathy but understanding of the author's style and subject—and, of course, artistic merit. It will be necessary to tell this artist how many illustrations, and of what size, will be needed, rather than leave it to him to send in whatever he feels is the right number. Artists who might benefit by such limitations are, however, often those who most ignore them, and sometimes there descends upon the bewildered publisher, not the twenty drawings asked for, but sixty or seventy, coming in one bunch or in a trickle spread over weeks. Such fecundity is the result of enthusiasm and lack of discrimination rather than of misplaced generosity; and for the typographer it means unnecessary work involved in detecting and discarding surplus drawings, which may make a re-reading of the text unavoidable, because the position of each drawing must bear some relation to its context. On the other hand, there are artists who appear reluctant to supply the full tally and have to be urged again and again. In fact, *some* of the artistic community is always a little bit rum, as the ordinary man has for a long time suspected.

Line drawings usually admit of only one means of reproduction, by line block, unless they are in pencil, when some form of tone reproduction is preferable; but pictures in tone may be reproduced by any of several processes, one of which will have to be decided on. Usually it is half-tone, but the fact that it is usual does not make consideration superfluous. One of the factors is cost, and in many cases this rules out the use of collotype or photogravure; expensive processes are confined to books on which the publisher is prepared to risk more money.

It is very unlikely that all, or indeed any, of the pictures used in any book are of the right size for that book, or the right shape either. Where they can be trimmed to a better proportion the task is made easier, but it is inadvisable, for obvious reasons, to take a slice off an old master, or a young one, for that matter. By means of photographic reduction or enlargement originals of the wrong size can be brought down or up to the size dictated by the area of the page, but this does not, of course, alter their proportions. Each picture must be dealt with separately, and perhaps each shows the result of a compromise.

Line illustrations may be printed in their appropriate places in the text, or as near as the exigencies of paging will allow. The positions of tone illustrations are restricted by the mechanics of binding, as I have already described, and some sort of compromise may be necessary. Whatever method is used, their positions have to be determined and the correct facing-page numbers inserted in the prelims.

The printer's cast-off shows the number of pages the book will make, and a dummy of the correct size and number of pages is made up of the kind of paper that will be used. This is bound in the proposed style, and the resulting bound dummy gives the precise dimensions of the finished book. With this information, the brass and jacket can be put in hand. When the brass has been cut, the binder uses it to block a case of the proper size and the selected cloth, in gold, silver, foil, or ink, as instructed by the typographer. When this specimen case has been approved or corrected, as may be, the binder will make up a number of complete books—perhaps a couple of dozen. These are the advance copies. They are used by the publisher as sales samples; but they are also equivalent to proofs, showing how the binder has interpreted his instructions throughout. On approval of these advance copies, binding of the bulk is proceeded with.

The dummy is also used for fitting the jacket, which is made to measure. Jacket designs may be divided into two main classes, those done by a typographer using type and those done by an artist with or without type. There is no distinct dividing line, and the two classes merge and overlap. If the typographer feels that an artist's jacket is preferable he must choose an artist capable of producing the effect he wants and inform him how many colours he can afford to use, and what process he means to apply. On either flap there may be details of other publications, and there will almost certainly be a blurb. Custom has made the front flap the position for the blurb, though occasionally it is to be found on the back board, or running over from the front flap either on to the back flap or the back board. Advertisements must be laid out in a suitable style and the blurb arranged so that it will look attractive and readable.

Finally, and it will have been done before this, the question of paper for the text must be settled. There are hundreds of different kinds of paper, varying from mill to mill and according to weight—an antique paper of 90 gsm looks and feels very different from a 140 gsm paper of the same kind. And kinds are complicated by colours: dazzling white, dead white, and off-white; blue-white, green-white, toned, and deep toned. All these can be obtained in standard papers from one mill or another, though they do not necessarily go by these names; and in addition the typographer can have any kind or colour of paper specially made for him if his orders are large enough to warrant it.

The various details of production do not necessarily follow the order I have outlined here. No continuous period is spent in the design and production of any one book, and cannot be, because of the time over which it is spread. Other books are in hand simultaneously, in diverse stages, and one is attended to in the intervals between the others or as publication dates dictate. A score or more of books may easily be in progress together, and if the typographer is fortunate enough to possess a good memory his work will be made easier; but the details of book production are apt to be so numerous that it is not a simple matter to keep abreast of them without some competent system of filing and reference.

No easy or joyous part of his work lies in dealing with authors, who can prove the most incompetent and exasperating of persons. Some are business-like and know what they are doing, and some are very much the reverse. It is an extraordinary thing that many of those people whom one would expect to know their own minds—planning authorities, architects, and soldiers, for example—are exactly those who present manuscripts incomplete and illogical, and illustrations that do not fit and cannot be made to, and are generally irritating, exasperating, and exhausting in their correspondence. On the other hand, farmers and doctors appear to fall into authorship with very little trouble and with their minds made up.

A curse is the author who swamps his unfortunate publisher in repeated second thoughts, sending in perhaps half a dozen distinct prefaces each intended to supersede its predecessor; or additional copy with uncertain indication where it should go in the text of the book. Every author is anxious that his book should be published soon and most of them are anxious to know the publication date; that is understandable. But the man is a pest who writes daily to his publisher to urge him to press on with the work, because, he may say, topical affairs make it absolutely essential that the book should come out at once; these things are always 'absolutely essential'; indeed, if the book doesn't come out to-morrow then it may as well never come out at all, because it will be too late and will then inevitably be a flop!

In this welter of humour, exasperation, detail, and mundane labour the typographer must see that printer, author, blockmaker, bookbinder, and anyone else concerned all work in concert, each delivering his quota in time to allow printed and bound copies to be ready for the sales manager when he wants them.

Receiving a worn and sometimes almost indecipherable manuscript, the typographer at length puts into the sales manager's hands a book sparkling with newness, attractive in appearance and to handle, and inviting to the eye. It is a first edition. It may be the book that will make its author famous; or the first effort of a new genius; or it may be forgotten shortly and never be heard of again. The typographer, even if he is a judge of literature, cannot tell, because he has neither the time nor the opportunity to read everything that passes through his hands, though he may gather some idea of the substance of a book by glancing through it. Certainly he should know something of it before he begins to work on it; and if there is something special about the book or it is on a subject that interests him, he may spend some time browsing through the pages, finding as he does so that a pattern grows in his mind ready for his pencil and the printer. If it doesn't, he may have to fall back on that debatable quality of guesswork that some men like to call instinct.

Throughout this account the typographer has been described as though he controlled all phases of production; some typographers do, but many do not. Increasingly today the typographer is a servant of the production manager. The latter controls all the clerical and progress side of the operation, including selection of printers, binders, etc., and decides the processes to be used; corresponds with artists and decides on costs and fees; and is responsible to the publisher for delivery dates and quality. He employs a typographer or typographers, either on his staff or as free-lances, and the typographer's contacts are with him or his department and not with the printer and other trades involved in printing, binding, etc. The typographer is left free to concentrate on design. This is simply specialization and has its advantages as well as its disadvantages.

XV

TEXT TYPES OF TO-DAY

No foundry type is comprised within the subject of this chapter, for text sizes of foundry types are no longer of importance to the book printer. The printer has emancipated himself from the founder, and has delivered himself into the hands of the manufacturers of composing machines, each of whom is the source of supply of matrices for his particular machine. To-day the text of a book must be set by machine if the cost of the setting is to be a commercial proposition; hand-setting cannot compete on anything like equal terms. So if a printer wishes to use a particular type face, he must possess the composing machine and the appropriate accessories that provide it, or persuade another printer or a typesetter who has the equipment to set it for him.

It is no real hardship, however, if the printer finds himself confined within the covers of the type list of the manufacturers of his composing machine. All of them contain faces of good quality, and there is ample variety; for the matter of that, it is altogether too ample. The manufacturers of composing machines sometimes seem to be setting out to satisfy every possible sort of taste. Every one of their lists contains monstrosities that should never have been brought into the open in this self-styled enlightened twentieth century. But they do also contain fine types, both new and old.

The accent lies chiefly upon the word 'old'. The book faces of to-day are nearly all derived from the past; though they may suffer some adaptation to suit the exigencies of modern machines, it is no sea-change, and the faces remain the same as or closely related to those our ancestors used in a more laborious time. Is it that we have lost the faculty of type design, that we should have to depend so much upon the dead? I do not think so. Though in the past many types were cut and used, it does not require many fingers to count the number of great types in the history of printing; few types have proved of sufficient value to survive the wrack of time, and those that have survived did so in a state of suspended animation, waiting, like the Sleeping Beauty, for the percipient Prince to awaken them. We cannot expect, then, a plethora of superlative new type faces when former centuries have produced only a handful between them. We may, if we wish, advance our own period as the peer of other ages, believing that this face or that is as good as its predecessors, that Shaw is the equal of Shakespeare, or John or Moore of Holbein or Michelangelo. While we live we are entitled to our opinion, but even as we breathe time is at work upon our candidate, and we may find before we die that it or he has preceded us to the grave.

It has been argued that because we depend on the past for our type faces our typography must be anachronistic: modern books should be set in types of contemporary design, and if they do not exist, and few do, then one must encourage budding genius to produce them. No doubt typography would benefit if we were less satisfied with what is available and if the letter designer had more scope and outlet for his work than he has at present. Nevertheless, the suggestion that all fine types that are also old types should be relegated to museums seems to me just as sensible as to contend that we should make no use of Shakespeare's plays or Wagner's music because their authors are dead and done with. We are never like to be so rich that we can bury our inheritance with those who bequeathed it. It is not the inheritance that matters, but the use we make of it, and even here pastiche and imitation have their occasions of value; after all is said, modern man must make use of the past in his own way for the benefit of the future, and by this let him be judged.

There is a vast variety of book faces available to the printer to-day, not only the spoil of dead centuries, but the undiscriminated issue of this century also. Too many printers show an extraordinary aptitude, if left to themselves, for choosing the worst of them. The majority are of little value and might without any sense of loss be annihilated in the melting-pot. And in fact in recent years composing-machine companies, although they have issued new faces, have drastically pruned their lists. Of those types that remain some are inconvenient for the publisher because very few printers possess the apparatus for setting them. Only a score or so of good faces are readily available and a printer who has a complete range of half a dozen of them is distinctly well equipped. The range of faces of which I am going to show specimens is therefore not to be brought up against a printer as an indication of what he ought to possess; it is a synthesis compiled from the type lists of composing-machine manufacturers.

To the lay reader it may seem that I place too much emphasis on the varieties of type design. The difference between one type face and another is not apparent to someone who has not stopped to consider it before, and he may indeed be surprised to learn that any difference exists—he has been 'type blind'; if he does see that there is a difference, it is unlikely that he will be able to say exactly where the difference lies, and may consider it of no real importance. And yet the difference is as plain as day to the printer and typographer, who can tell at a glance, without pausing to consider the peculiarities of individual letters, but merely by the effect in the mass, what a particular type is. For the ordinary man type is apt to be so many letters that may be combined to form words, and the letters of any type are very much like those of another. Why, then, all this fuss? In this belief the ordinary man is the equivalent of Lewis Carroll's Humpty-Dumpty: ' "That's just what I complain of," said Humpty-Dumpty. "Your face is the same as everybody has—the two eyes, so—" (marking their places in the air with his thumb) "nose in the middle, mouth under. It's always the same. Now if you had two eyes on the same side of the nose, for instance—or the mouth at the top—that would be *some* help." ' Type faces are, like human faces, the same in essentials, but vastly different in detail; and the difference in detail is an expression of that indefinable quality called character. They may be ugly or beautiful, commonplace or memorable; and may possess attributes that make them typical of particular countries (though types nearly always become cosmopolitan, and cosmopolitanism blurs nationality). Many are ordinary types, whose characters are characterless; others have characters that mark them out as individuals; some are 'characters', with all the eccentricity the quotation marks suggest. To appreciate the qualities of type it is necessary to be sensitive to atmosphere; and atmosphere is something of which, if you are insensitive or untrained, you become aware only by accident.

It has been suggested more than once that books of a particular period, or written about a period, should be set in contemporary types. It is a charming idea, and sometimes it can be put into practice with success, but it imposes too many limitations on the typographer. Logically, according to this argument, no type other than one designed in this century should be used for books written to-day, and if we were to accept that theory we should raise unnecessary difficulties for ourselves. Nor, if a period effect is wanted, is the best way always to use a type of the period: much more recent faces might conceivably be of more assistance.

None the less, I have thought it desirable to arrange the types of the specimen list that follows in a kind of chronological order, because to do so helps to show the development of type design and reinforces chapter 13. I say a 'kind of chronological order', because in fact it is a chronology that has been subjected to artificial resuscitation. Some of the types I show represent older types that should occupy that position in the list, but the representative is not in every case an exact copy of its master; the master is not there because it no longer exists as type. Thus I have ignored dates of redesigning or revival, which would make Poliphilus and Centaur subsequent to Bodoni and Walbaum, which is chronologically absurd. Centaur is first in the list because it is claimed to be a recutting of Jenson's fifteenth-century roman.

The list shows the progression from Jenson to Bodoni very well, and shows what did happen in typographical history; but only up to the end of the eighteenth century. The wilderness of the nineteenth century is represented by a single modern face. Afterwards there was a revival of old faces, and this can only be represented by turning at the end of the list and coming back to the beginning again, remembering that each type passed on the return journey is gathered up and remains currently in use.

After Scotch Roman comes a sequence of twentieth-century typefaces, all of which owe their inspiration more or less to past centuries, but which possess qualities that identify them rather with our century than with any previous one. These represent the contribution of our time to the history and development of types for continuous reading. The achievement is notable.

Bold and semi-bold companion faces designed to go with the romans are a modern development, that is since the nineteenth century.

New text types continue to be designed and older ones to be introduced and there is nothing to suggest that these innovations will cease. Many of these new types are interesting and excellent in their own right, as for example Monotype Berling and Melior, Monophoto Albertina, and Linotype Telegraph-Modern. But some printers argue that we have enough, that new type faces serve only to titillate the jaded palates of typographers without notable benefit to the reading public. It is true that we have at our command today a wider range of excellent type faces than at any time in the history of books, it is true that the public has little understanding or perception of the differences or advantages of one type face compared with another: but to cease to make and to use new designs would be to stagnate.

A glance through the lists of the manufacturers of the three principal composing machines shows a remarkable unanimity in the nomenclature of revived type faces. The Monotype, Linotype, and Intertype companies each provide Baskerville, Caslon, Garamond, Bodoni, Plantin, etc. This nomenclature is misleading; the same name does not always indicate exactly the same face. Linotype Baskerville is very different from

Monotype Baskerville, and Intertype Baskerville is different again; but all three are descendants of Baskerville's type, and their common parentage is plainly seen. With varying success, each of the children tries to be exactly like its father, and the only way to distinguish them is to give them Christian names, and to call them Monotype Baskerville, Linotype Baskerville, or Intertype Baskerville, and so forth. It is cumbersome, and the more one has to do with them, the farther one is from 'Tom, Dick, or Harry' or other terms of familiarity.

The confusion is confounded by the ranges of type faces produced for the many photo-composition machines on the market. No composing machine is of much use if it does not offer a satisfactory range of type faces. Each manufacturer has therefore made up a range of faces copied or derived from those already existing in metal type of one kind or another. Monotype, Linotype, and Intertype already had their extensive catalogues on which to draw. Other photo-composition manufacturers have had to come to an arrangement with hot-metal composing-machine manufacturers or with typefounders. The same type names are therefore to be found in photo-composition as in metal types. A few, a very few new types have been specifically designed for photo-composition, principally with the object of producing a letter that will withstand all the required sizes of reproduction from a single size of photo-matrix.

It is necessary to point out that type-faces produced by the English and American Linotype companies are not interchangeable between the two countries. Differences in the mould structure and the manufacture of the matrices preclude the running of matrices of one country in machines of the other. As, however, publishers in America and in Britain sell printed sheets and bound books to each other, American Linotype faces appear in Britain and British ones in the United States.

Type faces that have been discontinued by the manufacturers do not disappear at once, but may continue in use for many years, until the matrices wear out.

Note on the specimens of text types shown on the following pages. Large initials are shown where they are available in the same series or in a series designed for use with the text type. Where no sufficiently large size exists the text begins with a text capital. The main headings are examples of larger sizes of the type named; where no such type exists Baskerville has been used. Bold faces do not exist for all types, nor, where bold faces do exist, do all of them have italics. This explains apparent inconsistencies in the range for each specimen. It should not be understood that the alphabets shown represent all the characters available in the founts concerned, nor the existence or absence of special sorts.

CENTAUR AND ARRIGHI

Monotype

ABCDEFGHIJKLMNOPQRSTUVWXYZÆŒ

ABCDEFGHIJKLMNOPQRSTUVWXYZÆŒ

12345) abcdefghijklmnopqrstuvwxyzæœ (67890

&fiflffffiffl?!,.:;£

ABCDEFGHIJKLMNOPQRSTUVWXYZÆŒ

12345] *abcdefghijklmnopqrstuvwxyzæœ* *[67890*

&fiflffffiffl?!,.:;£

DESIGNED by Bruce Rogers, the American typographer, Centaur is a redrawing of Jenson's famous roman of 1470, but it has, unfortunately, turned out weaker than the original, having lost much of the quality and sturdy common sense of Jenson. It is lighter and more feminine, and is inclined to be self-conscious where Jenson was self-sufficient. Nevertheless, Centaur is an excellent type, and well fitted for certain kinds of bookwork. It should be set with close and even spacing and preferably in sizes larger than 12 point, if it is to show at its best. It does show at its best in a large lectern Bible designed by Rogers for the Oxford University Press. Centaur 14 point set solid

Italic types did not exist in 1470 and some other source had to be found for a companion letter. Frederic Warde resorted for it to a script developed by the sixteenth-century calligrapher Ludovico degli Arrighi, and he made from it an italic type that consorts excellently with Centaur. Arrighi

BEMBO

Monotype

ABCDEFGHIJKLMNOPQRRSTUVWXYZÆŒ

ABCDEFGHIJKLMNOPQRSTUVWXYZÆŒ

12345) abcdefghijklmnopqrstuvwxyzæœ (67890

&fiflffffiffl?!,.:;£

ABCDEFGHIJKLMNOPQRSTUVWXYZÆŒ

12345] abcdefghijklmnopqrstuvwxyzæœ [67890

&fiflffffiffl?!,.:;£

ABCDEFGHIJKLMNOPQRSTUVWXYZÆŒ

12345) abcdefghijklmnopqrstuvwxyzæœ (67890

&fiflffffiffl?!,.:;£

Bembo 13 point set solid

THE original of this type appeared a few years before Poliphilus, but it seems to our eyes to be in a style nearer to our own time. It is claimed that Poliphilus was based on Bembo and that both were designed by Francesco Griffi for Aldus. This may be so, but it seems to me that Poliphilus is nearer in spirit to Jenson and that Bembo is akin to the fine French types that came later. It was first used in a book called *De Aetna* written by the poet and scholar, Pietro Bembo. The first type to which the term 'old face' may properly be applied, it shows, compared with Centaur and Poliphilus, greater variation of stroke and a different kind of serif formation. In general the effect is rounder and sharper.

Bembo italic

The italic is another version of the chancery types, but rather more orderly and finished than Arrighi and Blado. An alternative italic, Narrow Bembo, is very beautiful.

Bembo Bold

Bembo Bold may be the roman thickened, but it takes on thereby quite a different character. Rather heavy to work with the roman, it gives considerable punch to sub-heads and titles.

POLIPHILUS AND BLADO

Monotype

ABCDEFGHIJKLMNOPQRRSTUVWXYYZÆŒ

ABCDEFGHIJKLMNOPQRSTUVWXYZÆŒ

12345) abcdefghijklmnopqrstuvwxyzæœ (67890

&fiflffffiffl?!,.:;£

ABCDEFGHIJKLMNOPQRSTUVWXYZÆŒ

12345] *abcdefghijklmnopqrstuvwxyzæœ* *[67890*

&fiflffffiffl?!,.:;£

THIS is a copy, that is, a close facsimile, of a type cut for Aldus Manutius by Francesco Griffi of Bologna, which was first used in a fine edition of the *Hypnerotomachia Poliphili* published in 1499. The good quality of the presswork of the *Hypnerotomachia*, which allowed the facsimile to be made, is particularly fortunate, because Poliphilus depends for much of its charm on its eccentricities of design. Notice, for example, the M. Poliphilus 12 point leaded 1 point

An italic was provided for Poliphilus by recutting that used by Antonio Blado, printer to the Holy See from 1549 to 1567. It is probable that this letter was designed by Arrighi, to whom Frederic Warde went for an italic for Centaur.

The originals of Arrighi and Blado were not intended as assistants to roman, but as book faces in their own right, and they possess individuality and strength instead of the weakness and lack of character that later convention imposed on italic letters. Blado italic

GRANJON

Linotype

ABCDEFGHIJKLMNOPQRSTUVWXYZÆŒ

ABCDEFGHIJKLMNOPQRSTUVWXYZÆŒ

12345) abcdefghijklmnopqrstuvwxyzæœ (67890

ctstff,f.f-ff ff,ff.ff-fafefofrfsftfufyffaffeffoffrffsffy

fiffflffiffl&£?!,.:;

ABCDEFGHIJKLMNOPQRSTUVWXYZÆŒ

ABCDEGJMNPRTY

12345) abcdefghijklmnopqrstuvwxyzææ (67890

ctstff,f.f-ff ff,ff.ff-fafefofrfsftfufyffaffeffoffrffsffy

fiffflffiffl&£?!,.:;

Granjon 12pt leaded 2 point

GRANJON was produced in 1924 by George W. Jones for the Linotype. This face has been described as 'a true Garamond design', and it is probably the nearest we have to the elusive letter of that acknowledged master. It is a magnificent letter, clear, clean, and dignified, with an enviable timeless quality. Granjon has proved popular. At its best in sizes over 12-point, like most fine types, Granjon should be printed on a rougher paper than this, as should all old faces.

Granjon italic

The italic is a mere auxiliary, like all later italics, with little of the richness of the roman. It does for the occasional word or line, but it will not serve well for whole paragraphs.

GARAMOND

Monotype

ABCDEFGHIJKLMNOPQRSTUVWXYZÆŒ

ABCDEFGHIJKLMNOPQRSTUVWXYZÆŒ

12345) abcdefghijklmnopqrstuvwxyzæœ (67890

&fiflffffiffl?!,.:;£

ABCDEFGHIJKLMNOPQRSTUVWXYZÆŒ

A B C D E F G H J M P T V

12345] abcdefghijklmnopqrstuvwxyzææ [67890

&fiflffffiffl?!,.:;£

ABCDEFGHIJKLMNOPQRSTUVWXYZÆŒ

12345) abcdefghijklmnopqrstuvwxyzæœ (67890

&fiflffffiffl?!,.:;£

FOR long this type was thought to have been designed by Claude Garamond at Paris in the sixteenth century; but in fact it was cut by Jean Jannon a century later. None the less, it may be placed here because the mistake is not as egregious as it might appear; Jannon's letter is certainly derived from Garamond's, though it is inferior to it. Jannon Garamond is a type of immense popularity, and nearly every printer has one version or another of it. Garamond 12 point leaded 1 point

The italic is unusual in its independent variation of angle and the free sweep of the kerned letters. The capitals show two or three distinct slopes and will not combine satisfactorily; but the conjunction of the erratic capitals with the erratic lower-case is charming. However, a regularised italic has also been cut. Garamond italic

Garamond Bold is, like most of the earlier companion bold faces, on the heavy side, *contrasting strongly* with the wayward delicacy of the roman. The larger sizes make good display faces. Garamond Bold

SABON

Linotype, Monotype, and Stempel

ABCDEFGHIJKLMNOPQRSTUVWXYZÆŒ

ABCDEFGHIJKLMNOPQRSTUVWXYZÆŒ

12345) abcdefghijklmnopqrstuvwxyzæœ (67890

&fiflffffiffl?!,.:;£

ABCDEFGHIJKLMNOPQRSTUVWXYZÆŒ

12345] abcdefghijklmnopqrstuvwxyzæœ [67890

&fiflffffiffl?!,.:;£

ABCDEFGHIJKLMNOPQRSTUVWXYZÆŒ

12345) abcdefghijklmnopqrstuvwxyzæœ (67890

&fiflffffiffl?!,.:;£

Sabon 12 Didot on 13 point

Sabon is unique among type faces in having been conceived, or rather redesigned, as a type to be cast for hand-setting by a type foundry as well as for composition on Monotype and Linotype machines. The type was designed and cut for the three methods at the request of a group of German master-printers. The exigencies of the self-contained Linotype matrix may be perceived in the lower-case roman f and in the italic *f* and *j*, which are carried through into the Monotype and founders' versions, but in every respect the face is a laudable success as a type to be read and to be admired. The designer was Jan Tschichold. Sabon is derived from a type in the foundry of a sixteenth-century Frankfurt typefounder called Jacques Sabon. The relation to Garamond is clear.

Sabon italic

The italic is a redrawing of a fount cut by Robert Granjon.

Sabon Semi-bold

The semi-bold has enough weight to make its presence felt but is not too heavy to be used on its own in a paragraph or two.

VAN DIJCK

Monotype

ABCDEFGHIJKLMNOPQRSTUVWXYZÆŒ

ABCDEFGHIJKLMNOPQRSTUVWXYZÆŒ

12345) abcdefghijklmnopqrstuvwxyzæœ (67890

&fiflfffffiffl?!,.:;£

ABCDEFGHIJKLMNOPQRSTUVWXYZÆŒ

12345] abcdefghijklmnopqrstuvwxyzæœ [67890

&fiflfffffiffl?!,.:;£

Christoffel van Dijck was regarded by his contemporaries as a type designer of excellence. He was a goldsmith who began to cut letters and to found types some time after 1643, supplying various Dutch printers and notably the Elzevirs. Yet, despite the reputed excellence of his work, no type specimen issued by him has survived and there is no type that can be attributed to him with certainty. Enschedé, the famous Dutch founders, apparently received much of his material; in 1810, when what van Dijck represented was out of fashion, they melted it down. Van Dijck's influence was widespread, and among his imitators was William Caslon. The type to which Monotype has given the name Van Dijck comes, for the roman, from a volume of Ovid's *Metamorphoses* published in Amsterdam in 1671, which may reasonably be said to be Van Dijck's, and for the italic from punches still in the possession of Enschedé. The roman is a handsome old face, rather small on the body, and therefore at its best in sizes from 12 point up.

Van Dijck 12 point leaded 1 point

The italic has some of the irregularity and charm of italics derived from Garamond through Jannon, but it is not for reading in the mass.

Van Dijck italic

PLANTIN

Harris-Intertype

ABCDEFGHIJKLMNOPQRSTUVWXYZÆŒ

ABCDEFGHIJKLMNOPQRSTUVWXYZÆŒ&

12345) abcdefghijklmnopqrstuvwxyzæœ (67890

&fiflffffiffl?!,.:;£

ABCDEFGHIJKLMNOPQRSTUVWXYZÆŒ

12345] abcdefghijklmnopqrstuvwxyzæœ [67890

&fiflffffiffl?!,.:;£

ABCDEFGHIJKLMNOPQRSTUVWXYZÆŒ

12345) abcdefghijklmnopqrstuvwxyzæœ (67890

&fiflffffiffl?!,.:;£

Plantin 11 point leaded 2 points

Plantin, introduced by Monotype in 1913, has become a popular face on line-casting machines also. The original of the type was one associated with Plantin's printing-house in Antwerp late in the sixteenth century. Its qualities are not very obvious at first sight, and indeed the heaviness of the letter is initially deterrent; but it proved a most useful type for printing on art paper and smooth super-calendered papers, and from that it came to be regarded as a kind of bread-and-butter type suitable for anything. Because of its weight it needs leading to make it pleasant to read, and the large x-height stands up very well to generous leading.

Plantin italic

The italic shows the merits and faults of the roman in weakened form.

Plantin Bold

Intertype Plantin is duplexed with Plantin Bold, in which the weight is added to the insides of the letters, and gives a heavy, condensed appearance. The Linotype version is similar, the Monotype wider and more open.

PLANTIN LIGHT

Monotype

ABCDEFGHIJKLMNOPQRSTUVWXYZÆŒ

ABCDEFGHIJKLMNOPQRSTUVWXYZÆŒ

12345) abcdefghijklmnopqrstuvwxyzæœ (67890

&fiflffffiffl?!,.:;£

ABCDEFGHIJKLMNOPQRSTUVWXYZÆŒ

12345] *abcdefghijklmnopqrstuvwxyzæœ* [*67890*

&fiflffffiffl?!,.:;

ABCDEFGHIJKLMNOPQRSTUVWXYZÆŒ

12345) abcdefghijklmnopqrstuvwxyzæœ (67890

&fiflffffiffl?!,.:;£

The Harris-Intertype Plantin on the previous page resembles Monotype Plantin series 110. Monotype Plantin Light series 113 is a lightened version with more elegance than 110 and, on anything other than art papers and such smooth surfaces, it offers greater legibility and comfort to the eye. In all respects other than weight Plantin Light resembles its bolder parent. A few sizes of Plantin Light appeared many years ago, but the whole series of sizes is now available.

Plantin Light 11 point leaded 2 points

The italic is close-fitting and regular and rather dominated by its heavier strokes, but it makes a good hand-maiden to the roman.

Plantin Light italic

Plantin Semi-bold is *decidedly lighter and crisper* than the heavier bold made to work with the older Plantin; it goes well with both weights of Plantin roman.

Plantin Semi-bold

CASLON OLD FACE

Monotype

ABCDEFGHIJKLMNOPQRSTUVWXYZÆŒ

ABCDEFGHIJKLMNOPQRSTUVWXYZÆŒ

12345) abcdefghijklmnopqrstuvwxyzæœ (67890

&fiflfffffiffl?!,.:;£

ABCDEFGHIJKLMNOPQRSTUVWXYZÆŒ

A B C D E G K M N P R T V Y

12345] *abcdefghijklmnopqrstuvwxyzæœ* *[67890*

&fiflfffffiffl?!,.:;£

Caslon 12 point leaded 1 point

THIS type was one of the first-fruits of the foundry set up by William Caslon at the beginning of the eighteenth century. It is closely related to the Dutch types contemporary with it, but exhibits differences that English printers found much to their liking, and it at once achieved popularity in this country, so much so that the type has been claimed to be typically English, which it certainly is not. It became *the* old face ; and even to-day 'old face' is as likely to mean Caslon as any other type on which that label may be fastened. Since its revival in the middle of the nineteenth century Caslon has increased in popularity everywhere, and few printers are without it.

Caslon italic

Caslon italic is a meet helpmate for the roman, but it is nothing more. By the eighteenth century the degradation of italic was complete and no subsequent italic until recent years possesses value as a text type.

BASKERVILLE

Monotype

ABCDEFGHIJKLMNOPQRSTUVWXYZÆŒ

ABCDEFGHIJKLMNOPQRSTUVWXYZÆŒ

12345) abcdefghijklmnopqrstuvwxyzæœ (67890

&fiflfffiffl?!,.:;£

ABCDEFGHIJKLMNOPQRSTUVWXYZÆŒ

12345] abcdefghijklmnopqrstuvwxyzæœ [67890

&fiflfffiffl?!,.:;£

ABCDEFGHIJKLMNOPQRSTUVWXYZÆŒ

12345) abcdefghijklmnopqrstuvwxyzæœ (67890

&fiflfffiffl?!,.:;£

CASLON appears to have fallen into typefounding almost by accident, but Baskerville set out consciously to make his mark upon the craft of printing, to reshape it nearer to his own conception of what it should be. His type is sharper, more graceful, more disciplined than its predecessors, and was intended by Baskerville to be used without the aid of ornament or decoration. In his hands it produced very fine results, and is still capable of doing so when printed, as it should be, on paper with a smooth surface. It is a popular type, to be found in most printing houses, and is more often used without discrimination than otherwise, for any and every kind of purpose on any and every kind of paper.

Baskerville 12 point leaded 1 point

The vagrancies and the eccentricities of earlier italics are avoided in Baskerville italic, which follows the roman in the matter of discipline. It is, perhaps, a little cold, but it has dignity.

Baskerville italic

Monotype Baskerville Bold is a thunderous face more appropriate to clamorous publicity than to bookwork of the general kind. The Intertype and Linotype versions are crisper and less weighty.

Baskerville Bold

BASKERVILLE

Linotype

ABCDEFGHIJKLMNOPQRSTUVWXYZÆŒ

ABCDEFGHIJKLMNOPQRSTUVWXYZÆŒ

12345) abcdefghijklmnopqrstuvwxyzæœ (67890

&fiflffffiffl?!,.:;£

ABCDEFGHIJKLMNOPQRSTUVWXYZÆŒ

12345] *abcdefghijklmnopqrstuvwxyzæœ* *[67890*

&fiflffffiffl?!,.:;£

Baskerville 12 point leaded 1 point

Comparison of Monotype and Linotype versions of Baskerville's types shows how much two types of the same name and descent may differ; but there is good warrant for each version in the work of the eighteenth-century printer. Linotype Baskerville has more contrast in the thicks and thins, more sharpness in the serifs, and the capitals are lower in height than the ascenders. It is based on types cast from Baskerville's own matrices, which after his death were bought by Beaumarchais for a projected fine edition of the works of Voltaire. The matrices are now in the possession of the Cambridge University Press. Linotype Baskerville appeared in 1931.

Baskerville italic

The italic is a little loose fitting, its width, as in other line-cast type-faces, being governed by the roman.

FOURNIER

Monotype

ABCDEFGHIJKLMNOPQRSTUVWXYZÆŒ

ABCDEFGHIJKLMNOPQRSTUVWXYZÆŒ

12345) abcdefghijklmnopqrstuvwxyzæœ (67890

&fiflffffiffl?!,.:;£

ABCDEFGHIJKLMNOPQRSTUVWXYZÆŒ

12345] abcdefghijklmnopqrstuvwxyzæœ [67890

&fiflffffiffl?!,.:;£

PIERRE SIMON FOURNIER, or Fournier le Jeune, was a notable French typefounder in the eighteenth century. Incredibly industrious, he cut more than eighty faces. In this present type he depended for inspiration on the Romain du Roi made for the Imprimerie Royale at the beginning of the century. He condensed the design a little, made the capitals the same height as the ascenders, and gave less variation to the stroke, but adopted the vertical stress of his original. In short, Fournier's type, following the Romain du Roi, is transitional, pointing the way to the moderns. The Monotype version was issued in 1925. It proved moderately popular and many books have been printed in it since. Yet according to Stanley Morison the cutting of Fournier was a mistake made in his absence; he had intended that the type now called Barbou should have been cut in its stead.

Fournier 12 point leaded 1 point

The italic is even and regular, and shows the curiosity of romanized serifs on certain letters, e.g. the m, n, and p, instead of the usual commencing loop.

Fournier italic

BARBOU

Monotype

ABCDEFGHIJKLMNOPQRSTUVWXYZÆŒ

ABCDEFGHIJKLMNOPQRSTUVWXYZÆŒ

12345) abcdefghijklmnopqrstuvwxyzæœ (67890

&fiflfffffiffl?!,.:;£

ABCDEFGHIJKLMNOPQRSTUVWXYZÆŒ

12345] *abcdefghijklmnopqrstuvwxyzæœ* [*67890*

&fiflffffiffl?!,.:;

Barbou 12 point leaded 1 point

Barbou has many similarities to Monotype Fournier, and in fact both types are derived from types issued by the mid-eighteenth-century typefounder and publisher Pierre Simon Fournier, who died in 1768. Books set in the original of Barbou were printed for Fournier by Joseph Gérard Barbou, member of a notable French printing family. Barbou is a better letter than Monotype Fournier, a little clearer, less blunted, and it can serve well on a wide range of paper surfaces. Points that help to distinguish Barbou from Fournier are the crossed w and the slightly splayed legs of the M. Barbou is a transitional letter.

Barbou italic

The revival of Barbou began with the issue of the 12 point size by the Corporation in 1959.

FONTANA

Monotype

ABCDEFGHIJKLMNOPQRSTUVWXYZÆŒ

ABCDEFGHIJKLMNOPQRSTUVWXYZÆŒ

12345) abcdefghijklmnopqrstuvwxyzæœ (67890

&fiflffffiffl?!,.:;£

ABCDEFGHIJKLMNOPQRSTUVWXYZÆŒ

12345] *abcdefghijklmnopqrstuvwxyzæœ* *[67890*

&fiflffffiffl?!,.:;£

Fontana was designed in 1935 by Dr. Giovanni Mardersteig for the exclusive use of Collins' Clear Type Press in Glasgow and for twenty-five years it was to be seen only in the books of one publisher, Collins. The name Fontana is derived from Collins' trade-mark, a fountain. The type was released for general use in 1961 but has not been much taken up by other publishers. It is a good, clear, crisp letter derived faithfully from a type cut by Alexander Wilson at his Glasgow Letter Foundry about 1760. Wilson followed in the steps of Baskerville, but made his letters rather wider and more open, producing a transitional face with the sharpness of a modern and the comfort of an old face. The thins grow gradually into thicks and there is a slight obliqueness in the stroke of the O. *Dr. Mardersteig's principal alteration has been the slight lowering of height of the capitals.*

Fontana 12 point leaded 1 point

Fontana italic

The italic is regular and legible, but the curly T, w, and v catch the eye.

Linotype Georgian is also based on the same type cut by Wilson.

BELL

Monotype

ABCDEFGHIJKLMNOPQRSTUVWXYZÆŒ

ABCDEFGHIJKLMNOPQRSTUVWXYZÆŒ

12345) abcdefghijklmnopqrstuvwxyzæœ (67890

&fiflffffiffl?!,.:;£

ABCDEFGHIJKLMNOPQRSTUVWXYZÆŒ

ACJKNQRSTV

12345] abcdefghijklmnopqrstuvwxyzæœ [67890

&fiflffffiffl?!,.:;£

Bell 11 point leaded 2 point

BASKERVILLE foreshadowed Bodoni, but between these two there are a number of types that are clearly transitional in design, though in fact some of them appeared after the transition was complete. Bell is a transitional face that appeared at its proper time. It was brought out in 1788 by John Bell, and was cut for him by Richard Austin. In Bell's type the revolution initiated by Baskerville may be seen advancing: the fine lines are finer still and the contrast is enhanced; the serifs are more lightly bracketed. Like a great many compromises, it has achieved success, and its appearance is one of brilliance and power, eminently readable.

Its revival is due to Bruce Rogers. Appreciating the quality of an old fount of type, he rescued it from the melting pot and printed some books in it without knowing its origin. Its history *was discovered shortly afterwards by Stanley Morison, who found the original punches still in the possession of Stephenson, Blake, the English firm of letter founders, by arrangement with whom the type was cut for machine composition on the Monotype.*

Bell italic

WALBAUM

Monotype

ABCDEFGHIJKLMNOPQRSTUVWXYZÆŒ

ABCDEFGHIJKLMNOPQRSTUVWXYZÆŒ

12345) abcdefghijklmnopqrstuvwxyzæœ (67890

&fiflffffiffl?!,.:;£

ABCDEFGHIJKLMNOPQRSTUVWXYZÆŒ

12345] *abcdefghijklmnopqrstuvwxyzæœ* *[67890*

&fiflffffiffl?!,.:;

ABCDEFGHIJKLMNOPQRSTUVWXYZÆŒ

12345) abcdefghijklmnopqrstuvwxyzæœ (67890

&fiflffffiffl?!,.:;£

THIS is a German transitional type that appeared in 1810, a little late in the day. It was revived first in England by the Curwen Press, and then by the Monotype Corporation. It is an exceptionally wide letter, and this contributes to its excellent legibility. So far it has been preserved from too common use, but it is capable of being used for almost any kind of book without incongruity, and that is a property that may increase its popularity and may one day make us tired of it. But for the present Walbaum has all the adaptability of the bread and butter type, with the added charm of novelty.

Walbaum 12 point leaded 1 point

Although placed in the transitional class, it is rather out of the main stream of design, as of time. The variation of stroke is not carried so far, and the width of the letter is counter to every influence proceeding from Baskerville.

Walbaum italic

Walbaum Medium is unusual among bolds in its faithful reflection of the roman while yet achieving a strong individuality. Its weight in relation to the roman is excellent.

Walbaum Medium

BODONI

Monotype (Bodoni No. 3)

ABCDEFGHIJKLMNOPQRSTUVWXYZÆŒ

ABCDEFGHIJKLMNOPQRSTUVWXYZÆŒ

12345) abcdefghijklmnopqrstuvwxyzæœ (67890

&fiflfffiffl?!,.:;£

ABCDEFGHIJKLMNOPQRSTUVWXYZÆŒ

12345] *abcdefghijklmnopqrstuvwxyzœæ* [*67890*

&fiflfffiffl?!,.:;£

ABCDEFGHIJKLMNOPQRSTUVWXYZÆŒ

12345) abcdefghijklmnopqrstuvwxyzæœ (67890

&fiflfffiffl?!,.:;£

Bodoni 12 point leaded 1 point

GIAMBATTISTA BODONI watched with interest the work of his English contemporary, Baskerville, who appeared to be proceeding the way Bodoni himself wished to go. But Bodoni went further, to extremes, and all at a bound, for though transitional types exist, they were not necessarily part of Bodoni's evolution. Bodoni's type reflects the brilliance, the contrast between white light and black shadow, of the Italian day. It is wonderful in appearance, but, one is apt to suspect, a little too wonderful. The Italian has brought us definitely into the age of reason, and not only that, he has landed us on the edge of the machine *age. For there is something rather machine-made about Bodoni; it is inhuman and cold and perfect. To the eye it is ultimately unsympathetic and exhausting.*

Bodoni italic

Bodoni Bold

Walbaum Medium and Bodoni Bold show how much easier it is to make a companion bold face for a type with modern characteristics than it is for an old face. Bodoni Bold *is a good companion* for Bodoni No. 3 and also an excellent display face.

CALEDONIA

Linotype

ABCDEFGHIJKLMNOPQRSTUVWXYZÆŒ

ABCDEFGHIJKLMNOPQRSTUVWXYZÆŒ

12345) abcdefghijklmnopqrstuvwxyzæœ (67890

&fiflffffiffl?!,.:;£

ABCDEFGHIJKLMNOPQRSTUVWXYZÆŒ

12345] abcdefghijklmnopqrstuvwxyzæœ [67890

&fiflffffiffl?!,.;:£

Caledonia was designed by the American type-designer W. A. Dwiggins and first appeared in 1939. Classed as a modern by the manufacturers, it has in fact considerable old-face qualities and falls stylistically into the transitional bracket. It owes some of its character to William Martin's type (see Bulmer) and something to Scotch Roman—from which comes the name 'Caledonia'. Caledonia avoids the excessive contrast of out-and-out moderns and is all the more readable for that. The ascenders are moderately tall, the descenders rather curtailed; but alternative longer descenders are available and these improve the appearance and help the eye.

Caledonia 11 point leaded 1 point

The italic is irregular and a little heavy, but close-fitting.

Caledonia italic

BULMER

Monotype

ABCDEFGHIJKLMNOPQRSTUVWXYZÆŒ

ABCDEFGHIJKLMNOPQRSTUVWXYZÆŒ

12345) abcdefghijklmnopqrstuvwxyzæœ (67890

&fiflffffiffl?!,.:;£

ABCDEFGHIJKLMNOPQRSTUVWXYZÆŒ

12345] *abcdefghijklmnopqrstuvwxyzæœ* [*67890*

&fiflffffiffl?!,.:;£

Bulmer 12 point leaded 1 point

This type was originally cut by William Martin for the printer William Bulmer, who founded the Shakespeare Printing Office in London in 1790. William Martin was a brother of Robert Martin, John Baskerville's foreman, and William's type derives from Baskerville's through the sharper, narrower letters of Bodoni and the Didots. It is still a transitional face, but it is clear that it leans more in the direction of the moderns than the old faces. It was used by Bulmer for his edition of Shakespeare in 1791 and in our time has been used for such fine editions as the Nonesuch Dickens and the Folio Society Shakespeare. Bulmer needs careful use and it is not happy if set solid.

Bulmer italic

The italic is a logical derivative of the roman, but it dazzles a little.

SCOTCH ROMAN

Monotype

ABCDEFGHIJKLMNOPQRSTUVWXYZÆŒ

ABCDEFGHIJKLMNOPQRSTUVWXYZÆŒ

12345) abcdefghijklmnopqrstuvwxyzæœ (67890

&fiflfffffiffl?!,.:;£

ABCDEFGHIJKLMNOPQRSTUVWXYZÆŒ

12345] *abcdefghijklmnopqrstuvwxyzæœ* [*67890*

&fiflfffffiffl?!,.:;£

IN THE early nineteenth century Scotland occupied an important position in the history of typography in this country, and about that time there was in use there a kind of modern face peculiar to Scotland. Bodoni is an excellent letter, but capable of great degeneration, and in Scotch Roman we see the degeneration commencing. The contrast and the sharp serifs may appear fine at first, but here they are a mannerism that gets in the way of the reader. The page has a tendency to resolve itself into a series of dazzling, unrelated strokes in various *directions, made less, rather than more, lucid by the knife-edged fine lines. Scotch Roman pointed forward into the slough of the nineteenth century. Yet, though Scotch is a portent, it is not itself as poor as its descendants became, and in the right place it will perform well.*

Scotch Roman 12-pt. on 13-pt.

Scotch Roman italics

IMPRINT

Monotype

ABCDEFGHIJKLMNOPQRSTUVWXYZÆŒ

ABCDEFGHIJKLMNOPQRSTUVWXYZÆŒ

12345) abcdefghijklmnopqrstuvwxyzæœ (67890

&fiflfffffiffl?!,.:;£

ABCDEFGHIJKLMNOPQRSTUVWXYZŒÆ

12345] *abcdefghijklmnopqrstuvwxyzæœ* *[67890*

&fiflfffffiffl?!,.:;

ABCDEFGHIJKLMNOPQRSTUVWXYZÆŒ

12345) abcdefghijklmnopqrstuvwxyzæœ (67890

&fiflfffffiffl?!,.:;£

Imprint 12 pt. leaded 2 pt.

THIS face, like Times, is a type face made for a specific commercial use. It was designed for the magazine *Imprint* and was cut by the Monotype Corporation in 1912. It is in effect an old face regularized and made larger on the body, and its parentage lies in the old faces of the eighteenth century. An unassuming type face, it is legible and widely used; a wide range of accented and other special characters makes it applicable to foreign languages and various specialized publications.

Imprint italic

The italic, regular, and dark in colour, is evidently designed as a simple adjunct to the roman.

Imprint Bold

Imprint Bold is bold and blunt and rolling, a wide letter that makes its presence felt against the strong letter of text roman.

PERPETUA

Monotype

ABCDEFGHIJKLMNOPQRSTUVWXYZÆŒ

ABCDEFGHIJKLMNOPQRSTUVWXYZÆŒ

12345) abcdefghijklmnopqrstuvwxyzæœ (67890

&fiflffffiffl?!,.:;£

ABCDEFGHIJKLMNOPQRSTUVWXYZÆŒ

12345] *abcdefghijklmnopqrstuvwxyzæœ* *[67890*

&fiflffffiffl?!,.:;

ABCDEFGHIJKLMNOPQRSTUVWXYZÆŒ

12345) abcdefghijklmnopqrstuvwxyzæœ (67890

&fiflffffiffl?!,.:;£

PERPETUA is evidence of the sincerity of our revival of old face types: for it is an old face of our own time, designed by Eric Gill and cut by the Monotype Corporation in 1928. It has no typographical predecessor, as have all the other types we have so far examined. The capitals are derived from the lettering of the Trajan column and other Roman monuments, and the lower-case has been designed to work in sympathy with the capitals; and very brilliantly it does so. The type, especially in the capitals, possesses the dignity and clarity of the stone-cut letter.

Perpetua 13 point leaded 1 point

Perpetua italic is unusual among later italics in that it has a strength and charm of its own. I do not know whether it could sustain a whole book, for I have never seen it tried; but I do not believe that it is quite good enough for that. It is rather a sloped roman than a true italic.

Perpetua italic

Perpetua Bold is bold indeed, a somewhat mechanical weighting of the roman that loses much of the nobility of Eric Gill's original letter.

Perpetua Bold

DANTE

Monotype

ABCDEFGHIJKLMNOPQRSTUVWXYZÆŒ

ABCDEFGHIJKLMNOPQRSTUVWXYZÆŒ

12345) abcdefghijklmnopqrstuvwxyzæœ (67890

&fiflfffffiffl?!,.:;£

ABCDEFGHIJKLMNOPQRSTUVWXYZÆŒ

12345] abcdefghijklmnopqrstuvwxyzæœ [67890

&fiflfffffiffl?!,.:;

ABCDEFGHIJKLMNOPQRSTUVWXYZÆŒ

12345) abcdefghijklmnopqrstuvwxyzæœ (67890

&fiflfffffiffl?!,.:;£

Dante 12 Didot on 13 point

Dante was cut by the noted punch-cutter Charles Malin to the design of Giovanni Mardersteig, who founded the Officina Bodoni and the Stamperia Valdónega in Italy to produce respectively hand-printed books and machine-printed books. The type first appeared in 1954 in an edition of Boccaccio's *Trattatallo in Laude di Dante*, and six years later the first sizes for machine-composition in Monotype were issued. Dante is a beautiful old-face letter sufficiently self-effacing not to interrupt the reader with its charms, but sufficiently strong in character to appeal to the knowledgeable. It is splendidly legible. There is a titling series.

Dante italic

The italic has chancery characteristics and it therefore has more personality than have many old-face italics.

Dante Semi-bold

The semi-bold is sufficiently strong to mark its distinction from the roman. *It has a crisp clarity* not common in old-face bolds.

SPECTRUM

Monotype and Enschedé en Zonen

ABCDEFGHIJKLMNOPQRSTUVWXYZÆŒ

ABCDEFGHIJKLMNOPQRSTUVWXYZÆŒ

12345) abcdefghijklmnopqrstuvwxyzæœ (67890

&fiflffffiffl?!,.:;£

ABCDEFGHIJKLMNOPQRSTUVWXYZÆŒ

12345] abcdefghijklmnopqrstuvwxyzææ [67890

&fiflffffiffl?!,.:;£

ABCDEFGHIJKLMNOPQRSTUVWXYZÆŒ

12345) abcdefghijklmnopqrstuvwxyzæœ (67890

&fiflffffiffl?!,.:;£

Spectrum was designed in 1941–3 by the Dutch typographer Jan van Krimpen for the publishing house of Het Spectrum, who planned a series of Bibles in different sizes of the type. Consequently the type was intentionally made robust in colour for the best legibility in text sizes, and rather on the narrow side for economy of space. The Bible has a lot of capital initials and to avoid spottiness on the printed page the capitals of Spectrum were designed to be lower in height than the lower-case ascenders. Van Krimpen's success in producing a dignified and legible type is clearly evident. The war killed the Bible project and Spectrum, cut by Monotype in 1952, is now available as a general book face.

Spectrum 12 Didot on 13 point

The narrow and regular italic, rather upright, has chancery characteristics. It is good enough to be readable in the mass, carrying the eye along at high speed.

Spectrum italic

TIMES ROMAN

Linotype

ABCDEFGHIJKLMNOPQRSTUVWXYZÆŒ

ABCDEFGHIJKLMNOPQRSTUVWXYZÆŒ

12345) abcdefghijklmnopqrstuvwxyzæœ (67890

fiflffffiffl?!:;,.£&

ABCDEFGHIJKLMNOPQRSTUVWXYZÆŒ

12345] *abcdefghijklmnopqrstuvwxyzæœ* [*67890*

fiflffffiffl?!:;,.£&

ABCDEFGHIJKLMNOPQRSTUVWXYZÆŒ

12345) abcdefghijklmnopqrstuvwxyzæœ (67890

&fiflffffi?!,.:;£

Times Roman 11-pt. on 13-pt. short descenders

THE TIMES newspaper was printed in a modern face from 1799 until 1932. In the latter year the newspaper appeared in a new type especially designed for it by Stanley Morison, which was cut for Monotype, for Linotype, and later for Intertype. It was called The Times New Roman. This page is printed from Linotype. Basically a weighted old face, Times Roman proved very suitable for its purpose and its qualities were such that it soon became popular with book printers and book publishers. Bold enough to withstand wear, the type has no delicate kerns to break under the weight of the press. The unusually large size of the lower-case in relation to the capitals is noticeable. Long descenders are available on a body 1 point larger and these are an improvement for bookwork.

Times Roman 11-pt. on 13-pt. long descenders

Times Roman italic

Times Roman has proved inadequate, however, for the greater press speeds and cheaper papers of present-day newspaper printing and in 1972 it was superseded in The Times *by Times-Europa.*

Times Roman bold

Times Bold is thickened inside the letter and so looks more condensed than does the roman. Roman and bold match very well. The Monotype version has a bold italic.

EHRHARDT

Monotype

ABCDEFGHIJKLMNOPQRSTUVWXYZÆŒ

ABCDEFGHIJKLMNOPQRSTUVWXYZÆŒ

12345) abcdefghijklmnopqrstuvwxyzæœ (67890

&fiflffffiffl?!,.:;£

ABCDEFGHIJKLMNOPQRSTUVWXYZÆŒ

12345] abcdefghijklmnopqrstuvwxyzæœ [67890

&fiflffffiffl?!,.:;

ABCDEFGHIJKLMNOPQRSTUVWXYZÆŒ

12345) abcdefghijklmnopqrstuvwxyzæœ (67890

&fiflffffiffl?!,.:;£

Narrow letters such as this were in use in central Europe about the end of the seventeenth century. The designer of this example is not certainly known, but may have been a Hungarian called Nicholas Kis. The type appeared in a specimen sheet of the Ehrhardt foundry of Leipzig early in the seventeenth century, and it was on this showing that Monotype based the present design, which they first issued in 1938. The series of text sizes was not completed until after 1945 and it was not until then that Ehrhardt began to be much used. It combines large x-height with economy of space and excellent legibility.

Ehrhardt 12 point leaded 1 point

The italic is conventional, with less distinction than the roman, but it is close fitting and economical.

Ehrhardt italic

Ehrhardt Semi-bold is a companion letter *that does not overwhelm* the roman with excess weight.

Ehrhardt Semi-bold

Linotype also have a version of the type. It is called Janson and this paragraph is set in it. *Rather wider than Ehrhardt and larger on the body*, it is a handsome and readable letter. Its attribution to Anton Janson, a Dutch punch-cutter, is mistaken. Janson is based on punches that have survived in the possession of the Stempel foundry in Frankfurt.

Janson 12 point leaded 1 point

ROMULUS

Monotype and Enschedé en Zonen

ABCDEFGHIJKLMNOPQRSTUVWXYZÆŒ

ABCDEFGHIJKLMNOPQRSTUVWXYZÆŒ

12345) abcdefghijklmnopqrstuvwxyzæœ (67890

&fiflffffiffl?!,.:;£

ABCDEFGHIJKLMNOPQRSTUVWXYZÆŒ

12345] *abcdefghijklmnopqrstuvwxyzæœ* [*67890*

&fiflffffiffl?!,.:;£

ABCDEFGHIJKLMNOPQRSTUVWXYZÆŒ

12345) abcdefghijklmnopqrstuvwxyzæœ (67890

&fiflffffiffl?!,.:;£

Romulus 12 Didot on 13 point

THIS ROMAN was the first of a series begun by Jan van Krimpen for Enschedé en Zonen of Haarlem in 1931. The series, all cut by Enschedé, is unusually comprehensive and includes the roman, with a sloped italic, Romulus Semi-bold, a *Cancelleresca Bastarda* designed to work with the roman (when leaded), and four weights of sanserif that aline with the roman but do not otherwise appear to have much relation to it. The semi-bold is unusual in possessing small caps. The roman and the semi-bold were cut by Monotype from 1936 onwards. Romulus roman is a squarish letter with old-face characteristics but with the flat serifs of a modern. It is not often seen.

Romulus sloped roman

The sloped roman is clearly unsuccessful, its width contradicting the speed of the italic and its weight and design making it too similar to the roman.

Romulus Bold

The semi-bold (called 'bold' by Monotype) avoids the blunder of too much weight and retains the sharpness of the roman.

JULIANA

Linotype

ABCDEFGHIJKLMNOPQRSTUVWXYZÆŒ

ABCDEFGHIJKLMNOPQRSTUVWXYZÆŒ

12345) abcdefghijklmnopqrstuvwxyzæœ (67890

&fiflfffffifl?!,.:;£

ABCDEFGHIJKLMNOPQRSTUVWXYZÆŒ

ABCDEFGHIJKLMNOPQRSTUVWXYZÆŒ

12345] *abcdefghijklmnopqrstuvwxyzæœ* [67890

&fiflffffiffl?!,.:;

THOUGH a design of the mid-twentieth century, Juliana has been inspired by the style of sixteenth-century Italian letters. Its lateral compression and bigness on the body follow a modern trend also evident in Times, Pilgrim, and Electra, and the result is a pleasant economy and legibility. Juliana was designed by S. L. Hartz in Holland in 1958, specifically for the Linotype. **Juliana 12 point leaded 1 point long descenders**

The paragraph above is set with alternative long descenders, which are preferable for many kinds of book printing, but require a body one point larger. This paragraph uses the standard short descenders. **Juliana 12 point short descenders**

The italic has neither the regularity nor the close fitting of the roman, but it is a true italic and distinct from the roman despite its upright character. Notice the existence of italic small capitals which are available in several Linotype and Intertype faces. **Juliana italic**

PILGRIM

Linotype

ABCDEFGHIJKLMNOPQRSTUVWXYZÆŒ

ABCDEFGHIJKLMNOPQRSTUVWXYZÆŒ

12345) abcdefghijklmnopqrstuvwxyzæœ (67890

&fiflffffiffl ? ! ,. : ;£

ABCDEFGHIJKLMNOPQRSTUVWXYZÆŒ

ABCDEFGHIJKLMNOPQRSTUVWXYZÆŒ

12345] abcdefghijklmnopqrstuvwxyzæœ [67890

&fiflffffiffl?!,.:;£

Pilgrim 12 point leaded 1 point

The original of this type was designed by Eric Gill and was cut in 1934, under the name Bunyan, in 14 point size for a limited edition of Sterne's *Sentimental Journey*. From that time until 1953 it was seldom seen. In this latter year it was made available for composition on the Linotype and almost at once became popular. This classical, highly legible type serves well in both books and periodicals. The x-height is large, and the characters, upper and lower-case alike, have almost the same weight of stroke throughout. Minerva, designed by Reynolds Stone, is intended as a display face to serve with Pilgrim.

Pilgrim italic

Gill drew only six lower-case and two capitals of the italics, but these were sufficient to show that he intended the fount to be sloped roman; from these eight letters the Linotype designers have produced a sloped roman that consorts well with its parent letter.

JOANNA

Monotype

ABCDEFGHIJKLMNOPQRSTUVWXYZÆŒ

ABCDEFGHIJKLMNOPQRSTUVWXYZÆŒ

12345) abcdefghijklmnopqrstuvwxyzæœ (67890

&fiflfffffiffl?!,.:;£

ABCDEFGHIJKLMNOPQRSTUVWXYZÆŒ

12345] *abcdefghijklmnopqrstuvwxyzæœ* [67890

&fiflfffffiffl?!,.:;£

Designed by Eric Gill and named after his daughter, this type was for long reserved for the exclusive use of the printing-house of Joanna's husband René Hague. It was cast for hand-composition from punches cut by H. W. Caslon & Co. The publishers J. M. Dent Ltd. acquired the rights and had the type cut for machine-composition by Monotype for their sole use. The type was generally released in 1958. Joanna, with small variation of stroke, is almost monotone, and it has some curious idiosyncrasies in individual letters, but it is legible and handsome. Joanna 12 point leaded 1 point

The italic is a sloped roman, with not much slope, and exceptionally compressed laterally. Joanna may be compared with Pilgrim, also by Gill. Joanna italic

u

LECTURA

Typefoundry Amsterdam and Harris-Intertype

ABCDEFGHIJKLMNOPQRSTUVWXYZÆŒ

ABCDEFGHIJKLMNOPQRSTUVWXYZŒÆ

12345) abcdefghijklmnopqrstuvwxyzææœ (67890

&fiflffffiffl?!,.:;£

ABCDEFGHIJKLMNOPQRSTUVWXYZÆŒ

12345] abcdefghijklmnopqrstuvwxyzææœ [67890

&fiflffffiffl?!,.:;£

ABCDEFGHIJKLMNOPQRSTUVWXYZÆŒ

12345) abcdefghijklmnopqrstuvwxyzææœ (67890

&fiflffffiffl?!,.:;£

Lectura 11 point leaded 1 point

Designed by Dick Dooijes for Typefoundry Amsterdam and Intertype, Lectura is available both as founders' type in a range of display sizes and as matrices for line-casting composition on the Intertype. Its inspiration seems to come from what was called the *gôut hollandais* of such type designers as Christoffel van Dijck and Nicholas Kis as reflected in the narrower letters of Fournier, with the addition of a calligraphic emphasis that is seen particularly in the italic. The result is an attractive face large on the body and with strong colour suitable for a wide range of papers. Old-face hanging figures are happier with Lectura, but ranging figures are also available.

Lectura italic

The italic has about the same colour as the roman with a stress and line that owe something to chancery italics.

Lectura Bold

The bold face looks more condensed than the roman, though it is in fact identical in width.

CORNELL

Harris-Intertype

ABCDEFGHIJKLMNOPQRSTUVWXYZÆŒ

ABCDEFGHIJKLMNOPQRSTUVWXYZÆŒ&

12345) abcdefghijklmnopqrstuvwxyzæœ (67890

&fiflffffiffl?!,.:;£

ABCDEFGHIJKLMNOPQRSTUVWXYZÆŒ

12345] abcdefghijklmnopqrstuvwxyzæœ [67890

&fiflffffiffl?!,.:;£

Cornell, designed by the American typographer George Trenholm for Intertype and introduced in the U.S. in 1949, takes its name from Cornell University. It follows a present-day trend for types with both old-face and modern characteristics, without, however, looking like a period transitional face. There are some odd little peculiarities that contribute to the personality of the face, such as the forward tilt of the bowls of b, d, and q, the slight scallop of the horizontal bar serifs of the capitals, and the curl of the horizontal strokes of such letters as B and G. The general effect is of an easy, wide-set, close-fitting letter particularly suitable for bookwork.

Cornell 12 point 1 point leaded

The round italic follows the roman in width and fitting, but the tilt of the bowls of b, d, and q, becomes a mannerism interrupting the general slope.

Cornell italic

APOLLO

Monophoto

ABCDEFGHIJKLMNOPQRSTUVWXYZÆŒ

ABCDEFGHIJKLMNOPQRSTUVWXYZÆŒ

12345) abcdefghijklmnopqrstuvwxyzæœ (67890

&?!,.:;£

ABCDEFGHIJKLMNOPQRSTUVWXYZÆŒ

12345] *abcdefghijklmnopqrstuvwxyzæœ* [*67890*

&?!,.:;£

ABCDEFGHIJKLMNOPQRSTUVWXYZÆŒ

12345) abcdefghijklmnopqrstuvwxyzæœ (67890

&?!,.:;£

Apollo 12 point leaded 1 point The Swiss Adrian Frutiger's Apollo, issued in 1964, was the first typeface specifically designed for photo-setting on the Monotype Corporation's Monophoto machine. The problem to be solved was to produce a letter that would be satisfactory in all composition sizes from 6 point to 24 point reproduced from a single set of matrices. Apollo can certainly be counted as a success in this respect. It is a clear, open face, of medium x-height and set, producing a pleasant and legible text. Some of Apollo's antecedents lie in the designer's earlier type Méridien, made for Lumitype.

Apollo italic *Apollo's slight mannerisms or idiosyncrasies are exaggerated in the less satisfactory italic.*

Apollo Semi-bóld **Apollo Semi-bold is a sharp letter rather bolder than the name suggests.**

TELEGRAPH-MODERN

Linotype

ABCDEFGHIJKLMNOPQRSTUVWXYZÆŒ

ABCDEFGHIJKLMNOPQRSTUVWXYZÆŒ

12345) abcdefghijklmnopqrstuvwxyzæœ (67890

fiffflffiffl?!,.:;&£

ABCDEFGHIJKLMNOPQRSTUVWXYZÆŒ

12345) abcdefghijklmnopqrstuvwxyzæœ (67890

fiffflffiffl?!,.:;&£

ABCDEFGHIJKLMNOPQRSTUVWXYZÆŒ

12345) abcdefghijklmnopqrstuvwxyz (67890

fiffflffiffl?!,.:;&£

Telegraph-Modern takes its name from the newspaper for which it was designed, the *Daily Telegraph*; it also appears in the *Sunday Telegraph*. It is a legible and distinctive and superbly practical face, produced by Walter Tracy to take account especially of the problems of high-speed stereotyping and of printing in thin ink on newsprint from type set on line-casting machines. A slightly rectangular letter with open counters and strong strokes, its modern character is most apparent in the lightly emphatic, unbracketed serifs, which carry the eye comfortably along the base line. Telegraph-Modern will certainly be used in books, where it will serve well if it is leaded a point or two. Telegraph-Modern 12 point 1 point leaded

The italic, a little lighter in weight, is a fit companion for the Roman. Telegraph-Modern italic

The bold face is adapted from Linotype Bold No. 2. Its emphasis is considerable, but it is not noticeably wider than the roman. Telegraph-Modern bold

OPTIMA

Stempel, Linotype and Monophoto

ABCDEFGHIJKLMNOPQRSTUVWXYZÆŒ
12345) abcdefghijklmnopqrstuvwxyzæœ (67890
&fiflfffffiffl?!,.:;£

ABCDEFGHIJKLMNOPQRSTUVWXYZÆŒ
12345] abcdefghijklmnopqrstuvwxyzæœ [67890
&fiflfffffiffl?!,.:;£

ABCDEFGHIJKLMNOPQRSTUVWXYZÆŒ
12345) abcdefghijklmnopqrstuvwxyzæœ (67890
&fiflfffffiffl?!,.:;£

Optima 12 point leaded 1 point

If one has to use a sanserif in continuous text it seems reasonable to use one with the variation of stress to which our eyes have become accustomed in roman letters. Optima, designed by Herman Zapf in 1958 for the Frankfurt companies of Stempel and Linotype, was introduced as a Monophoto face in 1969. It was by no means the first such letter – see for comparison Ludlow Stellar, 1929, ATF Lydian, 1938, Ludwig & Mayer's Colonia, 1938, and Deberny & Peignot's Touraine, 1947. There have also been others since – Amsterdam's Pascal could well serve as a bold for Optima. As a text type Optima is attractive and, if not held too long, readable.

Optima italic

The italic does not possess legibility equal to that of the roman and is therefore best used for emphasis.

Optima Semi-bold

The Semi-bold is too heavy for the name and loses the old-face charm of the roman.

UNIVERS

Deberny & Peignot, Monotype, Monophoto

ABCDEFGHIJKLMNOPQRSTUVWXYZÆŒ

12345) abcdefghijklmnopqrstuvwxyzæœ (67890

&?!,.:;£

ABCDEFGHIJKLMNOPQRSTUVWXYZÆŒ

12345] abcdefghijklmnopqrstuvwxysæœ [67890

&?!,.:;£

ABCDEFGHIJKLMNOPQRSTUVWXYZÆŒ

12345) abcdefghijklmnopqrstuvwxyzæœ (67890

&?!,.:;£

Sanserifs are not the ideal types for text composition, but they are often used, especially in books with less text than illustration. Univers stands here for many other sanserifs because it has become the most popular, not because it is necessarily the best. Designed by Adrian Frütiger, designer of Apollo, the concept was for a whole range of related sans in various weights and widths, *which over a period of ten years have one by one come into being*, and are available **as founders' type, as metal Monotype, and as photo-composition matrices.** The original aim was for twenty-one related faces, but there seems no reason why additional varieties should not occur in the future.

Univers Light 10D on 11 point leaded 1 point

Univers Light italic

Univers Medium

Univers may be compared with Linotype Helvetica and Intertype Galaxy.

The types shown in these specimen pages are arranged below in order to demonstrate two modes of difference: x-height and set. It may be remarked, on looking through the following table, that the types appear to be of different sizes, Times, for example, appearing several sizes larger than the Perpetua shown. Actually, all of the specimens, unlike those in the preceding pages, are set in the same point size. The eye measures type size, not by the point size, but by the x-height, and x-height, demonstrably, varies greatly from type to type.

Types also vary in width, or set, as I have already explained, the set controlling the number of letters that may be got into a given line. It is shown comparatively in the table.

Types are made in different point sizes, as I have shown, and there are few text types that are not cast in sizes large enough to be used as display faces. Many Monotype faces go up to 72 point. The large initial in most of the specimens in the list is an example of a larger size of the same face. Thus a book may be, and some are, set in one kind of type throughout, different sizes being used as required for chapter headings, part titles, and title-pages, and for the jacket.

TABLE OF VARIATIONS OF SET WIDTHS

The alphabets shown opposite, all set in 12 point, demonstrate the variation in set widths of the types shown on pages 275 sqq. and give a good idea of the relative x-heights.

TEXT TYPES OF TODAY

VAN DIJCK	abcdefghijklmnopqrstuvwxyz
CENTAUR	abcdefghijklmnopqrstuvwxyz
PERPETUA	abcdefghijklmnopqrstuvwxyz
FOURNIER	abcdefghijklmnopqrstuvwxyz
BARBOU	abcdefghijklmnopqrstuvwxyz
POLIPHILUS	abcdefghijklmnopqrstuvwxyz
BEMBO	abcdefghijklmnopqrstuvwxyz
TIMES	abcdefghijklmnopqrstuvwxyz
JOANNA	abcdefghijklmnopqrstuvwxyz
GRANJON	abcdefghijklmnopqrstuvwxyz
BULMER	abcdefghijklmnopqrstuvwxyz
EHRHARDT	abcdefghijklmnopqrstuvwxyz
CALEDONIA	abcdefghijklmnopqrstuvwxyz
JULIANA	abcdefghijklmnopqrstuvwxyz
ROMULUS	abcdefghijklmnopqrstuvwxyz
CASLON	abcdefghijklmnopqrstuvwxyz
WALBAUM	abcdefghijklmnopqrstuvwxyz
OPTIMA	abcdefghijklmnopqrstuvwxyz
GARAMOND	abcdefghijklmnopqrstuvwxyz
BELL	abcdefghijklmnopqrstuvwxyz
PLANTIN	abcdefghijklmnopqrstuvwxyz
SPECTRUM	abcdefghijklmnopqrstuvwxyz
PILGRIM	abcdefghijklmnopqrstuvwxyz
CORNELL	abcdefghijklmnopqrstuvwxyz
IMPRINT	abcdefghijklmnopqrstuvwxyz
PLANTIN LIGHT	abcdefghijklmnopqrstuvwxyz
BASKERVILLE (*Linotype*)	abcdefghijklmnopqrstuvwxyz
DANTE	abcdefghijklmnopqrstuvwxyz
BASKERVILLE (*Monotype*)	abcdefghijklmnopqrstuvwxyz
FONTANA	abcdefghijklmnopqrstuvwxyz
APOLLO	abcdefghijklmnopqrstuvwxyz
BODONI	abcdefghijklmnopqrstuvwxyz
SABON	abcdefghijklmnopqrstuvwxyz
SCOTCH ROMAN	abcdefghijklmnopqrstuvwxyz
TELEGRAPH-MODERN	abcdefghijklmnopqrstuvwxyz
UNIVERS	abcdefghijklmnopqrstuvwxyz

XVI

PAGE

AT an early date in the history of books certain rules concerning the treatment of the page were formulated by the scribes and calligraphers, who did not overlook minutiae, and gave to those details that in sum are important in effect the care and thought they lavished on the whole. Some of their practices have descended to us as fixed conventions and affect the printed book of to-day exactly as they did the manuscript of the dark ages. To the scribe, for example, we owe our ideas concerning the apportionment of margins. Other of our conventions have arisen from the printing house, to become equally strongly part of the design of books. Thus we are indebted to the printer for page headlines and the regular use of page numbers.

Manuscripts and early printed books show that their designers were concerned with the problems of 'colour' and atmosphere, and their solutions of these problems remain valid. Though indifferent printers have been ignorant of any problem or its solution, competent printers and typographers are aware of the value of their inheritance.

The kind, or design, of letter is important to the appearance of the page, for it contributes its own individual colour and atmosphere. Atmosphere is something difficult of explanation, the cumulative effect of type design and typography; it must accord with the atmosphere of the book of which it is part. To give a limited and extreme example, it might be out of keeping to set the *Canterbury Tales* in Bodoni (though they have more than once been set in a degraded modern); Chaucer may be set without offence in Caslon, and there is no reason for any attempt to confine his work to faces that may be supposed to have a contemporary flavour, which could only be gothics. But Chaucer should not be set in types that are contrary in inspiration and alien in sympathy. Choice of face, the treatment it receives at the hands both of the typographer and the printer, and the kind of paper it is printed on, all contribute to the effect of atmosphere. It even has national characteristics, for it is possible to take a page set in a type available on both sides of the Atlantic and to say that that page must have been set in America. Even the period is indicated more or less clearly to an experienced eye. Atmosphere is therefore something definite and recognizable, if difficult of description.

Colour is more easily definable. It has nothing to do with the colours of the palette, but means simply the shade of grey represented by the mass of type on the printed page. The colour of type is of importance both aesthetically and practically; but it is not absolute. It is not possible to state that such and such a type of such and such a size will produce colour of such and such a sort. It will do so only under certain conditions of leading and spacing and machining.

I have already dwelt upon the modern practice of light impression. For certain kinds of faces, such as Bodoni and Walbaum, a light impression on smooth paper is correct—they depend for their brilliance and contrast on a true rendering of the hair-lines. Too heavy an impression thickens the hair-lines, without proportionately increasing the stresses, and a rough-surfaced paper has the same effect, so that the design of the face is seriously affected and the colour of the page is altered. On the other hand, Venetians and old faces were primarily intended for printing with a more vigorous impression on rougher paper, and if they are printed lightly on smooth paper they appear thin and poverty-stricken and the colour is false.

Spacing between words should be close and approximately equal throughout the book; if it is allowed to vary, an unpleasant unevenness of colour is the result. This effect is enhanced by some undiscriminating printers who believe that a full stop does not live up to its name and choose to emphasize the end of each sentence by inserting a larger space, usually totalling an em, after the stop. It is this sort of printer who also likes to emphasize every punctuation mark other than the comma by inserting a thin space before it and a double space after it. Occasionally one comes across a printer who to these sins adds a disinclination to break words, with results that shout for themselves to anyone but those of the same persuasion. The total effect is unlovely and undesirable, but that does not perturb this printer or disturb his conviction that it is what his customer wants.

It is not difficult to define good spacing, and it is not difficult to achieve it. Most competent typographers consider that there should be no extra space anywhere; as far as possible the spaces between words should be of approximately the same width throughout, and that is the width of the letter i. Some typographers like to have a slight extra space at the end of a sentence.

Two other kinds of space occur in printed matter, the paragraph indention and the space in the short line at the end of the paragraph. Paragraph indention is, or should be, invariable throughout the book, and usually it will be found to equal one em of the type size in use. An em of a large size is, however, a good deal, and in a book in which the text type is large it is often better to indent rather less. It is rarely advisable to indent more than an em, but there are times when a larger indention is more successful—in conjunction with very wide leading, for example. The space at the end of the paragraph is largely uncontrollable, and little attempt need be made to control it; it is part of our convention of writing and gives relief to the eye, which tends to find solid pages heavy and exhausting. This last line of the paragraph should be spaced in the same degree as the other lines; and care should be taken that it is not too short—the word 'it' on a line all by itself looks a little silly.

Some manuscripts and some of the early printed books avoided paragraph divisions and ran all paragraphs on, indicating the commencement of each by means of a paragraph mark, which sometimes was printed in colour. Gothic types will stand up to this manner very well, and in an age in which people probably read more slowly and certainly read less it perhaps did

125. Opening page (*Incipit*) of Euclid's *Elementa*, Ratdolt, Venice, 1482

Preclarissimus liber elementorum Euclidis perspi/
cacissimi: in artem Geometrie incipit quãfoelicissime:

Punctus est cuius ps nõ est. ¶ Linea est
lõgitudo sine latitudine cui⁹ quidẽ ex/
tremitates sũt duo pũcta. ¶ Linea recta
ẽ ab vno pũcto ad aliũ breuissima extẽ/
sio ĩ extremitates suas vtrũq3 eoꝶ reci
piens. ¶ Supficies ẽ q̃ lõgitudinẽ ⁊ lati
tudinẽ tm̃ hꝫ: cui⁹ termi quidẽ sũt linee.
¶ Supficies plana ẽ ab vna linea ad a/
liã extẽsio ĩ extremitates suas recipiẽs
¶ Angulus planus ẽ duarũ linearũ al/
ternus ꝯtactus: quaꝶ expãsio ẽ sup sup/
ficiẽ applicatioq3 nõ directa. ¶ Quãdo aũt angulum ꝯtinẽt due
linee recte rectiline⁹ angulus noiat̃. ¶ Qñ recta linea sup rectã
steterit duoq3 anguli vtrobiq3 fuerit eq̃les: eoꝶ vterq3 rect⁹ erit
¶ Lineaq3 linee supstãs ei cui supstat ppendicularis vocat̃. ¶ An
gulus vo qui recto maior ẽ obtusus dicit. ¶ Angul⁹ vo minor re
cto acut⁹ appellat̃. ¶ Termin⁹ ẽ qd vniuscuiusq3 finis ẽ. ¶ Figura
ẽ q̃ termino vl' termis ꝯtinet̃. ¶ Circul⁹ ẽ figura plana vna q̃dem li/
nea ꝯtẽta: q̃ circũferentia noiat̃: in cui⁹ medio pũct⁹ ẽ: a quo oẽs
linee recte ad circũferẽtiã exeũtes sibiinuice3 sũt equales. Et hic
quidẽ pũct⁹ cẽtrũ circuli dr̃. ¶ Diameter circuli ẽ linea recta que
sup ei⁹ centꝶ trãsiens extremitatesq3 suas circũferẽtie applicans
circulũ ĩ duo media diuidit. ¶ Semicirculus ẽ figura plana dia/
metro circuli ⁊ medietate circũferentie ꝯtenta. ¶ Portio circu/
li ẽ figura plana recta linea ⁊ parte circũferẽtie ꝯtẽta: semicircu/
lo quidẽ aut maior aut minor. ¶ Rectilinee figure sũt q̃ rectis li/
neis cõtinent̃ quarũ quedã trilatere q̃ trib⁹ rectis lineis: quedã
quadrilatere q̃ q̃tuor rectis lineis. q̃dã mltilatere que pluribus
q̃3 quatuor rectis lineis continent̃. ¶ Figurarũ trilaterarũ: alia
est triangulus hñs tria latera equalia. Alia triangulus duo hñs
eq̃lia latera. Alia triangulus triũ inequalium laterũ. Haꝶ iterũ
alia est orthogoniũ: vnũ .s. rectum angulum habens. Alia ẽ am/
bligonium aliquem obtusum angulum habens. Alia est oxigoni
um: in qua tres anguli sunt acuti. ¶ Figurarũ autẽ quadrilateraꝶ
Alia est q̃dratum quod est equilaterũ atq3 rectangulũ. Alia est
tetragon⁹ long⁹: q̃ est figura rectangula: sed equilatera non est.
Alia est helmuaym: que est equilatera: sed rectangula non est.

De principijs p se notis: ⁊ pmo de diffinitionibus earundem.

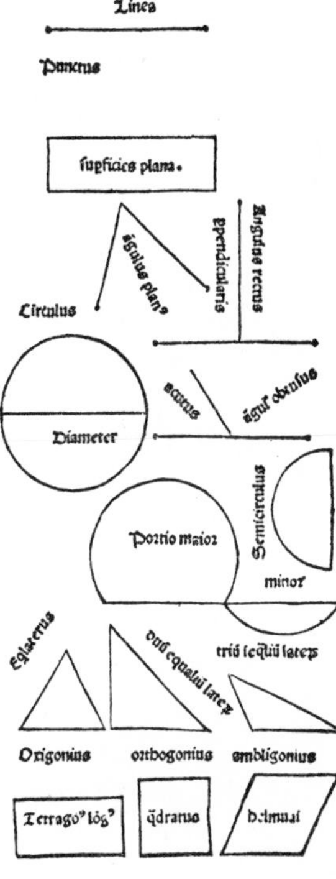

not matter that this fashion imposed some difficulty. The colour of the page was not affected, as gothic is a heavy face and the paragraph mark merges with it; or the page was diversified by marks in red or some other hue. William Morris revived the fashion and was followed in it by some others of the private presses, but they did not achieve the same success as the older printers. They were working, not with gothic, but with roman or romanized faces, the paragraph marks for which are invariably too heavy.

It is a custom, amounting almost to a rule, with many publishers that quotations in a book should not be set in the text size, but in a smaller size of type; and the practice is so common that often an author will ask specifically that it should be followed. It seems to me a custom without reason. It certainly destroys the unity of the page by imposing upon it a colour of a different kind from that of the text; but that is by no means the only objection to it, nor the most serious. Presumably the writer does not mean to belittle the author from whom he quotes, but that is what he is doing; usually he quotes from him in order to enhance his own point, and if that is the case it is surely better that the authority should speak in a normal voice rather than in a repressed whisper. We do not want the reader to miss the quotation, but if it is subdued it surely suggests that he need not bother with it.

There is another way of setting quotations that is also unsatisfactory. It is to set them in the text type, but to indent each line one em or more. The result is a ragged page that cannot but look uncomfortable.

A variant of indention is the use of quotation marks at the beginning of each line of the quotation. This method gives the lines the appearance of indention and at the same time so thoroughly emphasizes the alien quality of the matter that the reader can have no excuse for confusing it with the author's own work. The effect on the page is disastrous, and the longer the quotation is, the worse the effect. The printers of Dr. Johnson's day did not boggle at several consecutive pages all eroded down the left side by orderly but subversive phalanxes of measles.

126. Page from *Hypnerotomachia Poliphili*, Aldus, Venice, 1499

POLIPHILO INCOMINCIA IL SECONDO LIBRO DI LA SVA HYPNEROTOMACHIA. NEL QVALE POLIA ET LVI DISERTABONDI, IN QVALE MODO ET VARIO CASO NARRANO INTERCALARIAMENTE IL SVO INAMORAMENTO.

NARRA QVIVI LA DIVA POLIA LA NOBILE ET ANTIQVA ORIGINE SVA. ET COMO PER LI PREDECESSORI SVI TRIVISIO FVE EDIFICATO. ET DI QVELLA GENTE LELIA ORIVNDA. ET PER QVALE MODO DISAVEDVTA ET INSCIA DISCONCIAMENTE SE INAMOROE DI LEI IL SVO DILECTO POLIPHILO.

LE MIE DEBILE VOCE TALE O GRAtiose & diue Nymphe absone peruenerãno & inconcine alla uostra benigna audiẽtia, quale la terrifica raucitate del urinante Esacho al suaue canto dela piangeuole Philomela. Nondimeno uolendo io cum tuti gli mei exili conati del intellecto, & cum la mia paucula sufficiẽtia di satisfare alle uostre piaceuole petitione, non ristaro al potere. Lequale semota qualũque hesitatione epse piu che si congruerebbe altronde, dignamente meritano piu uberrimo fluuio di eloquentia, cum troppo piu rotunda elegantia & cum piu exornata politura di pronũtiato, che in me per alcuno pacto non si troua, di cõseguire il suo gratioso affecto. Ma a uui Celibe Nymphe & adme alquãto, quantũche & confusa & incomptamẽte fringultiẽte haro in qualche portiuncula gratificato assai. Quando uoluntarosa & diuota a gli desii uostri & postulato me prestaro piu presto cum lanimo nõ mediocre prompto humile parendo, che cum enucleata tersa, & uenusta eloquentia placẽdo. La prisca dunque & ueterrima geneologia, & prosapia, & il fatale mio amore garrulando ordire. Onde gia essendo nel uostro uenerando conuentuale conspecto, & uederme sterile & ieiuna di eloquio & ad tanto prestãte & diuo ceto di uui O Nymphe sedule famularie dil acceso cupidine. Et ĩtanto benigno & delecteuole & sacro sito, di sincere aure & florigeri spiramini afflato. Io acconciamente compulsa di assumere uno uenerabile auso, & tranquillo timore de dire. Dunque auante il tuto uenia date, o bellissime & beatissime Nymphe a questo mio blacterare & agli femelli & terrigeni, & pusilluli Conati, si aduene che in alchuna parte io incautamente

Such folly invited the denunciation of the forthright Samuel, but unfortunately that very bookish man saw nothing in typography, and seems to have been able to distinguish merely the difference between big print and little print.

I prefer to set quotations in the text type, exactly as an ordinary paragraph of the text, but quoted at the beginning and end, as they should be, to show that they are quotations. Set in this way they do not stand out from the page or disturb its even tenor, and there is no doubt for the reader that what he is reading is a quotation. If this is not considered sufficient distinction a half-line of space may be left before and after the quotation.

Quotation marks (or 'inverted commas', as they are mistakenly called) can be a nuisance, principally because of our inexplicable habit of using double quotation marks on every occasion. The common usage is to commence a quotation with double quotes and to single-quote any quotation within the main quotation. That does not seem to be logical, and to-day many printers, the Oxford University Press among them, reverse the practice. The O.U.P. style is certainly better for the appearance of the page, for quotation marks occupy only a fraction of the body of the type, and double quotes leave an unpleasant gap below them that should be avoided wherever possible.

Capitals are destructive of even colour, and where an author calls for a word in capitals it is usually better to set it in small capitals, or in capitals a couple of points smaller than the text type. This is particularly so when founts are in use in which the capitals are the full height of the ascenders. Some faces (Bembo is an example) have capitals that are shorter than the lower-case ascenders and the improvement in appearance this brings about is noticeable.

The amount of leading to be used is fixed not only in relation to appearance but also in relation to the extent of the book. There are several reasons why it should be desirable to increase or decrease the number of pages a book occupies—the difficulty of binding a very thin book, for example, or the convenience of making the extent a multiple of sixteen pages. Whatever the reason for leading may be, if it is not done for its

127. Page from *Horae*, with borders by Geofroy Tory, printed by Simon de Colines, Paris, 1539

aut filius hominis, quoniã viſitas eũ?
M inuiſti eum paulominus ab ange=
lis, gloria, & honore coronaſti eum,
& conſtituiſti eum ſuper opera ma=
nuum tuarum.
O mnia ſubiecisti ſub pedibus eius, o=
ues, & boues vniuerſas, inſuper & pe=
cora campi.
Volucres cęli, & piſces maris, qui per=
ambulant ſemitas maris.
D omine dominus noſter, q̃ admirabi-
le eſt nomen tuum in vniuerſa terra.
G loria patri, & filio, & ſpiritui ſancto
S icut erat in principio & nunc, & ſem
per. aña. Benedicta tu in mulieribus,
& benedictus fructus ventris tui. ãn.
Sicut myrrha. Pſalmus.
C Aeli enarrant gloriam dei, & o=
pera manuum eius annũciat fir=
mamentum.

own sake it has to be remembered that it alters the colour and the atmosphere of the page; apart from considerations of convenience, and no less important, leading is of value to the typographer because it puts into his hands a means of controlling the effect of the page. Further, types like Times and Plantin, which are so large on the body that they are crowded when set solid, become useful and legible when they are suitably leaded. Leading should be equal throughout the book. Extra leads between paragraphs are unnecessary and undesirable.

Authors often mark a pause in their argument by means of a line of space. The typographical equivalent need not be the same. It may be any number of lines of space that best accords with the design of the book, though usually it is best to keep the white to a minimum of one line. On the other hand it need not be a blank at all, but may be a line of three or four stars or some other non-committal ornament chosen to accord with the spirit of the type face.

The colour of the page is, of course, affected by the quality and the quantity of the ink used, and to some extent by the shade of the paper it is printed on. No amount of poor ink will give a satisfactory result. The ink should be capable of giving a sharp and clean impression, and should be truly black and matt. Glossy inks are best avoided in the printing of books.

The last factor we need consider bearing on the colour of the page may appear at first sight not to have any importance at all. It is the area of the margins. The human eye is inveterate in synthesis and will practise it upon every occasion, presenting to the brain, sometimes a useful generalization, sometimes a mere illusion. It is an illusion that a page of type in the middle of a large white space is lighter in colour than the same page in a smaller space, but it is an illusion of which we cannot disembarrass ourselves. The page must be designed in relation to the margins it is known that it will have, and in the end the result is empiric.

128. Page from Basinius, *Opera*, Albertiniana, 1793

CANDIDO ET BENEVOLO
LECTORI
LAVRENTIVS DRVDIVS
PHIL. ET MED. ARIMINENSIS
S. P. D.

Prodeunt tandem in lucem, Lector benevole, praestantiora Basinii Parmensis Opera, publico Programmate dudum promissa, diu expectata, ac conviciis prope dixerim efflagitata. E re quidem nostra fuisset maturius, ut animo conceperamus, ea in lucem emittere: plurima vero interciderunt, quae non evitabilem interponerent moram; quaeque ut te rescire supervacaneum, sic de operis totius oeconomia tibi rationem reddere ducimus pernecessarium: paucioribus tamen, quam fieri poterit, verbis, ne operis ipsius legendi voluptatem diutius differamus.

SUB-HEADS

In many books chapters are divided into sections by means of sub-heads, and in some books this division is elaborated into a scheme calling for many sub-heads of different values or grades of importance—an arrangement more frequently found in textbooks or technical books than elsewhere. Sub-heads may be set in a number of different ways and in different types, but they should be assimilated to the general style of the book. Where there are many kinds of sub-heads it is useful on occasion to be able to use a bold-face version of the text type; unfortunately many perfectly good text types possess only mediocre or downright bad bold-faces, and this is particularly true of revived faces for which companion bolds have had to be designed. Garamond is an example, and so is Baskerville. Times New Roman, on the other hand, has a bold face that goes excellently with it. There is, however, no reason why the typographer should restrict himself to types of one family when he may better achieve his end by using a different face—except that extra cost may follow.

Grades of importance of sub-heads are expressed by position as well as by use of type, and position may be assisted by discriminatory leading. It is an accepted convention that a centred sub-head is superior to one set to the side, for example.

There are five main varieties of sub-heads.

CROSS HEADS

are centred across the measure, and may have one or more lines of space above them and perhaps half a line below. They form a definite division in the page, partitioning the chapter into its major parts. There may in one book be cross heads of more than one value, one subsidiary to the other. Variations of emphasis can be obtained by variations of type and of leading.

SIDE HEADS

are subsidiary to cross heads and almost as flexible in variety of emphasis. They may have leads above and below, as a cross head, or only above.

129. Page from Davison's *Poetical Rhapsody*, Lee Priory Press, 1814

ADVERTISEMENT

TO

THE FIRST PORTION OF THIS EDITION.

HE Collection of Elizabethan Poetry, which is now again introduced to the curious through the Lee Priory Press, has long been a desideratum among the lovers of our old English literature: for, though it passed through four editions in the reign of King James I. (1602, 1608, 1611, 1621,) it has for at least a century been so rare, that very few have had an opportunity of being gratified with the perusal of it.

The intrinsic merit of the pieces, which it contains, is intended to form the subject of an Introduction, which is kept back till the printers have had time to complete the impression of the original work.

Francis Davison, the collector, and in part author, of these poems, was the son of

Afloat again

CHAPTER XXIV. UP THE THAME THE SECOND DAY.

HEY were not slov take my hint; & ind as to the mere tim day, it was best for to be off, as it was p seven o'clock, & the promised to be very h So we got up and w down to our boat; El thoughtful and abstr ed; the old man very kind and courteous, as i make up for his crabbedness of opinion. Clara cheerful & natural, but a little subdued, I thoug and she at least was not sorry to be gone, and of looked shyly and timidly at Ellen and her stra wild beauty. So we got into the boat, Dick say as he took his place, "Well, it is a fine day!" a the old man answering "What! you like that, you?" once more; and presently Dick was send the bows swiftly through the slow weed-check stream. I turned round as we got into mid-strea and waving my hand to our hosts, saw Ellen le ing on the old man's shoulder, and caressing healthy apple-red cheek, and quite a keen pa smote me as I thought how I should never see beautiful girl again. Presently I insisted on taki the sculls, and I rowed a good deal that day; wh no doubt accounts for the fact that we got very l

SHOULDER HEADS are subsidiary to side heads. Variety of nphasis is limited, because whatever type is used should aline ıd work with the text type without discomfort or trouble. his generally means that the type used for the shoulder head ıust be of the same size as the text; more, it must aline with ıe text, a condition that does not apply to cross heads or side ɜads. Shoulder heads are not usually expected to give great nphasis and are often set in some variation of the text type— g. caps and small caps, even small caps, or upper and lower ıse italic. If they are expected to stand out more than this, ɔper and lower case of bold face may be used.

JT-IN EADS

Cut-in heads are not frequently met with, but they may be fective if they are properly used. They are especially useful when it is desired to have sub-heads and yet not obstruct the flow of reading. They must be well done and the types carefully chosen if they are to be successful and aintain the harmony of the page. An argument against them that they give more trouble to the printer and are corres- ɔndingly more expensive to set.

The Marginal Head

The marginal head should be set in a style that prevents its ɜing confused with the text type. It is placed in the foredge argin at the level required. If it has more than one line, the ıes are alined on the side next to the text. There is no inter- ıption of the text or of the colour of the page; but marginal ɜads do give a distinctive air, or atmosphere, if you like.

Any kind of sub-head may be ignored by the reader if he ants to ignore it, but none so easily as the cut-in head and the arginal head.

FOOTNOTES

Some authors are given to footnotes and some despise them. ertainly they are an excellent depository for second thoughts, ıd when used for that purpose they may be taken as evidence untidy writing or of dyspeptic digestion of the subject matter. 'hen they are used as a means of reference or to give authori- ɜs, there can be no doubt of their value for those readers who

o. Page from William Morris's *News from Nowhere*, elmscott Press, 1892

ODYSSEY II

Now red'ning from the dawn, the Morning ray
Glow'd in the front of Heav'n, and gave the Day.
The youthful Hero, with returning light,
Rose anxious from th'inquietudes of Night.
A royal robe he wore with graceful pride,
A two-edg'd faulchion threaten'd by his side,
Embroider'd sandals glitter'd as he trod,
And forth he mov'd, majestic as a God.
Then by his Heralds, restless of delay,
To council calls the Peers: the Peers obey.
Soon as in solemn form th'assembly sate,
From his high dome himself descends in state.
Bright in his hand a pond'rous javelin shin'd;
Two Dogs, a faithful guard, attend behind;
Pallas with grace divine his form improves,
And gazing crowds admire him as he moves.
His Father's throne he fill'd: while distant stood
The hoary Peers, and Aged Wisdom bow'd.
'Twas silence all: at last Ægyptius spoke;
Ægyptius, by his age and sorrows broke:
A length of days his soul with prudence crown'd,
A length of days had bent him to the ground.
His eldest hope in arms to Ilion came,
By great Ulysses taught the path to fame;
But (hapless youth) the hideous Cyclops tore
His quiv'ring limbs, and quaff'd his spouting gore.

wish for these things. That few people want to read footnotes may be deduced from the fact that convention dictates that they should be set in type a couple of sizes smaller than the text; and they are sometimes set smaller than that. None the less, some authors believe in them, and write footnotes so long that the compositor's struggle to get *some* text type, even if it is only one line, on to the page is painfully evident. The compositor is right in attempting to avoid pages all footnote, but if he and the text are swamped he cannot help displaying the torments of a drowning man. There is little the typographer can do in such a case, unless he can persuade the author to exercise restraint.

Long footnotes are usually set like ordinary paragraphs, but in the smaller size of type; short notes may be centred, unless they are accompanied at the foot of the page by notes of more than one line, when all have the ordinary paragraph indention. If a number of very short notes occur together they may be set two or more to a line, providing that no confusion results. Sometimes the whole of the notes at the foot of the page are run on in one solid block; set thus, it is not easy to see where each note begins, and no system, it seems, could be devised to try the reader's patience more severely or more ingeniously to interrupt his concentration on the text.

For references in the text and at the beginning of each note it is customary to use either superior figures or the range of signs supplied with the fount (asterisk *, dagger †, double dagger ‡ section §, parallel ||, and the paragraph mark ¶, in that order). Few types have entirely satisfactory reference marks, and no roman face possesses a paragraph mark that is not, in my opinion, too bold. A further disadvantage of using them is that there are only six, and the fecundity of notifiers often exhausts their variety: when that happens the seventh reference begins the series again, but doubled (**, ††, ‡‡, etc.). The effect is a blodge. On the other hand, in a suitable book in which the notes are few, reference marks may impart a pleasant flavour of antiquity.

In most books I prefer to see superior figures as note refer-

131. Page from *The Odyssey*, Nonesuch Press 1931

ences, because they are less blatant and do not interfere with the colour of the page. A small matter, but one that is worth stating, is that it would be more in harmony to use old-face (hanging) figures with old-face types and lining figures only with modern faces; but printers and typefounders appear to prefer lining figures, and old-face figures are seldom forthcoming even when asked for.

Some authors are aware of the interruption caused by footnotes, but yet desire to have notes somewhere, and consider they have solved the problem if they set their notes in a body either at the end of each chapter or all together at the end of the book. The walling off of each chapter by a structure of notes seems to me undesirable; and undesirable also is the undigested and indigestible mass at the end of the book. There is a disadvantage in the setting of the references in the text also. Signs cannot be used, as there are not enough of them, and superior figures are resorted to. Superior figures up to 9 cause no trouble; double figures show something of the gap beneath them; triple figures make the page look as though it has a hole in it—but triple figures are reached by people who put their notes at the end of the book. This may be avoided by abandoning superior figures altogether, and setting in the text in the appropriate place the phrase '(see note 234)', or words to that effect. The notes may run into hundreds with this scheme and the unity of the page is still preserved; but at what cost to the morale of the reader the reader himself must judge.

In some books notes are set in the margin. Ample margins must be allowed if this is to be done, and it is preferable that the notes should not be very long. When it is well done, in the few kinds of books this method suits, the result may be pleasantly decorative.

In some old books the problem of copious notes has been solved in a striking manner. Instead of relegating them to an inferior position at the foot of the page the printer has made them into a border running round all four sides of the double spread, set in a smaller size of type to give a different and slightly darker colour that acts as a frame for the text. This

132. Page from the Tiptoft Missal, English manuscript, before 1332

Incipit epistola sancti iheronimi ad
paulinum presbiterum de omnibus
divine historie libris. capitulū pͥmū.

Frater ambrosius
tua michi munus-
cula perferens. detulit
sil et suavissimas
lrās. q̄ a principio
amicitiaȝ. fidē pba
te iam fidei ⁊ veteris amicitie nova:
pferebant. Vera enim illa necessitudo ē.
⁊ xp̄i glutino copulata. quā non utili-
tas rei familiaris. nō p̄ntia tantum
corporꝝ. nō subdola ⁊ palpās adulatio.
sed dei timor. et divinaꝝ scripturarū
studia conciliant. Legim⁹ in veteribȝ
historijs. quosdā lustrasse pͥncias.
novos adijsse ppłos. maria transisse.
ut eos quos ex libris noverant: corā
q̄ȝ viderēt. Sicut pitagoras memphi-
ticos vates. sic plato egiptū. ⁊ architā
tarentinū. eandemq̄ oram ytalie. que
quondā magna grecia dicebat̄. labo-
riosissime peragravit. et ut qui athenis
mgr̄ erat. ⁊ potens. cuiusq̄ doctrinas
achademie gignasia psonabāt. fieret
peregrinus atq̄ discipulus. malēs aliena
verecūde discere: q̄m sua ipudent ingerē.
Deniq̄ cū lrās quasi toto orbe fugien-
tes psequit̄. capt⁹ a piratis ⁊ venūda-
tus. tyrāno crudelissimo paruit. duct⁹
captivus vinct⁹ ⁊ servus. Tamē quia
phūs maior emente se fuit. ad titum
livium. lacteo eloquētie fonte manantē.
de ultimis hispanie galliarūq̄ finibȝ.
quosdam venisse nobiles legimus. ⁊
quos ad contemplationē sui roma nō
traxerat: unius hoīs fama pduxit. Ha-
buit illa etas inauditū oībȝ seculis.
celebrandūq̄ miraculū: ut urbē tantā
ingressi: aliud extra urbem quererent.
Apolloni⁹ sive ille mag⁹ ut vulgus
loquitur. sive phūs. ut pitagorici tra-
dunt. intravit psas. ptransivit caucasū.
albanos. scithas. massagetas. opulē-
tissima indie regna penetravit. et ad
extremum latissimo phison amne
transmisso pervenit ad bragmanas. ut
hyarcam in throno sedentē aureo et de
tantali fonte potantem. inter paucos
discipulos: de natura. de moribȝ. ac de
cursu dierū et siderū audiret docentem.
Inde p elamitas. babilonios. chalde-
os. medos. assyrios. parthos. syros.
phenices. arabes. palestinos. reversus
ad alexandriā: perrexit ad ethiopiā.
ut gignosophistas ⁊ famosissimam
solis mensam videret in sabulo. In-
venit ille vir ubiq̄ qd disceret. et semp
pficiēs. semp se melior fieret. Scrip-
sit super hoc plenissime octo volumi-
nibus: phylostratus. II

Quid loquar de seculi hominibȝ.
cū apłus paulus: vas electionis.
⁊ magister gentiū. qui de conscientia
tanti i se hospitis loquebat̄. dicēs. An
experimentū queritis eius qui in me
loquit̄ xp̄c. Post damascū arabiāq̄
lustratā: ascēdit iherosolimā ut videret
petrū ⁊ mansit apud eū diebȝ quindecī.
Hoc enim mistio ebdomadis et ogdo-
adis: futur⁹ gentiū pdicator instruen-
dus erat. Rursūq̄ post ānos quatuor-
decim assumpto barnaba et tyto: expo-
suit cū apłis evāgeliū. ne forte in vacuum curreret aut cucurrisset. Habet
nescio qd latentis energie: vive vocis
actus. et in aures discipli de auctoris
ore transfusa: fortius sonat. Unde et
eschinus cū rodi exularet. ⁊ legeretur

method requires some expenditure of time and accurate calculation (and possibly the co-operation of an obliging author or editor). References are as usual, by figures or signs.

HEADLINES

The salient parts of a page may be said to be three: the text, including notes; the headline; and the folio, or page number.

The first thing to be said about the headline is that we are much too fond of it. Too often it serves no practical or aesthetic use, and does not earn in service the value of the labour it consumes. It is there because the printer or the publisher or the typographer considers that the public might be concerned by its absence; or because they believe that a page without a headline is too spartan and out of the ordinary; or simply because they are in the habit of having headlines.

There are times when a headline is of no practical use, but does act as a decoration, subserving the design, and there is then an argument for its presence that may be sustained.

On the other hand, the headline may be an invaluable part of a system of reference, a signpost on an involved network of roads and bypaths directing the reader quickly and efficiently towards the place he is looking for. In any book in which it can be of such use there is no doubt of its value, and there should be no question of omitting it; there should equally be no question of including it where it can have no possible value.

Headlines are mainly of three different kinds: running headlines, or title headlines; section headlines; and page headlines. The term 'running head' is in common use; the others I have had to invent because there is no satisfactory nomenclature. 'Page headline' and 'page heading' too often mean simply headline.

(*a*) RUNNING HEADLINES consist of the title of the book, appearing either on both left- and right-hand pages, or else on left-hand pages only, the right-hand page having a section headline. I can see no sense in the running headline, and in my opinion not even the plea of decoration can justify its use. If the

133. Opening page from the 42-line Bible, Mainz, 1456

reader needs to be reminded, at each opening, of the title of the book he is reading, he cannot be much interested in the book; if the publisher believes that it is necessary, either he has little faith in the intelligence of his readers, or believes that his book can make little mark upon the reader's mind. The truth, of course, is that it is a habit; many people, publishers and printers included, never *see* headlines, and the running head is there because no one thought of omitting it. The only recommendation I have heard for it is that it serves as an advertisement, enabling your neighbour in train or bus to see what you are reading.

(*b*) SECTION HEADLINES (including part headlines and chapter headlines). These consist of the titles of whatever subdivisions (chapters, books, parts, etc.) the book may have. If there are chapters only, and running headlines are not used, the chapter title may be set on both left- and right-hand pages; if the chapters are divided into sub-sections, the chapter title appears on the left-hand page and the wording of the sub-head on the right. When sub-heads are used as headlines there is the danger that a sub-section may commence on a new page, when the headline, repeating the wording above the sub-head, looks a little silly; the only thing to do is to readjust the pagination or abandon consistency and omit the headline. Books that are divided into parts or 'books' which are again divided into chapters have the part title as the left headline and the chapter title as the right headline, so that wherever he opens the book the reader knows in what part and in what chapter he is and may direct himself from that information. In an anthology the author's name may go on one side and the title of his contribution on the other. The variations of the section headline are limited only by the number of ways of dividing a book into parts, cantos, books, sections, fits, and so on; and it is because they signpost this diversity that they are valuable.

(*c*) The PAGE HEADLINE. This may appear on both left- and right-hand pages, or on one side only, in conjunction with a section headline on the other side. Its wording summarizes the contents of the page over which it appears; or indicates the

134. Page from *The Four Gospels*, with wood-engravings by Eric Gill, Golden Cockerel Press, 1931

that when Jesus had finished these parables, he departed thence. And when he was come into his own country, he taught them in their synagogue, insomuch that they were astonished, and said, Whence hath this man this wisdom, and these mighty works? Is not this the carpenter's son? is not his mother called Mary? and his brethren, James, and Joses, and Simon, and Judas? And his sisters, are they not all with us? Whence then hath this man all these things? And they were offended in him. But Jesus said unto them, A prophet is not without honour, save in his own country, and in his own house. And he did not many mighty works there because of their unbelief.

AT THAT TIME HEROD THE TETRARCH HEARD OF THE FAME OF JESUS, AND SAID UNTO HIS SERVANTS, THIS IS JOHN THE BAPTIST; HE IS RISEN FROM THE DEAD; & THEREFORE MIGHTY works do shew forth themselves in him. For Herod had laid hold on John, and bound him, and put him in prison for Herodias' sake, his brother Philip's wife. For John said unto him, It is not lawful for thee to have her. And when he would have put him to death, he feared the multitude, because they counted him as a prophet. But when Herod's

main topic of the page; or, and this is bad, pretends to be a witty or profound remark concerning it. The page headline is therefore different for every page. Its value is doubtful. It may provide an amusing diversion for a bored reader—he may even, by skimming through them, consider that he has got as much as he wants from the book without bothering to read the text; but the page headline cannot act as a guide, because it does not point the way in any direction. Some authors are addicted to page headlines as a mannerism, and it is a mannerism that costs them some time and trouble; indeed, no headline is as troublesome as this one. It cannot be provided by a mere instruction to the printer, as can others; each one must be written individually by the author. They cannot be written until the book is in page proof, and then their addition may make a revised proof necessary where otherwise it might not have been needed.

The style of setting headlines varies from book to book and from publisher to publisher. There is no 'right' way, and the only wrong way is that which fails to cohere in the general design. That they should cohere is a detail that is too often lost sight of. The style of headlines is subject to infinite nuances that affect the atmosphere and colour of the page very strongly, and may give to it either the right effect or the wrong one. The type used may be the same face as the text type, and even the same size, or something quite different. It should be remembered that the headline is a unit of a larger design, that it should therefore accord with such other units of that design as chapter heads and part titles, and of course, with the text above which it appears. A headline set in a comparatively large size of swashbuckling italic such as Garamond can give to a page an air of gaiety and freedom, while one set in, say, text capitals, is more serious and business-like.

The position of the headline is also subject to variations. It is not always centred across the measure. Often it is set to one side, opposite pages being set to opposite sides. The amount of space between the headline and the text is a matter of judgement, but it should not be enough to isolate the headline.

135. Page with engraved chapter-head illustration from d'Ussieux, *Le Décaméron françois*, Paris, 1774

ÉLIZENE,

ANECDOTE OTTOMANE.

LE mois le plus riant de l'année pour le peuple de Constantinople, c'est-à-dire, le mois d'avril venoit de renaître, & le ferrail du Grand-Seigneur s'apprêtoit à célébrer, avec tout le faste ordinaire aux orientaux, cette fête annuelle

128. Engraved chapter-head ornaments, eighteenth century

Decorations of various kinds are often used with the type, and may take the form of small ornaments incorporated in the headline itself, or of bands or ornament, or lengths of rule or border, between the headline and the text. Decoration is better if it is discreet; the ornament should not overcome the type.

FOLIOS

Folios, or page numbers, have not always been an indispensable part of a book, though nowadays we seem to be fixed in the habit of using them. There is no point in attempting to overcome the habit. In even the most ephemeral and slight of novels folios have their uses, and they are very necessary in any kind of serious book.

The position of the folio varies, but in most books it is placed either in the headline or at the foot of the page; in some modern (or modernistic) books, the designers of which appear to have thought it necessary to be different at all costs, the folios appear in the outer margin, perhaps in ultra-heavy type. If the purpose of reference were the only consideration the folio in the margin would be commendable, but it is no better, and perhaps rather worse, *for reference*, than the folio at the outer end of the headline. Both can easily be seen as the pages are flicked over. Bare utility is not, however, the only thing that matters; there is also the question of appearance.

When the folio is set in the headline it is usually set in the figures of the same type; but this should not be done where that type is much larger than the text. Eighteen-point figures are not likely to look well over an eleven-point text. In these cases it is better to set the folios in figures of the text type and aline them with the headline. The usual place for the folio is at the extreme outer end of the headline, but there is no reason why it should not be indented a little for a change.

Folios in the margin are not often seen, and then only in decorative or more pretentious books, for this use involves extra labour and therefore extra cost. Although the position is good from the point of view of reference, it is bad on almost every other count. The folio is isolated in space, and so draws an unreasonable amount of attention to itself; and it forms a distracting spot in the corner of the eye that is destructive of concentration, particularly when heavy figures are used.

At the foot of the page the folio is subject to more variation than elsewhere. It occupies a line to itself, and in most books it is centred on that line; but it may be set to one side, level with the edge of the type measure, beyond it, or indented within it. It may be separated from the text only by the normal leading of the page, or by any amount of leading that may be thought necessary. The figures used are usually of the text type, but they may be smaller or larger or in a different type. Sometimes the figure is flanked by ornaments or by square brackets or parentheses acting as ornaments.

Occasionally in books without headlines the folio is set at the head of the page in a style more commonly found at the foot.

In some books the preliminary pages are numbered in lower-case roman figures, otherwise treated in the same way as the arabic figures in the body of the book. Some printers and publishers do this regularly, others only when, for one reason or another, the number of pages the prelims will occupy is uncertain.

PROPORTION AND MARGINS

It is a convention, from which we depart comparatively seldom, that books should be upright oblongs. This is so much the rule that printing and binding machinery is adapted to the upright oblong and any other shape introduces problems. The horizontal oblong, which is a format sometimes employed, does not, if it is a standard size, introduce more than minor difficulties. In recent years, however, a number of square or squarish books have appeared on the market. The production of a square book involves either some waste of paper, or else a special making to the size required, probably some waste of machining capacity, and awkwardness in the bindery. All this may entail additional costs and a designer ought to look

Chap. 32 K{Charles Henry *The historie of* Book IV

224

The End of MAN 179

White Roads and Green Lanes

FORMER TIMES AND FORMER WAYS 69

THE MUTE IMAGE

[FANCY THOUGHTS]

Along the Stream

and Other Things and Places 153

137. A selection of headline styles

carefully at these matters before he decides that a square format is essential for a book in hand.

Paper from time immemorial has been manufactured in sheets of oblong shape; and though to-day paper sizes differ in different countries, the rule remains. These sheets when folded, as they are folded after printing, into folio, quarto, octavo, etc., give oblongs whose sides are in the proportion of 1 to $1\frac{1}{3}$ or $1\frac{1}{2}$.

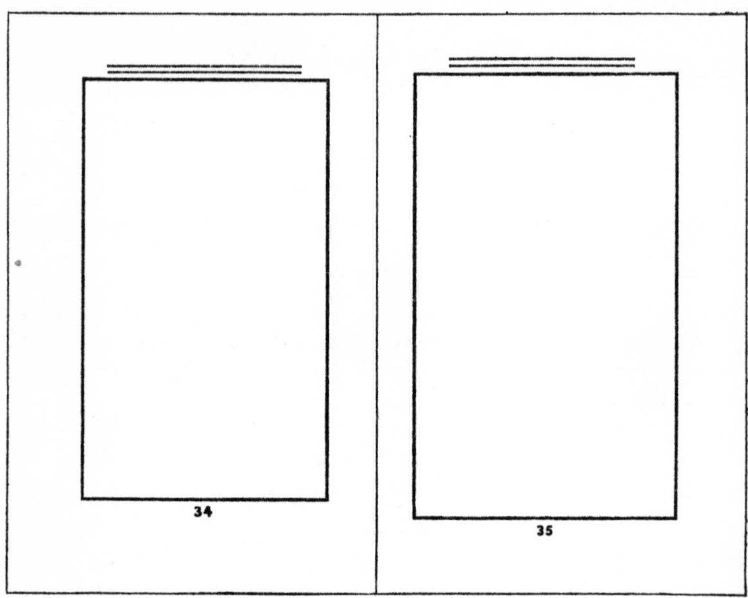

138. Diagram to show (left) 55 per cent type area and (right) 58 per cent type area

The type area follows approximately the shape of the page. In America paper is made in sizes different from European that produce squarer books, wider in proportion to their height.

The difference between the area of the type and the area of the page on which it is to be printed is a quantity of white space that must be apportioned between four margins. Proportion and margins are interdependent, and the one governs the other in some respects. How large the type area should be, and therefore how much white space should be left has been a matter of opinion at all times, but there is a theory that the type area should be about 50 per cent of the page area. That any page should consist of 50 per cent of white is apt to appear somewhat striking, suggesting an unnecessary waste of paper. Actually such a page is quite an ordinary one, as may be discovered by taking any book from the shelf and measuring it. In the second world war regulations designed to save paper stipulated a type area not less than 58 per cent, and the margins this left were

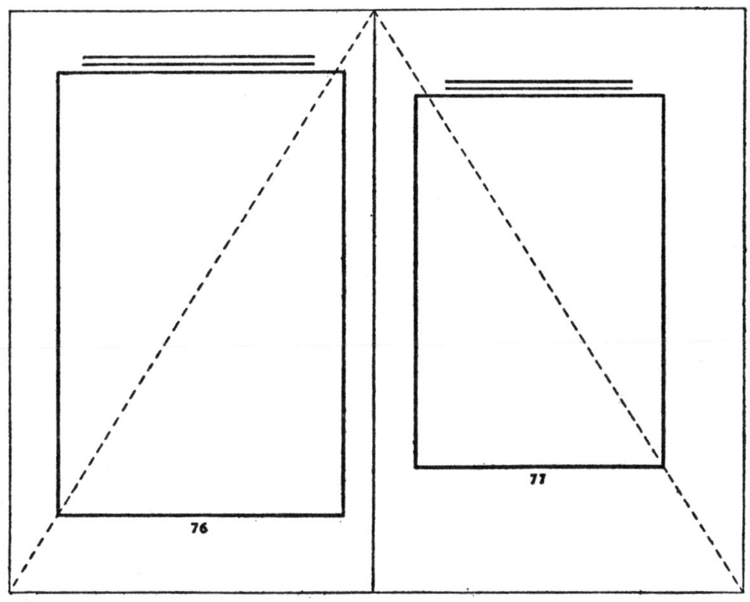

139. Diagram to show proportions and margins of pages calculated on the diagonal

considered somewhat skimpy. So-called large-paper editions may be as much as 80 per cent blank paper. A page with no more than 35 per cent blank looks decidedly crowded, and may be seen in many paperback books. The fifty-fifty basis may be taken as the norm, from which the exception departs. The exceptions, because they are abnormal, are not therefore bad; everybody likes ample margins and hates meagre ones. There is a vast amount of good on either side of the norm; what should be avoided are extremely narrow margins that give the impression that the book has been clumsily cut down in size; or over-large margins, in which the panels of type are two lost rafts in the middle of a desolate ocean.

Whatever the proportion of space may be, it is not simply space. From the first it can only be thought of as a frame or setting for the type panel; it must be divided into four strips called margins. The problem may be looked at in another way, not as the apportionment of margins, but as the setting of the type panel in a given space. It does not matter what point of view is taken if the result is successful.

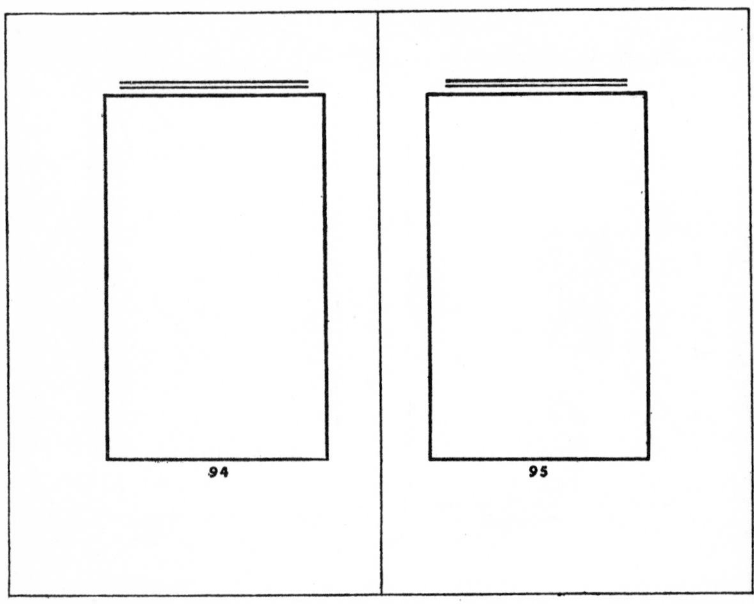

140. Diagram to show margins in the proportion 1½, 2, 3 and 4

There are rules for the apportionment of margins and various methods of achieving a satisfactory result. In one method advocated in textbooks the panel and the page must be of the same proportion. If this is agreed, the size of the panel and the dimensions of the margins can be obtained at once by making the diagonals of the two coincide, as in Figure 139.

Frequently, however, this method is unsatisfactory because the type area is not of the same proportion as the page, and it is not ideal that it should be. When this happens the type may be placed to give margins in the following proportions: inner, $1\frac{1}{2}$; top, 2; outer, 3; and foot, 4. It is an old rule, and good one, but it should not be too rigidly applied; there are times when for optical reasons, depending upon the kind of headline in use, it may be advisable to make the top margin larger or smaller, and there may be similar reasons for other variations.

It may have been remarked that the inner margin is, approximately, only half the width of the outer one, and the reason for this is that the unit of design is not the single page I have so far dealt with, but the two facing pages seen together at any opening of a book. If the unit were one page we should be right in making the margins on each side equal, like those of a mounted picture, and this is what some printers do if they are left to their own devices; it is a strange error, and one that originated, I think, in the nineteenth century—at least, I have never noticed it in any earlier book. But the unit is not one page, because we do not see the pages separately; therefore the two narrow inner margins combine to make a channel between the two pages of the same width, or a little less, as each of the margins on the foredges. The top margin is less than the bottom one fundamentally, perhaps, because the eye always sees the centre of a page rather higher than the actual centre; certainly a page with too small a margin at the foot looks as though it has slipped down.

A number of modern designers, anxious to re-examine every convention, have designed books with the margins directly contrary to the conventional arrangement, as though the diagram of Figure 140 were turned upside down. Other experiments with margins have occupied the minds of designers, and occasionally the effect is impressive. These experiments lead to success only if there is ample space to juggle with.

Good margins (not necessarily wide margins) are of importance in the design of a book and should be arranged with care, and as soon as possible in the course of book production. They contribute largely to the comfort and pleasure of reading, giving ease to the eye and dignity to the book. In production they form a basic frame on which everything else is built up. Chapter heads, half titles, and the title-page are, it will be noticed, placed, not in direct relation to the page area, but in relation to the position of the type area on the paper. Illustrations are placed in the same relation, whether line or tone. The proportions of the margins may even be echoed in the binding and the jacket, where lettering or ornament on the front board often looks better if it is placed a little nearer the inner edge than the foredge, and may look wrong if it is centred on the board.

XVII

PART TITLES AND CHAPTER HEADS

THE divisions of a literary work are more complex than at first they may appear to be. Within the text there are divisions between words, between clauses and phrases, between sentences, and between paragraphs, and those more emphatic paragraph divisions marked by a line of white or by a row of stars or asterisks; and further the divisions marked by sub-heads. We take these things for granted nowadays, but they were not always a matter of custom: some early manuscripts show such a passion for continuity that they dispense even with spaces between the words, the reader apparently being expected to make out the sense by context and patience. Little wonder, then, that major divisions were ignored or submerged.

It is difficult to say exactly how these major divisions developed. An early means of indication was a mark or tick that developed later into a paragraph mark; or the first line of the new section projected into the left-hand margin of the page. These devices appear to have been used inconsistently and became reduced in importance until they indicated only paragraphs.

Not until the numbering and entitling of chapters was practised may we say with certainty that a definite system of division had arrived, that, in fact, chapters existed. It is difficult to fix even that date. Chapter divisions had been developed by the end of the sixteenth century, yet as late as the eighteenth Defoe was capable of writing books without any chapter divisions of any kind.

We have come to expect chapter divisions in our books and

to take them for granted because as readers we have been brought up on them. Our childhood fairy tales showed that they were part of the accepted order of things, and later our school books unanimously confirmed the fact. Between the close of one chapter and the opening of the next we have learned to rest with the author; or to gather our energies in suspense for the leap into the next chapter and the release of tension. So a book is parcelled out into sections, as our lives are into days, convenient periods capable of being remembered and understood, and showing in the accumulation of what has passed a pattern of events and ideas.

We are so used to chapter divisions that the chapter head has become synonymous with that division, inseparable from it, exerting at times a tyranny that few writers have ventured to overthrow. James Joyce rebelled against it in *Ulysses*; but then James Joyce was 'odd'; and even he could not defy convention without losing something of value to the enemy. And yet the truth is that in a great many books—particularly novels—neither chapter number nor chapter title has any purpose of importance, and the paragraph mark or large initial of our ancestors, or commencing a new page, would serve just as well. How many readers of the popular novel ever notice the chapter numbers or have any use for them? How many ever read or remember the chapter titles?

Grouping of chapters into parts does not occur in every book and in those in which it does there is generally reason for it. I do not want it to appear that, because of what I have said above, I am attacking the institution of part titles and chapter heads indiscriminately. Chapter and part divisions often form a strong system of articulation with a definite and serious function; they may indeed be the frame on which the structure of the book rests, and where part titles and chapter heads help to elucidate that structure their value is obvious.

Sometimes a book is found with three kinds of divisions: chapters grouped into parts, parts grouped into 'books' or sections. Such a scheme is too often unwieldy. It may arise from a passion for orderliness, but too frequently it only leads the

141. Chapter head, from *La Mer des histoires*, Paris, 1488. Border and initial cut on wood

Selond les escriptures anciennes La .ve. aage du siecle commẽca en la destruction du roiaulme de iudee cestassauoir lan xie. de sedechias roy de iuda qui est lan du mõde iij M. iij C lxxiiij. du deluge. M. viij C xix. De la natiuite dabraham mil .iiij. cens et xxvij. Du cõmencement du regne de dauid et de la iiij e aage iiij C lxxxiiij. ãs. Et dura iusq̃s a laduenemẽt de nostre saulueur hiesucrist / q̃ fut lã xlij de octouiã auguste. contiẽt xiiij generations comprenãs v C ꝛ iiij xx ix ans Et est comparee a viellesse. Car cõe telle aage est fatigee et trauaillee de plusieurs maux: Ainsy fust le peuple des hebrieux quasse et rompu pour les persecutions quẽ ceste aage il endura.

Selond beda ꝛ eusebius ceste quinte aage cõmenca lan du monde iij M. v cens et. ix. cest. v. cẽs iiij xx ꝛ dix ans deuãt la natiuite de hiesucrist. Laquelle chose est prouuee en ceste maniere. Car se iceulx ans sont ioings ensẽble ilz font le nombre de v M. cent iiij xx. et xix ans / lesquelx sont depuis adã iusques a laduent de hiesucrist. donques le premier an de ceste. ve. aage est lan ensuiuãt le xie an du regne de sedechie / ou quel cõe est ia dit fust faicte la desolation du temple ꝛ de la cite de hierusalẽ. ꝛ du regne la exterminatiõ des iuifz Ceste desolation tesmoing hieremye dura lxx ãs cestassauoir iusq̃ au secõd an de darius filz de ydaspes. En ce lieu ne deuons point lesser lopinion daulcũs touchant lesdis lxx. ans. Car aulcũs historiens cõme comestor ꝛ africanus / les cõmencẽt lan xiije. de iosias pere de ioachim / ou q̃l an hieremie cõmenca prophetiser. Et ainsy durerent iusques au premier an de cirus Les autres cõmencerent lan iije. de ioachim filz de iosias / et les terminẽt lã xxe. de cirus: ou quel tẽps icelluy cirus acompaignie de dare prist et destruit babilone apres linterfectiõ de baltasar Les autres cõmencent lan ve. de la captiuite. cestassauoir quãt nabugodo/

author into disorder and disjunction, and the reader into bewilderment. Such triple division should be practised only where there is very good reason for it.

THE PART TITLE

The part title marks the major division, and consequently it is treated in a special way. To accord with its importance, and to impress upon the reader the fact that here is a serious pause in the argument, that, in fact, a new train of ideas or a new approach to the theme commences, it is usually given the dignity of a right-hand page to itself. Whether the last chapter of the preceding part ends on a right-hand page also is no matter; if it does, it merely means that the part title faces a blank.

There is here something of the function and of the opportunity of the title-page—a clear field with a simple purpose of announcement and a more subtle one of anticipation. While it should not pretend to compete with the title-page itself, the part title should be in harmony with it, and the typographer may do much with it. By its nature and circumstance, it should dominate the chapter head, and to this end the page can be set more monumentally, and if necessary decorated with flowers, borders, or rules. Generally the wording is extremely simple, consisting of nothing more than the number and the title of the part; or of the title only in some instances. In some books there is no title, the author considering that his purpose in division is sufficiently achieved by numbering the parts.

White space, properly used, cannot but add to the dignity and power of lettering, if that lettering is itself good. This property of space is utilized on many part titles, first by restricting the setting to the words only, eschewing all additions or ornament, and then by choice of type and placing of the lines. Whatever kind of face is selected, it should be one that is good of its kind. Some faces scarcely allow one to go wrong, and an example is Perpetua Titling. The setting should be carefully done, and where lines of capitals are used, they should be letter-spaced to improve their appearance and, what is important, to

142. Page from the *Works of Congreve*, Baskerville, Birmingham, 1761

THE
OLD BATCHELOR.

ACT I. SCENE I.

SCENE, *The Street.*

BELLMOUR *and* VAINLOVE *meeting.*

BELLMOUR.

VAINLOVE, and abroad ſo early! good Morrow; I thought a Contemplative Lover could no more have parted with his Bed in a Morning, than he could have ſlept in't.

VAINLOVE.

Bellmour, good Morrow—Why Truth on't is, theſe early Sallies are not uſual to me; but Buſineſs, as you ſee, Sir—— [*Shewing Letters.*] And Buſineſs muſt be follow'd, or be loſt.

obtain optically equal spacing. The lines will almost certainly require leading, but how much must depend on the effect aimed at. As for the position of the lines on the page, there is little one can say about it. Certainly no rules can be laid down. Generally, conventionally one may say, the lines are set in the upper half of the page, but at what height particularly depends on the circumstances. The only thing to do with these pages is to sit back and look at them and to alter them until they are right. That is good advice concerning any page of a book.

Part titles in which decoration is used are in a different category, not in the sense that they require any less stringent care in design, but because they impose on the typographer a different approach. The decoration may be slight, or it may be elaborate; in either case it must be in harmony with the general atmosphere and design of the book. Where it is used it is most often printed from fleurons, but new designs by artists are used sometimes. The decoration is in a sense added, but it should not appear so; indeed, it should never look as though it were superadded, as though it were something that might be imposed or subtracted at will. It must do something necessary, even if that thing is only to give pleasure; it must enhance the spirit of the book; it must join with the lettering in a unified and cognate whole.

Another kind of part title is that designed entirely by the artist. Wood-engravings notably, and also scraper-board drawings, have been used in this way, and auto-lithography has also been employed. The artist's part title, where it is suitably used, gives an added richness to a book, and experiments in this direction are worth while. Books in which they appear may demand a special form of title-page, and artist and typographer can here collaborate.

Part titles are usually blank on the reverse, the chapter commencing on the next right-hand page. Sometimes the blank is used for an introductory quotation or some such matter, and where this is short it is well to put it there; the alternative position on the part title itself is seldom satisfactory unless special arrangements are made for it.

THE CHAPTER HEAD

A chapter head is that collocation of chapter number, chapter title, and large initial with which, in most books, each chapter begins. To these three elements are added, in certain books, quotations, synopses, sub-titles, decorations, or illustrations, or whatever fancy may occur to author, typographer, or artist.

None of these elements is obligatory. As I have shown, there is no reason sometimes why any of them should be used. Some writers prefer to have only a chapter number and no title, a few a chapter title and no number. Large initials are a convention or a habit to which we are addicted, but there are times when they are unnecessary or undesirable and are omitted. Any possible arrangement of the elements of a chapter head may be found in one book or another, with or without reason, but it does not need elaborate statistical machinery to discover that in the majority of books only the three elements of chapter number, chapter title, and initial occur, and on this arrangement I have based this section.

The simplest thing to do with both the chapter number and the chapter title is to set each in some variation of the text type and to centre it across the text measure, and this is what is commonly done. The use of the same series as the text ensures homogeneity, and if the sizes are chosen with discretion the result is pleasant. The chapter number can be set in several ways, with or without the word 'chapter' and with the figure in arabic or roman numerals or spelled out. Below it, the chapter title may be set in capitals or in capitals and lower-case, or even in caps and small caps, usually of a size larger than the text type; rarely, the type used for the chapter title is smaller than the text type. Below the chapter title the text commences with or without a large initial.

Chapter heads seldom commence at the top of a page. They are started lower down than the first line of a full page, each chapter so many lines consistently throughout the book. They are, in printer's parlance, dropped, and the distance from the top of the page to the first part of the chapter head is called a chapter drop. It is not unimportant, this space at the head of the chapter, for it has some psychological value not easy to explain. It is not a case of the more the better; a deep chapter drop looks like a mannerism, but it may be right in relation to the book and its design—the word 'mannerism' is used too often in a derogatory sense excluding pleasure or utility. On the other hand, no chapter drop at all can be equally right. Between the two extremes variations of the chapter drop convey, together with the chapter head, many shades of expression.

There is no reason why the type of the chapter head should be confined to the series in which the text is set if a more suitable effect is obtained by using a different type. The mixing of types is only bad when it is done without reason or taste, as it was too often in the nineteenth century; that it can be done with equal success as failure is shown in the advertising columns of our newspapers; in the news columns of the popular dailies it is apt to appear at its worst.

Restriction to a single face throughout a book imposes limits on the variety and range of character that may be expressed by the typographer through the medium of type, and there are times and books and display faces, apart from his own roving imagination, that will suggest to him the use of a type different from that of the text. Immediately this principle of type mixing is allowed the horizon expands, until the only limits to an unending variety of design become the typographer's taste or ingenuity or the harassed printer's refusal to co-operate any further.

There is nothing good in searching far for strange type faces or extrarodinary ornaments or borders; these of themselves cannot make typography good, or endow it with that freshness or charm we always hope for. The best or the strangest of types is nothing until it is used, and it is in its use that the quality of design lies. There are harmonies and discords, subtle or apparent, in the relations between types, and these should be realized and exploited in the layout. Unfortunately, the ordinary reader, from lack of knowledge or perception, is tone-deaf as far as these harmonies and discords are concerned, and only the

143. Chapter head with printer's flowers, from P. S. Fournier, *Dissertation sur l'origine et les progrès de gravure*, etc., *c.* 1758–60

DISSERTATION

SUR

L'ORIGINE ET LES PROGRÉS

DE L'ART

DE GRAVER EN BOIS,

Pour éclaircir quelques traits de l'Hiſtoire de l'IMPRIMERIE, & prouver que GUTTEMBERG n'en eſt pas l'Inventeur.

DES erreurs ſoûtenues par des Auteurs célèbres, & long-temps accréditées, ſont de nature à en impoſer : elles ont tenu & ne tiennent encore que trop ſouvent la vérité captive. C'eſt une erreur de cette eſpèce qui me paroît avoir fait donner à Gut-

professional or the connoisseur seems to hear them consciously. They penetrate to the layman, perhaps, but certainly no more than the nuances of music; rather less. In this half-century we babble of our dreams of new design and hope for great things in a future of perpetual sunshine; but then, as now, it will remain true that ninety-nine people out of a hundred are unaware of design, though it has existed about them in diverse forms all their lives. It is recognized only when it is labelled in large letters. We are getting that habit of labelling now, and no doubt there will come a time, and soon, when we shall set out, like architects and town-planners in their subject, to tell the public what in typography is designed, in the hope that they will learn from each book enough to allow them to understand more of the typography of the next.

I said a few pages back that the usage was to centre the elements of the chapter head across the measure. That arrangement can be varied or abandoned, when necessary, and a new or different arrangement made. The chapter head may be set to one side; may be run on in a block, usually of capitals (a Morris idea); or, following the example of our respected grandfathers, it may be drawn in a delicate arch and festooned with roses and trailing vines. On occasion, if the chapters are sufficiently distinct and complete in themselves to warrant it, the chapter head may be set on a separate right-hand page, like a half-title, the chapter itself commencing with or without a heading on the following right-hand page.

There is no point in listing further possibilities of variation; description is apt to be wordy and after all bare of meaning when compared with the object itself; the few chapter heads reproduced here will serve to show something of what may be achieved; and any bookshelf will be found to hold both good and bad examples.

A chapter head may depend for its effect entirely upon the use of type, but on the other hand some kind of ornament or rule, plain or fancy, may be included as part of the design. Whether it is good or bad to do this is a matter of some controversy, in which I do not propose to take sides; neither side

144. Chapter-head from Bodoni's *Manuale Tipografico*, Parma, 1818

GIAMBATTISTA BODONI

A CHI LEGGE

Eccovi i saggi dell'industria e delle fatiche mie di molti anni consecrati con veramente geniale impegno ad un'arte. che è compimento della più bella, ingegnosa, e giovevole invenzione degli uomini, voglio dire dello scrivere, di cui è la stampa la miglior maniera, ogni qual volta sia pregio dell'opera far a molti copia delle stesse parole, e maggiormente quando importi aver certezza che

2A

is entirely right. Many excellent typographers, among them Baskerville and Bodoni, have on occasion thought it better to avoid ornament, and the quality of their work is beyond question. None the less, it does not prove that all ornaments and printer's flowers should be consigned to the melting-pot forthwith and no new ones designed; it proves only that in some circumstances and by some people a successful result may be achieved without them. It must, indeed, be a frigid world in which we cannot be allowed the smallest frill, as even the work of Baskerville and Bodoni will indicate; we may, on suitable occasion, indulge in elaborate ornamentation and get away with it. Success lies in more than one direction and can be achieved by purpose, but seldom by hazard. Both antis and pros have done fine work the quality of which cannot be doubted except by the fanatics of the opposite faction. Often both kinds are done by the same man with no feeling of faction at all; but there are others who elevate a personal preference to the status of a principle, and these must be any sensible man's abhorrence,

Where ornament is used it may be of two kinds, either drawn or engraved or painted and printed by some reproductive process, or built up from printer's flowers. The first kind is usually made especially for a particular book; the second is made up of standard elements of type the arrangement of which is subject to infinite variation. Frederic Warde's *Book of Monotype Ornaments* is a first-class demonstration of how printer's flowers can be used.

Even the most beautiful ornament or arrangement of flowers needs to be used with discretion and judgement. No ornament can of itself make a book design successful, but any ornament can, if it is not well used, prove an enemy that will ruin all. Ornament must contribute to the design, not strive to dominate it or impose disharmony or incongruity. If there are many chapters, and particularly if they are short, an ornamented chapter head may prove an irritation and an obstruction because it is repeated too often. There is always a danger in repeating an ornament, a danger that is more acute with freak or individual patterns, or with those that seem to incorporate something of illustration. That particular difficulty can be

145. Chapter head from *The Bible designed to be read as Literature*, Heinemann, 1937

THE ACTS OF THE APOSTLES

A HISTORY OF THE EARLY CHURCH

THE ASCENSION

THE FORMER TREATISE have I made, O Theophilus, of all that Jesus began both to do and teach, until the day in which he was taken up, after that he through the Holy Ghost had given commandments unto the apostles whom he had chosen: to whom also he showed himself alive after his passion by many infallible proofs, being seen of them forty days, and speaking of the things pertaining to the kingdom of God: and, being assembled together with them, commanded them that they should not depart from Jerusalem, but wait for the promise of the Father, which, saith he, "Ye have heard of me. For John truly baptized with water; but ye shall be baptized with the Holy Ghost not many days hence."

When they therefore were come together, they asked of him, saying, "Lord, wilt thou at this time restore again the kingdom to Israel?" And he said unto them, "It is not for you to know the times or the seasons, which the Father hath put in his own power. But ye shall receive power, after that the Holy Ghost is come upon you: and ye shall be witnesses unto me both in Jerusalem, and in all Judæa, and in Samaria, and unto the uttermost part of the earth."

And when he had spoken these things, while they beheld, he

avoided, of course, by making each chapter head different—if the designer has the time, the patience, and a store of invention.

The large initial with which in many books each chapter commences is a legacy from the manuscript. By the fifteenth century the calligraphy and especially the illumination of manuscripts had reached a high level, and on the best of them was lavished such care as few, very few printed books have

Um aiad
uerterem
Modernorum figmen
ta a doctrina Arestote
lis presertim in scia vni
uersaliū q̄ sunt cardies
et pncipia cuiuslibet ar:
tis z scie multiformiter
deuiare z antiq̄ꝝ cetum
q̄daȝ inter se pblemata
neutraliter volutare q̄ꝝ
pmū magne ꝯtrouersie
in sciaꝝ ꝯclusionibꝫ pbu
it occasionē Iuxta illud
Paruus error in princi
pio maximus fit in fine. zm sco nouelloꝝ in pbia arestotelis aliūpnorum

146. Wood-cut initial used by Johann Landen, Cologne, 1496

received. The treatment of initials was particularly remarkable. It is true that some of them were so elaborated that to us they no longer appear to bear the shape of letters, but whether there could be any doubt about them in the minds of our ancestors it is difficult for us, who have been nurtured on the roman letter, to judge. What we do know is that the tradition of the illuminated or decorative initial was of some importance, for it was carried over into the printed book; not as a printed letter, however, for it was difficult with the apparatus of the fifteenth century to print multicoloured initials in register—although by some means not certainly known, Peter Schoeffer, Gutenberg's successor, printed magnificent two-colour initials in perfect register. For a time after the introduction of printing, initials were drawn in the printed book by the illuminator, a space being left by the printer to receive them; or they were impressed, colour by colour, with hand stamps. In this space was printed a small letter, a capital or lower-case of the text type, to inform the illuminator what initial was required—a practice that seems to suggest that the illuminator could not read, or at least was unable to read the language in question. It was intended that the printed letter, the initial indicator, should be covered by the

Catho tzo duytzschem ·

Atho was eyn wijser man
Der sich wijsheyt versan
Was zo rome ī eren grois
Do hei sach dy werlt blois
Van eren jnd van zoichtē
Begünde hey zo soichten
Umb einē soen had hei do
Lerende jnd sprach also
Eyn gedangke mir jn myn hertzen quaem
Daer van ich in moide vernam
Dat veil der lude yr zijt verquüisten
Die güder seden noch nye engewusten

147. Wood-cut initial used by Ulrich Zell, Cologne, *c.* 1500

illumination, or so we may think, but in practice this did not always happen; apparently its continuing presence did not worry the artist or the reader. It is probable that the same illuminators supplied the initials of both manuscripts and printed books without distinction, despite the antagonism that developed between the scribes and the printers. It can have made little practical difference to the artist whether the book on which he worked had been written by hand or had been produced by the new mechanical means; though he may have found that with the advent of printing he had more work to do, because there were more books.

At what stage and by whose order books were thus embellished is not always clear. Sometimes, it seems, the printer had the work done (he may even have employed an illuminator in his printing-house), so that he could present a complete and finished book for sale; on the other hand, the purchaser of the book sometimes commissioned the illumination, and so obtained the kind of work he preferred. There appears to be no doubt that printed books were sold without illumination, perhaps for this reason, and some of them survive with the spaces provided still unfilled and others with the work partly done.

148. Initial used by Erhard Ratdolt, Augsburg, 1499

It was not until late in the fifteenth century that printed initials came into use. Their advent was one of many signs of independence of the manuscript and the illuminator that was slowly arising, though it was not to be complete until well on into the following century. These printed initials were by no means as grand or as complex as those done by hand, and some of them were embellished by the pen and the brush. The illuminator and also those who valued his work made here their last gesture. The art of illumination was dying in proportion as the craft of printing improved and as books increased in number and their price was reduced. Printing ceased to imitate the art of the scribe, and was applied to the production of less elaborate books in

149. Initial used by Johann Schoeffer, Mainz, 1518

greater numbers; in other words, it began to be realized that the press was an instrument of mass production, and painstaking and laborious illumination became impossible on the score of expense, if not incongruous aesthetically. The illuminator was compelled

150. Initial used for a title page by Pierre le Caron (*c.* 1489–1500), Paris

to find other work to make his living, and if he returned to illumination it was only to execute a commission for some single volume valued by its owner or intended, perhaps, to be used as a present or a prize. That is exactly his position to-day.

The printed initial could not pretend to compete with the illuminated one because it could be neither as rich in colour nor as elaborate in detail except by an expenditure of labour and time out of proportion with the result—which even then was likely to fall short of what was aimed at; but to our eyes those early initials seem to be complex and rich, even when they were printed in only one colour, for they remained overlaid with the tradition of gothic art. In these days, for ordinary books, we have abandoned colour and complexity, and the initials of most of our books are no more than plain letters of large size. The fifteenth- and sixteenth-century printers had more courage and more ingenuity than we in this matter, it seems—or was it that the world turned more slowly then and men did not so value haste? Plain initials were exceptional in their books, and were by no means the rule even as late as the Victorian era. This first letter of the chapter was subjected to every kind of decoration, it was superimposed upon line drawings or engravings or set among intricate patterns of arabesque or acanthus, cut to show white upon a black or white-line pattern, or set upon a criblé ground; or the letter itself, however staid, burgeoned and put forth tendrils and leaves and flowers in a convoluted and delicate pattern. All this, of course, was the work of the type designer and the punch-cutter; nine times out of ten the printer set his wonderful initials badly, where they never could fit, and so destroyed some of the glory.

151. Initial used by Erhard Ratdolt, Augsburg, 1486

152. Initial used by Robert Estienne, Paris, 1544

It is a pity that the art of the initial should so have declined in this, the twentieth century. We have technical means that far surpass those of any other period and could manufacture initials with greater ease; but that does not mean that we could do it with the same aesthetic success. There are, apparently, few artists interested in this branch of design, and I cannot recall anything of the kind among artist's specimens submitted over a number of years to a large publishing office. We are not entirely destitute: some excellent initials have been produced for particular books, or for a printer for use in his work alone, but they are not many. Among those made for particular books those of Eric Gill for the Gospels should be studied; both initials and illustrations, they stand upon the page aptly, and with dignity and power. Barnett Freedman designed a notable set for the Baynard Press; these, done in a technique derived from lithography, are not intended for any particular book, but they are, in fact, too individual in design to be of wide application, and need to be used circumspectly.

153. Initial from J. R. Wood's catalogue, U.S.A., 1869

154. Initial U, wood-engraved, from a nineteenth-century novel

No initial is complete in itself. Each is a unit, not only in the design of the chapter head but in the orthography of the word of which it is part. It should be integral in and congruous with the chapter head, which in turn should be in harmony with the typography of the book as a whole. A subtle or intricate design is out of place in a children's book; just as a masculine one is unsuitable for an essentially feminine book. There are relations and harmonies that are right, and others that are wrong; characteristics that are in agreement or in contradiction. More mechanically, there are right ways and wrong ways of placing the initial in the line. It must join with the word of which it is part without danger of misapprehension and without unsightliness; and it must agree with subsequent lines as though it were made to fit there, and not dropped haphazardly on the page.

These conditions have more often been ignored than observed, sometimes with unlooked for and unfortunate results. In English there are two one-letter words, the article 'a' and the pronoun 'I', and it is possible to split many words commencing with these letters so that they read like article and noun or pronoun and verb; for example, the word 'Ideal' becomes 'I deal'. This danger of disseverance is particularly present with some kinds of ornamental initials, especially the kind in which a wide border surrounds a comparatively small capital; they can seldom be made to fit, and most of them should never have been designed.

To fit well, an initial should equal an exact number of lines of text in depth and should fit as closely as possible to its word, with little more than ordinary letter-spacing, in fact. This is no difficult matter, but it is one that sometimes requires practice slightly out of the way of the ordinary compositor, and for that reason too often escapes attention; not to speak of the force of bad precedent some three hundred years old.

The simple initial of modern books is a letter larger than the text size and frequently, but not necessarily, of the text face. It is spoken of as of so many lines, a three-line initial, for example, being equal in size to three lines of the text type. This 'line' is not the 12-point line by which compositors measure poster types; it is an arbitrary term with no meaning if the text size is not known; thus, an 18-point titling letter will make a three-line initial for 6-point type set solid. Ideally, any initial should be of such a size that it equals exactly the distance from the top of the ascenders of the first text line to the base of the x-height of the second, third, or fourth line, as the case may be: this, of course, ignoring special cases aiming at special effects. An example will make this clear:

HERE is an initial that fits properly and which has also been used properly.

HERE is one that fits badly; an effect too often seen.

The H on the left is, theoretically, perfect; it is not, however, possible to find initials that will fit every variation of x-height and leading, for type is not made in as many gradations of size. When one cannot be had that is exactly the correct height, the effect on the right above is not the one to be aimed at. The initial should still be alined at the foot and allowed to project above the first line at the top, thus:

HERE is an initial of intermediate size alined at the foot and projecting above the line at the top.

Letters like H and I will stand close to the text type without alteration, but others may have to have the shank cut away to avoid an unsightly gap, otherwise the disseverance I spoke of earlier will occur. This is *not* the thing to do:

A BOUT set like this becomes two words and may be misunderstood; and it looks shoddy.

L OOK at this. L shows a larger gap than any other letter when set like this.

Other letters show similar effects when set badly, for example O or Q or B when its upper bowl is smaller than the lower one. The cure is to cut away the blank metal from the shank of the letter so that it fits like this:

AFTER the operation. The text is alined down the side of the sloping letter and gaps are avoided.

LOOK at this now. The initial becomes part of the text, instead of standing aloof.

The improvement is obvious; and yet some printers have a passion for spaces, and even where an initial is straight-sided, like H or I, prefer to insert an en or an em between the initial and the second and third lines; this is an old custom that is followed even with A and L, in spite of the ugliness of the result.

There is some difference of opinion concerning what should follow an initial: capitals, small capitals, or lower-case. The caps and small caps have the majority vote, but they are no more in the right because of that than any majority is. Personally I dislike seeing that odd word in capitals; the first word of the chapter is seldom worthy of stress, and capitals give too much emphasis. If they are used at all, they should be used for the whole of the first line at least, if not more; otherwise I prefer to use even small capitals or lower-case, or else capitals of a size intermediate between the text capitals and small capitals.

155. Initial designed by Eric Gill for the Golden Cockerel Press

Among other possible elements of the chapter head are quotations and synopses. Introductory quotations in this place annoy me as a reader, but apparently there are people who like them. They are commonly set in text italics or in a smaller size of roman, with the author's name and the source set to the right. It is a custom to treat them thus pianissimo, but there is no law about it, and if there is reason the quotation can be made much of and set monumentally.

156. Initial designed by Edward Bawden for the Curwen Press

I have never been able to see the point of the synopsis, unless it may be designed for those who do not want to read the book but would like to know roughly what it is all about—a supposition that the author surely does not foresee! None the less, many writers are addicted to synopses and for the typographer synopses are among the minor problems to be dealt with. A synopsis consists usually of a number of independent phrases, separated by some kind of punctuation mark or a dash; or it may be of the kind that begins 'In which the hero . . .' and so on. There is very little to say about the manner in which it is set. It should not be given too great prominence, and it should not be set so that it is confused with the text. It can be split off from the text by means of rules, or by setting it in a smaller or larger type. I make one plea—that the divisions between the sentences should not be marked by dashes; so many dashes together look untidy and sprawling, and a full point or colon will do the work just as well.

It is usual to commence each chapter on a new page, but in some books it will be found that this is not done, the head of the next chapter lying under the tail of the last. This style may follow as a measure of economy, because by this means a few pages are saved in each book, and that saving multiplied by the number of the edition may amount to a fair quantity of paper. It may also be done for other reasons. When the chapters are short and numerous (as *Tristram Shandy's* famous one-sentence or wordless chapters!) running on will prevent a sense of fragmentation of the text. Chapters may be run on, too, where they are merely conventional divisions in a continuous narrative.

157. Initial designed by Barnett Freedman for the Baynard Press

I remarked earlier that chapter heads could be set in the same series as the text. There is a school of typography that advocates that this principle should always be followed, and not so long ago it was a strong school; it has lost much of its influence now. The one-series notion was applied as a rule not only to chapter heads but to the whole book. There is no doubt whatever that the rule has achieved a great deal of good—indeed, it may be claimed that it has contributed more than any other to the improvement of typography we have witnessed in this century; but having achieved that improvement, its work is done, and it may be rubbed from the statute. It was the pleasant habit of Victorian printers to use in one job as many type faces as they could lay their hands on or find excuse for. This insensate passion for variety was indulged for fifty years or more, and its traces can still be seen in the work of some small and 'conservative' printing shops. In this chaos the one-job one-series rule was introduced as a salutary innovation, and it appeared as a new and somewhat revolutionary idea. There was really nothing new about it, for it had been practised, if not formulated, from the birth of printing to the early years of the nineteenth century. It was imperative to reduce chaos and confusion to order and harmony, and the best way to do it was undoubtedly to confine the layout of any job within the limits of one series or family. The idea was reinforced by the appearance of such type families as Cheltenham. For the printer unskilled in the niceties of typography it was a safe guide; for the typographer, when he appeared, it formed a firm base from which he could project his interest to latitude and variety. It remains a sound method by which pleasant and homogeneous and even noble books can be made when it is properly applied.

It is an elementary rule, and as such it still forms part of the teaching of art schools and schools of printing, where it is liable to be so impressed upon the budding printer or typographer that it becomes for him a dogma never to be refuted. That is a restriction from which, when he can walk firmly, he must escape, for it takes out of typography the idea of contrast and the spice of adventure.

XVIII

ODDMENTS

IN the printer's mind, it seems, a book properly commences with the introduction or first chapter and ends with the last page of the last chapter; all outside these limits is included, by long custom, under the term 'oddments'. It is a word of convenience, not of opprobrium. The oddments are a divided family, sundered in the middle and parted by the long and heaving seas of the text; the half at the front is known as the preliminaries, while the half at the back, having never succeeded to a decent name, is called, a little lamely, end-matter. There may be some other word for it, but I cannot remember having met with it.

The preliminaries, or prelims, as they are more generally called, may consist of some or all of the following:

(*a*) bastard title
(*b*) a list of other works by the same author, or books in the same series, or other similar announcement
(*c*) frontispiece
(*d*) title-page
(*e*) bibliographical note or imprint
(*f*) dedication
(*g*) preface or foreword
(*h*) acknowledgements (which may also go at the end)
(*i*) list of contents
(*j*) list of illustrations

This catalogue is not exhaustive; there is no limit to an author's genius or flights of fancy, and so there is no telling what he may or may not devise for inclusion in his prelims. He may feel, perhaps, that as they are they represent no more than the scraping of the violins before the show begins, and he may like to think that they will be converted into an overture by the addition of a page or two of apt quotations or a poem of his own, or some other inspiring matter calculated to put the reader in the right state of mind for what follows.

The order in which I have given the elements of the prelims above is not my own invention, but one that has been hallowed and fixed by custom and tradition, and it cannot be violated without incurring suspicion of ignorance of the art of the book. That it is not entirely an arbitrary or illogical order both the maintenance of the custom and new consideration may indicate, though in fact it must be admitted that it has become so settled that it is followed not so much of deliberate choice as of habit. It is a beneficial habit, because when it is known to everyone what the accepted order is, a great deal of rearrangement and correspondence and divergence of opinion is avoided.

Except for the title-page, which deserves a chapter to itself, and the frontispiece, which is covered by the chapter on illustrations, I propose to deal with the preliminaries in the order I have shown above, and the end-matter afterwards.

(A) THE BASTARD TITLE

This is page 1 of the book, unless, as in some books, it is preceded by blank leaves the purpose of which is to make the extent up to an even working convenient for machining. These blanks should not be confused with the free half of the endpaper, which is called the flyleaf, and on which some people have the amiable habit of writing their names.

It is curious that the word 'bastard' should be used for this purpose, but no more curious than that it should be used for anything that appears to be an imitation of or substitute for something else, or which is regarded as spurious. Our forebears saw something appropriate in the term, and did not mind these 'strong' words, as many people do now in a time that we like to think is more civilized, but is perhaps only more queasy. There has for many years been a tendency to say 'half-title' instead of 'bastard title', no doubt because of this objection to a 'strong' word, but it is a bad tendency in that it bans an exact term in favour of one that is inexact. There can be only one bastard title in a book, but there may be several half-titles, for this term is used, inexactly, for any part title that occupies a page of itself.

In most books the bastard title bears only the name of the book and nothing more, and the style of setting is usually simple and unostentatious. The page does very little real work, and it may appear to be useless. If it does not appear so, it may be wondered how it managed to become so inevitable among the elements of a book. There are several theories of its origin, and what is probably one of the most reasonable of them I shall give in the next chapter, because it purports also to explain the origin of the title-page. Commonly the title of the book is set on the bastard title in a smallish size of type in the upper part of the page, though it is not unusual to find it placed exactly in the middle. Whether it stands in any preconceived typographical relation to other parts of the book is, it seems, a point of so little importance that it is scarcely to be wondered at if it is overlooked, and overlooked it often is. It is a neglected page, because so little can be done with it if the traditional restraint of its character is to be preserved; not even the moderns, or the modernists, have succeeded in stamping their new individuality upon the bastard title.

I think it best to link it typographically with the body of the book by setting the wording in one of the types used for the chapter head, and more often than not it turns out that the type of the chapter title itself is the most suitable. If this is done the question of the drop settles itself, for the line should obviously have the same drop as the corresponding line in the chapter head.

The style of an elaborate chapter head may appear too pretentious in the open space of the bastard title, and this is especially so when ornament or decoration is used; then the alternatives are compromise, or a simpler setting that will nevertheless harmonize with the style of the book. Decoration is not necessarily banned, but because of the very modesty of the page, it should be discreet. The bastard title is not a competitor of the title-page; it is not an ambassador extraordinary, but a mere vassal going before a lord to announce his approach.

(B) THE ANNOUNCEMENT

There is no common name for this, the reverse of the bastard title. The word 'announcement' does not always fit, because the page is frequently left blank and announces nothing to anybody: but when it is used, it is, in effect, used as an announcement or advertisement. Here may be listed the titles of other works by the same author, or other books in the same series, or other such ancillary information. I find it also useful, when the author is replete with titles and distinctions and honours (of which, naturally, the reader must be informed), as a home for these details, which may make a whole block of type, and are an encumbrance and a nuisance on the title-page. They suffer no harm by this divorce, and it may be argued that in a more roomy space they can be made more legible, without being obtrusive.

In calling this page the announcement I have of purpose avoided the word 'advertisement' because of the blatancy of display that is commonly connected with the latter word. On no account should this page be displayed in any manner that makes it compete with the title-page opposite. The title-page is the main announcement of the book; what is printed on the announcement itself finds itself there only because that page is one that otherwise would be left blank. Any matter upon it must be set discreetly in type not larger than that of the text, and possibly smaller, if the text type is large. It depends a great deal on the amount of matter to be included. A prolific writer may feel that it is an advantage to have all his previous books announced, but fecundity can in this connection be a nuisance, and typographically he may be well advised to restrict his pride.

(E) THE BIBLIOGRAPHICAL NOTE OR IMPRINT

This is usually called the biblio, which is as good a name for it as another, provided that it is remembered that, although the word 'biblio' is an abbreviation for 'bibliography', a biblio should never be called a bibliography. A bibliography, which should never be called a biblio, is quite a different thing and is placed near the end of the book. A biblio may also be called an imprint, if this is where the printer puts his name and address, which by law he should include somewhere in the book. The law does not dictate where the imprint is to go, and some printers prefer to put it at the end, either on the last printed page or on any blank that may follow it. On the biblio, however, by requirement of foreign customs authorities, will be found the words 'Printed in Great Britain'. The page is also used for a statement of the date of publication and details of previous reprints or editions. The publisher's name and address may be included, and should be included if the title-page contains only his name. Yet another element is the statement of copyright.

These elements—publisher, printer, 'Printed in Great Britain', copyright, and the details of editions—they are too often set apart, scattered across the fair surface of the page, so many counters flung idly upon a table. It entails no great strain upon the mind to gather them together and to set them in some manner that shall at least be neat. There is nothing here that is of clamorous importance, and nothing that needs the emphasis of type larger than the text type. Indeed, if the text type is itself large, the biblio can very well be set in a smaller size. All the four elements can be gathered together in an orderly and grammatical paragraph and set like an ordinary paragraph of type, either to the text measure or narrower, perhaps in upper and lower-case italics or in even small capitals, or the paragraph may be made to tail off into a wedge; or each phrase may be set on a separate line, and centred, so that all together they make an irregular but not unpleasing shape; or there may be some other neat arrangement that satisfies and is not obtrusive. There is no great triumph to be won upon this field, but there is the minor pleasure of orderly existence.

In all but a very few books there is no indication of manufacture other than the printer's imprint (the publisher being not a manufacturer, but an agent or factor). This imprint is that of the printer of the text. Illustrations may well have been printed by another printer, and if they are printed by a different process it is likely that they have been; it is unfair not to designate any such printer. More serious, in my view, is the failure to name the binder. His omission was understandable, for his inclusion was impossible, when books were issued unbound or in temporary bindings, so that they could be rebound by hand; but to-day the binder plays an important part in the manufacture of a finished product and he is entitled to credit for his work. There are good binders and bad binders, and both might benefit by this publication of responsibility. For the good binder it would be a valuable advertisement; for the bad one it would be a public proclamation of his defects and might compel him to mend his ways.

(F) THE DEDICATION

A dedication is, I suppose, the result of paternal pride working upon the heart of the author, who here calls to the object of his admiration or affection to come and see what he has done, and suggests by including a name or other identifying phrase that it has all been done for the sake of or under the inspiration of the dedicatee.

There was a time when writers were fulsome in their dedications, but that time has passed, and we have become parsimonious of words. Nowadays we tend to say no more than 'To John Smith', although, if we are feeling loquacious, we may add a small quotation or a phrase suggesting the nature of the debt to Mr. Smith. Our predecessors were more adventurous, more careless of the hearts upon their sleeves; they did not count their words like so much small change. If they wished to honour the person to whom the dedication was made, they did it without feeling that the mere fact of dedication was in itself enough. Everyone knows the charming, if perplexing, dedication of Shakespeare's sonnets, which, perhaps in order not to lose any of the elements of the mystery, is still set in the double triangle arrangement in which it first appeared. Dedications were destined to become more fulsome and elaborate by far than T.T.'s tribute, and in the eighteenth century they attained the height (or depth) of absurdity. A mere dedication was not enough, not by any means; it was thought desirable, or perhaps advisable is the right word, to wrap it up in four or five pages of highfalutin and generally servile nonsense; the eighteenth-century author loved to have a noble name to grace his pages, and thought he knew how a lord should be treated by those of lesser estate. That the noble lord may have provided the means whereby the book came to be written seems little excuse for this larded flattery. Such dedications were a formality in their time, and the terser modern dedication is the formality of our time. We may think that we are more sincere than our ancestors in this matter, and that their fulsomeness was no more than their way of paying off a monetary obligation. The truth is perhaps that neither the eighteenth century nor ourselves know how to pay a compliment without being self-conscious, and prolixity and terseness are merely two sides of the same medal.

We still accord the dedication the honour of a right-hand page, but nowadays it is set very simply, probably in one of the variations possible within the limitations of the text type, and placed at about the level of the chapter drop or at the optical centre of the page. If it is rather more elaborate than the simple 'To John Smith', it may be treated monumentally but discreetly and set in capitals and in lines of varying length, each centred. The shape accidentally produced in this way is generally pleasing, and it needs only a little care in choosing the size of capitals and the amount of leading and in fixing the position upon the page to achieve a satisfactory result.

(G) THE PREFACE OR FOREWORD

It was once customary to set the preface in some manner distinct from that of the text, often in larger type or with wider leading, or even in italics throughout. When the preface was written by some notability, who had thus graciously condescended to boost the book, the flattery of large type perhaps struck home. We are plainer to-day and we have lost something of this local colour: the preface has come to be regarded as part of the book, and is set in the same type as the text.

I see no reason why the preface head should be treated differently from the chapter head, though examples are not difficult to find in which it appears to have been regarded as belonging to another class. It is good practice to treat each heading between the preface and the beginning of the text in the same manner as the chapter head, including the headings of the list of contents and the list of illustrations; they should appear in the same type and with the same drop as the chapter title (not the chapter *number*, which may be different). By this means a continuity is ensured that brings these trifles of the prelims within the unity of the book. But it cannot and should not always be done. Sometimes the repetition of the chapter-head style perhaps half a dozen times within as many pages proves as irritating and uncomfortable as a hoary joke. This may happen if the chapter head is elaborate or ingenious or is in some way unusual; the very point that makes for delight is blunted and spoiled by too frequent repetition.

The custom of placing the preface before the list of contents is old and tenacious, and in the main is right; but a reasonable objection is possible if the preface is a long one. It is an inconvenience and an annoyance to have to look through thirty or forty pages of preface before coming to the contents, and when the preface is so long that it makes the contents inaccessible in this manner, it is better to transpose the two and defy custom and tradition. If there is a list of illustrations, that should come along with the contents.

These long prefaces are often more truly introductions, and then the transposition is doubly warranted. Indeed, it is sometimes difficult to distinguish between a preface and an introduction, and as authors appear to have even more hazy notions about the matter than printers have, what they call them is of little importance. There are prefaces and there are introductions, and there are hybrids or mules that partake of both sides and in which both parents can be traced, with neither dominant. The publisher has no terminology or disposition for the mule, and when it turns up is willing to accept whatever label may be attached to it. If, however, he thinks that it is long enough to be better as an introduction and puts it after the contents, he may feel a twinge that it should still be called a preface.

This confusion of the true natures of preface and introduction is further confused by a widespread ignorance among all kinds of writers concerning the difference between a preface and a foreword. That there is a difference appears to be a conviction, and it is not uncommon for a book to have both a preface and a foreword. There is, in fact, no difference whatever. The pair should be either both prefaces or both forewords—which you choose may depend on whether you are by persuasion a latinist or a saxonist. It is, it seems, the fear of repetition that strikes terror and calls for a difference; let us not, for mercy's sake, I hear the author say, use the same word twice—is it not a cardinal crime in the calendar of authorship? They must be differentiated. And this notion is carried out to the extent of labelling three plain prefaces, preface, foreword, and introduction. One book I came upon had, besides a preface and a foreword, an 'ante-scriptum'!

(I) THE LIST OF CONTENTS

It may appear that there is little room for a display of individuality or virtuosity in so simple a thing as the list of contents, but it is in this page, together with the title-page, that bad design or no design does show obviously. Open any poorly made book and let us see what we shall find. There is wide spacing, with a large gap between the chapter number and the title. Between the chapter title and the page number there is a rash of dot leaders, placed there, apparently, under the impression that the reader must be an imbecile who cannot keep his eye on the line. Above one shoulder of the contents is the word 'chapter' in small letters, to inform the uninitiated that the figures below represent chapter numbers; above the other shoulder is the word 'page' with an equally essential function. Neither of these words is really necessary, and nothing is lost if they are omitted: if the word 'page' is thought essential or if it performs some small function in the pattern, as it may, it can be set in lower-case of roman or italics immediately before the first page number and on the same line, in type of the same size as the figures. Nor are the leaders desirable—white space is pleasanter; but the removal of the leaders may leave a large blank that really does make it difficult to keep one's eye on the line and to distinguish which page number belongs to which chapter. In that event the list can be set to a narrower measure and the difficulty will be gone.

Spacing on this page, as on any other, must be even. It is better to avoid the columnar effect achieved by inserting extra space after the chapter number; there should be no more than a normal space here, for the full point usually placed after the numeral is sufficient division without extra space. Chapter titles so long that they turn over on to a new line may produce unpleasantly wide spacing if an attempt is made, as it usually is, to space the first line out to the measure, and it is better to avoid this by sacrificing the straight alinement on the right and to leave the lines of varying length but with consistent spacing. Leading is important enough to deserve some consideration, for by means of it a measure of distinction and emphasis can be obtained that usefully distinguishes this page from any other without making it alien. Comparatively wide leading may be used with advantage, and particularly so if the page is set in capitals or small capitals. Variations in the leading should be avoided unless it is clear that variation performs some necessary duty: in a contents elaborated by the inclusion of part-titles and chapter summaries, it may be necessary to vary the leading.

Chapter numbers and page numbers should follow the text in the use of arabic or roman numerals. There is no sense in using arabic in the contents if the chapter heads have roman numerals, and there is no need to do so. All numerals set one under the other in a column must be alined on the right-hand side. Roman numerals running beyond xxx may prove awkward because of this, which is an argument against using them that reinforces the contention that people are unfamiliar with them and find it a nuisance to have to interpret. Roman numerals set in capitals, and any words in capitals, look better if they are letter-spaced one unit at least. This amount of space may be scarcely visible, and yet it is enough to make a difference, and a difference for the better, in the result.

The method of setting the contents with the chapter number on the left, then the chapter title, and finally, at the other end of the line, the page number, is usual, but not compulsory. There is no reason why any different method that will do the work required should not be tried. Involved typographical tricks are out of place in as much as they make the page, which is essentially a reference page, a nuisance to consult, but outside that limitation there is room for variety and experiment.

Not infrequently an author makes his contents a detailed and even elaborate guide to the book, including in it a résumé or list of heads of argument for each chapter and part. This may entail the use of several values of typographical emphasis, which can be provided for either by variations of type size or by means of leading, or in both ways together. It is better to avoid a multiplication of type sizes; the necessary emphasis can more often than not be achieved within the scope of the text size; even if other sizes are desirable for one reason or another, they will retain more of their value if they are used sparingly. In this kind of contents the aim should be lucidity; bungling produces only a forest of words, forbidding and trackless.

(J) THE LIST OF ILLUSTRATIONS

This, coming closely after the contents, is typographically closely related to it, and the layout of the one should be assimilated to that of the other. Where both are simple, they should be set in the same manner. There are, however, occasions when a difference is desirable, and a long or elaborate list following a short and simple contents is such an occasion. The expedients adopted to give value to a slight contents will make a large list of illustrations altogether too clumsy and some other form must be devised. This may mean nothing more than the setting of the contents in capitals and the list of illustrations in upper and lower-case of the same fount. It is customary to set in the list the full legends appearing below the illustrations themselves, and when these are brief it serves very well; but long legends are better abbreviated or digested in some manner, and the author should be persuaded to do this or to allow it to be done. In any event, such wording as '*left*, Mr. Johnson; *right*, Mr. Smith' is out of place in the list, and legends of this kind are better altered to read simply: 'Mr. Johnson and Mr. Smith'.

END-MATTER

The oddments at the end of the book are more unpredictable than those at the front, and while it is possible to draw up a list of what may occur, as I have done below, it is quite another matter to claim that it is traditional or complete. What appears at the end of the book is subject to no laws other than those of authorship, and what the author wishes to insert there is his own business. Among the useful functions the end-matter performs is that of acting as a place of relegation; here may be printed, for example, the foreign originals of documents translated in the text, or perhaps there will be set out the body of an Act of Parliament of which the organs have been dissected in the book. But there are items that occur over and over among books, and from these a list of common ingredients may be prepared. These are:

(*k*) appendixes
(*l*) bibliography
(*m*) notes
(*n*) supplements
(*o*) indexes
(*p*) imprint or colophon
(*q*) advertisements

There is little point in dealing with these in detail item by item. The first four, except in special cases, are better set in the text type, with headings after the manner of the chapter heads. The index is customarily set in a smaller size of type than that of the text, and generally in double column; the columns may be separated by a rule down the centre of the page, and some printers insert this invariably, as though the phrase 'double column' also signified 'rule'; but I think it is a bad practice—

the rule serves no good purpose and it might just as well be omitted.

The notes, too, are sometimes set in smaller type, and this is particularly so when they are no more than footnotes that have been transferred to the end, perhaps because the author is of the opinion that footnotes clutter up the text or because the typographer desires the effect of a clean and even rectangle of type. This, however, is no excuse for setting either the notes or the index so minutely that it requires an effort of the eye to be able to read them at all.

Explanatory notes that are in effect paragraphs outside the text may be set throughout in the text type, so that for those who wish to read them (and their inclusion is surely motivated by the notion that someone may wish to) there is no impediment. I remember one author who included some pages of notes and asked the publisher to have them set in very small type so that the reader should be discouraged from paying attention to them, an attitude of mind scarcely reasonable.

Bibliographies are boring things to compile, and the results of the boredom are all too often evident in the bibliography itself, expressed in uncertainties, hesitations, incompetencies, and inconsistencies. The compiler is frequently the author himself; it is a kind of work that he abhors and it is undertaken in the spirit of grim duty, whatever may have been the spirit in which the body of the book was written. Faced with a collection of minute bits of information, he is apt to become confused because he does not know how bibliographies are made. There are many authors, some have written more than one book, and for each book there is the following list of items: the name of the author, the title of the book, the name of its publisher, and the date of its publication; to these may be added volume, chapter, and page numbers for reference to particular passages. If the reference is to a magazine the number and the date of the issue and the titles of the article referred to ought to be given. It is necessary to get these items in some reasonable order, and to maintain it throughout the bibliography. I think it is best done as follows:

D'ALTON, D. A., *History of Ireland* (Gresham Publishing Co., 1910), vol. vi, ch. xvi, p. 371.

History of Meath (Eason, 1905), ch. iii, p. 75.

ANNERSLEY, RICHARD, 'The Rebellion of '97' (*Dublin Magazine*, vol. 76, no. 10, May 1927), p. 46.

Authors' names can be set in caps and small caps for extra emphasis and to help the reader to pick them out during reference. In the absence of any other arrangement, the order should be alphabetical under the author's name. Bibliographies are often divided up into sections corresponding with the chapters they refer to or to the subjects dealt with, and when this is done some simple form of crosshead must be devised to make the arrangement clear.

In a modern book the imprint, when it is placed at the end, is apt to be an inconspicuous line in small type. This inhibition contrasts with the boldness and self-assertion of the colophons used in the earlier days of printing, and still used at times, if a little self-consciously, by some printers and publishers who may feel that they are following in the steps of the private press. The Oxford University Press uses its coat of arms as a colophon, or, sometimes, following a later practice, sets it upon the title-page; it even uses it on jackets as the main decoration. Many early colophons were no more than a device incorporating the printer's initials, or were frankly monograms. They were printed on a separate page at the end of the book, often quite large, and not only suggested that the printer was proud of his work, but that he was pleased as Punch at having produced it, which often he had the right to be. Many of the colophon devices are decorative and charming, and it was not long before they graduated from the end of the book to the front, to become the chief ornament of the title-page, and imprint and advertisement to boot. Notably the Aldine printing house followed this practice, and examples of it will be seen among the illustrations in the next chapter.

But there were colophons more informative than the devices, which, with or without device, were set in type and gave details concerning the book; sometimes details concerning its production. Naturally their prime purpose was to give the name and address of the printer, but in addition they might give the date and the number of the edition, or other relevant information. The wording was frequently arranged to make some kind of pleasing shape, and might be embellished with flowers or borders. In some modern books the informative colophon reappears, and is extended to include details concerning the type and the paper it is printed on, and even the name of the typographer. I have already remarked that the name of the binder should appear, and where there is a colophon in a modern book he should be included in it. I would like to see the informative colophon used more widely than it is, because, or so it seems to me, it is desirable to make the reader conscious of the fact that there is more than one kind of type and more than one kind of paper, and to emphasize that books can and should be designed.

We have got away from the odious habit, common enough in the last century, of filling the last few pages of a book with commercial advertisements. When these advertisements consisted merely of a selected list of other books in the publisher's stock, some justification might be claimed; though against it there is the argument that a book is intended, in theory at least, to be permanent, and, no catalogue being anything of the kind, the two should not be confused. But the catalogue of books was a venial, even an amiable, thing compared with the advertisements for soap and sealing-wax or other desirable commodities that were inserted in books. There was no telling what one might come across. There might be something appropriate in concluding a sentimental novel, in which the hero and the heroine enter into connubial bliss in the last paragraph, with announcements for layettes and baby foods, but if it happened it was quite fortuitous; an advertisement for whisky, that ancient bogey and breaker-up of happy homes, was just as likely. It was perhaps, a useful source of income, but I doubt that it enabled the publisher to make any reduction in the price of the book.

There appears to be something of psychological importance

about a right-hand page. All the parts of a book other than the chapters are placed or begin on a right-hand page, to take advantage of the emphasis it confers. Bastard title, title-page, dedication, preface, lists of contents and of illustrations, all are normally placed or begin on right-hand (or recto) pages. After the preface the introduction and the first chapter, part-titles and the first pages of parts all begin on right-hand pages. Where illustrations are printed on one side of the paper only, they are made to face left-hand pages, that is, they are placed in the position of right-hand pages; they look wrong and unprofessional if they are placed otherwise. Only the frontispiece is an exception, and that may be said to derive its importance from the reflected glory of the title-page. All this may entail many blank left-hand pages, but if it does we accept them without discomfort as part of the effect of a book; as though a blank *left-hand* page scarcely mattered, where a blank *right-hand* one would matter very much.

What is the magic of a right-hand page? Is it anything more than that it is necessary to turn the first page of any book in order to find a left-hand page, and that therefore we regard the left-hand page as the back of a right-hand one? And who rates the back of anything at the same value as the front? This relation of back to front is not as obvious in the body of a book, but the idea is preserved in the terms 'recto' and 'verso', nowadays more in use with bibliophiles than printers.

XIX

THE TITLE-PAGE

We have become so accustomed to the title-page, its presence is now so inevitable, that a book without one would appear to us to be a book without a head. And yet the title-page has not always been indispensable; it is, in fact, a recent development in the history of books. No medieval manuscript possesses one in the sense that we understand it, and of the few that do allow a leaf for the purpose many have the title on the back of that leaf, on what we would call page 2. The majority start straightway into the text on page 1 or 2, though not without, in many cases, some such annunciatory phrase as 'Here beginneth the history of Arthur king of Britain . . .'. The custom was international, and 'Here beginneth' or 'Incipit' or 'Cy commence' appears often enough to be monotonous.

If the reader of manuscripts felt no need of a title-page, how is it that we have come to regard it as indispensable? How and why was the title-page developed? There is no definite answer to these questions. Certainly the modern title-page serves a purpose of information that is essential now, whatever may have been the case four or five hundred years ago, and the rise of the necessity must have played some part in its development. The increasing importance of the title as a means of distinction and identification, of the author's name as a commercial asset, and of the publisher's name as a brand of value, must early have made itself felt, and if it did not of itself suggest the wisdom of setting aside a separate page for the display of these items, it must have caused the suggestion to be seized upon when it was made.

One theory put forward implies that the title-page originated as a matter of utility, that it arose out of a commercial necessity rather different from the one I have suggested above. A manuscript was bound immediately the scribe had finished with it, and was thus at once protected from the soilure of dust and handling. It is probable that this was also the practice with the first printed books, but it did not continue so; books began to be sent out to the bookseller unbound, packed in bales or boxes, and many of them must have remained unbound in the shop for long periods before they were sold. In this state, the first page, taking the brunt of wear and handling, was particularly liable to damage. To protect the text the printer took to leaving the first leaf blank, so that it could be cut away by the binder when its function was over, leaving the book whole and in good condition. But this expedient was only partially effective, because in protecting the book it also obscured its identity, to the inconvenience of both the bookseller and his customer; the blank page had to be turned to discover what the book was, and the first page of the book was once again exposed and endangered. To avoid this the title or some identifying phrase was printed on the face of the blank, which then assumed something of the appearance of a bastard title. As the inclusion of other information became desirable it developed and became the title-page. As soon as the value of this was realized, it too required protection, and the process began again. Another blank was added, and on this the title was printed as before and for the same reason. In this way the present arrangement of bastard title and title-page was arrived at. When the practice was established of binding printed books at once, the original purpose of the bastard title had been forgotten, and it became, as it has remained, a traditional part of the book.

It is of interest to remark that this theory of the development of the bastard title and title-page appears to be supported by the peculiar name the Germans give to the bastard title—*Schmutztitel*, or dirt title.

The theory is neat and plausible—in fact it is too neat and too plausible. History is seldom so tidy, so naïve and uncom-

158. Typical 'Here beginneth', Cologne, 1485

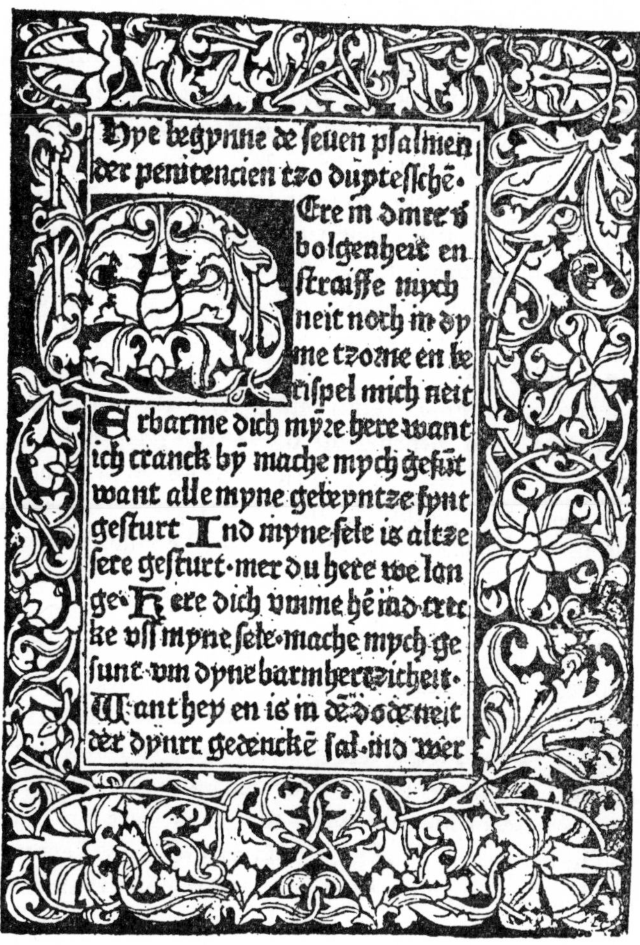

Hye begynne de seuen psalmen
der penitencien tzo duytesschē·
Here in dinre v
bolgenheit en
straiffe mych
neit noch in dy
me tzorne en be
rispel mich neit
Erbarme dich myre here want
ich cranck bȳ mache mych gesūt
want alle myne gebeyntze synt
gesturt Ind myne sele is altze
sere gesturt · mer du here we lan
ge · Here dich vmme hē ind trec
ke vss myne sele · mache mych ge
sunt vm dyne barmhertzicheit ·
Want hey en is in dē dode neit
der dynre gedenckē sal · ind wer

2C

plicated as this, and small research is needed to show that there were other factors that contributed largely to the development of the title-page. No history of books can be written without the word 'colophon' cropping up very soon, for whatever it may have been in the beginning, the colophon soon became an embryo title-page, and not only that, but at times a condensed preface and dedication as well. True, it appeared, not at the beginning of a book, but at the end, but the more it came to resemble a title-page, the more it tended to wander from its original home. As a title-page it took some time to settle down into what seems to us the logical position, and for a while it was apt to appear anywhere among the oddments, or even after a prologue. Caxton, for example, was notably undecided about what to do with it.

It was not until the sixteenth century that the fully developed title-page appeared, bearing the title of the book, the name of its author, and the name of the printer or bookseller who acted in the capacity of publisher, and even then it continued for a while to be the exception rather than the rule. The printer here proclaimed himself, for at this time the printer was a more important person than perhaps he was ever to be again; he was generally the publisher as well. The printer's device advanced from the colophon to take its place on the title-page, and on the score of decoration alone it not infrequently deserved its promotion. These devices had grown in size and grandeur and complexity, and it was not only for decorative reasons, or even for the purpose of identification, that they were brought forward. They were the equivalents of coats of arms, demonstrating the importance and the potency that the new craft of printing and its directors had acquired. They had become proud emblems, and the humble and hidden colophon was insufficient room for them. They spoke not only of the pride of the printer in himself, but also of his pride in his craft and in the example of his work that bore his mark.

The title-page of the sixteenth-century gothic book was often printed in the same size and face of type as that used for the text, at least in the early part of the century, and this

159. The first displayed title-page, Ratdolt, Venice, 1476

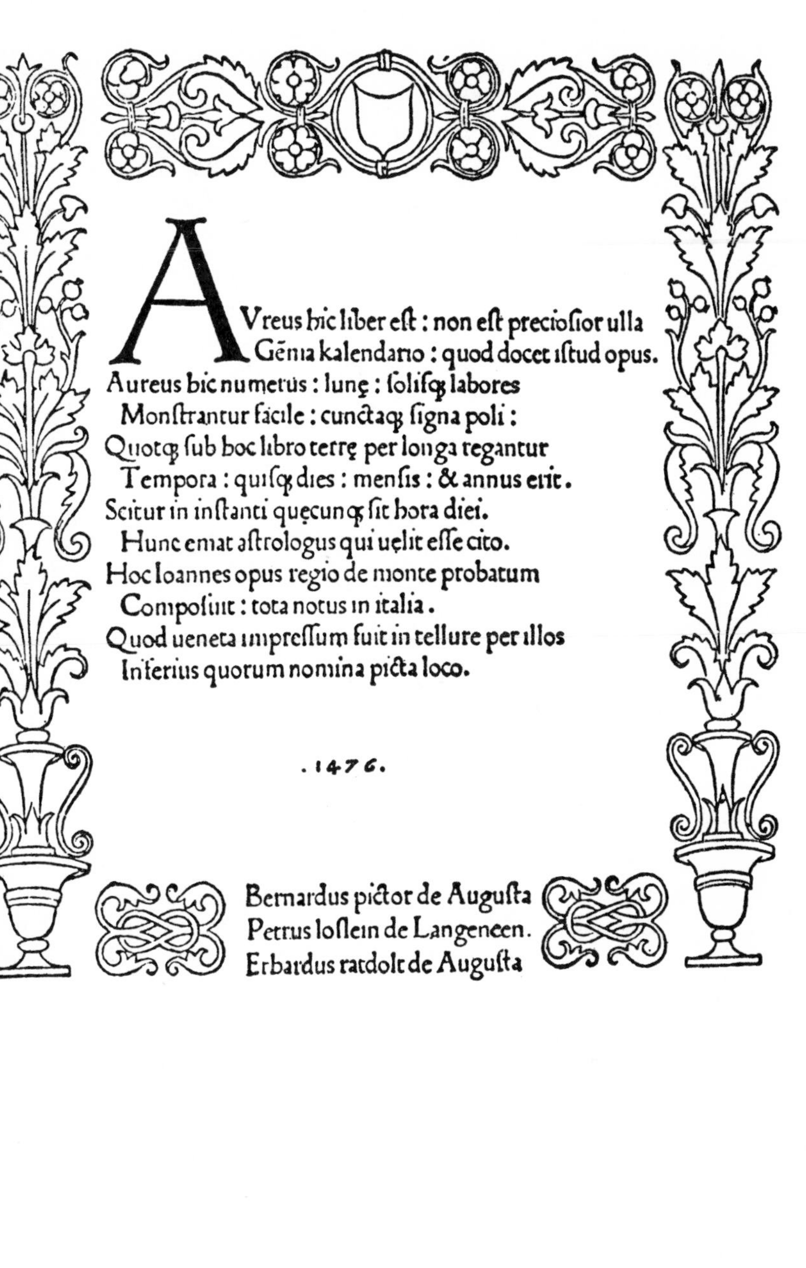

AVreus hic liber est: non est preciosior ulla
 Gēma kalendario: quod docet istud opus.
Aureus hic numerus: lunę: solisq; labores
 Monstrantur facile: cunctaq; signa poli:
Quotq; sub hoc libro terrę per longa regantur
 Tempora: quisq; dies: mensis: & annus erit.
Scitur in instanti quęcunq; sit hora diei.
 Hunc emat astrologus qui uelit esse cito.
Hoc Ioannes opus regio de monte probatum
 Composuit: tota notus in italia.
Quod ueneta impressum fuit in tellure per illos
 Inferius quorum nomina picta loco.

.1476.

Bernardus pictor de Augusta
Petrus loslein de Langencen.
Erhardus ratdolt de Augusta

practice is noticeable in the immature title-page of the previous century. The need for diversity soon made itself felt, however, and larger sizes of type, especially of the impressive *lettre de forme*, were brought in for the main line. This line was not necessarily the whole of the title; the pattern of the page seems to have occupied the designer more than any question of shades of emphasis, and what was set in the larger type was simply the first few words of the phrase that formed the title, as much, in short, as could be got into the line; the remainder was set in the following lines in a smaller size of type and even in a different face. The result apparently produced no sense of discomfort. Gothic types, and particularly *lettre de forme*, were used on title-pages otherwise set throughout in roman, in exactly the way I have described. Nothing odd was felt in having part of the title in a large size of gothic and the rest in a smaller size of roman, not even when the division came, as it often did, at a hyphen in the middle of a divided word.

The gothic line was in many instances cut in wood rather than set, and by this means the intricacy to which gothic lends itself was exploited to produce lettering delightfully decorative, if not always legible. It was carried to such lengths that the title became as much a decoration as a group of words. Then a fashion arose of cutting a device or illustration also, which caused little extra work for the printer, and enhanced the appearance of the page still further. Many of these woodcuts are remarkable for the understanding they show of the typographical problems concerned in the marriage of type and illustration, and problems that in our time are too often ignored. Elaborate and beautiful borders were also cut in wood with similar success, and there are examples designed by artists of such eminence as Dürer and Holbein. Many of these borders were designed for particular books and included scenes or symbols appropriate to particular trades, professions, or subjects. Theoretically their use was restricted to the subjects for which they were intended, but in practice there seem never to have been enough borders to suit the printer's purpose, and he did

160. Title-page showing typical mixture of gothic and roman, and division of words, and wood-cut border, 1545

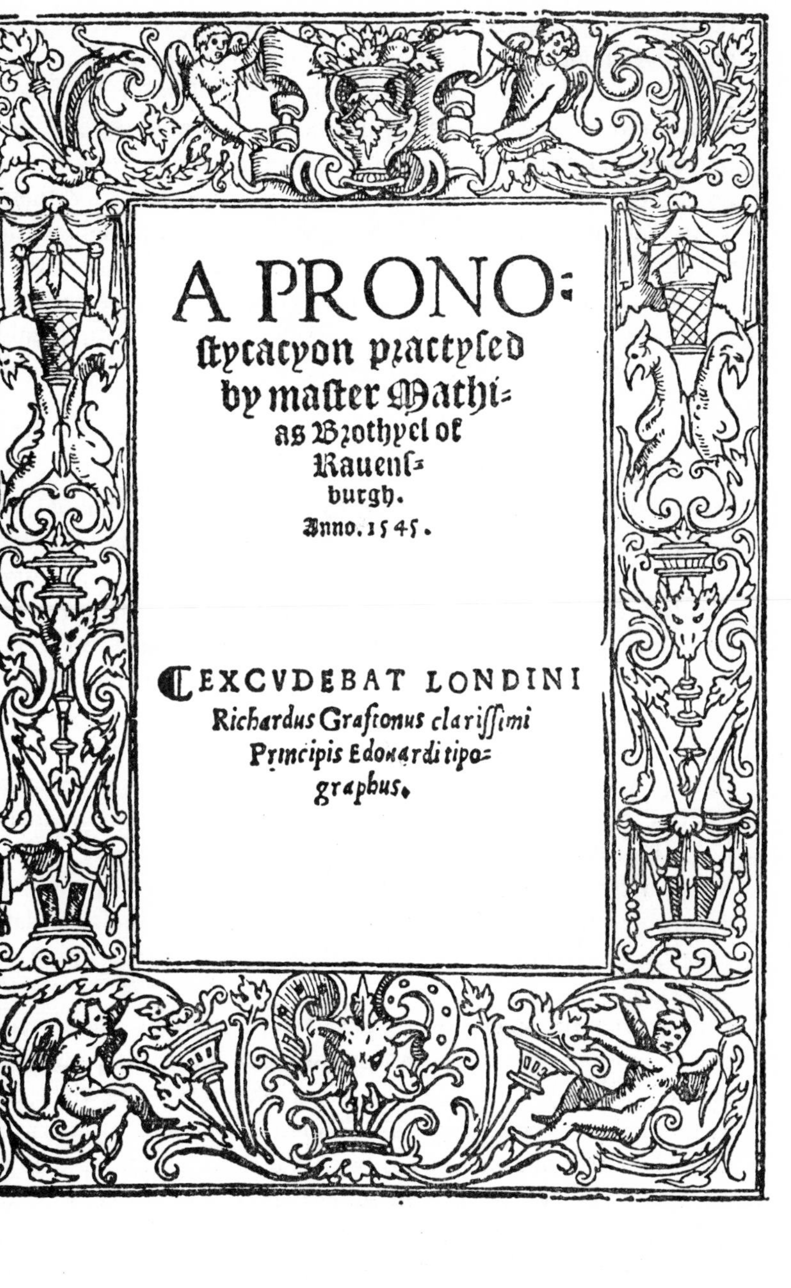

A PRONO-
stycacyon practysed
by master Mathi-
as Brothyel of
Rauens-
burgh.

Anno. 1545.

EXCVDEBAT LONDINI
Richardus Graftonus clarissimi
Principis Edonardi tipo-
graphus.

not hesitate to regard any border as merely decorative and to apply it in books for which it is, for us at least, incongruous.

Decorative arabesque borders built of type flowers appeared in the sixteenth century, and enjoyed considerable vogue. The patterns that could be made with them were limited in variety, however, and no doubt this was partly responsible for their disappearance eventually. They were revived in the eighteenth century with flowers capable of greater variety in assembly, only to be outmoded once more by a growing tendency towards purity, or puritanism, which eschewed all kinds of ornament. They soon reappeared, and never again lost their appeal completely.

The printer was not always immersed in the delights of woodcut illustrations and borders and type flowers, and at times he preferred to embellish his page by means of rules printed in black or in colour, or even to depend on the effect of type alone. With a little ingenuity—there was perhaps too much ingenuity—rules were formed into various patterns and frames, and were sometimes combined with woodcuts or other devices to give a new twist to an old border. When rules and borders and all such adventitious aids were dispensed with, ingenuity was applied to making shapes out of type masses. A common one was that of the hour-glass or the double triangle. It was no doubt a pleasant pastime, giving much innocent pleasure to the compositor when it was his own idea, or annoying him when it wasn't, but it soon palls on the reader. It was the fag end of the enthusiasm for experiment that always arises with a new process; and a similar progress was soon to start with a different method of printing—engraving.

Engraved title-pages were popular throughout the seventeenth century. In some instances only part of the title-page was printed by this means, but more commonly it was the whole of it. Later there were to be books printed throughout by engraving. The effect of an engraved page is pleasantly different, and no doubt the novelty was in some degree responsible for the increasing frequency of the use of the process. Many kinds of illustration or device or decoration in combination with lettering

161. Title-page from the Aldine press, 1545

IL LIBRO DEL CORTEGIANO DEL CONTE BALDESSAR CASTIGLIONE,

Nuouamente ristampato.

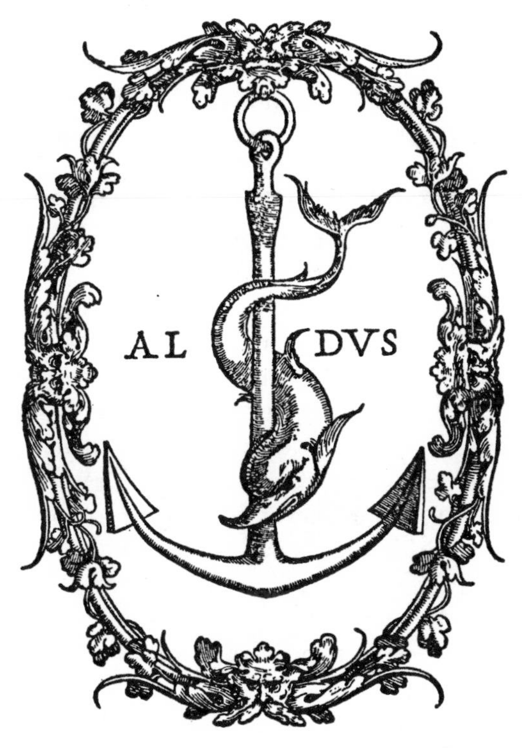

IN VENETIA, M. D. XLV.

can be printed by engraving, and engraved title-pages were often very beautiful while they remained comparatively simple. Later on they were developed in elaboration and virtuosity to such an extent that at last they became pompous and over-burdened, the lettering becoming of quite secondary importance. The word 'engraved' when applied to a title-page still suggests something of this pretentiousness. Engraving was a fashion that flourished and became rich and died of surfeit. Yet even at best it is true that there is something incompatible in its marriage with typography; and perhaps there is recognition of this in the common practice of providing a typographical title-page behind the engraved one. Nevertheless, it had another vogue in the eighteenth century.

Colour has at all times been used in typographical and woodcut title-pages, and the combination chosen has most commonly been black and red. This is again an inheritance from the manuscript, derived through the incunabula. It survives because of its peculiar effectiveness and adaptability. Green and black is another effective combination that continues to be used with success, but its popularity is much smaller.

The best examples of every period demonstrate the truth of the contention that colour, if it is to have its full effect, must be used with restraint, and early printed books show no exception of any importance. Frequently the colour was used for one line only, usually the main line, or it was used to heighten the effect of a decoration or border. In gothic books it was used more generously, even to the extent of printing alternate words of a paragraph title in red and black—a practice akin to that from which, because of the appearance of a rich textile that resulted, we have derived our word 'text'.

During the seventeenth century a peculiar sort of typographical title-page came into fashion the aim of which appeared to be to give a maximum amount of information concerning the book, its author, and its publisher, and also a conspectus of the types in the printer's office. The wording scrambled over the page, crammed and crowded and tautological, so that it is to be wondered what sort of mind deemed such a portal necessary for

162. Poster title-page, London, 1663

CABALA,
Sive SCRINIA SACRA,
Myſteries of State
AND
GOVERNMENT:
IN
LETTERS
OF
Illuſtrious Perſons and Great Miniſters of State
As well Forreign as Domeſtick,
In the Reigns of King *HENRY* the Eighth,
Q: *ELIZABETH*,
K: *JAMES*, and K: *CHARLES*:

WHEREIN
Such Secrets of Empire, and Publick Affairs, as were then in Agitation, are clearly Repreſented;
And many remarkable Paſſages faithfully Collected.

Formerly in Two Volumns.

To which is added ſeveral Choice LETTERS and Negotiations, no where elſe Publiſhed.

Now Collected and Printed together in One Volumn.

With two Exact Tables, the One of the Letters, and the Other of Things moſt Obſervable.

LONDON,
Printed for *G. Bedell* and *T. Collins*, and are to be ſold at their Shop at the Middle-Temple-Gate in Fleetſtreet.
M: DC: LXIII.

a plain book. These were pages of dual purpose: the printer struck off a number of copies of the title-page alone, to be used as posters and stuck up on hoardings or in shop windows for advertisement. Hence the wealth of wording: these people did not know, or did not heed, the notion that posters should be so managed that he who runs may read, and perhaps they were not wrong. But they did confound principles: a title-page is not an advertisement in this sense, and it serves a purpose the antithesis of that of the poster. The two cannot be combined.

With the eighteenth century there came some simplification in the design of title-pages, as of books as a whole, and in the latter part of the century this proceeded to its furthest extent —extreme would be the wrong word to use. It must not be thought that the result was bareness or aridity. That sense of proportion and excellence of taste evident in this period in so many things was not absent from books. On the contrary it was exhibited in what was perhaps its purest form, and as in other things, simplicity was more apparent than real. If to abandon ornament and decoration is to be simple, then the typography of the period was often simple; but subtlety may inform simplicity, and in the work of such men as Baskerville and Bodoni and Didot there was decided subtlety in exact spacing and the use of a limited range of type sizes and a more strictly limited range of type faces to achieve perfect proportion. In the best title-pages of Baskerville and Bodoni not the smallest alteration can be made without detracting from the perfection of the whole. Classical simplicity is never as simple as it looks.

These printers worked with types they had designed themselves and of which they had every reason to be proud. Their typography was intended to show off the merits of their types, and they adopted styles that only types of great excellence could support. Where there is ornament or decoration a defective type face may go unnoticed, but when these are made away with and typography is reduced to its bare essentials the lettering must be capable of supporting the whole emphasis.

The emergence of a classical formula should have proved a healthy corrective to extravagance, but its period proved in the event to be no more than an interval; for with the new century, the nineteenth, taste returned to a profusion of both ornament and wording. Ingenuity was applied to letter design as it never had been before, and great quantities of new faces appeared on the printed page. Ingenuity in the use of these letters was also abundant. We think of many things Victorian with a shudder and thank God we live in another and better time; as if to say, 'There but for the grace of my better taste go I.' Until very recently the word 'Victorian' was an epithet of pure disdain, and even our tardy appreciation of some of the notions and things of that rapidly receding period is not untinged with condescension. It is true that much Victorian typography is bad, and very bad indeed, in despite of the hours of labour lavished on it: either this or the springs of their aesthetic remain incomprehensible to us.

The blame has been put on the lithographer. Certainly that capable gentleman, his craft but lately perfected, was having his dog's day. The limitations of the rectangular type body, which had hitherto acted in some degree as a healthily corrective corset to the fancy of the letter designer, did not apply when he turned his attention to lithography. There his fancy expanded floridly and grotesquely. The typefounder followed in his steps to the best of his ability. The formula that resulted, in which both lettering and ornament are loaded and overloaded with sentiment, may to a more sober conscience and a sadder day appear to be bad in itself, yet it did achieve successes, even if of a minor kind. There is no longer any thrill in the title-page of, let us say, a Christmas story made up of letters contrived out of icicles or of twigs crowned with snow and robins. The title-page of a ladies' annual might well be enlivened (or smothered) by every kind of decorated letter the printer could lay his hands on or the artist invent—and in the latter case there might also be a sprinkling of half-naked (but discreet) graces and totally naked (but sexless) cherubs. Much of this work is indescribably vulgar and superficial, and yet it was not the formula that was wholly to blame. Some Victorian title-pages, and in particular those of some travel books, achieved charm of a kind impossible in any other period. Certainly it is sentimental and profuse and at times glib, but it is also delicate and even graceful. It is not great design, but the pleasure it gives has something of the quality of permanence.

Around about the seventies a remarkable idea arose that manifested itself particularly in posters but that also had its effect on the title-page—a conjunction that is reminiscent of the poster title of the seventeenth century. It was the doctrine that every line should fill the measure and be set in as large a type as possible, and, if it could be achieved, in a type face different from that of any other line on the page. I do not suppose that the doctrine was stated in this manner at that time, but I have heard it seriously so stated by an old comp in my time. There were now enough contracted and expanded types to make the idea capable of near fulfilment. A title of only one or two short words could be set in a type so expanded that it stretched from one end of the measure to the other, while below it the author's name, perhaps a triple-barrelled one, would be set in a type so tall and narrow as to be scarcely legible. The word 'by' between the two could not possibly be made to fill the measure, but the desire that it should could be expressed by setting it in the most expanded type the office possessed, with an ornament on each side of it to enhance the effect.

The riot could not last, and as with most riots it gave way to an unnatural peace of law and order. Responsibility for this, or at least part of it, is laid with the rest of the groceries at the door of William Morris. His passion for medieval things led him to abandon the nineteenth century and caused him to reiterate the past, in the hope, perhaps, that it would burgeon into a new life; and in his hands it did appear to live again, even if the appearance of life was achieved by continuous artificial respiration. Morris went back a long way, even beyond the earliest days of the title-page. His books are untraditional in that they have a bastard title, but no title-page in the modern sense; thereafter he reverted to the style of the ancient 'Here beginneth'. This appeared at the head of a page of text that was the most splendid thing in a splendid production. The

163. Baskerville title-page, Birmingham, 1761

D. JUNII JUVENALIS

ET

AULI

PERSII FLACCI

SATYRAE.

BIRMINGHAMIAE:

Typis JOHANNIS BASKERVILLE.

MDCCLXI.

two pages of Chaucer on pages 406–7 are from his finest work. The great decorated initials, the heavy, convoluted border, the close, almost crowded setting, these are marks of Morris's style. Now this page is not less decorative than the worst excess of the ingenious compositor, but it is decorative in a very different manner. Where the printer's work shows a hotch-potch of decorative vulgarities and unassimilated ideas of design, Morris's page is a carefully designed whole, with type, ornaments, and illustration contributing to and merged in a completely integrated unity. All this was quite different from what had for long been accepted as the proper thing, and the commercial printers of Morris's time neither understood what he was trying to do nor approved. They knew little or nothing of the distant days of their craft, and perhaps cared nothing for them, and in this as in other things in the making of books Morris's ideas seemed to them newfangled and irresponsible. Few, if any, of the established printers, followed Morris's lead, but many of the private presses that succeeded the Kelmscott in different parts of the country acknowledged Morris as their master and inspiration, in their work if not in words.

Something quite contrary to the richness of Morris's work has also come from the private press, and this is the style of title-page long used in the plays of Bernard Shaw. The title and the author's names and other details are set in capitals in the upper part of the page in the form of an ordinary paragraph without the initial indention. Sometimes the title begins with a large dropped initial letter. This over-simplified style is probably to be explained as a reaction against both the general excess of the latter half of the nineteenth century and also against the elaborate magnificence of Morris. The style soon died out, and in his adherence to it Bernard Shaw was, in this at least, old-fashioned.

There is no doubt that the influence of the private presses was useful and even salutary for commercial book design, despite the fact that many of them were so consciously odd in everything they did. Possibly they set a doddering book design on its feet again, as some enthusiasts claim, but if they did,

164. Bodoni title-page, Parma, 1791. Note the curled serifs on the word 'Flacci'

Q.

HORATII

FLACCI

OPERA

PARMAE

IN AEDIBVS PALATINIS

CIↃ IↃ CC LXXXXI.

TYPIS BODONIANIS

book design went its own way, and it was not and could not be the way of the private press.

Among the many styles of setting title-pages in force at the present time, a leaning towards simplicity and the elimination of unnecessary wording is evident. The verbal and typographical profusion of the Stuarts and Victorians is avoided, and in general the exemplars are Baskerville and Bodoni. The formula for the wording is basically: the title, the author's name, and the name and address of the publisher. To these essentials there may be added as necessary the name of any preface writer or illustrator, or a quotation, or a date, and so forth. Ornament and other typographical embellishment are indulged in at the typographer's inspiration, but we no longer fill the page with miscellaneous information and a typefounder's catalogue of faces and flowers.

It has, it appears, always been the custom to place the greatest weight of type, with the most important information, in the upper part of the page, even though much of the lower part is left blank, and this custom is still followed with very few exceptions. The reason for it is not far to seek. It is that the natural optical centre of the page is distinctly higher than the physical centre, appearing at approximately a third of the depth down, which corresponds with the painter's rule of the intersection of thirds. There are, as I have suggested, exceptions to this placing of the type mass at the optical centre, but they depend on some means of leading the eye from the optical centre to the position chosen for the type mass: which in effect means no abandonment of the rule. The title of the book and the name of the author are generally set in the upper part and the name of the publisher in the lower. The title usually comes first, but on occasion the author's name is found at the top with the title beneath it. The latter arrangement brings the title more nearly on the optical centre, and yet also places more emphasis on the author. If the author is to be emphasized, obviously he must be of some importance, and therefore the arrangement should not be adopted in books in which the point of authorship is no great matter—a state and a statement not as illogical as they may appear.

165. Bodoni title-page, Parma, 1806

ORATIO DOMINICA

IN

CLV. LINGVAS

VERSA

ET

EXOTICIS CHARACTERIBVS

PLERVMQVE EXPRESSA.

PARMAE

TYPIS BODONIANIS

MDCCCVI.

2D

This slight variety practically exhausts the possibilities of the title-page so far as the order of the items is concerned; even the unconventional scarcely ever depart from it. There is no need to quarrel with it, for this inflexibility is the rock on which all the modest and gaudy, good, bad, and middling title-pages of millions of books have been built. Variety is brought in by the endless subtleties of type faces and type sizes, by display and spacing, and further by the use of borders, ornaments, illustrations, rules, and whatever may be printed; and the addition of colour increases still further a scope already incalculable.

But there is little virtue in mere variety. Whatever kind of title-page may be conceived for any book, it must bear a relation to the design of the text. It is homogeneity that is here the virtue. The simplest way to achieve it is to set the title-page within the field of the text area and in the type face used for the text—a direction in which lie both the commonplace and the excellent. Where contrasting, or even clashing, type faces have been used to enliven or characterize the chapter headings, they can be adopted in the title-page: for the title-page is the introduction to the typography as well as to the subject of the book. I regard it as the most obvious test of the book typographer's ability. It is here that he may indulge his sense of design, but he must control himself, too, for it does not do to be carried away by enthusiasm for this or that type or fashion of typography. In the end it is by the total effect, including consonance with the subject and the literary style of the author, that a book must be judged.

Display is a term that covers all the means that are summed up in the result, and it is misleading to suggest that any one element of it is of primary importance; perfection is achieved only in the perfection of every detail. Of the elements of display, disposition and spacing are placed first in this account only because they are apt to present themselves first for consideration. It is plain that disposition of the words upon the page must be closely allied with their sense, and in any division of lines that becomes necessary this must be taken into account; and there is also to be taken into account their relative importance among themselves. The title is commonly set in a larger

166. Title-page from *The Holy War*, Pickering, 1840

·THE·HISTORY·OF·THE·
·HOLY·WAR·
BY·THOMAS·FULLER·
·D·D·

LONDON
WILLIAM PICKERING

1840

size than anything else on the page in order to give it the primary emphasis it is deemed to deserve, but this practice is not without exception. A title-page can be set in one size of type throughout and relative emphasis secured by position and spacing. Spacing is of importance, because by its means lines can be placed in exactly the position that best enhances and enforces them in relation to others, a matter in which Bodoni and Baskerville, with their nice sense of judgement, still remain excellent models.

There is an unfortunate tendency among compositors to put too much space between words in display lines, and this is particularly in evidence when the lines are set in capitals. The effect is a division of the line into so many segments and is destructive of unity. It is undesirable and unnecessary and can easily be avoided. Generally a thick space is sufficient for lower-case and an en space for capitals, but rather more is needed if the line is letter-spaced.

Letter-spacing is a simple and effective means of achieving emphasis and enhancing legibility, and even of obtaining variety, for in some subtle manner it alters the appearance of a face, the extent of the alteration varying with the amount of letter-spacing. But it is easily overdone. Capitals are nearly always better for slight letter-spacing, but many lines generously letter-spaced are trying to the eye, and prevent an instant grasp of word shapes. Yet single lines can be spaced very widely indeed without losing their identity as made up of words. Baskerville was particularly fond of generous letter-spacing, and Theodore de Vinne remarked of one of his title-pages that it looked as though the letters had been flung apart by an explosion—a criticism more unkind than useful. Heavy types, such as the fat faces, e.g. Falstaff, Ultra Bodoni, etc., look better and are more legible when generously spaced; and so too do the condensed or elongated types. Incidentally letter-spacing allows optically equal spacing of letters to be obtained much more easily than when they are set close.

Lines of upper and lower case are sometimes found letter-spaced. It should be done only with the very greatest care, because the result is apt to be more novel than pleasant—the spaces begin to look intrusive and the individual letters are over-emphasized. In my opinion the necessity for spacing lower-case characters occurs very seldom indeed, and even the little that is done nowadays is often too much.

For our own convenience we may divide the title-pages of the present day into five classifications, in one or other of which any title-page will be included. These five classifications are: plain; decorated; illustrated; coloured; and miscellaneous. The last heading may appear to have been included merely to gather up anything that could not be included under the others, but actually I have used it to cover the modern and the modernistic and the deliberately different.

I have already suggested that the plain title-page may not be as simple as it looks. By the word 'plain' I intend nothing derogatory, but merely the style that depends for its effect upon exploitation of the good qualities of a type face by means of display, eschewing the use of flowers, ornaments, or borders. No doubt the majority of title-pages of this century come within this category, but by no means all are included by right of merit. Like any classification, the present one is subject to division, in this case into the good, the bad, and the merely indifferent. In our time, in books at least, we are free of the notion that typography must depend on embellishment for its effect, but we do not always avoid the contrary danger of believing that any plain piece of typography must be successful. Too much of this kind of work is dull or insipid. There are many books that are of no more than ephemeral value, and intended as such; they are business-like and ordinary, and there is no reason why the typographer should exert himself unduly on their account. Their typography may with justice be left on the higher levels of mediocrity. These, the middling good, form the plain from which we may measure the mountains.

No formula is capable of producing good work automatically, whatever the branch of design, and fine typography as much as any needs individuality, imagination, and discrimination. The need of these qualities is perhaps more acute in the design of

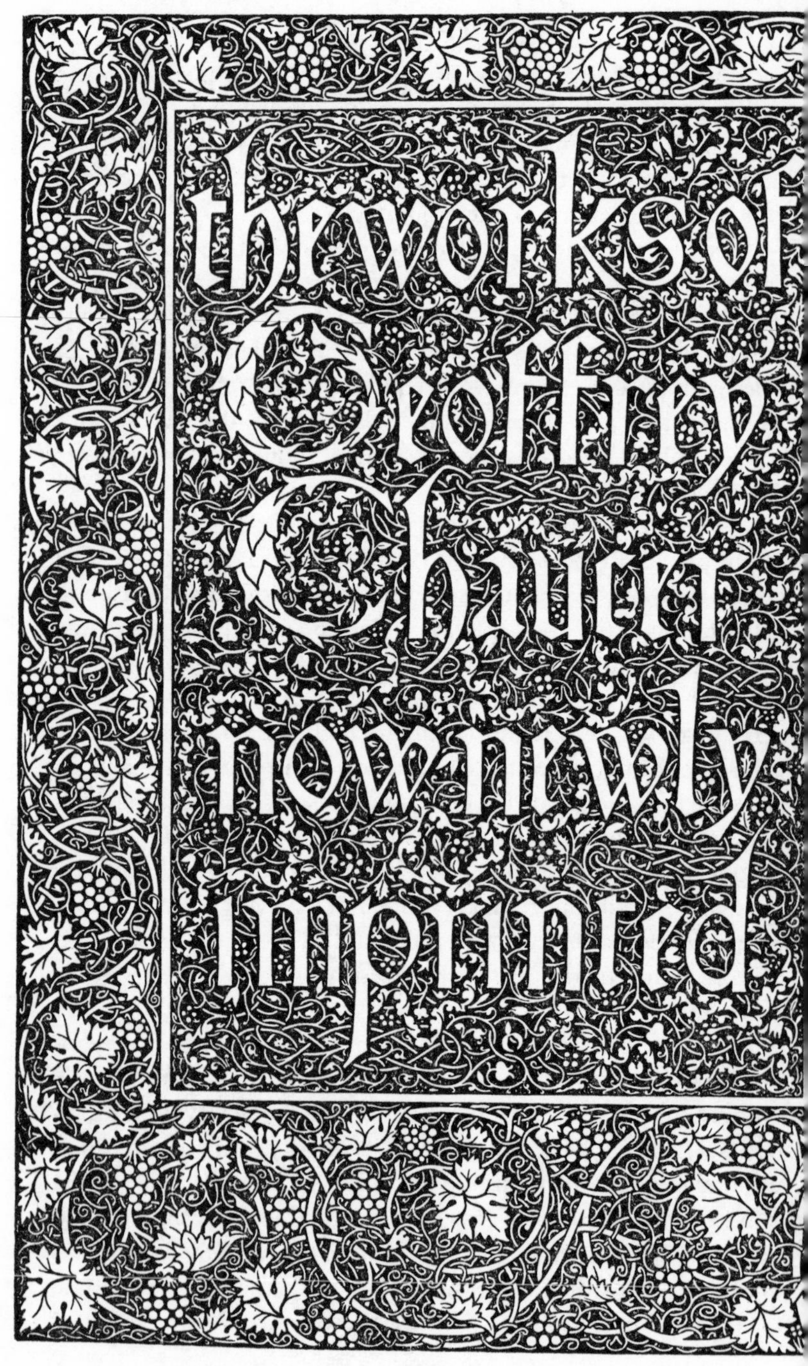
the works of
Geoffrey
Chaucer
now newly
imprinted

167. Title opening, Kelmscott Press, 1896; borders designed by William Morris; illustration by Sir Edward Burne-Jones.

THAT Aprille with his shoures soote
The droghte of March hath perced to the roote,
And bathed every veyne in swich licour,
Of which vertu engendred is the flour;
Whan Zephirus eek with his swete breeth
Inspired hath in every holt and heeth
The tendre croppes, and the yonge sonne
Hath in the Ram his halfe cours yronne,
And smale foweles maken melodye,
That slepen al the nyght with open eye,
So priketh hem nature in hir corages;
Thanne longen folk to goon on pilgrimages,
And palmeres for to seken straunge strondes,
To ferne halwes, kowthe in sondry londes;
And specially, from every shires ende
Of Engelond, to Caunterbury they wende,
The hooly blisful martir for to seke,
That hem hath holpen whan that they were seeke.

BIFIL that in that seson on a day,
In Southwerk at the Tabard as I lay,
Redy to wenden on my pilgrymage
To Caunterbury with ful devout corage,
At nyght were come into that hostelrye
Wel nyne and twenty in a compaignye,
Of sondry folk, by aventure yfalle
In felaweshipe, and pilgrimes were they alle,
That toward Caunterbury wolden ryde.

'plain' title-pages than when decoration is resorted to, for in the latter case the design may get away with it more on the strength of the decoration than on the ability with which it is used. Sound choice of face and nice judgement in its use are essential. In the relation of type sizes one to another, in the contrast or harmony of mixed faces, and in their placing upon the page, there is the possibility of immense variety; yet for any given combination there is, it often seems, only one final perfection, and to achieve it is not always an easy matter. It depends not only on the lay-out, but also on the paper and the ink and the printing, not only on the typographer, but also on the printer.

I have arbitrarily excluded from the plain class all title-pages containing rules or ornaments, but there is in practice no such clear-cut or natural division. If we cannot be arbitrary it would be difficult to say where the plain title-page ends and the decorated one begins, though it is easy enough to recognize specimens of either. It is reasonable to argue that plain rules may be entirely functional and therefore essential, but it is only a step from plain rules to swelled rules, and thence by a chain of nuances to the most elaborate decoration.

The simplest use of the rule is for emphasis or underlining; but rules can also be used for separation, or to divide space, to partition the field of the page into compartments. For these purposes the rule may be of any length required, and may even bleed at either or both ends, and it may be of any thickness that does not throw the page out of balance. Generally, but not invariably, the rule should not be heavier than the weight of the thickest stroke of lettering on the page, unless it is to be printed in colour. Rules of different weights lend themselves to combination, and such combined, or composite, rules are effective in the right places. Rule combinations make effective borders, particularly if a second colour is used. Indeed, there is more in the rule than is always realized, and a useful essay might be written on its function in typography.

The swelled rule, wide in the middle and reduced by a curved line to a point at each end, is a simple contrivance, but an effective one. The curved taper confers on it a quality quite

168. Title-page designed by D. B. Updike, The Merrymount Press, Boston, U.S.A., 1923

STEPHEN CRANE

BY

Thomas L. Raymond

NEWARK NEW JERSEY

The Carteret Book Club

1923

different from that of the plain rule; it gives it grace and elegance, but at the same time it restricts its potentialities. Even so, its value is greater than common use suggests. As a mere ornament upon the page, a petty adjunct, it has no great merit. Used with more imagination, it can convert what might otherwise have been an undistinguished piece of display into one possessed of some dignity and strength. On a title-page it may be used to give breadth where the wording otherwise makes the composition narrow. Essentially conventional and conservative, it possesses nevertheless an atmosphere peculiarly its own, and it will repay experiment.

Swelled rules, as I have said, point towards the decorative, and within their shape and that of the allied French rule there are many patterns, some of them complex. These patterned rules undoubtedly come under the heading of decoration or ornament quite as much as do printers' flowers or efflorescent or geometrical borders and so forth. In the employment of decoration on a title-page there are various considerations to be kept in mind. It should suit the character of the book, be in harmony with the subject and the style in which it is written—obviously literary and typographical expression must not be at variance. A book is not like the amorphous lump of stone or clay upon which the sculptor imposes his conception; on the contrary, before it comes to the typographer at all there is embodied in it deliberate design. It is not a graphic expression, but it does contain within it a germ, or direction, if you will, that influences typographic design applied to it, or at least should do so. Unwittingly, the shape of the book has been broadly and roughly indicated by the author (though it is nothing unusual to find that the author's conscious desire is for something totally and childishly incongruous), and it is the typographer's concern to bring the implied shape or pattern to the surface. If decoration is implied, there lies in the combination of type and decoration the exact shade of expression the typographer requires. He does not need to call in the artist, unless there is some special reason, for there is no limit to the new patterns that can be contrived out of existing units. A decoration or border

169. Title-page, *The Iliad*, Nonesuch Press, 1931

HOMER
THE ILIAD
POPE

THE NONESUCH PRESS MCMXXXI

made by an artist, however, has an effect different from that of one made up of type units, and possesses a freedom and continuity not otherwise readily obtainable. This is noticeable in the better examples of the woodcut borders and pieces to be found in old books, and it is a pleasant thing to reproduce them for use in another book of this later day; they can generally be reproduced without trouble by line block, though some may need retouching. This source of decoration has been very little explored from this angle, which is strange when it is remembered that many of the printers' flowers now in use are recuttings of older ones. There are many fine things in old books, and they are still capable of freshness and surprise.

I have so far laid especial stress on decoration, but it is essential to remember that the title-page has a job to do and that, though decoration may be used, the page does not exist merely for its display. The central motif must always be the type; the words are the real point. Though decoration and words be welded into a single design, a unity, and though the total effect be aesthetic as well as literary, yet the decoration is there only to subserve, or better, to enhance, the literary meaning of the page. If the details of authorship, title, and publisher are confused or overwhelmed, however fine the page may be as an example of decorative art, as a title-page it is a failure. That is inescapable, and yet it was sometimes forgotten or ignored by the Victorians and also by some of the private presses, not excluding the great Morris himself. But decoration is not often pushed as far as this in a typographical page—the uncompromising horizontals of lines of type are the salvation of many who are too fond of ornament. Type and type ornaments or flowers are made to go together, and with whatever measure of felicity they will cohabit even where they will not marry. It is in the partly or wholly drawn title-page that the danger of submersion of the wording is most likely to arise.

The drawn title-page is a comparative rarity. The equivalent was popular in the heyday of engraving, and it appeared again, this time through the medium of lithography, in the nineteenth century, and once more, either engraved on wood or reproduced by means of the line block, towards the end of the century. But it seems never to have achieved any permanent popularity, in spite of the rise of the drawn bookjacket. The artist has staked his claim in the field of jacket design, but has failed utterly to achieve any lasting influence on the design of the title-page. Some of the reasons, if not all, are fairly obvious. There is, of course, the extra expense of the artist's fee and the cost of reproduction; but the greatest obstacle in the way of any publisher who might like to experiment in this direction is the dearth of suitable artists. An artist capable of the work must have an intimate knowledge of letter design and good taste in its use. The fancy display lettering in use in advertising, which may be valuable when used on bookjackets, is nearly always out of place on a title-page; here the need is for a purer, less self-assertive form. Again, knowledge of process-engraving is necessary, the more expert the better. Few artists can both draw and letter well; fewer still know how their work will be reproduced, or how to make the most of their opportunities within the stringent limits of printing processes.

Pictures and devices of one kind or another have appeared on title-pages from the earliest times. Speaking generally, any picture used here serves the purpose of decoration, and should in justice be treated under that head. If the drawing is well done, with understanding and appreciation of the type face with which it is to be used, a picture may certainly contribute greatly to the beauty of a fine page. How the picture should be placed, and how large it should be, and what shape, are questions with more than one answer, and obviously depend on the design of the whole page, but the artist should know what is being done and should work in collaboration with the typographer. He may, indeed, subject to the typographer's direction, design the page and choose the types himself. How often these ideal conditions are fulfilled is another matter.

I have used the word 'picture' in this context because of its convenience, though it embraces a wide variety of graphic expression, but one sense I want to avoid is that of illustration. It is nearly always undesirable to use on a title-page a picture that is truly illustration in the sense that it depicts some definite action in a narrative. Such a picture is almost bound to have too strongly individualized or detailed an interest to join with the abstract qualities of the title-page, which represents, at least theoretically, the whole book.

Even when colour appears nowhere else in a book, it may be used with advantage on the title-page. It cannot make good typography out of bad, as some designers appear at times to believe, and it will not improve a page that is entirely satisfactory in black only. It should not be used for its own sake, and it should not be spread with too lavish a hand. Used discreetly and skilfully, it can bring with it a jewel-like quality that is not otherwise easily obtainable.

Colour has at all times been used on title-pages, and as in printing it entails an extra cost, it is in books of special interest or merit that it is most likely to be found, that is, in editions that are intended to be better than the common run. These conditions still hold, though it is now the publisher and not the printer who controls the use of colour—unless the reader, with a pen and a bottle of ink, chooses to add the colour for himself. Adding colour manually was popular in the seventeenth and eighteenth centuries, and perhaps earlier, and commonly took the form of inscribing red rules crossing at the corners in the manner of an Oxford border. So many books embellished in this way have survived that it is a little difficult to say who really did do the embellishing. Was it the printer, who found that it was easier and cheaper to draw coloured rules by hand than to print them (a questionable conclusion), or did there exist an army of indefatigable book-lovers who spent hours ruling books in this manner? Some books have every page ruled by hand, each page bearing six or seven different lines. Bibles were favourite subjects, and being rather long books offered ample scope to the practitioner. It is difficult even to say whether the printer foresaw the ruling and allowed for it, for every specimen I have seen would have been a perfectly normal book of the period without it. What the practice does show is the strength of the desire for colour in books, at that time at

170. Title-page cut on wood by Eric Gill for the Golden Cockerel Press, 1927

TROILUS
AND
CRISEYDE
BY
GEOF-
FREY
CHAUCER

least. For those who want to try it now, a little experiment with a pen and a ruler will show how much the effect can be varied.

To-day the addition of colour to a title-page, however small the amount, remains as it has always been, an additional expense. That is no doubt the main reason why colour is so little used in modern books, and it weighs seriously whether colour is worth while for the book in hand. It may also lurk behind the notion, not uncommon, that if colour is to be used, one might just as well have a lot of it as a little.

It is commonly considered that colour is emphatic, and that this is so may be most easily seen in the posters that come from the local jobbing printer—nearly always it is the important lines that are in colour. I believe it to be a fallacy, and that the truth is that, compared with black, colour is recessive, even when the colour is red. It forms as it were a second plane, a screen or level one step beyond the black. Thus, the introduction of colour gives a prominence, a sense of relief, to the black that is not observable when black alone is used. Colour therefore imports a new set of values into display. A page in two colours must be designed as such, because each size and face of type becomes endowed with characteristics it does not possess in the absence of colour. For example, where an important line, such as the title itself, is to be printed in colour, it must be set in a manner that will give it emphasis, that might indeed make it over-emphatic if it were printed in black. This can be done by setting it in a larger size of type, or in a bolder face, or by means of spacing or disposition. Colour and type must be interdependent, must rest in a state of suspended balance.

Emphasis may be gained by a restricted, even parsimonious, use of colour in other places than the main type line. I have said that colour introduces another plane, and that this must imply that it makes the black to stand forth. A small amount of colour will do this: one thin rule in red may be enough to give quite a different effect to the entire page. This is especially noticeable when the presswork is good and the quality of the inks high. So small a quantity of colour may be hard to defend when set

171. Title-page designed by Seán Jennett, London, 1945: the border is enlarged from the device in Figure 161

EDITH OLIVIER

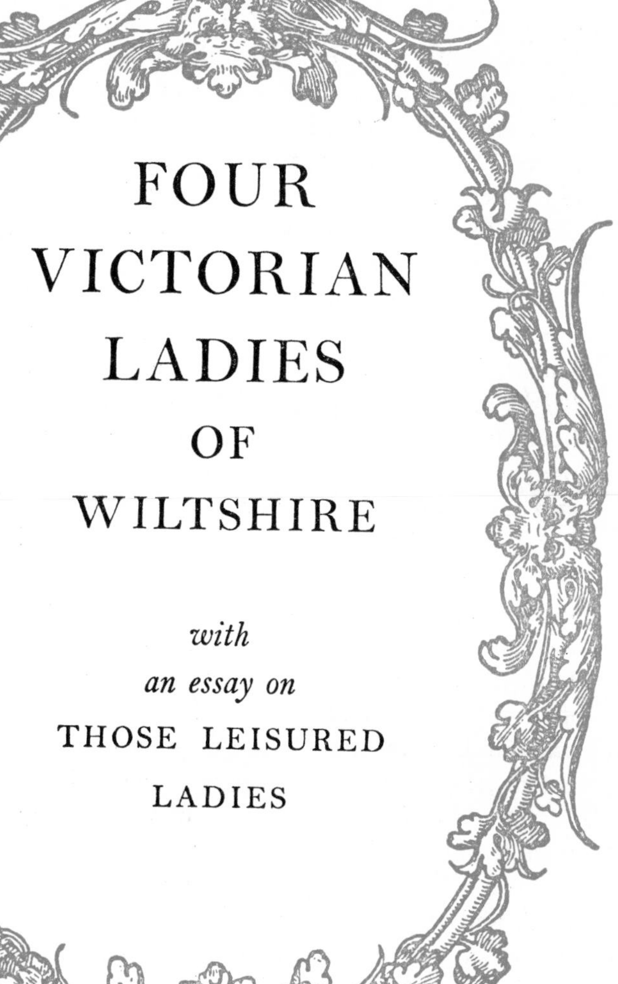

FOUR VICTORIAN LADIES OF WILTSHIRE

with

an essay on

THOSE LEISURED LADIES

FABER & FABER

2E

against the deal of trouble necessary to place it there, but it can be worth while in the end.

While emphasis is a function of colour, it is not in my opinion its most important function, at least on the title-page. It is the sparkle, the quality of the jewel, it brings with it that interests me more, and the feeling of depth, of perspective, that is implicit in the illusion of planes. Emphasis is inseparable from colour, however it may be used, but it is the wholeness or unity of the design in which it is used, and the aesthetic value of the design, that matter, not the force with which it impresses salient details on the eye or the mind.

Different colours naturally have different effects, and they must be used differently to achieve the best result. Red is potent, like an old liqueur, and a little is usually enough. Bright reds, like vermilion, have a tendency to rawness, particularly in the mass, even to the extent of offence, and I prefer reds that have something of brown in them, rusty reds and autumn reds. They are brilliant among the black, but with a soft, warm fire. Brown, on the other hand, is a dull colour with black, and must have a little red in its composition if it is to please. Blue appears to me to lack vigour, to be too languorous a colour to consort well with a rich black, even when the blue too is rich; but this is no doubt a personal reaction, for there are many who like blue. Green, if it is not too yellow a green on the one hand, or too blue-bottle a green on the other, is a good colour. It is in some senses opposite to red, because where red is bright and enlivens the page by its vividness, green is cool and restful; but it is like red in that it combines well with black. Diluted colours, like pink or Cambridge blue, are not much used, and when they are tend to give an impression of femininity. Mixed colours, such as magenta and lilac, may be precious, but effective and valuable where preciousness is not out of place. Yellow is valueless, unless it can be surrounded with black, as in a two-colour type face; otherwise it is practically invisible on white paper.

The colour of the paper on which colour is printed naturally influences the total effect. Pure white shows any colour at its

172. Title-page engraved in wood by Joan Hassall, London, 1940

CRANFORD
by
Mrs
Gaskell
George G. Harrap & Co. Ltd London.

best. Inks are more or less transparent, and the brilliance of white paper increases the brilliance of colours printed on it. Toned papers give a softer result, both because the contrast is reduced and because the brilliance is less, because the tone to some extent alters the colours.

The classification 'miscellaneous', which I cheerfully admit is no classification at all, is so capacious that I cannot pretend to deal with everything that may be consigned to it. I might with justice have allotted the modern title-page a heading of its own in this chapter, but it seemed to me more convenient to deal with it here under 'miscellaneous', without, however, allowing the word to suggest that there is something belittling or pejorative about it. What the word may suggest in connection with the modernistic I scarcely care. The modern and the modernistic are not by any means the same thing, though the dividing line is sometimes indistinct. Dogmatically, it may be stated, as of some assistance in detection, that the modern may be good, but that the modernistic is always bad. This dichotomy is apparent in every branch of design and in the fine arts, and it is probably most easily observable in furniture and architecture. Here the modern arises from the emergence of new materials and the impact of new needs, and desires to use the materials through design to satisfy the need without hindrance from useless convention. The result not infrequently appears self-conscious, and when it is so it must be counted a failure. The self-consciousness arises no doubt because modern design has sprung a little abruptly from the bases on which it has necessarily grown. No kind of art can be entirely new and independent of the past, but modern design and art are often perilously close to believing that they are rootless. It is a temporary phase, and will pass.

What is called modernistic is sham art that follows a mistaken or false use of the methods or materials of the modern—or what its practitioners believe are those methods or materials. Consciously or not, it is deficient in integrity and simple honesty. Its aim generally appears to be to ape the successes of the modern, which presumably appeal to the modernistically minded, not out

173. Engraved title-page from *Theatrum Praecipuarum Urbium*, Amsterdam, 1657

PRÆMIUM
bonis.
POENA
malis.
Discite
IVSTITIAM
moniti.
Religio
THEATRUM
PRÆCIPUARUM
URBIUM,
POSITARUM
AD
SEPTENTRIONALEM
EUROPÆ
PLAGAM.
Modus hodiernus exstruendarum Munitionum.
Nulla salus BELLO PACEM te poscimus omnes.
Cum privil. Sac. Cæs. et Reg. Mt.

LE

DÉCAMÉRON

FRANCOIS.

PAR M. D'USSIEUX.

TOME SECOND.

A PARIS

Chéz DUFOUR Libraire rue

St. Jean de Beauvais.

M DCC LXXIV.

of the necessity of the material or the need, but simply for commercial advantage. In furniture, at least, the intention appears to be to rope in customers who can be persuaded by superficial qualities to take the apparent for the genuine.

In typography there are no new materials and few new types that are not at least a hundred years old in original inspiration. The field may therefore appear to be somewhat unpromising. But there is new need; there is, in fact, enormous new need. The printed word is used in our day for purposes far more numerous and diverse than in any other period of its history. Advertising alone accounts for many new purposes, and it is out of advertising that the modern has grown, or so it seems to me, though the more obvious origin is the revolutionary example of the Bauhaus. The principles worked out in advertising and elsewhere have been applied to book production with undoubted success, though they had to suffer a sea-change first. It cannot reasonably be claimed that there is in book design the same need of a new aesthetic as may have been apparent in advertising, but there is no doubt that the modernists have contributed something worth while to books; and they have helped at all times to lift book design from the rut of complacency and self-satisfaction.

How should the modern be expressed typographically? Paper is still the material of books and type design must essentially be firmly rooted in the customs of the past. A man may live comfortably in a house that appears to have been built on principles different from any known before, but he cannot be comfortable with a book printed in type faces radically different from those he has become accustomed to. Even the mild revolution involved in the use of sanserif types for book texts proved a decided failure; success must have meant overturning the habits not only of a lifetime but of centuries. There have been only two such successful revolutions in the history of printed books: the first in the abandonment of gothic for the roman letter; and the second, far less drastic, that of Giambattista Bodoni.

None the less, though it was found that text types could not be

174. Title-page with engraved lettering, Paris, 1774

altered, the general layout of the book was made subject to experiment in the search for a different mode of expression. The Bauhaus led the way in the development of the modern, matching its revolutionary dogmas in this as in other branches of design, under the supervision of Walter Gropius, with Jan Tschichold in the role of typographical anarchist in chief. The Bauhaus was brought to an end by the fervid opponents of 'Kultur-bolschevismus', and it was succeeded by a number of isolated workers scattered throughout the world. Many of these were products of the Bauhaus, and the others were mostly dependent on it for inspiration.

The principles underlying the modern in typographical design may appear fairly simple, but they are in fact as subtle as those underlying any other kind of design. The aim, as in architecture, is to produce a clear and articulated whole the primary purpose of which is to be of service, but which exploits the aesthetic involved in the purpose. In typography experiment is conducted through the whittling away of what are considered to be inessentials, through contrast of type faces, and rearrangement of the elements of the page. No preconceptions, at least ideally, are allowed to deter experiment or to deflect the aim. This determination is indeed often in danger of confusion with the desire to be different, and that is the slough into which the modernist too often falls. It is apparent in the practice of mixing types that no-one had thought of mixing before. But if there were egregious failures that for a time passed as admirable, there have also been some astonishing successes.

A prominent characteristic is the use of space. It makes of space a forceful and yet subtle quality that is as important to the whole as the types that are more immediately obvious to the casual observer, though the effect of this use of space can scarcely be lost on anybody. There is a tendency to avoid the traditional centring of lines, and to set the type in blocks or areas related to one another by space rather than by their possession of a common axis. Flowers, decorations, and borders are avoided, but play is made with plain rules. Round blobs or stars in black or colour are sometimes used, but the tendency

175. Title-page designed by Seán Jennett, London, 1954

COMPTON MACKENZIE

REALMS OF SILVER

One hundred years of banking in the East

ROUTLEDGE & KEGAN PAUL
Broadway House, Carter Lane
London

seems to be towards severity, or, if you prefer it, towards purity. Type faces may in theory be of any kind in the catalogue, but in practice it is found that the variety is severely restricted. Those principally used are members of the sanserif group, for these are thought to represent the ultimate purity of type design—such things as serifs are excrescences and unnecessary. Later, and perhaps degenerate, practice has brought in members of the egyptian, script, and fat-face families—and of course the usual text faces.

Occasionally the dictum that the unit of design in a book is an opening of two pages has been applied to the design of title-pages over the double spread. The experiment offers interesting possibilities, but attempts seem to be seldom wholly satisfactory. Too often the fold between the two pages is ignored, but it cannot be discounted as though it does not exist. A successful design, it seems, must treat the fold as a kind of unemphatic vertical contrasting with the horizontals of the lines of type.

Perhaps the greatest disadvantage of the modern is an almost inescapable sense of fashion, which may be very well while the fashion lasts, but is undesirable when it has languished and died. The period of its production is too evident, and it may look as absurd as a woman in the style of thirty years ago. While the contents of the book may remain alive and valuable, its garb becomes that of an outworn mode.

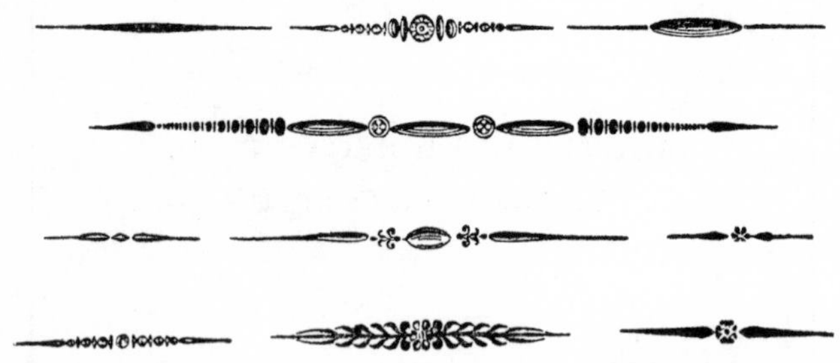

176. Nineteenth-century ornamental rules

XX

THE USE OF ILLUSTRATION

It is curiously interesting to consider how closely graphic action and speech are interwoven, how characterless of themselves are words that in speech are enforced by a lift of the eyebrow or a gesture of the hands. Sound and sight combine in the expression of an idea or an emotion. In literature this combination is paralleled in the relationship of the picture and the written word. In past ages the picture and the word were, indeed, the same thing, so close did they lie in the minds of men. Many languages recorded their literature by means of pictures, and the hieroglyphics of the Egyptians, the Hittites, and the Mayans, and the pictograms of the Chinese are only the most obvious examples that spring to mind. It seems certain that men drew or painted or incised pictures long before it occurred to them that there could be a visible symbol for sound, and when the symbol was needed it was to the artist that they turned for its form.

The Western world has passed beyond this stage of calligraphy. Though it appears evident that the letters of our alphabet are ultimately derived from pictograms or hieroglyphics, they are now wholly abstract, and the artist and the writer are different persons. It is not in the merging of their personalities but in their alliance that we are concerned in the literary expression of an idea. I suspect that this alliance is far more ancient than may be thought. It has been suggested that the remarkable series of wall paintings executed by Magdalenian man in the caves of Altamira and elsewhere were part of a magical rite to ensure good fortune in the chase. It seems to me that the archaeologist is too ready to imply that prehistoric man was of a kind inferior in common sense compared with the species that digs him up several thousands of years later. It does not follow. These pictures may have been made for whatever reason an artist makes a picture, and they can stand on their merits without excuse. They may also have been made as illustrations. As in other primitive societies, were not stories told around the fire at the end of the day, or when professional storytellers stopped by the way with stocks of heroic tales told many times before? In historical times, and still even to-day among primitive peoples, old stories were told repeatedly, perhaps by some gifted member of the household or by some such conscious artist as skald, minnesinger, troubadour, or seannchaidhe. The Magdalenians were a hunting people. Their stories must have been concerned with hunting, and what is more likely than that the artist joined with the storyteller to better the effect. Their spirited drawings of animals may have been illustrations valid from generation to generation.

This is speculation, and may be no more, but it is undoubtedly true that pictures have been joined with words from time out of knowledge. Self-sufficient as the artist and the writer in their purest form may be, they are not mutually repugnant. There have been periods when the artist apparently thought illustration his main business. The Pre-Raphaelites, to cite an example close to our own day, seem never to have thought of a picture divorced from a story. Indeed, the picture complete within itself seems for all practical purposes to have been an invention of the Renaissance.

The power of the picture and its popularity are such that it is not surprising that attempts should have been made to multiply pictures in the same way as attempts were made to multiply works of literature. What is surprising is that it was not done sooner. The Chinese were undoubtedly first in the field, but leaving China aside, even in Europe the art of wood-cutting antedated the mystery of type printing by some decades at least. Thus when printing did appear, it came complete with the ability to multiply pictures as well as words.

Copper engraving was also known before the invention of

177. A page from *Hypnerotomachia Poliphili*, Aldus, Venice, 1499

Hora quale animale che per la dolce esca, lo occulto dolo non perpende, postponendo el naturale bisogno, retro ad quella inhumana nota sencia mora cum uehementia festinante la uia, io andai. Alla quale quando essere uenuto ragioneuolmente arbitraua, in altra parte la udiua, Oue & quando a quello loco properante era giunto, altronde apparea essere affirmata. Et cusi como gli lochi mutaua, similmente piu suaue & delecteuole uoce mutaua cum cœlesti concenti. Dunque per questa inane fatica, & tanto cum molesta sete corso hauendo, me debilitai tanto, che apena poteua io el lasso corpo sustentare. Et gli affannati spiriti habili non essendo el corpo grauemente affaticato hogi mai sostenire, si per el transacto pauore, si per la urgente sete, quale per el longo peruagabondo indagare, & etiam per le graue anxietate, & per la calda hora, difeso, & relicto dalle proprie uirtute, altro unquantulo desiderando ne appetendo, se non ad le debilitate membra quieto riposo. Mirabondo dellaccidente caso, stupido della melliflua uoce, & molto piu per ritrouarme in regione incognita & inculta, ma assai amœno pa e. Oltra de questo, forte me doleua, che el liquente fonte laboriosamente trouato, & cum tanto solerte inquisito fusse sublato & perdito da gliochii mei. Per lequale tute cose, io stetti cum lanimo intricato de ambiguitate, & molto trapensoso. Finalmente per tanta lassitudine correpto, tutto el corpo frigescen-

printing, and when printers began to feel the need of illustrations, which was soon, for illustrations contributed greatly to the richness of the manuscripts they set out to emulate, engraving was a method they turned to. Apparently it proved too troublesome and too difficult for them. They wanted a process that allowed the illustrations to be printed with the same apparatus and at the same time as the text, and they turned back again to wood-cuts, even to the extent of printing with woodcuts second editions of books that had originally appeared with engravings.

Engraving remained the most suitable means of reproducing maps and diagrams in which fine detail was necessary, but until the seventeenth century wood-cuts were preferred by the printer. Then began a decided vogue for engraving. It was revived once more in the eighteenth and early nineteenth centuries. The best work seems to have been done in France, but there was no lack of good work in other countries, and artists of the first water set their hands to illustration. In England, for example, there were William Blake and J. M. W. Turner.

The engraver did not stop at title-pages and illustrations. In some instances the whole book was engraved, a curious return in principle to the block book. In spite of its vogue, engraving was not to endure. It declined in popularity and ceased to attract artists, until at last it became an unusual method of illustration, as it is to-day.

Various kinds of etching and engraving flourished and had their day. Mezzotint, aquatint, and steel engraving have all been used in books. None of them ever achieved the popularity of engraving on copper. They are undoubtedly capable of beautiful results, but they suffer from drawbacks of one kind or another from the point of view of the printer and publisher.

The later history of engraved and etched book illustration is a repetition of what happened in the fifteenth century. Fine as the results of these processes undoubtedly are, the printer hankered after something simpler, something more consonant with his own method of printing. Just as the fifteenth century

178. Engraved illustration by Moreau *le jeune*, from *Œuvres de Molière*, Paris, 1773

179. Engraving made for Rupert Brooke's poems by Ru van Rossem, 1948

returned to wood-cuts, the nineteenth returned to wood-engraving, and later to a new method of producing blocks for the letterpress machine—process engraving.

In his experiments with engraving the fifteenth-century printer had been seeking, not something better, but something different, something that promised a more ambitious or more luxurious result. He was defeated by the complexities arising out of the alliance of two distinct methods, complexities that did not bother him when he returned to the wood-cut.

The wood-cut was no despicable means—it needs only the name of Albrecht Dürer to show to what heights it could attain. Many printers in Germany did excellent work in the printing of wood-cut illustrated books, and they had at hand many excellent artists. Their blocks were cut with surprising vigour and also with considerable virtuosity in the use of the knife, so much so that it is sometimes difficult to believe that they are not wood-engravings.

The best work, however, was done in Italy. At Venice in 1499 was produced one of the finest illustrated books of all time. This is the *Hypnerotomachia Poliphili*, printed by Aldus Manutius with wood-cuts by an unknown artist. Its quality does not lie in any dazzling superlativeness of the wood-cuts, for it is questionable whether these, good as they are, are of themselves better than much work done elsewhere. It lies in the concord of the illustrations with the type, in the total effect.

It is generally conceded that, apart from this one great work of Venetian artist and printer, the best illustrated books were produced in Florence. Here distinct wood-cutting studios seem to have grown up to supply printers with blocks, and large numbers of illustrated books issued from the Florentine presses. There are two characteristics of Florentine work. One is that most of it is anonymous, and the other is that each illustration is surrounded by a decorative border, apparently cut on the same block. The best example is probably the *Quadriregio*, illustrated by Frezzi, and published in 1508.

The wood-cut declined with the general decline of printing, and was presently thrust out of favour by the increasing popularity

180. Wood-cut from *Quadriregio*, Florence, 1508

of copper engraving. When wood again appeared in the forefront it was not cut, but engraved. Bewick brought to wood-engraving remarkable technique and artistic ability, and in the books of the period his work appears frequently.

Henceforward wood-engraving was to have increasing importance in the growth of the press, but unfortunately not increasing aesthetic value. Technically, it achieved near perfection, but it became craftsmanship, not art, a mere means of reproduction of work done by artists with no knowledge of the medium. It could be delightful for all that, as the Dalziel brothers in particular showed. It was rescued from this state by William Morris and his private-press disciples, who used wood-cutting and wood-engraving to good effect, if anachronistically, in conscious emulation of the early masters.

In our time wood-engravings have been made for books by a number of notable artists, among whom may be mentioned Robert Gibbings, Eric Ravilious, John Farleigh, and Blair Hughes

Stanton. But it is to the versatile Eric Gill that we owe the finest work in this medium, in my opinion the best since the great days of the wood-cut in the fifteenth and sixteenth centuries. His engravings for an edition of the Gospels published by the Golden Cockerel Press are particularly fine.

The invention of line process engraving offered for the first time a means of reproduction by the camera and at once threatened the livelihood of those wood-engravers who had given themselves up to the copying of other people's drawings so that they might be printed. Publishers soon began to avail themselves of process engraving and a few artists began to draw with the conscious intention that their work should be reproduced by this means. In too many cases the artist thought, as he still thinks, that the camera had freed him from all obligations, that he could do now just as he pleased and the result would be faithfully reflected in thousands and thousands of copies issuing from the printing press. I shall deal with this fallacy shortly. There were artists who understood the medium, and among them the name that most immediately leaps to mind is that of Aubrey Beardsley. His work was not the first to do honour to the line block, but it was much the most startling and unexpected. If any doubt had existed concerning the value of photo-engraving, here was proof that it could be a sensitive and valid medium for the artist who knew what he was doing. Notable contemporary exponents of the line technique include Robin Jacques and the late Mervyn Peake, who have made of the press a successful medium for the expression of talents as personal as Beardsley's.

Four other methods of photographic reproduction have been developed and have attracted the attention of publishers. These are half-tone process engraving, photo-lithography, photogravure, and collotype. In monochrome or colour each is capable of a high standard of work, but in practice it is to process engraving that publishers most often resort. This preference is not based on the quality attainable by this process, but on its relative cost and convenience.

These processes are without ancestry in the history of the book

181. Wood-cut by Albrecht Dürer, from *The Great Passion*, Nuremberg, *c.* 1510

182. Wood-cut from *Theuerdanck*, 1517

and are the result of a desire to reproduce tones as they appear in a painting—or, it would be better to say, as they appear in a photograph. They are primarily processes for the reproduction of existing originals or of photographs, and have not been of great service to the artist who would do original work in book illustration. Half-tone engraving was for a while used by artists who tried to 'draw' photographs, and around the turn of the century this pseudo-photographic form of illustration was popular—see for examples books for boys of the period and such magazines as the *Strand*, in which many of the Sherlock Holmes illustrations were done in this way. Photo-lithography has been used with more imagination and more success, but even so it would appear that for the artist working in black and white there is just a little too much of the mechanical in screen processes.

An older process that appears from time to time is stencilling. This is not really a method of printing at all. The black or grey outline or 'key' is printed, either letterpress, litho, or intaglio, and then the colour is applied by hand through stencils. Never greatly used because of the expense of the handwork involved, it has on the other hand never died out, and perhaps the peculiarly individual character of the result, which has great charm, will ensure that the process will survive even this machine-ridden age. The Curwen Press strove to keep it in being, and many of the modern English examples will be found to have been stencilled by them. Most books with this kind of illustration are in the high-price class, and even so there are not as many of them as one might wish. At least one example was issued inexpensively, and this was Mervyn Peake's *Ride a Cock Horse*.

In the eighteenth century illustrations with a printed key and coloured by hand were used in certain kinds of books, particularly in books on botany, to the great delight of the collectors of to-day.

There are now many artists drawing for books, and many more who are ambitious to draw for them, and every publisher is constantly on the watch for work of an original character. It is true that we no longer illustrate books of the kind that used to be illustrated. Adult fiction is seldom given pictures now, except for classics appearing in special editions, and we seldom illustrate poetry either, although it was done by the Victorians and earlier. Technical books rely on the camera more than on the artist for their examples, and the photographer has replaced the artist in many other ways also. The most fruitful field remaining to the artist seems to be the children's book, a state of affairs that, however pleasant it is for children, is neglectful of adults. In a long history of notable illustrated books for children,

183. Wood-engraving from a drawing by F. Sandys, 1865

the standard to-day is high. Publishers now appear to vie with each other to produce the most charming and effective 'juveniles'. Books for the young have constantly attracted certain kinds of artist, and even drawn the best out of them. Who does not remember Tenniel's drawings cut on wood by the Dalziels for *Alice in Wonderland* and *Through the Looking-Glass*? Or the dream-world of Kate Greenaway interpreted by Edmund Evans through the medium of coloured wood-engraving? Or

184. Wood-engraving by Dalziel from a drawing by A. Hughes, 1872

Arthur Rackham's elves and hobgoblins, reproduced either by line block or colour half-tone? The accent has now shifted to auto- and photo-lithography, though good work is being done in other ways. There is no great outstanding figure, but there are many who are good and whose work is delightful.

In the wider field many artists of note have turned their hands to book illustration, too often, it is to be regretted, in limited editions. In this respect the name of Ambroise Vollard, of Paris, is famous. Apparently with no deterrent thought of expense, he set himself to produce illustrated books of the most

By courtesy of the Artist and Sir Laurence Olivier.

185. Laurence Olivier – oil-painting by Harold Knight. (Four-colour photo-offset reproduction from *Theatre*, Britain in Pictures series).

By courtesy of the Artist

186. Chiswick Reach at Low Tide – oil-painting by Gwen Herbert. (Photo-offset reproduction from *Ports of London*, Britain in Pictures series)

ambitious kind and he did not hesitate to approach the most notable artists of his time. Bonnard, Braques, Chagall, Degas, Rodin, Maillol, Derain, and Picasso were commissioned by him for particular books. Vollard's enthusiasm and his knowledge of painting seem to have led him into thinking of a book as a challenge to himself and the illustrator, as though the text were simply an excuse for illustration. This is the wrong approach, and the result is that, fine as Vollard's books undoubtedly are, they are picture galleries built on the text, rather than illustrated books in the true sense, in which illustrations and text join hands to produce a new unity. All the same, Vollard's achievement is wonderful enough, and tribute must be paid to his skill and courage. His example inspired others to like endeavour, to produce books illustrated by Matisse, Chirico, and Toulouse-Lautrec, among others. English publishers were more cautious and less enterprising, if we except the private presses, which did much good work in the employment of artists for books. The commercial book publishers perhaps could not afford to be as adventurous as the inspired amateur. One such amateur of particular ability, Francis Meynell, founded the Nonesuch Press and proceeded to show the trade how to produce fine books, mostly in limited editions, illustrated by many notable artists. The Golden Cockerel Press also did remarkable work in limited editions.

Despite the high quality of the best of the work done since the revival of printing and book design, it is questionable whether we have achieved the greatness evident among illustrated books in the fifteenth and early sixteenth centuries. If we are to achieve it I believe it must be through a return to unity of style derived from unity of method. The French, particularly during their great days under the tutelage of Vollard, used non-typographic methods of reproduction for illustrations, such as etching, engraving, and drypoint, and there is inevitably a feeling that their marriage with typography is not perfect. The artist is apt to judge an illustration for its quality as a drawing, but this is totally to ignore the reason for its existence. No illustration can have merit in itself; it can be judged only in the harmony of its

187. Wood-engraving from a drawing made by Gustave Doré for *The Rime of the Ancient Mariner*, 1877

alliance with the text and the type used for it. Text and illustration must co-exist not merely in amity, but in harmony and indivisible unity. I believe that this can only be achieved by unity of method, by understanding on the part of the artist of the technique involved in the whole book, and sympathy between his line and the spirit of the type face.

In the great days of the wood-cut this sympathy was evident. With both wood-cut and type, ink is impressed on paper by methods and with implements based on common mechanical principles—the idea and principle we now call letterpress. Because of this, mechanical unity in the result is assured. A further reason operated to give aesthetic unity also. From the beginning the printer secured in his type faces the feeling of impression as distinct from that of drawing, a distinction subtle enough but apparent to anyone who has compared a drawing with a print from a line block made from it. It is essential, if true unity is to be achieved, that the artist should realize the distinction and work towards impression. For Gutenberg and his successors there was small diversity of choice to impede success. If they were limited they were also safeguarded by the necessity of employing an artist who was expert in the cutting of wood. Such a man would understand not only the problems involved in cutting the block, but also the technicalities concerned in printing from it. His contribution to the book, a block or blocks from which prints could be taken directly, was as intimate as that of the typefounder.

Perhaps there was from the first impatience with the labour of wood-cutting, and there came to be men who for payment would cut blocks from other men's drawings, as happened later with wood-engraving. It seems certain that at an early date the actual cutting of the wood was left to an apprentice or workman in the artist's studio, or delegated to others outside. Despite any virtuosity the wood-cutter might have developed, the printed result must have begun to diverge more and more from the drawing, as the artist forgot or ignored the limitations of the medium or grew lax in his supervision.

This process is more noticeable in wood-engraving. Wood-cutting is a poor medium for the reproduction of an existing picture, but wood-engraving is more adaptable. Bewick had shown what white-line engraving was capable of doing, and his technique was improved by succeeding generations until it began to seem that there was nothing that wood-engraving could not do. Artists who drew for the press began to suppose that a knowledge of wood-engraving technique was unnecessary or would have liked to forget that engraving was anything but a mechanical process, a necessary medium between their work and the public. It had become a servant craft, a mere go-between. It is true that as such it attained astonishing heights of virtuosity in the hands of such people as the Dalziel brothers, but it lost the genius and originality of the true artist.

What the artist wanted, whether he knew it or not, was some method of transforming his drawing into a printing surface, a method that would free him from any worry concerning the technique and limitations of printing. And quite suddenly it appeared that such a method had been devised. The application of photography to the problems of typographical reproduction resulted in a process that, or so it appeared, was just what the artist wanted. The new process, miscalled photo-engraving, seemed to have solved the problem, to have provided a means of producing exact facsimiles of an artist's drawing. The offer was to prove not altogether as fair as it seemed.

Laziness is a fundamental quality of man: he will seize on anything that promises to enable him to avoid labour or trouble or even thought, and this propensity has cost him more in sweat and quality than can be imagined. Process engraving, the artist appears to think, for he continues to think so, has divorced him from the galling necessity of considering means of reproducing his work; for whatever he might do in the future, could not the magic eye of the camera discern the true contour of his line and the alchemical skill of the etcher transmute his vision into cunningly wrought metal from which any number of duplicates of the original drawing might be made in the press? To any discerning observer it was soon apparent that the answer was No; and the answer is still No in this blessed and clever twentieth

188. Line drawing by Aubrey Beardsley for *The Rape of the Lock*, 1896

century. Even if it were otherwise, the ideal of book illustration would not be achieved, as I shall shortly try to show.

Line engraving is a process very strictly limited. There is much that it is incapable of reproducing satisfactorily, but when its limitations are known to the artist and he works within them, it is capable of the very finest results. Unfortunately the majority of artists remain ignorant of any such limitations,

189. Scraperboard drawing by C. F. Tunnicliffe, 1949

ensconced in an invincible belief that anything can be reproduced. What we see is once more the result of that division of labour that we saw in wood-cutting and wood-engraving, but here, for the first time, is a process that the artist cannot learn to understand by learning to work it for himself. Nevertheless, with a little study and some experience, he can, if he wants to, learn what can be done and what cannot.

The problem remains unsolved. The artist making a drawing for its own sake cannot be blamed if it proves refractory from the point of view of the process engraver. We must do what we can if we are called upon to reproduce such a drawing, and if with the best of workmanship and materials we are unable to achieve good reproduction, it is the insufficiency of our means that is to blame, and not the artist. The artist who works specifically for the press is in a very different position. Whatever aesthetic merit his work may possess, it must be accounted a failure if it cannot be satisfactorily reproduced.

It is instructive to compare a typical drawing made for its own sake in, let us say, pen and ink, and one made with full knowledge for reproduction by line block. They are both composed of lines, but with an important difference. The lines of the first are not even in colour. The artist's hand varies the pressure of the pen, and this is most easily seen at the commencement and end of each line, especially if it is fine. The line begins and develops almost out of nothing, deepens in colour, and again diminishes and fades away. In the lightest parts there is scarcely any ink at all, and what there is is thin and grey and only on the surface of the paper—there is insufficient to fill up the pores and what may seem a continuous line shows up under a glass as a mere string of particles. There is, in short, tone in the line as well as disjunction. Such a drawing cannot be satisfactorily reproduced by line block. Tone is impossible and the line must be an even black. The fine particles either tend to vanish, or from the effort to preserve them become much coarser than in the original. A great deal of the character and charm of the drawing depend on this tone and disjunction in the line, and the reproduction, however well done, is bound to be unsatisfactory because the softness inherent in these peculiarities becomes in the print a harsh and strident statement that destroys the balance and quality of the original.

The artist drawing for the press must know what the printed result will look like, must be able to foresee it. This he cannot do if he produces work that does not conform to the exigencies of process engraving and letterpress printing. Ideally a drawing made for reproduction must look as though it were itself printed, with every line fully black and clear. A print derived from such an original may be almost indistinguishable from it, and is then a true reproduction. If, as often happens a reduction in scale is to take place, it must be allowed for in the thickness of the lines and in the closeness of their spacing. This does not mean that fine work is impossible—on the contrary, it is remarkable how tenuous a line can be brought out with fidelity. There is no ban on the fine pen; what is necessary is that the line shall be distinct and defined.

This is all very elementary, but would that the artist knew it and would practise it. It is only when it is mastered that he can come to a deeper and subtler knowledge, the feeling for the fact of impression. It is distinct from the feeling of drawing, and yet it is to be achieved through drawing. A pen-drawn letter preserves the sensation that it has been formed by a sequence of motion. A printed letter, on the other hand, is impressed all at once, and whatever flourish or script-like quality it may have, the sensation of sequence is lacking. It is the difference between two distinct methods of putting ink on paper, and it applies to a drawing with even greater force than it does to letters of the alphabet. It must be understood by the artist, and he must aim at expression through impression, he must subordinate and direct his inspiration according to the exigencies of the medium.

Is it too much to ask that the artist should also know something of type design and understand the spirit beneath the face? The differences in detail may be only minute, but in the mass they are distinctive. The artist's work is to be accompanied by type, and he should know before he commences to draw what the type face will be and how it will be used. But in this respect the typographer comes up against either solid ignorance or a dilettante appreciation worse than ignorance. It is only by the most intimate collaboration between the artist and the typographer that harmony and unity can be achieved in the illustrated book, and it is essential that the artist should know enough or learn enough to make collaboration possible. If this were done, if artists in general knew so much, we might achieve again that dignity and wonder in the printed page that was known in the childhood of printing, and which seems to have vanished for good.

In practice ideal conditions have a habit of never occurring,

190. Plastocowell drawing by Gordon Noel Fisher to illustrate *The Castle of Otranto* by Horace Walpole.

Irene in Montpelier Square

and failing them the typographer can do much by choosing the right artist for the kind of book he has in hand and the treatment he has tentatively decided on. Artists have different styles, just as types have different faces, and the typographer can try to bring the right artist and the right face together. If shrewd judgement or luck can hit on him, likelihood of a good result is greater than when the need must be explained. Words are not precise instruments, and it is always difficult to explain to anyone what you feel you want when what you want is a feeling.

Apart from line engraving and wood-cutting and engraving, the process of greatest interest to the artist and to the typographer who would use him is auto-lithography. This process shares with wood-cutting and wood-engraving the distinction that the artist himself prepares the printing surface and thus takes an intimate share in the commercial result. In no such work can success go to the ignorant or the shirker of technique. The artist must know his business, and must know a great deal of the process of printing, even though it will not be he who will prepare the press and feed the sheets to it.

As a means by which the artist may project his vision into a mass edition, methods of auto-lithography are of interest to publishers. The process is capable of infinite variety and we have come no further than the brink of what is possible. It is still not as widely used as it might be, perhaps because it is expensive. It is expensive first because it requires a good artist who has the requisite technical ability, and secondly because it is not a process for the indifferent printer, and the good printer is seldom a cheap printer. In adult books auto-lithography may more often be seen on the jacket than within the covers, publishers seeing nothing incongruous in employing a first-rate artist and a first-rate printer for an ephemeral dust-cover while the more permanent book is devoid of their work. To such a mistaken scale of values has advertisement brought us.

Auto-lithography has been widely used for children's books, and for adult books as well, both in monochrome and in colour. However, its use appears to be declining in face of the greater convenience of photo-offset. Auto-lithography tends to become

191. Plastocowell drawing by Anthony Gross for the *Forsyte Saga* (Heinemann)

192. Wood-engraving by Reynolds Stone for a part heading, 1946

a process for the illustration of fine books, but it does occasionally appear in less exalted, more mass-produced publications, and still occasionally in children's books.

A lithographic process introduced by W. S. Cowell Ltd., which allows the artist to draw on a plastic sheet instead of on stone or metal, has proved to be a very valuable addition to the artist's range. It is more convenient and easier to work than ordinary forms of auto-lithography, as far as the artist is concerned, and it requires less experience of lithography on his part. The plastic can be treated in several ways and is amenable to many different styles; and while it can be used as nothing more than a substitute for stone or metal, it can also be used to produce results that could not have been achieved by any other means. The drawing by Anthony Gross facing page 413 is an example of this process.

While I have deprecated the use of screen processes for the reproduction of drawings made for books, I must modify this opinion where work in colour is concerned. Otherwise I should close so many fields to the artist that books and the public would be the losers. Nevertheless, I would still say that what can be done well by half-tone process engraving can usually be done better by another process. Colour photogravure is not often used in this way, but colour lithography is. For this we may go for the most convenient examples to juvenile books, especially the early Puffins and King Penguins, and also to many children's books from various publishers.

So far I have written only of drawings especially prepared by an artist for book illustration, but among the assorted material that comes into a publishing office under the banner of illustration there is much more that has been gathered by the author from every sort of source. Diagrams, drawings, wood-cuts, wood-engravings, lino-cuts, etchings, paintings, prints, photographs—any kind of graphic representation that has ever appeared in the world may be brought at some time or other within the purview of the publisher. Whatever may be thought to illustrate the text of a book is liable to be presented confidently for reproduction. Thus it is not uncommon to find that the illustrative matter consists of an object or two, a selection of photographs of varied size and vintage, three or four paintings, and some drawings in line. Through the most miscellaneous collection runs a common thread, their relation to the text that has been the cause of their being gathered together. Their value lies not necessarily in themselves or in any aesthetic quality they may possess, but in their enforcement or extension of the author's message. From the point of view of reproduction they may not be ideal; if they are it is probably more due to fortune than intention. Though skilful men, when their abilities are challenged, may be able to perform apparent miracles, there remain some things that cannot satisfactorily be reproduced by any process, and when they occur they must be laid aside with whatever regret may be due.

It is not often that the material is completely unsuitable. Most people know a well made photograph from a bad one, not from any fund of technical knowledge, but simply because a good photograph looks better; and this is true of other kinds of picture. An author who takes the trouble to select material that

193. Line drawing by Mervyn Peake, from *The Rime of the Ancient Mariner*, 1

is technically competent is not likely to fail in his duty to his publisher. Sometimes, however, there is no choice, and then it remains to make the best of a bad job. Nothing is to be gained by rejecting a unique photograph, taken under difficulties or at serious risk, on the ground that it is unsharp or under-exposed.

Selection of the process to be used for the illustrations is complicated by matters not purely technical or aesthetic. The price at which the book is to be sold, the size of the edition, convenience in reprinting, the kind of illustration, are all factors, among others, that affect the decision. Line subjects that can be printed on the same paper as the text may be set down at once as line blocks, though not inevitably, but tone subjects are very different. In the majority of cases these will be reproduced by half-tone process engraving. This process is cheaper than others and the result is good—sharp, brilliant, and faithful, if a little factual in atmosphere. It can deal with all kinds of subjects from an agricultural implement to a famous painting. It is the process for all the ordinary run of books and for not a few of the extraordinary.

The other three of the four processes I have already mentioned—photogravure, photo-lithography, and collotype—have each a separate and individual effect and suit different purposes. Each complicates the economic factor. Photogravure is cheap enough if large editions can be printed, but it costs a lot to get going, and for the editions common for books at the present time may be prohibitive. This is a great pity, because it is capable of the finest work, and when it is done well (and it is too often done not so well) it possesses richness of light and shade foreign to process engraving.

Collotype, often regarded as a luxury process, is not too expensive for the finer qualities of books. Among its advantages is one that is unique—there is no screen to break up the tones, and for this reason it is used where accurate reproduction of fine detail is desirable. Its tonal range is great, delightful to the eye, and never harsh. The ink used is rather similar in shade to that commonly used in photogravure, a warm black or cold brown.

194. Etching by Henri Matisse, for *Poésies de Stéphane Mallarmé*, 1932

Photo-lithography is in effect an alternative method of printing images broken up by the familiar half-tone dot screen, but the result is not an imitation of process engraving. It lacks the crispness of half-tone, but gains in delicacy and softness. The loss of the air of mechanical precision is counterbalanced by a gain in an intangible quality that we may call 'humanity'. Conscientious and capable craftsmanship is essential, for without it the result will almost certainly be flat and degenerate.

When the illustrations are to be printed in colour, the question must be looked at rather differently. Aesthetically, I would place the processes I have mentioned in the following order: collotype, photo-lithography, photogravure, and process engraving. Full-colour collotype and photogravure are seldom seen in books because they are so costly that only a very expensive book could support their use. Collotype, especially, is astronomically expensive, and the magnificent colour work done in this way is best seen in the plates offered for sale by some museums and galleries at prices some artists would be glad to receive for original pictures.

Colour photo-lithography, once a neglected process in the making of books, is now frequently employed. The peculiar softness of the print gives to colour reproductions a distinct and engaging character. Deep rich colours and delicate tints are both possible, with every shade between.

Colour reproduction by half-tone process engraving, which I have placed last aesthetically, should practically be placed at the head of the list. In books this process is used more often than all the other three put together. It is not only because it is the cheapest that it is so, but also because it is the most convenient. It should be stated that, although my opinion is different, this process is thought by many to be the best and most accurate means of colour reproduction. It suffers, as half-tone always does, from the necessity of using art paper, and it has other disadvantages. For many subjects I think it is too assertive and too harsh. A serious disadvantage is that water-colour paintings and chalk drawings tend to lose their character and to look as though they had been done in some oil medium—an effect perhaps due to the oily ink sitting on the surface of the coated paper.

Whatever the process, the work of bringing an assortment of originals into a common relationship with the page remains essentially the same, and it should be understood that where in the following pages I speak of blocks and process engraving they stand as symbols to represent the printing surface of each process. Illustrations may be treated in many ways, and what is done with them must depend on the type of book, on the effect aimed at, and on the illustrations themselves. The questions that present themselves for answer concern the size and disposition of the margins, whether the pictures shall or shall not bleed, whether they are to be printed on one or both sides of the paper, whether to have more than one picture on a page, how to set the legends, and finally how to place the pages in the book.

Any photographer is aware of the importance of mounting in enhancing a picture, and the placing of a picture on a page is the equivalent of mounting. There is, however, an important difference between the practice of the photographer and that of the typographer: the first cuts the mount to fit the picture, while the other must make the picture fit the mount. The page is the typographer's starting point, and however greatly he may admire wide margins, it needs no demonstration to show that the wider the margins are the smaller must the picture be. Reduction may seriously affect its value, and certainly will do so when detail is of interest. On the other hand, unduly narrow margins are objectionable. In my opinion the best basis on which to settle the question of size is the type area of the text page. This is not to say that the margins of the illustrations must be the same as those of a wide-margined text page, but that the illustrations should be placed in relation to the text page, that is to say, the rectangle of the text panel becomes the foundation of the area of illustrations and determines what the margins shall be.

Whether there should be more than one or two pictures to the page is a moot point. It can be argued that if a picture is worth including, it should be made a reasonable size. Quarter-page illustrations, however, can be used effectively in books with pictures in which detail is not of paramount importance. It means that the author can get many more illustrations into a given number of pages, and it may be of value to his argument to do so.

It is necessary to deal with each picture individually in determining its size, unless—and it scarcely ever happens—all the originals are exactly the same size and to be reduced or enlarged in the same proportion. The new size must be calculated for each picture separately and recorded in some way convenient for the process engraver—usually the new measurement of one dimension is marked on the back of the original. One dimension automatically controls the other, and the typographer must be able to calculate what the other will be, for it is not the length of one side that matters to him, but the area. There are several methods of making the calculation. It can be done by arithmetic, by geometry, or by means of a vernier scale.

Pictures may vary considerably in proportion, from the fat or square to the long and narrow, and the variations naturally reappear in the plates, unless steps have been taken to prevent it. If the diversity is too great to be comfortable, it may be possible to trim the originals, or to reproduce only portions, and where these originals are photographs of, let us say, processes or people they can often be trimmed without harm to their composition. There is no need to strive for exactly the same proportions or the same size for every picture—the existence of diversity helps to prevent monotony. It must be kept in mind that the legend is optically part of the plate and must be allowed for.

Pictures of what is called landscape proportion, that is those that are wider than they are deep, are always unsatisfactory in a book unless they can be printed two on a page. If each one is given a page to itself, to allow of its being made a more useful size, it must be printed sideways. This means that the book must be given a ninety-degree turn every time one of these illustrations is encountered, and what a nuisance this is anyone who uses illustrated books understands only too well. It can keep a book with many plates constantly spinning, and with it the reader's head also. It may be argued that it is good for the neck muscles, even if it is bad for the temper, but fraying of temper and wasted muscular exertion are not the most serious aspects of the question. The turning and twisting have a bad effect on the book itself, and a heavy one may begin to show damage after the first bout. When illustrations are commissioned it is worth while to impress on the artist or photographer that none should be made that are intended to fit sideways on the page. In the majority of cases there is, I believe, no reason why the pictures should not be conceived and executed as upright ones. Just as the cinematographer has had to learn to confine himself to 'landscape' composition, the book illustrator can learn to confine himself to the upright picture in upright books.

In a naughty world legislation must be made to deal with the imperfect. When horizontal compositions do occur it must be considered how they shall be treated. It will not do to place the foot of the picture always to the foredge, for that means that left- and right-hand pictures will face different ways and only increases the swivelling and the annoyance. The best practice indicates that the foot of the picture should be always at the right. The margins should be based on those of the text page. The picture should not be placed in the centre of the field, because there it will undoubtedly look too low. It should be treated like a text page, with more space at the tail than at the head.

Upright or horizontal, the pictures must be brought into harmony with the rest of the book, and the first thing to be done is to reduce them all to a common basis of size related to the area of the text page. I have suggested that some may be trimmed to alter their proportions, but paintings and drawings and other originals that are presumed to have been carefully composed should never without good reason be interfered with by the typographer, and whatever diversity of proportion may exist must be made the best of.

The practice of running illustrations to the edge of the paper, known as bleeding, has increased considerably in recent years, particularly in magazines. It was considered a modernism once, but nowadays it has lost its daring look and become almost matter of fact. None the less, it has considerable use in book production, not only where it is desired to have the illustrations as large as possible; its peculiarly individual effect makes it of value in many kinds of book, just as it makes it unsuitable for others. It might not be applicable for illustrations of, say, Regency architecture, but it does suit modern architecture; it is excellent for machinery and its products, but not in many cases for *objets d'art.*

These, however, are not the only considerations that govern the decision whether illustrations should be bled. It is, for example, essential that a book with bled illustrations shall be trimmed on all sides that bleed, and this may not be desired; where the effect of a rough edge is required, illustrations should be arranged in the ordinary way, with margins.

The ideal may appear to be a picture that bleeds on all four sides, but in practice this seldom happens; it can only occur when the original is of exactly the same proportions as the page or when drastic trimming to make it so can be endured. When it does happen it poses the question of what to do with the legend. Obviously the simplest thing is to abandon the legend altogether, but this might cause not a little inconvenience to the reader, who may be puzzled to know how the illustration is related to the text—particularly if the subject is something not at once easily recognizable, such as a radiograph. Legends are usually necessary and must somehow be included. They can be incorporated into the block, as white lettering on a black ground or black lettering on a white ground, or even as mixed counterchange on a piebald ground. It may be amusing to experiment, but I don't think the result is satisfactory. The best thing to do with such a legend seems to be to print it at the foot of the facing page, either below the type area or included within it; in the latter case some device must be adopted to make the legend distinct from the text. Actually, since the proportions of picture and page seldom exactly coincide, there is usually a blank area in which the legend can be printed comfortably.

The success of bled illustration lies not in its harmony with the text pages, but in its contrast. The common relationship between the type panel and the illustrations is abandoned and everything is banked on the contrast of large, dark, frameless areas with the smaller framed areas of grey that are the text.

In this discussion of toned illustrations I have so far thought in rectangles. Many subjects are better reproduced in some other manner: some, such as medallions, are naturally round or oval, and there are other things whose shape is indeterminate. The latter description applies to such things as pencil or crayon drawings, silhouettes, and so forth. The background for these is the paper on which they are drawn, and it may be desirable as far as possible to preserve this effect in reproduction. In such cases the blockmaker will need special instructions.

A variety of finishes is available for the rectangular illustration, each incorporated in the block. It may be finished with a thin black rule round the edge to form a close frame within the margin, or it may be several rules, arranged thick and thin to form a pattern. More ambitious still, if one had a taste in that direction, there used to be many fancy borders in the engraver's catalogue, which were supplied on request. These may be encountered occasionally in books published before the first world war or in old-fashioned sales material, but their heyday is past. Now they are out of fashion, and like any outworn mode they appear a trifle ridiculous to the taste of the present time. Nowadays the general practice is to take the block as it is and to allow the screen itself to form the edge.

After the material has been sent to the engraver, the next stage is the engraver's proofs. The material is returned together with proofs of the blocks made from it. The proofs are checked to ensure that the blocks have been made the correct size and that the required part of the original has been reproduced, and to judge the quality of the reproduction. If any defects or shortcomings are discovered the engraver is expected to put them right, just as the printer is expected to correct his own errors in type.

So far the proofs resemble the originals in that they are no more than a bundle of pictures, without arrangement or order, but differ in that they possess a common basis of size in relation to the page. The printer must be instructed how to deal with them.

When the illustrations are line drawings to be printed with the text the printer is told where they are to be placed in the book and also where they are to be placed on the page. No-one can tell better than the artist what action in the story each drawing is intended to illustrate, and it is worth while to encourage him to indicate clearly on each drawing its position in relation to the text, so that when proofs do arrive the typographer may do his work on them without further reference. Sometimes there is no indication of position and no way of finding it short of reading through the book with the illustrations at hand, a process that anyone with other work to do fights shy of. The easiest thing is to send the galleys and block proofs to the artist and to ask him to pin the proofs in where they go. He may be asked to do more than this if he is willing and cares sufficiently for his idea of how the drawings should be presented. With the galleys and proofs may go a specimen page from which the artist can build a paste-up showing the exact position of each block on the page and in the text. The book thus becomes an even closer collaboration between the artist and the typographer. The author too may be called in, and if he has any ideas of his own may insist on being called in.

Those drawings that are intended to occupy whole pages are generally better on right-hand than on left-hand pages, and this is particularly so when the reverse of the illustration is blank I think it extremely objectionable to come upon a blank right-hand page and then to find an illustration on the back of it; but a blank left-hand page on the back of a right-hand illustration does not seem to matter at all. The position of the illustration on the page should be related to the text by its margins. Where the block is of the same size as the text panel the margins will be the same; where they differ the block is placed on the page within or on an imaginary rectangle representing the text area. This explanation is a little mechanical, and in practice there are factors that disturb it. For example, the balance of a drawing may not be in the drawing itself, but beside it, and mechanical placing of such a drawing will certainly make it look out of centre; it should be placed in relation to its balance.

It is questionable whether headlines and folios should appear on pages on which there are whole-page drawings. Some people appear to like them there, but I dislike them and choose to print the block as though it were on otherwise blank paper. Typographical details are apt to draw too much importance to themselves. The same remark applies to the legend, except that this is frequently essential. Where it can be dispensed with it should be; where it cannot it must be set in some manner that will make it part of the page and prevent it from being conspicuous or inharmonious.

Small line blocks may be put in the margin or as head or tail pieces or simply scattered throughout the chapter according to the references in the text. Margins permit of little more than thumbnail sketches, but if they are dealt with skilfully these are charming, importing into the rigid rectangle of the text a kind of unpredictable variety, almost of irresponsibility in some books; and yet they are also capable of gravity when the occasion demands it. Headpieces really belong to the chapter head, but come in here in the sense that they are illustrations and not merely decorations. Illustration or decoration, they form one whole with the chapter head, and their placing and spacing must be governed by the design made for that. Headpieces are seldom large and are nearly always narrow horizontal bands presenting the artist with problems in composition. They may incorporate the lettering of the chapter head or provide an island space in which to print it. Here more than anywhere else the question of relative weight is important and the artist should know what kind of type is being used before he starts to draw. Tailpieces may be practically anything that will go into the space, though there is a tendency to restrict choice to subjects that may be considered illustrative of the chapter or book as a whole rather than of any incident in it. This may have arisen because it may not be known until the book is in page what tailpieces will be needed, and if they are to be drawn in advance a general subject is a safe bet. Tailpieces are sometimes used as pendants at the tip of a typographical arrangement of the last page in the form of an inverted triangle. Small drawings in the text may be placed in practically any position one can think of, but one, the dead centre of the page, should be avoided, because a block so placed looks too low on the page. Apart from this, they are placed at the foot, at the head, at the sides with the type run round, if they are small enough, or near the optical centre of the page. Legends are not really necessary for illustrations of a story, but may be necessary for diagrams or technical drawings. The space that separates the block from the text should not be large, and usually it should not be greater than the equivalent of a line and a half of text; if it is, it tends to become a gap and the colour and unity of the page are spoiled.

Illustrations in tone, printed on a paper different from the text, are treated differently. The printer must be told the order in which they will appear, how each will be placed upon the page, the position of the legends and the size and face of type in which to set them, and how the plates are to be fixed in the book. None of these are things he can be expected to know or to decide for himself, and the information is conveyed in the form of a paste-up, which is made in the publisher's office or to his instruction.

One of the first things to be settled is whether the plates shall be printed on one or both sides of the paper. It is not entirely or even mainly, a question of economy. It depends on the number of plates, on the importance of their relation to chapters or parts, and on the effect the typographer wants to produce. The effect of printing on one side only is more spacious and generous, and for that reason this method may be adopted. When it is adopted, the plates should be printed, for the reasons, I have already stated, so that they occur on right-hand pages. When the illustrations are numerous the recurring blanks begin to look a little silly, and then it is better to print on both sides of the paper; and this should also be resorted to when there are many illustrations to go into one chapter, for then there are less interruptions of the text. The two methods may be used concurrently in one book, but this is better avoided.

There are several ways of making a paste-up, but the best way, even though it entails some trouble, is the most precise way. First a blank dummy of the correct number of pages and the correct size is made, with the pages grouped as they will finally have to be printed—i.e. if the plates are to be wrapped round text signatures, then the dummy will be made in units of four pages; if they are to appear in groups of eight or sixteen, then the dummy is made up of sections of eight or sixteen pages. The proofs are then cut out and pasted into the dummy in the positions in which it is intended they shall appear when finally printed, so that the completed paste-up shows the arrangement page by page, the correct order, and also the imposition required. Pasting-in of the block proofs also makes identification of the blocks by the printer as nearly foolproof as possible. Each page needs individual attention to determine the margins, which, as I have already said, are calculated in relation to the text margins, and the block proofs should be pasted down exactly in the positions required to give the margins stated; in addition, it is useful for the printer, and removes any possibility of doubt, if the amounts of the head and inner margins are stated for each page, preferably in ems for half-tone, because a type scale is a commoner tool in a letterpress office than an inch rule, and anyway the printer finds it handier to work in ems and points rather than in fractions of an inch. In determining the margin an allowance must be made for the binder's trim of the pages.

Provision is made in the paste-up for legends, copy for which should accompany it, together with instructions concerning the type and its disposition. Some means of keying legends and illustrations is essential, and it need only be parallel numbering of the legends and the plates. This is a small point that is too easily overlooked, and bungling it only means a puzzled and querulous printer—if the publisher cannot make up his mind, the printer cannot be expected to know that one of two portraits is Mrs. Smythe and the other Mrs. Browne.

The method of inserting the plates in the book may have to be decided in collaboration with the author. Most authors plump more or less uncompromisingly for having each plate precisely opposite some predetermined mention in the text, which is all right ideally, but in practice raises a number of snags. In the end the author usually proves amenable to persuasion, cajolery, or hard facts. There are various considerations that govern the insertion of plates, and among them are ease and speed of binding, and the importance of physical strength in the finished book—which may almost be said to be the pole opposite to the placing of the illustrations against their references in the text. If the juxtaposition of plate and reference is essential, then each plate must be printed on a single leaf, which is pasted-in in the bindery. From the author's point of view there is no better method, for he can juggle with his pictures as he likes and put them exactly where he wants them. From the point of view of the publisher and binder, it is not as satisfactory as it appears to the author. The leaf is held in the book by a narrow line of paste along the edge, and while it may be surprising how strong a little paste can be, it does give way in the end and the plate comes out. That with a little ill usage it can give way very quickly most librarians are aware. A stronger method is to hook the plate in, that is to print it on paper rather wider than the page, fold the surplus round a text section, and stitch in the ordinary way. As far as strength is concerned, this is satisfactory, but it is also ugly, because the stubs show up on the other side of the section and give the impression that either a vandal or a censor has been at work. The stubs are less obvious if they are pasted down, and though this is bothersome to the binder, it can be done.

In my opinion the best and cheapest way is that in which the plates are arranged to wrap round and stitch in with the signatures. It is true that by this method they can fall against any particular reference only by chance, and that the position of one plate dictates the position of another, but it is unlikely that the gap between plate and reference will be very great. In many books there is, indeed, no real point of reference at all, each illustration applying to several pages of text or even illuminating a whole chapter; in such cases it cannot matter greatly where the plate is placed, provided it does not fall in a section of the book that is foreign to it.

The method is simple. The plates are printed in four-page sections, and each section is wrapped round a section of text. If the text is printed in sixteen-page sections, and a section of plates is wrapped round signature B, there will then be a plate facing page 16 and, if the plates are printed on both sides of the leaf, another facing page 17; then follow sixteen pages of text and another plate facing page 32; the reverse of this plate will face the first page of the next section, page 33. When the plate sections are wrapped round alternate text sections, a leaf of illustrations occurs every sixteen pages. In books with many illustrations and a comparatively short text, this may not be enough, and then a larger number may be accommodated by inserting four-page plate sections inside the alternate text sections, which in section C gives plates facing pages 36, 37, 44 and 45. By wrapping round and inserting, every thirty-two pages of text can be made to accommodate eight pages of illustrations, with each leaf standing alone. Actually, plates occurring so frequently may be a serious interruption of the text, and it may be wiser to print the plates of a lavishly illustrated book in sections of eight or sixteen pages, to be bound in between the sections of text.

Particularly in books of the more expensive kind, plates, and especially colour plates, may be cut out and mounted, perhaps on paper of colour and quality different from that of the text. The effect is pleasing and a little luxurious, the texture of the mount adding richness and variety to the book. This method has some disadvantages, among which are the problems of fastening the mounts in the book, the risk that the plates, which are attached at only two corners, may be creased or damaged in handling, and increased cost. The purchaser of a luxury book is willing to pay more than usual, so that the question of cost need not detain us. Fastening is usually done by hooking in, of the disadvantages of which I have spoken already: the effect is worsened when a coloured mount is used, for then the stub is also coloured, and consequently more noticeable. The method of attaching the print to the mount by two blobs of paste is most inefficient and dangerous, though I have known it defended on the ground that a plate lightly attached can easily be detached if the purchaser wants to take it out and adorn his walls with it—an unreasonable argument, because books are not, or should not be, made to be taken to pieces in this way. The only satisfactory mounting is one that will stick the print down all over and yet will not cockle either the print or the mount. Dry mounting is satisfactory as far as cockling is concerned, but I am not sure that it is as permanent as its advocates assert. Rubber solution is probably better, but again the question of permanence is one that requires investigation. Glue, paste, and gum tend to cockle any mount that is not very stout.

The completed paste-up, together with the copy for the legends and instructions for setting them, is sent to the printer, whose business it is to impose the blocks and set the legends and submit proofs of the forme. These proofs should be, but very often are not, in flat sheets properly backed up in register, but not necessarily made ready—all that is necessary is to be able to read the legends and to be able to recognize the blocks. One of the sheets should be ruled up by the printer to show how he has interpreted the margin instructions. Alternatively, the printer may insert a short fine rule to show where the fold or cut will come, and ruling up will then be unnecessary. The ruled-up sheet allows the margins to be checked and alterations can be marked on it if any are required. Collotype, photogravure, and lithography do not allow of correction of the margins at this stage, for that would entail a new plate or cylinder; the margins must be right in the paste-up.

Legends will need reading and correcting and should be shown to the author for this purpose. All corrections from all sources are next gathered together and collated on to one proof, which is then ready to be returned to the printer, either for press, or if the number of corrections warrants it, for a revised proof.

The list of illustrations in the prelims will need checking against the legends below the pictures, and the facing-page numbers must be supplied. This is a point that is easily overlooked, and bungling it results in an irritated binder trying to make plates face impossible pages before he at length announces that it is all wrong and he won't do it!

Colour illustrations offer essentially the same problems as monochrome in regard to margins, etc., and need not be treated in any way differently. But the colour itself brings in a new element in checking the proofs and provides a new problem for the printer. It may not matter greatly if, let us say, the colours of a children's book of inferior quality do not correspond exactly with the colours in the originals of its inferior artist; it appears that there are printers and publishers who believe that colour is the main thing and that any kind of colour is good enough for a gullible public. Accurate reproduction of good work is a very different matter, and an artist fails himself if he does not demand that the printed colours shall correspond as nearly to his own as the process allows. Where the original has been made for its own sake, as for example a painting, the engraver and printer must strive to achieve the utmost they can within the limits of the process, and if those limits preclude complete success the present stage of that process must be considered unsatisfactory as far as that particular painting is concerned. An original made for reproduction by an artist who knows his business is a different matter; engraver and printer are expected to produce a *reproduction* in the exact sense of the word, and if they fail it is they themselves who must be blamed and their skill considered insufficient.

These are harsh statements, and suggest that there are men infallible as judges. Unfortunately, the case is very different. No two people seem to see colour in the same way, and what one person considers an accurate match another may decry. This and carelessness or imperfection in the process produce between them diversities of colour in reproduction that are quite surprising and perfectly visible to anyone when two prints of the same subject from different sources are compared. This state of affairs does not apply only to indifferent or cheap printing; even good printing is frequently in error, and there can be no certainty that an expensive reproduction preserves exactly the colours of the original. There are so many stages at which differences may creep in, and if at the first stage in the engraver's works the original has been available for comparison, it is rarely available at the final stage in the printer's machine-room.

Certainly there are people, artists and others, who have trained themselves towards a true appreciation of colour, and such a person should be in charge or should have the final decision in all questions of colour, from the engraver to the printer. Only in this manner is it likely that the result will approximate to the original. The typographer is not necessarily such a person, and it may be wiser for him to lean upon a more expert judgement.

A final word may be addressed to the author. He of all persons connected with the making of books should know something about their manufacture, though it need be no more than will suffice to present his material in a reasonable manner. The astonishing untidiness, the incredible ignorance of the business of books exhibited by writers is nowhere so much in evidence as in the matter of illustrations. It is not uncommon for a publisher to receive a collection of dog-eared, foxed, creased, hazed, fogged, or faded material that turns out on examination to be three or four times as large as is required. There is no suggestion of order, no list by which the material may be checked. There are no legends, but there may be scribbled notes intended to inform some members of the publishing house that this is Bill and that is a dog—but whether it is Bill's dog who shall say? In short, there is nothing to suggest that the author has had any vision whatsoever of the pictures as part of a book.

Naturally, not all authors are like this, thank heaven, but even those who are orderly in mind and in their works might learn a lesson. Originals of any kind should possess at least technical competence in their medium. Photographs should be sharp and clear and properly developed and printed; the reiterated statement that photographs for the press should be contrasty is bunk, the truth being that they should be good photographs as photographs. Where there is choice they should be black and white and glossy, but matt or sepia will do as second best if nothing else can be had. Contact prints from small negatives will not do; wherever possible the original should be larger than the reproduction will be. Selection of the pictures is the author's job, and their arrangement in sequence should also be done by him. In short, what the publisher likes to receive is a set of good originals complete in one batch, with a list in duplicate of the legends numbered to agree (one of which is for the list of illustrations in the prelims), an indication of the relative importance of the pictures, and where necessary a list of owners of copyright and necessary acknowledgements. Any of these things may mean extra trouble for the author, but if they are left undone they mean much more trouble for the publisher and more likelihood of delay in the publication of the book.

XXI

ENDPAPERS

In spite of the prevalence of blank ends in modern books it may with reason be claimed that the purpose of endpapers is mostly aesthetic. They contribute little to the mechanical perfection of the book and scarcely anything to the strength of the binding; they are placed where they are to hide the works that unite the stitched sections to the case and to mask the turned-in edges of the cloth or other substance used to cover the boards.

Aesthetically their qualities have been enhanced and extended by the artist and the decorator. The two-page spread is an excellent field for their work, and at various times it has been used in one way or another to strike an additional note in the chord that is the design of the whole book. Many examples are elaborate and involved, while others achieve their effect, which may be none the less rich, through simplicity and reiteration. Colour printing finds a use here, and it is possible to achieve both discreet beauty and sumptuousness by means of coloured inks and coloured paper.

The simplest but not necessarily the least effective pattern is that made by the repetition of a simple motif in a simple arrangement, as for example a fleur-de-lys arranged on a chequer-board; and variety may be introduced into this by the addition of a second colour used alternately with the first. The principle of counterchange introduces still further possibilities, either in one colour or more. In counterchange patterns there are usually heavy solids, and these can be lightened and enlivened by imperfect printing, that is by starving the plate of ink so that the solids print grey and broken and with something of variety of tone. The variations are not under complete control and every impression will be different, but that does not matter—on the contrary, it may be considered an advantage.

Simple or intricate patterns suitable for endpapers could very well be built up out of printers' flowers and ornaments, or even out of types, and that there are considerable possibilities in this direction Frederic Warde has demonstrated in his book on Monotype printing ornaments. Unfortunately the example he has set has been scarcely heeded, perhaps partly because of the strength of the modern tradition of blank ends, partly because some ingenuity and some expenditure of time are necessary, both of which are expensive commodities in publishing and printing offices.

Another form of pattern, the arabesque, has by no means been neglected in the design of endpapers. It is scarcely necessary to say that the arabesque is capable of as great degeneration as excellence, and the book, while it has not missed the excellent, has also not escaped the degenerate. Arabesque patterns have at various times been in vogue, and were popular in the early part of this century, perhaps as undulations from the splash of the high dive of Aubrey Beardsley into the seas of art, or from the frolics and churnings of William Morris in the same waters. It is understandable that they should have been adopted by publishers of popular series of the classics, and the reader will remember the elaborate twinings of sinuous branches in the endpapers of the Everyman series in the format that was used for many years. The pattern was sometimes made to incorporate a plaque or a symbolical figure, or a little device with blank spaces for the owner to write his name and address in—a built-in book-plate, in fact, though at a time before the phrase 'built-in' had acquired the magic it has to-day.

Marbled papers, which are available in great variety, must be included under the heading of patterned papers. They were used more in former times than they are to-day, and I think it a pity that they have vanished from the ordinary run of books. Cost is the reason, for good marbled papers are necessarily hand-marbled papers. They are still made, and appear in the occasional book that the publisher wants to make much of. Some patterns are delightful in their restrained use of colour and pattern. Good marbled paper can be pleasant as ends, if not for the common book, and even for the more expensive one it must be used with care and with awareness of the pitfalls and misuse which have perhaps been responsible more than anything else for its rarity in books to-day. It is easy with these materials to produce a sense of anachronism. Imitations of marbled papers have been made by photo-lithography and process engraving, and though in theory there may appear to be no objection to such change in the method of producing the pattern, in practice the imitations are generally too much like imitations to be successful.

Maps and diagrams sometimes appear on the endpapers, and maps in particular may be pleasantly decorative even when they have been made from a completely utilitarian point of view. It may be argued that the endpaper, being a part of the binding and liable to destruction in rebinding, is no place for matter essential to an understanding of the author's message; it is a somewhat old-fashioned argument now, and the answer is that modern books issued in cases are not intended to be rebound, but to be permanent in the form in which they leave the publisher's office.

Endpapers are sometimes made the vehicles of illustrations, or of illustrative decoration. True illustration, that is a picture of some transitory action or event in the story, should not be used as an endpaper if its local value outweighs its value in relation to the story as a whole; endpaper illustration, because of its detached position, should represent or symbolize the general theme or trend of the text.

Colour is always desirable, because black alone is inclined to be dull, and where there is to be only one printing it is better to print in colour. A two-colour effect can be obtained by using coloured paper.

Half-tone blocks are not suitable for the printing of endpapers because they generally necessitate the use of art paper, which is neither strong enough nor suitable for the purpose. Indeed, reproduction in tone by photo-litho or half-tone may appear out of key, perhaps because of the somewhat factual atmosphere of the processes. Line blocks are excellent, and so are non-screen forms of lithography. One form of lithography, indeed, strikes me as eminently applicable, but it is not used as often as it might be, outside children's books. It is auto-lithography, which can convey those idiosyncrasies and eccentricities of the artist that are often a great deal of what matters in decoration.

Coloured papers might be used for ends more than they are, though here again a nineteenth-century surfeit has perhaps affected their value for us. Everyone has come across Victorian books with dark and dismal endpapers in blue or brown or black, with the colour laid on so thickly that the paper has something of the feel and a good deal of the properties of carbon paper. This kind of paper was, it appears, purposely made for endpapers, but who invented it in the first place and why, no-one seems to know, nor why it was used. It could not have served to prevent scribblers from making notes on the ends, for you can write on it with a fingernail. However, the use of coloured papers need not be as unsubtle as that. There is great variety of coloured papers, even when choice is restricted to the more delicate shades suitable for our purpose, and failure to achieve the effect aimed at can seldom be attributed to the papermaker.

Selection of paper is, indeed, a matter that requires attention. No loose or fluffy paper should be used—featherweight antique, however specious its appearance, is out of place. There is no need to stint quality, for the amount of paper required is so small that cost is of slight importance. It certainly should not be of worse quality than the paper used for the text. Preferably it should be of a kind and substance sufficient to make a tangible difference in stiffness and strength.

I have emphasized that what is printed on the endpapers should be representative of the whole book, but this does not mean that the endpaper should be merely decorative or symbolical; on the contrary, it can perform a very useful function, as for example when it is the vehicle of a map or chart. It is easy and it is a common fallacy, to believe that the word 'decorative' entails a goodly amount of elaboration and ornament, surrounding what utility there may be in a riot of intricacy or colour, as though the useful could not be handsome in its own right. This error leads inevitably to excess of subtlety and ingenuity. Arabesques and even counterchange motifs may fail from lack of simplicity in design or of honesty in conception; and where decoration is used to embroider utility it may smother it with the weight of its encumbrance. None the less, it is true that greater latitude is possible in the treatment of the endpaper than is usually allowable in the text, and a boldness of design which would be out of place in the body of the book may here be very pleasant.

What colours are used, whether of inks in the pattern or of the paper on which it is printed, should not be selected without reference to the design of the book as a whole. The colour scheme characteristic of the general design may be repeated literally in the pattern of the endpaper, or be merely echoed, or there may be a deliberate contrast intended to enhance both parties to it. This can be stated simply and practically in the suggestion that where there is a colour-washed head, the endpapers should be either the same colour or a shade of it; or else a contrast, which should not be violent—one half of the endpaper, it should be remembered, will be framed in the margin of the binding cloth.

XXII

BINDING DESIGN

PERHAPS no aspect of the book shows greater divergence between the old and the new, between hand work and machine work, than the binding. Bibliophiles may lament the vanished skill that produced the masterpieces of the dark and middle ages and deplore the poverty of our resources to-day. Yet are we so poor, who work for a different end? When for one book that was then bound so sumptuously for the pleasure of the great, we now produce a million in cheaper and more sober garments for the use of the multitude? We are not all dukes and princes, with large estates and noble revenues, nor their modern versions, rich industrialists; and our temper is different and would be not a little impatient of a process that by the loving care and skill of hand it entailed limited our property in books.

That is not to deny that among old books there are bindings that are wonderful achievements. No-one in his senses can deny it. The best deserve reverence analogous to that inspired by a good painting or a cut jewel and give the same deep pleasure; the craftsmen who made them were not merely craftsmen, but artists. In the making of some of them, indeed, the professed artist played a part. Such bindings were made to order and could be commissioned by no mean customer, to enclose what were then treasures of great esteem. The precious binding was the shrine of a rare and precious possession.

A few of those old bindings were precious in the real sense, involving the co-operation of the silversmith, the goldsmith, the jeweller, and the artist. The boards were inlaid with silver or gold and encrusted with jewels set in them like the stones in a king's crown, mere units in a whole design of which a part might be the arms of the man who had ordered the binding. Perhaps no printed book was ever bound so munificently as this, and indeed few manuscripts were, but rich and elaborate workmanship continued after the invention of printing. Nevertheless the clatter of Gutenberg's press was the knell of the binder who worked in rich materials for rich customers. In the end the printer made books cheap, and made them commonplace possessions no longer thought worthy of the sumptuous fanes in which they had been set when they were rare and costly things. It became incongruous to set a book costing the equivalent of a few shillings in a binding worth a king's ransom, and consequently as the presses flourished bindings became cheaper and more sober. The binder did not willingly relinquish his traditions of richness and magnificence, even though all that was left to him that was precious was gold and his own taste and skill. On the less sumptuous sort of binding gold was used in abundance, but it was after all only leaf gold, and a little gold goes a surprisingly long way when the beater has dealt with it. What was incalculable was the patience and the skill of the binder, who might labour on one book for weeks or even months together, building up piece by piece the intricacies and the complexities of an elaborate design. There was no easy way round in his labour, there was no substitute for his skill.

Binding design is a subject of wide variety. I have already indicated how craftsmen and artists have contributed to the beauty of precious books, but beauty does not lie only in expensive or rare materials. It is always the workmanship and the power of design behind it that matter most, and many binders have been content with comparatively humble materials. Velvet was one of these, and silk, satin, canvas, and brocade have also been used. Velvet bindings were made for Henry VIII, who seems to have been fond of them. Embroidery was used for decoration, usually in thread, but sometimes in fine silver wire. Tooling on leather seems to have begun about the twelfth century, in Europe at least; this tooling was blind, the manner of applying gold leaf not being introduced until the end of the fifteenth century, when it was brought into Italy apparently from the East. Gold did not, and never has, completely dispossessed blind tooling; the two have continued to exist side by side, frequently appearing together on the same book. Very beautiful work has been done by tooling, in particular, in England, by Samuel Mearne, binder to Charles II, and Roger Payne in the eighteenth century. The bindings made for Jean Grolier in France or Italy in the sixteenth century are regarded by many as the finest of all.

The binder's materials were principally wood, cardboard, leather, silk, velvet and gold leaf, wood or cardboard for the boards, leather, silk, or velvet for the cover, and gold for the tooling. Wooden boards were not always covered, but were sometimes smoothed and polished to reveal the decorative qualities of the grain; or they were inlaid with metal or with contrasting woods, or carved in low relief or intaglio. Most books, however, were covered, the majority in leather of one kind or another. Leather, with its capacity for taking dyes of fine colour, is capable of infinite variety of expression and is among the best of all surfaces for the tool. There is a peculiar satisfaction in leather; fine leather is a joy to the hand and to the eye. And there is additional pleasure when a beautiful material is made the basis of a beautiful design.

The binder might find among the tools in his shop all that he needed for his purpose, or he might cut new tools or have them cut for him to enable him to carry out some special design. In a previous chapter I described these tools and showed that they could be divided into a small number of categories. Wide variety of patterns is not necessary for any one book, for it must be understood that a tooled binding is nearly always an example of closely repetitive pattern. The symbols or patterns recur and some of them will very likely be found on a whole series of bindings issuing from one bindery. Each tool is separately and individually impressed in the leather, each impression separately and individually gilded. Because the hand can never exactly repeat itself, the many slight variations that creep into the design, however trivial, are in some way responsible for that feeling of humanity, of *manu*facture, inherent in the work.

Most of the designs applied to books are based on organic patterns in nature—they are, in short, arabesques. Others are built up of rules or other abstract units. There is, of course, no distinct dividing line. The binder using arabesques did not scruple, and need not scruple, to use rules and geometrical shapes, or whatever else he found useful, to complete his design. No purist doctrine hindered him or detracted from his satisfaction in the result.

An element of common occurrence is the coat of arms or other indication of the owner's identity, which was usually made to occupy the centre of the field.

The leather was carefully moulded over the cords on the spine, dividing the length into compartments, four, five, or six, according to the number of cords. No attempt was made to disguise the cords; on the contrary, the bars they formed and the spaces between them were made the basis of the design applied to the spine. The value of the cords became a convention, and when, as did happen later, the cords were reduced in size and became too thin to make their mark through the leather, they were packed out until they showed sufficiently. The spaces between them are rectangles, and in these, designs were built up, either with the patterns that had been used on the boards or with others that could be used in harmony. The leather over the cords themselves was often left untouched, but on some books it was given a fillet or a combination of tiny flowers, or it was stained a darker colour. Not all the rectangles between the cords were filled. One at least was left, usually the second one down, for the title and the author's name, and perhaps another one at the foot to take any other information that might seem relevant. The spine thus became a dazzling intricacy of gold that presented on the shelf a richness of a kind to stir the heart.

Such bindings, with all the skill and expense they represented, were made to last as enduring possessions, but they were soon to be succeeded by bindings of a plainer and less ambitious character. As books grew cheaper, so binding too must become cheaper, and one way of doing it was to abandon the elaborate tooling of the earlier day. In the process, binding acquired perforce a new aesthetic based on the qualities of leather. It began to be realized that leather possesses beauty of its own, and perhaps the binder was no longer sorry to leave the boards partly or wholly plain. And yet artifice was not altogether abandoned. Methods of patterning the leather were introduced, as for tree calf, for example, which became very popular, or to give it a mottled or variegated appearance. Even so, boards were seldom wholly plain. They were given a rule border at least, blind or in gold, and more often a border made up of ornaments; and there was tooling round the edges of the boards also, and perhaps some more inside where the leather was turned in. The inside of the board, known among bibliophiles as the doublure, was sometimes tooled very elaborately, usually having a rectangular space in the centre. The spine tended to retain much of its complexity, if not all of its quality, of design.

With the nineteenth century came a different conception of binding in which three revolutionary ideas were blended. These were the introduction of a cloth as a covering instead of leather, the application of the machine, and the discovery that bindings could be embossed in one piece. The introduction of cloth was of importance not only because it made the machine possible and edition binding feasible, but also because it introduced a new aesthetic of which we have not even yet explored the limits. The development of the embossing process, what is known as 'blocking', dispensed at one stroke with the hours and hours of labour that formerly had to be spent on each book. It was now possible in seconds to block a cover with as much gold ornament as it would have taken a hand worker days to tool.

It rather went to the heads of some people—of most people, it would perhaps be fairer to say. The idea seems to have been that, since it made no difference to the speed of binding, one might just as well have a lot of gold or blind tooling as a little.

The more recent and more chaste examples of binding design were ignored and a return was made, perhaps in intention but certainly not in fact, to the ideas of the binders of earlier masterpieces. The boards were covered with blocking, blind or gold, or in several colours, and the whole length of the spine. There are no cords in machine binding and it would be difficult to fake them, but the desire for them was indicated by parallel blocked rules in approximately the right positions. Aesthetically it was a bad period, but from the point of view of workmanship it is of the greatest interest because standards were not necessarily lowered by the advent of the machine. For strength and durability the cloth-covered edition binding of the nineteenth century is sometimes a better piece of work than the individual, hand-bound, leather-covered book of the later eighteenth century; but it is inferior in taste.

The two kinds of book are different in every way. The eighteenth-century book represented all the past ages of book binding, though it was a shrunken and emasculated representative; the cloth edition-bound book represented the future and the increasing domination of the machine. While one was a product of the hand, individual, bespoke, and capable of infinite variety of personal expression, the other was mass-produced, subject to the limitations of mass-production, and based on a method of construction radically different and which conditioned its appearance. Some of the results of mechanization were negative, there were things that the machine could not do: tooling vanished from the edges of the board, for example.

The craze for all-over blocking of cloth cases was perhaps not entirely without utility. To our eyes, at least, many of the cloths in use at the time were unpleasant and incapable of a satisfactory effect in their own right; all-over blocking, even if it was blind, gave a poor or unpleasant cloth a different character and helped to disguise its deficiencies.

Before the introduction of cloth it had been the custom of publishers to issue books in what are known as paper boards. This kind of cover was intended as a temporary protection to serve until the purchaser could have the book bound to his own taste in leather. Binding, it will be noted, was not the publisher's business; it was the introduction of cloth that permanently fixed the responsibility of binding on the shoulders of the publisher in England and America. These paper boards, plain, with the title, if it was shown at all, printed on a label pasted on the spine, were destined for a colourful future. While cloth gained headway rapidly for most kinds of books, novels continued to be published in boards, particularly for cheap issues in single volumes; and as the century proceeded their treatment became more and more elaborate. It is easier and cheaper to print on paper than it is to block on cloth, and wider variety is possible. The bookshops, and more particularly the bookstalls, of the period must have seemed gaudy and garish to our eyes—although what the Victorians did with their paper boards we now do with our jackets. The last fling of paper boards was expended on what have come to be called 'yellow-backs', which showed the craft of printing in decline, but which did for Victorian fiction what the cheap edition does to-day.

HALF-BINDING AND QUARTER-BINDING

If it is true that these forms of binding originated in a purpose of utility, it is also true that even at an early period utility was confounded or overlaid by aesthetics. It is a little difficult now to see what useful purpose is served by half- or quarter-binding, because, except in hand-binding, the trouble and expense incurred may possibly outweigh the cost and convenience of covering entirely in the stronger of the two materials used. There is argument for them in the case of ledgers, each of which might require a whole skin, but there are certainly many books that could just as well, for the price at which they are sold, have been bound entirely in leather. I think it safer to assume that half- and quarter-binding are resorted to more for the sake of effect than otherwise. There have at different periods been fashions in one or the other form. Many late eighteenth- and early nineteenth-century books are half-bound in leather and marbled paper. Comparatively, quarter-binding is less popular, but it has its devotees especially for limited and private press editions.

THE MODERN BOOK

Limited editions, especially those from the private presses, are sometimes bound by hand even to-day, partly for the pleasure and durability of good hand-binding, and partly, it is to be suspected, for the value of the peculiar kind of snob appeal involved. Single copies of machine-bound editions also come the way of the hand-binder, when the purchaser desires a better binding or a different one—it should be noted that it is no good sending such books to the publisher, because machine-binding has so far ousted hand-binding that publishers make no provision for the latter. There is still work for the hand-craftsman, but as a figure he becomes rarer every day, and there is the sadness and nostalgia in his passing that arise from all things that are old and valued and vanishing. The machine has vanquished him and he cannot dispute with it; if he will survive it he must serve it and work within the new aesthetic it has introduced. That the machine has altered and to some extent controls the appearance of our books, does not mean, however, that any lack of variety has supervened. On the contrary, it seems that the possibilities of variety are greater than ever. Cloth may be had in dozens of different kinds and qualities and in as many surfaces and colours, and great play may be made with these and with blocking in coloured inks and foils instead of gold, or in combinations of gold and colours. Gilt, nevertheless, remains the most popular colour for blocking.

Choice of cloth is a matter of taste, and publishers tend to select the kind they prefer and to stick to it. Thus it is noticeable that the books of one publisher are mostly bound in glazed or smooth cloths, while those of another are bound in matt or rough cloths; one prefers dark, even drab colours, another brighter and gayer colours. There is room for every kind of taste, however good, and, unfortunately, however bad. For the imitationist there are cloths embossed with the grain of leather, though what kind of leather the manufacturers of some varieties might find difficult to say. Other cloths bear definite patterns of indefinite origin, but intended to disguise the nature of the cloth itself under the appearance of some other material. To this end some are coated with plastics of one sort or other. To the extent that it is intended to conceal or mislead, any disguise of materials is fundamentally dishonest, and what is dishonest cannot be part of sound design. It may be part of sound manufacture; for example, many coated cloths possess considerable powers of endurance, and they are the only kinds of cloth that really can be washed when they are on the book; but not all of them are pleasant to handle.

I submit that it is preferable to use a cloth that proclaims itself, that relies for its effect on its material, texture, and dye. Cotton should show as cotton, linen as linen; variety may be introduced by the mixture of materials, but for the most part it is obtained by different methods of weaving and of dyeing. Many cloths are now so distinct and individual in their characteristics that proper use of them will produce a book in its own way as pleasant to the hand and to the eye as a book bound in leather. I personally find matt or slightly rough cloths preferable, of clear and clean colour, and without any adventitious embossings, fillings, or dope. They should have certain qualities that are necessary to any binding cloth: they must be opaque and impermeable enough to prevent the adhesive from coming through, they must not be easily soiled, they must not fade or change colour, and they must have a pleasant feel.

Buckram as a binding material is almost in a class by itself. It feels different from the common run of cloths, and it is different. Good buckram is strong. Some kinds are expensive and most varieties cost more than ordinary cloths. A book well bound in good buckram is a book on its best behaviour; it is as sleek and as quietly efficient and as modestly rich as a Rolls-Royce. It is a delight to the hand and a pleasure to the eye, and full of the satisfaction of fine material and fine manufacture. It seems to be almost a convention that buckram should be blocked in gold, and nothing, no, not even leather, takes gold better; but

195. Fourteenth-century jewelled gold binding, of German origin, for a manuscript of the Gospels written in letters of gold between A.D. 1000 and 1020

196. Binding made for Grolier, for *Origenis Adamantii Directa in Deum*, *c.* 1535; brown calf, outer borders and corners stained black, central inlay of citron morocco; tooled in gold

it also takes coloured foils and inks excellently and they can be made to combine well with one another and with the peculiar, slightly drab colours typical of buckram.

I do not think that I have ever seen a cloth-bound book blocked quite as luxuriantly or as elaborately as the leather-bound books of former times were tooled, though there are no technical difficulties in the way. For many reasons, blocking, in spite of early attempts at imitation or emulation, was not destined to follow tamely in the wake of the tool. In the main, development has been towards increasing simplicity, until in our time we have reached the limits of ingenuousness, and have begun to turn back. The majority of modern books bear nothing more than the minimum, which is the names of the author and the publisher and the title of the book; there is no ornament and the boards are left plain. There is nothing necessarily bad in this; even with so little, considerable variety is available in competent hands, and results of great beauty and dignity may be obtained. Further, such simplicity, though it requires fine and delicate taste to achieve the best result, is not subject to great degradation, as in the wrong hands elaborate ornament is. None the less, we have on too many occasions been a little too cautious in the design of the brass, too stereotyped and satisfied with the commonplace, and some experiment in richness is overdue. Such experiment has been made within the last few years, showing no desire to reiterate ancient successes, but aimed at a new kind of design through use of modern materials and the machine. Books have appeared from some of the better publishers that have achieved a fresh delight by fresh means; a new twentieth-century style, but backed by the force of tradition, has emerged.

Essentially it consists of the exploitation of the possibilities of colour provided by the great ranges of cloth and inks and of coloured foils and gold. Gold is still, and seems likely to remain, the most important material in use in blocking, and in most examples of the sort of work I am about to discuss colour is used to emphasize or to enhance the gold. The foundation of the colour scheme of any cloth binding is necessarily the colour of the cloth itself, and it should be selected with care and purpose, and with the general colour scheme of the book in mind. The literary content of the book must also be remembered, because there are relations between colour and literature that make a crashing discord or even subtle insult too easy. For example, a book on Conservative politics need not be bound in blue, but it should not be bound in communist red; a poet may reasonably object to being bound in pink or a greenish-yellow; and I have known more than one Irishman object to being bound in green, on the ground that every English publisher appears to think green appropriate for every Irish author. With a little sense and a little knowledge, and perhaps a little tact, it is not difficult to avoid such errors.

On the basic colour of the cloth are imposed what other colours are to go to the whole scheme. The simplest way to use two colours on the cloth is to block, let us say, the title in one colour and the author's name in another. The result may be pleasing but it makes no departure in principle from the simplest form of blocking. Colour can be employed differently and to much better effect by using a solid panel of colour and blocking in gold on top of it. The effect is bolder and richer and capable of considerable exploitation. The panel may be blocked in foil or ink, either material having its own advantages and drawbacks: ink does not give as good a surface as foil, but it can be mixed to any shade desired; foil, on the other hand, gives an excellent surface, but the shades are restricted to those manufactured. The panel need not be rectangular. The brass for it is cut to order, and there is nothing to prevent its being made any shape the designer thinks will show to the best advantage, the only important restriction being the dimensions of the area on which it is to be used. The panel may be enforced by a rule or ornamental border in gold or a different colour. Within the panel all or a selected part of the lettering is blocked in gold or otherwise. When foil is used for the panel and gold for the lettering the effect is magnificent; by no other means can gold lettering be made so brilliant and so sharply cut. Thus with two colours and the colour of the cloth a three-colour effect is obtained.

Some cloths, particularly buckram and more coarsely woven cloths, can be panelled effectively without the use of ink or foil, the brass being used blind simply to crush and polish the surface of the material. As a result of the difference in the reflection of light the panel appears of a slightly different colour and the difference is sufficient to mark out the panel distinctly. Within it the lettering is blocked in gold or colour, and the panel itself may be emphasized by rules or borders blocked in the same material as the lettering.

The size and number and disposition of these panels is not to be decided carelessly because there are few restrictions upon them. In practice there are not usually more than two panels on a spine, and in most examples there is only one. Where there are two, one is placed near the head and contains the title and perhaps also the author's name, and the other is at the foot with the publisher's imprint or a date in it. The upper one is usually larger, not only because it may have to contain more wording, but also because that wording is the more important and because the general effect aimed at may dictate the difference. A single panel invariable appears at the head.

Panels are sometimes made separately, of a different material, usually leather, but sometimes paper, and glued on to the binding. This is an old practice revived, and it has sometimes been followed in standardized book-club bindings. There are many disadvantages, of which not the least is that the panels are not always permanent and with handling or ill storage will begin to peel off. That they can be repaired or a new panel made is no excuse. Some publishers who used this method apparently recognized its unsoundness and provided a spare panel tipped on to the endpaper.

This use of panels has to some extent been accompanied by an increased use of ornament. The ornament is not, however, strictly analagous to that used by the hand-binder or to the fleurons and unit borders of the printer. There is not in the modern bindery a corpus of ornaments and flowers from which an infinite variety of designs can be built up—brass type for blocking does exist, but it is neither as good nor as rich in variety as the range available to the printer. This state of affairs has arisen because the almost invariable recourse of publishers to the specially cut brass has tended to cancel any demand there may have been for binder's brass type. If a brass is cut for each new title, it may be designed distinctively and individually to suit the character or typographical style of the book. It may be designed by anyone capable of design, but not without some knowledge of the process. There are pitfalls, and in some ways they are similar to those encountered in making drawings for reproduction by line block, but with further restrictions derived from the materials used and the manner of impression. No very fine lines should be attempted, for obvious reasons, and delicacy of feeling, where it is desired, should be achieved through firm lines that will withstand a firm impression. Then, it is essential to remember, and it is too often forgotten, it seems, that when gold is used, any solid area or shaded portion will appear, not dark, as in a print from a line block, but light; in short, there are effects in gold blocking analogous to the effects of both negatives and positives in photography, and these not separately but present at the same time. The designer may make his drawing for the brass-cutter in black ink for convenience, but if he forgets for a moment that what he is working in is a brilliant, shimmering metal he is lost. To some extent, but not completely, a light-coloured cloth compensates because against it, in ordinary light, the gold appears darker. Indeed, the quality of gold of appearing light on a dark cloth and dark on a light one, though it may seem treacherous to an inexperienced designer, is of the greatest interest, and in expert hands may be an advantage.

Design applied to the brass, though our successors may perceive in it a distinctive period style, does not to our eyes follow any well-worn path. The design may be completely abstract, as many are, or it may be symbolical either of the book or its subject generally, or it may even be illustrative. Whatever it is, it must combine with the lettering that is always the main element of the whole; and it must be kept in mind that it is not a design *in vacuo*, existing like a painting within itself, but is part

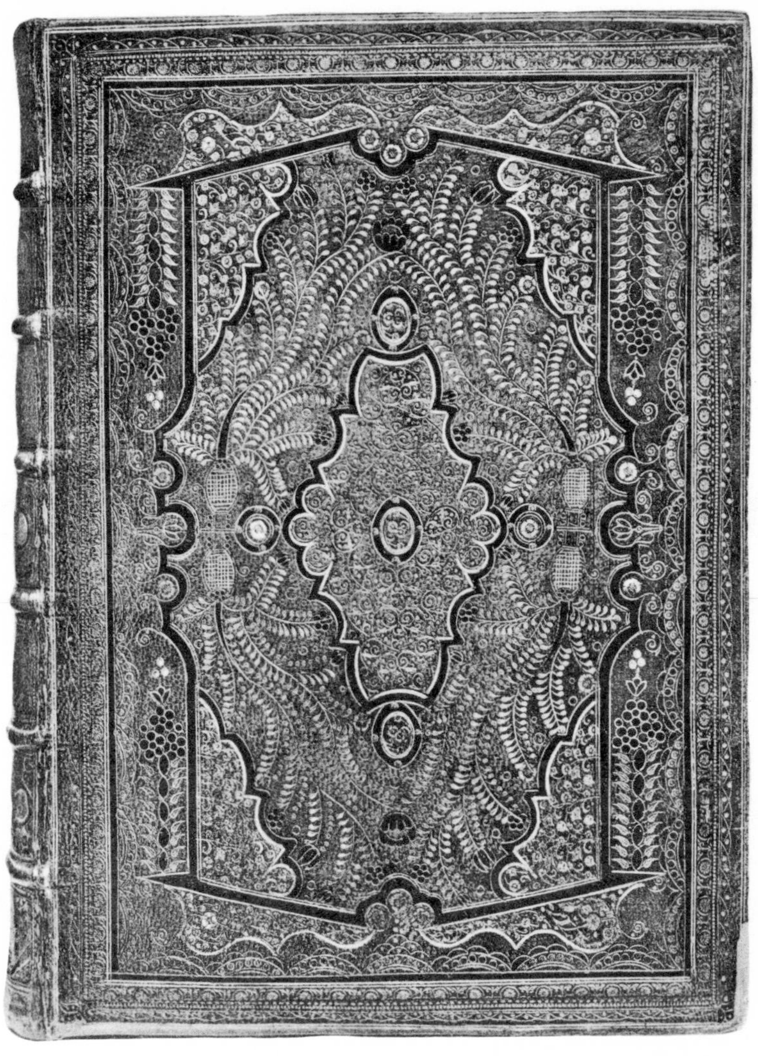

197. Cottage binding: Book of Common Prayer, 1678; red calf, tooled in gold, lines stained black

198. Binding by Monnier: Baudello, *La Prima Parte de le Novelle*, 1740; scarlet morocco, gilt and inlaid

of the larger design that is the totality of the binding, and beyond that of the whole book.

The front and the back boards receive comparatively little attention nowadays, not because of any technical difficulty in the way, but simply because we have fallen out of using them. It is a pity. Relatively few books have blocking of any kind on either board, and most of those that do have it show timidity and lack of imagination. In many of them the blocking consists of nothing more than a narrow blind rule border, of which the best that can be said is that it is innocuous; its absence would make no difference to anyone. Certainly it costs more to block the boards, but the difference is so small that I find it difficult to believe that this factor is a serious deterrent to a more venturesome policy. Perhaps the argument, which is a valid one, that blocking here has no basis in utility, as it has on the spine, but is entirely in the nature of decoration, has some power to affect the question, but that is to enunciate a principle that would deprive us of a great deal of pleasure in life. I like my useless pleasures, and I would like to see much more originality and more courage and determination applied to the design of the boards, not for every book, for that would be wearisome, but for those books that are intended to be a little better than the usual run, and certainly for more books than receive this attention to-day.

Where blocking of the boards is practised at present, it tends to follow well worn grooves. Either the title is repeated on the front board, or a decoration or illustration from the text is used, or some decorative motif, which may be the house sign of the publisher. These are confined to the front board; in modern usage the back board is seldom utilized.

By means of lithography or a special adaptation of process engraving the whole binding may be printed with an all-over design or even a reproduction of a picture, which may include the necessary lettering or leave it to be blocked separately. If the design or picture requires several printings for colour, it adds considerably to the cost of the book, and no ordinary book will bear the expense; which is just as well, perhaps, because, though there is no doubt that this method has achieved some success, it is capable of great degradation, and even at best would be wearisome if it were too frequently repeated. The yellow-backs of the Victorians and some of the earlier fiction series illustrate the horrors that lie in wait.

A similar thing may be seen more frequently on books bound in paper-covered boards, where, perhaps because the substance is paper and not cloth, the effect is less startling. With such books it is a common practice to make the binding the same as the jacket, and, of course, it may be printed by any process that is commonly applied to paper.

Though out of sight between the cover and the endpaper, the boards on which the cloth or other covering is laid play a more important part in the aesthetics of the book than might at first be realized; for it must be stressed that the pleasure to be had from a book, though primarily intellectual, is also visual and sensual. To me at least the feel of a book is of great importance, and the boards contribute a great deal towards the satisfaction of the sense of touch. Obviously they should be free from any tendency to warp, but their weight and density and hardness also matter. Hand-binders reject strawboard as unsuitable, and I think they are right, though it is the material generally used in machine-binding. Common qualities may be too soft, for any slight knock will dent them, while frequent use causes the corners to become limp—a phenomenon too well known to need any description. This objection might be overcome by subjecting the boards to greater pressure in manufacture, but that must inevitably make boards of equivalent thickness more expensive, and publishers, like anyone else, have to consider their costs. It is possible that plastics may eventually supply a better material.

Sometimes books are given very thin boards and announced as having flexible bindings. I personally do not like them, but others do, and it is entirely a matter of opinion. Very definitely such flexible bindings should not be used for large or thick books, or even for books likely to receive much handling. They cannot satisfactorily be blocked on the boards without risk of the blocking showing through on the inside. The thinness of the board should not be made an economy; the thinner it is, the better should be the material of which it is made, and a really flexible case should not be built on strawboard at all, as it often is, but upon millboard or some other substance that is tough and will bend without cracking.

In the majority of books the boards are cut with square edges, which are softened in outline by the folding of the cloth round them, but there are two other effects that are occasionally resorted to. These are bevelled edges and yapp edges. Both of these involve extra costs and are therefore applied to books that pretend to be a little better than usual. Perhaps this explains the conjunction of bevelled edges and buckram, which is not uncommon. The general effect is pleasant and for the present at least is too uncommon to lose its novelty.

Yapp edges, in my opinion, are unpleasant. There are two kinds, those that are soft and floppy and those that are stiff and permanently turned at a right angle to the board. Both professedly serve the purpose of keeping the edges of the pages clean, and both, in my opinion, are a confounded nuisance to the reader, and from the aesthetic point of view are pretentious and ugly. For some unknown reason, they are used more for Bibles than for anything else. Concerning the kind of yapp edge that is provided with a zipp fastener to turn the book into an imitation of a handbag or a tobacco pouch, the less said the better.

The better class of book may be given a headband, or perhaps two bands, the second one at the tail. The colours of these gay little pieces should be chosen to harmonize with the colours of the binding and with the washing or gilding of the edges of the pages.

Part of the effect of a bound book is attributable to the treatment the edges of the pages receive. In my experience the majority of readers, without thinking, plump for clean, smoothly guillotined edges on all three sides. There is no reason why they should be right, and among publishers and book designers who do think about it there are many who prefer rough edges of one kind or another. Books that are intended to give only ephemeral pleasure, as novels and so forth, are usually guillotined on all three sides, but in the better class of literature there are many books that are treated differently. In any kind of book the head is, and should be, guillotined, because otherwise it would be impossible to keep this surface, on which dust is so apt to settle, clean and neat. The other two edges should also be guillotined for any book that is to receive much use, as a reference book, or for one, as a text book, for which it is important that any fussy or distracting demands on the user should be avoided. Guillotined edges are clean and easy to keep clean, and they make the rapid turning of the pages a simple matter. These conditions do not matter so much for a book that it is expected will be read in comfort and at leisure and which will be treated with respect.

Rough edges probably originated in the deckle of hand-made paper. When this was the only paper available the deckle seems to have been regarded as a disfigurement and was almost invariably cut off; now we have come to prize it as a mark of real hand-made paper, and books printed on such paper retain the deckle and also the bolts. As a result the margins of these books may vary a good deal, sometimes as much as half an inch. Such extreme variation strikes me as precious and pretentious in the worst sense, and it should be avoided. As for the bolts—they are a sore point with some people, while others find a satisfaction in slitting the folds. Books printed on machine-made paper are also given rough edges, either by leaving the book entirely untrimmed, except at the head, or else by folding the sheets so that the bolts project slightly, when they can be trimmed off without affecting the edges of the sheets. This latter method is particularly useful and pleasant, as it leaves an edge that is not unpleasantly rough, but on the other hand is not mechanically smooth, and it also does away with the need for a paper-knife.

Guillotined edges can be treated in several ways to produce particular effects, gilding and washing being the most usual. Gold, being a metal, does not absorb dirt, and books with gilt edges are easily cleaned; but this is not the only, or even the main, reason why gilding is used. The aesthetics of the question are much more important than the utility. Gilding is valued for its appearance, and it can help to give to a book a special air of richness and distinction. Bibles are sometimes gilded on all three edges, in an attempt, perhaps, to make them superior to any other kind of book. The effect, in my opinion, is meretricious and unpleasant, and calculated to appeal to the vulgar. Washed edges also should be used only on the head, where, if the colour is wisely chosen, it contributes much to the sum total of effect. Any colour may be used, and obviously it must be selected to harmonize with the colour scheme of the book as a whole.

It is interesting here to remark that in the middle ages books were kept on their sides and the foredge was used as a surface on which to write the title and paint whatever decoration was required. Long after the spine had come to be the place for the title, foredge painting continued as a means of decoration, and some examples are elaborately and skilfully treated. Samuel Mearne invented a peculiar variation of foredge painting in the nature of an optical trick. The book was slightly fanned out and the painting was then done on the sloping foredge; afterwards the edges were gilded in the normal way. The result is that a minute fraction of the picture is contained on the foredge side of the face of each page. When a book so treated is closed in the ordinary manner the painting is invisible; it becomes visible when the leaves are again fanned out as before.

While the work of the binder, like that of the printer, has under modern conditions become more and more restricted to the technicalities of his business, and the power of design has passed out of his hands into those of the publisher, the success of a well designed binding still depends a great deal upon him. The designer can do nothing without his co-operation, and if he is a poor craftsman or a careless one the design cannot be successful. The furthest flights of fancy in the end rest on solid, competent workmanship, which indeed makes its own powerful contribution to the satisfaction of hand and eye.

XXIII

THE BOOKJACKET

No part of the book is as young in history as the jacket or wrapper. It is a product, and a symptom, of modern publishing, if we assume, and it is a reasonable assumption, that modern publishing commenced at some date early in the nineteenth century. Before that time books were issued in paper covers or paper boards, which were intended merely as a protection to suffice until the purchasers could have the books bound to their taste in a more permanent manner. The increased demand which was one of the results of the industrial revolution, and which was assisted by an industrial revolution within the pressroom itself, arising first from the introduction of metal into the manufacture of presses and then, and much more important, the application of steam power, tended at once to reduce the price of books and to enlarge editions. The category of bookbuyers was swollen by persons who had no desire for or could not afford the practice of rebinding which had hitherto held the field. Temporary bindings in paper or boards began to disappear, and in their place came edition bindings intended to be permanent. Books were now bound in quantity for the publisher and sold as finished products.

Any book is handled by many persons before it is sold in the bookshop, and it must soon have become clear that if the binding was to be in immaculate condition when the book reached the purchaser some kind of protection from soiling was necessary. A temporary paper cover of some sort was the obvious answer. Perhaps the same problem had presented itself to the hand-binder who desired to protect the finished book until it was called for. If it did it is likely that he found it useful to wrap books in such a manner that they could be opened without removing the wrapper. Paper was always to hand, and it was easy to cut a piece to cover the boards and spine and to turn in over the foredge: the physical principle of the bookjacket needed no great inventive genius. Schoolboys who cover books with brown paper use a much more elaborate kind of wrapping than the bookjacket.

A wrapper of plain paper has the unfortunate effect of converting a book into an anonymous block that must be unwrapped or opened if its identity is to be known, and this necessity not unnaturally detracts from the protective value of the wrapper. A modern binder wrapping advance copies overcomes this by using transparent paper or cellophane. But the simplest thing to do where large number of books are concerned is to print the title on the wrapper.

If the title is to be printed, other things can be printed with it without much extra trouble or expense. The author's name and the publisher's imprint would naturally be included. Further, it might be recorded as an inducement to the reluctant, that the author's previous book had been received with rapture by the public and hysterics by the critics, and a paragraph could be added to explain the argument and laud the quality of the present one. And there was still space left to suggest that the publisher had other interesting books for sale and to describe some of them. This century has never been slow to discover any medium of advertisement, and here was a hoarding that did not sit still, but travelled into the very homes of potential customers. It was seized upon, and to such effect that the original reason for having a jacket was lost sight of beneath the superimposed aims of advertisement. The jacket as hoarding came to stay, and in future it was to vary only in the amount and kind of advertising used and according to the wavering dictates of taste and fashion.

Bookjackets are of their nature ephemeral things. Despite all the attention they now receive from artists, printers, and publishers, they are still regarded as temporary coverings, to be cast away when they have served their purpose. This makes their history difficult to trace. Each one of the many works on the history and design of books that I have consulted either ignores jackets altogether or else by-passes the subject with a phrase or two. It is as though bookjackets were Topsies; or even creatures whose birth must never be mentioned in polite society. *The Growth of the Bookjacket* by Charles Rosner has illustrations of a number of early jackets and recounts the scanty details that are available.

Whatever their origin, it seems clear that bookjackets soon began to be made much of in the sacred name of publicity and sales. They began to be designed, decorated, illustrated. Perhaps we learned something from the Americans here—and yet I wonder. There are more than the elements of jacket design in the covers of the part issues of the early years of Victoria's reign; and again, to modern eyes, the garishly coloured illustrated paper boards of Victorian novels such as those of some of the popular series and the yellow-backs look like jackets that have somehow got stuck on to the books. It is in this direction that we should look for one of the sources from which the modern jacket has been derived.

Before proceeding further it will be useful to describe the anatomy of the jacket. Its substance is paper, and may be of any kind or colour. Folded as it appears on the book, it has the following surfaces, on any or all of which there may be printed matter. The front and back boards and the spine are the parts first seen, as they are on the outside. Inside there are two flaps, by means of which the jacket is held on the book. Finally, there is the reverse of the sheet.

It is desirable that the paper should be substantial, but not so stout that it cracks when folded; it should hold a fold easily and yet be tolerably stiff. Thin paper offers no firm surface to the hand and tends to crinkle, and, crinkling, it refuses to hold on the book, which slips about inside it. Besides, it tears easily and soon ceases to afford the protection it is primarily intended to give. This consideration does not prevent thin paper from being used by some publishers, with results of which any bookseller will tell

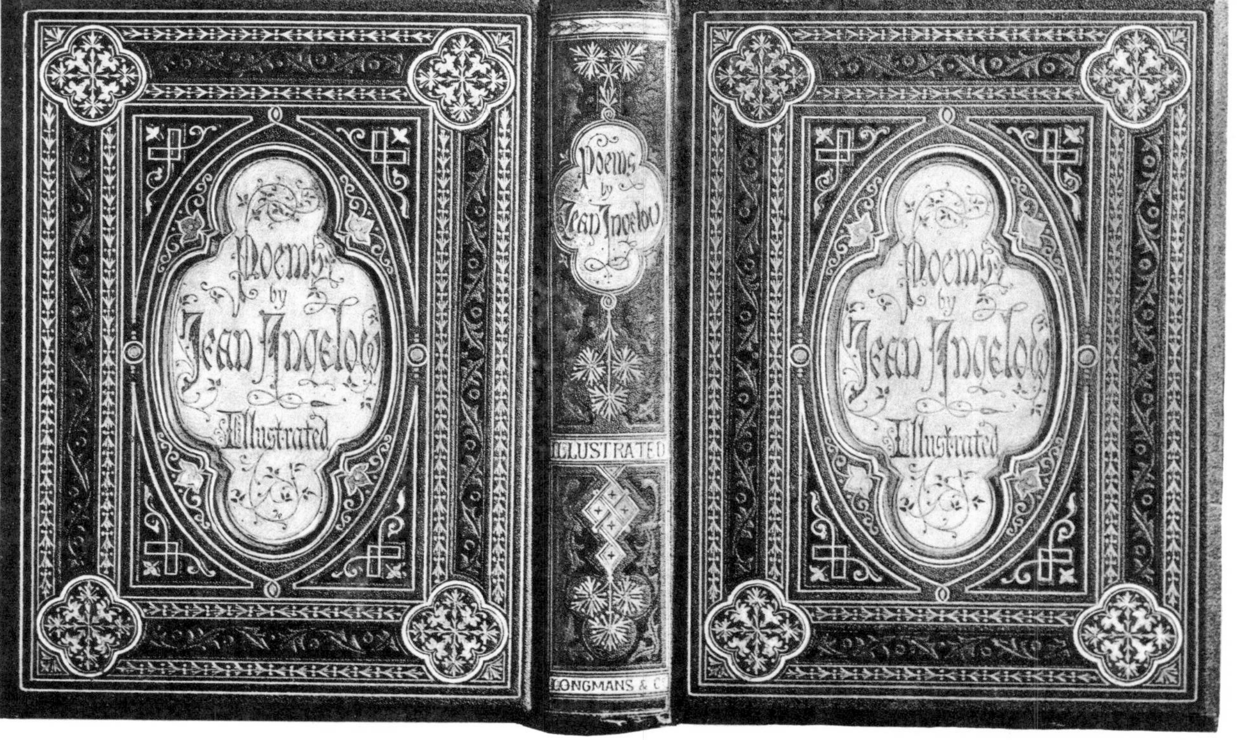

199. Cloth binding: dark blue cloth, grained, blocked in gold and black with cream vellum inlay blocked in gold; *Poems of Jean Ingelow*, 1867

200. Modern fine edition binding by Paul Bonet: black morocco, with

you in more or less heated language. It is also preferable that the side of the paper that comes next to the book should not have a smooth or slippery surface, because this also causes the jacket to slip. Double-sided art is such a paper, and should be avoided. The bookseller is not the only person who may be irritated. The protective function extends beyond his shop, and many readers who are careful with books like to leave the jacket on while they read; it is a nuisance, and an exhausting nuisance, if the book has to be held tightly to prevent it from slipping about.

Adequate flaps, together with the ability of the paper to retain a fold, contribute as much as friction to the hold of the jacket on the book. The flaps should extend at least to half the width of the board, and if the sheet from which the jackets are cut allows it, there is no harm in their being even wider than this, though it is not necessary.

Any kind of paper that fulfils the requirements stipulated above can be used for jackets, which means in effect that a vast variety of surfaces and colours is available. The scope for expression in the combination of texture and colour of paper with the colours of the inks printed on it is beyond computation. Texture and colour are indeed important, texture not only to the eye but to the hand also.

The front board and the spine are appropriated to advertisement of the book on which the jacket is used. The front board bears the title and the name of the author writ comparatively large, and may also have the publisher's imprint. In addition there may be decoration or a diagram or an illustration intended to enhance the book's appeal and perhaps in part to explain its content or kind. On the spine the same information is given, rather more discreetly because of the exigencies of space; and similar elaboration by decoration or illustration is practised. A further item that sometimes appears on the spine is the price, but to speak of money here is, it seems, a sort of gaucherie, and the better class of publishers reserve the statement for the hidden front flap. The publisher's imprint almost invariably appears on the spine, even if it is also printed on the front board.

In the majority of jackets the back board is used for the advertisement of other books in the publisher's stock, the list being usually one of books of the same class; thus, a volume of poetry is likely to have on the back a list of other volumes of poetry. Sometimes, however, it is used for a list of other books by the same author, perhaps with an appropriate blurb for each. Occasionally there appears here, reprehensibly, an advertisement for something, such as soap or soda water, not in any way connected with the book—the use of advertisement pushed to a logical and tasteless conclusion. At other times the back board is appropriated to the book to which the jacket belongs and either repeats the front board or continues the design begun there or else has a separate design linked with the front by the spine.

The front flap is by custom reserved for the blurb. There may also be some quotations from reviews here, and sometimes such quotations are used instead of a blurb. At the foot of the flap is printed the price of the book.

The back flap is often left blank, but occasionally it is printed to continue a blurb that is too long to be accommodated entire on the front flap, or it may be used for more reviews or for more advertisements.

Rarely, the reverse of the sheet is also printed, sometimes in the past with a collection of advertisements reminiscent of the old-fashioned theatre drop, but more usefully to present a catalogue of other books in the series. Printing the reverse side of the jacket involves extra cost, of course.

Admitting that any advertising matter or blurbs should at least be pleasantly set and will repay simple care in layout, it is the front board and the spine that will occupy further discussion in this chapter.

The problem of jacket design is to set forth the essential details of title, author, and publisher in such a way that the result shall be appropriate to the book, in its general layout and in its literary style, and at the same time attractive and effective in salesmanship. On the whole publishers understand very well the axiom that advertisement cannot afford to be verbose and restrict the wording on the jacket to the bare essentials. The aim is to influence potential purchasers, and elaboration and verbosity are least likely to succeed.

We may for convenience divide jacket design into two broad categories, typographical and artist, which is to say those that are printed from type, with perhaps a block or two, and which are designed by the typographer, and those that are reproduced from a drawing or painting made specifically for the purpose.

That the services of an artist are frequently engaged does not mean to say that there is any lack of variety or opportunity in typography applied to jacket design. Every type face in existence is potentially a jacket face and any mixture of type faces that is effective and successful is justifiable. A typographical design may be attractive by sheer simplicity; and it may be none the less attractive and yet complex. There are latent possibilities in the use of coloured inks on coloured papers that can never be exhausted, and two, three, or four, and even more printings may be used. All kinds of blocks are introduced, from tint plates designed to print a solid mass of colour in any shape required, either as a background or as decoration, to line blocks and half-tones. Type reversal by means of line blocks, resulting in a light-coloured letter against a mass of darker colour, is often effective. In short, qualities of display are called into use that have no place in the body of the book, and in general a broader, bolder, and less subtle technique is required.

It is too commonly supposed that emphasis is synonymous with large type, a vulgarity of which I shall have more to say later. I prefer to think the use or disposition of space of greater importance than size or even design of type; further I would say that it is by his use of space that a good designer may be distinguished from an inferior one. A sheet of printing paper is, it may be said, a means of capturing space; and that space is not simply amorphous or anonymous: it derives distinction first from the texture of the paper and then from its colour. It is a denial of its value to relegate it to the position of a mere backdrop or ground support. It can be used more actively, to give emphasis subtly but positively where emphasis is needed, to change the character of a letter or a drawing or of coloured ink, and to bind and unify the whole design; and all this it does without proclaiming itself, without self-importance or vanity.

We begin then with a field of space, and upon this must be set the wording that is to be the verbal message of the jacket. This field possesses a band of focus, or, it is better to say, our senses superimpose a band of focus upon it, which is called, for want of a better term, the optical centre. It might equally well be called the psychological centre. This, as we saw earlier in connection with the title-page and text pages, lies in the upper half of the area and is conventionally said to lie at about a third of the depth from the top, but in fact its position is considerably affected by the design. It is a natural point of emphasis. Points of subsidiary emphasis lie at the intersection of thirds. These are generalizations drawn from an acknowledged optical or psychological phenomenon, abstractions from past experience the value of which lies in the fact that they are generalizations. They are not rules of conduct, for generalizations are made to be applied, not to be obeyed. And they may be applied in a manner not at all obvious. To particularize, the simplest manner of application is to place the phrase it is intended to emphasize on or near the optical centre, but on the other hand emphasis may be gained by using the optical centre less obviously, as a starting point to lead the eye to the message, and it is possible to do this by placing there some illustration or decoration that will serve that purpose, or even by leaving that part of the area blank.

The arrangement most frequently encountered places the title first near the optical centre and follows it with the author's name and any other necessary matter, such as the name of an illustrator or the writer of an introduction, and last, if it is included at all, the publisher's name. Thus the less important the information, the farther it is from the main point of emphasis. That this arrangement is a common one does not mean that it is not subject to variety, or that it is commonplace. It is the manner in which the designer uses it that matters, his choice of types and his use of colour and space. Indeed there is only one alternative arrangement of the details, and that is to place

201. Printed bindings: *A Book of English Clocks*, printed in black and yellow on cream paper, designed by Clifford and Rosemary Ellis; *Poems of Death*, cloth binding printed lithography in three colours on white cloth, designed by Michael Ayrton

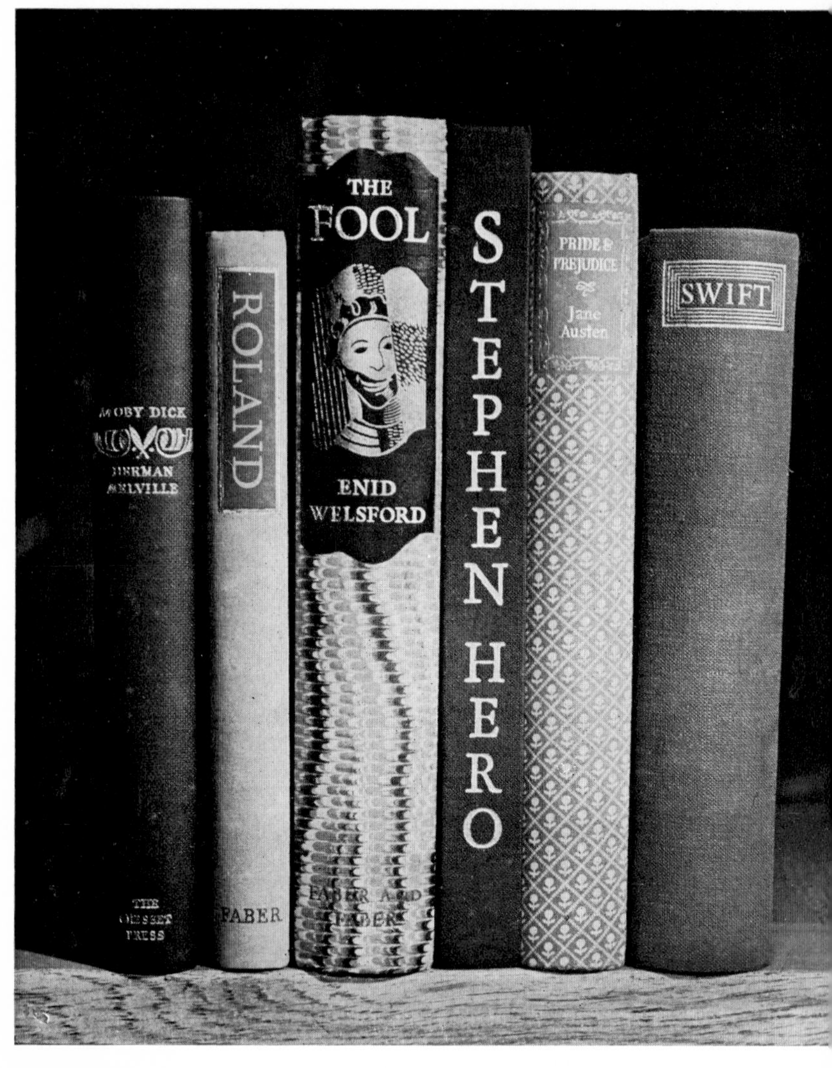

202. Cloth bindings: *Moby Dick*, gold on smooth dark-blue cloth; *Roland*, gold and blue on grey cloth; *The Fool*, gold and black on patterned cloth; *Stephen Hero*, gold on black cloth; *Pride and Prejudice*, gold and blue on cloth with lithographed brown all-over pattern; *Swift*, gold on rough brown cloth

the author's name first. This can be done where it is desired to give extra emphasis to the name or simply for the purposes of design.

Simplicity, or it is better to say, apparent simplicity, in my opinion produces the best jackets. Good types, unencumbered by ornament or superfluous additions, can be made, when used with discretion and ability and full awareness of their qualities, to produce effective and pleasing, and even beautiful, results. Such design may, from some people's point of view, have a tendency to severity, and there are books to the literary style of which it cannot be said to be suited. These things cannot be ignored, for it must be remembered that jacket design is design with a distinct purpose.

For some lighter books pleasanter, gayer, and even foolish effects may be aimed at, depending on the sort of book that is to be contained within the jacket, and all sorts of decorative device or illustration may be brought into play. Do not let it be thought that the mere use of decoration or illustration connotes frivolity: there are plenty of examples to show that it is not so. But just as frills in dress design make an impression of gaiety easier of attainment, so they do also in typography; and there are shades of gaiety from that which is merely not severe to that which is frankly frivolous.

Printer's flowers, rules, and borders, all have their uses. Rules can be used singly and simply or in combinations of different weights, and either kind make very good borders to corral and enclose space. Borders can also be made out of flowers, and there are also special border designs available.

Blocks of one kind or another are frequently used, either as decorative motifs or as points of attraction for the eye and mind. An illustration, perhaps selected from the body of the book, may well occupy the most prominent position on the jacket and be intended, by drawing attention to itself, to draw attention to the book. On the other hand, it may be used as a mere accessory or detail. Care is needed in choosing an illustration from the book for use on the jacket, and the same principles apply to this as to the title-page. Whatever the picture, it should in some way be capable of representing the book as a whole; an illustration comprehensible only in relation to some isolated action in the narrative is not suitable, and may even be misleading.

The spine is usually treated in a manner harmonious with the front board, and frequently the front board design is used again here, modified or reduced in size for the narrower space. Where the wording runs across the spine, the title of the book and the author's name are placed at the head, and at the foot the publisher's imprint. Between the two groups the price is sometimes printed; when it is placed on the spine it should not be, as it usually is, the most important item in the display—the price of a book is not the first thing about it that matters. Although, when a book is put on the shelf, the spine is the only part of it that remains visible, it should not be designed without reference to the front board; there are other occasions when both the spine and the front board are visible at once. And yet the spine must be capable of sustaining attention alone and of attracting it from other books on the shelf. Blatancy is not the best way to do this, any more than it is the best in any other part of book design. What the quality is that is sought after is not easy to describe, and it scarcely seems sufficient to claim that it is good design; sales psychology also enters into the question.

The wording can seldom be effectively run across the narrow spine of a slim book, and then there arises the old controversy that goes on perennially between the runners-up and the runners-down.

The adherents of each method stick contentiously to their opinions. Publishing houses adopt one way or the other as their house style. The argument was exacerbated during the second world war, when paper rationing caused books to be slimmer and lengthwise spines to become more numerous. It has receded since, but there are still many books with too few pages to give a spine wide enough to set the lettering across it in a size sufficiently legible in the bookcase—volumes of verse are only one example. The lack of a uniform practice remains an inconvenience for both booksellers and book-buyers.

Who is right? It can only be he whose method agrees more

with normal reading habits and is in accord with practical common sense. I cannot pretend to be impartial on this question, and strive as I may I cannot think of any reasonable argument to support the practice of running spines up. I can think of several against. It is surely desirable that when a book is laid on a table, it should be face up—this is the way people normally lay a book down; if this is admitted, it seems equally desirable that the spine should be the right way up, but if the lettering has been run upwards, it will now be upside down. It cannot be argued that it is necessary to be able to read the spine when the front board is in full view, but it should not defy reading. Running the lettering down the spine settles this question at once.

Runners-up are apt to find themselves in difficulties concerning the order of the items on the spine. The usual order on a cross spine is title, author, publisher, but if this is followed on a spine running up, the publisher must be placed at the head. Even the runners-up have a sneaking feeling that this is not right, and attempt to improve matters by transferring the publisher's name to the tail. But then it becomes the first item to be read, and still draws more attention to itself than it deserves. If, however, the spine is run down, all these difficulties vanish; the title commences at the head, is followed by the author, and finally by the publisher in his place at the tail. To me, a partisan of the runners-down, it all seems so simply and incontrovertibly right that it is difficult to understand why those who are not of like mind differ. It may be added that to run a spine up, and thus to compel the eye to move from bottom to top, is contrary to the reading habit of the whole of our hemisphere.

The same problem occurs in the blocking of the bindings of thin books.

It may be possible to use a bolder style on the jacket than was used on the binding, and a wider range of colours may be available, which can be used to give variety and richness and also to emphasize or differentiate one part of the wording from another. There is little room for anything other than the wording on a narrow spine, but single ornaments or other items may be used to separate the author from the title and from the imprint. The type itself can be reversed to make narrow panels of colour with the lettering showing in the colour of the paper, and these panels can be made to any shape that seems suitable.

Artist jackets in their arrangement of details are in general subject to the same conventions as the typographical jacket, but there is naturally much greater freedom possible in the use of these details and in the treatment of the design. Unless he is given a free hand it will be necessary for the artist to know how many colours the publisher is prepared to use, and also the process by which he intends to reproduce. Both matters can quickly be settled in collaboration, though in the latter case the choice of artist may more or less automatically decide the process. There are some artists who have made reputations for themselves through particular processes and a call upon their services implies use of their processes. It may be assumed that the typographer, working within the publishing office, though he may not have read the book, is at least familiar with it to the extent of knowing its category and general style. This is not true of the artist, who is usually a free lance outside the office, and he should be given proofs of the book so that he may know what he is doing. He can hardly be expected to produce a suitable design if he does not know what it is for.

Greater variety of lettering is available to the artist, since he may redraw and adapt not only any letter in the catalogue but also invent others for himself. Invention has given birth to some fine lettering and also to some exotic styles that little deserve the name; it is sometimes necessary for the publisher to exercise his prerogative of control. But what the artist can do with ease is to make his lettering a part of the structure of his design in a manner that the typographer can never do; he can give to it the motif of the whole design and make it grow from it. That is if, besides being a capable artist, he is also a capable letterer—the combination is not as common as it may be thought to be.

A great many artist's jackets come under the heading of

TORSTEN
FOGELQVIST

POST
LUDIUM

Norstedts

TORSTEN
FOGELQVIST

Postludium

NORSTEDTS

203. Lettered jacket by Dr. Akke Kumlien; lettering black, ornaments brown, on rough, stone-coloured paper; P. A. Norstedt & Söner, Stockholm, 1946

204. Design by Morgens Zieler, reproduced by two-colour line block; lettering black, lions sandy brown, white paper; Gyldendal, Copenhagen, 1945

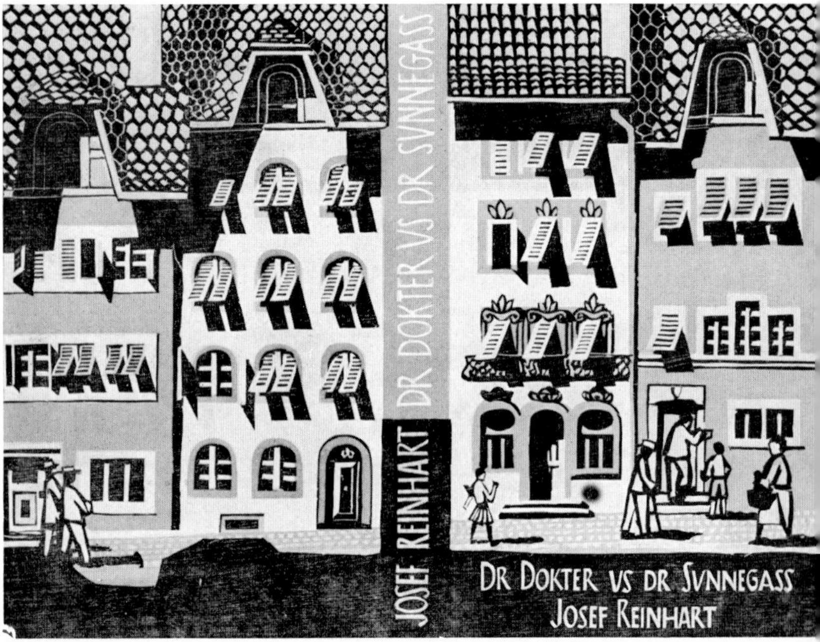

205. Wood-cut jacket design by Robert Sessler, printed in two colours direct from the wood; pink and black on white paper; H. R. Sauerlender & Co., Aarau, 1945

picture jackets, which try to tempt the public by displaying a picture of some incident in the narrative. They are commonly used for novels. Some good ones of this kind have been made, but I think it is true to say that the majority are not good. The picture jacket, indeed, is capable of infinite degradation. We have become satiated with the gaudiness and even salaciousness of some jackets put out by less reputable publishers, with startling pictures in startling colours to goad the appetite of a jaded public, but apparently they still do their business with some people, for they appear in droves and bookstalls may be lurid with them. The trouble is that if you want good quality in a picture jacket and are prepared to sacrifice low-class sales appeal, you very soon find that what you want is a first-class painter to paint it for you. And the services of a good painter are not likely to be cheap, even if he will condescend to a bookjacket.

Far more satisfying results have been achieved by artists who are prepared to use the picture, even when it is illustration, in an idealized or abstract manner that takes it out of the realm of illustration and more into that of design. A portrait of a hero or a heroine, for example, may be used in a manner that makes of it a symbol of the book without pretending to be a veracious picture of a man or a woman. Objects or scenes can be treated in the same way. There is some restriction in the sense that, while many unnecessary ideas or details may be whittled away in abstraction, the artist must avoid in his conception anything that is mistaken or inaccurate or liable to convey a wrong impression: there are pitfalls that the artist, not possessing the specialized knowledge of the author, may easily fall into.

But the artist is not confined to the picture jacket. He can also use pattern, abstract or geometrical or otherwise, and incorporate or superimpose the lettering on it.

The jacket spine must be designed in relation to the front board. It may have a picture or a pattern separate from those on the board, but they must be related and in harmony. Picture jackets are frequently so designed that the picture spreads from the board over the spine, and this is a very good method provided it is kept in mind that spine and board must be capable of being viewed separately without discomfort or any sense of incompleteness. It is not as difficult to achieve this as it may seem, although it must be admitted that spines so treated are liable to be weaker in effect than the board or the whole of the picture.

I have remarked that the back board is sometimes appropriated to the design, and this may be done in several ways, both in typographical and artist jackets. The simplest thing to do is to repeat the front board, either as it is or reversing it from left to right (but not reversing the lettering!). On the other hand it may be treated differently, but harmoniously, and given a different design. When this is done it should be regarded whole, and not as a place to which some discarded idea or superfluous ornament can be relegated. I see no point or purpose in using the space for the display of a bunch of daisies in a small oval frame or a lonely printer's or publisher's sign. Where the back board is used to continue the design, the spine becomes a link between the two boards, and it must perform its function of conjunction adequately without losing its own identity. Just as the spine and the front board can be contrived out of one continuous picture, so too can one picture be used to cover the back board as well. Such a picture must be capable of being divided into three parts so that each part is satisfactory in itself, if not complete in itself. Neither board should look as though it were only half the game; nor on the other hand should it look as though it were all the game. A picture that cannot be divided into other than incomprehensible remnants must fail as an all-over jacket design, even if as a picture it is among the best made by man. The only way of looking at such a picture is to view it whole and the bookseller is the last person to appreciate his customers' taking the jackets off his books to get the whole view. It is still the business of the jacket to protect the book, and since it has become an advertisement as well as a protection it must itself remain immaculate if its power of attraction and persuasion is not to be impaired.

The broad technique of poster design has been applied to

jackets with interesting results. The approach of those who work in this manner has certainly some backing in logic; if they argue at all, it is reasonable to argue that if the jacket is in effect an advertisement, a hoarding intended to inform, attract, and persuade the potential customer, it should have applied to it the principles that have been worked out in the design of posters. Advertising design, which has produced poster technique, is not entirely an haphazard growth, but the result of specialized knowledge and ability applied to a specialized purpose, and the publisher no more than anyone else with wares to sell can afford to dismiss the ideas of the specialist. On the contrary, a case can be made out to show that publishers avail themselves too little of that corpus of empiric knowledge that is miscalled the science of advertising. Nevertheless the poster is not the only means. Valuable as the poster technique undoubtedly is in jacket design, there are other things that enter into it that are not the result of thinking along those lines, or even of thinking at all; rather there is something of instinct and inspiration. A mere glance around any bookshop will show that there are more principles than one on which successful jacket design may be founded; the criterion is not conformity to any school or method, but aesthetic pleasure combined with practical success.

Lettering is a factor of the greatest importance. While it is undoubtedly true, as some people argue, that even bad types can be used well, and that an artist can get away with indifferent lettering if his draughtsmanship or drawing is good, it must be recognized that these are occasions and only to be used by those who know perfectly well what they are doing. It is easy to point out that good lettering is more likely to improve such designs rather than otherwise. There are qualities that make one kind of lettering more suitable than another for particular uses, and they must not be lightly ignored, and there are qualities that enter into any criterion of excellence. Legibility is a part of the criterion. There is a belief, which has some prevalence, that the larger and bolder the lettering the more it must be legible and generally successful; and coupled with this belief is a dogma that the lettering must cover the jacket. There is a grain of truth in it, but not a large grain. It strikes me as essentially a salesman's idea, and a rather unthoughtful salesman's too. The intention is, I suppose, that the book when displayed shall draw attention to itself by means of the thunder on the jacket. A very cursory examination of a bookshop window will show that the theory does not work: where many shout, few are understood. Even if it is admitted that the thunder does attract attention, that is not the sole end: attention must be kept, and blatancy repels more often than it attracts. Worse, it is most likely to repel the very people the publisher wants to attract. Now some jackets with large bold lettering are successful, and equally successful are others on which the lettering is much smaller and more reticent. No question involving psychological factors, as this one does, is easy to answer adequately, and there are apt to be numerous partly satisfactory answers, some in direct conflict with others. It is certainly a gross error to affirm that either practice is exclusively the right one. I suggest that the secret lies in design, that if the design is good, and of a kind suited to the book, it will be successful in despite of faction.

Besides being large or small, lettering may also be simple or complex. It may indeed be so complex that it is difficult to read. It is arguable that a jacket design may be made that is successful by sheer force of design, and that such a design will attract the customer closer and persuade him to make out the meaning of even difficult letters. There is no reason why such an argument should not be true provided that it is not applied too frequently in practice; if it were to become popular, it must also become fallacious. Victorian type design died of this surfeit and remained dead for a good long time, until in our own day the nineteenth century began to be recognized as a source from which precious or intricate or decorated letters might be drawn in abundance, to extend a range of feeling that was beginning to find itself a little restricted after the comparative sobriety of the early years of this century. There was no servile imitation in the use to which these stolen sweets were put; on the contrary, it appeared that it had been left to the typographers of the twentieth century to demonstrate how they should be used. If it was presumption on the part of the men of a younger time to pretend to teach their grandfathers how to manage their own faces, it could go unreproved; there were few grandfathers left to resent the lesson. One of the minor pleasures of history is to observe how the sons deride the notions of their fathers, while their grandsons scarcely credit them with sense; but the great-grandsons find that there was something in the old fellows after all, but that they never quite knew what was what. Victorian type designs were seized upon and reshaped where it was thought necessary, and sometimes, it must be admitted, they were vastly improved. Typographers and artists took up the inheritance that had so long remained in chancery and used it in a manner not at all Victorian, and not amended or adapted only but pure and undiluted from the spring. Discrimination might have been more in evidence than it has been, but in spite of that this neo-victorianism has been no bad thing. Perhaps the fashion for decorated letters will pass, for it certainly depends to a considerable extent on the meretricious charm of novelty, but it does seem to have come to stay in this generation as permanently as anything founded on the sands of man's capricous taste.

Experiment is always useful and to be encouraged, even when it fails, but there is no doubt that the bookjacket has been too much the home of queer and cranky letter design. In spite of the successes of decorated faces, there is something to be said for plain and honest letters. They are the basis of all letter design, and decorated letters are only successful by contrast with them, and even then not for ever. The primary purpose of lettering is to be read and not to form part of decoration; the pleasure it may give, the beauty of its appearance, are secondary to its quality of legibility, however inseparable they may in practice appear to be. Actually, good design and beauty of design are in lettering the same thing: a letter that has been well designed cannot avoid being a beautiful letter. Whether that beauty is retained on the jacket and made full use of depends entirely on the designer of the jacket.

There is something to be said for the contention that

lettering on jackets should wherever possible be confined to type if the artist is not a good letterer. Lettering is not an art as easily acquired as many believe, and if type is used there is at least the likelihood that it will be a better letter and a more suitable and legible letter than the artist can invent or draw. And there is, heaven knows, sufficient variety of types to please all kinds of tastes.

While it is usual to give the title of the book the greatest emphasis, there are occasions when it may appear more desirable to emphasize the author's name. The name may be the selling point, and famous authors may find their names appearing in huge letters, with the title in something comparatively small. There is a taint of vulgarity in this, something of the suggestion that the author is a sausage-maker and that all his sausages are guaranteed to taste alike, that if you enjoyed the last one you are sure to enjoy the next. On the other hand, the obscure writer who has produced an interesting book may find himself overshadowed by someone more famous who has condescended to write a preface or a foreword, and the publisher, anxious to cash in on the celebrity, pushes the author into the background. This too is the wrong approach, and one that savours a little of false pretences. After all, it is not the preface that matters, but the book, and the author wrote it, not the celebrity.

Truth in jacket design, which includes suitability of the design to the book, cannot be ignored, for the jacket plays an important part in the creation and preservation of good will. It is true, and it deserves emphasis, that any book is aimed at a particular section of the population, at a particular stratum or at strata of society, if you will, and it is the publisher's business so to clothe and present his book that its appeal to those for whom it is intended shall be enhanced and reinforced. A mistake in psychology or a wrong design merely means that we shall be trying to sell the book to the wrong people, and some may be persuaded to buy it who will not care to read it, and may be annoyed when they find out what they have spent their money on.

How widely publishers' estimates of the public's intelligence and taste vary is very evident in jacket design. At the bottom of the scale are the lurid and vulgar picture jackets so frequently used for inferior novels, and even for some that are not so inferior. Presumably the publishers who put out this kind of jacket have found out by experience that their low estimate is correct and is good business; but it does not mean that they have the right to degrade public taste still further. It is certainly more commendable, and it might very well be better business, to try to improve it by example and practice. There is no doubt that a higher estimate has on more than one occasion proved very good business indeed. The general level of taste may appear to be poor, or we may believe that it is so; but appearance and beliefs are not necessarily true. There is evidence that the ordinary man is surprisingly sensitive to good design and will react towards it positively enough to confound his detractors. He may not be able to say wherein lies the superiority of one design over another, but he can state his preference, and that preference can be enlightening.

The printing processes used for jackets are the same as those used in the printing of books. The majority are printed letterpress, from type or blocks. Occasionally collotype is used to print an illustration or similar detail. It is through the medium of lithography, however, that some of the most interesting developments have taken place, and it is indicative of the importance that publishers have come to attach to jackets that they are willing to resort to so comparatively expensive a process as colour lithography. Whatever the process, the scope is enormous and there need be no end to originality and variety in book jackets for as long as we continue the making of books.

A few books, usually limited or fine editions, are issued in slip-cases instead of in jackets. A slip-case is a box made to fit the book, and into which the book goes foredge first, exposing the spine. Sometimes the tailoring of the slip-case is too tight and then it is difficult to get the book out again. Slip-cases are always better if they have small semi-circles cut out of the open edges, as finger grips. The case is built of card covered with paper or cloth. The closed-side may be labelled, or even tooled like the spine of the book, so that the case may be put into the bookcase the other way round, and so give increased protection to its contents. Occasionally one comes upon double slip-cases, one nesting inside the other to enclose the book completely.

Very elaborate boxes may be made to enclose very rare and valuable books; these, of course, are one-off jobs made only to special order by hand-bookbinders.

206. Lithographic jacket, drawn on the stone by Pierre Gauchat; light brown with maroon patches strengthened with black and green, on white paper; Eugen Rentsch, Zurich, 1946

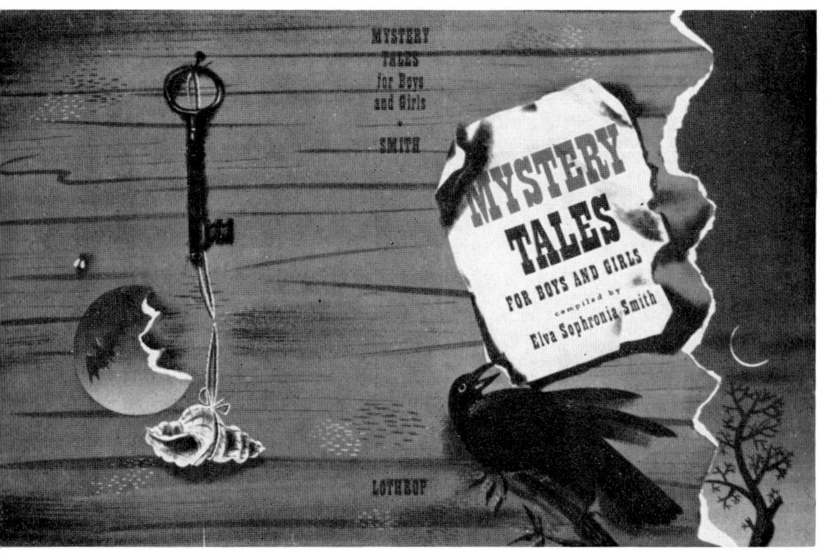

207. Jacket by Leonard Weisgard, printed in six colours by photo-lithography; background brown, with dark grey-blue sky; label white with lettering in red and black; on white paper; Lothrop, Lee & Shepherd Co. Inc., New York, 1946

208. Jacket reproduced by six-colour photo-lithography from a print made by Thomas Malton in 1800; Batsford, London, 1949

209. Jacket design by Mariette Lydis, reproduced by four-colour half-tone; background solid black, lettering white; Hachette, Paris, 1946

XXIV

HARMONY AND THE WHOLE

THE method of apportioning a chapter to each component of a book, which I have adopted in Part Two, is not without its dangers. It is a literary convenience and has simplified my work, but it should not be allowed to suggest that a book is so many separate pieces individually designed and jointed together at a later stage, without integration or overriding sense of unity. I do not deny that too many books from even reputable and sensible publishers are put together in a somewhat haphazard manner; where such books are successful in design, it is only by good fortune, and luck is not a lady to be depended on. However, scrap-book typography, as it may be called, is not always an offence of indolence or wilfulness. The typographer in a busy publishing office, struggling, among the multifarious details of several score or more of books concurrently in hand, to achieve an integrated unity for each, is a figure for sympathy and not condemnation; and if he does succeed in creating for each of his works its own typographical personality he has done well enough, though it may be no more than is expected of him. But it is important. Though the various elements of a book may be dealt with separately and at different times, and will certainly be interspersed with work upon other books, there should be kept in mind a distinct vision of the whole, and every part should contribute to it.

The starting point of typography in book design is the subject, the author, and his style. These three produce a character, atmosphere, spirit, or what you will, that may be inexplicable but is certainly there, and this is the key in which the typographer will play his piece. It may or may not be subtle. It needs very little imagination to suggest that a book on, let us say, the city of Bath by a professional historian is likely to be a very different thing from one on the same subject by Sir John Betjeman, and what would be typographically suitable for the one would not be suitable for the other. In short, each book needs a costume in accord with its character. But the character of a book is not always as obvious as this, particularly in a period when ambiguous or merely symbolical titles are popular, and it is necessary for the typographer to be able to recognize it. However desirable it may be ideally, he cannot afford to read through every book he handles, for if he did he would have no time for anything else and typography could go hang. He must be able to judge character by dipping here and there, and if necessary by picking the brains of anyone who has read the typescript—for despite persistent belief to the contrary, there is nearly always someone in a publishing office who *has* read it. Usually this is sufficient. But when a book arrives that is to be treated with more care and which deserves the best he is capable of doing, he must, if he possibly can, find time to read it; and if he feels then that he would like to read it a second time, all the better, for the more he is interested in it the more he is likely to produce the perfect book. If it can hold him so much that he is captured by it, he may easily find that when he comes to design it the work has already been done for him by his subconscious mind. But in his surrender to the spirit of the writer he must not lose his sense of objectivity. Obviously only a comparatively small number of books are worth this amount of attention; no-one should expect an ephemeral popular novel to be a masterpiece of typography, but there is no reason why it should not be a piece of good workmanship.

Text faces and display types and the general use of display and the treatment of the page are marshalled towards the completion of the typographer's conception. The design should constantly enforce the message of the text, without intruding itself in front of it. Ornaments and flowers, where they are used, must be used in this spirit, but it is safe to say that most books are better without this kind of decoration. There is no need for the result to be frigid or stiff. Indeed, there are occasions when apparent abandon is justified—the emphasis is on the word 'apparent'—bacchic art is not created by drunkards.

Throughout the book should run one motif or related group of motifs expressed in the use of type, colour, and texture. This is no limiting or restrictive condition, because at all points new conditions and new requirements arise that extend the application of the motif. A jacket, for example, is quite different from the title-page in the purpose it serves, and the difference of purpose necessarily dictates a difference in appearance; but it does not imply design or expression in opposition to the character of the book itself.

Problems concerned with the use of colour, either in harmony or in contrast, are comprised within the scope of book design, even when, as in most books, no colour is used in the printing of the text. Other places where colour may be found are the endpapers, the binding case, and edges, and of course the jacket. Wherever it appears, colour must be used in the service of a coherent design aimed at a complete whole. Any discord or clash of colours must be the result of intention, and to be successful must achieve its purpose and at the same time add something essential to the whole. This is not to say that any book must be designed within a narrow range of colours or shades; just as in a painting many colours may be embraced within a single scheme, so too in a book may several colours contribute to the total effect aimed at.

To me at least the sense of touch is in many ways as important as the sense of sight, and it is catered for in the choice of paper for the text, of boards and cloth for the binding, and in the treatment of the jacket. Touch should definitely be a factor in the choice of cloth for the case. There is as wide a variety of textures as there is of shades, and among them there are always some that are right for a particular book and some that are equally wrong, and others that are neutral and innocuous. There are cloths that have the harsh texture of a silk stocking or a fine file and that make the fingers numb after a while, and these are wrong for any book. Others have the texture masked by a thick coating of filling material, on which a glaze may be laid, and these are also undesirable, because what comes into contact with the finger is not the character of the cloth, which is used merely as a base, but the soft and characterless filler. Others again, quite different, offend like a liar or a man in disguise, because they are not themselves, having been treated to counterfeit other materials.

I do not pretend that even at best a great deal of attention is paid to the sense of touch, certainly not as much as I would like. The tendency is simply to pick on a cloth the colour of which suits the selector's idea, and not to worry about the texture if it is not downright objectionable. I think this is a wrong approach. There lies a subtle relation between the sense of touch and the atmosphere created by the literary style and typography of a book, and that relation should be one precisely attuned to complete the orchestration of book design.

Touch is peculiarly important in connection with the jacket, which is the first part of a book to come into contact with the hand. A jacket is paper, and should feel like paper, and like good sound paper too. Varnishes, which look so fine to the eye, are mere impediments to the finger; worse, may feel definitely unpleasant in warm weather. Coated papers have a similar effect, and while they may be necessary if half-tones are to be used, are none the less undesirable for that.

Indeed, the question of paper texture throughout the book deserves consideration. The kind and quality of paper may contribute a great deal to the total impression, and to ignore this is to ignore a useful ally. Among the many grades, surfaces, and textures, there is somewhere a combination peculiarly suitable to the purpose in view. The effect of the right paper when it is found is as strong and decisive as the effect of the wrong paper that turns up without search. There are, or it appears so, a great many people who like the feel of a soft, fluffy paper, for the manufacturers send out and publishers use large quantities of paper of this nature. I prefer papers of closer structure and harder surface and with some evidence of size in their feel. The difference is not only manifest on the surface; it is even more so in the feel of the book itself. Light, fluffy papers make light floppy books, while a more solid paper makes a book that may be thinner and may even be lighter in actual weight, but that yet feels as though it has been manufactured to endure. Featherweight antiques may be exactly the thing for some of the featherbrained stuff that finds its way into print. On the other hand, no paper is more solid or more heavy than art paper, and no paper makes a book that feels more like an ingot of lead; but it is no guarantee of the intellectual weight of the message it bears.

Whatever the typographer may do, however competent he may be, and however carefully he may direct all who are engaged in the manufacture of books, if he cannot depend on the craftsman, the man at the frame, the machine, or the bench, he must be defeated. Sound and conscientious craftsmanship is the rock upon which all industrial design is based, and without it the edifice must totter. Printers and binders, by which I mean the workmen and not their masters, call themselves craftsmen, and this proud title they should deserve. All too often they do not deserve it. The remarkable renaissance of typography that has taken place in this century began and has continued from outside the printing trade, and to no small degree it has been achieved in the teeth of the prejudices of the 'craftsman'. This is indefensible. And yet it is not fair to blame the workman entirely: if the master does not care, or is sunk in ignorance, it is very hard for the workman to do good work. Such conditions are common enough to make the search for good workmanship heartbreaking. What the workman is paid and the length of his working day is reflected in the estimate, and need not delay us here; it is the interest and pleasure he finds in his work that matter, for out of these arises good workmanship, and good workmanship means good quality in the product. The workman who is careless and watchful for the relaxation of supervision, who cannot be trusted to do a thing properly, who sees the hands of the clock creep round like lazy snails, and works only because he would not starve, this man is not a craftsman, though he serve an apprenticeship of seven times seven years; he is a mere labourer, and the sooner he is replaced by an efficient machine, the better it will be for all except himself—and why should we care about him? The trade unions remain convinced that all their members are worth their salt, and they spend their energies on the achievement of higher wages and better conditions, neglecting the quality of the workman. A renaissance of craftsmanship is overdue; without it we shall lose one of the greatest satisfactions in the world—the thing that is beautiful because it is well made, because it embodies within it the care and interest of all concerned in the making of it.

Finally, a word of warning. Because the subject of this book is typography, it looms large over that other aspect of the book, its literary value, and the reader may be left with the impression that typography is all that matters. Such an impression cannot be left undisturbed. No book should be treated merely as an excuse for typographical display or virtuosity, and in no book should the typographer allow his personality to obtrude in front of that of the author. To do so is unwarrantable egoism. The typographer cannot do without the author, and the author should not be made, as he too often is, to do without the typographer. The two are collaborators in the production of a book, but the author is the senior; it is his book, and contains his message, and it is this that matters. The typographer is an interpreter and his business is to present the message in its most attractive and suitable light, to interest and captivate the reader beforehand so that he will be drawn to the book, and when that has been done to make his reading easy and delightful. The reader may, and preferably should, know enough of the qualities of typography to know a well designed book when he sees one, but if while he is reading he is constantly compelled to exclaim, mentally or even subconsciously, upon the design of the book, the typographer has failed at his job. Forceful typography is not typography that forces itself on the attention to the detriment of the literary message. Such typography is in bad taste, just as the literary style that gets in front of the idea, rather than elucidates it, is also in bad taste.

On the other hand there are those who assert that the typographer should be completely self-effacing, even to the point of refusing any claim upon the gratitude of the book-lover. For these people the appearance of a typographer's name in an imprint or colophon is a red rag that incites them immediately to charges of egoism. They do not see that they perceive only the extremes of the question. The work of a good typographer is characteristic, and is itself a form of signature writ plain for the discerning; a literal signature conveys to the layman information that is as much his right as the name of the printer and the publisher.

And now I have come to the end of my book on books. If I have enabled the reader to enjoy books with a more understanding eye and wider and keener appreciation, because he now knows how they are made and how they are designed, I shall feel that I have been successful.

A SELECTION OF BOOKS
FOR FURTHER READING AND REFERENCE

ALDIS, HARRY G., *The Printed Book* (Cambridge University Press, 3rd ed., 1951)

AUDIN, MARIUS, *Histoire de l'imprimerie par l'image*, 4 vols. (Jonquière, Paris, 1928–9)

BARLOW, T. D., *Woodcuts of Albrecht Dürer* (King Penguin Books, London, 1948)

BIGGS, JOHN R., *An Approach to Type* (Blandford Press, 1949; 2nd ed., 1961)

BLADES, WILLIAM, *The Biography and Typography of William Caxton* (facsimile reprint of 1877 ed., Muller, 1971)

BLAND, DAVID, *The Illustration of Books* (Faber & Faber, 1962)
A History of Book Illustration (Faber & Faber, London, 2nd ed., 1969)

BRINKLEY, JOHN, *Design for Print* (Sylvan Press, London, 1949)

CARTER, JOHN, *Publishers' Cloth, 1820–1900* (Constable, London, 1935)

CARTWRIGHT, H. M., *Process Engraving* (Ilford Ltd., Ilford)
Photolithography (Ilford Ltd., Ilford)

A Catalogue of English and Foreign Bookbindings offered for sale by Bernard Quaritch (Quaritch, London, 1921)

CAVE, RODERICK, *The Private Press* (Faber & Faber, 1971)

CLAPPERTON, R. H., *Paper: an historical account of its making by hand from the earliest times down to the present day* (Shakespeare Head Press, Oxford, 1934)

COCKERELL, DOUGLAS, *Bookbinding and the Care of Books* (Pitman, London, 4th ed., 1939)

CURWEN, HAROLD, *Processes of Graphic Reproduction in Printing* (Faber & Faber, London, new ed., 1963)
Printing (Penguin Books, 1948)

DARLEY, LIONEL, *Bookbinding Then and Now* (Faber & Faber, London, 1959)

DAY, FREDERICK T., *An Introduction to Paper: its manufacture and use* (George Newnes, 1963)

DAY, KENNETH, ed., *Book Typography 1815–1965 in Europe and the United States of America* (Ernest Benn, 1966)

DE VINNE, THEODORE LOW, *A Treatise on Title-pages* (in series *The Practice of Typography*, Century Co., New York, 1904)

The Invention of Printing (New York, 1877)

DIRINGER, DAVID, *The Illuminated Book* (Faber & Faber, London, 1958)

DOWDING, GEOFFREY, *An Introduction to the History of Printing Types* (Wace & Co., London, 1961)

ETTENBERG, EUGENE M., *Type for Books and Advertising* (Van Nostrand, New York, 1947)

FAIRBANK, ALFRED, *A Book of Scripts* (King Penguin Books, London, 1949)

FOSTER, JOANNA, *Pages, Pictures and Print* (for young people; Constable, London, 1962)

FRANKLIN, COLIN, *The Private Presses* (Studio Vista, 1969)

GILL, ERIC, *An Essay on Typography* (re-issue, Dent, 1941)

GOUDY, FREDERIC W., *Typologia: studies in type design and type making* (University of California Press, 1940)

GRAY, NICOLETE, *Nineteenth-Century Ornamented Types and Title-pages* (Faber & Faber, London, 1938)

A Guide to the Exhibition in the King's Library (British Museum, Department of Printed Books, London, 1939)

HEWITT, GRAILY, *Lettering* (Seely, Service, London)

HIGHAM, ROBERT R. A., *A Handbook of Papermaking* (O.U.P., 1963)

HOBSON, G. D., *English Bindings, 1490–1940, in the Library of J. R. Abbey* (privately published, 1940)

HOWE, ELLIC, *The London Compositor: documents relating to wages, working conditions, and customs of the London printing trade, 1785–1900* (Bibliographical Society, London, 1947)

HUNTER, DARD, *Papermaking: the history and technique of an ancient craft* (Pleiades, London, 2nd ed., 1948)

JACKSON, HOLBROOK, *The Printing of Books* (essays on books, not a technical work; Cassell, London, 2nd ed., 1947)

JAMES, PHILIP, *English Book Illustration, 1800–1900* (King Penguin Books, London, 1947)

JENNETT, SEÁN, *Pioneers in Printing* (Routledge & Kegan Paul, London, 1958).

JOHNSON, A. F., *A Catalogue of Engraved and Etched English Title-pages* (Bibliographical Society, London, 1934)

German Renaissance Title Borders (Bibliographical Society, London, 1929)

One Hundred Title-pages, 1500–1800 (Bodley Head, London, 1928)

Type Designs, their history and development (Grafton, London, 1934; 3rd ed., 1966)

JOHNSTON, EDWARD, *Writing and Illuminating and Lettering* (Pitman, London, 21st imp., 1945)

KRIMPEN, J. VAN, *On Designing and Devising Type* (Sylvan Press, London, 1957)

LAMB, LYNTON, *Drawing for Illustration* (O.U.P., 1962)

LEWIS, JOHN, *A Handbook of Type and Illustration* (Faber & Faber, London, 1956)

MACKERROW, R. B., *Printers' and Publishers' Devices in England and Scotland, 1485–1640* (Bibliographical Society, London, 1913)

MACKERROW, R. B., and F. S. FERGUSON, *Title-page Borders used in England and Scotland, 1485–1640* (Bibliographical Society, London, 1932)

MCLEAN, RUARI, *Modern Book Design* (Faber & Faber, London, 1958)

Victorian Book Design (Faber & Faber, London, 2nd ed., 1971)

MCMURTRIE, DOUGLAS C., *The Book* (O.U.P., London, 3rd ed., 1943)

MADDOX, H. A., *Paper: its history, sources, and manufacture* (Pitman, London, 1945)

MEYNELL, SIR FRANCIS, *English Printed Books* (Britain in Pictures series, Collins, London, 1946)

MORAN, JAMES, *Stanley Morison: his typographic achievement* (Lund Humphries, 1971)

MORISON, STANLEY, *First Principles of Typography* (Cambridge, 1950)

Four Centuries of Fine Printing (Benn, London, 2nd ed., 1949)

The Typographic Arts (Sylvan Press, London, 1949)

Type Designs of the Past and Present (The Fleuron, London, 1926)

OSWALD, JOHN CLYDE, *A History of Printing: its development through five hundred years* (Library Press, 1929)

A Picture Book of Bookbinding (Victoria and Albert Museum, 1933)

Printing in the Twentieth Century (The Times Publishing Co., London, 1930)

PHILLIPS, ARTHUR, *Computer Peripherals and Typesetting* (H.M.S.O., 1968)

PLANT, MARJORIE, *The English Book Trade* (George Allen & Unwin, 1965)

Printing and the Mind of Man, catalogue of exhibition at British Museum, 1963

RANSOM, WILL, *Private Presses and their Books* (Bowker, New York, 1929)

RAYNER, JOHN, *Wood Engravings by Thomas Bewick* (King Penguin Books, London, 1947)

REED, TALBOT BAINES, *A History of the Old English Letter Foundries* (London, 1887; new edition, Faber & Faber, London, 1952)

REINER, IMRE, *Modern and Historical Typography: an illustrated guide* (Zollikofer, Switzerland, 1946)

ROSNER, CHARLES, *The Art of the Book-Jacket* (Stationery Office, London, 1949)

The Growth of the Book-Jacket (Sylvan Press, London, 1954)

SADLEIR, MICHAEL, *The Evolution of Publishers' Binding Styles, 1780–1900* (Constable, London, 1930)

SIMON, OLIVER, *An Introduction to Typography* (Faber & Faber, London, 1945; 2nd rev. ed., 1964; also Penguin Books, 1954)

Printer and Playground (Faber & Faber, 1956)

A SELECTION OF BOOKS

SMITH, JANET ADAM, *Children's Illustrated Books* (Britain in Pictures series, Collins, London, 1948)

STEINBERG, S. H., *Five Hundred Years of Printing* (Penguin Books, London, 1955; and Faber & Faber, London, 1959)

SYMONS, A. J. A., DESMOND FLOWER, and FRANCIS MEYNELL, *The Nonesuch Century: an appraisal, a personal note, and a bibliography of the first hundred books issued by the press, 1923–1934* (Nonesuch Press, London, 1936)

TAYLOR, JOHN RUSSELL, *The Art Nouveau Book* (Methuen, 1966)

TOWN, LAURENCE, *Book Binding by Hand* (Faber & Faber, London, 1951)

TSCHICHOLD, JAN, *An Illustrated History of Writing and Lettering* (Zwemmer, London, 1946)

Meisterbuch der Schrift (Otto Maier, Ravensburg, 1952)

UNWIN, STANLEY, *The Truth about Publishing* (Allen & Unwin, London, 7th ed., 1960)

UPDIKE, DANIEL BERKELEY, *Printing Types; their history, forms, and use* (Harvard University Press, 2nd ed., 1937)

WARDE, FREDERIC, *Monotype Printing Ornaments* (Monotype Corporation, London, 1928)

WALKER, R. A., editor, *The Best of Beardsley* (Bodley Head, London, 1948)

WHETTON, HARRY, editor, *Practical Printing and Binding* (Odhams, London, 1946)

WILLIAMSON, HUGH, *Methods of Book Design* (O.U.P., London, 2nd ed., 1966)

YOUNG, J. L., *Books from the Manuscript to the Bookseller* (Pitman, London, 3rd ed., 1947)

TYPE CATALOGUES

Those marked with a star are or have been on sale to the public

**Book Types from Clowes* (William Clowes & Sons, Beccles)

**A Handbook of Printing Types*, by John N. C. Lewis (W. S. Cowell, Ipswich)

**A Handbook of Printing Types for use at the Shenval Press* (Shenval Press, Hertford)

A SELECTION OF BOOKS

*Jaspert, W. P., Berry, W. Turner, and Johnson, A. F., *An Encyclopedia of Type Faces* (Blandford Press, 4th ed., 1971)

Monotype Desk Book (Monotype Corporation, Redhill)

*Monotype Alphabet Tracing Sheets (Monotype Corporation, Redhill)

**Philips' Old-fashioned Type Book* (a collection of nineteenth-century type faces; shockingly printed: Frederic Nelson Philips Inc., New York)

Printing Types (catalogue of Stephenson, Blake & Co., Sheffield)

Type Cabinet (catalogue of C. & E. Layton, London)

**Type for Books: a designer's manual* (W. J. Mackay & Co. Ltd., Chatham, 1959)

Type Specimen Book (nv Drukkerij G. J. Thiene, Nijmegen, 1959)

PERIODICALS

Alphabet and Image, quarterly from 1946 to 1948 (Shenval Press, London)

Book Collector, The, quarterly (Shenval Press, London)

Book Design and Production, quarterly, 1958–1965

British Printer, The, every month (MacLean Hunter, London)

Fleuron, The, seven issues, 1923 to 1930 (The Fleuron, London, later the Cambridge University Press)

Graphis (Amstutz & Herdeg, Zurich)

Image, 1–8, 1949–1952 (Shenval Press, London)

Journal of the Printing Historical Society, edited by James Mosley, 1965, annually

Library, The, Transactions of the Bibliographical Society, fifth series (O.U.P.)

Linotype Matrix, irregular (Linotype & Machinery, London)

Monotype Recorder, quarterly to 1940; recommenced 1949 (Monotype Corporation, Redhill)

Motif, irregular from 1958 to 1970 (Shenval Press)

Penrose Annual, The, yearly to 1940; recommenced 1949 (Lund, Humphries, London)

Print, quarterly (Rudge, Woodstock, U.S.A.)

Print in Britain, monthly (Print in Britain Ltd.)

Print Design and Production, bi-monthly, 1965 onwards (Cox & Sharland)

Signature, 1935 to 1940; new series, 1–18, 1946 to 1954 (Signature, London)

Typographica, three times a year from 1949 to 1970 (Lund, Humphries, London)

Typography, quarterly from 1937 to 1939 (Shenval Press, Hertford)

DICTIONARIES AND CHRONOLOGIES OF PRINTING AND PUBLISHING

ALLAN, E. M., ed., *Harper's Dictionary of the Graphic Arts* (Harper & Row, New York, 1966)

ARCHAMBEAUD, P., *Dictionnaire des Industries Graphiques* (Edition de la Revue Caractère, Paris, 1966)

BERRY, W. TURNER, and POOLE, H. EDMUND, *Annals of Printing* (Blandford Press, 1966)

CLAIR, COLIN, *A Chronology of Printing* (Cassell, 1969)

COLLINS, F. HOWARD, *Authors' and Printers' Dictionary* (O.U.P.)

Coordinamento Grafico (Societe Editrice Internationale, 1964)

Dictionary of Printing Terms (Porte Publishing Co., Salt Lake City, U.S.A., 5th ed., 1950)

HOSTETTLER, RUDOLF, *The Printer's Terms* (Redman, London, 3rd ed., 1959)

KENNELSON, W. C., and SPILMAN, A. J. B., *Dictionary of Printing, Papermaking and Bookbinding* (George Newnes, London, 1963)

Polygraph Wörterbuch der graphischen Industrie in sechs Sprachen. German, English, French, Spanish, Italian, Swedish (Polygraph Verlag GMBH, Frankfurt, 1967)

Rules for Compositors and Readers at the Oxford University Press (O.U.P.)

WIJNEKUS, F. J. M., *Elzevier's Dictionary of the Printing and Allied Trades*, in English, French, Dutch, German (Elzevier Publishing Co., Amsterdam, 1967)

A POLYGLOT GLOSSARY OF TECHNICAL TERMS

The English term is given first, followed by American (A), French (F), German (G), and Italian (I). Where the American is the same as the English it has been omitted. The gender is indicated in italics.

adhesive binding, unsewn binding
F reliure sans couture *f*
G Klebebindung *f*
I legatura a colla *f*

alinement, alignment
A alignment
F alignement *m*
G Schriftlinie *f*
I allineamento *m*

alloy
F alliage *m*
G Schriftlegierung *f*, Zeug *m*
I lega tipografica *f*

ampersand
F 'et' commercial *m*
G Et-Zeichen *n*
I congiunzione commerciale *f*

antique paper
F papier non apprêté *m*
G Werkpapier *n*
Werkdruckpapier *n*
I carta antica avoriata *f*

art paper
A coated paper, enamel paper
F papier couché *m*
G Kunstdruckpapier *n*
I carta patinata *f*

asterisk
F asterisque *m*
G Stern *n*
I asterisco *m*

bastard title
F faux-titre *m*
G Schmutztitel *m*
I occhiello *m*

bands (or cords) of hand-bound book
F nerfs *m*, nervures *f*
G Bünde *m*
I nervatura *f*

beard (of type)
A beard or neck
F talus de pied *m*
G Fleisch am Fuss *n*
I bianco alla base *m*

bed (of a press)
F marbre *m*
G Fundament *n*
I carro *m*

bibliography
F bibliographie *f*
G Bibliographie *f*
I bibliografia *f*

to **bind** (books)
F relier
G einbinden, binden
I rilegare

binder, bookbinder
F relieur *m*
G Buchbinder *m*
I rilegatore *m*

binders' tools
A binders' stamps
F fers à dorer *m*
G Stempel *m*
I ferri da rilegatura *m*

bindery
F atelier de reliure *m*
G Buchbinderei *f*
I legatoria *f*

binding (of a book)
F reliure *f*

G Einband *m*
I rilegatura *f*

black-letter, gothic
A blackletter, Old English, text type
F caractère gothique *m*
G Textur *f*, Gotisch *f*
I carattere gotico *m*

to **bleed** (illustrations)
F couper franc-bord
G anschneiden
I illustrare a vivo

blind blocking
A blind stamping, blind tooling, blanking
F gaufrage à sec *m*
G Blindprägung *f*
I stampa a secco *f*, ornamenti a secco *m*

block, printer's
A cut
F cliché *m*
G Klischee *n*
I cliché *m*

blockmaker, photo-engraver, process engraver
A photo-engraver
F clicheur *m*
G Chemigraph *m*
I fotoincisore *m*, zincografo *m*

body size (of type), **point size**
F force de corps *f*, corps de caractère *m*, corps, *m*
G Kegel *m*
I corpo *m*

bold (type)
A bold-face
F mi-gras
G halb-fett
I nero

bolt, fold
F pli *m*
G Bruch *m*
I piega *f*

book
F livre *m*
G Buch *n*
I libro *m*

book jacket, wrapper
A book jacket, dust jacket
F couverture de protection *f*
G Schutzumschlag *m*
I copertina *f*, copertura protettiva, *f* sovra coperta *f*

book plate, ex libris
A bookplate
F ex-libris *m*
G Exlibris *n*, Bücherzeichen *n*
I ex-libris

book sizes

16mo
A 16mo, sixteenmo, sextodecimo
F in-16, in-seize *m*
G 16°, Sedezband *m*
I in-16, in sedecesimo *m*

8vo
F in-8, in-octavo *m*
G 8°, Oktav *n*
I in 8°, in ottavo *m*

4to
F in-4, in-quarto *m*
G 4°, Quartband *m*
I in 4°, in quarto *m*

folio
F in-folio *m*
G Folio *n*
I in folio *m*

border
F bordure *f*, cadre *m*
G Rand *m*
I fregio *m*

brass, binder's
A binder's die
F fer à dorer *m*
G Messinggravur *f*
I bronzi per trancia *m*

bulk (of a book) *see also* spine
F dos *m*, millième *m*, grosseur *f*
G Stärke *f*
I dorso *m*

calender
F calendre *f*
G Kalander *m*
I calandra *f*

to **calender** (paper)
F calandrer, glacer
G kalandrieren
I calandrare

capitals, caps
F majuscules *f*, capitales *f*
G Versalien *f*, Grossbuchstaben *m*
I lettere maiuscole *f*

caption (*see* underline)
F légende *f*
G Legende *f*
I leggenda *f*

cardboard, strawboard
A board
F carton *m*
G Karton *m*
I cartone *m*
cartridge paper
F papier cartouche *m*
G Zeichenpapier *n*
I cartoncino Bristol avorio *m*
case (typecase)
case
A job case, case
F casse *f*, bardeau *m*
G Setzkasten *m*, Schriftkasten *m*
I cassa *f*
upper case
F haut de casse *m*
G oberer Teil des Schriftkastens *m*, Oberkasten *m*
I alta cassa *f*
lower case
F bas de casse *m*
G unterer Teil des Schriftkastens *m*, Unterkasten *m*
I bassa cassa *f*
double case
F casseau *m*
G Akzidenzschriftenkasten *m*
I cassettina *f*, cassa per la spaziatura *f*
case (of a book)
F plat *m*, couverture *f*
G Deckel *m*
I copertina *f*
casing-in (of machine-bound books)
F finissure *f*, endossage *m*
G Einhängen *n*
I finitura *f*
caster (Monotype)
F fondeuse *f*
G Giessmaschine *f*
I fonditore *m*
casting-off (copy)
F calibrage *m*
G Umfang des Manuskripts ausmessen *m*
I calibratura *f*, tipoconteggio *m*
chancery script
F cancellaresca *f*
G Cancellaresca *f*
I cancelleresca *f*
chapel
F chapelle *f*
G Verein der Setzer und Drucker *m*
I capello *m*
chase
F châssis *m*
G Rahmen *m*
I telaio *m*
clicker
A case overseer
F metteur en pages *m*
G Metteur *m*
I impaginatore *m*
clump (metal)
A slug
F plomb *m*, reglette *f*
G Regletten *f*
I lingotto *m*
collotype
F phototypie *f*
G Lichtdruck *m*
I collografia *f*, fototipia *f*
colophon
F colophon *m*
G Kolophon *m*, Druckvermerk *m*
I colofon *m*
to **compose** (type)
F composer
G setzen
I comporre
composing machine
F machine à composer *f*, composeuse
G Setzmachine *f*
I compositrice *f*, macchina a comporre *f*
composing room, case room
F atelier de composition *m*
G Setzersaal *m*
I sala de composizione *f*
composing stick, setting stick
F composteur *m*
G Winkelhaken *m*
I compositoio *m*
compositor
A compositor, typesetter
F compositeur *m*
G Setzer *m*
I compositore *m*
computer
F ordinateur *m*
G Computer *m*

I calcolatore elettronico *m*

contact screen
F trama de contact *f*
G Kontaktraster *m*
I retino per contatto *m*

contents page
A table of contents
F table des matières *f*
G Inhalt
I tavola delle materie *f*

copyright (international term)
F droit d'auteur *m*, droits réservés *m*
G Urheberrecht *n*
I diritti d'autore *m*

cords *see* bands

counter (of type)
F contre-poinçon *m*, profondeur centrale *f*
G Punzen *m*
I profondità d'occhio *f*, contro-punzone *m*

dandy roll
F rouleau égoutteur *m*, filigraneur *m*
G Wasserzeichenwalze *f*
I ballerino *m*

deckle edge
F barbes *f*, bord barbé *m*
G Büttenrand *m*
I frastagliatura della carta a mano *f*

deckle (paper maker's)
F bord de la cuve *m*
G Schöpfrahmen *m*
I barba *f*, frangia *f*

dedication
F dedicace *f*
G Widmung *f*
I dedica *f*

delete
F supprimer
G deleatur, herausnehmen
I sopprimere

display type
F caractères de fantaisie *f*
G Zierschrift *f* Akzidenzschriften *f*
I carattere fantasia *f*

distribute (of type)
F distribuer
G ablegen
I scomporre

doctor or ductor blade (gravure)
F racle *f*
G Rakel *m*
I racla *f*, racletta *f*

dummy
F maquette en blanc *f*, livre spécimen *m*
G Skizze *f*, Probeband *m*
I volume di saggio *m*

edition
F édition *f*
G Auflage *f*
I edizione *f*

editor
F rédacteur *m*
G Redaktör *m*
I redattore *m*

Egyptian (slab serif)
A square-serif letter, slab-serif letter
F égyptienne *f*
G Egyptienne *f*
I egiziano *m*

electronic colour-scanner
F appareil de selection des couleurs *m*
G Farbscanner *m*
I scannare cromático *m*

electronic engraver
F machine à graver électronique *f*
G elektronische Kilschier-maschine *f*
I macchina per incidere i clichés *f*

electrotype
F galvano *m*, électrotype *m*
G Galvano *n* Kupferniederschlag *n*
I galvano *m*

endpaper
A end-paper, end-sheet
F feuillet de garde *m*, gardes *f*
G Vorsatzpapier *n*
I risguardi *f*

engine sizing
A beater sizing, engine sizing
F collage en pâte *m*
G im Stoff geleimt
I incollamento a macchina

engrave
F graver

G gravieren, stechen
I incidere

engraver
F graveur *m*
G Graveur *m*
I incisore *m*

engraving, copper
F gravure à l'eau forte *f*
G Kupferstich *m*
I incisione su metallo *f*

engraving (picture or proof of)
F gravure *f*
G Stich *m*
I incisione *f*

esparto
F alfa *m*
G Alfa *m*, Esparto *n*
I alfa *f*

estimate (cost of printing, etc.)
F devis *m*
G Kostenanschlag *m*
I preventivo *m*

etching
F eau forte *f*
G Radierung *f*
I acqua forte *f*

face (design of type)
F caractère *m*
G Schrift *f*
I carattere tipografico *m*

face (printing surface of letter)
F œil du caractère *m*
G Buchstabenbild *n*, Gesicht *n*, Auge *n*
I occhio *m*

fat face
F caractère gras *m*
G Fette Schrift *f*
I romano nerissimo *m*

featherweight paper
A featherweight paper, bulking paper
F papier bouffant *m*
G Federleichtpapier *n*
I carta riso *f*

feeder, automatic
F margeur automatique *m*
G Anlege-apparat *m*, Bogen anleger *m*
I mettifoglio automatico *m*

fillet, bookbinder's
F roulette *f*
G Roulett *f*
I rotella *f*

fleuron, printer's flower
A flower, fleuron, floret
F fleuron *m*
G Schmuck *m*, Zierat *m*
I svolazzo *m*

flong
F flan *m*
G Mater *f*, Stereomater *f*
I matrice *f*, flano *m*

folding machine
F plieuse *f*
G Falzmaschine *f*
I piegatrice *f*

folding (paper)
F pliage *m*
G Falzen *n*
I piegatura *f*

folio (page number)
F numéro de page *m*
G Pagina *f*, Seitenzahl *f*
I numerazione *f*

footnote
F note *f*
G Fussnote *f*
I nota a piede di pagina *f*

foot (of type)
F pied *m*
G Fuss *m*
I piede *m*

foredge, fore-edge
A fore edge
F marge extérieure *f*, tranche extérieure *f*
G aüsserer Papierand *m*
I margine di taglio *m*

foreman or overseer (of printing house or department)
F prote *m*
G Faktor *m*
I proto *m*

foreword, preface
F avant-propos *m*
G Vorwort *n*
I prefazione *f*

format
F format *m*
G Format *n*
I formato *m*

forme (of type)
F forme *f*
G Form *f*, Druckform *f*

I forma *f*
fount (of type)
A font
F fonte *f*, police *f*
G Satz *m*, Giesszettel *m*
I fondita *f*, polizza *f*
frame, composing
F rang *m*
G Setzregal *n*
I scaffale *m*
French-sewn binding
F emboitage *m*, points de brochure à la machine *m*
G gehollandert mit Buchfadenheftmaschine
I punti per brossura *m*
frontispiece
F frontispiece *m*
G Titelbild *n*
I frontespizio *m*
furniture, printers'
F garnitures *f*, blancs *m*, lingots *m*
G Hohlstege *m*
I marginatura *f*

galley proof (slip)
A galley proof, slip proof
F placard *m*, épreuve en placard *f*
G Fahne *f*
I vantaggio *m*
to **gather, collate**
F assembler
G zusammentragen
I raccogliere le signature
gathering (collation)
F assemblage *m*
G Lage zusammentragung *f*
I rismare *m*
gild, gilding
F dorer, dorure *f*
G Vergolden, Vergoldung *f*
I dorare, doratura *f*
gilt edges
F tranches dorées *f*
G Goldschnitt *m*
I taglio dorato *m*
gothic (black-letter)
A text or black letter
F gothique *m*
G Textur *f*, Gotisch *f*
I gotico *m*
groove (type)
F gouttière *f*
G Anguss *m*
I scanalatura *f*
guillotine
F massicot *m*
G Schneidemaschine *f*
I tagliacarte *m*
gutter (two inner margins)
F marge de fonde *f*
G Bundsteg *m*
I crocetta *f*

half-binding
F demi-reliure *f*
G Halbfranzband *m*
I rilegatura tre quarti pelle *f*
half-tone
F simili *f*
G Halbton *m*, Autotypie *f*
I mezza-tinta *f*
half-tone screen
F trame *f*
G Raster *m*
I retino *m*
hand press
F presse à main *f*
G Handpresse *f*
I torchio a mano *m*
headband (binding)
F comète *f*, tranche-fil *f*
G Kapitalband *n*
I capitello *f*
headline
F ligne de tête, manchette *f*
G Hauptzeile *f*, Uberschrift *f*, Schlagzeile *f*
I linea *f*, riga di testa *f*
hyphen
F division *f*, trait d'union *m*
G Bindestrich *m*, Divis *m*
I divisione *f*

illuminator
F enlumineur *m*
G Illuminator *m*
I miniatore *m*
illumination (of MSS, etc.)
F enluminure *f*
G Illuminierung *f*
I miniatura *f*
illustration
F illustration *f*
G Abbildung *f*, Illustration *f*

I illustrazione *f*

imitation art paper
F papier couché en pâte *m*
G Illustrationsdruckpapier *n*
I carta uso mano per illustrazione *f*

imposing surface, stone
A imposing stone, imposing table
F marbre *m*
G Schliessplatte *f*
I marmo *m*, piano per serrare le forme *m*

imposition
F imposition *f*
G Ausschiessen *n*
I impostazione *f*

impression (of printing press)
F impression *f*, foulage *f*
G Druck *m*
I impressione *f*, pressione *f*, stampa *f*

incipit, here begins
A incipit
F incipit *m*, ci commence
G Anfangsworte *n*
I incipit *m*

incunable
A incunabulum
F incunable *f*
G Inkunabel *f*
I incunabulo *m*

indentation
A indention
F renfoncement *m*
G Einzug *m*
I a capo

index
F index *m*
G Register *n*, Index *m*
I indice *m*

india paper
F papier bible *m*
G Bibeldruckpapier *n*
I carta pelure *f*, carta biblia *f*

initial
F initiale *f*
G Initiale *f*
I iniziale *f*

ink, printer's
F encre *f*
G Druckfarbe *f*
I inchiostro da stampa *m*

intaglio
F impression en creux *f*
G Tiefdruck *m*
I intaglio *m*

italic
F italique *m*
G Kursiv *f*
I corsivo *m*

jobbing printing
A job printing
F bilboquet *m*, travaux de ville *m*
G Akzidenzdruck *m*
I lavori commerciali *m*

justification (of lines of type)
F justification *f*
G Ausschliessung *f*
I giustificazione *f*

to **justify** (lines of type)
F justifier
G ausschliessen
I giustificare

kern
F cran *m*
G Überhang *m*
I crenatura *f*, sporgenza *f*

kerned letter
F lettre débordante *f*
G überhängender Buchstabe *m*
I lettera sporgente *f*

keyboard
F clavier *m*
G Tastatur *f*
I tastiera *f*

laid lines (in paper)
F vergeures *f*
G Wasserlinien *f*
I colonelli *m*

laid paper
F papier vergé *m*
G geripptes Papier *n*
I carta vergata *f*

lay of case
F modèle de casse *f*
G Kastenschema *n*
I schema di cassa *f*

layout
F maquette *f*
G Entwurf *m*
I bozzetto *m*

lead (metal)
F plomb *m*
G Blei *n*
I piombo *m*
lead (for spacing)
F interligne *f*
G Durchschuss *m*
I interlinea *f*
to **lead**
F espacer, interligner
G durchschiessen
I interlineare
legend (*see* caption, underline)
letterpress
F typographie *f*
G Hochdruck *m*, Buchdruck *m*
I tipografia *f*
letters (i.e. type)
caps, u.c.
F lettres majuscules *f*, haut de casse *f*, capitales *f*
G Versalien *m*
I lettere maiuscole *f*
lower-case
F lettres minuscules *f*, bas de casse *f*, minuscules *f*
G Gemeine *m*
I lettere minuscole *f*
small caps
F petites capitales *f*
G Kapitälchen *n*
I maiuscolletto *m*
roman
F romaine *m*
G Antiqua *f*
I tondo *m*
italic
F italique *m*
G Kursivschrift *f*
I corsivo *m*
bold face
A boldface
F grasse *f*
G fette Schrift *f*
I nero *m*
light face
A lightface
F maigre *f*
G Mager *f*
I chiaro *m*
lino-cut
A linoleum block
F gravure linoleum *f*
G Linolschnitt *m*
I incisione in linoleum *f*
lithography
F lithographie *f*
G Lithographie *f*
I litografia *f*
ligatures (fi, ff, etc.)
F ligatures *f*
G Ligaturen *f*
I legature *f*
line block
A cut, line cut
F cliché au trait *m*
G Strichklischee *n*, Strichätzung *n*
I cliché al tratto *m*
loading (of paper)
F charge *f*
G Füllstoff *m*, Zusatz *m*
I carica *f*
to **lock up** (a forme)
F serrer la forme
G schliessen
I chiudere la forma
logotype
F logotypie *f*
G Logotype *f*
I logotipia *f*
look-through (of paper)
F épair *m*
G Transparenz *f*
I trasparenza *f*
lower-case letters
F minuscules *f*, bas de casse *m*
G Gemeine *m*
I lettere minuscole *f*

machine-minder
A pressman
F conducteur de machine *m*
G Maschinenmeister *m*
I macchinista *m*
machining
F tirage *m*
G Druck *m*
I tiratura *f*
make-ready
F mise en train *f*
G Zurichtung *f*
I avviamento *m*
make-up
F mise en page *f*
G Umbruch *m*
I impaginazione *f*

manuscript
F manuscrit *m*
G Manuskript *n*
I manoscritto *m*
marbled paper
A marble paper, marbled paper
F papier marbré *m*
G marmoriertes Papier *n*
I carta martellata *f*
margins
F marges *f*
G Ränder *m*
I margini *m*
back or inner
A back margin
F marge de fond *f*
G Bund *m*
I margine di cucitura *m*
foredge
A fore edge
F marge extérieure *f*
G äusserer Papierrand *m*
I margine di taglio *m*
head
F blanc de tête *m*, marge de tête *f*
G Kopf *m*
I margine di testa *m*
tail
F marge de pied *f*
G Fuss *m*
I margine di piede *m*
mask
F cache *m*
G Abdeckshablone *f*
I maschera *f*
matrix
F matrice *f*
G Matriz *f*
I matrice *f*
matrix case, die case
F châssis porte-matrice *m*
G Matrizenrahmen *m*
I telaio per matrici *m*
measure
F justification *f*
G Satzbreite *f*
I giustezza di riga
mechanical tints
F procédé Benday *m*
G Rastern *m*
I punti aghi formi
mezzotint
F mezzo-tinto *m*
G Mezzotinto *n*, Schabblatt *n*
I mezzatinta *f*
mill finish or machine finish (MF)
F apprêté sur machine
G maschinenglattes Papier *n*
I calandratura *f*
modern
F didot *m*
G moderne Schrift *f*, Klassizistische *f*
I romano moderno *m*
monochrome
F monochrome
G einfarbig
I monocromo
mould (for type)
A mold
F moule *m*
G Giessform *f*
I forma a fondere *f*
mould (paper-making)
A mold
F forme *f*
G Form *f*, Papiersieb *n*
I forma *f*
mould-made paper
A moldmade paper
F papier à la cuve á la machine *m*
G Maschinenbüttenpapier *n*
I tina di macchina *f*
movable types
F caractères mobiles *m*
G bewegliche Typen *f*, Buchstaben *m*
I caratteri mobili *m*
mull
A crash
F tissu *m*
G Gaze *f*
I tela-garza *f*

newsprint
F papier journal *m*
G Zeitungspapier *n*
I carta di giornale *f*
nick (type)
F cran *m*
G Signatur *f*
I tacca *f*
nickel-facing
F nickelage *m*
G Vernickelung *f*

I nichelatura *f*

nonpareil
F nonpareille *f*
G Nonpareille *f*, 6 Punkt *m*
I nonpariglia *f*

offset deep-etch
F offset en creux *m*
G Offset-tiefdruck *m*
I offset-inciso *m*

offset printing
A offset *m*
G offsetdruck *m*
I stampa offset *f*

old face
A Old Style
F elzévir *m*
G Mediaeval *f*
I elzeviro *m*

overlay
F bequet *m*, mise en train *f*
G Zurichtung *f*
I rivestimento del cilindro *m*

overs (surplus of paper for spoilage)
F passe *f*
G Zuschuss *m*
I fogli aggiunti *m*

page
F page *f*
G Seite *f*
I pagina *f*

page, left-hand, even, verso
F page paire *f*
G gerade Seite *f*, linke Zeite *f*
I pagina pari *f*

page, right-hand, odd, recto
F page impaire *f*
G rechte Seite *f*
I pagina impari *f*, pagina dispari *f*

pagination (numbering)
F pagination *f*
G Paginierung *f*
I impaginatura *f*

paging (type of a book)
A make up, paging
F mise en pages *f*
G Umbrechen *n*
I messa in pagina *f*, impaginazione *f*

paper
F papier *m*
G Papier *n*
I carta *f*

art
A coated paper
F papier couché *m*
G Kunstdruckpapier *n*
I carta patinata *f*

hand-made
A handmade paper
F papier à la main *m*
G handgeschöpftes Papier *n*
I carta a mano *f*

imitation art
F papier couché en pâte *m*
G Illustrationsdruckpapier *n*
I carta uso mano per illustrazione *f*

laid
F papier vergé *m*
G geripptes Papier *n*
I carta vergata *f*

machine-made
F papier méchanique *m*
G Maschinenpapier *n*
I carta a macchina *f*

MF
F papier apprêté sur machine *m*
G maschinenglatt Druckpapier *n*
I carta da stampa calandratura *f*

mould-made
A moldmade paper
F papier à la cuve à la machine *m*
G Maschinenbuttenpapier *n*
I tina di macchina *f*

rag
F papier de chiffons *m*
G Hadernpapier *m*
I carta di stracci *f*

wove
F vélin *m*, bouffant
G leicht gekornt
I carta granulosa

paperback book
F livre de poche *m*
G broschiertes Buch *n*
I libro tascabile *m*

paper-making machine
A paper machine
F machine à papier *f*

G Papier maschine *f*
I macchina continua per carta *m*

papyrus
F papyrus *m*
G Papyrus *m*
I papiro *m*

paragraph indent
A paragraph indention
F alinéa *m*
G Alinea *n*, Absatz *m*
I capoverso *m*

parchment
F parchemin *m*
G Pergament *n*
I pergamena *f*

part-title
A divisional title, part title
F titre divisionaire *m*
G Abteilungstitel *m*
I occhiello *m*

paste
F colle *f*
G Kleister *m*
I colla *f*

perfect binding
A reliure sans couture *f*
G Klebebindung *f*
I rilegatura senza file *f*

perfecter
F machine à retiration *f*
G Schön- und Widerdruckpresse Maschine *f*
I macchina a ritrazione *f*

perfecting
F retiration *f*
G Widerdruck *m*
I stampa in volta *f*

photo-composition
A photocomposition
F photo-composition *f*
G Photosatz *m*, Lichtsatz *m*
I foto composizione *f*

photogravure
F héliogravure *f*
G Phototiefdruck *m*, Heliogravüre *f*
I foto incisione *f*

photo-lithography
A photolithography
F photolithographie *f*
G Photo Lithographie *f*
I fotolito *f*

photosetter
A phototypesetting machine, photocomposition machine
F photo-composteur *m*, machine à photo-composition *f*
G Photosetzmaschine *f*
I fotocompositrice *f*

pi, printer's
A pie
F pâté *m*
G Zwiebelfische *m*
I fascio *m*

to **pi**
A to pie
F mettre en pâte
G verfischen
I mandare in fascio, refusare

pica (12 pts)
F cicéro *m*
G Cicero *f*
I cicero *m*

pin mark
F repère *m*
G Giessmarke *f*
I marchio di fabbrica *f*

planer
F taq *m*, taquoir *m*
G Klopfholz *n*
I battitoio *f*

platen machine
A platen press
F presse a platine *f*
G Tiegeldruckpresse *f*
I macchina a platina *f*, a pressione piana *f*

point (for type size)
F point *m*
G Punkt *m*
I punto *m*

point size
F force de corps *f*
G Kegelstärke *f*
I forza di corpo *f*

poster
A poster, bill
F affiche *f*
G Anschlag *m*, Plakat *m*
I cartellone *m*, manifesto *m*

powderless etching
F gravure sans poudre *f*
G Einstufenätzung *m*
I incisione senza polvere *f*

prelims
A front matter
F feuilles de titre *f*
G Titelbogen *m*, Titelei *f*
I preliminario *m*

pre-make-ready
A pre-makeready
F pré-mise-en-train *f*
G Vorzurichtung *f*
I preavviamento *m*

press, printing
F presse méchanique *f*
G Druckpresse *f*
I macchina da stampa *f*

press room, machine room
F salle des machines *f*
G Maschinensaal *m*
I sala di macchine *f*

to **print**
F imprimer
G drucken
I stampare

printer
F imprimeur *m*
G Drucker *m*
I stampatore *m*

printer's devil (apprentice)
F apprenti *m*
G Lehrling *m*
I apprendista *m*

printer's error
F coquille *f*
G Druckfehler *m*
I refuso *f*

printer's flower (*see* fleuron)

printer's ornaments
F vignettes typographiques *f*
G Typenornamente *n*, typographische Ornamente *n*
I fregi tipografici *m*, ornamenti *m*

printer's reader, proof-reader
A proofreader
F correcteur *m*
G Korrektor *m*
I correttore *m*

printing, art of
F imprimerie *f*
G Buchdruckerkunst *f*
I stampa *f*

printing house
F imprimerie *f*
G Druckerei *f*
I stamperia *f*

printing machines

cylinder
F machine à forme ronde *f*, machine en blanc *f*
G Zylinderpresse
I macchina a stampa cilindrica

platen
F presse à platine *f*
G Tiegeldruckpresse *f*
I macchina a platina *f*, a pressione piana *f*

rotary
F rotative à bobine *f*
G Rotationsmaschine *f*, Hochdruck-Rollenrotation *f*
I rotativa *f*

stop-cylinder
F presse machine à arrêt de cylindre *f*
G Stopzylinder maschinepresse *f*
I macchina ad arresto del cilindro *f*

two-revolution
F presse deux tours *f*
G Zweitourenmaschine *f*
I doppio-giro *m*

process camera
F camera de reproduction *f*
G Reproduktionskamera *f*
I macchina fotografica riproduzione *f*

process engraving
F photogravure *f*
G Photochemigraphie *f*
I fotoincisione *f*

progressive proofs
F épreuves gammes *f*
G Skalenandrucke *m*
I selezione progressiva *f*

proof (of type)
F épreuve
G Andruck *m*
I bozza di stampa *f*

publisher
F éditeur *m*
G Verleger *m*
I editore *m*

pulp (for paper)
F pâte *f*
G Papiermasse *f*
I pasta *f*

punch (type founder's)
F poinçon *m*
G Schriftstempel *m*
I punzone *m*
punch-cutter
F graveur de poinçons *m*
G Stempelschneider *m*
I incisore di punzoni *m*

quad, 1 em (mutton)
A em quad, mut, mutton
F cadratin *m*
G Geviert *n*
I quadratino *m*
quad, quadrat
F cadrat *m*
G Quadrat *n*
I quadrato *m*
quire
F main *f*
G Lage *f*
I quinterno di carta *m*
quoin
F coin *m*, serrage *m*
G Schliesszeug *n*
I serraforma *f*
quotation marks
F guillemets *m*
G Gänsefüsschen *n*, Anführungzeichen *n*
I virgolette *f*
quotations (spacing)
A quotation quads, quotations
F cadratins creux *m*
G Hohlwürfel *m*
I quadratoni *m*

reader's marks
A proofreader's marks
F signes de correction *m*
G Korrekturzeichen *n*
I segni per la correzione *m*
ream
F rame *f*
G Ries *n*
I risma *f*
recto (*see* verso)
F recto, page impaire *f*
G Vorderseite *f*
I recto *m*
register (in printing)
F repérage *m*
G Register *n*
I registro *m*
reglet (wood)
F réglette *f*
G Reglette *f*
I lingotto *m*
to **remainder** (books)
F solder
G verramschen
I liquidare
reproduction
F reproduction *f*
G Vervielfältigung *f*, Reproduktion *f*
I riproduzione *f*
roller, inking
F rouleau *m*, toucheur *m*
G Auftragwalze *f*
I rullo *m*
roman type
F romain *m*
G Antiqua *f*
I romano *m*
rotary press
F presse rotative *f*
G Rotationspresse *f*, Rotationsmaschine *f*
I macchina rotativa *f*
routing machine
A router
F fraiseuse *f*
G Fräser *m*
I fresatrice *f*, contornitrice *f*
rule (brass)
F filet *m*
G Messinglinie *f*
I filetto *m*
rule, swelled
A Bodoni dash, French rule
F filet anglais *m*
G englische Linie *f*
I filetto inglese *m*
running head
F titre courant *m*
G Lebender Kolumnentitel *m*
I titolo corrente *m*

sanserif
A gothic, sansserif
F sans empattements
G Grotesk *f*
I carattere lineare *m* senza grazie
scraperboard
A scratchboard, scraperboard

F papier procédé *m*, carte à gratter *f*
G Schnabkarton *m*, Papier Gillot *n*
I carta Gillot *f*

section, signature (of a book)
A signature, section
F cahier *m*
G Lage *f*
I segnatura *f*

serifs
F empattements *m*
G Serifen *m*
I grazie, terminazioni *f*

set (type width)
F largeur *f*
G Dicke *f*
I spessore *m*

to **set type**
F composer
G setzen
I comporre

set-off
A offset, set-off, setting off
F maculage *m*
G Abschmutzen *n*, Abschmieren *n*
I controstampa *f*

setting rule, composing rule
F lève lignes *m*
G Setzlinie *f*
I cavarighe *f*

sewing (a book)
F brochage *f*
G Broschieren *n*, Heften *n*
I legature in brossura *f*

sewing-machine
F couseuse *f*
G Heftmaschine *f*
I cucitrice *f*

sheet, of paper
F feuille *f*
G Blatt *n*, Bogen *m*
I foglio *m*

shoulder note, side note, marginal note
A marginal note
F manchette *f*, addition *f*
G Marginalie *f*
I postilla *f*, nota marginale *f*

signature
F signature *f*
G Unterschrift *f*
I firma *f*

size (for paper)
F collage *m*
G Leimung *f*
I collatura *f*

slug (of type)
F lingot *m*, ligne *f*
G Setzmaschinenzeile *f*
I riga di macchina da comporre *f*

small capitals, small caps
F petites capitales *f*
G Kapitälchen *f*
I maiuscoletto *m*

sorts (type)
F sortes *f*, assortiment *m*
G Defekte *m*
I rappezzi *m*

spaces (type)
F blancs *m*, espaces *f*
G Ausschluss *m*, Füllmaterial *m*
I bianchi *m*, spazi *m*

em (mutton)
A em quad, mut, mutton
F cadratin *m*
G Geviert *n*
I quadratone *m*

en (nut)
F demi-cadratin *m*
G Halbgeviert *n*
I quadratino *m*

hair
F espaces fines *f*
G Haarspatien *f*
I spazio finissimo *m*

middle
F espace moyenne *f*
G Viertelspatien *f*
I spazio mezzano *m*

thick
F espace forte *f*
G Drittelspatien *f*
I spazio di tre *m*, terziruolo *m*

thin
F espace mi-fines *f*
G starke Spatien *f*
I spazio fino *m*

spacing material
A spacing material, space metal
F espaces *m*, blancs *m*
G Ausschluss *m*
I bianchi *m*, marginatura *f*

spine (of a book) *see also* bulk
A spine, shelfback, backbone
F dos *m*

G Buchrücken *m*
I dorso *m*
fast spine
F dos rigide *m*
G fester Rücken *m*
I dorso rigido, dorso a scatto *m*
flexible spine
F dos brisé *m*
G biegsamer Rücken *m*
I legatura flessibile *f*
hollow back
A hollow back or open back
G hohler Rücken *m*
I dorso a soffietto *m*
standing type
F conservation *f*
G Stehsatz *m*
I composizione da conservare *f*
stereotype plate
F stereotype *m*, cliché *m*
G Stereo *n*
I stereo *f*, cliché *m*
stereotyping
A stereotypy
F stereotypie *f*, clichage *m*
G Stereotypie *f*
I stereotipia *f*
stet
F bon
G bleibt stehen
I cancellare correzione
to **supercalender**
F glacer, supercalandrer
G hochsatinieren
I calandrare, cilindrare
swash letters
F lettres ornées *f*
G Schwungbuchstaben *m*
I iniziale ornata *f*
synopsis
F argument *m*
G Inhaltsangabe *f*
I sommario *m*

tail-piece
A tailpiece
F cul-de-lampe *m*
G Schlussstück *n*
I fregio di fondo *m*, finalino *f*
tang (type)
F jet *m*
G Gussbart *m*
I boccame *m*
text (of a book)
F texte *m*
G Text *m*
I testo *m*
thicks and thins (type design)
F pleins et déliés *m*
G Abstich *m* and Haarlinie *f*
I gambi e fuscellini *m*
tin
F étain *m*
G Zinn *n*
I stagno *m*
title-page
F grand titre *m*
G Titelseite *f*, Haupttitel *m*
I titolo principale *m*
tooled binding
F reliure ciselée *f*
G Buchdeckenverzierung *f*
I rilegatura cesellata *f*
trim (edges of a book)
F rogner
G beschneiden
I rifilare
tub-sizing
F collage en cuve *m*
G in der Bütte geleimt
I collatura alla gelatina
type
F type *m*
G Type *f*, Schrift *f*
I tipo *m*, carattere *m*
type casting
F fonte de caractères *f*
G Schriftguss *m*
I fusione dei caratteri *f*
type family
F familles de caractères *f*
G Schriftfamilie *f*
I famiglia di caratteri *f*
type foundry
F fonderie *f*
G Schriftgiesserei *f*
I fonderia *f*
type height to paper (0·918 in.)
F hauteur du caractère, hauteur en papier *f*, 23·56 mm
G Schrifthöhe *f*, 23·56 mm
I altezza tipografica *f* 23·56 mm
type scale
A type measure
F typomètre *m*

G Typometer *m*, typographischer Zeilenmesser *n*, Zeilenmass *n*
I tipometro *m*
type size (point size)
F force de corps *f*, corps *m*
G Kegelstärke *f*
I forza di corpo *f*, corpo *m*
typography
F typographie *f*
G Typographie *f*
I tipografia *f*

uncials
F onciales *f*
G Uncialschrift *f*
I unciali *f*
underlay
F hausse *f*
G Klischeeunterlage *f*
I tacco *m*, rialzo perclichés *m*
underline, legend
A legend
F légende *f*
G Unterschrift *f*, Erklärungen *f*
I sotto titolo, leggenda *f*
upper-case
F haut de casse *m*
G Oberkasten *n*
I alto *m*

vat
F cuve *f*
G Bütte *f*
I tinozza *f*
vellum
F vélin *m*
G Jungfern-Pergament *n*, Velin *m*
I velina *f*
Venetian (type face)
F venetienne *f*
G Frühform der Antiqua *f*
I veneziano *m*
verso (*see* recto)
F verso *m*, page paire *f*
G Rückseite *f*
I verso *m*

water-mark
A watermark
F filigrane *m*
G Wasserzeichen *n*
I filigrana *f*, marchio d'acqua *m*
wayzgoose (printers' annual outing)
F balade *f*
G Betriebsausflug *m*
I gita sociale *f*
woodcut
F gravure sur bois *m*
G Holzschnitt *m*
I xilografia *f*
wood-engraving (block)
F gravure sur bois *f*
G Holzstich *m* (Hirnholz)
I incisione su legno *f*
wood pulp
chemical
A chemical fiber, chemical wood pulp
F pâte chimique de bois *f*
G Holz-zellstoff *m*
I fibbra chimica *f*
mechanical
F pâte mécanique de bois *m*
G Holzschliff *m*
I pasta di legno *f*
wove paper
F vélin *m*, bouffant
G leicht gekörnt
I carta granulosa *f*
wrong font
F lettre d'un autre œil *f*, coquille *f*
G Fisch *m*
I refuso *m*

x-height
F œil de la lettre *m*
G Mittelänge *f*
I lunghezza media *f*

ACKNOWLEDGEMENTS

In the preparation of this book I have received a great deal of assistance and advice, freely and generously given, from friends, colleagues, and strangers, and I acknowledge it gratefully. To the care of Mr. David Bland and the indefatigable research of Mr. R. S. Atterbury I owe the solution of a number of problems and the provision of some of the illustrations. I am grateful for advice and suggestions to the following gentlemen, who kindly read the typescript or proofs of various sections of the book: Mr. Lionel Darley, Mr. James Shand, Mr. R. G. Hawkins, Mr. John Easton, Mr. T. E. Griffits, Mr. L. C. Smith, Mr. T. A. Hartnup, Mr. W. A. J. Blaker; and also for similar assistance given by the Cotswold Collotype Company, the Monotype Corporation Ltd., and John Dickinson & Co. Ltd.; and for advice to Mr. J. O. T. Howard of Quaritch's and Mr. F. F. Patrick of Birmingham Public Libraries.

I am indebted to the following firms for allowing me to take photographs in their factories; the numbers against their names refer to the illustrations concerned: W. S. Cowell Ltd., 67, 68; James Burn & Company, 91, 92, 93–6; C.W.S. Printing Works, Reddish, 10, 28; Fine Art Engravers, 54, 56, 60, 61; Harrison & Sons, 65–6; Hazell, Watson & Viney, 37, 38, 47; King & Jarret, 46; and I am glad to acknowledge the assistance of the compositors, machine-minders, and others who appear in these photographs.

I am deeply grateful to the Cotswold Collotype Company for supplying the collotype plates for this book, 173, 174, 178, 179, 197–200; to W. S. Cowell Ltd. for the photo-litho and Plastocowell plates, 185, 186, and 190, 191; and to Clarke & Sherwell for the gravure plates, 132, 133, 135, 136; and to Intertype Ltd., the Linotype & Machinery Co. Ltd., and the Monotype Corporation Ltd. for type for the text type specimen pages.

I owe thanks to Mr. T. E. Griffits for the litho plate drawn on the stone, 72; to Mr. Anthony Gross and Heinemann & Co., for the Plastocowell drawing made for John Galsworthy's *Forsyte Saga*, 191; to Mr. George Woodman, who drew several of the line diagrams, 5, 13, 15, 17, 22, 23, 38, 39, 41, 79–81, 88–90, 138, 139, 140; and to Mr. B. J. Palmer, who also made drawings for line diagrams, 38, 64.

I also acknowledge with thanks the various contributions that have made Figure 114 possible; type, electros, or proofs have been supplied by Amsterdam Type Foundry, the Curwen Press, Dellagana & Co., Intertype Ltd., Mardon, Son & Hall, Foister & Jagg, Latimer Trend & Co., Odham's Press, the John Roberts Press, the Shenval Press, and Stephenson, Blake & Co.

I am indebted to Major J. R. Abbey for allowing me to consult his magnificent library and to reproduce photographs of his books, 186, 190; to the National Book League for the use of its growing library and permission to reproduce photographs, 195, 198; to the St. Bride Foundation Institute and its librarian for giving me facilities for research and photography, 12, 14, 16, 44, 50, 98, 99, 121, 140, 141, 143, 146, 147, 149, 150; to the British Museum for photographs of books in the library, 1, 3, 5, 98, 100–107, 111, 113, 114, 125, 126, 128–30, 132, 134, 141, 143, 144, 160, 161, 163–7, 174, 188, 197; and also to the Bodleian Library, 127, 162, 182, 183.

I thank the following for permission to reproduce photographs, books, bookjackets, etc.; *The Ambassador*, 82–4; Mr. R. S. Atterbury for the decorated rules in Figure 176; Mr. Charles Batey, 11; B. T. Batsford Ltd., 208; the Baynard Press, 157; Bowater Sales Co., 73–6; Chatto & Windus, 202, and Mr. Mervyn Peake, 193; Collins Ltd., 186; W. S. Cowell Ltd., 201; the Cresset Press, 202; the Curwen Press, 156; Faber & Faber, 171, 189, 192, 202, and for lending the blocks for Figures 48, 49; Mr. Charles Wrey Gardiner for lending a copy of Baskerville's *Works of Congreve*, 110, 142; the Golden Cockerel Press, 134, 155,

170; George G. Harrap & Co., 172; the Harvard University Press and the Oxford University Press, 2, 97, 120; William Heinemann Ltd., 145; Mr. Ellic Howe, 18, 45; C. & E. Layton Ltd., 54; Lothrop, Lee & Shephard Co. Inc., 207; Sir Francis Meynell and the Nonesuch Press, 131, 169, 202; Linotype & Machinery Ltd., 19, 20, 25; the Monotype Corporation, 6, 22, 24, 25, 29, 30, 31, 33; New Directions, New York, 202; Mrs. Tirzah Swanzy (Mrs. Ravilious) and the Oxford University Press, 52; Penguin Books, 51, 53, 183, 184, 201; Perez (London) Ltd. for lending the carpet block used for Figure 63; Eugen Rentsch Verlag, Zurich, 206; Routledge & Kegan Paul, 175; Mr. Ru van Rossem, 179; Albert Skira, Lauzanne, 194; Stephenson, Blake & Co., 7; Victoria & Albert Museum, 85–7; Mrs. Beatrice Warde and the Cambridge University Press, 108; Mr. William Webb, 122; Mr. J. W. Thomas, A.R.P.S., 196.

For additional photographs in this fifth edition I owe thanks to: the Monotype Corporation Ltd., Figures 29–33; K. S. Paul & Associates Ltd., Figure 35; Linotype & Machinery Ltd., Figure 36; Frank F. Pershke Ltd., Figure 57; and Crosfield Electronics Ltd., Figures 32 and 58.

I also thank the Monotype Corporation Ltd., Linotype & Machinery Ltd., and Intertype Ltd., for information about photosetting and computers and especially Mr. Rowley Atterbury and Rocappi Ltd. for allowing me to visit the general-purpose computer typesetting installation at Otford, Kent.

I am indebted for help with the glossary to Mr. Germano Facetti; Mr. Aldo Novarese of Societa Nebiolo; Frederick A. Praeger Inc. of New York; Dr. Konrad F. Bauer of the Bauer Typefoundry, Frankfurt; and Mr. Berthold Wolpe.

If I have failed to acknowledge any material I have used, or have not returned thanks where thanks are due, I hope my apologies will be accepted.

INDEX

Figures in italics refer to illustrations

Adastra, type, 250
address on tape, 95
advance copies, 264
advertisements, 378, 381
Albertina, type, 272
Albertus, type, 251, *255*
albumen, 164, 196
Aldine italics, *225*, 226
Aldus Manutius, *225*, 226, 276, 277, *319*, 381, *391*, *427*, 429
Alice in Wonderland, 436
alloy, 31, 36
America, 33, 40, 71
American Civil War, 173
Amman, Jost, *174*
Amsterdam, 281
Ancient Mariner, The Rhyme of the, *438*, *448*
announcement, 370
antiqua, 226
Antique No. 3, type, *254*
antique papers, 181
anti-set-off sprays, 125
Antwerp, 229, 282
Apocalisse, L', *493*
Apollo, type, *308*
appendixes, 378
aquatint, 428
area-composition, 93–4
Arlin, 202
Arrighi, Ludovico degli, 275
Arrighi, type, *275*
Ars Memorandi, *27*
artists, 444–5
art paper, 146, 183
ascenders, 41 seq.
Ashendene Press, 241, *243*
asterisk, 329
Austin, Richard, 290
authors, 265
auto-lithography, 159 seq., *168*, 436, 445–6

Babylon, 23
Baghdad, 172
Balacuir, 202
Balatron, 202
Bamberg, 28
Barbou, type, 287, *288*
Barbou, Joseph Gérard, 288
Baskerville, John, 34, 172, *232*, 236, 346, 354, 394, *397*, 400, 404
Baskerville, Linotype, *286*
  Monotype, 232, *285*
Basle, 228
Bassinius, *Opera*, *323*
bastard title, 367, 368–70, 382–4
Bauer typefoundry, 30
Bauhaus, 421, 422
Bawden, Edward, *364*
Baynard Press, 258, 361
beard, of type, *37*, 39
Beardsley, Aubrey, 431, *441*
beater, 176
Beaumarchais, Pierre Augustin Caron de, 286
Bell, type, 236, *290*
Bell, John, 234, 290
Bembo, Cardinal Pietro, 228, 276
Bembo, type, *276*
Bensley, Thomas, 237
Benton, Linn Boyd, 80
Berling, type, 272
Bernhard Cursive, type, 250
Bessemer, type, 250
Beton, type, 248
Bewick, Thomas, 133, *134*, 430, 440
Bible, 230, 245, 299, *331*, *333*, *355*, 480

Bible *cont.*
  42-line, 28, 256, *331*
  designed to be read as Literature, *355*
bibliographical note, 367, 370–72
bibliography, 378, 379–80
bichromate, 163, 167–8
bi-metallic litho plates, 164–5
binding, book, 188 seq., *189*, *190*, *193*, *196*, *197*, *198*, *199*, *204*, *205*, 474
  automation in, 312 seq.
  bevelled edges, 481
  blocking, 476
  blocking machine, 210–11
  case, 209
  casing machine, 211
  case-making machine, 209
  cloth, 476, 479–80, *492*, *497*
  cottage style, *484*
  design, 172 seq.
  examples, *480*, *481*, *484*, *485*, *492*, *493*, *496*, *497*
  flexible, 486
  folding, 192
  half-, 478
  hand-, 189–200
  jewelled, *480*
  leather, *474*, *481*, *484*, *485*, *493*
  lettering and tooling, 195–7, 473–5
  lining machine, 208–9
  machine-, 200 seq.
  materials, 477
  mechanization, 477
  perfect, 214
  pressing unit, 205, *213*
  printed, 485–6, *496*
  quarter-, 478
  raised bands, 475
  rounding spine, 194
  sewing, 193
  theoretical evolution, 188–90
  tools, *199*
  trimming, 194
  wrappering machine, *205*, 213
  yapp edges, 487
  unsewn, 214
Blado, Antonio, 277
Blado, type, *277*
Blair Hughes Stanton, 430–31
Blake, William, 428
blank pages, 101
bled illustration, 454–6
blind tooling, 196, 212
block books, 24–5, *27*
blocking, 476, 481
blocking machine, 210–11, 212
blurbs, 264–5, 494
Boccaccio, 298
Bodoni, Giambattista, 226, *234*, 236, 292, 354, 394, *399*, *401*, 404, 421
Bodoni, type, 233–4, 292
bold faces, 272
Book of Kells, 213
bolts, 488
Bonet, Paul, *493*
Bonnard, Pierre, 437
bookbinding, *see* binding
bookjackets, *see* jackets
Book of English Clocks, *496*
book sizes, 186, 260
borders, 388, 390
Braques, Georges, 437
brass, binder's, 209–10
Brook, Rupert, poems, *429*
buckram, 480
Bulmer, William, 237, *294*
Bulmer, type, 294
bumping machine, 206
Bunyan, type, 304
Burne-Jones, Sir Edward, *406–7*
buying paper, 186–7

Cabala, *393*
Cable, type, 248
Cairo, type, 248
Caledonia, type, *293*
Cambridge University Press, 286
Cancelleresca Bastarda, type, 302
carbon tissue, 154–5
Carolingian script, 220–21
Carroll, Lewis, 270
case, binding, 209
case, double, type, *64*
case-making machine, 209
casing machine, 211
Caslon, William, 231, 281, *284*
Caslon, type, *45*, 231, 237, *284*
Caslon & Co., 305
cartridge paper, 181–2
Castellar, type, 250, *252*
caster, Monotype, 77–9
cast-off, 264
CaT, computer-aided typesetting, 88
cathode-ray tube, 93–4
Catholicon, 28
Caxton, William, 386
Centaur, type, 224, *275*

INDEX

Chagall, Marc, 437
chancery italics, 221, 224, 226, 298, 299
chapel, 64–5
chapter divisions, 343 seq.
chapter heads, *334*, *335*, 343 seq., *345*, *347*, 349 seq., *351*, *353*, *355*
chapter titles, 100, 261
Charlemagne, 220
chase, *102*, *103*, *105*, 106, *108*
Chaucer, Geoffrey, works, 398, *406–7*
Chaucer type, *239*
Cheltenham, type, 244, 248, 366
chemical wood pulp, 175–6
children's books, 436, 445
China, 23–4, *32*, 425, 426
Chirico, Georges de, 437
Chisel, type, 248
Chiswick Press, 237, 238
Chromograph, 151
civilité types, 251
classification of typefaces, 251
cloth, binding, 195, 201, 476, 479–80
  substitutes for, 201–2
clumps, 48
coated papers, 182–3
coatings, 164
codex, 188, *189*
Colines, Simon de, *321*
Collins' Clear-Type Press, 289
collotype, 167 seq., 431, 449
  machines, *165*
Cologne, *31*, *356*, *357*, *385*, *387*
Colonna, type, 250
colophon, 378, 380–81, 386
colour reproduction, 140–41
colour printing, in auto-lithography, 160
  in photogravure, 157
  in collotype, 169
  in photolithography, 165–6
colour separation, 140–41, 147–8, 151
Common Prayer, Book of, *484*
companionship, 63–4
composing machines, 63, 66 seq.
  Linotype, *68*
  Monotype, *73*, 75, *76*, *77*
  photo-composition, *84*, *85*, *92*
  Young Delcambre, *67*
composing stick, 54
composition, 31, 49 seq.
compositor, 49 seq.
Compuscan, 97–8
computers, 87 seq.
  general-purpose, 88–90
  keyboards, *92*
  installation, *92*
  special purpose, 90, 91
  tape, *86*
Congreve, works, *232*, *347*
Consort, 248, *254*
contact screen, 150
contents list, 367, 375, 382
copper engraving, *334*, *335*, *420*, *421*, 426–8, *428*, 429
copyright, 262
cords, 190
Cornell, type, *307*
corrections, 90, 109
  in photo-composition, 94–8
corrector of the press, 111 seq.
Coster, Janzoon, 24, 25–6
costs, 261
cottage binding, *484*
Cowell, W. S., Ltd, 161, 446
Cranford, *419*
Craw Modern, type, *254*
cross heads, 324
cross-line screen, *see* half-tone screen
C.R.T. (cathode-ray tube), 93–4
Curwen Press, 258, 291, *346*, 434
cut-in heads, 327

dagger, 329
Daily Telegraph, 309
Dalziell brothers, 430, *436*
Daniel, Rev. C.H.O., 238
Dante, type, *298*
data-processing, 88
De Aetna, 227
Décaméron François, Le, *421*
deckle, 179–80, 488
decoration, 348, 353, 388, 410–12
  on bookbindings, 472 seq.
dedication, 367, 372–3, 382
deep-etch process, 164
Defoe, Daniel, 343
Degas, Edgar, 437
delete, 114–15
Dent, J. M., Ltd, 305
Derain, André, 437
descenders, 40 seq.
Deutsche Industrie Normen (DIN), 185
development, in photo-composition, 83
Diamond Sutra, *32*
Diary of Lady Willoughby, 237, 238

INDEX

Diascan, 151
dichromate, 164
Didot family, 229, 234, 236
Digiset, 93
Dijck, Christoffel van, 281, 306
direct lithography, 161
direct-screen process, 150
display faces, 244
Dissertation sur l'origine et les progrès de gravure, 351
distribution, 32, 62
divisions of a book, 344
doctor blade, 156
Dominus, type, 250
Dooijes, Dick, 306
Doré, Gustave, *438*
double case, 63–4
double column, 378
double dagger, 329
doublure, 476
Doves Press, 241, *243*
dragon's blood, 138
drawings for binding design, 484
drawings, *see* illustrations
driographic plate, litho, 165
dry offset, 166
dummy, 264
Duralin, 202
Dürer, Albrecht, 388, 429, *432*
Dwiggins, W. A., 293
Dycril, 140, 143

edges, boards, bevelled, 487
  yapp, 487
edges, paper, coloured, 197, 489
  gilt, 197, 488–9
  guillotined, 207, 487–8
  painted, 489
  rough, 488
  trimmed, 207
edition binding, 476
editorial department, 259
Egyptians, 171, 425
egyptians, types, 248
Ehrhardt, type, 301
electronic engraving, 138–40, *141*, 143
electronic scanner, *141*, 150, 157
electrotype, *133*, 134–5
Elizabeth Roman, type, 251
Elongated Roman, type, 250
Elzevir, 281
em, 54, 69
end matter, 378 seq.
endpaper, 190, 195, 467 seq.
  coloured, 469
  maps and diagrams, 469
  marbled, 468
  patterned, 467–8
  printed, 469–70
  suitable papers, 470
England, 29, 40, 42, 64, 71
engraving, *335*, 390–92, *420*, *421*, 426, *428*, *429*
engraving machine, electronic, *141*, 143
Enschedé van Zonen, 281, 302
Eragny Press, 241
Erbar, type, 248
esparto grass, 173, 176
Estienne, *360*
estimate, 261
etching, 132, 155
Euclid, *Elementa*, 317
Eusebius, *De Praeparatione Evangelica*, 224
Evans, Edmund, 436
examples of printing processes, 170

Fabriano, 172
Fabroleen, 202
Falstaff, type, *255*
Farleigh, John, 430
fat faces, 245, 404
featherweight antique paper, 181
feeding, 123, 124
  automatic, 126
Fell, Dr. John, 238
Fell types, 238
fillets, 196
filters, 141, 147
flax, 172
fleurons, 348, 352–3, 390, 412
flong, 109
Florence, 429
folding, 192, 203–4
folios, 335 seq.
Fontana, type, *289*
footnotes, 99, 100, 327
  references, 329
foredge, *190*
foreword, 367, 373–5
forme, *93*, *102*, *103*, *105*, *107*, *108*, 109, 119
Forum Titling, 251
Fototronic, 91
  CRT, 93
fount of type, 51

INDEX

Fourdinier, Henry, 174
Four Gospels, The, *333*
Fournier, Pierre Simon, 229, *287*, 288, *351*
Fournier, type, *287*, *351*
Four Victorian Ladies, 417
Fraktur, *219*
frame, composing, 54
France, 227, 229, 234, 428
Francesca Ronde, type, 250
Freedman, Barnett, 161, 361, *365*
French grooves, 213
French sewing, 206
frontispiece, 367
Frutiger, Adrian, 308, 311
Fry's Ornamented, type, 250, *252*
Fundamentbuch, *218*
furniture, *48*
Fust, Johann, 28, 217, 229

Galaxy, type, 311
galley, *59*, 60, 99
galley proof, 59–60, 99, 111–12
Garamond, Claude, 228, 229, 279
Garamond, type, *228*, 278, *279*, 280
gathering, 192, 205
  machine, *204*, 205–6,
Gauchat, Pierre, *508*
gelatine, 167–8, 155
Georgian, type, 289
Gibbings, Robert, 430
Gill, Eric, 134, 298, 304, 305, 361, *415*, 431
Gill Sans, type, 248
glair, 196
Glindura, 202
glueing, 194,
gold, 196, 211, 473, 481–2
  imitation, 211
Golden Cockerel Press, 241, *333*, *364*, *415*, 431, 437
Golden type, *239*, 240
Gospels, *333*, 361, 431
gothic types, 217–20, *218*, *219*, 224–6, 240, 316–17, *333*, 388
Goudy Hand-tooled, type, 250
gouges, 196
Grandjean, Philippe, 229
graining litho plates, 161
Granjon, Robert, 230, *278*, 280
gravure, *see* photogravure
Greece, 220
Greenaway, Kate, 436
Griffi, Francesco, *225*, 226, 276
Grolier, Jean, 474, *481*
Gropius, Walter, 422
Gross, Anthony, 161, *445*, 446
gsm (grammes per square metre), 187
guillotine, 207
Gutenberg, Johann, 23 seq., 132, 217, 229, 256, *331*, 439, 473
Guyot, François, 230

Hadego, 98
Hague, René, 305
half-titles, 100
half-tone, *133*, 141 seq., 431, 449
  in colour, 146 seq.
half-tone screens, 141 seq., *142*, 144–5, *145*, 148, 162
hand-binding, 188 seq., *189*, *190*, *193*, *196–7*, *198*, *199*
hand-press, 30, 119, *120*
hard copy, 92, 96
harmony, 509 seq.
Haroun al Raschid, Caliph, 172
Harris-Intertype, 306, 307
Hartz, S. L., 303
Hassall, Joan, *419*
headband, 190, 487
headlines, 331 seq., *337*
headpieces, 458
height to paper, 40–41
Helvetica, type, 311
Herbert, Gwen, *437*
'Here beginneth', 383, *385*
hieroglpyhics, 425
high-speed printer, 90
Hittites, 425
Holbein, Hans, 388
Holmes, Sherlock, 433–4
Holy War, The, *403*
Horace, *Opera*, *399*
Horne, Herbert, 241
Hughes, A., *436*
hyphenation, 88–91
Hypnerotomachia Poliphili, *225*, 226, 277, *319*, *427*, 429

idiot tape, 89
illumination, 356, 357–9
illustrations, list of, 367, 377–8, 382
illustration, 132 seq., 154 seq., 262–4
  bled, 454
  in colour, 451–2, 464–5
  margins, 452

inserting, 459 seq.
landscape, 453–4
mounting, 462–3
paste-up, 460
placing in text, 457 seq.
sizing, 453
use of, 425 seq.
imitation art paper, 183
imposing surface, 104–6
imposition, 99 seq., 101, *102*, *103*, *105*, *107*, *108*, 203
impression, 130
Imprimerie Royale, 287
Imprint, *296*
imprint, 367, 370–71, 378, 380
'Incipit', 383
indention, 316
indexes, 378
India paper, 183–4
indulgences, 28, *33*
Ingelow, Poems of Jean, *492*
initials, 356, *356*, *357*, *358*, *359*, *360–65*
indicator, 337
placing, 361–4
ink, 126 seq., 129
inking, 119, 123, 127
inlay, 197
ISO (International Standards Organization), 185
Intertype, 71, 272, 273
italic, chancery, 221, 224, 226, 298, 299
intaglio process, 154 seq.
half-tone, 157
invert half-tone, 157
Italy, 234

jackets, book, anatomy, 492
arrangement of lettering, 496, 506
artist-designed, 500 seq.
backboard, 502
blurb, 494
design, 492 seq.
evolution, 490–1
flaps, 493
illustration, 497
lettering, 503–6
picture, 501
poster technique, 502
printing processes, 507
spine, 498, 501–2
typographical, 495 seq.
examples, *500*, *501*, *508*, *509*
Jacno, type, 251
Jacques, Robin, 431
Jannon, Jean, 229, 279
Janson, Anton, 301
Janson, type, *301*
Játiva, 172
Jennett, Seán, *417*, *423*
Jenson, Nicolas, 222, *223*, 227, 240, 241, 275
Joanna, type, *305*
Jones, George, W., 278
Joyce, James, 344
Juliana, type, *303*
June, type, *252*
justification, 31–2, 56–7, 66, 82, 88
jute, 172
Juvenal, *223*, *237*
Juvenalis, *397*

Karnak, type, 248
Keere, Henric van der, 230
Keller, 173
Kells, Book of, 218
Kelmscott Press, *239*, *326*, *406–7*
kerns, *40*
keyboard, counting and non-counting, 91–2
Linotype, 32, 68 seq.
Monotype, 72 seq., *73*, 76; electronic, 76
King's Fount, *243*
Kis, Nicholas, 301, 306
Klang, type, 251, *253*
Klischograph, *141*, 143
Knight, Harold, *436*
Koenig and Bauer, 30, *121*, 121–2
Koops, Matthias, 173
Krimpen, Jan van, 299
Kumlien, Dr. Akke, *500*

laid papers, 172, 180
Landen, Johann, 356
Lanston, Tolbert, 32, 71
lay of the case, *52*, 52–4, *64*
leading, 57, 100, 320
leading, articles, 101
leads, *48*, 100, 101
leather, for binding, 195, 198–9, 474
patterned, 476
tree calf, 476
Lectura, type, *306*
Lee Priory Press, *325*
Legend, type, 250, 253
legends, or underlines, 263–4

INDEX

Lèpre morale, La, 30, *31*
lettering and tooling, 195–6
blind, 196, 212
gold, 196
letter-spacing, 404
lettre bâtarde, *219*, 388
lettre de forme, *219*, 388
lettre de somme, *219*
libel, 111, 117
Libro del Cortegiano de Conte Baldessar Castiglione, *391*
ligatures, 72
limestone, 158, 159
limited editions, 131, 479
Linasec, 90
line advance, 91
line block, 40, *133*, *136*, *137*
line drawing, 443
linen, 172
lining machine, 208–9
Linofilm, 87
Linoscan, 151
Linotron 505c, 87, 91, *92*, 93
Linotron 1010, 93
Linotype, 32, 63, *68*, 242, 272, 273
Linson, 202
lithographic plates, 164–5
stone, 159–60
lithography, 158 seq., *164*, *168*, 395, 431, 434, 445–6, *508*
auto-, 159 seq., 431, 445–6
direct, 161
invention of, 166–7
machines, 44
offset, 162 seq.
photo-, 162 seq., 431, 434
web-offset, 166
lower-case, 54
Ludlow, 34
Lumitype, 87, 91
Lydian, type, 310
Lydis, Mariette, 509

machine-finished papers, 182
machine proof, 112
Madonna Ronde, type, 250
Magdalenian man, 425, 426
Magnacolor, *140*, 150
Magnascan, *141*, 151, 153
Magnaset, 87, 93–4
magnetic tape, 86, 90, 96
Maillol, Aristide, *437*
Mainz, 23, 28, 358
make-ready, 128–31, 144
make-up, 99 seq.
Malin, Charles, 298
Malton, Thomas, *509*
Manuale Tipografico, *234*, *353*
manuscripts, 217, 218, 222, 259, 262, 265, 316, *330*, 357, 384
Manutius, *see* Aldus
Marathon, type, 251
Mardersteig, Dr. Giovanni, 289, 298
marginal head, 327
margins, 106, 261–2, 314, 336 seq.
Martin, William, 234, 293
masks, photographic, 148, 150, 152
Matisse, Henri, 437, *450*
matrix, 26, 34, 69 seq., *69*, 77, *84*, *85*
matrix case, Monotype, *84*
Mayans, 425
Mearne, Samuel, 474, 489
mechanical wood process, 175
Melior, type, 272
Mercurius, type, *255*
Mer des Histoires, La, *345*
Mergenthaler, Ottmar, 63, 68, 79
Meriden, type, 308
Merrymount Press, 409
metric paper sizes, 186
Metro, type, 248
Meynell, Sir Francis, 437
mezzotint, 132, 428
M.F., machine-finish, 182
Miehle, 125, *132*
Minerva, type, 304
minnesinger, 426
Mistral, type, 250, *253*
modern faces, 234–6, 244
Molé Foliate, type, *252*
Molière, *Oeuvres*, *428*
Monnier of Baudello, *485*
Monophoto, 76, 82, seq., *84*, *85*, 272
Monophoto 600, 86, 87
Monotype, 32, 36 seq., 46, 71 seq., 272, 273
Monotype Corporation Ltd., 82, 86, 226, 242
Monotype Ornaments, Book of, 354
Moreau le Jeune, *428*
Morison, Stanley, 287, 290, 300
Morris, William, 224, 238–40, 318, *326*, 396–8, *406–7*, 430
mould-made paper, 182
mould, type, 26, 30, 32, 69
movable types, 25 seq.

multi-colour presses, 125
Musée Plantin-Moretus, 50–51

Netherlands, 29, 230
News from Nowhere, *326*
newspapers, 145
newspaper presses, 122
newsprint, 173, 180
Nicholson, William, 121
nick, 38, *48*, 56
nipping machine, 206
nomenclature of type-faces, 272
Nonesuch Press, *328*, *411*, 437
nonpareil, 43
non-woven binding materials, 202
notes, 378, 379
numerals, arabic, 376; roman, 376
Nyloprint, 140

octavo, 104 seq.
oddments, 367
Odyssey, The, *328*
Officina Bodoni, 298
OCR (optical character recognition), 97
offset machines, 162–3
old faces, 234–6, 276
Old Face Open, type, 250, *252*
Onyx, type, 250
Optima, type, *310*
Oratio Dominica, 401
orihon, 188–9
ornament, 395, 400
overlays, 144
Ovid, *Metamorphoses*, 281
Oxford University Press, 238, 275, 320, 380

paging, 99 seq.
page, 99 seq., 314 seq.
  examples, *317–40*
  headings, 100, 314, *337*
  numbers, 314
  left-hand (verso), 382
  margins, 106, 261–2, 314, 336 seq., *339*, *340*
  proofs, 60, 112
  proportions, 336 seq.
  right-hand (recto), 382
pair of cases, *52*
paperback books, 214
paper, 171 seq.
  antiques, 181
  art, 183
  buying, 186–7
  cartridge, 181–2
  coated, 182–3
  featherweight, 181
  India, 183–4
  imitation art, 183
  laid, 172, 180
  mould-made, 182
  offset, 182
  sizes, 185–6
  twin-wire, 181–2
  varieties, 180–83
  wove, 172, 180
paper-making, *172*, *173*, 173 seq., *174*, *179*
  chemical wood process, 175–6
  hand-making, 176–8, 179
  loading, 183
  mechanical wood process, 175
  pulp, 175 seq.
  sizing, 179
  supercalendering, *173*, 182
papyrus, 171
paragraph indention, 316–17
paragraph mark, 316, 329
parallel mark, 329
parameters, 74, 88, 89
parchment, 172
Parma, 233
part titles, 261, 343 seq., 346
Pascal, type, 310
paste-up, 460
Payne, Roger, 474
Peake, Mervyn, 431, 434, *448*
perfect binding, 214
perfectors, 125
peripherals, 88, 90
Perpetua, type, *297*, 346
Perpetua Titling, type, *255*
Pharos, type, 250
photo-composition, 34, 82 seq.
  machines, 83, 86–7
  type faces for, 272
photo-engraving, 440 seq.
photography, 135–6, 440, 447, 449, 465–6
photogravure, 154 seq., 431, 449
  screen, 157, *160*
  machines, 161
photo-lettering machine, *85*, 98
photolithography, 162 seq., 431, 436, 449

bi-metallic plates, 164–5
coatings, 164
pre-sensitized plates, 164–5
tri-metallic plates, 164–5
photo-matrices, 82 seq., *84*, *85*, 87, 94
photopolymers, 140, 143
pica, 43, 48
Picasso, Pablo, 437
Pickering, William, 237, *403*
pictograms, 425
Pilgrim, type, *304*
pi, printers', 59
Pi-Sheng, 24
pin-mark, *37*, 39
pi-system, 93
planetary system, 166
planographic processess, *see* lithography *and* collotype
Plantin, Christopher, 50, 227, 229, *230*, 231
Plantin, type, *282*
Plantin Light, type, *283*
plastic printing plates, 140
Plastocowell, 162, *444*, *445*, 446
plates, litho, 161–6
platen, 120
Playbill, type, 250, *254*
Plinth, type, 250
Poems of Death, *496*
point sizes, 41 seq., 45, 69
Poliphilus, type, 226, 276, *277*
poster types, 44
powderless etch, 138, 143, *144*, 157
preface, 367, 373–5
preliminary pages, (prelims), 261, 367
pre-make-ready, 144
Pre-Raphaelites, 426
press, 118 seq.
hand-, 30, 34, 119–21
Miehle, 125
stop-cylinder, 30, 122 seq.
two-revolution, 124 seq.
Wharfedale, 122
pressman, 118
primary colours, 148–9
Prima Parte de le Novelle, 485
primary tape, 89, 91
primitive word string, 89, 91
printers' flowers, 348, 351, 352, 390, 412
printers' pi, 59
printing houses, early, 50
sixteenth century, 55
seventeenth century, 61
printing machines, 118 seq.
collotype, *165*, 168–9
gravure, 156, *161*
letterpress, 118 seq., *132*
lithographic, 163 seq., *164*
print-out, 90
Prisma, type, 250
private presses, 240, 241, 318, 430, 437
process camera, 137
camera-enlarger, *140*, 150
Magnacolor, *140*, 150
process colours, 146 seq.
process engraving, 132 seq., *137*, *139*, *140*, *141*, *142*, *144*, *145*, *148*, 431, 440
production department, 262
production manager, 267
Profil, type, *252*
programming, 88
progressive proofs, 148
Pronostycacyon, *389*
proofs, 109
proof-reader, 111, 117
proof-reading, marks, 114–15
punch-cutting, 79–80
punch-cutting machine, *69*
punches, 26, 74 seq.

Quadriregio, 429, *430*
quads, 47, 57
quoins, 59, *102*, *103*, *105*, 106, *107*, *108*
quotations (spaces), *48*
quotations, in chapter heads, 364
quotation marks, 320
quotations, style of setting, 318

Rackham, Arthur, 436
rags, 172, 175
raised bands, *190*, *193*, 195, 475
Rape of the Lock, *441*
Ratdolt, Erhard, 317, 358, 360
Ravilious, Eric, 430
Raymond of Navarre, 172
reader, proof-, 111 seq.
Realms of Silver, *423*
reams, 186
recto page, 382
reference signs, 329
register, 149
reglets, 48
Reiner Script, type, 250, *253*
Renaissance, 218, 426
Riccardi Press, 241

Riccardi type, *242*
right-hand page, 382
Robert, Louis, 174
Rockwell, 248
Rodin, Auguste, 437
Rogers, Bruce, 224, 275, 290
rollers, inking, 127
Romain du Roi, 287
Rome, 220, 222
Romulus, type, *302*
Rosner, Charles, 492
Rossetti, Christina, *436*
rotogravure, 157
routing, 138, *144*
rules, 390, 408, 414–16, *424*
Rusch, Adolf, *220*, 222

Sabon, type, *280*
Sabon, Jacques, 280
Salto, type, 251
Sandys, Frederick, 435
Sans 215, type, 248, *255*
Sans 216, type, 248
sanserifs, 246, 310, 311
scanner, electronic, *141*, 150
Schmutztitel, 384
Schoeffer, Johann, 228
Schoeffer, Peter, 28, 217, 229, 356, *358*
Schwabacher, type, *219*
Scotch Roman, type, *295*
Scotland, 295
scraperboard, *442*
screens: half-tone, *142*, *145*, *148*
  photogravure, *160*
scribes, 24, 217, 314
scripts, 217, 222, 250
scroll, 188
seals, 23
seannchaidhe, 426
section mark, 329
Senefelder, Alois, 166–7
serifs, 39, 41
Sessler, Robert, *501*
set measurement, 46
  table of widths, 313
set-off, 125, 129
sewing, 192, 206
  sewing-frame, *193*
  French, 206
  machine, *204*
Shakespeare, William, *Poems*, *239*
Shakespeare Printing Office, 294
Shaw, G. B., 398
Shenval Press, 258
shoulder heads, 327
side heads, 324
signatures, 192
silver, 197, 211
sizing, 179
skald, 426
Slimblack, type, 250, *254*
slip case, 507–8
slip proof, 59–60, 99
slugs, 33 seq., 68 seq., 71
small capitals, 320
smashing machine, 206
Society Script, type, *252*
space-bands, 69 seq.
spaces, 46–8
spacing, 46 seq., 56–7
  word-, 315–16
specimen page, 261
Spectrum, type, 299
Speculum Vitae Humanae, *221*
spine, *190*
  flexible, fast, hollow, *198*
  glueing, 207
  lining maching, 208–9
  rounding, 194, 207
Spira, Johann and Wendelin da, 222, *223*
sprays, 125
square books, 336–7
Stamperia Valdónega, 298
Stanton, Blair Hughes, 430–31
star chamber, 231
Starsettograph, 98
steampower, 30
Steel, type, 251
steel-engraving, 132, 428
Stellar, type, 310
Stempel typefoundry, 280, 310
stencil, 434
Stephen Crane, *409*
Stephenson, Blake, Ltd, 250, 290
stereotyping, 109
stone, 104–6
stonehand, 106
Stone, Reynolds, *133*, 304, 446
Stop, type, 251, *252*
stop-cylinder press, 122–4
Story of the Glittering Plain, 239
Strasbourg, 222
Studio, type, 252
studio lettering machine, *84*, 98
Subiaco, 220, *221*, 222

sub-heads, 324 seq.
supercalendered paper, 182
super-caster, 33
superior figures, 329–30
supplements, 378
surface, imposing, 104
Sweden, 29
Sweynheim and Pannartz, 220–22, *221*, 227, 241
Switzerland, 29
synopsis, 364
Szechuan, 23

tail-pieces, 458–9
Talbot, Henry Fox, 136
tang, 37, 78
tape: magnetic, 86, 96
  paper, *34*, 34 seq., 45
tape converter, 90
tape-merging, 95
tape-reader, 89
Telegraph-Modern, type, 272, *309*
Tempo, type, 248
Tenniel, Sir John, 436
text types, 268 seq.
Theatrum Praecipuarum Urbium, *420*
thermoplastics, 109
Theurdanck, *433*
Thorne Shaded, type, *252*
Thorowgood, type, 250
Through the Looking-Glass, 436
Times, The, 30, 33, 66, 122, 124, 300
Times Extended Titling, type, *255*
Times Roman, type, 41, 46, 244
  Linotype, *300*
Times Titling, type, *255*
tints, mechanical, *139*, 141
Tiptoft Missal, *330*
title-page, 260, 367, 382, 383 seq.
  as posters, 392–4
  classification, 405
  drawn, 412–13
  engraved, 390, *420*, *421*
  examples, *393–423*
  illustration on, 413–14
  use of colour on, 392, 414–18
tooling, 195
  blind, 196
  gold, 195
  silver, 197
Tory, Geofroy, *321*
Toulouse-Lautrec, Count Alphonse de, 437
Touraine, type, 310
Tracy, Walter, 309
Trafton, type, 250
Trajan column, 297
transitional faces, 236, 290
Trenholm, George, 307
trichromatic half-tone process, 146 seq.
tri-metallic litho plates, 164–5
trimming, 194
Tristram Shandy, 365
troubadour, 426
Tschichold, Jan, 280, 422
tub-sizing, 179, 181
Tunnicliffe, C. F., 442
Turner, J. M. W., 428
twin-wire papers, 182
two-revolution press, 124–5, *132*
tympan, 119
type, movable, invention of, 24–6
type, parts of, *37*
type areas, *338*, *339*, *340*
type, shape of, 31
type sizes, 42–3, *45*
type cases, 51
  double case, 63–4
  pair of, *52*
type designer, 257
type faces, *see under individual names*
  antiqua, 226
  bold faces, 272
  classification, 251, 449
  development from gothic to roman, 222
  display, 244
  design, 36, 70
  first true roman, *222*
  family of, 248, *249*, 366
  fat faces, 245
  gothic, 217–20, *218*, *219*, 224–6, 240
  modern faces, 244
  nomenclature, 272–3
  old faces, 228 seq., 237 seq., 272
  in photo-composition, 273
  roman, 226
  recognition of, 270–71
  text types, 268 seq.
typefounding, 29, 68, 78
typefounders, 36 seq., 257
Typefoundry Amsterdam, 306
type height, 40
Typis Literarum, *245*
typographer, 256 seq.
typography, 256 seq.

INDEX

Ultra Bodoni, type, 250
Ulysses, 344
under-colour removal, 152–3
Union Pearl, type, 250, 252
Univers, type, 248, *311*
unsewn binding, 214
unsharp masking, 152
Updike, D. B., 239, *409*
upper-case, 54

Vale Press, 241, *243*
Van Dijck, type, 281
vellum, 172, 195
Vendôme, type, 251, *254*
Venice, 429
verso page, 382
Vinne, Theodore de, 404
vinyl, 202
Virgil, *225*, 232
Vogue, type, 248
Vollard, Ambroise, 436–7

Walbum, type, 236, *291*
Walter, John, 122
Warde, Frederic, 275, 354
water-marks, 180
wayzgoose, 65
webb-offset, 166
Weisgard, Leonard, *508*
Weiss Roman, type, 251
Westminster Abbey, 64
Wharfedale, 122
whirler, 167
Whittingham, Charles, 237
Wilson, Alexander, 289
Woman, 158
Wood, J. R., 361
wood-cut, 49, 132–3, *133*, *426*, 428, 429, 430, *432*, *433*, 439, *501*
  on title-page, 388, *415*
wood-engraving, 132–4, *133*, *134*, *135*, 430–31, *435*, *436*, *438*, 439–40
wood pulp, 175
word spacing, 315–16
wove paper, 172, 180
wrappers, *see* jackets

x-height, 46

yellow-backs, 478
Young-Delcambre composing machine, 67

Zapf, Hermann, 310
Zell, Ulrich, 357
Zieler, Morgens, *501*
zinc, 161